SolidWorks 2013
Part II - Advanced Techniques

Advanced Level Tutorials
Parts, Surfaces, Sheet Metal, SimulationXpress,
Top-Down Assemblies, Core & Cavity Molds

Written by: Sr. Certified SolidWorks Instructor
Paul Tran, CSWE, CSWI

Schroff Development Corporation
P.O. Box 1334
Mission KS 66222
(913) 262-2664
www.SDCPublications.com

Publisher: Stephen Schroff

Examination Copies:

Books received as examination copies are for review purposes only and may not be made available for student use. Resale of examination copies is prohibited.

Electronic Files:

Any electronic files associated with this book are licensed to the original user only. These files may not be transferred to any other party.

Disclaimer

The author makes a sincere effort to ensure the accuracy of the material described herein, however the author makes no warranty, expressed or implied, with respect to the quality, correctness, reliability, currency, accuracy, or freedom from error of this document or the products it describes.

The author disclaims all liability for any direct, indirect, incidental or consequential, special or exemplary damages resulting from the use of the information in this document or from the use of any products described in this document. Data used in examples and sample data files are intended to be fictional.

Trademarks

SolidWorks is a registered trademark of Dassault Systems.
Microsoft Excel / Word are registered trademarks of Microsoft Corporation.
All other brand names or trademarks belong to their respective companies.

Acknowledgments

Thanks as always to my wife Vivian for always being there and providing support and honest feedback on all the chapters in the textbook. I would like to give a special thanks Lani for her editing and corrections. Additionally thanks to Dave Worcester and Peter Douglas for writing the forewords.

I also have to thank SDC Corp. and the staff for its continuing encouragement and support for this edition of *SolidWorks 2013 Part 2 Advanced Techniques*. Thanks also to Zach Werner for putting together such a beautiful cover design

Finally, I would like to thank you, our readers, for your continued support. It is with your consistent feedback that we were able to create the lessons and exercises in this book with more detailed and useful information.

ISBN: 978-1-58503-770-4

Printed in the USA.

Foreword

I first met Paul Tran when I was busy creating another challenge in my life. I needed to take a vision from one man's mind, understand what the vision looked like, how it was going to work and comprehend the scale of his idea. My challenge was I was missing one very important ingredient, a tool that would create a picture with all the moving parts.

A vision born in the mind of man, only becomes a reality when seen through that man's eyes, and that man was blind. Over time and many conversations, mostly with him talking and me asking endless questions, I came to understand his idea and adopt his vision. The challenge now became, how do I make it real, *how do help a blind man build his dream?*

Research led me to discover a great tool, SolidWorks. It claimed to allow one to make 3D components, in picture quality, on a computer, add in all moving parts, assemble it and make it run, all before money was spent on bending steel and buying parts that may not fit together. I needed to design and build a product with thousands of parts, make them all fit and work in harmony with millimeters tolerance. The possible cost implications of failed experimentation were daunting.

To my good fortune, one company's marketing strategy of selling a product without an instruction manual and requiring one to attend an instructional class to get it, led me to meet a communicator who made it all seem so simple.

Paul Tran has worked with and taught SolidWorks as his profession for more than 25 years. Paul knows the SolidWorks product and manipulates it like a fine musical instrument. I watched Paul explain the unexplainable to baffled students with great skill and clarity. He taught me how to navigate the intricacies of the product so that I could use it as a communication tool with skilled engineers. *He teaches the teachers*.

I employed Paul as a design engineering consultant to create the thousands of parts for my company's product. Paul Tran's knowledge and teaching skill has added immeasurable value to my company. When I read through the pages of these manuals, I now have an "instant replay" of his communication skill with the clarity of having him looking over my shoulder - *continuously*. We can now design, prove and build our product and know it will always work and not fail. Most important of all, Paul Tran helped me turn a blind man's vision into reality and a monument to his dream.

Thanks Paul.

These books will make dreams come true and help visionaries change the world.

Peter J. Douglas – CEO, Cake Energy, LLC

Images courtesy of C.A.K.E. Energy Corp., designed by Paul Tran

Preface

The modern world of engineering design and analysis requires an intense knowledge of Computer Aided Design (CAD) tools. To gain this deep understanding of unique CAD requirements one must commit the time, energy, and use of study guides. Paul Tran has invested countless hours and the wealth of his career to provide a path of easy to understand and follow instructional books. Each chapter is designed to build on the next and supplies users with the building blocks required to easily navigate SolidWorks 2013. I challenge you to find a finer educational tool whether you are new to this industry or a seasoned SolidWorks veteran.

I have been a part of the CAD industry for over twenty five years and read my share of instructional manuals. I can tell you Paul Tran's SolidWorks books do what most promise; however what others don't deliver. This book surpasses any CAD instructional tool I have used during my career. Paul's education and vast experience provides a finely tuned combination, producing instructional material that supports industry standards and most importantly, industry requirements.

Anyone interested in gaining the basics of SolidWorks to an in-depth approach should continue to engage the following chapters. All users at every level of SolidWorks knowledge will gain tremendous benefit from within these pages.

Dave Worcester
System Administer
Advanced Sterilization Products - A Johnson & Johnson Company

Author's Note

SolidWorks 2013 Basic Tools and Advanced Techniques are comprised of lessons and exercises based on the author's extensive knowledge on this software. Paul has over 27 years of experience in the fields of mechanical and manufacturing engineering; 17 years were in teaching and supporting the SolidWorks software and its add-ins. As an active Sr. SolidWorks instructor and design engineer, Paul has worked and consulted with hundreds of reputable companies including; IBM, Intel, NASA, US- Navy, Boeing, Disneyland, Medtronic, Guidant, Terumo, Kingston and many more. Today, he has trained more than 6500 engineering professionals, and given guidance to nearly ½ of the number of Certified SolidWorks Professionals and Certified SolidWorks Expert (CSWP & CSWE) in the state of California.

Every lesson and exercise in this book was created based on real world projects. Each of these projects have been broken down and developed into easy and comprehendible steps for the reader. Learn the fundamentals of SolidWorks at your own pace, as you progress form simple to more complex design challenges. Furthermore, at the end of every chapter, there are self test questionnaires to ensure that the reader has gained sufficient knowledge from each section before moving on to more advanced lessons.

Paul believes that the most effective way to learn the "world's most sophisticated software" is to learn it inside and out, create everything from the beginning, and take it step by step. This is what the **SolidWorks 2013 Basic Tools & Advanced Techniques** manuals are all about.

About the CD

This text includes a CD containing copies of the various files that are used throughout this book. They are organized by the file names that are normally mentioned at the beginning of each chapter or exercise.

In the Built Parts folder you will also find copies of the parts, assemblies and drawings that were created for cross references or reviewing purposes.

It would be best to make a copy of the content to your local hard drive and work from these documents, and then safely store the original CD.

Who this book is for

This book is for the mid-level user, who is already familiar with the SolidWorks program and its add-ins. It is also a great resource for the more CAD literate individuals who want to expand their knowledge of the different features that SolidWorks 2013 has to offer.

The organization of the book

The chapters in this book are organized in the logical order in which you would learn the SolidWorks 2013 program. Each chapter will guide you through some different tasks, from navigating through the user interface, to exploring the toolbars, from some simple 3D modeling and move on to more complex tasks that are common to all SolidWorks releases. There is also a self-test questionnaire at the end of each chapter to ensure that you have gained sufficient knowledge before moving on to the next chapter.

The conventions in this book

This book uses the following conventions to describe the actions you perform when using the keyboard and mouse to work in SolidWorks 2013:

Click: means to press and release the mouse button. A click of a mouse button is used to select a command or an item on the screen.

Double Click: means to quickly press and release the left mouse button twice. A double mouse click is used to open a program, or showing the dimensions of a feature.

Right Click: means to press and release the right mouse button. A right mouse click is used to display a list of commands, a list of shortcuts that is related to the selected item.

Click and Drag: means to position the mouse cursor over an item on the screen and then press and hold down the left mouse button; still holding down the left button, move the mouse to the new destination and release the mouse button. Drag and drop makes it easy to move things around within a SolidWorks document.

Bolded words: indicated the action items that you need to perform.

Italic words: Side notes and tips that give you additional information, or to explain special conditions that may occur during the course of the task.

Numbered Steps: indicates that you should follow these steps in order to successfully perform the task.

Icons: indicates the buttons or commands that you need to press.

SolidWorks 2013

SolidWorks 2013 is program suite, or a collection of engineering programs that can help you design better products faster. SolidWorks 2013 contains different combinations of programs; some of the programs used in this book may not be available in your suites.

Start and exit SolidWorks

SolidWorks allows you to start its program in several ways. You can either double click on its shortcut icon on the desktop, or go to the Start menu and select the following: All Program / SolidWorks 2013 / SolidWorks, or drag a SolidWorks document and drop it on the SolidWorks shortcut icon.

Before exiting SolidWorks, be sure to save any open documents, and then click File / Exit; you can also click the X button on the top right of your screen to exit the program.

Using the Toolbars

You can use toolbars to select commands in SolidWorks rather than using the drop down menus. Using the toolbars is normally faster. The toolbars come with commonly used commands in SolidWorks, but they can be customized to help you work more efficiently.

To access the toolbars, either right click in an empty spot on the top right of your screen or select View / Toolbars.

To customize the toolbars, select Tools / Customize. When the dialog pops up, click on the Commands tab, select a Category, and then drag an icon out of the dialog box and drop it on a toolbar that you want to customize. To remove an icon from a toolbar, drag an icon out of the toolbar and drop it into the dialog box.

Using the task pane

The task pane is normally kept on the right side of your screen. It display various options like SolidWorks resources, Design library, File explorer, Search, View palette, Appearances and Scenes, Custom properties, Built-in libraries, Technical alerts and news, etc,.

The task pane provides quick access to any of the mentioned items by offering the drag and drop function to all of its contents. You can see a large preview of a SolidWorks document before opening it. New documents can be saved in the task pane at anytime, and existing documents can also be edited and re-saved. The task pane can be resized, close or move to different location on your screen if needed.

Table of Contents

Table of Contents

Table of Contents

Table of Contents

Table of Contents

Table of Contents

Sheet Metal Topics

Table of Contents

Table of Contents

Table of Contents

Top-Down Assembly Topics

Introduction

Introduction

CSWP Core Preparation Practice

Glossary

Index

SolidWorks 2013 Quick-Guides:

Quick Reference Guide to SolidWorks 2013 Command Icons and Toolbars.

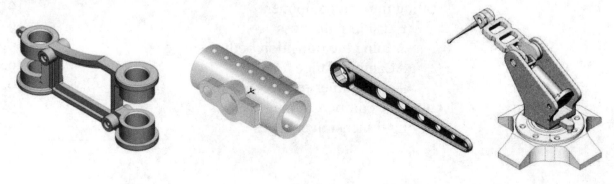

Introduction

SolidWorks User Interface

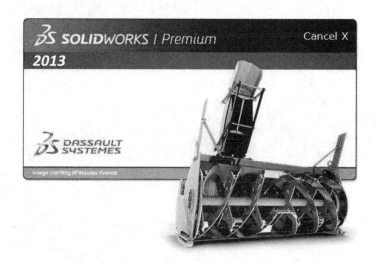

The SolidWorks 2013 User Interface

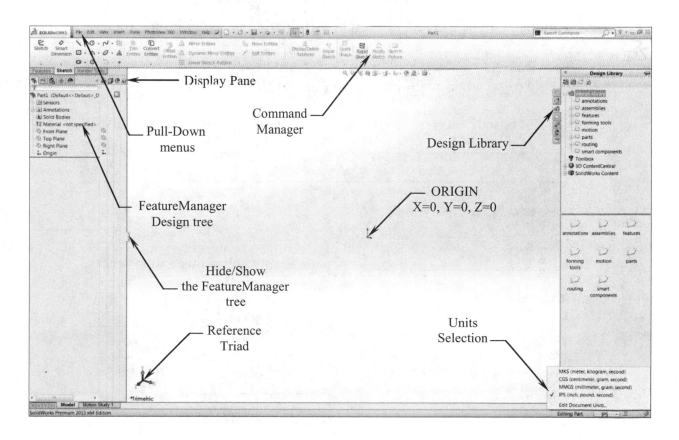

Display Pane

Command Manager

Design Library

Pull-Down menus

FeatureManager Design tree

ORIGIN
X=0, Y=0, Z=0

Hide/Show the FeatureManager tree

Reference Triad

Units Selection

The 3 reference planes:

- The Front, Top and the Right plane are 90°apart. They share the same center point called the Origin.

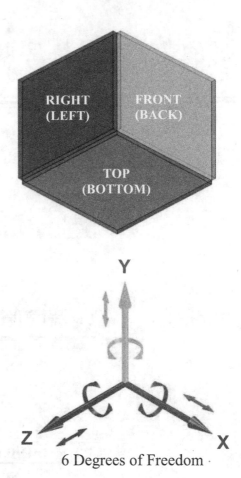

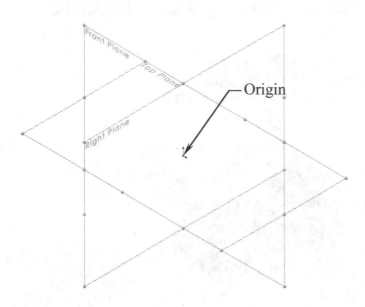

—Origin

6 Degrees of Freedom

The Toolbars:

- Toolbars can be moved, docked or left floating in the graphics area.

- They can also be "shaped" from horizontal to vertical, or from a single to double rows when dragging on their corners.

- The CommandManager is recommended for the newer releases of SolidWorks.

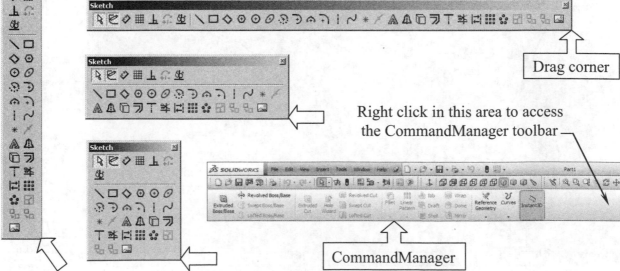

Drag corner

Right click in this area to access the CommandManager toolbar

CommandManager

Introduction

- If CommandManager is not used, toolbars can be docked or leave floating.

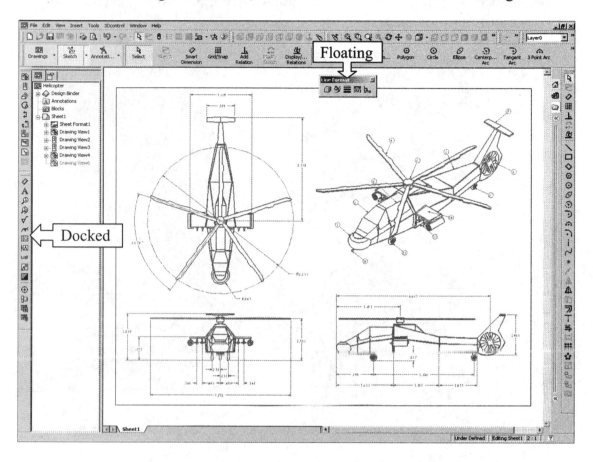

- Toolbars can be toggled off or on by activating or de-activating their check boxes:

- Select **Tools / Customize / Toolbars** tab.

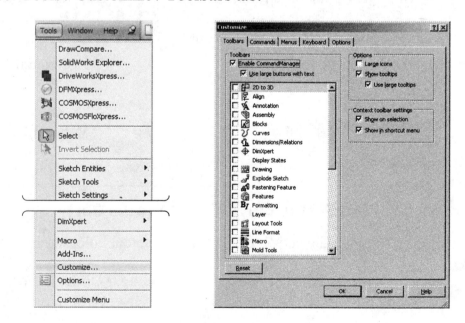

- The icons in the toolbars can be enlarged when its check box is selected ☐ Large icons

The View ports: You can view or work with SolidWorks model or an assembly using one, two or four view ports.

View Orientation

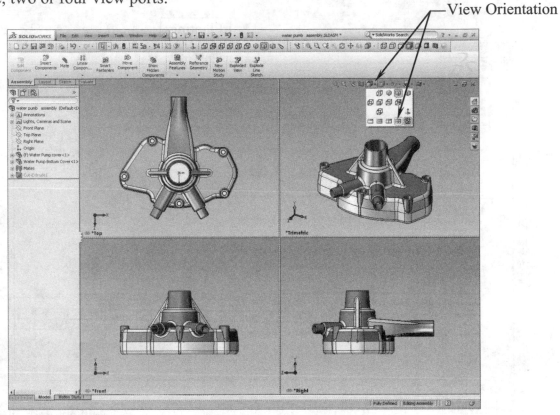

- Some of the **System Feedback symbols** (Inference pointers):

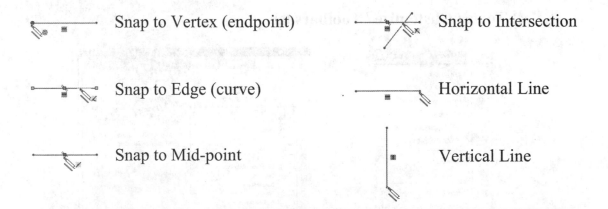

Snap to Vertex (endpoint)	Snap to Intersection
Snap to Edge (curve)	Horizontal Line
Snap to Mid-point	Vertical Line

The Status Bar: (View / Status Bar)

Displays the status of the sketch entity using different colors to indicate:

Green = Selected   **Blue** = Under defined
Black = Fully defined   **Red** = Over defined

2D Sketch examples:

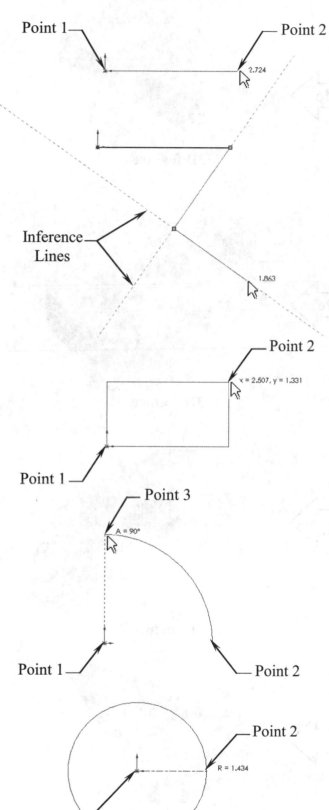

Click-Drag-Release: Single entity.

(Click Point 1, hold the mouse button, drag to point 2 and release).

Click-Release: Continuous multiple entities.

(The Inference Lines appear when the sketch entities are Parallel, Perpendicular or Tangent with each other).

Click-Drag-Release: Single Rectangle

(Click point 1, hold the mouse button, drag to Point 2 and release).

Click-Drag-Release: Single Centerpoint Arc

(Click point 1, hold the mouse button and drag to Point 2, release; then drag to Point 3 and release).

Click-Drag-Release: Single Circle

(Click point 1 [center of circle], hold the mouse button, drag to Point 2 [Radius] and release).

3D Feature examples:

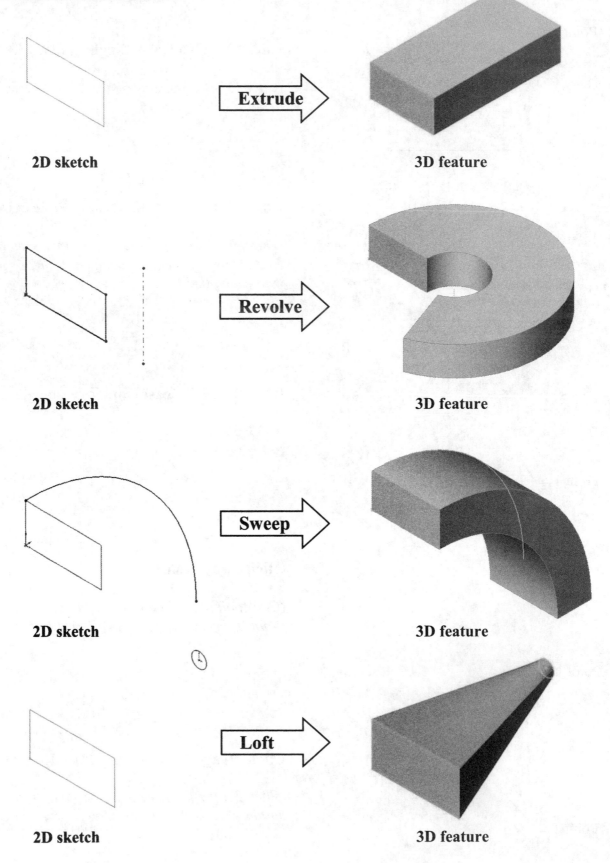

Extrude

2D sketch   3D feature

Revolve

2D sketch   3D feature

Sweep

2D sketch   3D feature

Loft

2D sketch   3D feature

Introduction

Box-Select: Use the Select Pointer 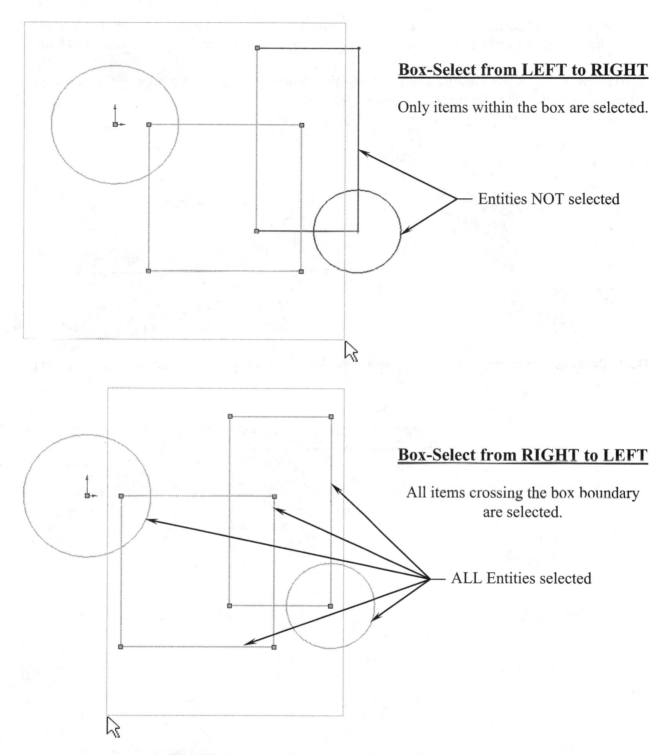 to drag a selection box around items.

Box-Select from LEFT to RIGHT

Only items within the box are selected.

Entities NOT selected

Box-Select from RIGHT to LEFT

All items crossing the box boundary are selected.

ALL Entities selected

The default geometry type selected is as follows:

* Part documents – edges * Assembly documents – components * Drawing documents - sketch entities,
dims & annotations. * To select multiple entities, hold down **Ctrl** while selecting after the first selection.

The <u>Mouse Gestures</u> for Sketches, Drawings and Parts

- Similar to a keyboard shortcut, you can use a Mouse Gesture to execute a command. A total of 8 keyboard shortcuts can be independently mapped and stored in the Mouse Gesture Guides.

- To activate the Mouse Gesture Guide, **right-click-and-drag** to see the current eight-gestures, then simply select the command that you want to use.

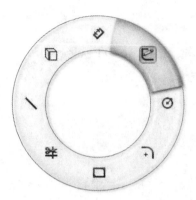

Mouse Gestures for Sketches

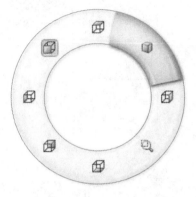

Mouse Gestures for Parts & Assemblies

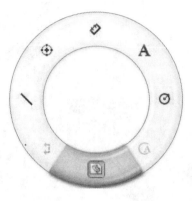

Mouse Gestures for Drawings

- To customize the Mouse Gestures and include your favorite shortcuts, go to:

Tools / Customize.

- From the **Mouse Gestures** tab, select **All Commands** and enable the **Show only commands with Mouse Gestures assigned** checkbox.

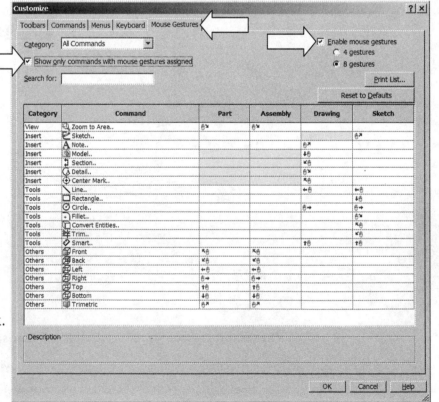

Introduction

Fit to Left display —| |— Fit to Right display

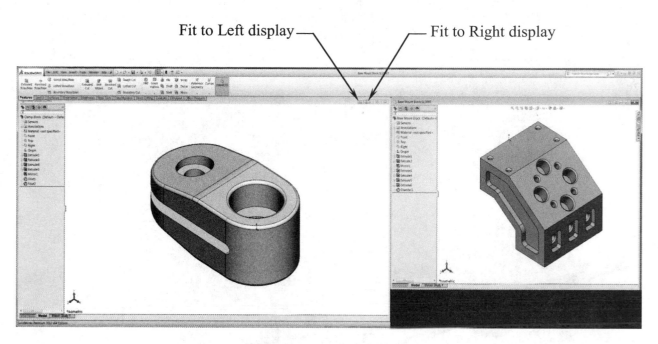

Dual monitors display

Image courtesy of ABCO Automation, Inc.

Text and images created using Windows 7 SP1 and SolidWorks 2013 64bit SP0

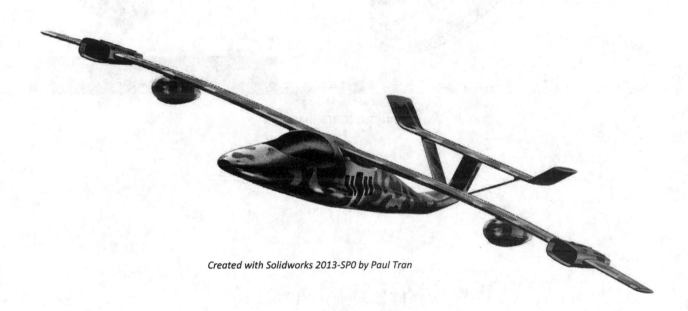

Created with Solidworks 2013-SP0 by Paul Tran

CHAPTER 1

Introduction To 3D Sketch

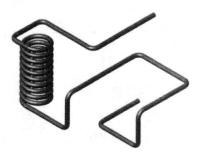

Introduction to 3D Sketch

Using SolidWorks enables you to create 3D sketches. A 3D-sketch consists of lines and arcs in series and splines. You can use a 3D sketch as a sweep path, as a guide curve for a loft or sweep, a centerline for a loft, or as one of the key entitics in a piping system. Geometric relations can also be added to 3D Sketches.

Parameters

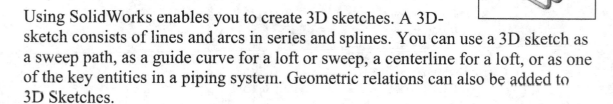

- **X Coordinate**

- **Y Coordinate**

- **Z Coordinate**

- **Curvature** (Spline curvature at the frame point)

- **Tangency** (In the **XY** plane)

- **Tangency** (In the **XZ** plane)

- **Tangency** (In the **YZ** plane)

Space Handle

When working in a 3D sketch, a graphical assistant is provided to help you maintain your orientation while you sketch on several planes. This assistant is called a *space handle*. The space handle appears when the first point of a line or spline is defined on a selected plane. Using the space handle you can select the axis along which you want to sketch.

Introduction to 3D Sketch

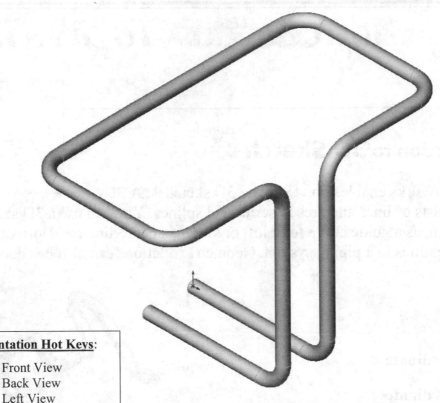

View Orientation Hot Keys:

Cntrl + 1 = Front View
Cntrl + 2 = Back View
Cntrl + 3 = Left View
Cntrl + 4 = Right View
Cntrl + 5 = Top View
Cntrl + 6 = Bottom View
Cntrl + 7 = Isometric View
Cntrl + 8 = Normal To
          Selection

Dimensioning Standards: **ANSI**
Units: **INCHES** – 3 Decimals

Tools Needed:

3D Sketch	2D Sketch	Sketch Line
Circle	Dimension	Add Geometric Relations
Sketch Fillet	Tab Key	Base/ Boss Sweep

1. Starting a new part file: Select **File / New / Part / OK**.

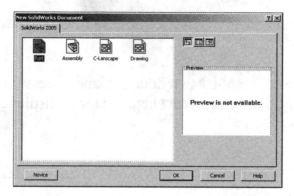

2. Using 3D Sketch:

- Click  or select **Insert / 3D Sketch**, and change to **Isometric view** .

- Select the Line tool and sketch the first line along the **X** axis.

Reference Axis
Indicator

- Sketch the second line along the **Y** axis as shown.

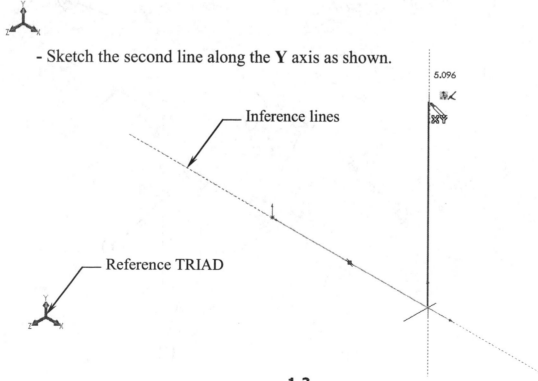

Inference lines

5.096

Reference TRIAD

3. Changing direction:

- By default your sketch is relative to the default coordinate system in the model.

- To switch to one of the other two default planes, press the **TAB** key and the reference origin of the current sketch plane is displayed on that plane.

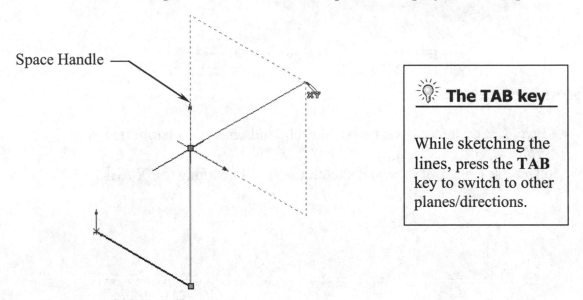

Space Handle ——

> ### The TAB key
>
> While sketching the lines, press the **TAB** key to switch to other planes/directions.

4. Completing the profile:

- Follow the axis as labeled; press **TAB** if necessary to change the direction.

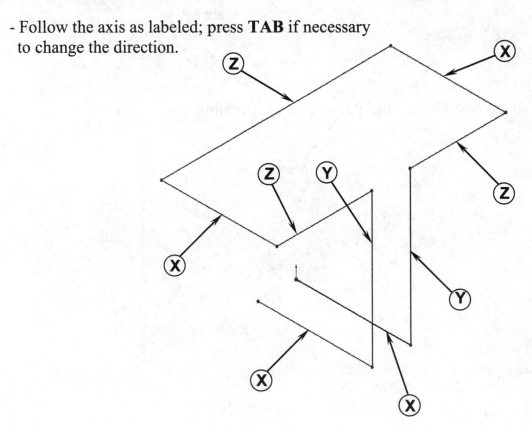

5. Adding dimensions:

- Click 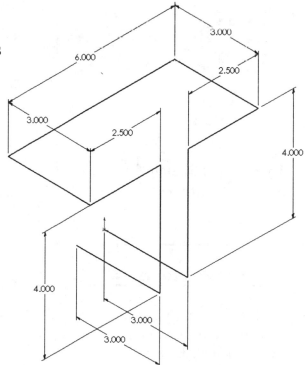 or select **Tools / Dimensions / Smart Dimension**.

- Click on the first line and add a dimension of **3.00"**.

- There is not a general sequence
  to follow when adding dimensions,
  so for this lesson, add the dimensions
  in the same order you sketched the lines.

- Continue adding the dimensions
  to fully define the 3D sketch
  as shown.

- Re-arrange the dimensions so
  they are easy to read, which
  makes editing a little easier.

6. Adding the Sketch Fillets:

- Click or select **Tools / Sketch Tools / Fillet**.

- Add **.500"** fillets to <u>all</u> the intersections as indicated.

- Enable the **Keep Constrained Corner** check box (Maintains the virtual intersection point if the vertex has dimensions or relations).

- Click **OK** when finished.

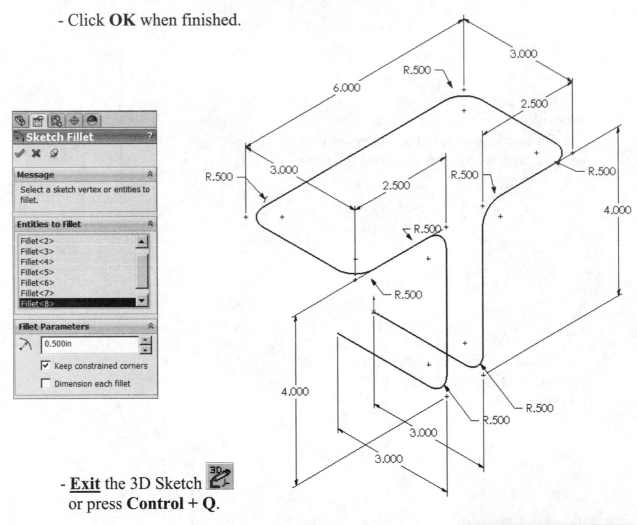

- **Exit** the 3D Sketch or press **Control + Q**.

💡 **Geometric Relations**

Geometric Relations such as Along Z and Equal can also be use to replace some of the duplicate dimensions.

7. Sketching the Sweep Profile:

- Select the <u>Right</u> plane from the FeatureManager tree.

- Click 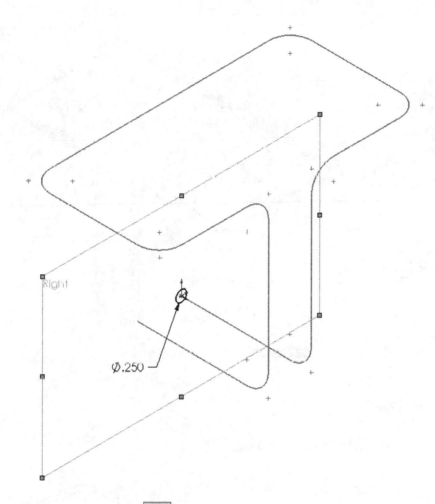 to open a new sketch or select **Insert / Sketch**.

- Sketch a Circle ⊕ using the Origin as the center. (The system automatically creates a Coincident relation between the Center of the circle and the Origin.)

Ø.250

- Add a **Ø.250** dimension ⬦ to fully define the circle.

- **Exit** the Sketch ✏ or select **Insert / Sketch**.

<u>Note:</u>

- *The Sweep Profile should be Pierced or Coincident with the Sweep Path.*
- *The Swept Boss/Base command is only available when the sketch pencil is off.*

8. Creating the Swept feature:

- Click 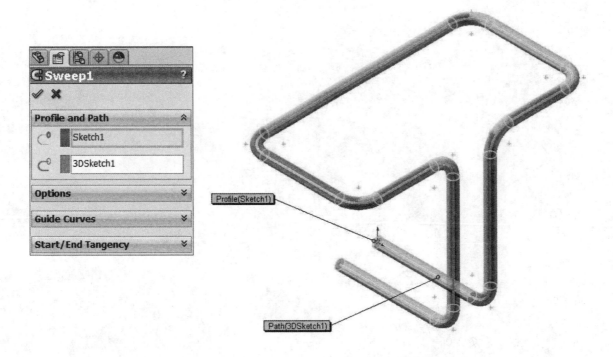 or select **Insert / Boss-Base / Sweep**.

- Select the Circle as Sweep Profile ⌒⁰ (Sketch1).

- Select the 3D Sketch to use as Sweep Path ⌒⁰ (3Dsketch1).

- Click **OK** ✓.

9. Saving your work:

- Select **File / Save As / 3D Sketch / Save**.

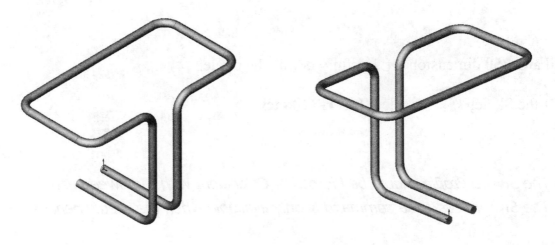

Questions for Review

1. When using 3D Sketch you do not have to pre-select a plane as you would in 2D Sketch.
   - a. True
   - b. False

2. The space handle appears only after the first point of a line is started.
   - a. True
   - b. False

3. To switch to other planes in 3D Sketch mode, press:
   - a. Up Arrow
   - b. Down Arrow
   - c. TAB key
   - d. CONTROL key

4. Dimensions cannot be used in 3D Sketch mode.
   - a. True
   - b. False

5. Geometric Relations cannot be used in 3D Sketch mode.
   - a. True
   - b. False

6. All sketch tools in 2D Sketch are also available in 3D Sketch.
   - a. True
   - b. False

7. When adding sketch fillets, the option Keep Constrained Corner will create a virtual intersection point, but will not create a dimension.
   - a. True
   - b. False

8. 3D Sketch entities can be used as a path in a swept feature.
   - a. True
   - b. False

7. FALSE   8. TRUE
5. FALSE   6. FALSE
3. C   4. FALSE
1. TRUE   2. TRUE

Exercise: Sweep with 3D Sketch

1. Create the part shown using 3D Sketch.

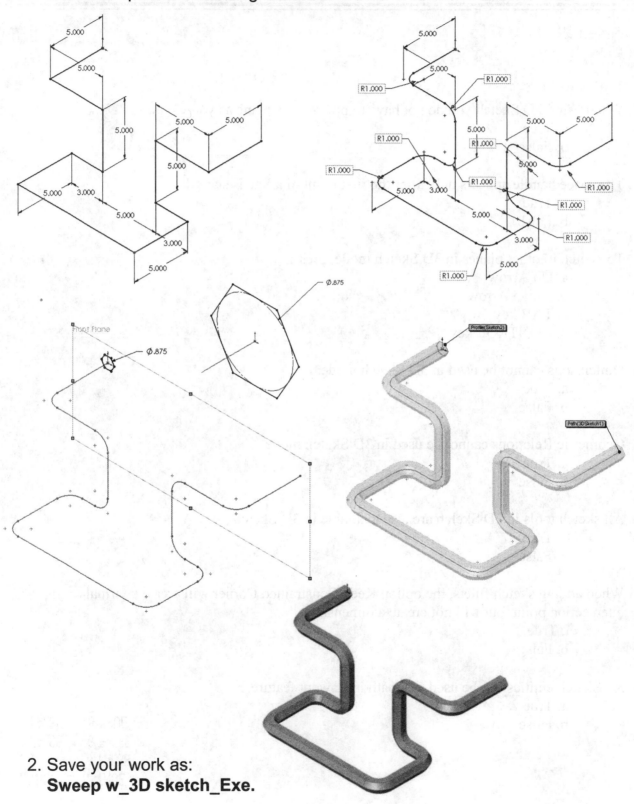

2. Save your work as:
   Sweep w_3D sketch_Exe.

Exercise: 3D Sketch & Planes

A 3D sketch normally consists of lines and arcs in series, and splines. You can use a 3D sketch as a sweep path, as a guide curve for a loft or sweep, a centerline for a loft, or as one of the key entities in a routing system.

The following exercise demonstrates how several planes can be used to help define the directions of 3D Sketch Entities.

1. Sketching the reference Pivot lines:

- Select the <u>Top</u> plane and

 open a new sketch 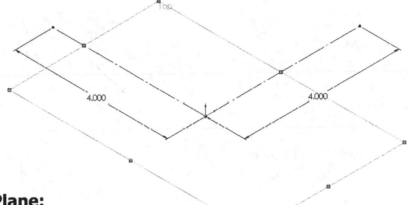 .

- Sketch **2** Centerlines

 and add Dimensions
 as shown.

2. Creating the 1st 45º Plane:

- Select **Insert/Reference Geometry/Planes** .

- Click the **At Angle** option and enter **45** for Angle .

- Select the **top** plane and the **vertical line** as noted.

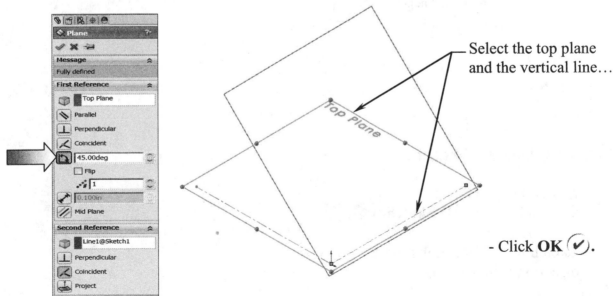

Select the top plane and the vertical line…

- Click **OK** .

3. Creating the 2nd 45° Plane:

- Select **Insert/Reference Geometry/Planes** 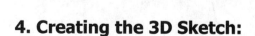.

- Click the **At Angle** option and enter **45** for Angle .

- Select the **front** plane and the **horizontal line** as noted.

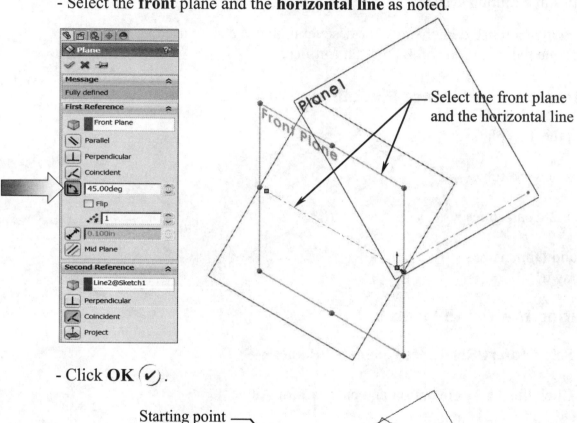

Select the front plane and the horizontal line

- Click **OK** .

Starting point
(At the endpoint
of the centerline).

1st line

1.534

4. Creating the 3D Sketch:

- Select the Top plane
  and click **Insert/3D Sketch** .

- Sketch the 1st line along the **Y**
  direction as noted.

- Select the **Plane2** (45 deg.) from the Feature Manager tree and Sketch the 2nd line along the **Y** direction (watch the cursor feedback symbol).

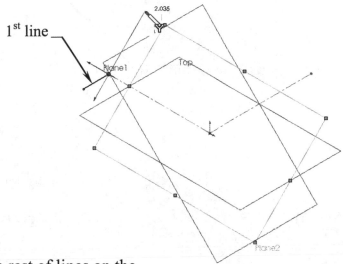

- Sketch the rest of lines on the planes as labeled.

- For clarity, hide all the planes (select the **View** menu and click off **Planes**). We will select the planes from the FeatureManager tree when needed

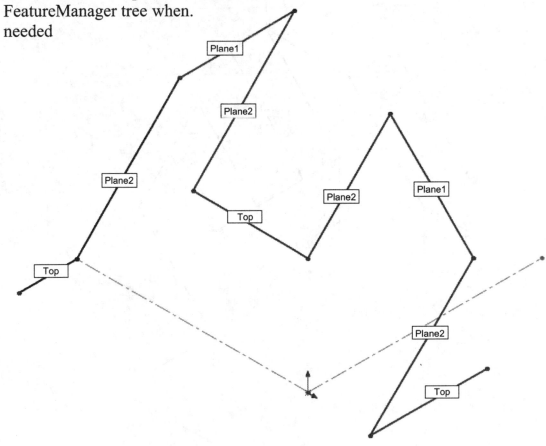

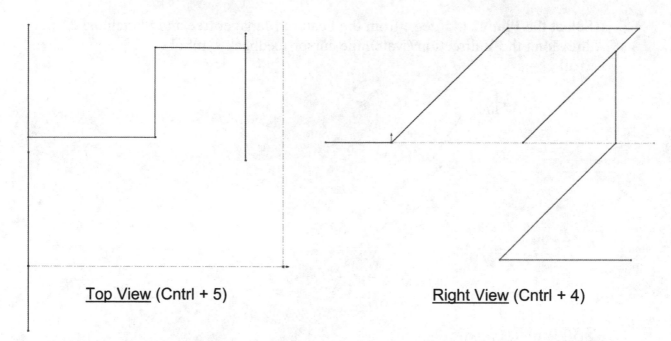

<u>Top View</u> (Cntrl + 5)   <u>Right View</u> (Cntrl + 4)

- Add Dimensions 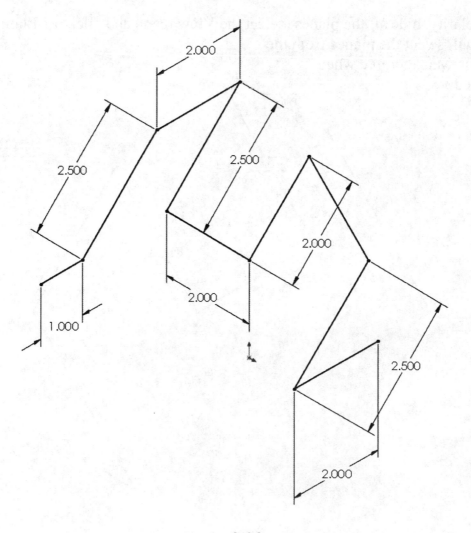 to fully define the sketch.

- Add **Sketch Fillets** 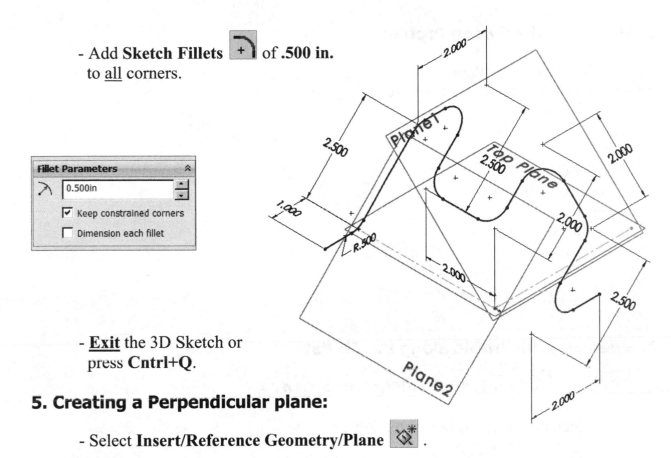 of **.500 in.** to <u>all</u> corners.

Fillet Parameters

0.500in

☑ Keep constrained corners

☐ Dimension each fillet

- **Exit** the 3D Sketch or press **Cntrl+Q**.

5. Creating a Perpendicular plane:

- Select **Insert/Reference Geometry/Plane**.

- Select the **line** and its **endpoint** approximately as shown.

- The **Perpendicular** option should be selected by default.

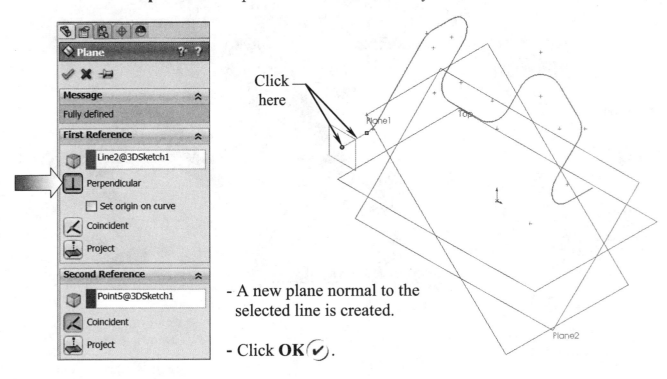

Plane

Message ⌃

Fully defined

First Reference ⌃

Line2@3DSketch1

⊥ Perpendicular

☐ Set origin on curve

Coincident

Project

Second Reference ⌃

Point5@3DSketch1

Coincident

Project

Click here

- A new plane normal to the selected line is created.

- Click **OK**.

6. Sketching the Sweep Profile:

- Select the <u>new plane</u>
(Plane3) and open a new sketch 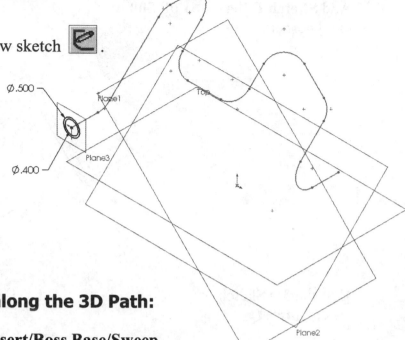 .

- Sketch 2 Circles ⊕
on the same center and
add the dimensions as
shown to fully define
the sketch.

7. Sweeping the Profile along the 3D Path:

- Click 🗗 or Select **Insert/Boss Base/Sweep**

- Select the Circles as the Sweep Profile ⌐⁰ .

- Select the 3D Sketch as the Sweep Path ⌐⁰ .

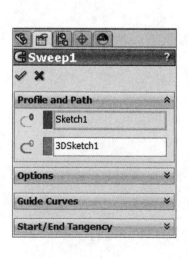

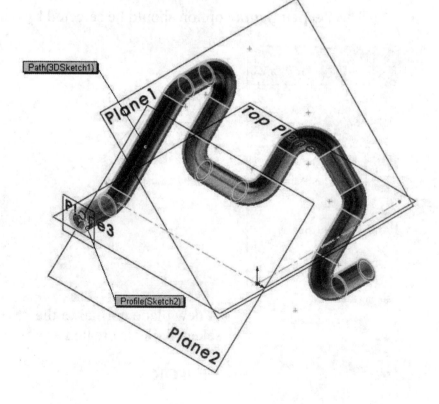

- Click **OK** ✅ .

- The resulting Swept feature.

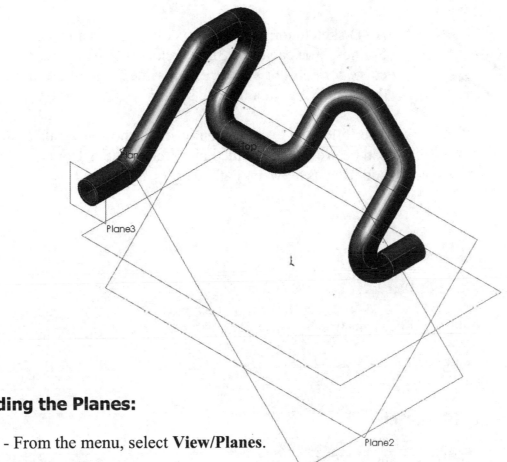

8. Hiding the Planes:

- From the menu, select **View/Planes**.

- The planes are temporarily put away from the scene.

9. Saving your work:

- Click **File/Save As: 3D Sketch_Planes**.

- Click **Save**.

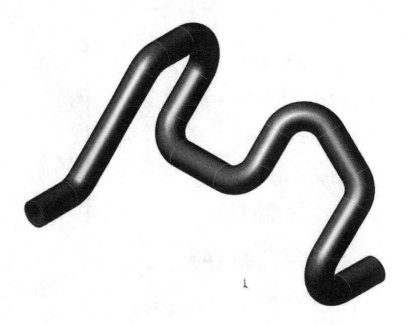

Exercise: 3D Sketch & Composite Curve

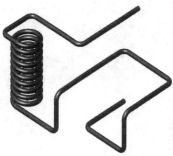

A 3D sketch normally consists of lines and arcs in series and Splines. You can use a 3D sketch as a sweep path, as a guide curve for a loft or sweep, a centerline for a loft, or as one of the key entities in a routing system.

The following exercise demonstrates how several 3D Sketches can be created, combined into 1 continuous Composite Curve, and used as a Sweep Path.

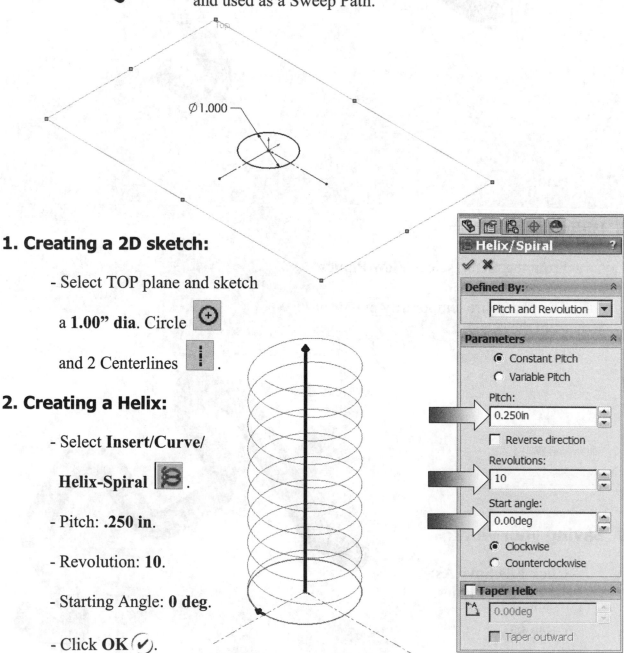

Ø1.000

1. Creating a 2D sketch:

- Select TOP plane and sketch

a **1.00" dia**. Circle ⊕

and 2 Centerlines ⋮ .

2. Creating a Helix:

- Select **Insert/Curve/**

Helix-Spiral 🗷 .

- Pitch: **.250 in**.

- Revolution: **10**.

- Starting Angle: **0 deg**.

- Click **OK** ✔ .

Helix/Spiral

Defined By:

Pitch and Revolution

Parameters

○ Constant Pitch
○ Variable Pitch

Pitch:
0.250in

☐ Reverse direction

Revolutions:
10

Start angle:
0.00deg

○ Clockwise
○ Counterclockwise

☐ **Taper Helix**
0.00deg

☐ Taper outward

3. Creating the 1st 3D sketch:

- Select **Insert/3D Sketch**

- Select the Line command
and sketch the 1st line
along the X direction.

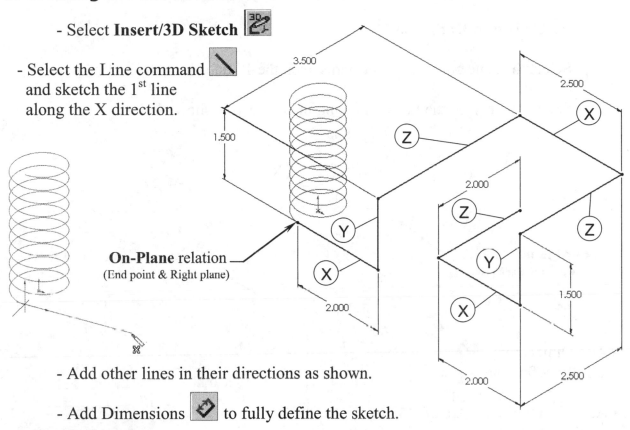

On-Plane relation
(End point & Right plane)

- Add other lines in their directions as shown.

- Add Dimensions to fully define the sketch.

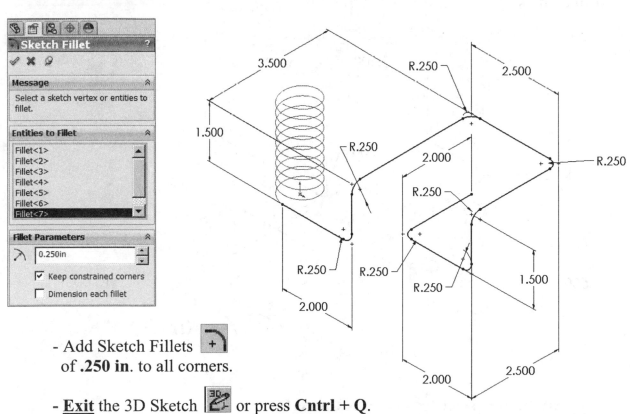

- Add Sketch Fillets
of **.250 in**. to all corners.

- **Exit** the 3D Sketch or press **Cntrl + Q**.

4. Creating the 2nd 3D sketch:

- Select **Insert/3D Sketch** .

- Select the Line command and sketch the 1st line along the X direction.

- Sketch the rest of the lines following their direction shown below.

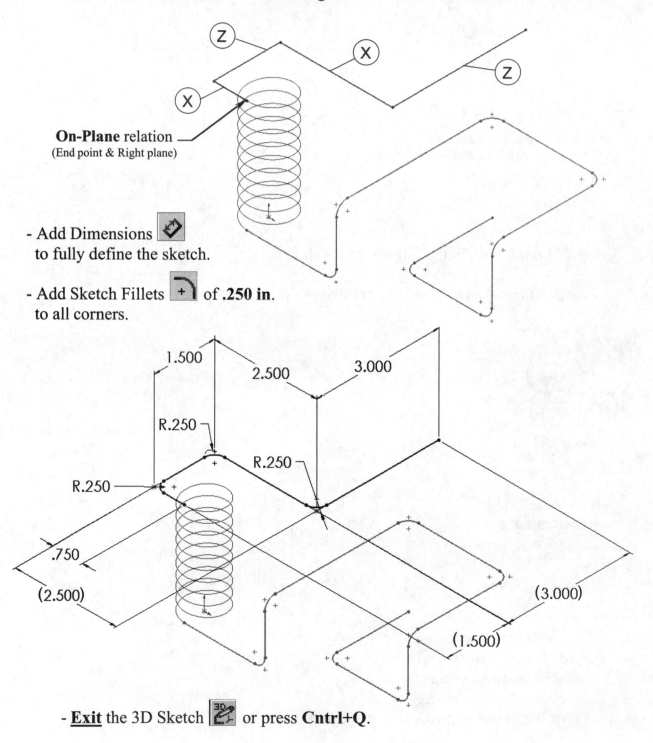

On-Plane relation
(End point & Right plane)

- Add Dimensions
  to fully define the sketch.

- Add Sketch Fillets of **.250 in**.
  to all corners.

1.500
2.500
3.000
R.250
R.250
R.250
.750
(2.500)
(3.000)
(1.500)

- **Exit** the 3D Sketch or press **Cntrl+Q**.

5. Combining the 3 sketches into 1 curve:

- Select **Insert/Curve/Composite** 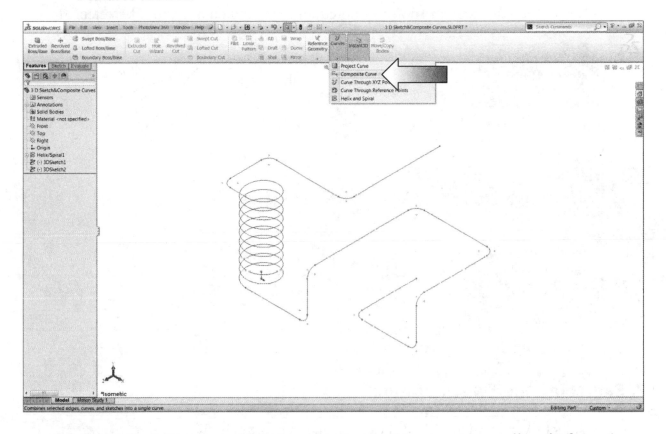 or select it from the Curves button on the Features toolbar.

- Select the 3 Sketches either from the Feature Manager tree or directly from the graphics area.

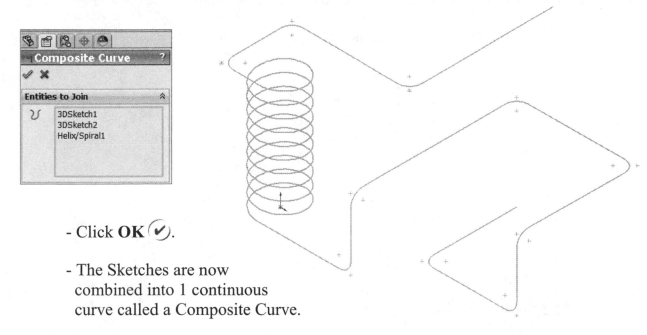

- Click **OK** ✓.

- The Sketches are now combined into 1 continuous curve called a Composite Curve.

6. Creating a new work plane:

- Select **Insert/Reference Geometry/Plane** .

- Select the **edge** and **endpoint** as noted, the Perpendicular should be selected.

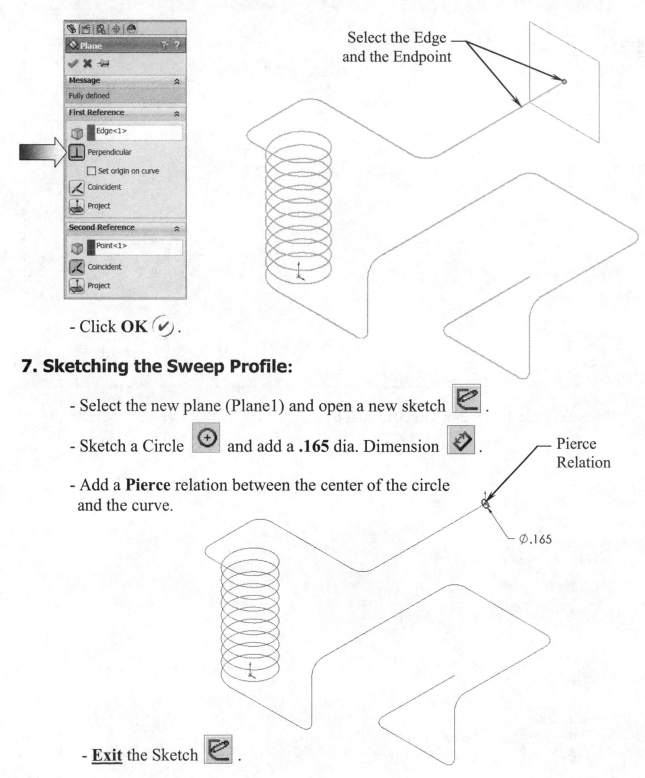

Select the Edge
and the Endpoint

- Click **OK** ✅ .

7. Sketching the Sweep Profile:

- Select the new plane (Plane1) and open a new sketch ✏️ .

- Sketch a Circle ⊕ and add a **.165** dia. Dimension ⬧ .

- Add a **Pierce** relation between the center of the circle
  and the curve.

Pierce
Relation

∅.165

- **Exit** the Sketch ✏️ .

8. Sweeping the Profile along the Path:

- Select **Insert/Boss Base/ Sweep**  .

- Select the Circle as the Sweep Profile.

- Select the Composite Curve as the Sweep Path.

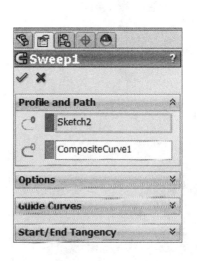

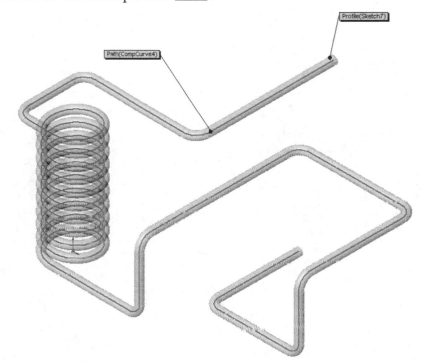

- Click **OK**.

9. Saving your work:

- Click **File/Save As**.

- Enter **3D Sketch_ Composite Curve**.

- Click **Save**.

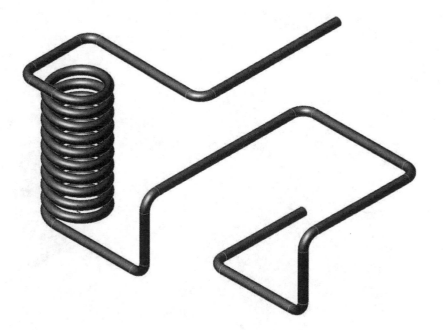

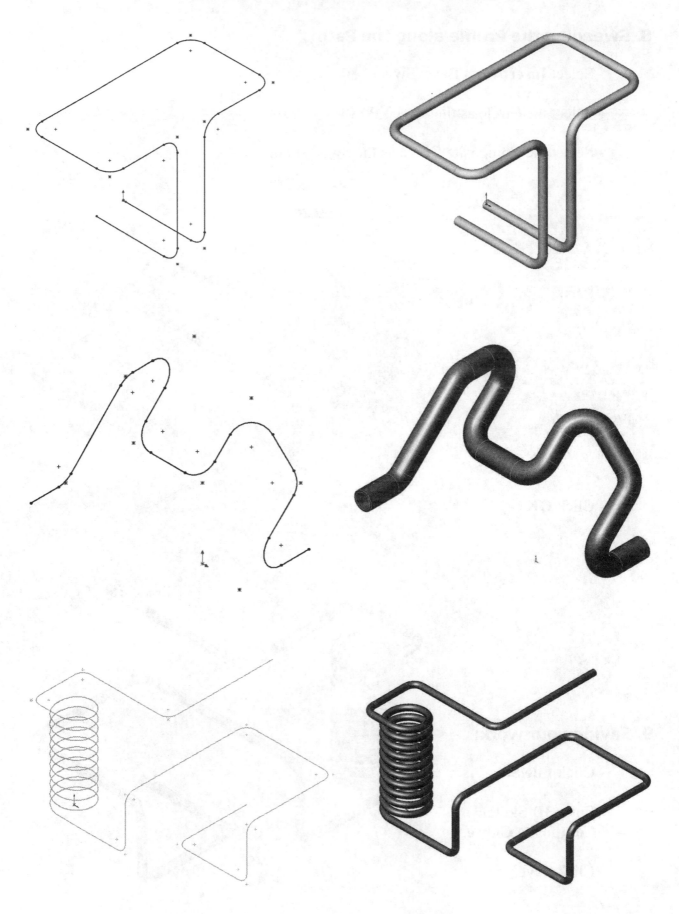

CHAPTER 2

Plane Creation

Planes
Advanced Topics

- In SolidWorks, planes arc not only used to sketch geometry, but also used to create section views of a model or an assembly. Planes are also used as cnd conditions to extrude features and as neutral planes to define the draft angles, etc.

- There arc several options to create planes:

 Parallel Plane.   At Angle Plane.

 Perpcndicular Plane.   Offset Distance Plane.

 Coincident Plane.   Mid Plane.

 Project Plane.

- Each plane requires slightly different types of references, some of them may require only one and some others may require two or three.

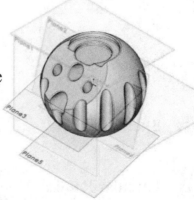

- This chapter discusses how planes are created using sketch geometry and other features that are available in the model, as references.

Plane Creation

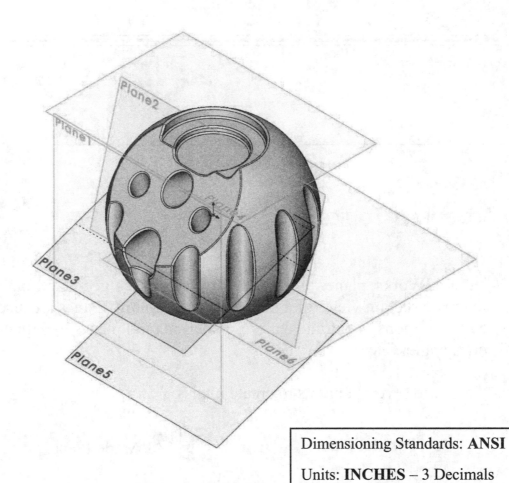

Dimensioning Standards: **ANSI**

Units: **INCHES** – 3 Decimals

Tools Needed:

Insert Sketch	Rectangle	Circle
Planes	Add Geometric Relations	Dimension
Sketch Mirror	Offset Entities	Boss/Base Revolve
Circular Pattern	Extruded Cut	Fillet/Round

1. Starting with a new Part document:

- Select **File / New / Part** and click **OK**.

- Select the <u>Front</u> plane from the FeatureManager tree.

- Click 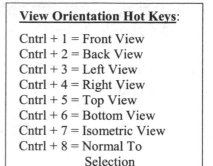 or select **Insert / Sketch**.

- Sketch the profile below and add dimensions 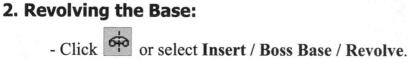 as shown. (It might be easier to sketch a circle, instead of a centerpoint arc, add the 2 centerlines, and then trim away the bottom half of the circle).

<table>
<tr><td><u>View Orientation Hot Keys</u>:</td></tr>
<tr><td>Cntrl + 1 = Front View</td></tr>
<tr><td>Cntrl + 2 = Back View</td></tr>
<tr><td>Cntrl + 3 = Left View</td></tr>
<tr><td>Cntrl + 4 = Right View</td></tr>
<tr><td>Cntrl + 5 = Top View</td></tr>
<tr><td>Cntrl + 6 = Bottom View</td></tr>
<tr><td>Cntrl + 7 = Isometric View</td></tr>
<tr><td>Cntrl + 8 = Normal To
Selection</td></tr>
</table>

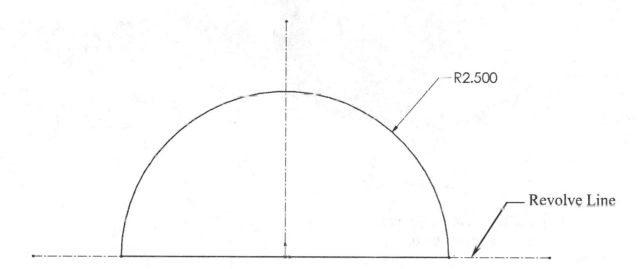

R2.500

Revolve Line

2. Revolving the Base:

- Click 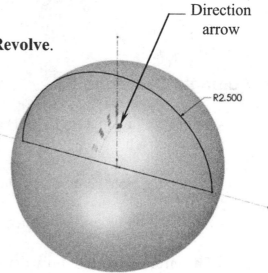 or select **Insert / Boss Base / Revolve**.

- Set Revolve Type to: **Blind** .

- Set Revolve Angle to: **360 deg.** .

- Click **OK** .

- *Note: Drag the Direction arrow to see the preview of the rotate angle.*

Direction arrow

R2.500

3. Creating a Tangent plane: (Requires a cylindrical face and a parallel plane).

- Click 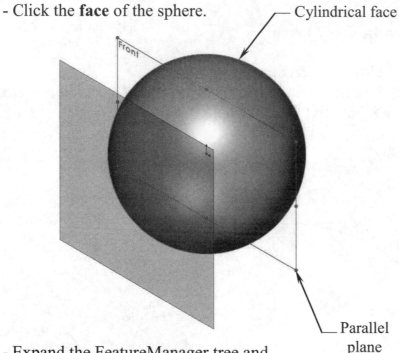 or select: **Insert / Reference Geometry / Plane**.

- Click the **face** of the sphere.

Cylindrical face

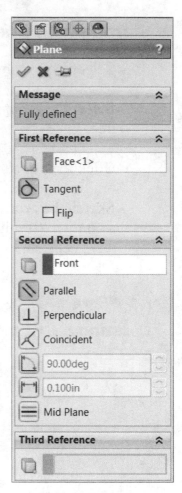

Parallel plane

- Expand the FeatureManager tree and select the **Front** plane.

- The **Tangent** option is selected automatically.

- Click the **Parallel** option in the Second Reference section.

- Click **OK** ✓.

4. Adding a Center hole:

- Select the <u>new plane</u> (Plane1) and open a new sketch.

- Sketch a Circle centered on the origin.

- Add a **1.000"** diameter dimension.

- The circle should be fully defined at this point.

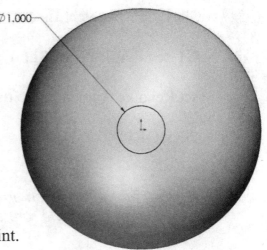

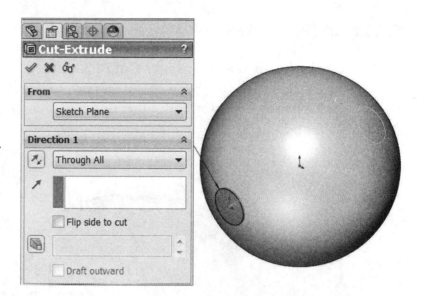

- Click or select:
  Insert / Cut / Extrude.

- Select **Through All** for
  Direction 1.

- Click **OK** ⊘.

5. Creating a flat surface:

- Select the <u>Right</u> plane from the FeatureManager tree.

- Click 🖉 or select **Insert / Sketch** and switch to the right view (Ctrl+4).

- Sketch a Line and add the Relations 🔳 as shown.

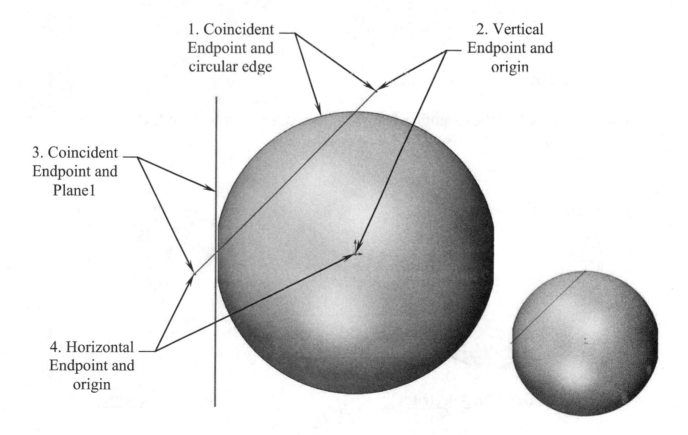

1. Coincident
Endpoint and
circular edge

2. Vertical
Endpoint and
origin

3. Coincident
Endpoint and
Plane1

4. Horizontal
Endpoint and
origin

6. Extruding a Cut:

- Click 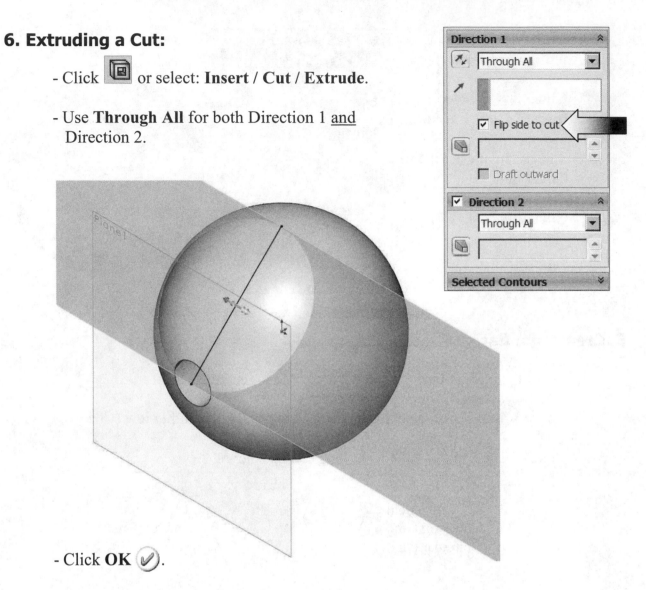 or select: **Insert / Cut / Extrude**.

- Use **Through All** for both Direction 1 <u>and</u> Direction 2.

- Click **OK** ✓.

- Take a look at the examples below for the option **Flip Side to Cut**.

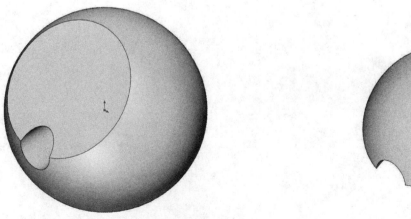

Flip Side to Cut <u>**Selected**</u>   Flip Side to Cut <u>**Cleared**</u>

7. Creating an At-Angle plane: (Requires a Reference Plane, a Reference Axis, and an Angular Dimension).

    - Select the u plane from FeatureManager tree.

    - Click 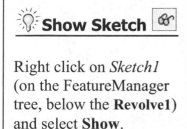 or select **Insert / Reference Geometry / Plane**.

    - Select the horizontal centerline as ref. axis.

    - Select the **At Angle** option.

    - Enter **15 deg**. in the dialog box and click **Flip**.

    - Click **OK** ✓.

Right click on *Sketch1* (on the FeatureManager tree, below the **Revolve1**) and select **Show**.

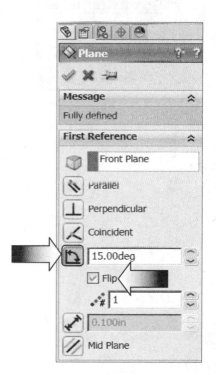

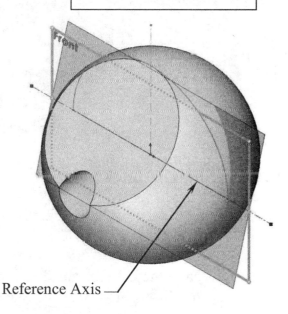

Reference Axis

8. Creating a Ø.750 hole:

- Select the new plane (Plane2).

- Click ✏ or select **Insert / Sketch**.

- Sketch a Circle ⊕ and add the dimensions and a vertical relation as shown.

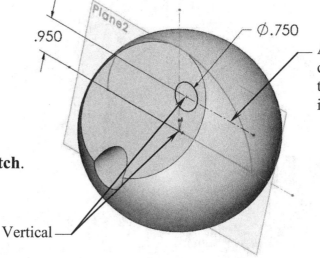

.950

Plane2

Ø.750

Add a ref. centerline to use later in step 10.

Vertical

- Click 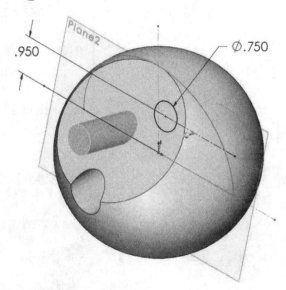 or select **Insert / Cut / Extrude**.

- Direction 1: **Through All**.

- Direction 2: **Through All**.

- Click **OK** ⊘.

9. Showing the Sketches:

- On the FeatureManager tree expand the Cut-Extrude1 (click the + symbol), right click on **Sketch2**, and select **Show**.

- Expand the Cut-Extrude2 (click the + symbol), right-click on **Sketch3**, and select **Show**, also Hide the Sketch1.

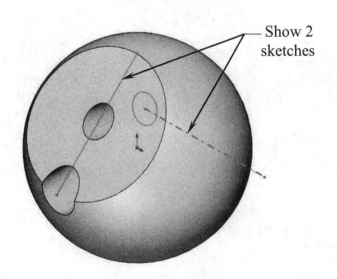

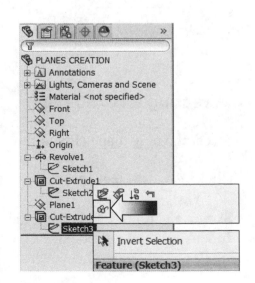

10. Creating a Coincident plane: (Requires a Reference Line and a Sketch Point or a Vertex).

- Click 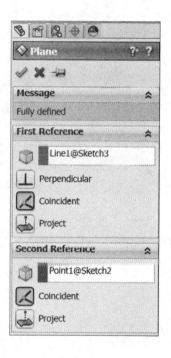 or select **Insert / Reference Geometry / Plane**.

- Select the Centerline and the End point as indicated.

- The **Coincident** option should be selected automatically.

- Click **OK** ✓.

1. Select the centerline (from step 10)

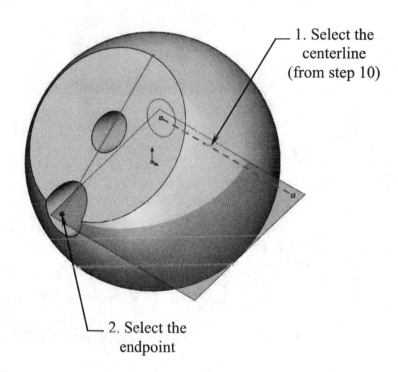

2. Select the endpoint

11. Creating the Ø.500 holes:

- Select the new plane (Plane3).

- Click or select **Insert / Sketch**.

- Sketch a Circle ⊕ and Mirror it ⚠ (Use either Dynamic Mirror or Mirror Entity to mirror the circles).

- Add Dimensions as shown to fully define the sketch.

Mirror Centerline

1.000

1.000

Ø.500

- Click  or select **Insert / Cut / Extrude**.

- Direction 1: **Through All**.

- Direction 2: **Through All**.

- Click **OK** ✅.

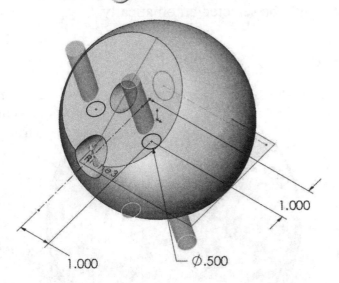

12. Creating a Parallel plane: (Requires a Reference Plane and Reference Point).

- Click or select **Insert / Reference Geometry / Plane**.

- Select the <u>Top</u> plane and the End point as indicated.

- Based on your selection, the system selects the **Parallel Plane** option.

- Click **OK** ✅.

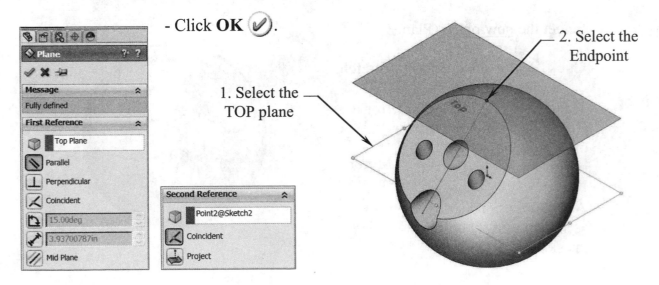

13. Creating the Ø2.500 Recess:

- Select the <u>new Plane</u> (Plane4) and insert a new sketch

- Sketch a Circle ⊕ and add Dimension ◈ .

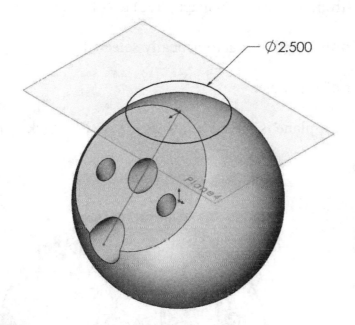

Ø2.500

- Click 🗗 or select **Insert / Cut / Extrude**.

- End Condition: **Blind**.

- Extrude Depth: **.625** in.

- Click **OK** ✓.

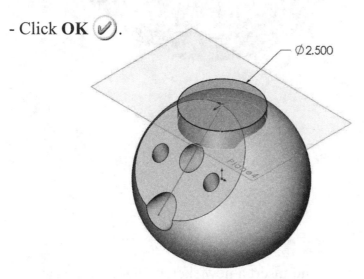

Ø2.500

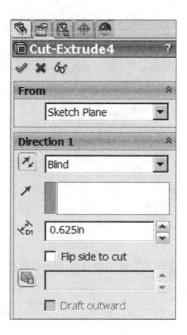

- Hide 👓 the Sketch2, Sketch3 and all planes.

14. Creating an Offset-Distance plane: (Requires a Reference Plane and a Distance dimension).

- Click  or select **Insert / Reference Geometry / Plane**.

- Select Plane2 (from the FeatureManager tree) to offset from.

- The **Offset Distance** option is automatically selected.

- Enter **3.375** for offset value.

- Make sure the new plane is placed below the PLANE2 (click Flip if needed).

- Click **OK** ✓.

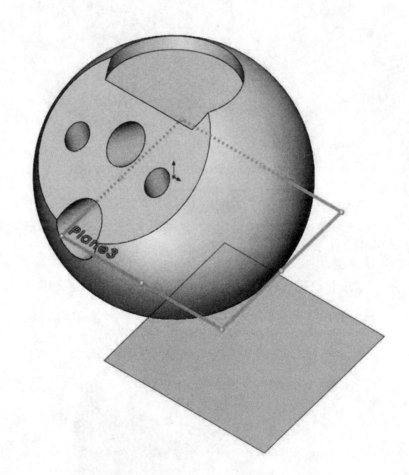

15. Creating the Bore holes:

- Select the <u>new plane</u> (Plane5) and insert a new sketch.

- Select the **circular edge** of the hole and press **Offset-Entities**.

- Enter **.100 in**. for Offset Distance (Only one offset can be done at a time, since the 2 circles are not connecting to each other).

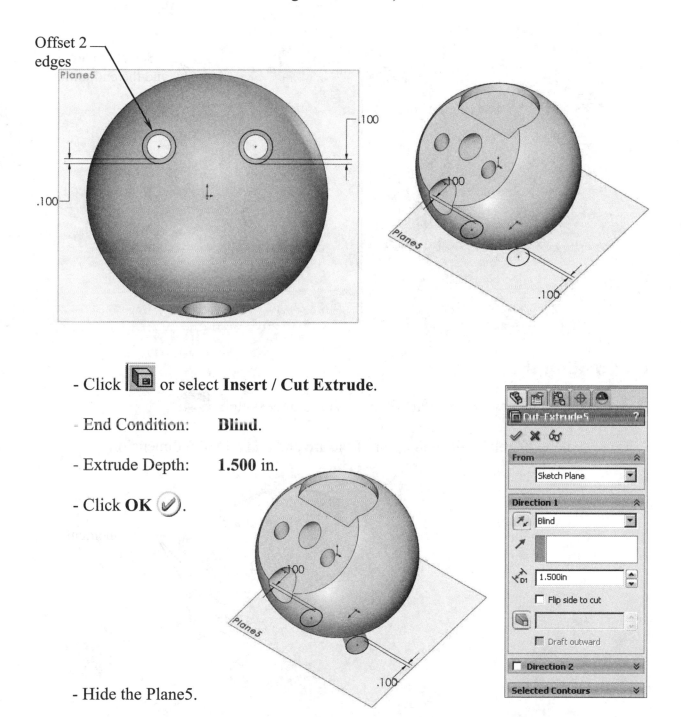

Offset 2 edges

- Click [icon] or select **Insert / Cut Extrude**.

- End Condition: **Blind**.

- Extrude Depth: **1.500** in.

- Click **OK** [icon].

- Hide the Plane5.

16. Creating a Perpendicular plane: (Requires a Reference Line or Curve & a Point).

- Click [icon] or select **Insert / Reference Geometry / Plane**.

- **Show** the Sketch1 and select the Arc and the Endpoint as noted.

- The **Perpendicular** option should be selected automatically.

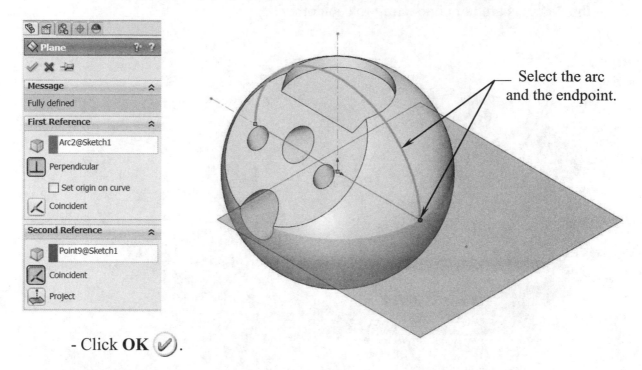

Select the arc and the endpoint.

- Click **OK** ✓.

17. Creating the side-grips:

- Select the <u>new plane</u> (Plane6) and insert a new sketch .

- Sketch a Circle at the end point of the arc and add a **Ø.625** dimension.

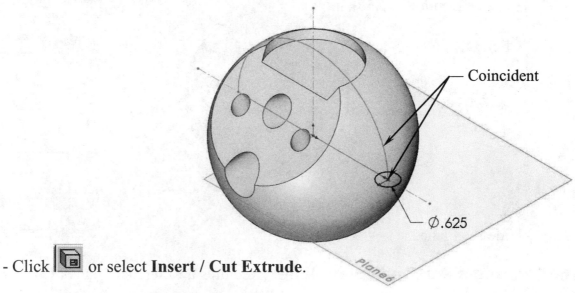

Coincident

Ø.625

Plane6

- Click or select **Insert / Cut Extrude**.

- Direction 1: **Through All**.

- Direction 2: **Through All**.

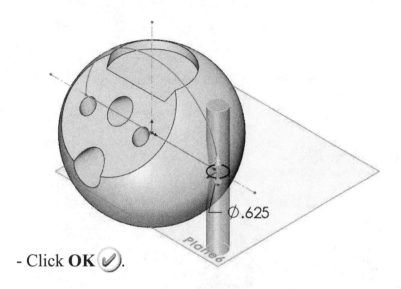

- Click **OK** ✅.

- Hide the Sketch1 and the Plane6.

18. Creating a Circular Pattern of the Grips:

- Click 🔲 or select **Insert / Pattern Mirror / Circular Pattern**.

- Click **View / Temporary Axis** and select the center axis as indicated.

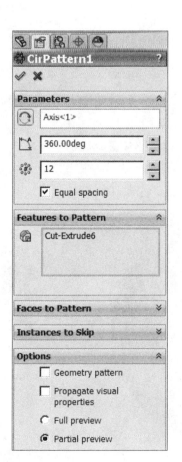

- Equal Spacing: **Enabled**.

- Total Angle: **360 deg**.

- Number of instances: **12**.

- Select the Cut-Extrude6 as Feature To Pattern.

- Click **OK** ✅.

Select this axis ⟶

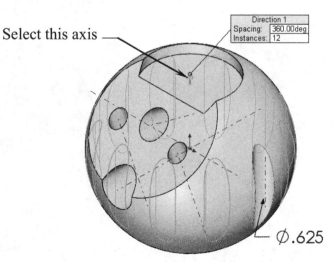

19. Adding another recess:

- Select the <u>upper face</u> of the recess and insert a new sketch .

- Sketch a circle centered on the Origin.

- Add a **1.750 diameter** dimension.

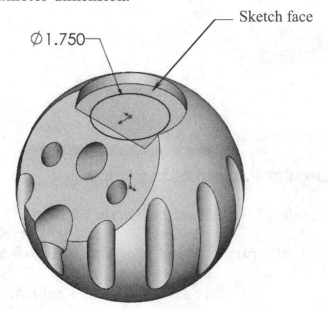

Ø1.750

Sketch face

- Click  or select **Insert / Cut Extrude**.

- End Condition: **Blind**.

- Extrude Depth: **.175** in.

- Click **OK** .

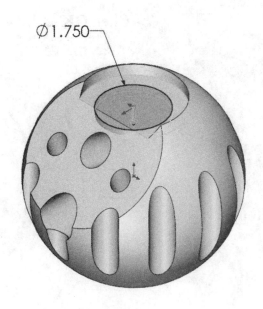

Ø1.750

20. Creating a Mid-Plane: (Requires 2 parallel planes or 2 planar faces).

- Click  or select:
**Insert / Reference
Geometry / Plane**.

- Expand the Feature-
Manager and select the
Plane3 and the **Plane5**
to use as the first and
second references.

- The **Mid-Plane** option
is selected automatically,
if not, click the mid plane
button (arrow).

- A preview of the new
plane appears in
the middle of the
two selected
planes.

- Click **OK** ✓.

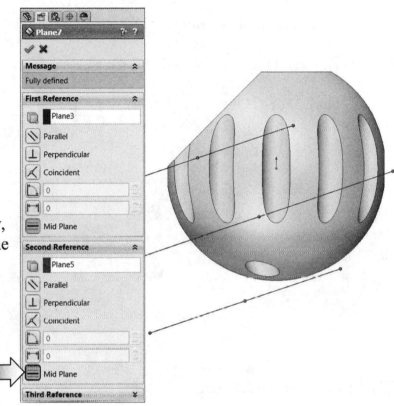

21. Creating a rectangular pocket:

- Select the <u>new plane</u> (Plane7) and insert a new sketch ⬚.

- Sketch a **Center Rectangle** that is centered
on the origin.

- Add the width and
height dimensions
to fully define the
sketch.

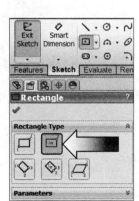

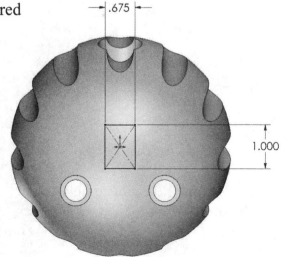

.675

1.000

- Click 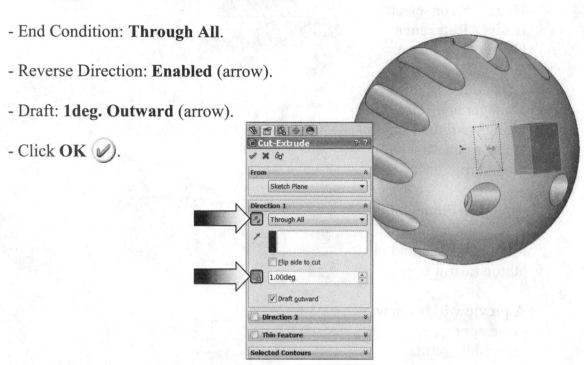 or select **Insert / Cut Extrude**.

- End Condition: **Through All**.

- Reverse Direction: **Enabled** (arrow).

- Draft: **1deg. Outward** (arrow).

- Click **OK** .

22. Adding fillets to the pocket:

- Click 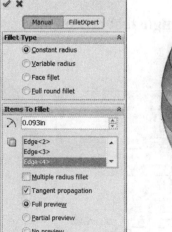 or select **Insert Features / Fillet-Round**.

- Use the default **Constant Radius** option.

- Enter **.093"** for radius.

- Select the **4 edges** of the pocket as noted.

Select 4 edges

- Enable the Full Preview checkbox.

- Click **OK** .

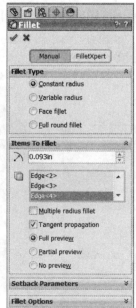

23. Adding Fillets to all edges:

- Drag a box around the part (drag select), to group all of its edges.

- Click or select **Insert Features / Fillet-Round**.

- Enter **.040** for Radius ⟍ | 0.040in | ▲▼ .

- Tangent Propagation: **Enabled**.

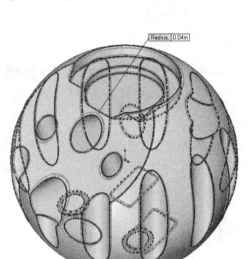

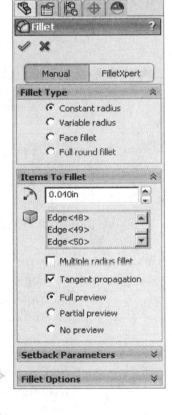

- Click **OK** ✅.

- Hide the planes before saving the part.

24. Saving your work:

- Click **File / Save As / Planes Creation / Save**.

Questions for Review

Plane Creation

1. Planes can be used to section a part or an assembly.
   - a. True
   - b. False

2. A sketch can be extruded to a plane as the end condition by using the Up-To-Surface option.
   - a. True
   - b. False

3. Which one of the options below is not a valid command?
   - a. Parallel plane at Point.
   - b. Offset plane at Distance.
   - c. Perpendicular to another plane at Angle.
   - d. Normal to Curve.

4. To create a plane at Angle, you will need:
   - a. The Angle and a Reference plane.
   - b. The Angle and a pivot Line.
   - c. The Angle, a pivot Line, and a Reference plane.

5. To create a plane through Lines/Points, you will need at least:
   - a. One line and a point
   - b. Two lines and a point
   - c. Two lines and Two points

6. To create a Parallel Plane At Point, you will need a reference plane and a point.
   - a. True
   - b. False

7. When creating a Plane Normal To Curve, you can select:
   - a. A linear model edge
   - b. A straight line.
   - c. A 2D or 3D curve
   - d. All of the above

7. D
5. A   6. TRUE
3. C   4. C
1. TRUE   2. TRUE

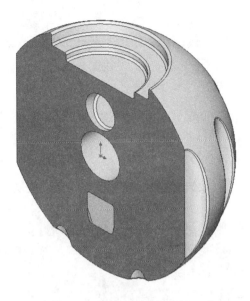

Section with Front plane

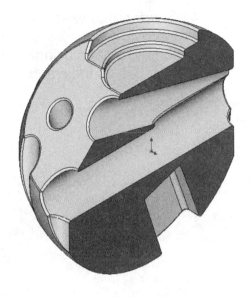

Section with Right plane

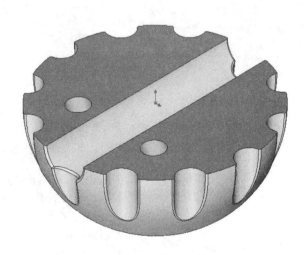

Section with Top plane

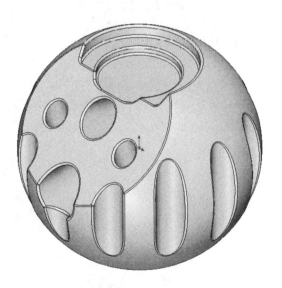

Isometric View

Exercise: Create new Work Planes

1. Create a reference sketch as shown.

2. Create 3 new planes using the references as indicated.

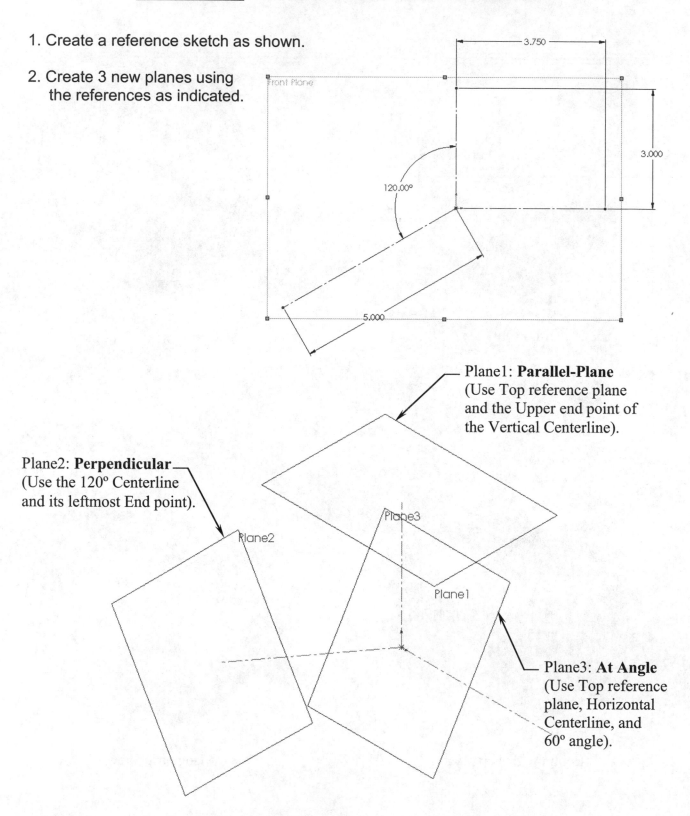

Plane1: **Parallel-Plane**
(Use Top reference plane and the Upper end point of the Vertical Centerline).

Plane2: **Perpendicular**
(Use the 120° Centerline and its leftmost End point).

Plane3: **At Angle**
(Use Top reference plane, Horizontal Centerline, and 60° angle).

3. Save your work as: **New Work Planes_Exe**.

CHAPTER 3

Advanced Modeling

Advanced Modeling – 5/8" Spanner

- The draft option is omitted in this lesson to help focus in other areas.

- The arc conditions Min / Max are options that help when placing dimensions on tangents of arcs or circles. Once a dimension is created, the arc conditions can be changed by right clicking on the dimension and selecting the Leaders tab. Only two conditions can be specified at a time. Either Center/Center, Min/Max, Max/Max, or Min/Min, etc.

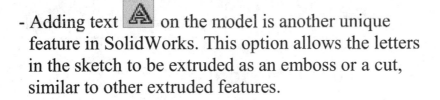

- Adding text 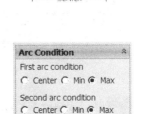 on the model is another unique feature in SolidWorks. This option allows the letters in the sketch to be extruded as an emboss or a cut, similar to other extruded features.

- All letters in the same sketch are considered one entity, they will be extruded at the same time and will receive the same extrude depth.

- This chapter and its exercise will guide you through some of the advanced modeling techniques as well as learning to use the Text tool to create the straight or curved extruded letters.

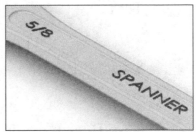

5/8" Spanner
Advanced Modeling

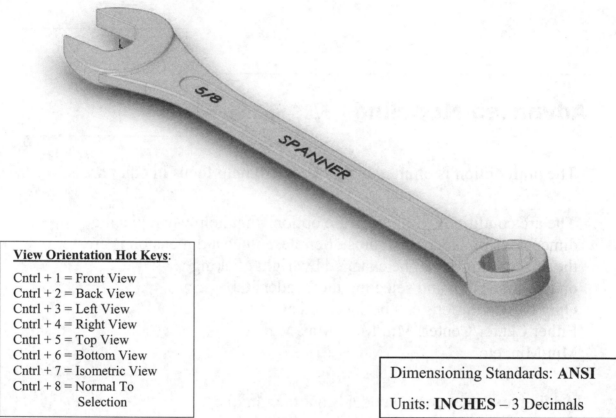

View Orientation Hot Keys:

Cntrl + 1 = Front View
Cntrl + 2 = Back View
Cntrl + 3 = Left View
Cntrl + 4 = Right View
Cntrl + 5 = Top View
Cntrl + 6 = Bottom View
Cntrl + 7 = Isometric View
Cntrl + 8 = Normal To
        Selection

Dimensioning Standards: **ANSI**

Units: **INCHES** – 3 Decimals

Tools Needed:

Insert Sketch	Line	3 Point Arc
Text	Add Geometric Relations	Dimension
Sketch Fillet	Polygon	Plane
Base/Boss Extrude	Extruded Cut	Fillet/Round

1. Opening the Spanner sketch document:

- From the Training CD, locate and open the document named: **Spanner Sketch**.

- **Edit** the **Sketch1**. This is the open end of the spanner.

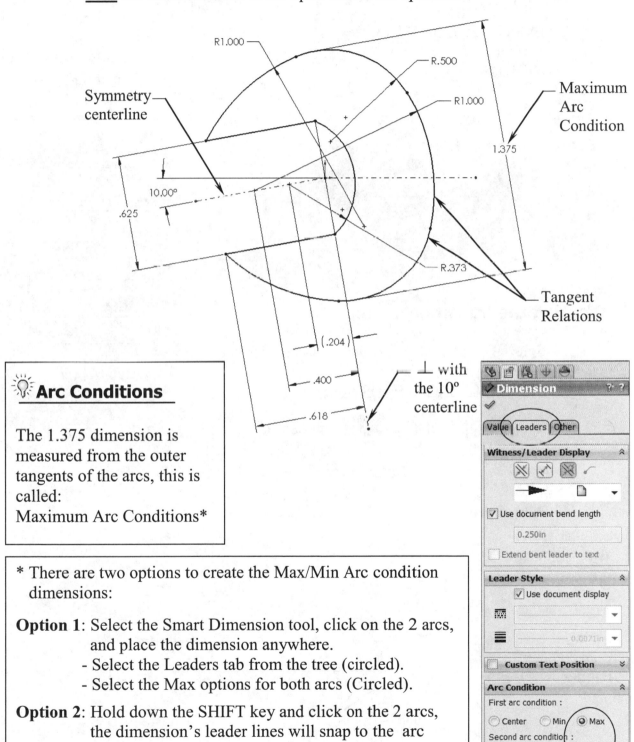

Symmetry centerline

Maximum Arc Condition

Tangent Relations

⊥ with the 10° centerline

☀ Arc Conditions

The 1.375 dimension is measured from the outer tangents of the arcs, this is called:
Maximum Arc Conditions*

---

* There are two options to create the Max/Min Arc condition dimensions:

Option 1: Select the Smart Dimension tool, click on the 2 arcs, and place the dimension anywhere.
- Select the Leaders tab from the tree (circled).
- Select the Max options for both arcs (Circled).

Option 2: Hold down the SHIFT key and click on the 2 arcs, the dimension's leader lines will snap to the arc tangents automatically.

2. Extruding the base feature:

- Click 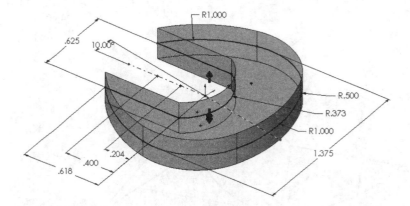 or select **Insert / Boss-Base / Extrude**.

- End Condition: **Mid Plane**.

- Extrude Depth: **.250 in**.

- Click **OK** ✅.

> 💡 **Renaming Features**
>
> Slow double click on each feature's name and rename them to something more descriptive like: Open-End, Transition-Body, Closed-End, etc...

3. Creating the transition sketch:

- Select <u>Top</u> plane from the FeatureManager tree.

- Click ✏️ or select **Insert / Sketch**.

- Sketch the profile below using Lines \\ .

<u>Note:</u> only add the Sketch Fillets after the sketch is fully defined.

- Add dimensions 🔷 or Relations ⊥ as needed.

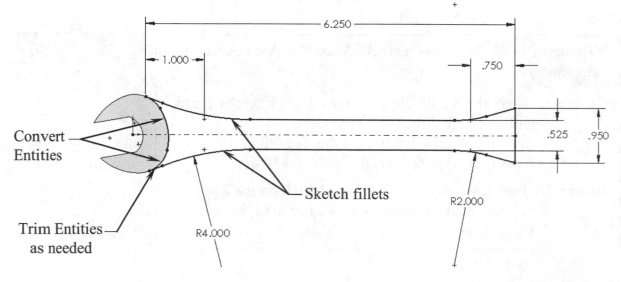

4. Extruding the Transition feature:

- Click 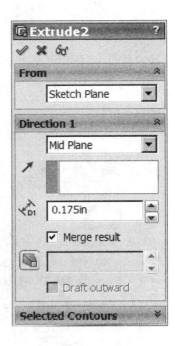 or select **Insert / Boss-Base / Extrude**.

- End Condition: **Mid Plane**

- Extrude Depth: **.175 in**.

- Click **OK** ✅.

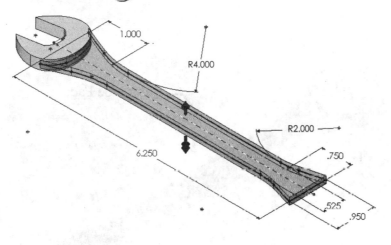

5. Adding the reference geometry:

- Select the <u>face</u> as indicated.

- Click ✏ or select **Insert / Sketch**.

- Sketch a Centerline ⫶ at the mid-point of the two vertical edges.

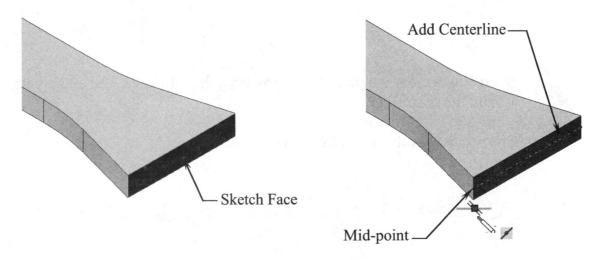

Sketch Face

Add Centerline

Mid-point

- Exit the Sketch ✏ or select **Insert / Sketch**.

6. Creating a new work plane: Plane at Angle

- Click 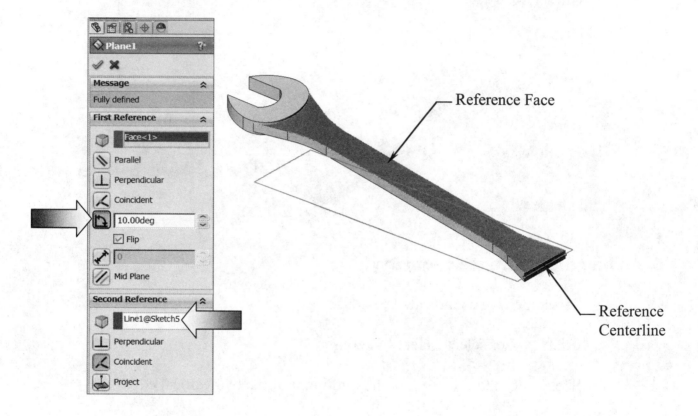 or select **Insert / Reference Geometry / Plane**.

- For Reference Entities ⬡ Select the **Sketch4** (centerline) and the **upper face** of the Transition.

- Enter **10 deg**. (arrow), click **Flip** (if needed) to place the plane on the bottom.

Reference Face

Reference Centerline

- Click **OK** ✓.

- SolidWorks creates a plane that starts from the reference face and pivots around the centerline.

- The preview of the new 10 degrees plane.

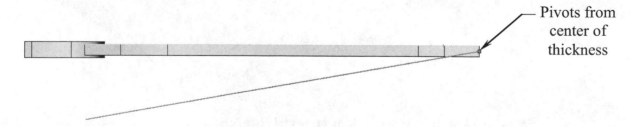

Pivots from center of thickness

7. Creating the Closed-End sketch:

- Select the new **10° plane** from the FeatureManager tree.

- Click 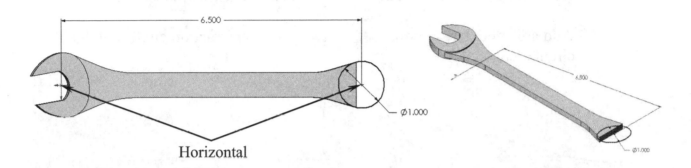 or select **Insert / Sketch**.

- Sketch a circle ⊕ and add dimensions ✏ as shown.

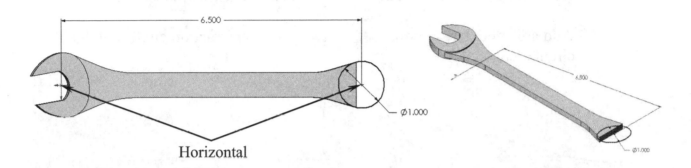

Horizontal

8. Extruding the Closed-end feature:

- Click 🗔 or select **Insert / Boss-Base / Extrude**.

- **Direction 1:**   **Blind**.

- Extrude Depth: **.200 in**.

- **Direction 2:**   **Blind**.

- Extrude Depth: **.130 in**.

- Click **OK** ✅.

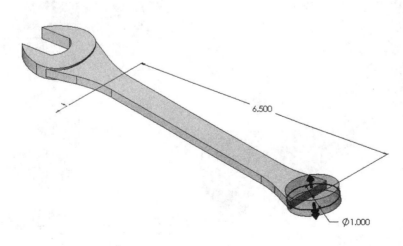

9. Adding a 12-Sided polygonal hole:

- Select the face indicated as sketch plane.

- Click or select **Insert / Sketch**.

- Sketch a Polygon with **12 sides** (arrow).

- Add a **.625 Dia**. Dimension to the inside construction circle.

- Add a **Concentric** relation between the construction circle and the circular edge.

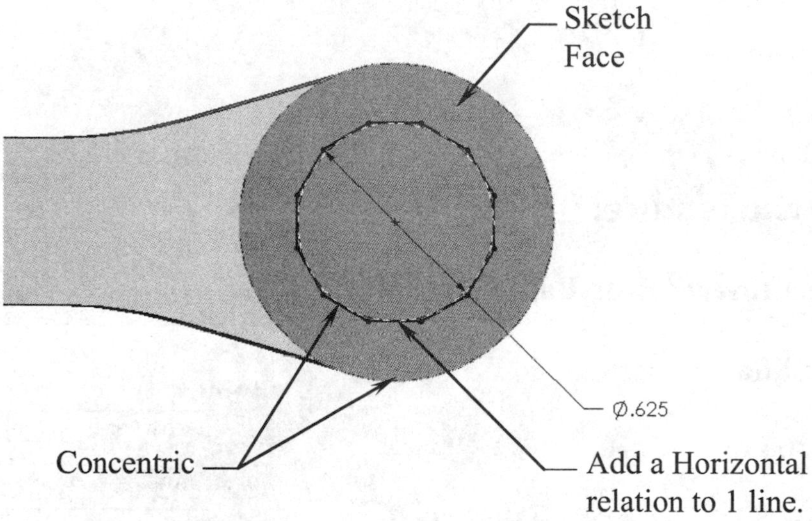
Sketch
Face
Ø.625
Concentric
Add a Horizontal
relation to 1 line.

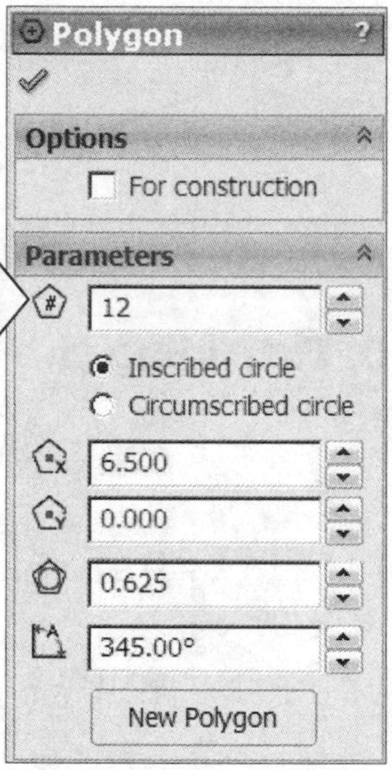
Polygon
Options
For construction
Parameters
12
Inscribed circle
Circumscribed circle
6.500
0.000
0.625
345.00°
New Polygon

10. Extruding a cut:

- Click or select **Insert / Cut / Extrude**.

- End Condition: **Through All**.

- Click **OK**.

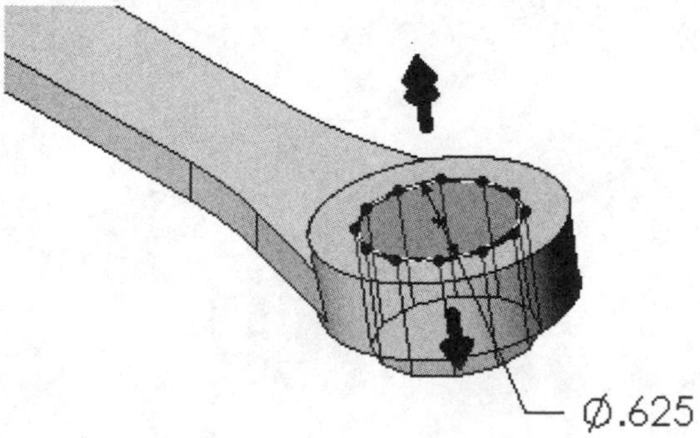
Ø.625

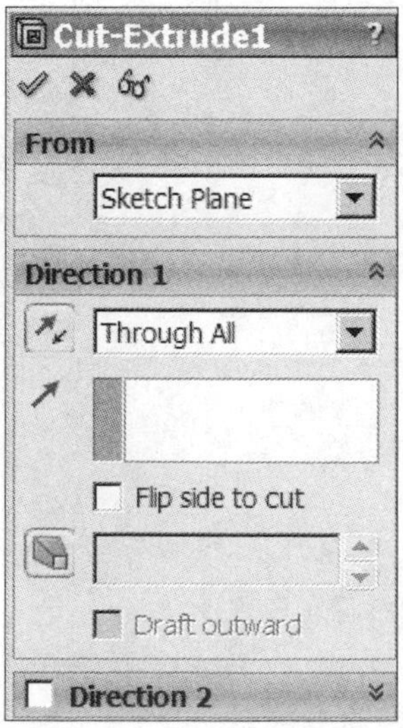
Cut-Extrude1
From
Sketch Plane
Direction 1
Through All
Flip side to cut
Draft outward
Direction 2

11. Creating the Recess profile:

- Select the <u>face</u> indicated as sketch plane.

- Click 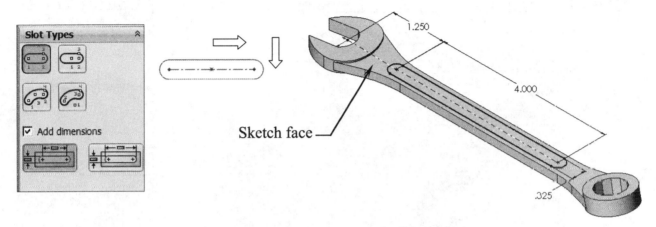 or select **Insert / Sketch**.

- Sketch the profile shown below using the **Straight-Slot** command .

Sketch face

- Add Dimensions and Relations to fully define the sketch.

12. Extruding the Recessed feature:

- Click or select **Insert / Cut / Extrude**.

- End Condition: **Blind**.

- Extrude Depth: **.030 in**.

- Click **OK** .

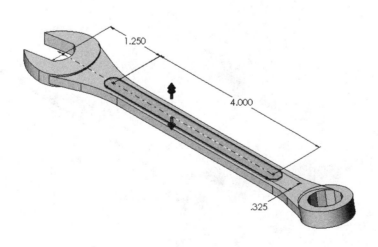

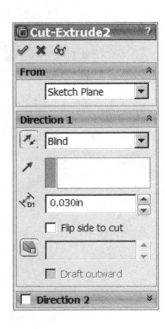

13. Mirroring the Recessed feature:

- Hold the CONTROL key, select the Top reference plane, and the Recessed feature from the FeatureManager tree.

- Click 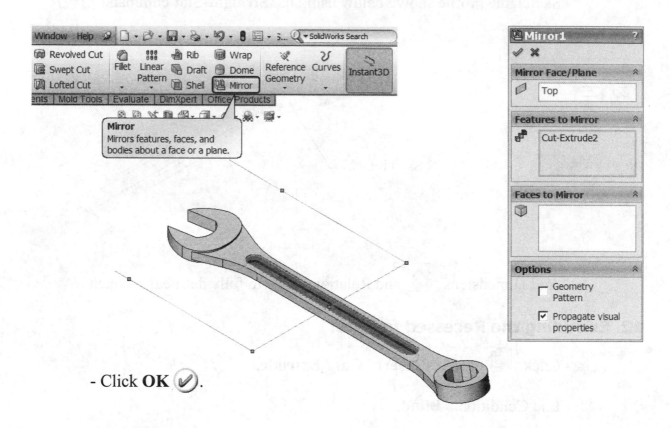 or select **Insert / Pattern Mirror** menu, then select **Mirror**.

- Click **OK** ✓.

- Rotate ⟳ the model to verify the results.

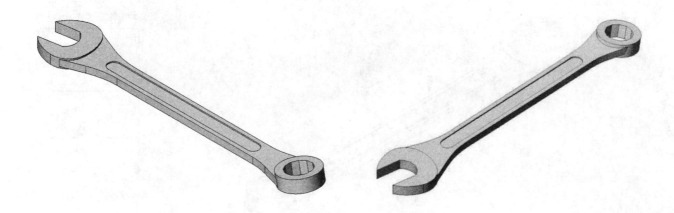

14. Adding the .030" fillets:

- Click 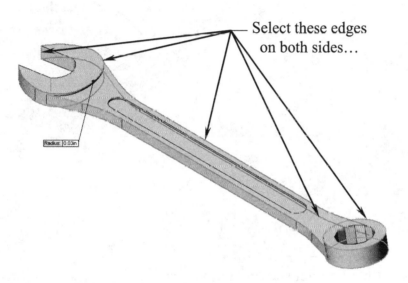 or select **Insert / Features / Fillet/Round**.

- Enter **.030 in**. for Radius.

- Select the edges as shown for Edges to fillet.

- Tangent Propagation: **Enabled**.

- Click **OK** ✓.

Select these edges on both sides...

15. Adding the .050" fillets:

- Repeat step 14 and add a **.050"** fillet to the 4 edges shown below.

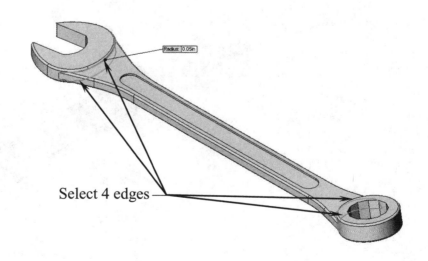

Select 4 edges

16. Adding the .015" fillets:

- Click 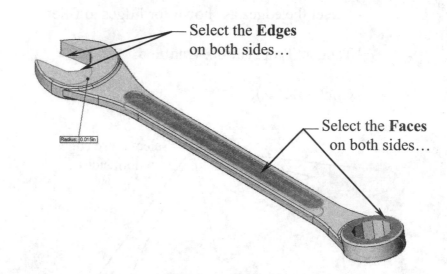 and add a **.015"** fillet to the edges and faces shown below.

Select the **Edges**
on both sides…

Select the **Faces**
on both sides…

- Click **OK** .

- Verify your fillets with the model shown below.

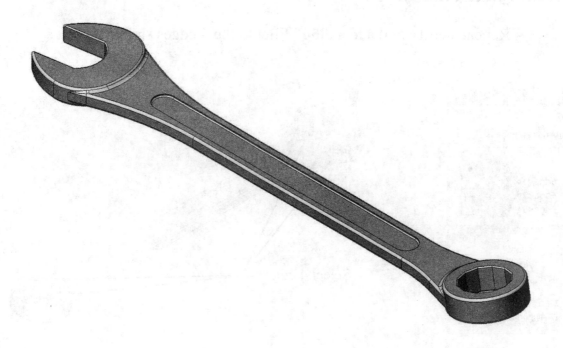

17. Adding text:

- Select the <u>face</u> indicated as sketch plane.

- Click  or select **Insert / Sketch**.

- Click ![A icon] and type **5/8** in the text dialog box.

- Click **OK** ✓.

- Add dimensions ✎ to position the text.

> 💡 **Positioning Text**
>
> Each set of sketch text comes with a Manipulator Point, dimensions can be added from this point to position the text.

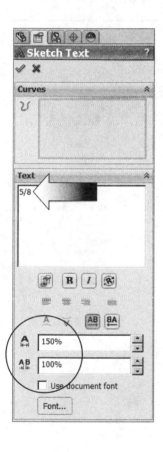

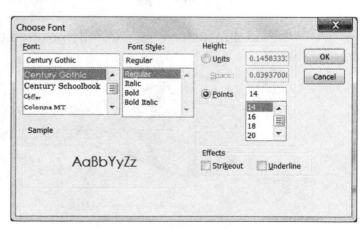

Sketch Face

Manipulator Point

- Clear Use document's font check box ☐ Use document's font .

- Change Width factor to **150%** ![A icon] .

- Leave Spacing at **100%** ![AB icon] .

- Font: **Century Gothic** [Font...] .

- Style: **Regular** - Points size: **14 pt**.

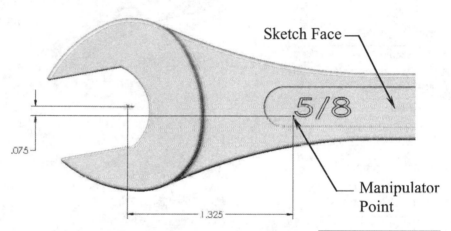

NOTE:
Use the Curves option when you want your sketch letters to wrap along a curve.

It will work better if the curve is created in the same sketch, as construction geometry.

18. Extruding the text:

- Click 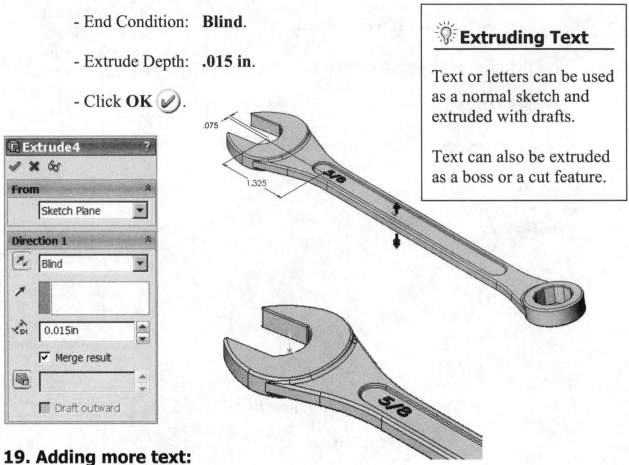 or select **Insert / Boss-Base / Extrude**.

- End Condition: **Blind**.

- Extrude Depth: **.015 in**.

- Click **OK**.

> **Extruding Text**
>
> Text or letters can be used as a normal sketch and extruded with drafts.
>
> Text can also be extruded as a boss or a cut feature.

19. Adding more text:

- Select the indicated face as sketch plane.

- Click or select **Insert / Sketch**.

- Click and type SPANNER in the Text dialog box.

- Add dimensions to fully position the text.

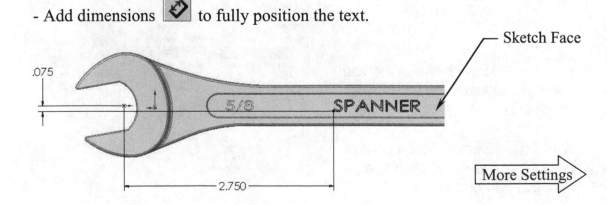

Sketch Face

.075

2.750

More Settings

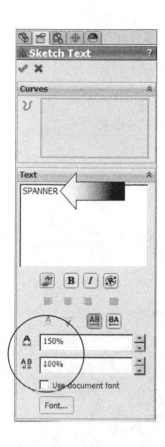

- Clear Use document's font check box 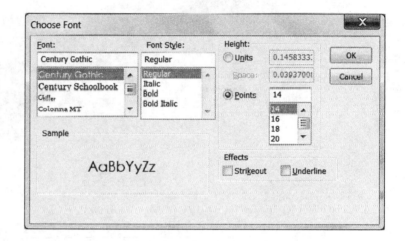 .

- Change Width factor to **150%** .

- Keep Spacing at **100%** .

- Font: **Century Gothic** Font... .

- Style: **Regular**.

- Points size: **14 pt**.   - Click **OK** .

20. Extruding the text:

- Click or select **Insert / Boss-base / Extrude**.

- End Condition: **Blind**.

- Extrude Depth: **.015 in**.

- Click **OK** .

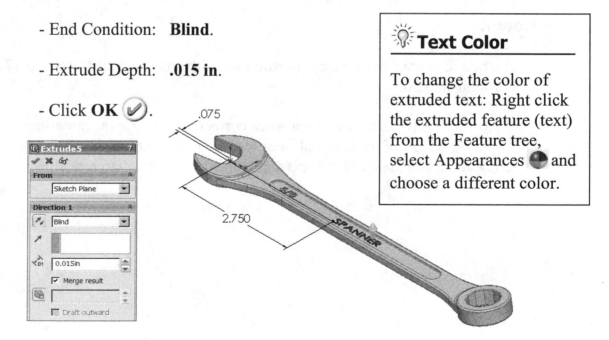

> 💡 **Text Color**
>
> To change the color of extruded text: Right click the extruded feature (text) from the Feature tree, select Appearances and choose a different color.

21. Saving your work:

- Select **File / Save as / Spanner / Save**.

22. Optional:

- To add the same text on the opposite side of the part, repeat from step 17 through step 20.

- Since the mirror option will not work correctly for text, you can either copy the sketch of the text, edit it, re-position, and extrude it again - OR - copy and paste the extruded text and then edit it's sketch to reposition.

Questions for Review

Advanced Modeling

1. The Min / Max conditions can be selected from the dimensions properties, under the Leaders tab.
   a. True
   b. False

2. The Mid-Plane extrude type protrudes the sketch profile to both directions equally.
   a. True
   b. False

3. It is sufficient to create a plane at an angle with a surface and an angular dimension.
   a. True
   b. False

4. When sketching a polygon, the number of sides can be changed on the Properties tree.
   a. True
   b. False

5. A 3D solid feature can be mirrored using a centerline as the center of mirror.
   a. True
   b. False

6. Text cannot be used to extrude as a boss or a cut feature.
   a. True
   b. False

7. Extruded text can be mirrored just like any other 3D features.
   a. True
   b. False

8. Text in a sketch can be extruded with drafts, inward or outward.
   a. True
   b. False

7. TRUE   8. TRUE
5. FALSE   6. FALSE
3. FALSE   4. TRUE
1. TRUE   2. TRUE

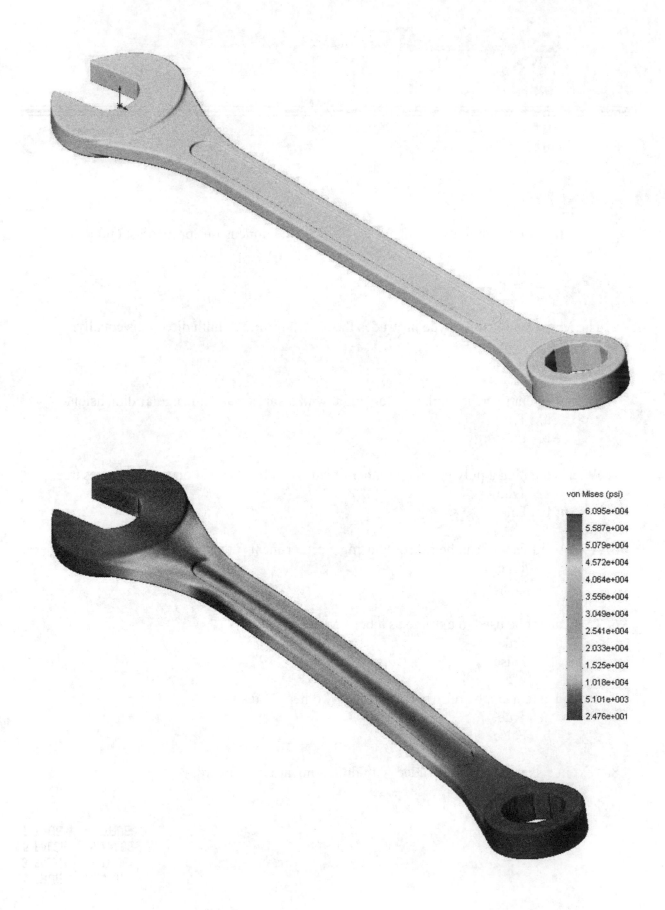

von Mises (psi)

6.095e+004
5.587e+004
5.079e+004
4.572e+004
4.064e+004
3.556e+004
3.049e+004
2.541e+004
2.033e+004
1.525e+004
1.018e+004
5.101e+003
2.476e+001

Exercise: Circular Text Wraps

1. Opening a part file:

- From the Training CD, open an existing part named: **Text Wrap**.

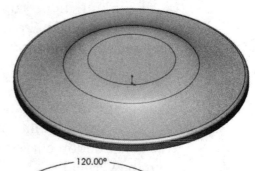

2. Adding Text:

- Select the <u>Top</u> plane and open a new sketch.

- Sketch a circle at Ø**5.500**" and convert it into construction geometry.

- Sketch the other centerlines, trim, then add the dimensions and relations as indicated.

- Click the **Text** command.

- Enter the word: **SolidWorks**.

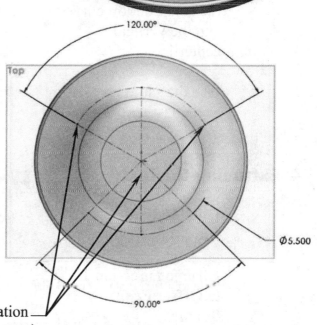

Symmetric relation (both top and bottom) between the endpoints and the centerlines

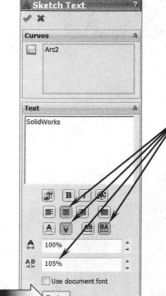

- Select the upper construction curve to bend the text around it.

Select these options

- Click the **Font** button and set the size to **72 points.**

Select this curve

- Select all other options as noted to align the text.

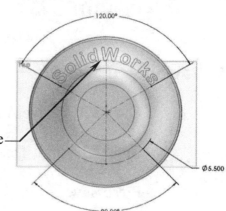

3. Repeating:

- Still working in the same sketch, repeat step 2 and add the number: **2013**.

- Add a Symmetric relation between the endpoints of the construction curve and the vertical centerline.

- Use the same text setting as the last text.

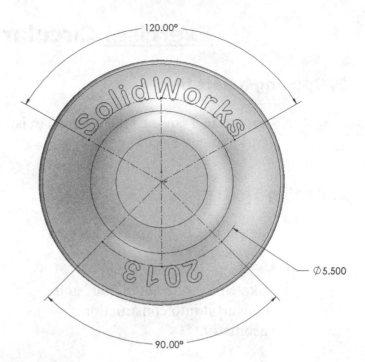

4. Extruding the text:

- Click **Extruded Boss-Base**.

- Change Direction 1 to **Offset From Surface**.

- Enter **.030"** and click **Reverse Offset**.

- Select the **face** as indicated.

- Click **OK** ✔.

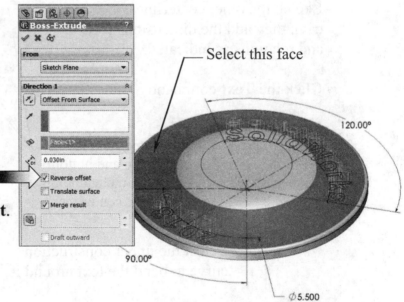

Select this face

5. Saving your work:

- Click **File / Save As**.

- Enter **Circular Text Wrap**.

- Press **Save**.

CHAPTER 4

Sweep with Composite Curves

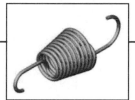

Sweep ⌐ with Composite Curves

Unlike extruded or revolved shapes, the sweep option offers a more advanced way of creating complex geometry, where a single profile can be swept along 2D guide paths or 3D curves to define the shape.

To create a sweep feature the Sweep Path gets created first, then and a single closed sketch Profile.

The Profile will be related to the Sweep Path with a PIERCE or a coincident relation.

When the Profile is swept, the Sweep Path and Guide Curves help control the shape and its behaviors such as twisting, tangencies, etc.

The Composite Curve ⌐ option allows multiple sketches or model edges to be jointed into one continuous path for use in sweep features. (The sketches must be connecting with one another in order for the composite curve to work.

This lesson will guide you through the creation of a helical extension spring; where several 2D sketches will be combined with a 3D helix to create one continuous curve.
This curve is called: **Composite Curve**.

Ø.080

Helical Extension Spring
Sweep with Composite Curves

View Orientation Hot Keys:

Cntrl + 1 = Front View
Cntrl + 2 = Back View
Cntrl + 3 = Left View
Cntrl + 4 = Right View
Cntrl + 5 = Top View
Cntrl + 6 = Bottom View
Cntrl + 7 = Isometric View
Cntrl + 8 = Normal To
         Selection

Dimensioning Standards: **ANSI**

Units: **INCHES** – 3 Decimals

Tools Needed:

Insert Sketch	Line	Circle
Tangent Arc	3 Point Arc	Add Geometric Relations
Dimension	Composite Curve	Sweep

1. Sketching the first profile:

- Select the <u>Front</u> plane from the FeatureManager Tree.

- Click 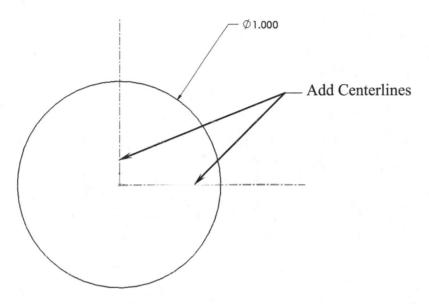 or **Insert / Sketch**.

- Sketch a circle and two centerlines then add the dimension as shown:

Ø1.000

Add Centerlines

2. Converting the circle into a Helix:

- Select **Insert / Curve / Helix / Spiral**.

Defined by:	**Pitch and Revolution**
Pitch:	**.100**
Revolution:	**10**
Starting angle:	**0°**
Taper helix:	**Enabled**
Taper angle:	**10°**

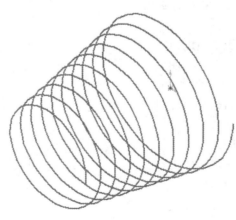

- Click **OK**.

3. Creating a 2-degree plane:

- Show the previous sketch (Sketch1).

- Click or select **Insert/Reference Geometry/Plane**.

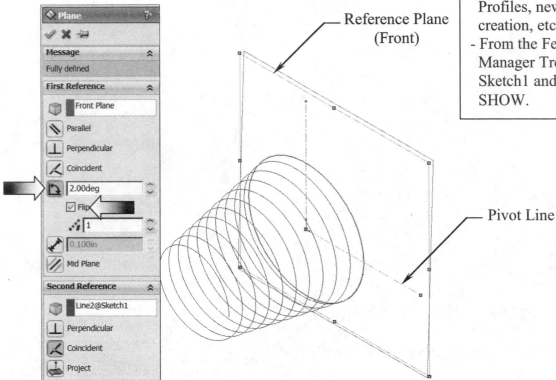

Reference Plane (Front)

Pivot Line

- Select the **Horizontal Centerline** as the Pivot Line.

- Select the **at Angle** option .

- Enter **2.00deg.** for Angle.

- Enable the **Flip** option. (Make sure the new plane leans to the right. Change to the Right view Cntrl+4).

- Click **OK** .

- Hide the Sketch1.

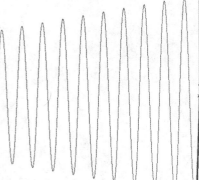

Plane1

2° Plane

4. Sketching the large loop:

- Select the <u>Plane1</u> from the FeatureManager Tree.

- Click [icon] or select **Insert / Sketch**.

- Sketch a 3-point Arc [icon] and add dimension as shown:

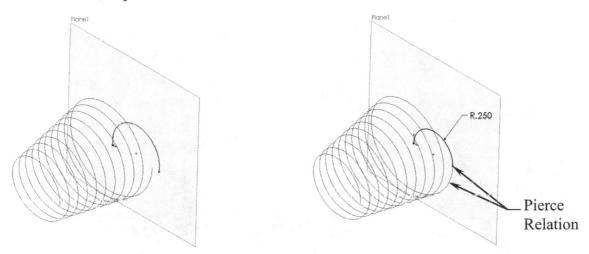

- Add a **Pierce** relation between the end point of the Arc and the Helix.

- **Exit** the sketch [icon] or select **Insert / Sketch**.

5. Sketching the large hook:

- Select the <u>Right</u> plane from the FeatureManager Tree.

- Click [icon] or select **Insert / Sketch**.

- Sketch the profile and add dimension and relations as shown below:

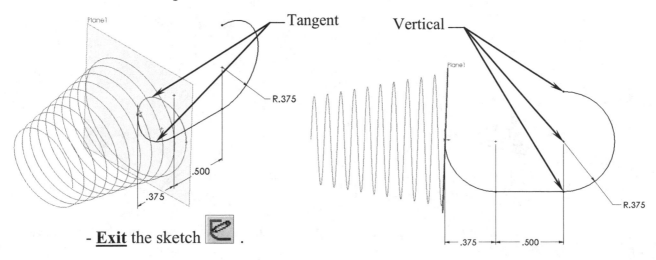

- **Exit** the sketch [icon] .

6. Creating a Parallel plane:

- Select the Plane1 from the FeatureManager Tree.

- Click 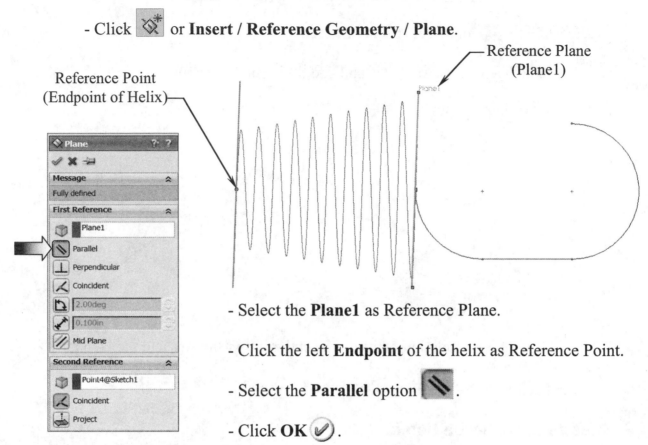 or **Insert / Reference Geometry / Plane**.

- Select the **Plane1** as Reference Plane.

- Click the left **Endpoint** of the helix as Reference Point.

- Select the **Parallel** option .

- Click **OK** .

7. Adding the small loop:

- Select the new plane (Plane2) from the FeatureManager Tree.

- Click 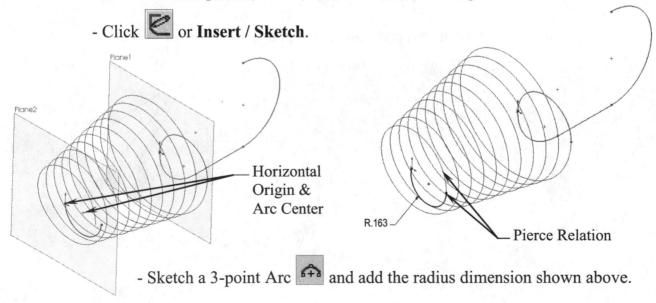 or **Insert / Sketch**.

- Sketch a 3-point Arc and add the radius dimension shown above.

- Add a **Pierce** relation ⬛ between the endpoint of the Arc and the Helix.

- **Exit** the sketch ⬛ or **Insert / Sketch**.

8. Creating a small hook:

- Select the <u>Right</u> plane from the FeatureManager Tree.

- Click ⬛ or **Insert / Sketch**.

- Sketch the profile and add the dimensions shown.

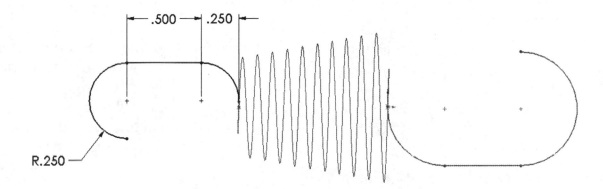

- Add the relations Vertical and Tangent to the indicated entities.

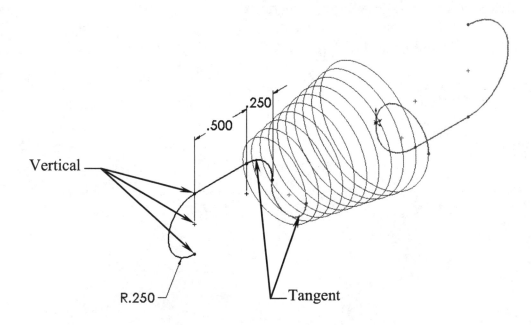

- **Exit** the sketch ⬛ or click **Insert / Sketch**.

9. Combining all sketches into one, using Composite Curve option:

- Click  under the Curves button or select: **Insert / Curve / Composite**.

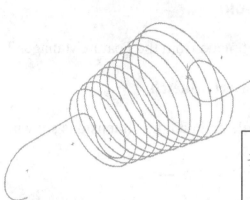

- Select all sketches as indicated.

- Click **OK** .

Composite Curve

Composite Curve option allows multiple sketches or model edges to be jointed into one continuous path for use in swept features.

---

10. Creating a Perpendicular plane:

- Click or **Insert / Reference Geometry / Plane**.

- Click the **edge** and the **endpoint** as noted.

- Select the **Perpendicular** option.

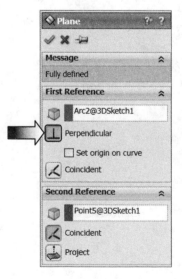

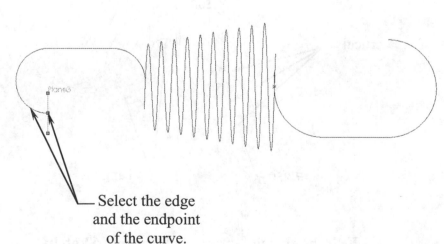

Select the edge and the endpoint of the curve.

- Click **OK**.

11. Sketching the sweep profile (the wire diameter):

- Select the new plane (**Plane3**) from the FeatureManager Tree.

- Click 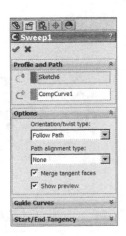 or select: **Insert / Sketch**.

- Sketch a circle at the end of the hook.

- Add a **Piece** Relation to fully define the sketch.

- **Exit** the sketch or **Insert / Sketch**.

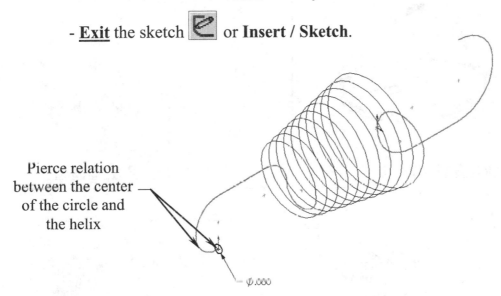

Pierce relation between the center of the circle and the helix

12. Sweeping the profile along the path:

- Click on the Features toolbar or select: **Insert / Boss-Base / Sweep**.

- Select the small circle as sweep profile .

- Select the composite curve as sweep path .

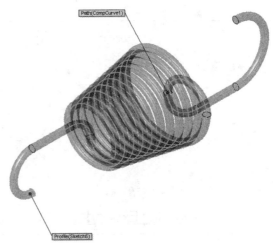

- Click **OK** .

13. Saving your work:

- Click **File / Save As / Helical Extension Spring / Save**.

<u>Other Examples:</u>

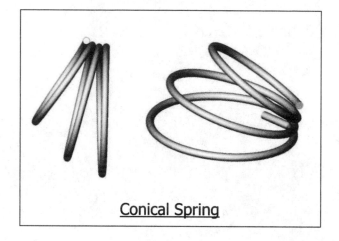

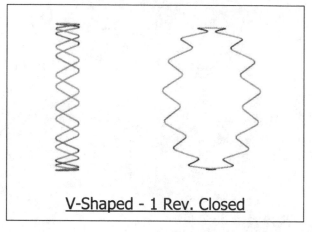

Conical Spring

V-Shaped - 1 Rev. Closed

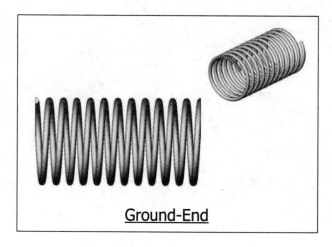

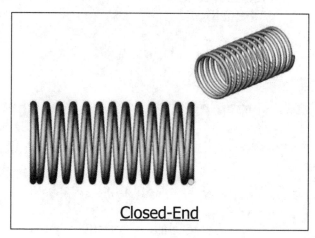

Ground-End

Closed-End

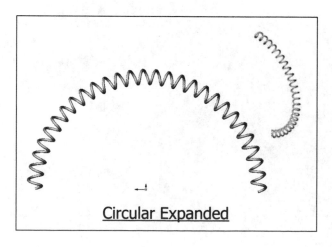

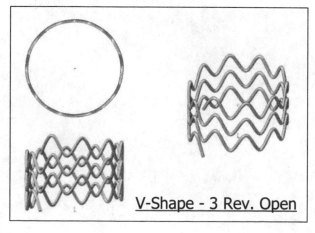

Circular Expanded

V-Shape - 3 Rev. Open

Questions for Review

Sweep with Composite Curve

1. Beside the Pitch and Revolution option, a helix can be defined with Pitch and Height.
   a. True
   b. False

2. It is sufficient to create an Offset Distance plane using a reference plane and a distance.
   a. True
   b. False

3. The sweep profile should have a Pierce relation with the sweep path.
   a. True
   b. False

4. Several sketches or model edges can be combined to make a Composite curve.
   a. True
   b. False

5. A Composite curve cannot be used as a sweep path.
   a. True
   b. False

6. The composite curve combines all sketches and model edges into one continuous curve, even if they are not connected.
   a. True
   b. False

7. In a sweep feature, SolidWorks allows only one sweep path, but multiple guide curves can be used.
   a. True
   b. False

8. Several sketch profiles can be used to sweep along a path.
   a. True
   b. False

7. TRUE   8. FALSE
5. FALSE   6. FALSE
3. TRUE   4. TRUE
1. TRUE   2. TRUE

Exercise: Circular Spring - Expanded

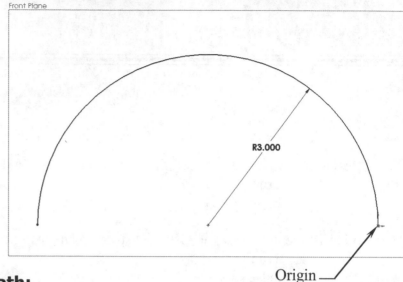

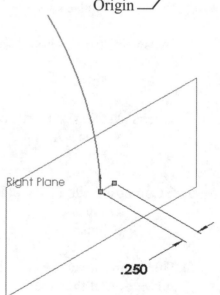

1. Sketching the Sweep Path:

- Select the <u>Front</u> plane and open a new sketch.

- Sketch an Arc as shown and add a Horizontal relation between the left and the right endpoints; then add a radius dimension.

- **Exit** the sketch.

2. Sketching the Sweep Profile:

- Select the <u>Right</u> plane and open a new sketch.

- Sketch a Horizontal line towards the right.

- Add a **.250 in**. dimension.

- **Exit** the sketch.

3. Creating a Swept <u>Surface</u>:

- Click 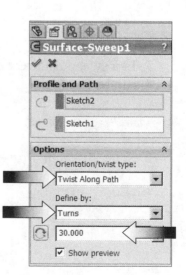 or select **Insert / Surface / Sweep**.

- Select the **Horizontal-Line** for use as the Sweep Profile.

- Select the **Arc** as the Sweep Path.

- Expand the **Optios** dialog box.

- Select **Twist Along Path**, under Orientation / Twist Type.

- For Define By: Select **Turns**.

- For number of Turns: Enter **30**.

- Click **OK** 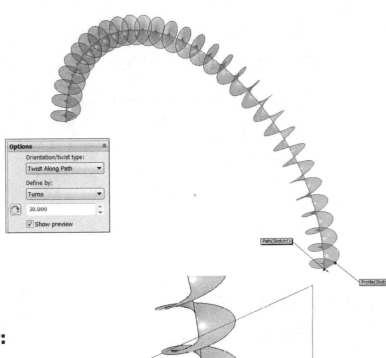.

4. Sketching the Wire-Diameter:

- Select the <u>Right</u> plane and open a new sketch.

- Sketch a Circle at the right end of the swept surface.

- Add a **Ø.125 in**. diameter dimension.

- **Exit** the sketch.

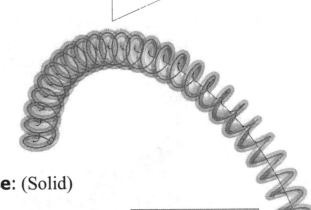

5. Creating a Swept Boss-Base: (Solid)

- Click 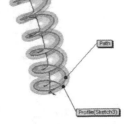 or select **Insert / Bose-Base / Sweep**.

- Select the **Circle** for use as the Sweep Profile.

- For Sweep Path, select the **Edge** of the Swept-Surface.

- Click **OK** .

6. Hide the Swept-Surface:

- Right click over the Swept-Surface

and select Hide 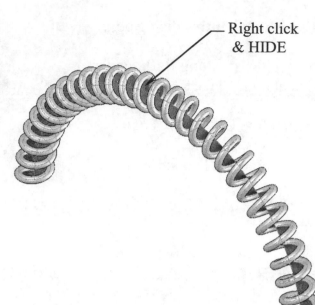.

Right click
& HIDE

7. Save your work:

- Select **File / Save As.**

- For file name, enter **Expanded Circular Spring**.

- Click **Save**.

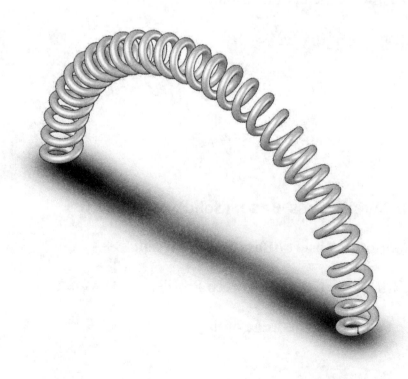

CHAPTER 4 (cont.)

Using Variable Pitch

Sweep 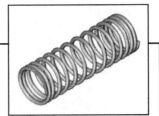 with Variable Pitch Helix

- In a Sweep feature, there is only one Sweep Profile, one Sweep Path, and one or more Guide Curves.

- The Sweep Profile describes the feature's cross-section; the Sweep Path helps control the twisting and how the Sweep Profile moves along the path.

- The Sweep path can either be a 2D or a 3D sketch, the edges of the part, or a Composite Curve.

- Beside the Pitch and Revolution option, the Helix and Spiral command offers other options to create more advanced curves such as:

> * Height and Revolutions.
> * Height and Pitch.
> * Spiral.
> * Constant Pitch.
> * Variable Pitch.

Region parameters:

	P	Rev	H	Dia
1	0.115in	0	0in	1in
2	0.115in	1.5	0.1725	1in
3	0.375in	6.5	1.3975	1in
4	0.25in	11.5	2.96in	1in
5	0.115in	12.5	3.1425	1in
6	0.115in	14	3.315i	1in
7				

- We will take a look at the option Variable Pitch in this lesson and learn how a helix with multiple pitch is created using a table, to help control the changes of the dimensions.

- To create the flat ground ends, an extruded cut feature is added at the end of the process.

Multi-Pitch Spring with Closed Ends
Using Variable Pitch

Dimensioning Standards: **ANSI**

Units: **INCHES** – 3 Decimals

Tools Needed:

 Insert Sketch

 Composite Curve

 Add Geometric Relations

 Dimension

 Base/Boss Sweep

 Extruded Cut

1. Creating the base sketch:

- Select the <u>Front</u> plane from the FeatureManager tree.

- Click 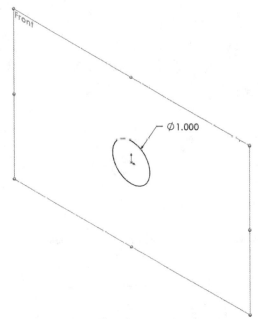 or select: **Insert / Sketch**.

- Sketch a circle ⊕ centered on the origin.

- Add a diameter dimension of **1.000"**.

Ø1.000

2. Creating a helix using Variable Pitch:

- Click ⧔ or select **Insert / Curve / Helix-Spiral**.

- Under Define By, select:
  Pitch and Revolution.

- Under Parameter, select:
  Variable Pitch.

- Under Region Parameters,
  enter the values for the **Pitch**,
  Revolutions, and **Diameters**.
  (Ignore the Height column, SolidWorks will
  fill in the values automatically).

- Set Angle to **0 deg** and **Clockwise** direction.

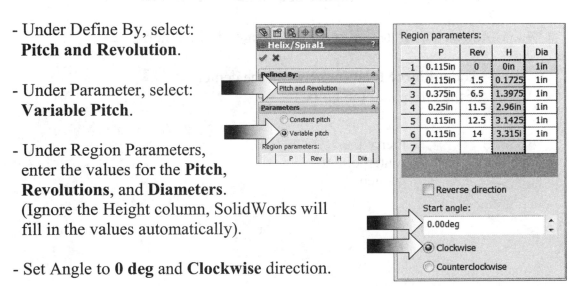

Region parameters:

	P	Rev	H	Dia
1	0.115in	0	0in	1in
2	0.115in	1.5	0.1725i	1in
3	0.375in	6.5	1.3975i	1in
4	0.25in	11.5	2.96in	1in
5	0.115in	12.5	3.1425i	1in
6	0.115in	14	3.315i	1in
7				

☐ Reverse direction

Start angle:
0.00deg

◉ Clockwise
○ Counterclockwise

- Your Variable Pitch helix should look like the image shown below.

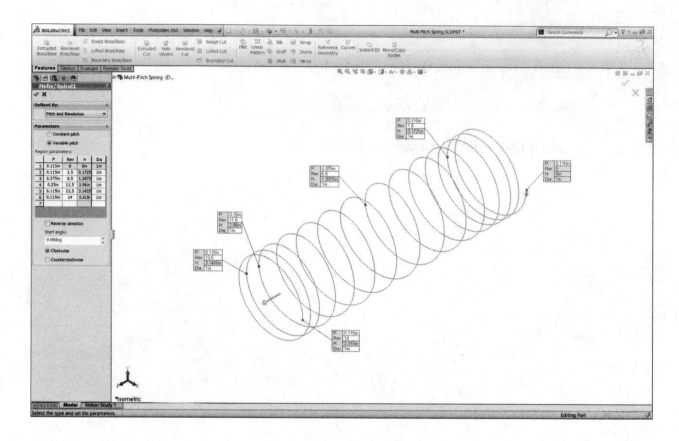

- Click **OK** ✅.

3. Sketching the sweep profile (the wire diameter):

- Select the <u>Top</u> plane and open a new sketch ✏️.

- Sketch a circle ⊕ near the right end of the helix.

- Add a **Pierce** relation between the center of the circle and the helix.

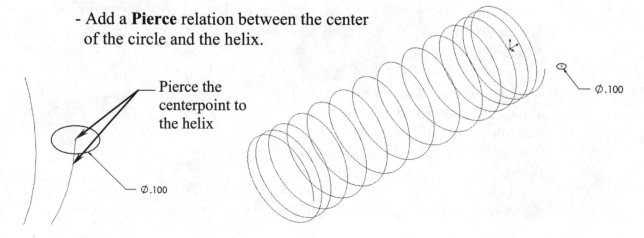

Pierce the
centerpoint to
the helix

Ø.100

Ø.100

- **Exit** the sketch. The Sweep command isn't available while the sketch is active.

4. Sweeping the profile along the path:

- Click [icon] or select: **Insert / Bose-Base / Sweep**.

- Select the small circle for sweep profile [icon] .

- Select the helix for sweep path [icon] .

- Click **OK** ✅ .

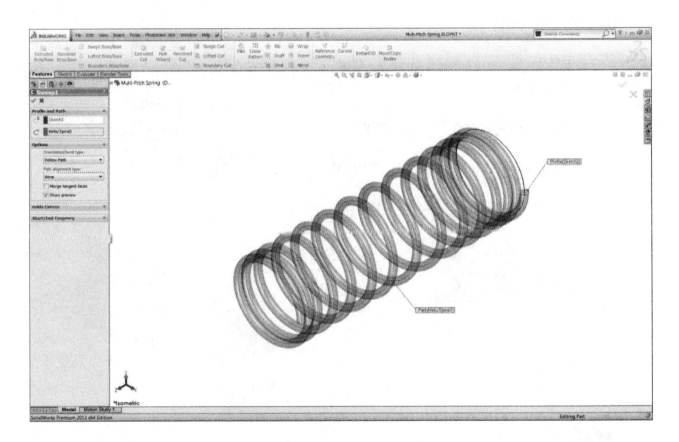

- The resulting Swept feature.

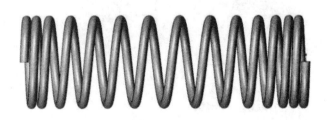

5. Creating a trimmed sketch:

- Select the <u>Top</u> plane from the Feature-Manager tree and open a new sketch.

- Sketch a rectangle and add a Midpoint relation between the line on top and the origin.

- Add a width and a height dimension. The sketch should now be fully defined.

6. Extruding a cut:

- Click 🔲 or select: **Insert / Cut / Extrude**.

- Set the Direction 1 to **Through All**.

- Set the Direction 2 to **Through All**.

- Enable the **Flip Side to Cut** checkbox.

- Click **OK** ✅.

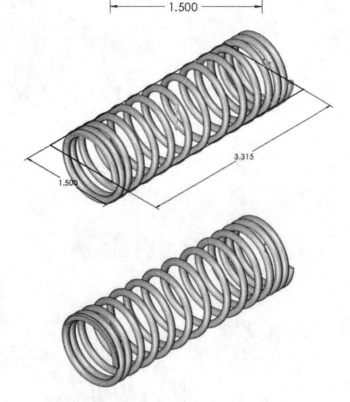

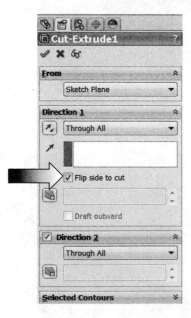

7. Saving your:

- Click **File / Save As / Variable Pitch Spring / Save**.

Questions for Review

Sweep w/Composite Curve

1. Multiple Sweep Profiles can be used in a sweep feature.
   a. True
   b. False

2. Multiple Sweep Paths can be used in a sweep feature.
   a. True
   b. False

3. Only one Sweep Profile and one Sweep Path can be used in a sweep.
   a. True
   b. False

4. A Helix can be defined by:
   a. Pitch and Revolution
   b. Height and Revolution
   c. Height and Pitch
   d. Spiral
   e. All of the above

5. Several connected Helixes can be combined into one single Composite Curve.
   a. True
   b. False

6. The Sweep Profile sketch should be related to the Sweep Path using the relation:
   a. Perpendicular
   b. Parallel
   c. Coincident
   d. Pierce

7. The Sweep Path controls the twisting and how the Sweep Profile moves along.
   a. True
   b. False

8. The Edges of the part can also be used as the Sweep Path.
   a. True
   b. False

7. TRUE	8. TRUE
5. TRUE	6. D
3. TRUE	4. E
1. FLASE	2. FALSE

<u>Exercise:</u> Projected Curve & Composite Curve

1. Create the part based on the drawing as shown.
2. Dimensions are in inches, 3 decimal places.
3. Focus on Projected Curve & Composite Curve options.

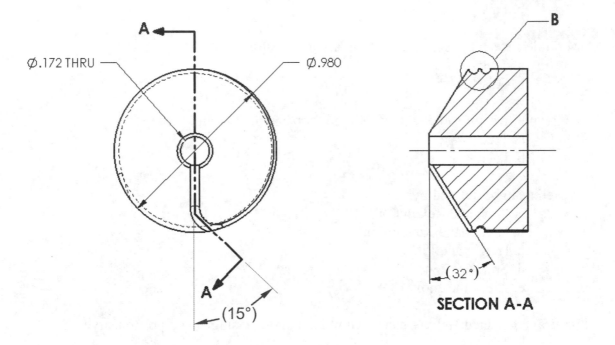

Ø.172 THRU   Ø.980

A

A

(15°)

B

(32°)

SECTION A-A

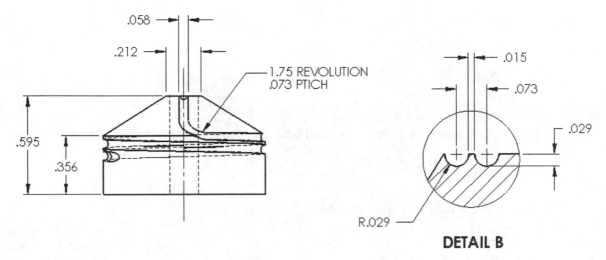

.058

.212

1.75 REVOLUTION
.073 PTICH

.595

.356

.015

.073

.029

R.029

DETAIL B

4. Follow the instructions on the following pages, if needed.

1. Opening a part document:

- From the Training CD, locate and open a part document named: **Project and Composite Curves**.

- This is an actual die to form the shape of a catheter. We will create the groove that wraps around this block, using the Project and Composite Curve options.

2. Creating a helix:

- Select the <u>Top</u> plane and open a new sketch.

- Select the bottom edge (for clarity) and press **Convert- Entity**.

- Click or select:
Insert / Curve / Helix-Spiral.

- Enter the following:

      * **Constant Pitch**.

      * Pitch: **.073"**

      * **Reverse Direction**.

      * Revolutions: **1.75**

      * Start Angle: **15deg**.

      * **Counterclockwise**.

- Click **OK**.

- Notice the helix starts at a 15° angle? This way the end of the helix will match up with the bend radius in the next step.

Convert the edge into a circle

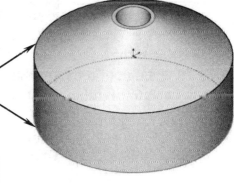

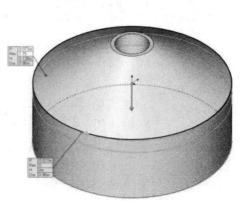

3. Sketching the upper transition:

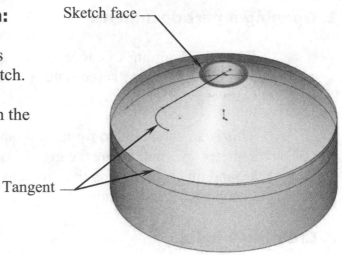

Sketch face

Tangent

- Select the small <u>upper face</u> as indicated and open a new sketch.

- Sketch a **Line** that starts from the origin and connects with a **Tangent Arc**.

- Add a **Tangent** relation between the arc and the circular edge of the part.

- Sketch a **centerline** that starts from the origin and connects to the right endpoint of the arc.

- Add a **Coincident** relation between the right endpoint of the arc and the circular edge of the part, then add a **15°** angular dimension.

Coincident

- The sketch should be fully defined at this point. **Exit** the sketch.

4. Creating a projected Curve:

Select 2 faces

- Click [icon] or select: **Insert / Curve / Projected**.

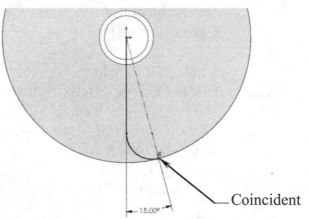

- Select the **Sketch on Faces** option.

- For Sketch to Project, select the **Sketch3**.

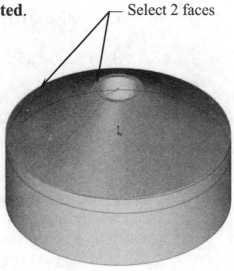

- For Projection Faces, select the **2 faces** as noted.

- Click **OK** [icon].

5. Adding a sketch line:

- We want the cut to start from the origin, a sketch line is needed to connect the projected curve to the origin.

- Sketch a line that starts from the origin to the endpoint of the projected curve.

- **Exit** the sketch.

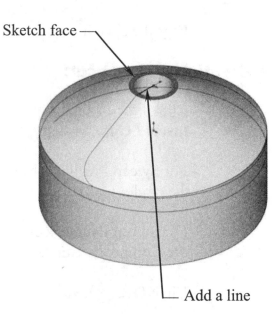

Sketch face

Add a line

6. Creating a Composite Curve:

- Click 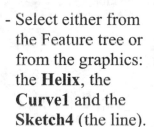 or select: **Insert / Curve / Composite**.

- Select either from the Feature tree or from the graphics: the **Helix**, the **Curve1** and the **Sketch4** (the line).

- Click **OK** ✓.

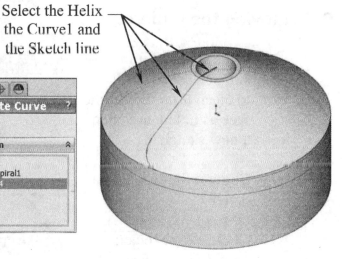

Select the Helix the Curve1 and the Sketch line

7. Sketching the sweep profile:

- Sketch a small circle on the **Front** plane and add the dimension/relation shown.

Pierce relation

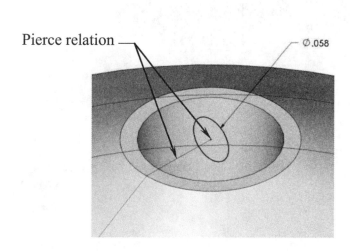

Ø.058

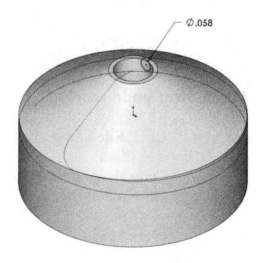

Ø.058

- **Exit** the sketch.

8. Creating a swept cut:

- Click ▣ or select:
Insert / Cut / Sweep.

- For Sweep Profile, select
the circle.

- For Sweep Path, select
the Composite Curve.

- Click **OK** ✔.

9. Removing the undercut:

- **If** the swept feature
stopped short, we'll need
to clean it up. Select the
face as noted and open
a new sketch.

- Convert the face into a
sketch.

- Click ▣ or select:
Insert / Cut / Extrude.

- Set Direction 1 to:
Through All.

- Click **OK** ✔.

Sketch face

Convert entities

10. Saving your work:

- Click **File / Save As**.

- Enter **Project and Composite Curves** for
the name of the file.

- Press **Save**.

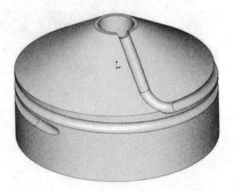

Exercise: Using Curve Through Reference Points

1. Creating the Base sketch:

- From the Top plane sketch a circle and a horizontal Centerline then switch them to Construction lines.

- Add a diameter dimension of **.100"**.

- Select the Horizontal Centerline and click **Circular Sketch Pattern**.

- Enter **16** instances, **Equal Spacing**.

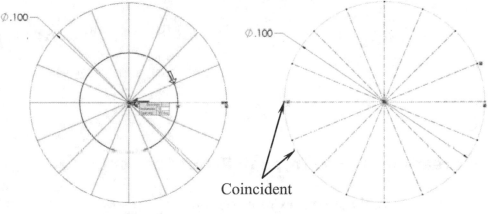

Coincident

- Add a couple of Coincident relations between the endpoints of any of the instances and the circle, to fully define the sketch.

- **Exit** the sketch (or **press +Q**).

2. Creating an offset plane:

- Create a new plane that is **.020"** above the **Top** plane.

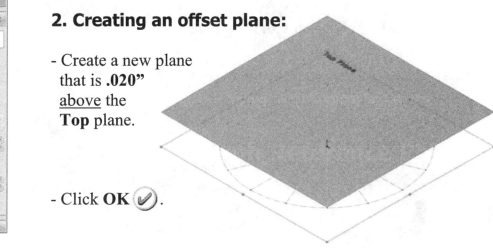

- Click **OK** ✅.

3. Creating a Derived sketch:

- Hold the **Control** key and select the **Sketch1** and the **Plane1**.

- Click **Insert / Derived Sketch**.

- Add a coincident relation between the centers of the 2 circles and a vertical relation between any 2 endpoints.

- **Exit** the sketch.

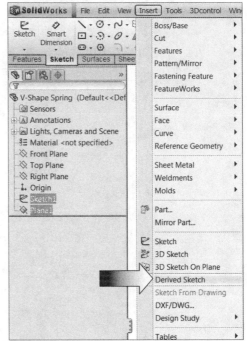

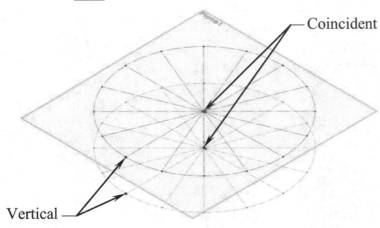

Coincident

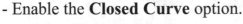

Vertical

4. Creating a Curve Through Reference Points:

- From the **Features** toolbar, click:
Curves / Curve Through Reference Points.

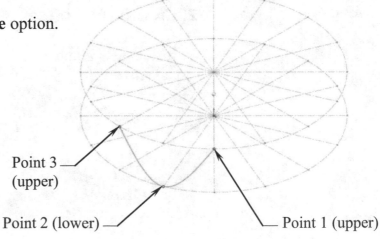

- Click the starting point (point 1), move clockwise and click point 2, then point 3 so on. Continue around.

- Enable the **Closed Curve** option.

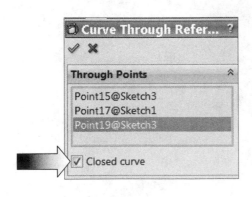

Point 3 (upper)

Point 2 (lower)

Point 1 (upper)

- Continue going around a full revolution and select all the connecting points in the 2 sketches.

- At the end of the path, do not click point 1 again as the **Closed Curve** option will joins the 2 ends together automatically.

- Click **OK** ✓.

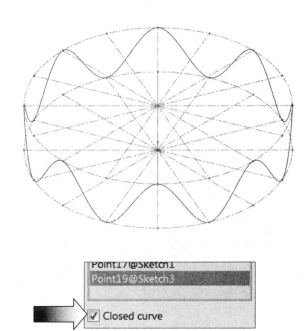

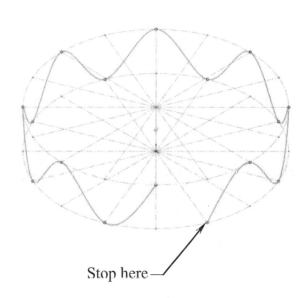

Stop here —

Point17@Sketch1
Point19@Sketch3

✓ Closed curve

5. Sketching the sweep profile:

- Select the <u>Front</u> plane and open a new sketch.

- Sketch a circle and add a diameter dimension of **.003"**.

- Add a Pierce relation between the center of the circle and the 3D curve.

- **Exit** the sketch.

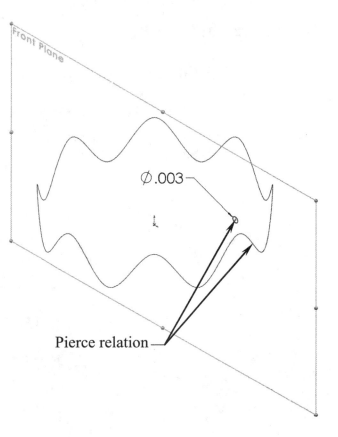

Ø.003

Pierce relation —

6. Creating a swept feature:

- From the **Features** toolbar, click **Swept Boss Base**.

- Click the small circle as the Sweep profile.

- Select the 3D curve as the Sweep path.

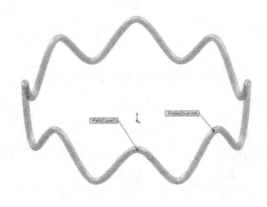

- Click **OK** .

7. Saving your work:

- Click **File / Save as**:

- Enter: **Curve Through Reference Points** for the name of the file.

- Click **Save**.

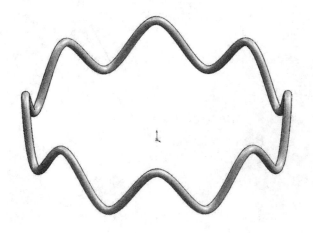

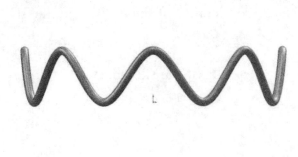

CHAPTER 5

Sweep & Loft

Advanced Modeling with Sweep & Loft

- The Sweep option creates a solid, thin, or surface feature by moving a single sketch profile along a path and guiding with one or more guide curves.

- In order to create a sweep feature properly, a set of rules should be taken into consideration:

- o The Sweep option uses only one sketch profile and it must be a closed non-intersecting contour for a **solid** feature.
- o The sketch profile can be either closed or open for a **surface** feature.
- o Only one path is used in a sweep and it can be open or closed.
- o One or more guide-curves can be used to guide the sketch profile.
- o The sketch profile must be drawn on a new plane starting at the end point of the path.

- The Loft option creates a solid, thin, or surface feature by making a transition between the sketch profiles.

- Keep in mind the following requirements when creating a loft feature:

- o The Loft option uses multiple sketch profiles that must be closed, and non-intersecting for a **solid** feature.
- o The sketch profiles can be either closed or open, for a **surface** feature.
- o Use the Centerline Parameter option to guide the profiles from the inside.
- o Use Guide Curves option to guide the sketch profiles from the outside.
- o The Guide Curves can be either a 2D or a 3D sketch.

Water Pump Housing
Advanced Modeling - Sweep & Loft

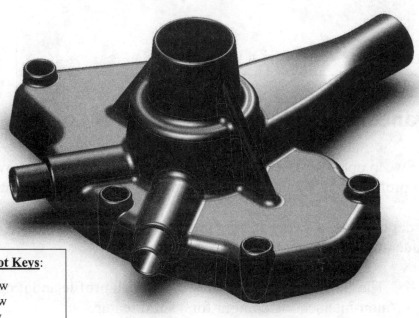

View Orientation Hot Keys:

Cntrl + 1 = Front View
Cntrl + 2 = Back View
Cntrl + 3 = Left View
Cntrl + 4 = Right View
Cntrl + 5 = Top View
Cntrl + 6 = Bottom View
Cntrl + 7 = Isometric View
Cntrl + 8 = Normal To
         Selection

Dimensioning Standards: **ANSI**

Units: **INCHES** – 3 Decimals

Tools Needed:

Insert Sketch	Split Entities	Add Geometric Relations
Rib	Plane	Revolved Boss/Base
Extruded Boss/Base	Swept Boss/Base	Lofted Boss/Base

Understanding the Draft Options

- Drafts are normally required in most plastic injection molded parts to ensure proper part removal from the mold halves.
- The Draft option in SolidWorks adds tapers to the faces using the angles specified by the user.
- Drafts can be inserted in an existing part or added to a feature while being extruded.
- Drafts can be applied to solid parts as well as the surface models.
- There are several types of draft available:

  * Neutral Plane
  * Parting Line
  * Step Draft

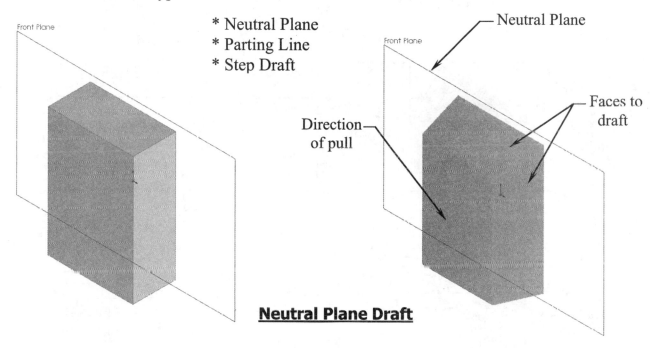

Neutral Plane Draft

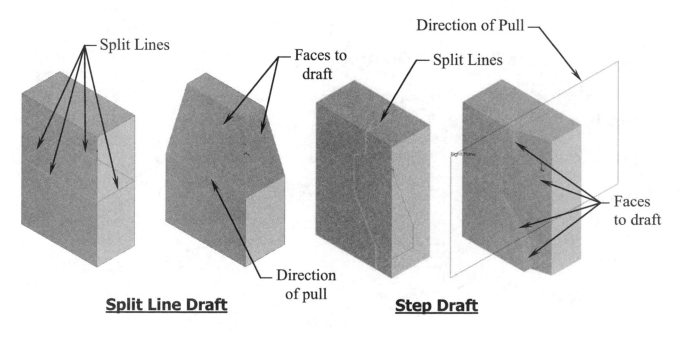

Split Line Draft   **Step Draft**

1. Opening a part document:

- From the Training CD, locate and open a part document named:
  Water Pump Sketch.

- The sketch was created ahead of time to help focus on the key features of this lesson: Sweep and Loft.

- **Edit** the Sketch1.

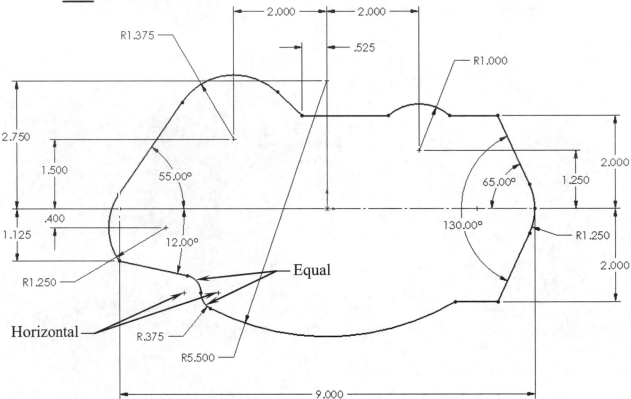

2. Extruding the Base with Draft:

- Click 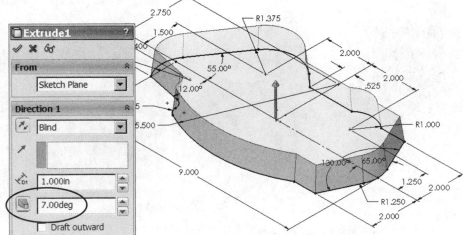 **Extruded Boss/Base.**

- End Condition: **Blind**.

- Depth: **1.00 in**.

- Draft: **7 deg. inward**.

- Click **OK** ✓.

3. Sketching the upper Inlet Port:

- Select the <u>Front</u> plane and open a new sketch.

- Sketch the profile as shown.

- Add the dimensions and relations as indicated.

- Add a vertical Centerline from the Origin and use it as the center of the revolve in the next step.

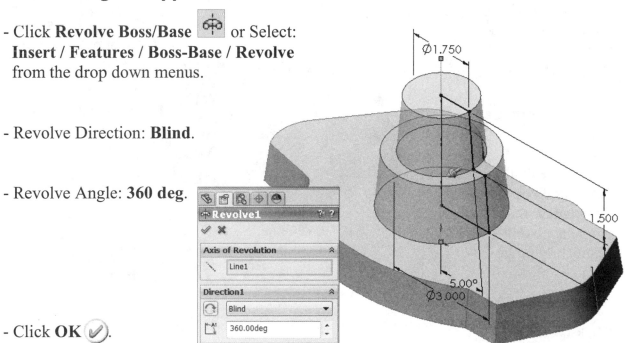

4. Revolving the upper Inlet Port:

- Click **Revolve Boss/Base** or Select: **Insert / Features / Boss-Base / Revolve** from the drop down menus.

- Revolve Direction: **Blind**.

- Revolve Angle: **360 deg**.

- Click **OK**.

5. Adding the .500" Fillets:

- Click **Fillet**  or select **Insert / Features / Fillet-Round.**

- Enter **.500 in.** for radius value.

- Select the **7 edges** as shown.

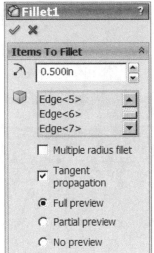

Select 7 edges

- Click **OK** .

6. Adding the .275" Fillets:

- Click **Fillet** 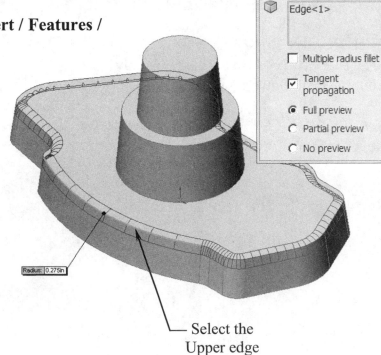 or select **Insert / Features / Fillet-Round.**

- Enter **.275 in.** for radius value.

- Select the **upper edge** of the base.

- Make sure that the option: **Tangent Propagation** is **Enabled** so the fillet can propagate itself to all connecting edges.

Select the Upper edge

- Click **OK** 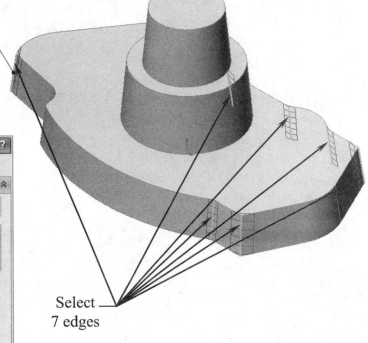.

7. Creating the 1st Offset-Distance Plane:

- Click **Plane** ◇ or select **Insert / Reference Geometry / Plane.**

- From the Flyout FeatureManager tree, select the **Front** plane to offset from.

- Enter **3.000 in**. for distance.

- Place the new plane on the **right side**.

- Click **OK** ✓.

Click here to bring out the FeatureManager tree (Flyout)

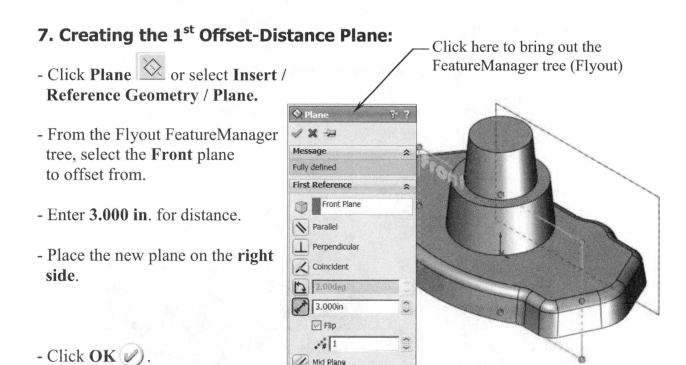

8. Creating the 2nd Offset-Distance Plane:

- Click **Plane** ◇ or select **Insert / Reference Geometry / Plane.**

- Select the <u>Front</u> plane again from the Flyout FeatureManager tree to offset from.

- Enter **5.000 in**. for offset distance.

- Place the new plane also on the **right side**.

- Click **OK** ✓.

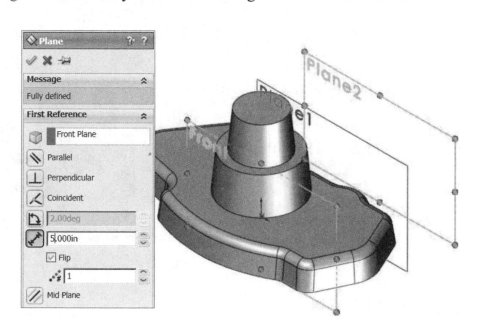

9. Creating the 3rd Offset-Distance Plane:

- Click **Plane** 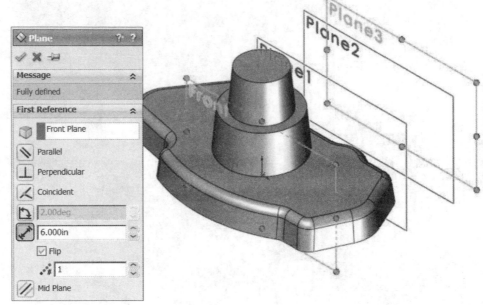 or select **Insert / Reference Geometry / Plane.**

- Select the <u>Front</u> plane once again from the Flyout FeatureManager tree to offset from.

- Enter **6.000 in**. for offset distance.

- Place the new plane also on the **right side**.

- Click **OK** ✓.

10. Sketching the 1st loft profile:

- Select the <u>Front</u> plane and open a new sketch

- Sketch a Rectangle ▢ that's just **.125 in**. above the bottom edge of the part.

- Add the dimensions and relations as shown to fully define the sketch.

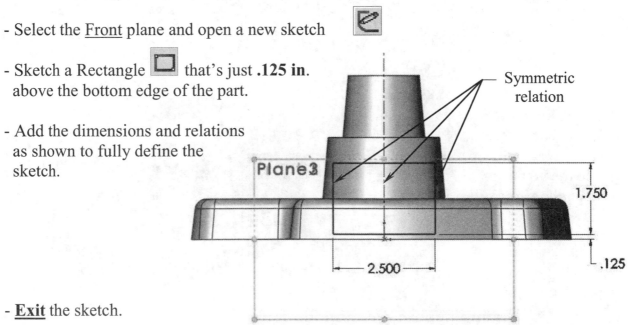

Symmetric relation

Plane3

1.750

2.500

.125

- <u>**Exit**</u> the sketch.

11. Sketching the 2ⁿᵈ loft profile:

- Select the Plane1 and open a new sketch ✎ .

- Sketch another Rectangle ▢ as shown.

- Add the dimensions and relations needed to fully define the sketch.

- **Exit** the sketch.

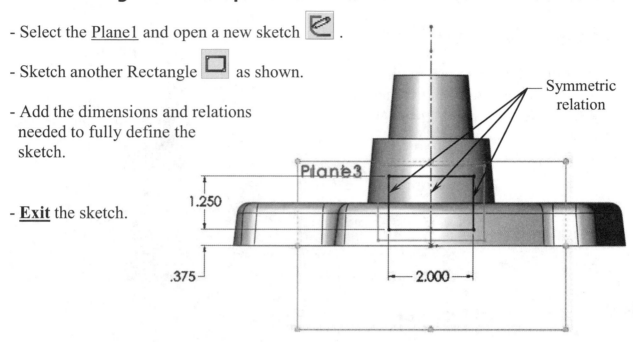

12. Sketching the 3ʳᵈ loft profile:

- Select the Plane2 and open a new sketch ✎ .

- Sketch a Circle ⊕ just above the Origin as shown below.

- Use the **Split-Entities** ✎ command and split the circle into **4 segments**.

- Add Vertical and Horizontal relations between the split points.

- The Split Entities command is used to split the entities in each sketch to an even number of connecting points for use within a loft feature.

- Add the dimensions and relations needed to fully define the sketch.

- **Exit** the sketch.

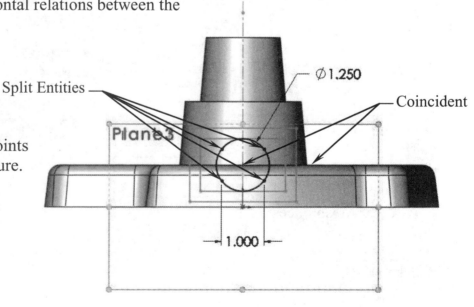

13. Sketching the 4th loft profile:

- Select the <u>Plane3</u> and open a new sketch 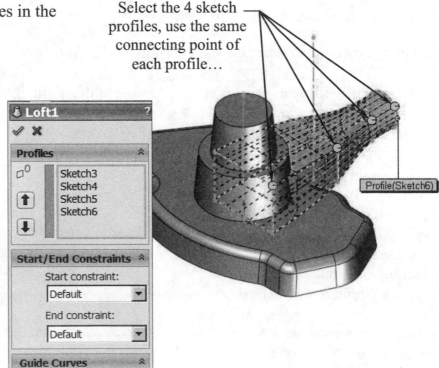 .

- Convert the circle from the previous sketch, this creates an On-Edge relation between the 2 circles and they will update at the same time when the first circle is changed.

Convert from the previous sketch…

- **Exit** the sketch.

14. Creating a loft feature:

- Click Loft 🔩 or select: **Insert / Boss-Base / Loft** from the drop down menus.

- Select the 4 sketch profiles in the graphics area.

Select the 4 sketch profiles, use the same connecting point of each profile…

(Since there are no guide curves to help control the loft, the profiles should be selected from the same side each time to prevent them from twisting.)

- For clarity, right click in the yellow shaded area and select the following options:

  - Transparent
  - Opaque
  - Clear Mesh Faces

- Click **OK** ✅.

15. Creating the mounting bosses:

- Select the <u>bottom face</u> and open a new sketch.

- Sketch **5 Circles** as shown.

- <u>Avoid</u> the hidden entities. (When sketching, your circles may snap to some of the hidden edges of the model causing over defined when adding the dimensions. To overcome this, hold the control key every time a hidden edge highlights, this will cancel the Auto-Relation snapping).

- Add a **Tangent** relation for each circle, to the outer edge of the part.

- Add an **Equal** relation to all 5 circles.

- Add dimensions to fully position the 5 circles.

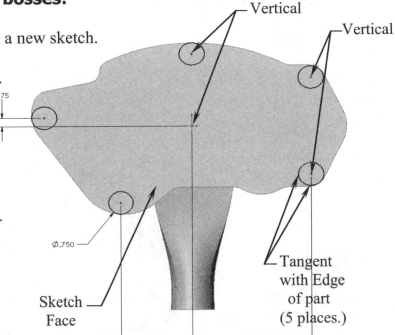

Vertical

Vertical

.275

Ø.750

Sketch Face

Tangent with Edge of part (5 places.)

2.100   3.450

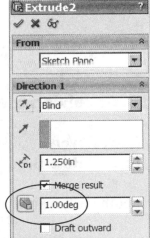

Extrude2

From
Sketch Plane

Direction 1
Blind

D1   1.250in

Merge result
1.00deg

Draft outward

16. Extruding the 5 mounting bosses:

- Click **Extrude Boss-Base** or select: **Insert / Extrude / Boss-Base**, from the drop down menus.

- Set the following:

  - End Condition: **Blind**

  - Depth: **1.250 in**.

  - Draft: **1 deg. Inward.**

- Click **OK** .

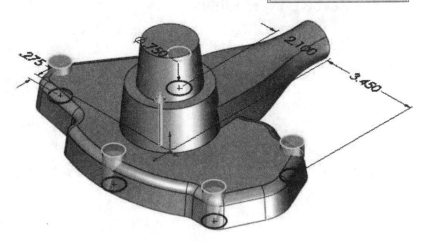

17. Sketching the rear Inlet Port:

- Select the <u>upper face</u> and open a new sketch.

- Sketch the profile of the Inlet at a 30° angle, one end of the profile locking to the Origin.

- Add dimensions and other relations to fully position the sketch.

- Select the Vertical centerline before clicking the Revolve command.

Sketch Face

.500

4.000   30.00°   .750

.375

18. Revolving the Rear Inlet Port:

- Click **Revolve** or select: **Insert / Boss-Base / Revolve**.

- Set the following:

    - Revolve Type: **Blind**.

    - Revolve Angle: **360 deg**.

Revolve2

Axis of Revolution

Line1

Direction1

Blind

360.00deg

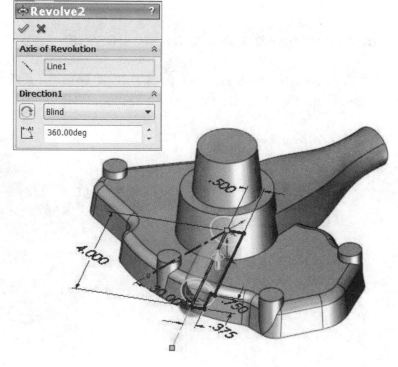

- Click **OK** .

19. Adding the 1st Face Fillet:

- Click **Fillet** or select:
  Insert / Features / Fillet-Round.

- Enter **.250 in.** for radius value.

- For **Face Set 1**, select the
  upper face of the lofted feature.

- For **Face Set 2**, select the **side
  face** of the lofted feature.

- Click **OK** .

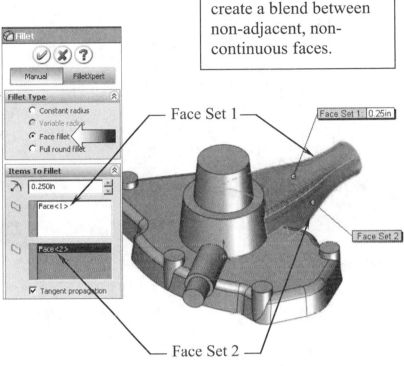

Face Set 1

Face Set 2

Face Set 2

> 💡 **Face Fillet**
>
> A Face Fillet a used to
> create a blend between
> non-adjacent, non-
> continuous faces.

20. Adding the 2nd Face Fillet:

- Click **Fillet** or select: **Insert / Features / Fillet-Round.**

- Enter **.250 in.** for radius value.

- For **Face Set 1**, select
  the **upper face** of the
  lofted feature.

- For **Face Set 2**, select
  the **side face** of the
  lofted feature.

- Click **OK** .

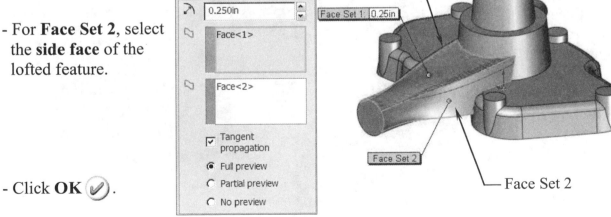

Face Set 1

Face Set 2

21. Adding the 3rd Face Fillet:

- Click **Fillet** 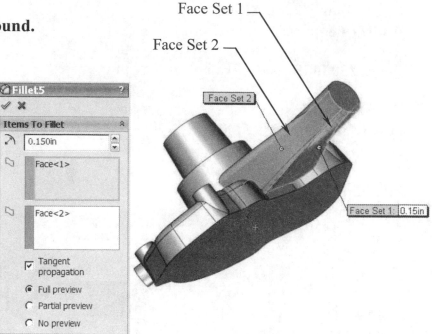 or select:
  Insert / Features / Fillet-Round.

- Enter **.150 in.** for radius
  value.

- For **Face Set 1**, select the
  lower face of the lofted
  feature.

- For **Face Set 2**, select the
  side face of the lofted
  feature.

- Click **OK** .

22. Adding the 4th Face Fillet:

- Click **Fillet** 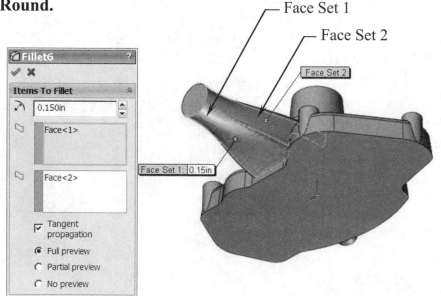 or select:
  Insert / Features / Fillet-Round.

- Enter **.150 in.** for radius
  value.

- For **Face Set 1**, select the
  lower face of the lofted
  feature.

- For **Face Set 2**, select the
  Side face of the lofted
  feature.

- Click **OK** .

23. Mirroring the rear Inlet Port:

- Click **Mirror** 📇 or select:
**Insert / Pattern Mirror /
Mirror.**

- For Mirror Face/Plane, select
the **Right** plane from the
flyout FeatureManager tree.

- For Features to Mirror, select
the **Rear Inlet Port** either
from the Graphics area or
from the Feature tree.

- Click **OK** ✅.

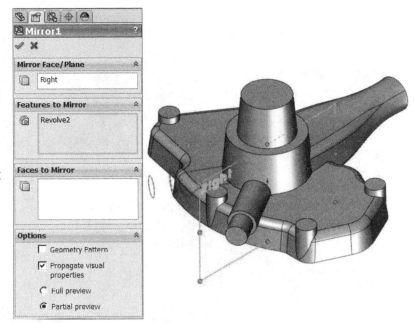

24. Adding the .175" Fillets:

- Click **Fillet** 🔲 or select: **Insert / Features / Fillet-Round.**

- Enter **.175 in.** for radius value.

- Select the edges as shown
to add the fillets.

- The option Tangent-
Propagation should be
on by default.

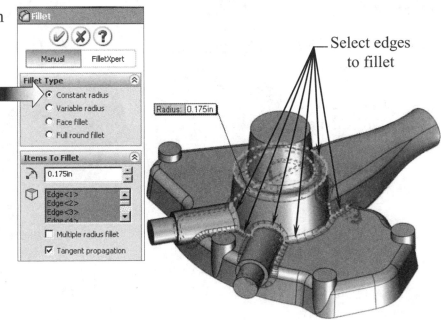

Select edges
to fillet

- Click **OK** ✅.

25. Shelling the part:

- Click **Shell** 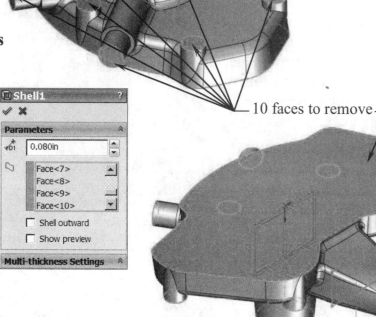 or select:
Insert / Features / Shell.

- Under the Parameters
section, enter **.080 in**. for
wall thickness.

- Select the total of **10 faces**
to remove.

- Click **OK** ✔.

10 faces to remove

26. Adding the .0625" Fillets:

- Click **Fillet** or select:
Insert / Features / Fillet-Round.

- Enter **.0625 in**. for
radius value.

- Select the edges as
shown to add the
fillets.

- Click **OK** ✔.

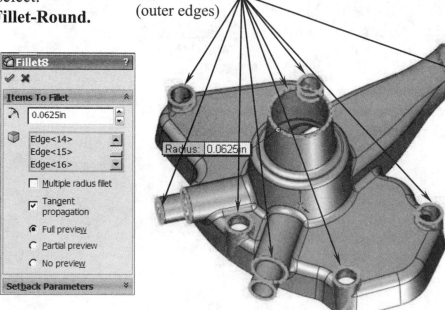

Edges to fillet
(outer edges)

27. Adding a Rib:

- Select the <u>Front</u> plane from the FeatureManager tree

  and open a new sketch .

- Sketch a Line as shown.

- Add Coincident relations between the
  endpoints of the line and the
  edges of the part.

> 💡 **Rib Features**
>
> A rib is an extruded
> feature which adds
> material of a specified
> thickness in a specified
> direction. Drafts can
> also be added to the
> faces of the rib.

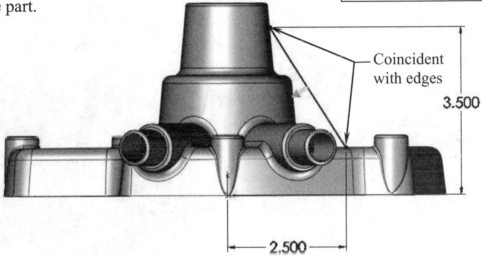

— Coincident
with edges

3.500

2.500

28. Extruding the Rib:

- Click **Rib** or select: **Insert / Features / Rib.**

- Select **Both Directions** under the Thickness section.

- Enter **.275 in**. for the
  thickness of the rib.

- Enable the Draft option
  and enter **1.00 deg**.

- Enable the **Draft
  Outward** check box.

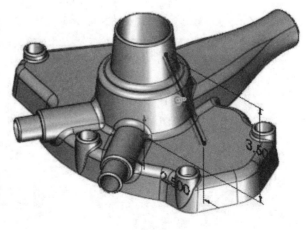

- Click **OK** .

29. Creating a Full-Round fillet:

- A Full-Round creates fillets that are tangent to three adjacent face sets.

- Click **Fillet** or select: **Insert / Features / Fillet-Round.**

- Select the **Full Round** fillet option.

- For Face 1, select the **left surface** of the Rib.

- For Face 2, select the **right surface** of the Rib.

- For Face 3, select the **middle surface** of the Rib.

- Click **OK** .

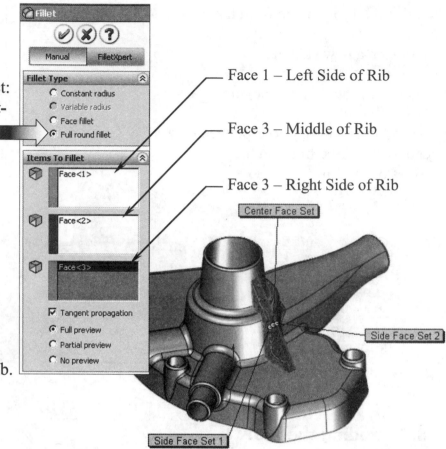

Face 1 – Left Side of Rib

Face 3 – Middle of Rib

Face 3 – Right Side of Rib

30. Mirroring the Rib:

- Click **Mirror** or select: **Insert / Pattern Mirror / Mirror.**

- For Mirror Face/Plane, select the **Right** plane.

- For Features to Mirror, select the **Rib** and its **fillet.**

- Click **OK** .

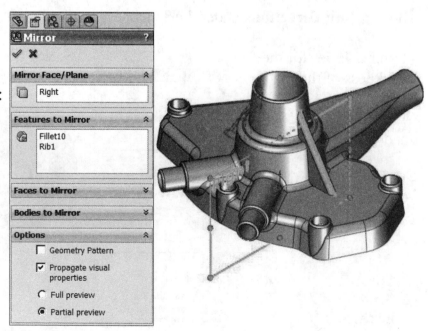

31. Adding the .025" fillets:

- Click **Fillet** [icon] or select: **Insert / Features / Fillet- Round.**

- Select the **Constant Radius** fillet option.

- Enter **.025 in.** for radius Value.

- Select the edges as indicated to add the fillets.

- Enable the Tangent-Propagation check box.

- Click **OK** [icon].

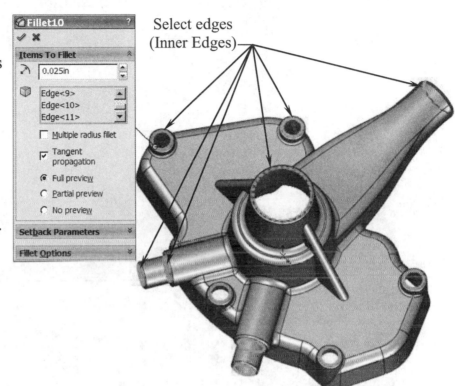

Select edges (Inner Edges)

32. Adding the .175" fillets:

- Click **Fillet** [icon] or select: **Insert / Features / Fillet-Round.**

- Enter **.175 in.** for radius value.

- Select the edges of the 2 ribs as shown.

- Click **OK** [icon].

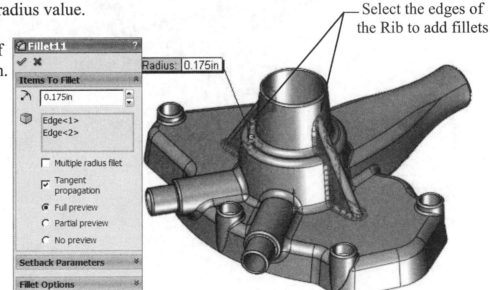

Select the edges of the Rib to add fillets

33. Saving your work:

- Click **File / Save As**.

- Enter **Water Pump Cover** as the name of the file.

- Click **Save.**

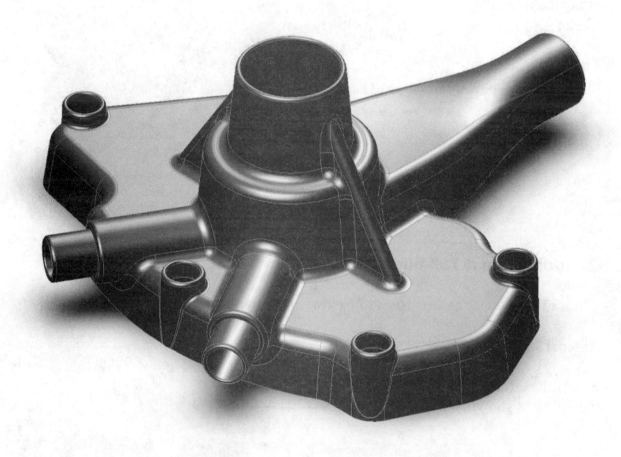

CHAPTER 6

Loft Vs. Sweep

Loft  vs. Sweep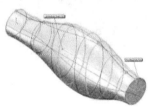

- The Loft and the Sweep commands are normally used to create advanced, complex shapes. The differences between the two are:

    • Sweep uses a single sketched profile to sweep along a path and is controlled by one or more guide curves.

Sweep uses one profile, one path and multiple guide curves

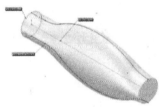

    • Loft uses multiple sketched profiles to loft between the sections and is controlled by 1 or more guide curves or 1 Centerline Parameter.

Loft uses multiple profiles, one centerline parameter, or multiple guide curves

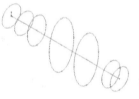

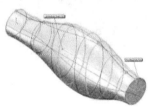

- In order to create a solid feature, each sketch profile must be a single, closed, and non-intersecting shape.

- The guide curves can be either a 2D sketch or a 3D curve.

- The sweep path and guide curves must be related to the sketch profiles with either a Coincident or Pierce relation.

- The loft profiles should have the same number of entities or segments. The Split-Entities ✗ commands can be used to split the sketch entities and add the necessary connectors to helps control the loft more accurately.

Water Meter Housing
Loft vs. Sweep

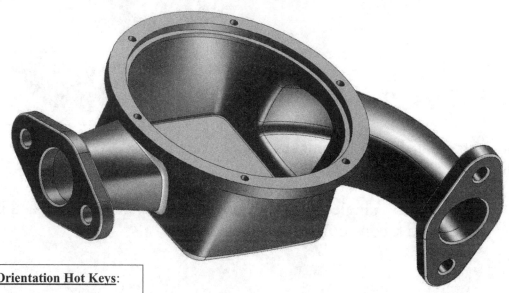

Dimensioning Standards: **ANSI**

Units: **INCHES** – 3 Decimals

Tools Needed:

Insert Sketch	Line	Split Entities
Sketch Fillet	Mirror	Add Geometric Relations
Dimension	Base/Boss Extrude	Extruded Cut
Plane	Base/Boss Sweep	Base/Boss Loft

1. Sketching the 1ˢᵗ Loft Profile:

- Select the <u>Top</u> plane from the FeatureManager tree.

- Click 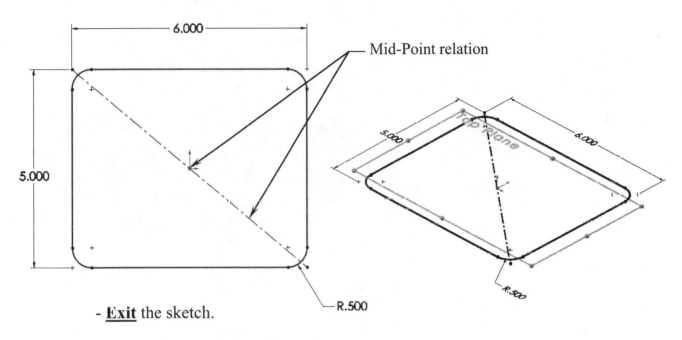 or select **Insert / Sketch**.

- Sketch a rectangle centered on the Origin and add the dimensions as shown.

Mid-Point relation

- **Exit** the sketch.

2. Creating a new plane:

- Click or select **Insert / Reference Geometry / Plane**.

- Select the <u>Top</u> reference plane from the FeatureManager tree.

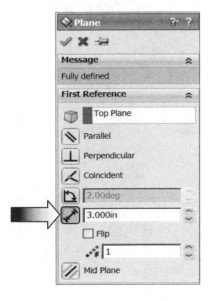

- Select **Offset Distance** option and enter **3.000** in.

- Click **OK**.

New Plane

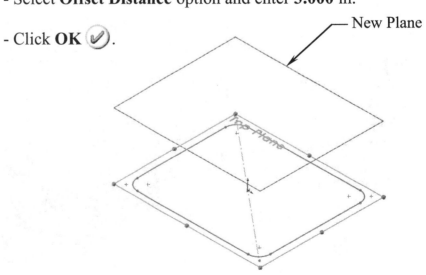

3. Sketching the 2ⁿᵈ Loft Profile:

- Select the <u>new plane</u> (**Plane1**) and open a new sketch  .

- Sketch a Circle ⊕ and add dimensions ◇ and Relations ⊥ as needed.

- Select the **Split Entities** command under: **Tools / Sketch Tools**.

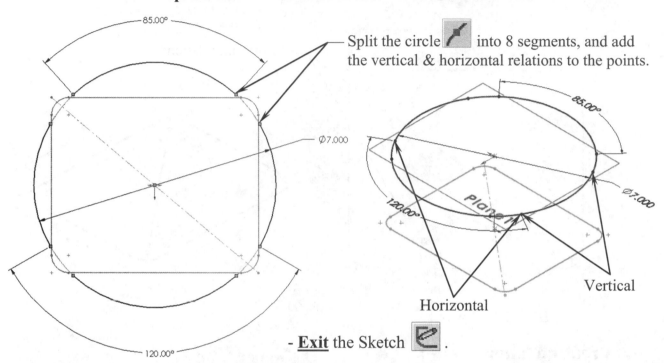

Split the circle ⤵ into 8 segments, and add the vertical & horizontal relations to the points.

Vertical

Horizontal

- **Exit** the Sketch  .

4. Creating the Lofted Base feature:

- Click 🗑 or select **Insert / Boss-Base / Loft**.

- Profiles: Select the 2 sketches as indicated.

- Move the Connector Points as needed to make a smooth transition between the 2 profiles.

- Click **OK** ✓.

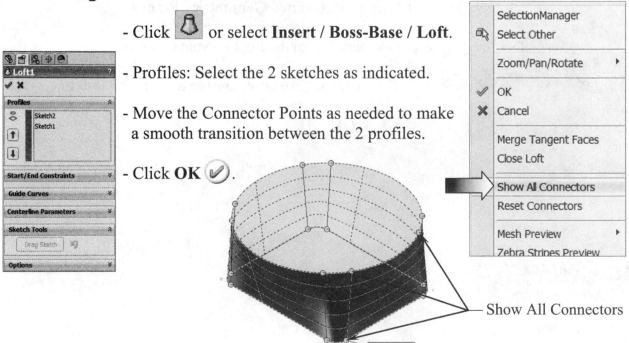

Show All Connectors

5. Creating an Offset Distance plane at 5.500":

- Click 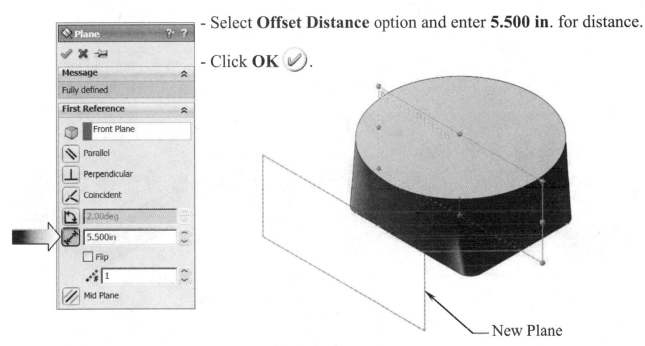 or select **Insert / Reference Geometry / Plane**.

- Select the **Front** reference plane from the FeatureManager tree.

- Select **Offset Distance** option and enter **5.500 in**. for distance.

- Click **OK**.

New Plane

6. Constructing the Inlet's 1st Loft Profile:

- Select the <u>Front</u> plane and open a new sketch.

- Sketch a Rectangle, add Dimensions, and Sketch Fillets.

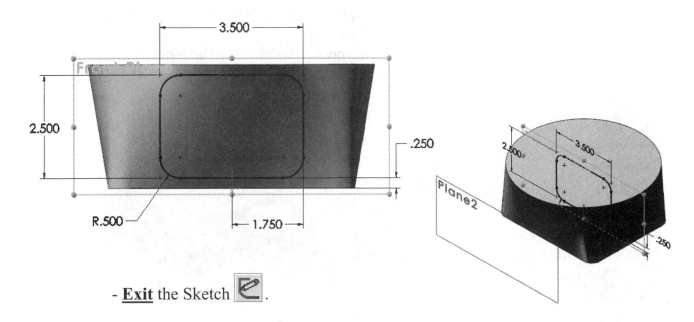

- **Exit** the Sketch.

7. Constructing the Inlet's 2nd Loft Profile:

- Select the Plane2 and open a new sketch

- Sketch a Circle ⊕ and add Dimensions to fully define.

- Click Split Entities 🖊 and split the circle into 8 segments.

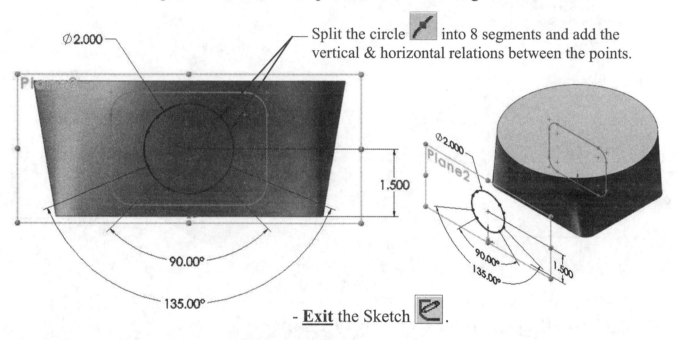

Split the circle 🖊 into 8 segments and add the vertical & horizontal relations between the points.

Ø2.000

Plane2

1.500

90.00°

135.00°

Ø2.000

Plane2

90.00°

135.00°

1.500

- **Exit** the Sketch 📝 .

8. Creating the Inlet solid feature:

- Click 🗗 or select **Insert / Boss-Base / Loft**.

- For profiles: Select the **2 sketches** from the graphics area.

- Show all connector points to make sure a smooth transition between the 2 profiles. Enable the **Merge Tangent Faces** option.

- Click **OK** ✅ .

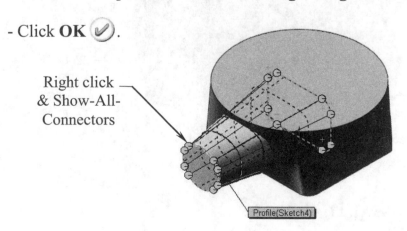

Right click & Show-All-Connectors

Profile(Sketch4)

9. Creating an Offset Distance plane from the Right:

- Click 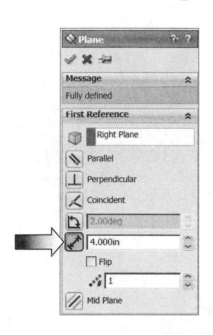 or select **Insert / Reference Geometry / Plane.**

- Select the **Right** reference plane from the FeatureManager tree.

- Select **Offset Distance** option and enter **4.000 in**. for distance.

- Click **OK** ✓.

New Plane

10. Constructing the Outlet's 1st Loft profile:

- Select the <u>new plane</u> (Plane3) and open a new sketch .

- Sketch a Circle ⊕ split it ✂ into 8 segments. Add dimensions ⌀ as noted.

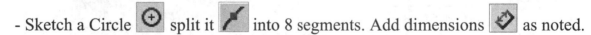
Split the circle ✂ into 8 segments and add the
vertical & horizontal relations to the split points.

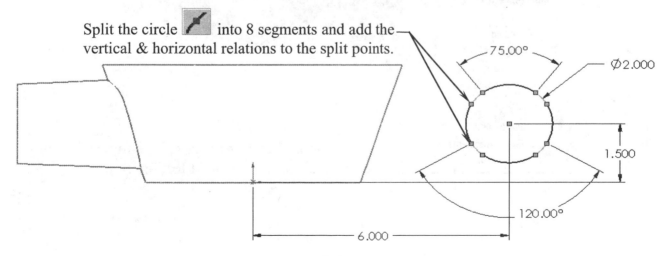

- Add the Vertical and Horizontal relations to the endpoints of the arcs to fully define them.

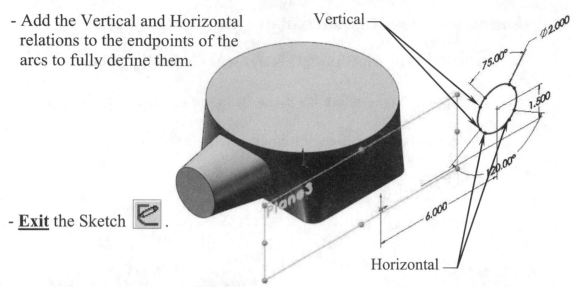

- **Exit** the Sketch.

11. "Re-Using" the previous sketch*:

- Expand the feature **Loft2** from the FeatureManager tree (click the + sign).

- Locate the sketch of the Rectangle (**sketch3**), Right click and select **SHOW**.

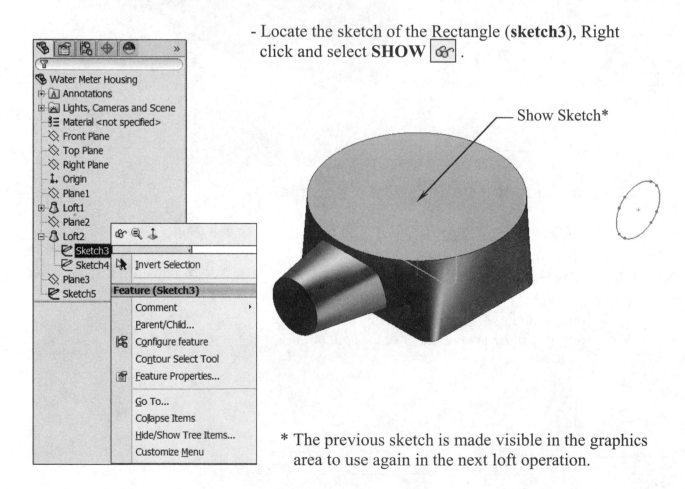

* The previous sketch is made visible in the graphics area to use again in the next loft operation.

12. Creating a plane Parallel:

- Click ⬦ or select **Insert / Reference Geometry / Plane**.

- Select the **Top** reference plane from the FeatureManager tree.

- Select the **Parallel** plane option.

- Click the **Center Point** of the Circle.

- Click **OK** ✓.

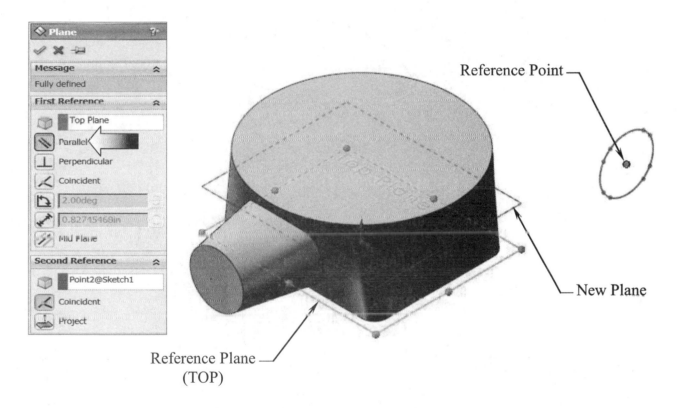

Reference Point

New Plane

Reference Plane
(TOP)

- The new plane is
  created (Plane4).

13. Constructing the Centerline Parameter:

- Select the <u>new plane</u> (Plane4) and open a new sketch .

- Switch to the Top view orientation (Cntrl+5) .

- Sketch the profile as shown below.

- Add Dimensions and Sketch Fillet as shown.

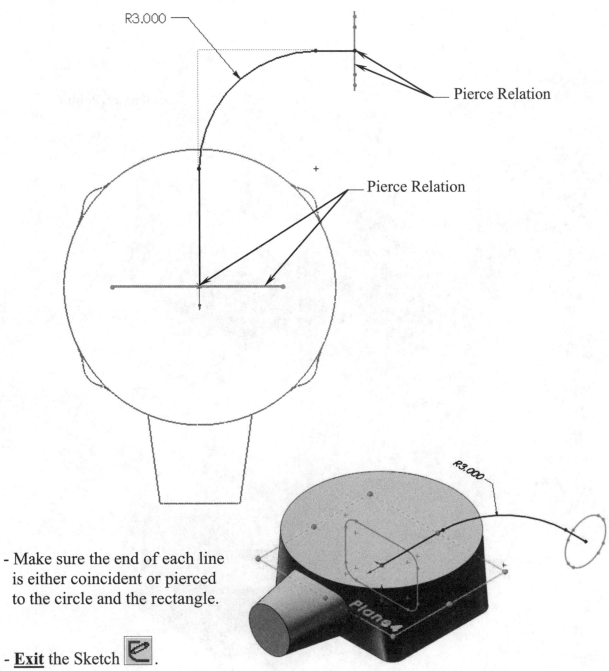

R3.000

Pierce Relation

Pierce Relation

R3.000

Plane4

- Make sure the end of each line
  is either coincident or pierced
  to the circle and the rectangle.

- **Exit** the Sketch .

14. Creating the Outlet loft feature:

- Click ⌂ or select **Insert / Boss / Loft**.

- Select the **2 Sketch Profiles** (Rectangle and Circle) from the graphics area.

- Expand the **Centerline Parameters** option and select **Sketch6** from either the graphics area or from the FeatureManager tree.

- Using the Centerline Parameter to guide the loft will cause the sketch planes of all the intermediate sections to be normal to the centerline.

- After the preview appears, check the connectors to ensure a proper loft transition.

- Click **OK** ✔.

> ### 💡 Centerline Parameters
>
> If the number of entities in each sketch is the same, a "Centerline Parameter Sketch" can be used instead of the guide curves.

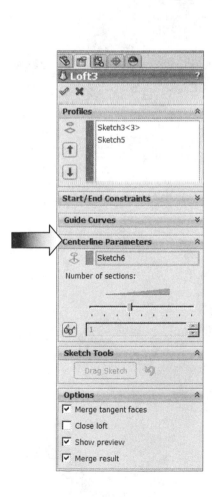

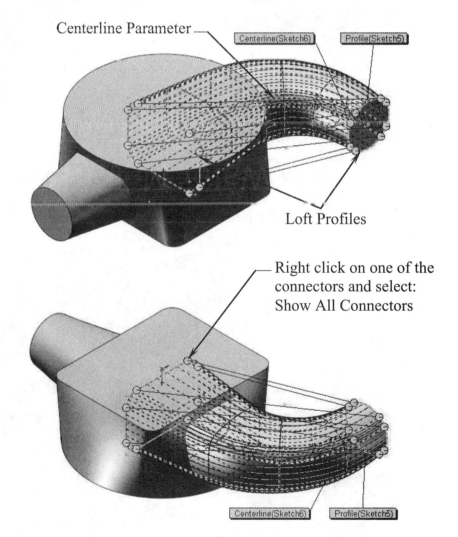

Centerline Parameter — Centerline(Sketch6)   Profile(Sketch5)

Loft Profiles

Right click on one of the connectors and select:
Show All Connectors

Centerline(Sketch6)   Profile(Sketch5)

15. Adding .250" fillet to the Bottom:

- Click 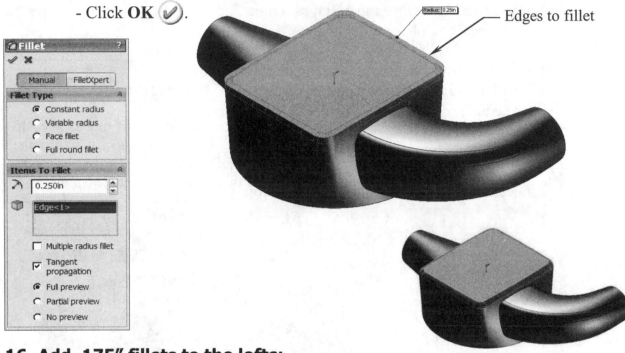 or select **Insert / Features / Fillet-Round**.

- Enter **.250 in**. for radius value and select the **bottom edges** as indicated.

- Click **OK** ✓.

16. Add .175" fillets to the lofts:

- Click or select **Insert / Features / Fillet-Round**.

- Enter **.175 in**. for Radius and select <u>all</u> side edges as noted.

- Click **OK** ✓.

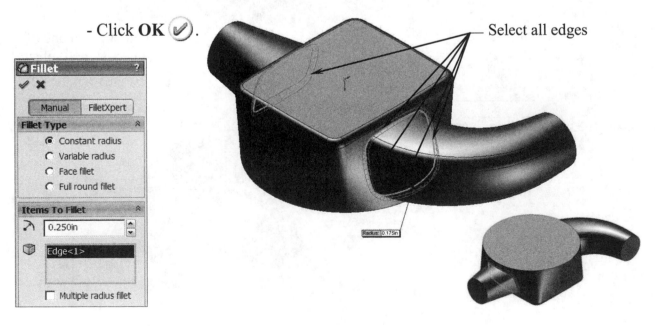

17. Shelling the part:

- Click  or select **Insert / Features / Shell**.

- Enter **.175** for wall thickness and select the 3 faces as shown.

- Click **OK** ✓.

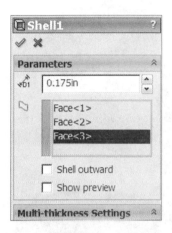

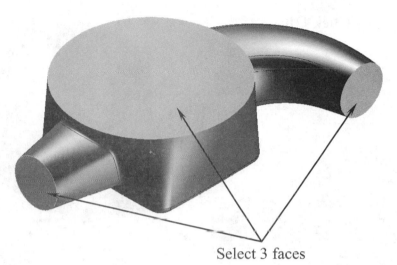

Select 3 faces

18. Creating the 1st Mounting bracket:

- Select the <u>Face</u> as noted and open a new sketch.

- Sketch the profile as shown below, use Convert Entities where applicable.

- Add Dimensions and Relations needed to fully define the sketch.

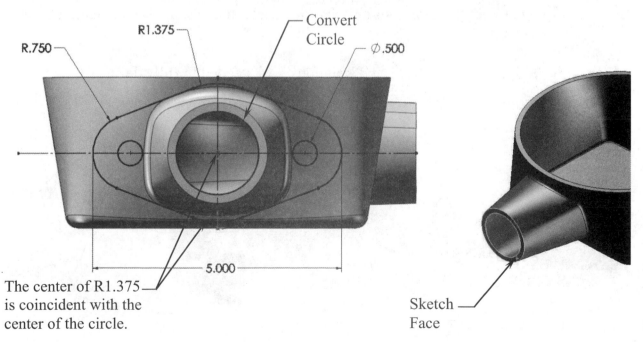

R1.375

R.750

Convert Circle

∅.500

5.000

The center of R1.375 is coincident with the center of the circle.

Sketch Face

19. Extruding the Left bracket:

- Click 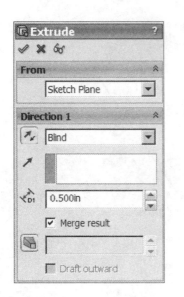 or select **Insert / Boss-Base / Extrude**.

- End Condition: **Blind**   - Depth: **.500 in**.

- Click **OK** ✓.

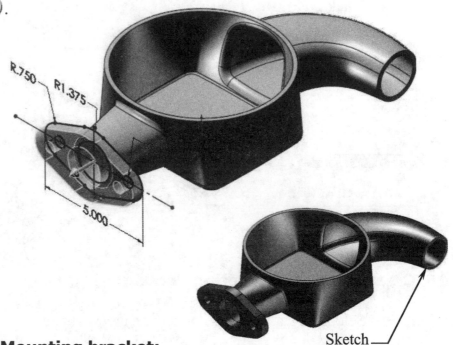

Sketch Face

20. Creating the 2nd Mounting bracket:

- Select the <u>Face</u> as noted and open a new sketch .

- Either copy the previous sketch – or – recreate the same sketch again on the right side.

- Add Dimensions ✏ and Relations ⊥ needed to fully define the sketch.

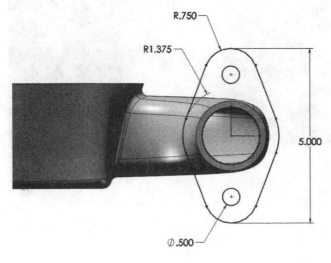

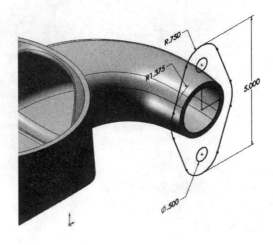

21. Extruding the Right bracket:

- Click ⬛ or select **Insert / Boss-Base / Extrude**.

- End Condition: **Blind**.   - Depth: **.500 in**.

- Click **OK** ✅.

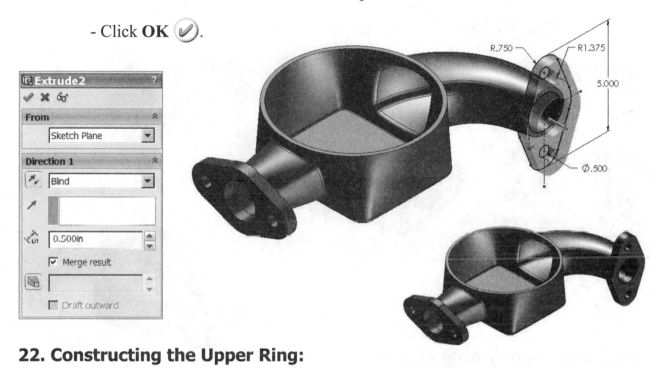

22. Constructing the Upper Ring:

- Select the <u>Face</u> as indicated and open a new sketch ⬛ .

- Sketch the profile below, using Convert Entities ⬛ where needed.

- The centers of the Ø.250 Circles are coincident with the Ø7.375 bolt-circle.

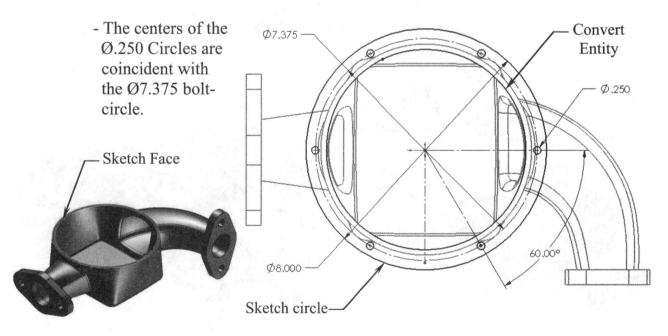

23. Extruding the Upper Ring:

- Click  or select **Insert / Boss-Base / Extrude**.

- End Condition: **Blind**.   - Depth: **.400 in**. (upward)

- Click **OK** ✓.

24. Adding a Seal-Ring bore:

- Select the <u>Face</u> as noted and open a new sketch 📝 .

- Select the Inside Circular Edge and click **Offset Entities** ⤵ .

- Enter **.150 in**. for Offset Value (offset to a larger diameter).

- Click **OK** ✓.

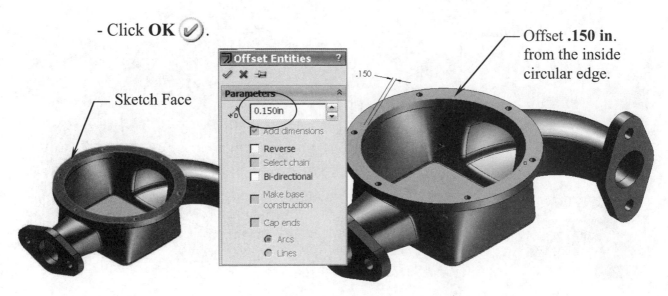

Offset **.150 in**. from the inside circular edge.

Sketch Face

25. Extruding Cut the Seal Ring bore:

- Click  or select **Insert / Cut / Extrude**.

- End Condition: **Blind**.

- Depth: **.250 in**.

- Click **OK** .

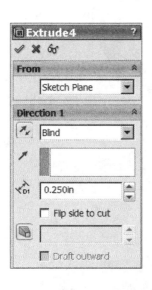

26. Adding fillets:

- Click or select **Insert / Features / Fillet-Round**.

- Enter **.0625 in**. for radius value.

- Select the 7 edges as noted.

- Click **OK** .

Edges to fillet

27. Adding Chamfers:

- Click 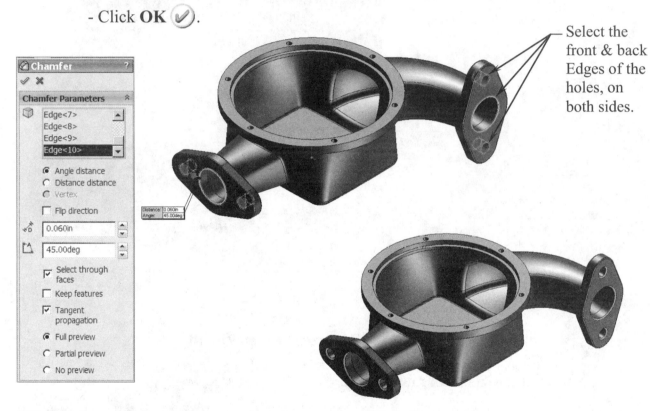 or select **Insert / Features / Chamfer**.

- Enter **.060 in**. for Depth.

- Enter **45 deg**. for Angle.

- Select the edges of the 6 holes.

- Click **OK** .

Select the
front & back
Edges of the
holes, on
both sides.

Chamfer

Chamfer Parameters

Edge<7>
Edge<8>
Edge<9>
Edge<10>

- Angle distance
- Distance distance
- Vertex

Flip direction

0.060in

45.00deg

Select through faces

Keep features

Tangent propagation

- Full preview
- Partial preview
- No preview

Distance: 0.060in
Angle: 45.00deg

28. Saving your work:

- Select **File / Save As / Water Meter Housing / Save**.

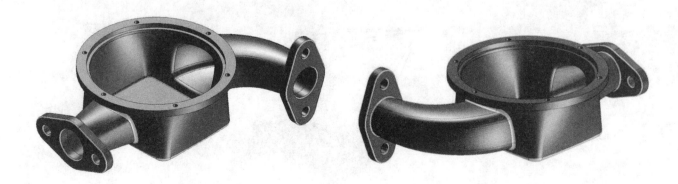

Questions for Review

Loft Vs. Sweep

1. In a new part mode, when the Sketch Pencil is selected first, SolidWorks will prompt you to select a sketch plane.
   a. True
   b. False

2. It is sufficient to create a Parallel-Plane-At-Point with a Reference Plane and a Reference Point.
   a. True
   b. False

3. A loft feature uses multiple sketch profiles to define its shape.
   a. True
   b. False

4. Only one guide curve can be used in each loft feature.
   a. True
   b. False

5. Multiple guide curves can be used to connect and control the loft feature.
   a. True
   b. False

6. The guide curves can be either a 2D sketch or a 3D curve.
   a. True
   b. False

7. The loft profiles and the guide curves should be related with Coincident or Pierce relations.
   a. True
   b. False

8. The loft profiles should be created before the guide curves.
   a. True
   b. False

7. TRUE	8. TRUE
5. TRUE	6. TRUE
3. TRUE	4. FALSE
1. TRUE	2. TRUE

Exercise: Loft

There are several different ways to model this part; but this exercise focuses on the Loft command.

1. Create the part below, using the Loft and the Circular Pattern features.

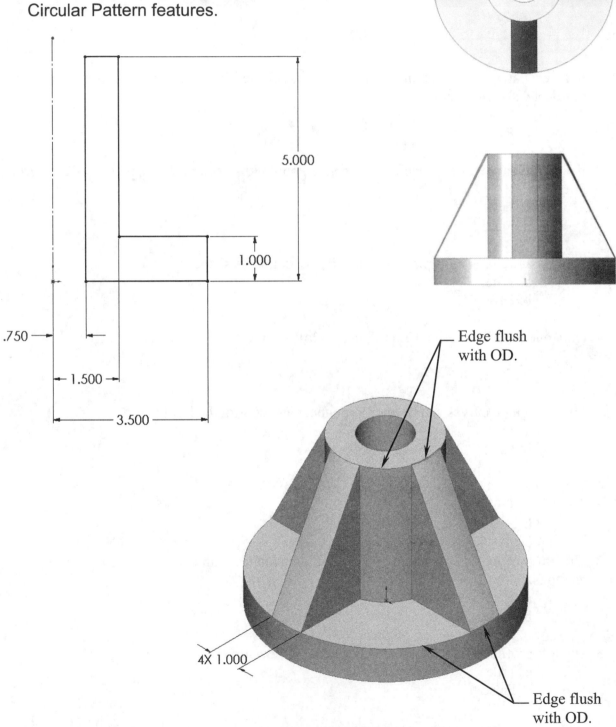

5.000

1.000

.750

1.500

3.500

Edge flush with OD.

4X 1.000

Edge flush with OD.

2. Use the instructions on the following pages, if needed.

1. Starting with the base sketch:

- Select the <u>Front</u> plane and open a new sketch.

- Sketch the profile shown.

- Add the dimensions to fully define the sketch.

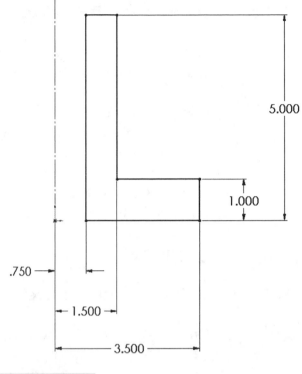

5.000

1.000

.750

1.500

3.500

2. Revolving the base:

- Click  or select **Insert / Boss-Base / Revolve**.

- Direction 1: **Blind**.

- Revolve Angle: **360deg**.

- Click **OK** ✅.

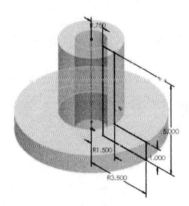

3. Creating the 1st loft profile:

- Select the <u>face</u> indicated and open a new sketch.

- Sketch the profile shown by converting the 2 circular edges then add 2 vertical lines.

- Trim the circles to form one continuous profile.

- **Exit** the sketch.

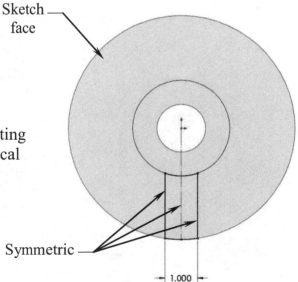

Sketch face

Symmetric

1.000

4. Creating the 2nd loft profile:

- Select the <u>upper face</u> as indicated and open a new sketch.

- Using the same techniques as in the previous sketch, construct this new sketch the same way.

- Add the Collinear relations to both sides, between the 2 sketches.

- **Exit** the sketch.

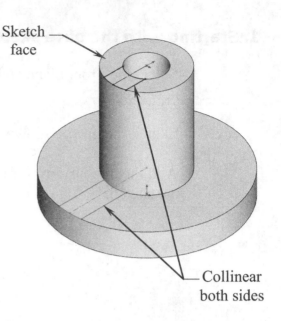

Sketch face

Collinear both sides

5. Creating the 1st loft feature:

- Click 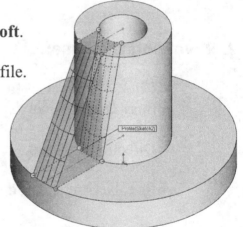 or select: **Insert / Boss-Base / Loft**.

- Select the outer corner of the 1st sketch profile.

- To prevent the loft from twisting, select the outer corner of 2nd loft profile, also from the same side as the 1st.

- Click **OK** ✅.

6. Pattern and save:

- Create a circular pattern of the lofted feature with a total of 4 instances, then save the part as: **Loft_Exe**.

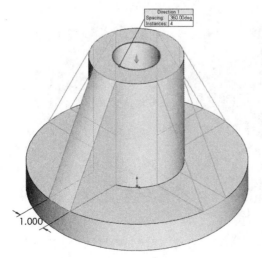

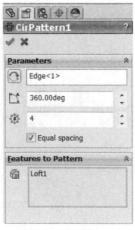

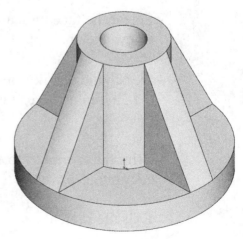

CHAPTER 7

Loft with Guide Curves

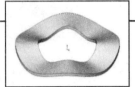

Loft with Guide Curves

- This lesson was developed to demonstrate how a loft feature is created using 4 sketch profiles and a single 3D guide curve.

- A loft feature normally contains several sections and one or more guide curves.

- In this exercise, four identical profiles will be used as the loft sections and a single guide curve will be used to connect the sections.

- Since the sections are identical, the derived-sketch option will be used to show how the sketches can be derived or copied.

- A derived sketch is driven by the original sketch. It can only be positioned with relations or dimensions, but its sketched entities cannot be changed.

- When the Original sketch is changed, the derived-sketch will be updated automatically; however the derived sketches can be Un-derived to break their associations with the Original sketch.

- The loft profiles are connected with a 3D curve; the 3D curve will be generated through some defined points called: Curve-Through-Reference-Points, and Pierced to the loft profiles.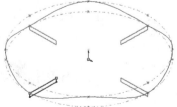

- The Curve-Through-Reference-Points will then be used to guide and control the transition between the loft sections.

Waved Washer
Loft with Guide Curves

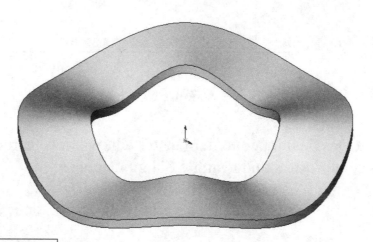

Dimensioning Standards: **ANSI**

Units: **INCHES** – 3 Decimals

Tools Needed:

Insert Sketch	Line	Circle
Sketch Point	Add Geometric Relations	Dimension
Derived Sketch	Curve Through Reference Points	Base/Boss Loft

1. Creating the 1st Construction profile:

- Select the <u>Top</u> plane from the FeatureManager tree.

- Click 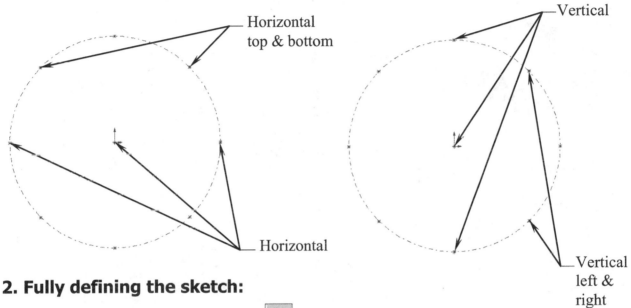 or select **Insert / Sketch**.

- Sketch a Circle and convert it into a construction circle .

- Add **8** sketch points approximately as shown.

2. Fully defining the sketch:

- Select the dimension tool and add dimensions to the sketch points.

- Add a vertical and a horizontal relation as indicated.

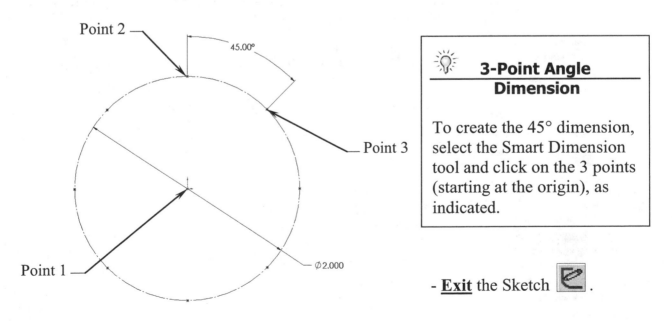

> 💡 **3-Point Angle Dimension**
>
> To create the 45° dimension, select the Smart Dimension tool and click on the 3 points (starting at the origin), as indicated.

- **Exit** the Sketch .

3. Creating an Offset Distance plane:

- Click 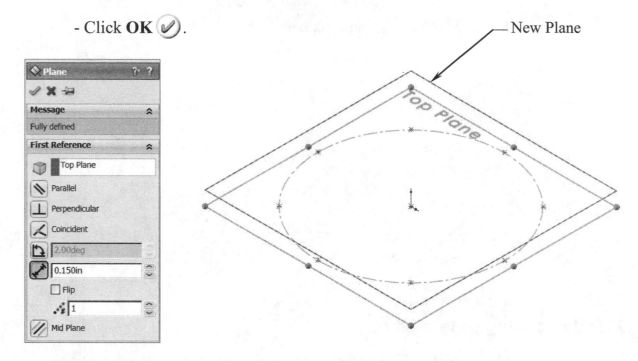 or select **Insert / Reference Geometry / Plane**.

- Select the **Top** plane as Reference Entities.

- Select **Offset Distance** option and enter **.150 in**.

- Click **OK** .

New Plane

4. Creating the 2nd construction profile using Derived Sketch:

- Hold the CONTROL key, select the **new Plane** (plane1) and the **Sketch1** from FeatureManager tree.

- Click **Insert / Derived Sketch**.

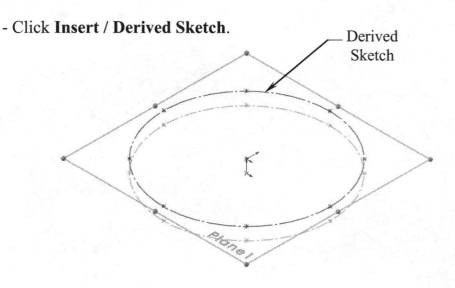

Derived Sketch

5. Positioning the Derived Sketch:

- Add a Vertical & Coincident relation 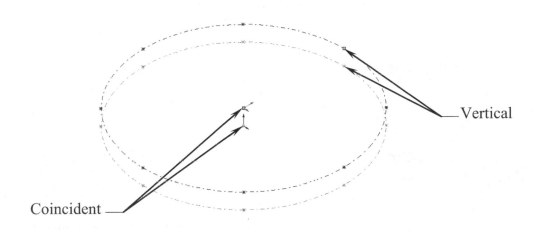 between the indicated points.

Vertical

Coincident

- **Exit** the Sketch or select **Insert / Sketch**.

6. Creating a Curve Through Reference Points

- Click or select **Insert / Curve / Curve-Through-Reference-Points**.

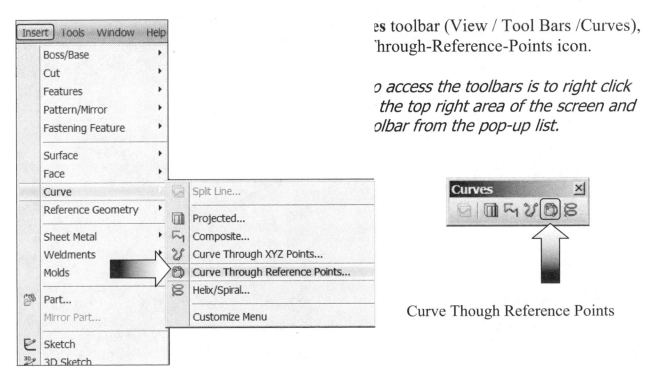

es toolbar (View / Tool Bars /Curves),
'hrough-Reference-Points icon.

o access the toolbars is to right click
the top right area of the screen and
olbar from the pop-up list.

Curve Though Reference Points

- Select the sketch points in the order as shown (required for this lesson only). (Point 1 is on top, 2 is on the bottom, 3 top, 4 bottom, and so on).

- Click [☑ Closed curve] to close the curve.

- Click **OK** ✓.

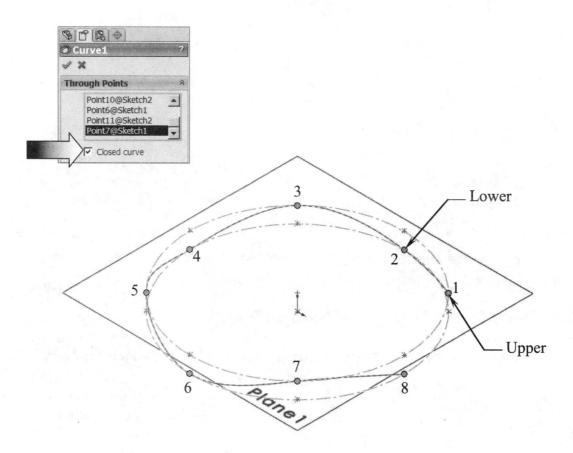

- The resulted 3D curve.

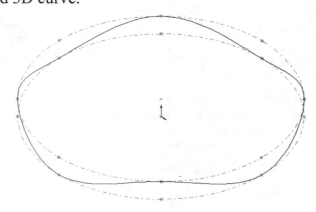

7. Sketching the 1st loft section:

- Select the <u>Front</u> plane from the FeatureManager tree.

- Sketch a rectangle ⬜ add Dimensions ◇ and Relations ⊥ as shown.

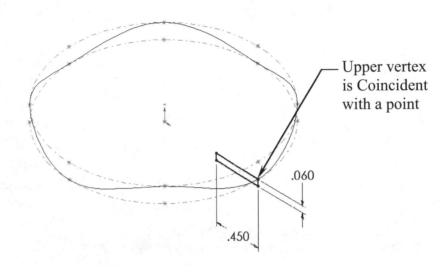

Upper vertex
is Coincident
with a point

.060

.450

- **Exit** the sketch 🖉 or select **Insert / Sketch**.

8. Creating the 2nd loft section using Derived-Sketch:

- Hold the CONTROL key, select the **Front** plane and the sketch of the **rectangle** from the Feature tree.

- Select **Insert / Derived Sketch**.

- The derived sketch is created and placed on top of the original sketch; drag it to the left side then add a coincident relation to the point on the bottom.

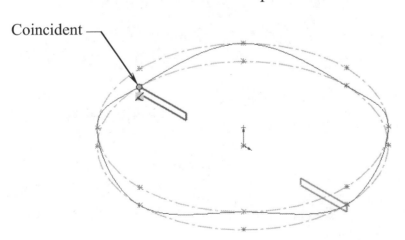

Coincident

9. Fully defining the Derived Sketch:

- Add a Collinear relation  between the 2 lines as indicated.

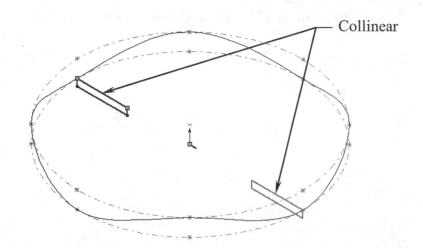

Collinear

> **Derived Sketch**
>
> A derived sketch is a dependent copy of the original sketch. It can only be moved or positioned on the same or different plane with respect to the same model.

- **Exit** the Sketch or select **Insert / Sketch**.

10. Sketching the 3rd loft section: (or use the Derived Sketch option)

- Select the <u>Right</u> plane from the FeatureManager tree.

- Sketch a rectangle (or copy and paste the previous sketch).

- Add Dimensions and Relations needed to fully define the sketch.

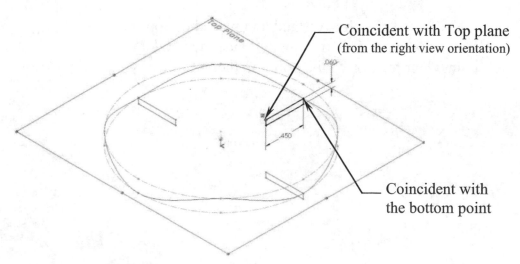

Coincident with Top plane
(from the right view orientation)

Coincident with
the bottom point

- **Exit** the Sketch or select **Insert / Sketch**.

11. Creating the 4th loft section using Derived-Sketch:

- Hold the CONTROL key, select the RIGHT plane <u>and</u> the sketch of the 3rd rectangle, from the FeatureManager tree.

- Select **Insert / Derived Sketch**.

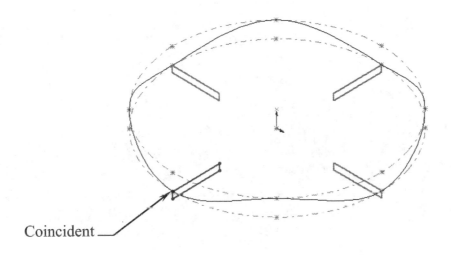

Coincident

12. Constraining the Derived sketch:

- Add a Collinear relation 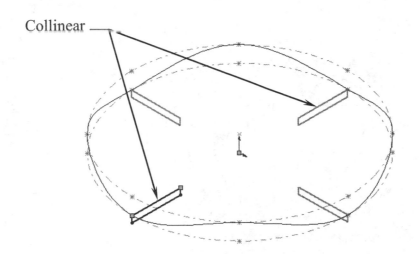 between the 2 lines as shown.

Collinear

- <u>Exit</u> the Sketch or select **Insert / Sketch**.

13. Creating a Loft with Guide curve:

- Click 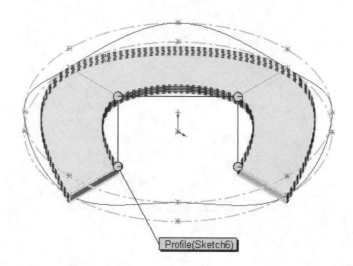 or select **Insert / Boss-Base / Loft**.

- Select the <u>four</u> rectangular sketches as Loft Profiles.

Profile(Sketch6)

- Select the <u>3D curve</u> as Guide Curve.

- Click **Close Loft** ☑ Close loft under Options (arrow).

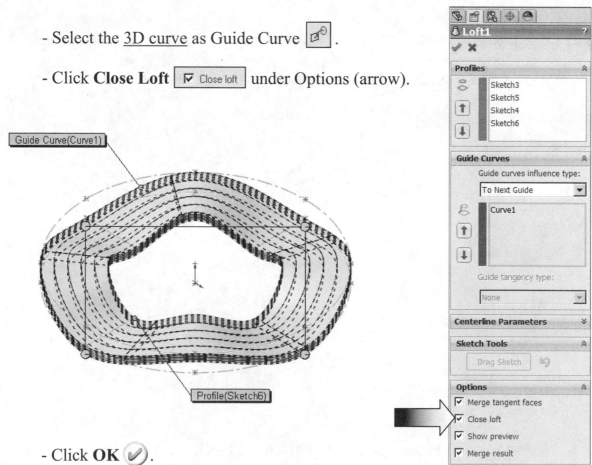

Guide Curve(Curve1)

Profile(Sketch6)

- Click **OK** ✓.

- The completed Waved Washer (with the construction sketches still visible).

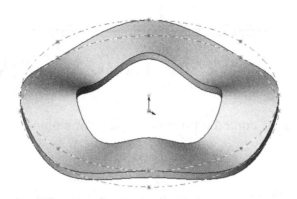

14. Hiding the construction sketches:

- Right click on the construction sketches and select **Hide** .

Hide sketch

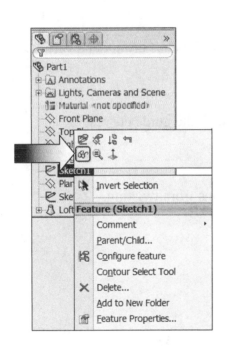

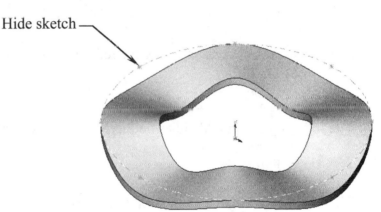

15. Saving your work:

- Select **File / Save As / Waved-Washer / Save.**

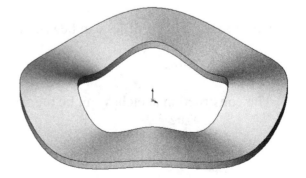

Questions for Review

Loft with Guide Curves

1. A sketch profile can be copied onto another plane or a planar surface.
   a. True
   b. False

2. Sketch points can be added in any sketch to help define the sketch geometry or locations.
   a. True
   b. False

3. If a derived sketch is driven by the original sketch, its entities cannot be changed.
   a. True
   b. False

4. A 3D curve can be created using the reference points in the sketches or model's vertices.
   a. True
   b. False

5. The loft sections should either be Pierced or Coincident with the guide curves.
   a. True
   b. False

6. The guide curves can also be used to control the loft sections from twisting.
   a. True
   b. False

7. Only two guide curves can be used in each loft feature.
   a. True
   b. False

8. Up to four sketch profiles can be used in a loft feature.
   a. True
   b. False

9. The construction sketches can be toggled (Show/Hide) at any time.
   a. True
   b. False

9. TRUE
7. FALSE   8. FALSE
5. TRUE   6. TRUE
3. TRUE   4. TRUE
1. TRUE   2. TRUE

Exercise: V-Shaped – 3 revolutions

1. Creating the Base sketch:

- From the Top plane sketch a circle that is centered on the origin.

- Add a diameter dimension of **.100"**.

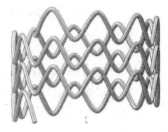

2. Activating the Surfaces toolbar:

- Right click on the **Sketch Tab** and click on **Surfaces** to enable it.

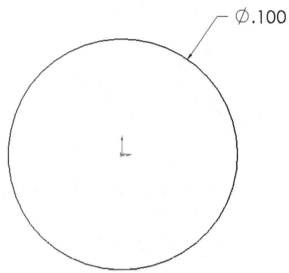

Ø.100

3. Extruding a surface:

- From the Surfaces toolbar click: **Extruded Surface**.

- Use the **Blind** type and enter **.060"** for extrude depth.

- Click **OK**.

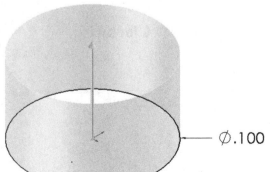

Ø.100

4. Creating a helix:

- Select the <u>Top</u> plane and open a new sketch.

- Select the bottom edge of the extruded surface and press **Convert Entities**.

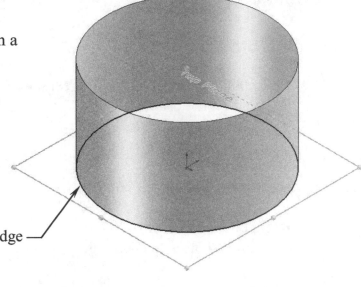

Convert edge ——

- From the Features toolbar click: **Curves / Helix and Spiral**.

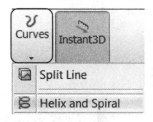

- Enter the following:

   * Defined by: **Pitch and Revolution**

   * **Constant Pitch**

   * Pitch: **0.020"**

   * Revolutions: **3**

   * Start Angle: **0**

   * **Clockwise**

- Click **OK** .

5. Creating a surface profile:

- Select the <u>Top</u> plane and open a new sketch.

- Sketch a vertical line and add a **.010"** linear dimension.

- Add a **Pierce** relation between the endpoint of the line and the helix.

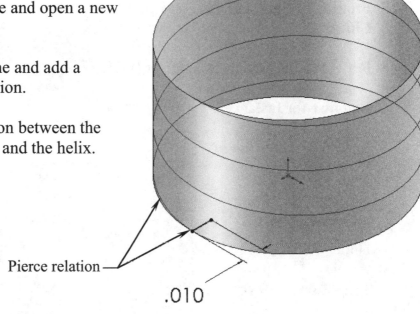

Pierce relation⎯

.010

- Switch to the **Surfaces** toolbar and click **Extruded Surface**.

- For extrude type, use the default **Blind** type.

- Enter **.020"** for extrude depth.

- Click **OK** ✓.

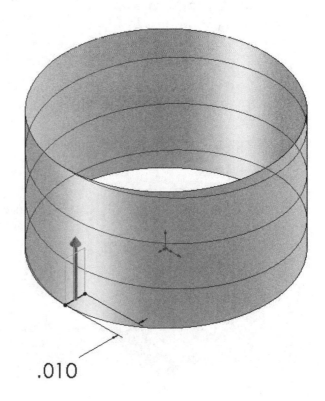

.010

6. Creating a Curve Driven Pattern:

- From the Features toolbar and click:
  Linear Pattern / Curve Driven Pattern.

- For Direction 1, select the **Helix** (Edge 1).

- Enter **61** for Instances.

- Enable **Equal Spacing** checkbox.

- Under Curve Method select:
  Transform Curve.

- Under Alignment-Method select:
  Tangent to Curve.

- Under Face Normal Select:
  the **Cylindrical surface** of the cylinder.

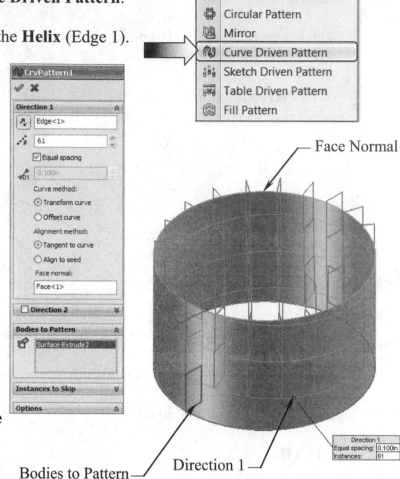

Bodies to Pattern —   Direction 1 —

Face Normal

- Expand the **Bodies to Pattern** section and select the **Extruded Surface** in step 5.

- Click **OK** ✓.

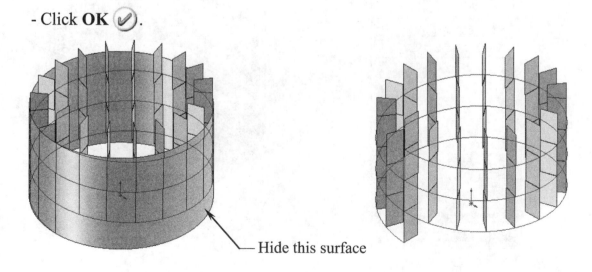

— Hide this surface

7. Creating a Curve Through Reference Points:

- From the Features toolbar select:
Curves / Curve Through Reference points.

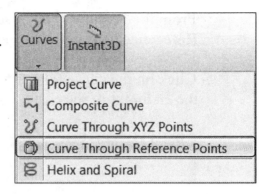

- Click the starting point (point 1) at the end of the helix and go clockwise to point 2, then point 3 as indicated.

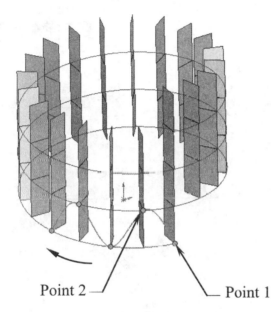

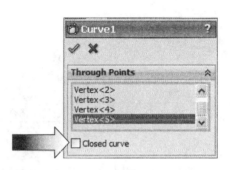

Point 2 ⎯⎯⎯   ⎯⎯ Point 1

- Continue going around and select all connecting points. Simply delete any mistakes from the Through Points dialog box.

- Be sure to **uncheck** the Close Curve checkbox since the two ends of this curve are not supposed to connect.

- Click **OK** ⊘.

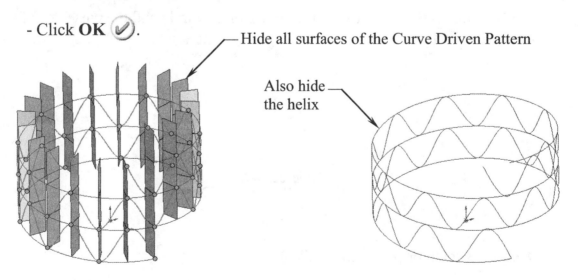

⎯ Hide all surfaces of the Curve Driven Pattern

Also hide ⎯
the helix

8. Creating a Perpendicular plane:

- From the Features toolbar select:
Reference Geometry / Planes.

- Click on the curve (closer to the end) AND also click the endpoint of the curve, as noted.

- Click **OK** 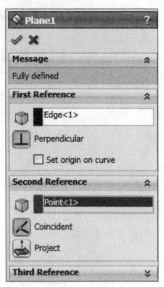.

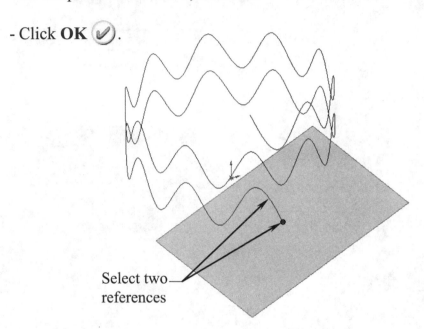

Select two references

9. Sketching the sweep profile:

- Select the <u>new plane</u> and open a new sketch.

- Sketch a **small circle** next to the curve and add a diameter dimension of **.002"**.

- Add a **Pierce** relation between the center of the circle and the curve to fully define the sketch.

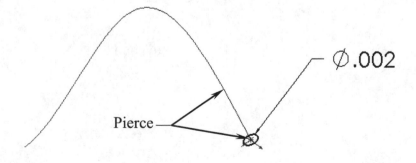

Pierce

Ø.002

- **Exit** the sketch or press Control + Q.

10. Creating the final sweep:

- Switch to the Features toolbar and click: **Swept Boss Base**.

- Select the small circle to use as the sweep Profile.

- Select the 3D curve as the sweep path.

- Click **OK** 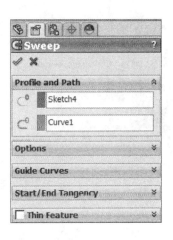.

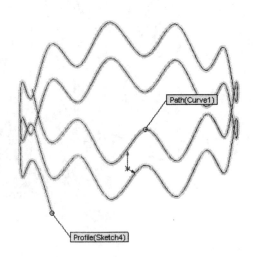

11. Saving your work:

- Click **File / Save As**.

- Enter **V-Shape Spring** for the name of the file.

- Click **Save**.

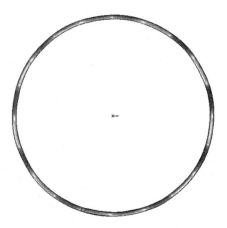

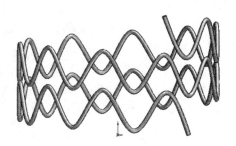

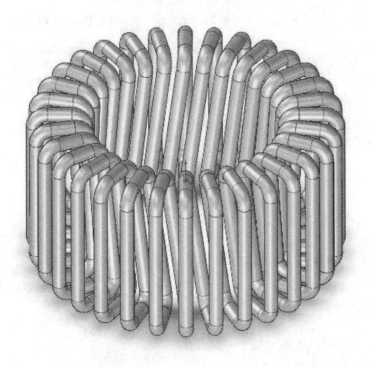

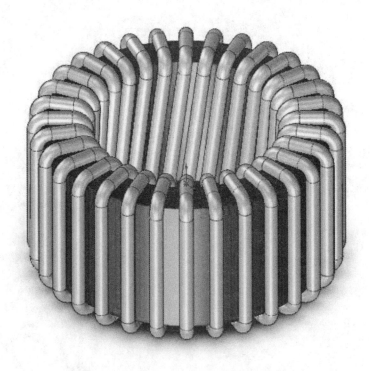

CHAPTER 7 cont.

Using Deform

There are 3 options in deform: Deform with a Point, Curve-To-Curve deform, and Surface Push. Curve to curve deform is a more precise option to deform a complex shape. You deform the part by starting with an initial curve to a set of target curves.

We will take a look at the Curve-To-Curve option and learn to deform a solid and a surface body, using a 2D sketch curve to control the deform shape.

1. Opening a part document:

- From the training CD, locate and open the document named: **Deform Solid**. Click **NO** to bypass the Feature Recognition options.

- This part document comes with a 2D sketch curve. Change to the Front view orientation (Control+1).

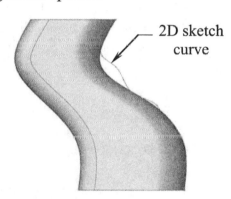

2D sketch curve

2. Creating a Curve-to-Curve deform:

- Click **Insert / Features / Deform**.

- Click the **Curve to Curve** option.

- For Initial Curve, click the **right edge** of the part as shown.

- For Target Curve, select the **2D curve sketch** as noted.

(more on next page...)

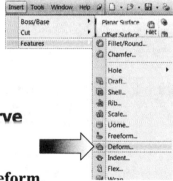

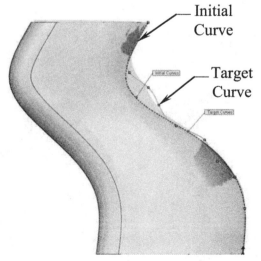

Initial Curve

Target Curve

- Click in the **Anchor** section.

- Select the 3 faces on the left side plus the top and bottom faces of the part. There should be a total of 5 faces selected.

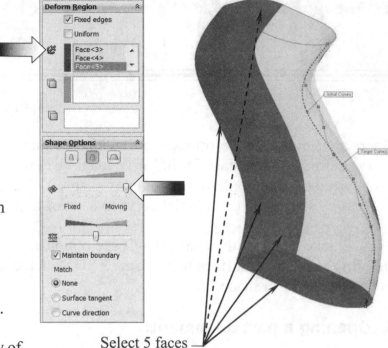

- The 5 selected faces will remained locked, they will not be affected by the deform feature.

- Under the **Shape Options*** section, drag the Accuracy slider all the way to the right.

Select 5 faces

***Stiffness**: Controls the rigidity of the deform shape in the deformation process.
***Stiffness minimum**: Least amount of rigidity.
***Stiffness medium**: Medium amount of rigidity.
 ***Stiffness maximum**: Largest amount of rigidity

- Click **OK** ✅.

- Change to the Front orientation to examine the results (Cntrl+1).

3. Save and close.

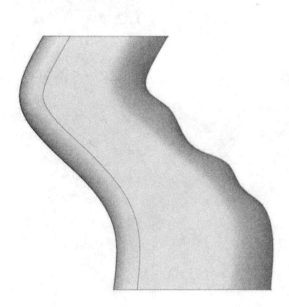

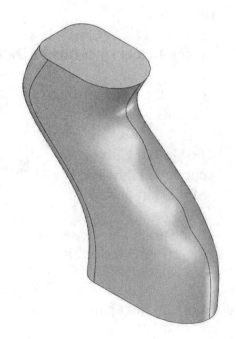

1. Opening a part document:

- For the 2nd half of this deform exercise, open a
  part document named: **Deform Surface**.

- Click <u>NO</u> to bypass the Feature Recognition options.

- This document contains 1 half of the surface body
  part. After it is deformed, we will mirror it to make
  a complete surface body part.

2. Creating a Curve to Curve deform:

- Select **Insert / Features / Deform**.

- Click the **Curve to Curve** option, if not yet selected.

- Change to the Front orientation (Cntrl+1).

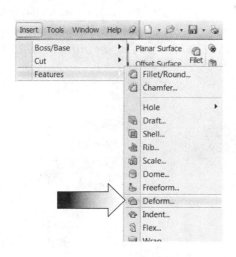

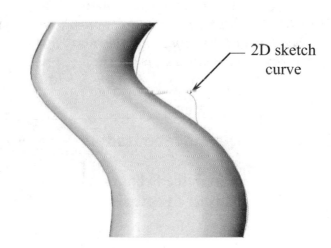

2D sketch
curve

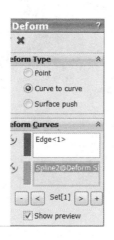

- For Initial Curve, select
  the **right edge** of the part
  as indicated.

- For Target Curve, select the
  2D curve sketch as noted.

(more on next page...)

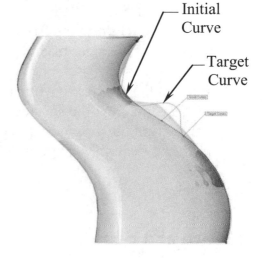

Initial
Curve

Target
Curve

- Click in the **Anchor** section.

- Select the 3 edges as indicated to keep fixed.

- Under the Shape Options drag the Accuracy slider all the way to the right.

(Note: Increasing the surface accuracy decreases the computer performance).

- Click **OK** ✓.

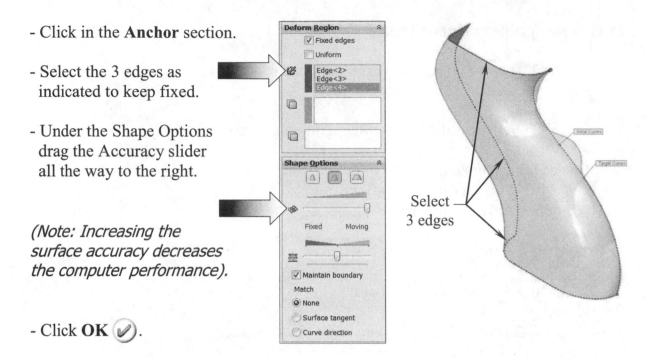

Select 3 edges

Shape accuracy: *Controls the surface quality.*
Weight: *Controls the degree of influence between two options: Fixed Edges and Moving Curves.*
Maintain boundary: *Ensures that boundaries selected for Fixed curves/edges/faces are fixed.*
Surface tangent: *Matches target edges of faces and surfaces with a smooth transition.*
Curve direction: *Matches Target curves by mapping Initial curves to Target curves using the normal of the Target curves to shape the deform.*

3. Mirroring a surface body:

- Click 🔲 from the Features toolbar or select: **Insert / Features / Mirror**.

- For Mirror Face / Plane, select: the **Right** plane from the FeatureManager tree.

- Expand the **Bodies to Mirror** section and click the surface body either from the graphics area or from the FeatureManager tree.

- Click **OK** ✓.

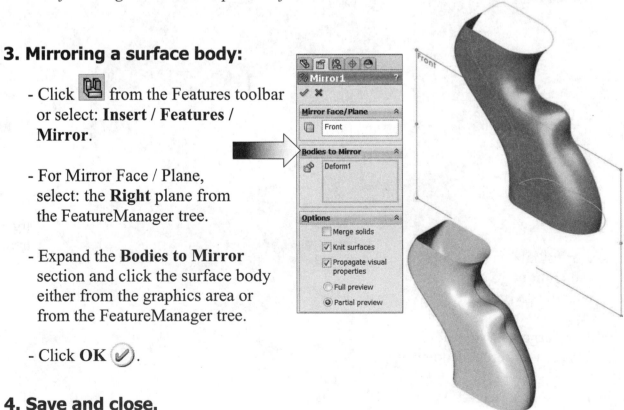

4. Save and close.

CHAPTER 8

Using Surfaces

Advanced Modeling - Using Surfaces

- Surfaces are a type of geometry that can be used to create solid features.

- The surface options are used to form complex free-form shapes and to manipulate files imported from other Cad formats.

- Unlike solid models, surfaces can be opened, overlapped, and have no thickness. Each surface can be constructed individually and then knitted together. A solid feature is created by thickening the surfaces that have been knit into a closed volume.

- Surfaces can be modeled in any shape and their sketches can either be extruded, revolved, swept, or lofted into a surface. These surfaces can also be replaced and filled with other surfaces.

- Edges of the surfaces can be extended and trimmed. Surfaces can be moved, rotated, and copied.

- The angle between the faces of a surface can be calculated using the Draft-Analysis tool; Positive Drafts, Negative Drafts, and Required Drafts are reported on screen.

- This 1st half of the chapter discusses the use of some surfacing tools in SolidWorks 2012.

Advanced Modeling
Using Surfaces

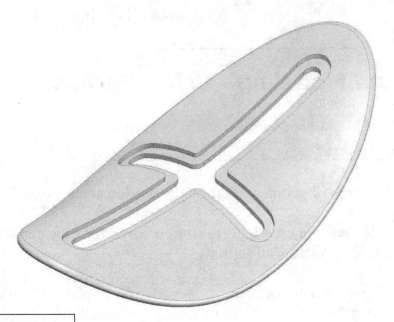

Dimensioning Standards: **ANSI**

Units: **INCHES** – 3 Decimals

Tools Needed:

✎ Insert Sketch	⌒ 3 Point Arc	⬯ Ellipse
◈ Dimension	⊥ Add Geometric Relations	▣ Split Line
✹ Plane	⎍ Lofted Surface	▣ Surface Thicken

1. Constructing a new work plane:

- Select the <u>Front</u> plane from the FeatureManager tree.

- Click 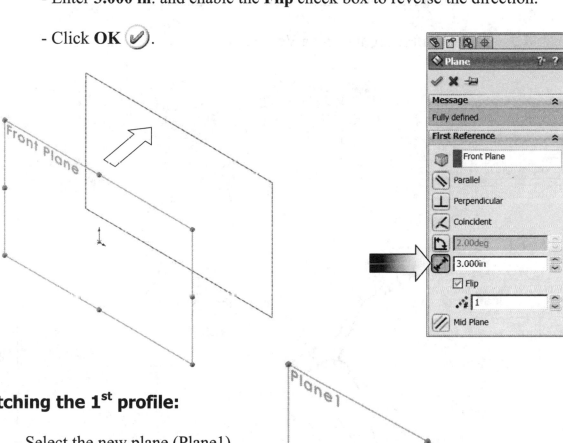 or select **Insert / Reference Geometry / Plane**.

- Select the Front plane and click the **Offset Distance** button.

- Enter **3.000 in**. and enable the **Flip** check box to reverse the direction.

- Click **OK** ✓.

2. Sketching the 1st profile:

- Select the <u>new plane</u> (Plane1).

- Click ✎ or select **Insert / Sketch**.

- Sketch a 3-Point-Arc 🔼 and add the dimensions as shown.

- Add a **Vertical** relation between the center of the arc and the origin point.

- <u>**Exit**</u> the Sketch ✎.

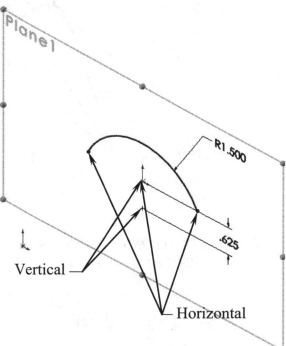

3. Sketching the 2ⁿᵈ profile:

- Select the <u>Front</u> plane from the FeatureManager tree.

- Click ✏️ or select **Insert / Sketch**.

- Sketch a 3-Point-Arc ⌒ as shown.

- Add a **.750** radius dimension ⬦ to the arc.

- Add a Horizontal and a Vertical relation ⊥ as indicated.

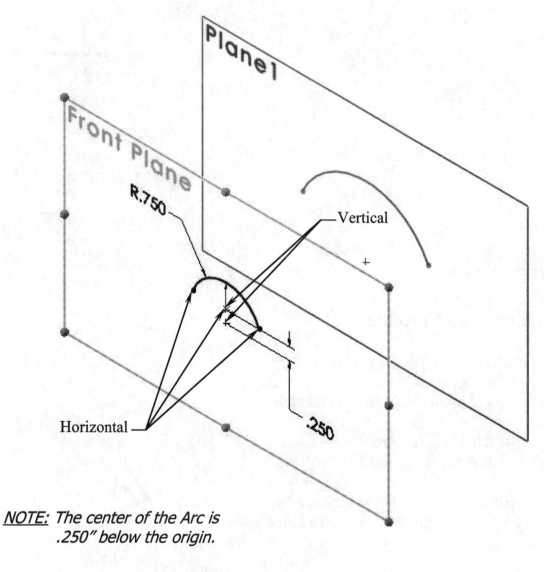

NOTE: The center of the Arc is
.250" below the origin.

- **Exit** the sketch ✏️ .

4. Sketching the Guide Curve:

- Select the <u>Right</u> plane from the FeatureManager tree and open a new sketch.

- Sketch a 3-Point-Arc 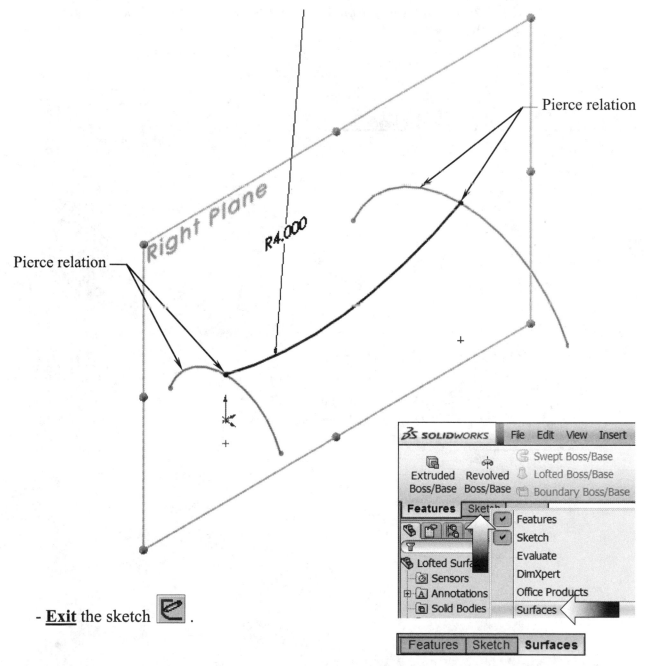 and add a **4.00** in. dimension .

- Add the Pierce relations as noted .

Pierce relation

Right Plane

R4.000

Picrce relation

- **Exit** the sketch .

Features | Sketch | **Surfaces**

Activating the Surfaces toolbar: *Right-click on one of the tabs (Features, Sketch, etc.)*
and select Surfaces. The new Surfaces toolbar appears next to the other tabs.

5. Creating a Surface-Loft:

- Click 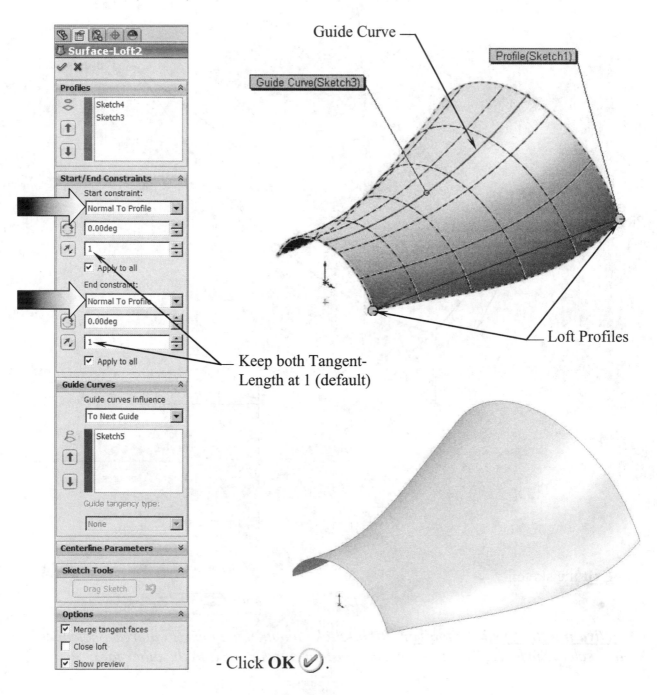 or **Insert / Surface / Loft**.

- Select the 2 Sketched Profiles by clicking on their ***right-most endpoints***.

- Expand the Guide-Curve section and select the sketched Arc as noted.

- Set <u>both</u> ***Start/End Constraints*** to ***Normal-To-Profile***. Set both Tangent Length to 1 (default).

Guide Curve

Keep both Tangent-Length at 1 (default)

Loft Profiles

- Click **OK** ✅.

6. Sketching the Split profile:

- Select the <u>Top</u> plane from the FeatureManager tree.

- Click 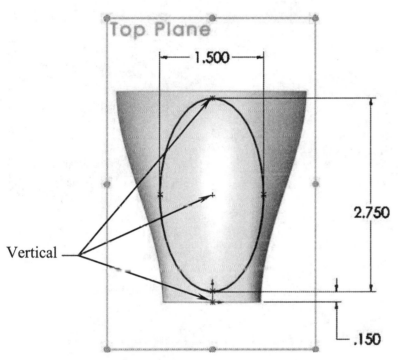 or **Insert / Sketch**.

- Change to Top view orientation .

- Sketch an Ellipse and add Dimensions/Relations as shown.

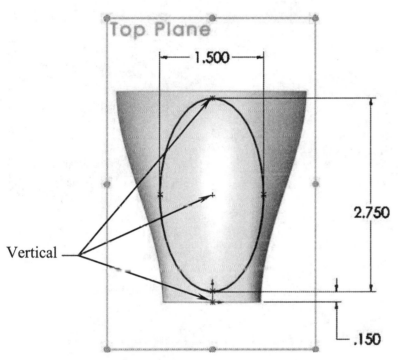

> ### 💡 Split Lines
>
> The Split Lines command projects a sketch entity onto a face (or a set of faces) and divides a selected face into multiple separate faces, enabling you to select and work with each face.

7. Splitting the surface:

- Click on the Curves toolbar OR select **Insert / Curve / Split Line**.

- Select the Ellipse as Sketch-to-Project .

- Select the Surface-Loft1 as Faces-to-Split .

- Click **OK** .

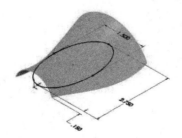

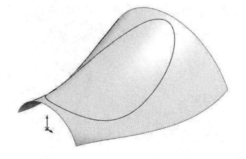

8. Deleting Surfaces:

- Right click on the outer portion of the surface.

- Select **Face** / **Delete** from the menu.

- Click **Delete** under Options (circled).

- Click **OK** .

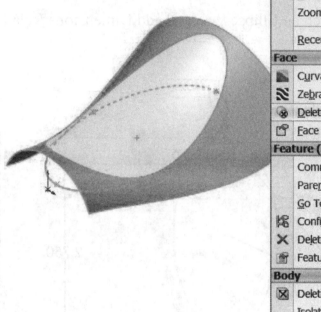

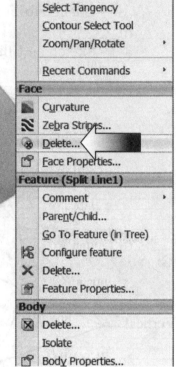

💡 Delete Face

This command deletes one or more faces from a surface or solid body.

Other options are:
* Delete and Patch, which automatically patches and trims the body.
* Delete and Fill, which generates and fills any gap.

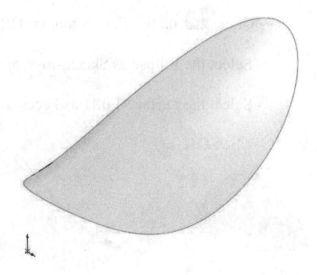

- The resulting surface.

9. Thickening the surface:

- Click 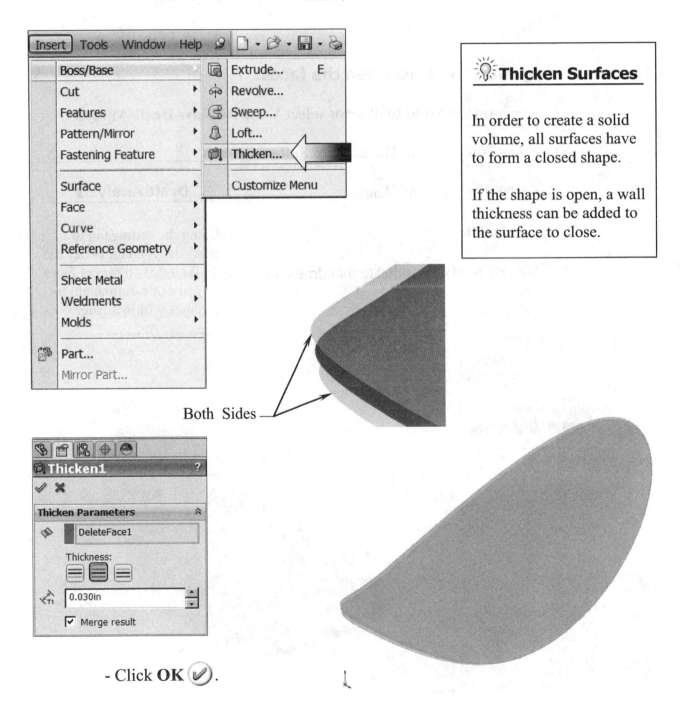 or select **Insert / Boss-Base / Thicken**.

- Click on the surface as Surface-To-Thicken .

- Choose **Thicken Both Sides** option .

- Enter **.030** in. as Thickness (.060 total thickness).

Thicken Surfaces

In order to create a solid volume, all surfaces have to form a closed shape.

If the shape is open, a wall thickness can be added to the surface to close.

Both Sides

Thicken1

Thicken Parameters

DeleteFace1

Thickness:

0.030in

☑ Merge result

- Click **OK** .

- The surface turns into a solid model.

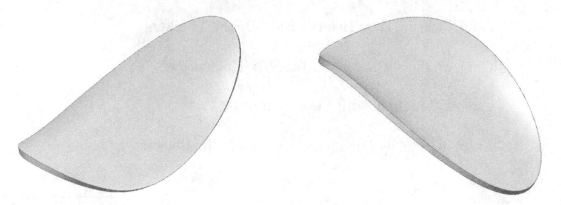

10. Calculating the angles between the faces:

- Click  on the **Mold toolbar** or select **View/Display/ Draft Analysis**.

- Select the **Top** plane for Direction of Pull.

- Enter **1.00** deg. for Draft Angle.

- Click **Calculate**.

- The **Yellow Surfaces** indicate that drafts are required.

> 🔆 **Draft Analysis**
>
> Using the settings in draft analysis, you can verify the draft angles on model faces or you can examine angle changes within a face.

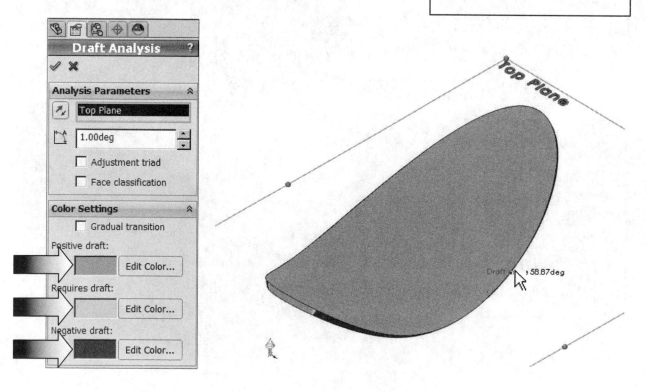

Draft Analysis

The **Draft Analysis** is a tool to check the correct application of draft to the faces of each part. With draft analysis, you can verify draft angles, examine angle changes within a face, as well as locate parting lines, injection, and ejection surfaces in parts.

Draft analysis results listed under Color Settings are grouped into four categories, when you specify Face classification:

Positive draft: Displays any faces with a positive draft based on the reference draft angle you specified. A positive draft means the angle of the face, with respect to the direction of pull, is more than the reference angle.

Negative draft: Displays any faces with a negative draft based on the reference draft angle you specified. A negative draft means the angle of the face, with respect to the direction of the pull, is less than the negative reference angle.

Draft required: Displays any faces that require correction. These are faces with an angle greater than the negative reference angle and less than the positive reference angle.

Straddle faces: Displays any faces that contain both positive and negative types of draft. Typically, these are faces that require you to create a split line.

*Note: When analyzing the draft for surfaces, an additional **Face classification** criterion is added: **Surface faces with draft**. Since a surface includes an inside and an outside face, surface faces are not added to the numerical part of the classification (**Positive draft** and **Negative draft**). **Surface faces with draft** lists all positive and negative surfaces that include draft.*

- Mouse cursor over the upper surface to see the read out draft angle for that particular area.

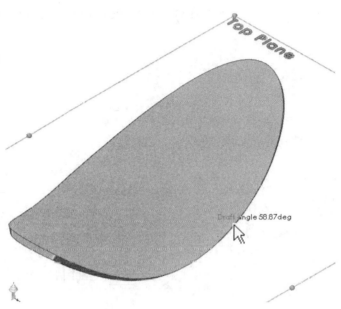

- Position the mouse cursor over the yellow areas (required drafts) and check the draft angles to see if they meet your draft requirements.

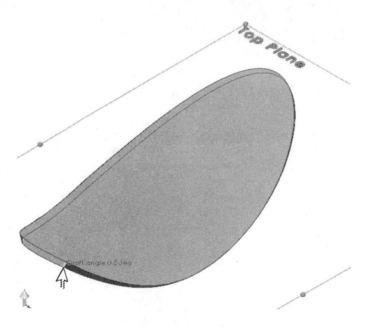

- Click **OK** .

11. Adding a Full Round Fillet:

- Click 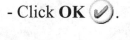 or select **Insert / Features / Fillet-Round**.

- Select the Side-Face-Set1, Center-Face-Set, and Side-Face-Set2 as noted.

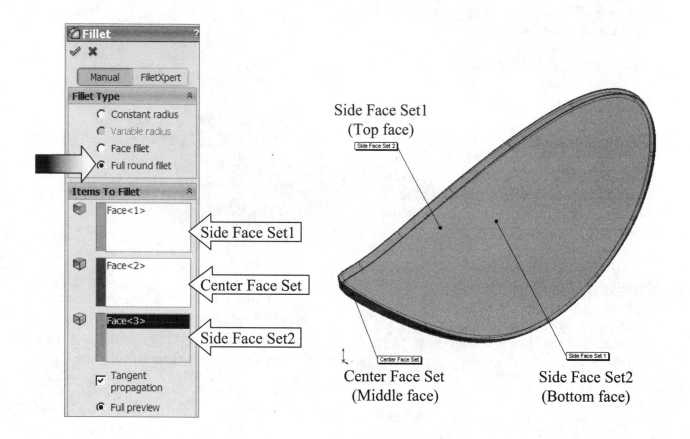

- Click **OK** .

- The resulting full round fillet.

12. Creating an Offset Distance plane:

- Select the Top plane from the FeatureManager tree and click ⬦*, or select **Insert / Reference Geometry / Plane**.

- Enter **.850 in**. for Distance and place the new plane above the Top plane.

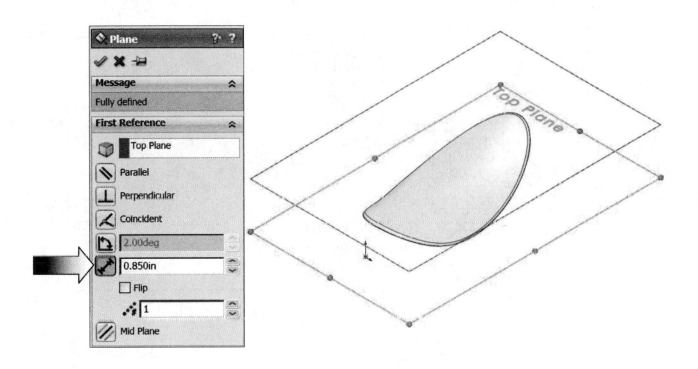

- Click **OK** ✓.

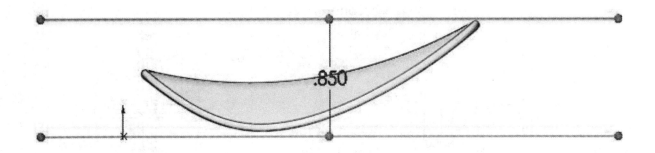

13. Sketching the Slot Contours:

- Select the new plane (**Plane2**) and open a new sketch ✏.

- Create the sketch using either **Mirror** or **Offset** options.

- Sketch the profile as shown, add dimensions to fully position the sketch.

- Create an offset ⫐ of **.0625** in. from the 2 sketch lines, using the settings below.

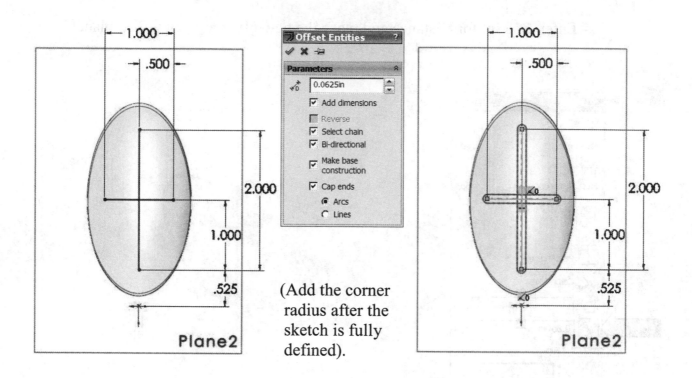

(Add the corner radius after the sketch is fully defined).

- Trim the inner intersections and create a second offset as shown.

- Clean up the corners and add the .031 radius as indicated.

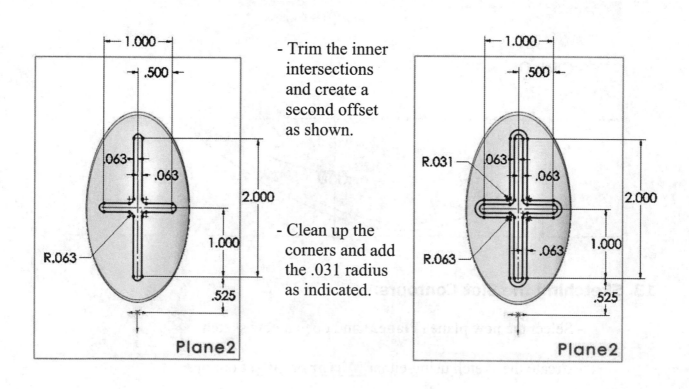

14. Extruding Cut the 1st Contour:

- Click 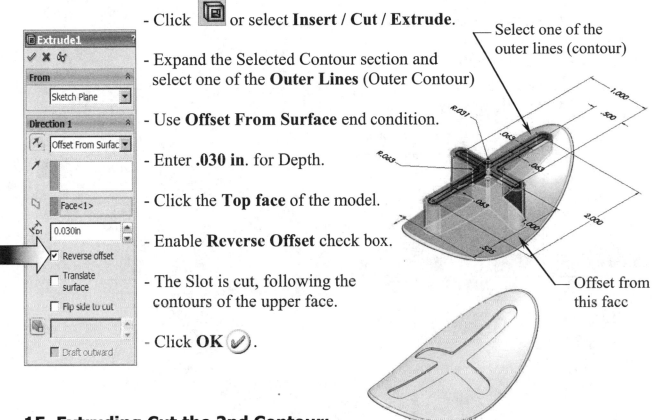 or select **Insert / Cut / Extrude**.

- Expand the Selected Contour section and select one of the **Outer Lines** (Outer Contour)

- Use **Offset From Surface** end condition.

- Enter **.030 in**. for Depth.

- Click the **Top face** of the model.

- Enable **Reverse Offset** check box.

- The Slot is cut, following the contours of the upper face.

- Click **OK** ✓.

Select one of the outer lines (contour)

Offset from this face

15. Extruding Cut the 2nd Contour:

- Expand the Cut-Extrude1 from the FeatureManager tree, right click on the

Sketch5 and select **SHOW** 👓 .

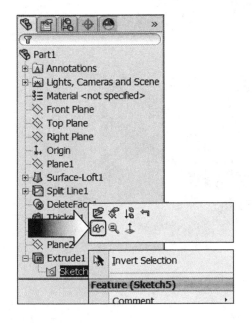

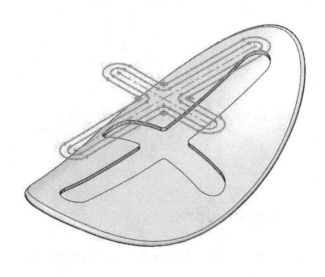

- Right click on one of the <u>inner lines</u> and pick **Select Chain**.

- Click 🔲 or select **Insert / Cut / Extrude**.

- Select **Though Al**l for end condition.

- Click **OK** ✅.

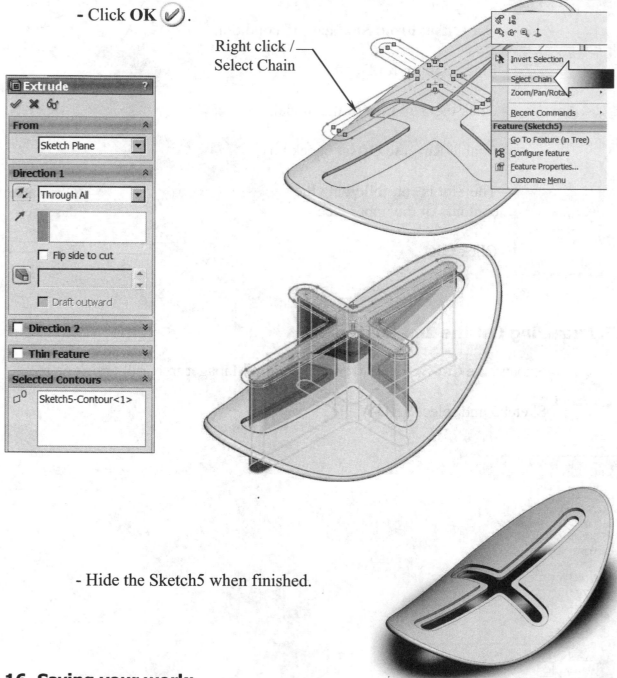

Right click /
Select Chain

- Hide the Sketch5 when finished.

16. Saving your work:

- Select **File / Save As / Lofted-Surface / Save**.

Questions for Review

Advanced Modeling – Using Surfaces

1. Surfaces are a type of geometry that can be used to create complex shapes.
   - a. True
   - b. False

2. Surfaces can be opened, overlapped, and have no thickness.
   - a. True
   - b. False

3. Surfaces can be modeled into any shape and can be extruded, revolved, swept, or lofted.
   - a. True
   - b. False

4. The split line option can be used to "divide" a surface into two or more surfaces.
   - a. True
   - b. False

5. Several surfaces can be lofted together to form a solid feature.
   - a. True
   - b. False

6. Surfaces cannot be moved or copied in a part document.
   - a. True
   - b. False

7. Each surface can be created individually and then knitted together as one surface.
   - a. True
   - b. False

8. The same Sketched profile can be Re-used to create different extruded contours.
   - a. True
   - b. False

9. Offset From Surface (extrude option) only works with surfaces, not solid features.
   - a. True
   - b. False

9. FALSE
7. TRUE   8. TRUE
5. TRUE   6. FALSE
3. TRUE   4. TRUE
1. TRUE   2. TRUE

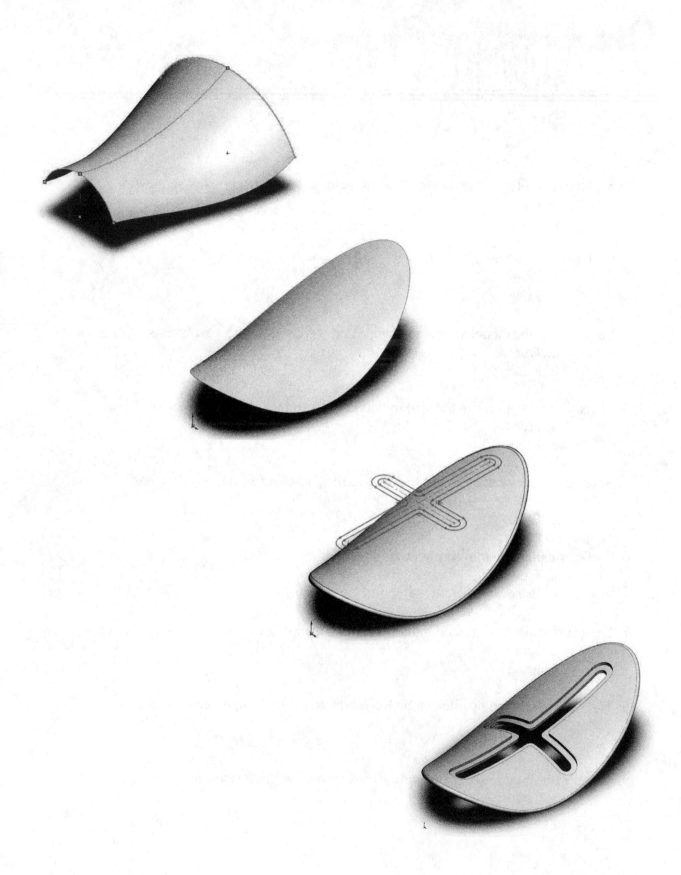

CHAPTER 8 cont.

Lofted Surface

Let's take a look at a couple of techniques when modeling these parts.

We will start out by creating some surfaces using various surfacing tools. These surfaces will get knitted into one surface; this surface will then get thickened into a solid part. Finally the part is split into two halves and gets assembled in an assembly document.

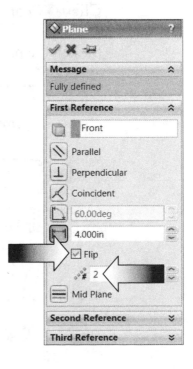

1. Creating new offset planes:

- Select the <u>Front</u> plane from the FeatureManager tree.

- Click 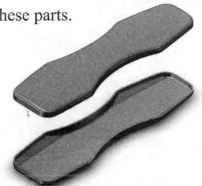 or select **Insert / Reference Geometry / Plane**.

- Choose **Offset Distance** and enter **4.00 in**.

- Use **Flip** direction if needed to place the new plane on the *back side*.

- Enter **2** for number of instances.

- Click **OK** ✅.

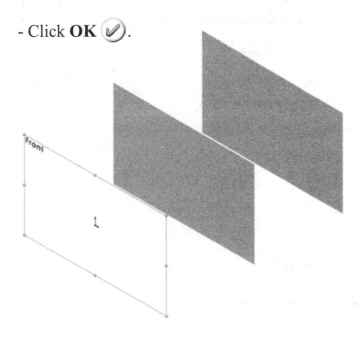

2. Sketch the first profile: (the front section)

- Select the <u>Front</u> plane from the FeatureManager tree.

- Click or select **Insert / Sketch**.

- Sketch the profile and add the dimensions shown.

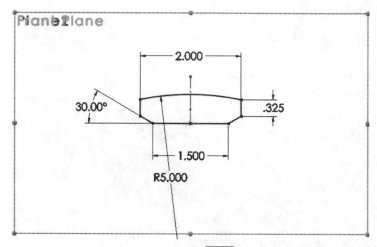

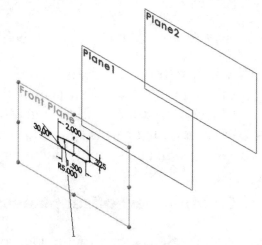

- **Exit** the Sketch or select **Insert / Sketch**.

3. Sketching the second profile: (the middle section)

- Select the <u>Plane1</u> from FeatureManager tree.

- Click or select **Insert / Sketch**.

- Sketch the profile and add the dimensions shown.

☼ Copy & Paste

The 1st profile can be copied and pasted to make the next 2 sketches. The dimensions will then be adjusted to size.

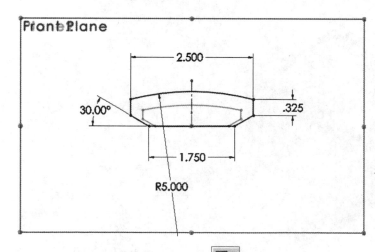

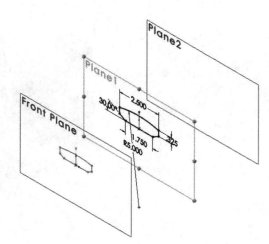

- **Exit** the Sketch or select **Insert / Sketch**.

4. Sketching the third profile: (the end section)

- Select the <u>Plane2</u> from the FeatureManager tree.

- Click 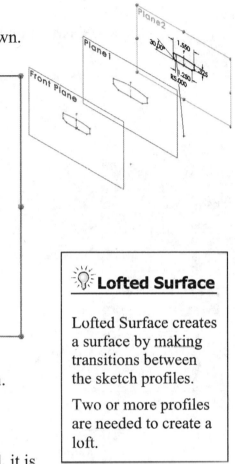 or select **Insert / Sketch**.

- Sketch the profile and add dimensions as shown.

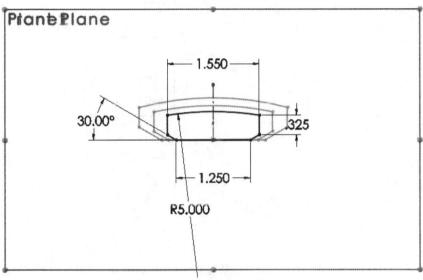

Plane Plane

1.550

30.00°   325

1.250

R5.000

- **Exit** the Sketch or select **Insert / Sketch**.

> ### ☼ Lofted Surface
>
> Lofted Surface creates a surface by making transitions between the sketch profiles.
>
> Two or more profiles are needed to create a loft.

5. Selecting the loft profiles:

- To prevent the loft feature from being twisted, it is recommended that all sketch profiles should be selected from the same side.

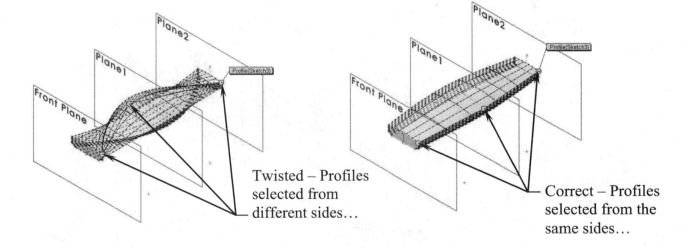

Twisted – Profiles selected from different sides…

Correct – Profiles selected from the same sides…

6. Lofting between the profiles:

- Click 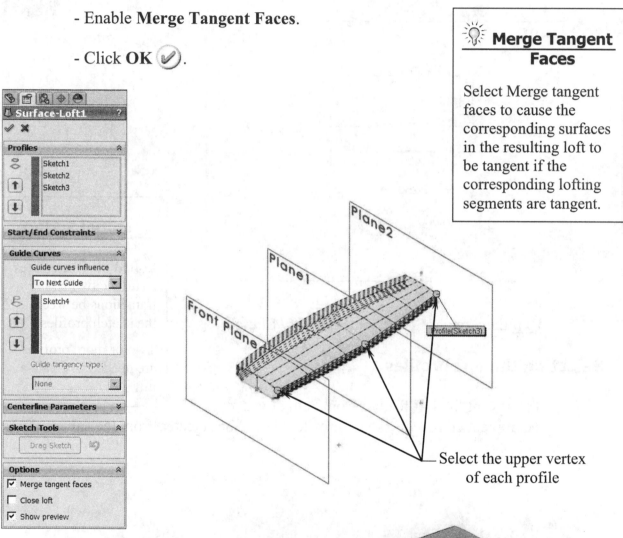 or select **Insert / Surface / Loft**.

- Select the upper-right vertex of each profile.

- Expand **Centerline Parameters** option and select Sketch5.

- Enable **Merge Tangent Faces**.

- Click **OK**.

> ☀ **Merge Tangent Faces**
>
> Select Merge tangent faces to cause the corresponding surfaces in the resulting loft to be tangent if the corresponding lofting segments are tangent.

Select the upper vertex of each profile

- The resulting Surface-Loft.

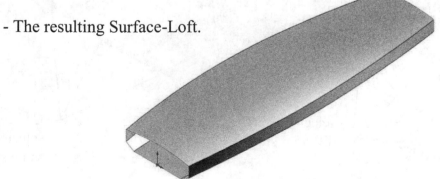

7. Creating a Revolved sketch:

- Select the <u>Top</u> plane from the FeatureManager tree.

- Click  or select **Insert / Sketch**.

- Sketch the revolve profile and add dimensions as shown.

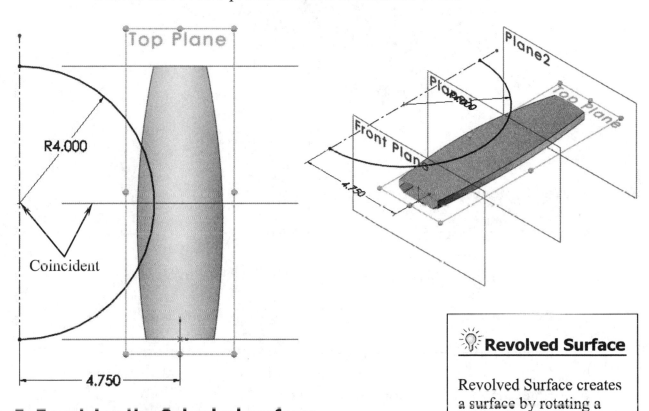

R4.000

Coincident

4.750

8. Revolving the Spherical surface:

- Click  or select **Insert / Surface / Revolve**.

- Revolve Type: **Blind**.

- Revolve Angle: **360 deg**.

- Click **OK**.

> 💡 **Revolved Surface**
>
> Revolved Surface creates a surface by rotating a sketch profile around a centerline (or the Axis of Revolution).

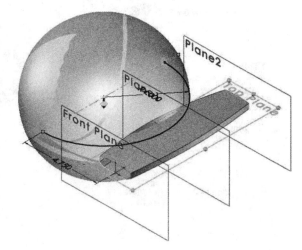

Surface-Revol...

Axis of Revolution
Line1

Direction1
Blind
360.00deg

- The Revolved Surface.

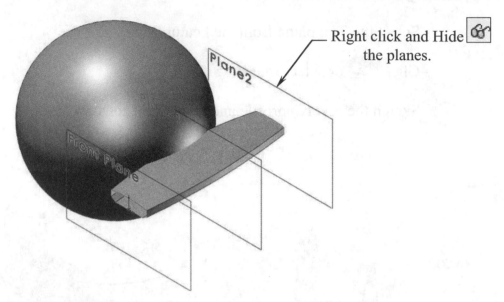

Right click and Hide the planes.

Plane2

Front Plane

9. Copying the Revolved Surface:

- Click 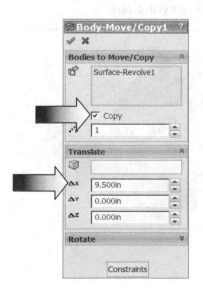 or select **Insert / Surface / Move/Copy**.

- Under Surfaces to Move/Copy, select the Surface-Revolve1 .

- Enable the **Copy** check box.

- Enter **1** for Number of Copies.

- Enter **9.500** in the **Delta X** distance box.

- Click **OK** .

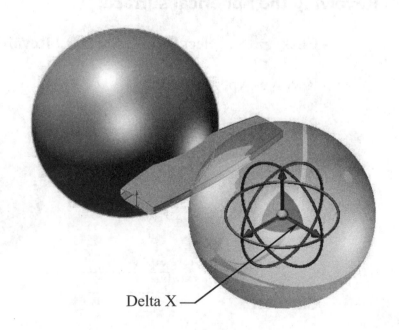

Delta X

10. Trimming the Base part:

- Click 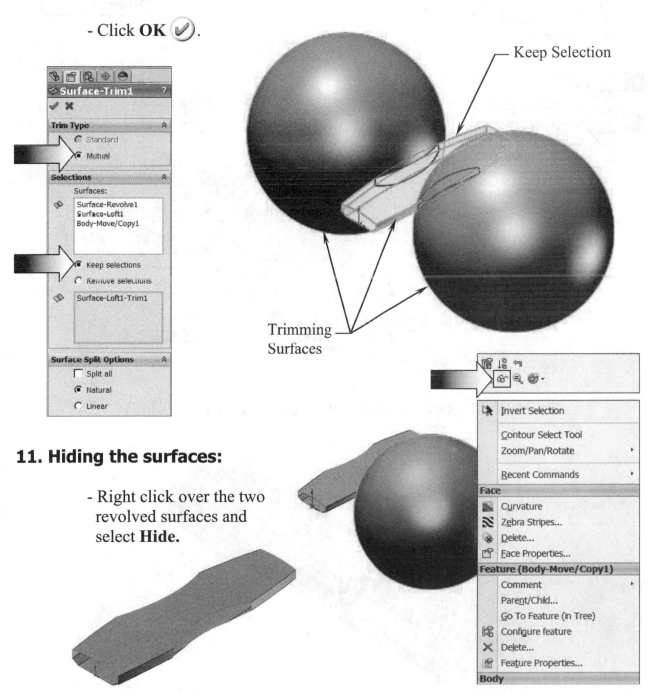 or select **Insert / Surface / Trim**.

- For Trim-Type, click **Mutual Trim** `⊙ Mutual trim` .

- For **Trimming-Surfaces**, select all **3 surfaces** .

- For **Keep Selection**, select the Surface-Loft1 .

- Click **OK** .

> ### Trim Surface
>
> A surface or a sketch can be used as a trim tool to trim the intersecting surfaces.

Keep Selection

Trimming Surfaces

11. Hiding the surfaces:

- Right click over the two revolved surfaces and select **Hide.**

12. Filling the openings with Surface-Fill:

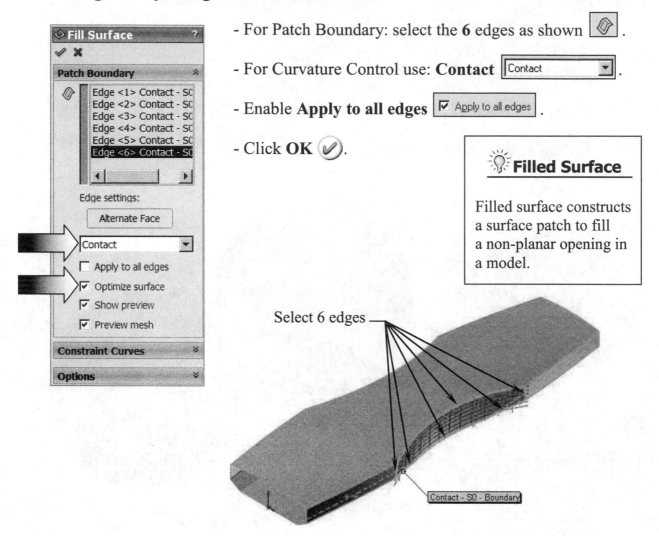

- For Patch Boundary: select the **6** edges as shown .

- For Curvature Control use: **Contact** | Contact | .

- Enable **Apply to all edges** ☑ Apply to all edges .

- Click **OK** .

> ### Filled Surface
>
> Filled surface constructs a surface patch to fill a non-planar opening in a model.

Select 6 edges

Contact - S0 - Boundary

- The right side cutout is filled with a new surface (Surface-Fill1).

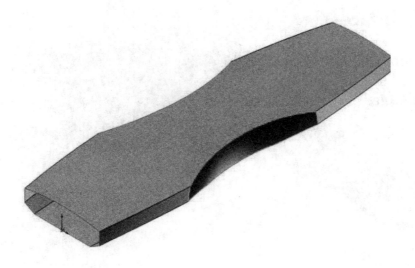

13. Filling the left side cutout:

- Rotate the view 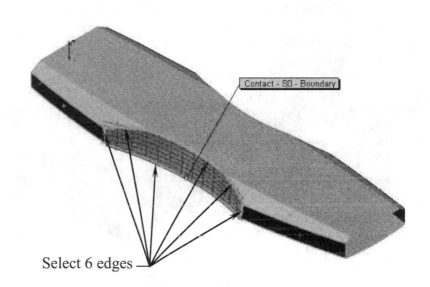 to the other side (or Hold the Shift key and press the Up arrow key twice (rotate 90° per key stroke).

- Repeat step 13 to fill the left side cutout with a new surface.

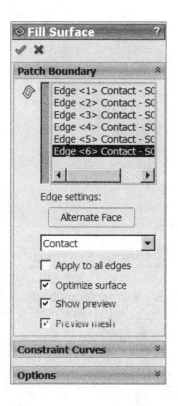

Select 6 edges

Contact - S0 - Boundary

- The left side cutout is filled with a new surface (Surface-Fill2)

14. Filling the front opening using Planar Surface:

- Click ▭ or select **Insert / Surface / Planar**.

- For Boundary Entities: select all **6** edges in the front opening ◇.

- Click **OK** ✓.

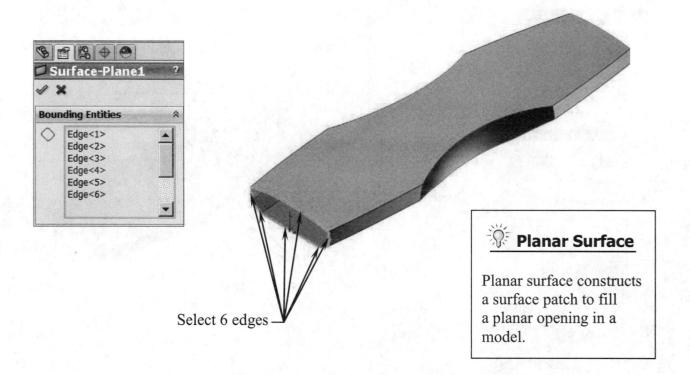

Select 6 edges

Planar Surface

Planar surface constructs a surface patch to fill a planar opening in a model.

- The front opening is filled with a planar surface (Surface-Plane1).

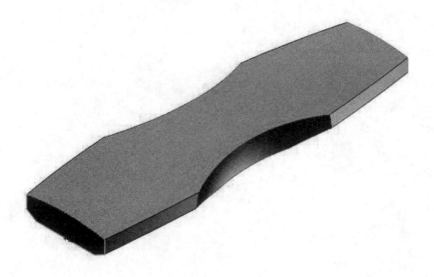

15. Filling the rear opening using Planar Surface:

- Click 🔲 or select **Insert / Surface / Planar**.

- For Boundary Entities: select all **6** edges in the back opening ◇ .

- Click **OK** ✅ .

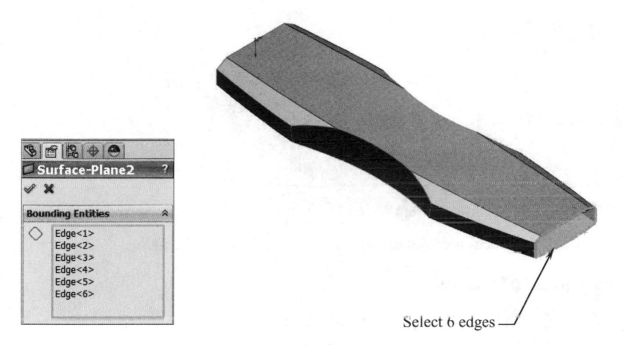

Select 6 edges

- The back opening is filled with a planar surface (Surface-Plane2).

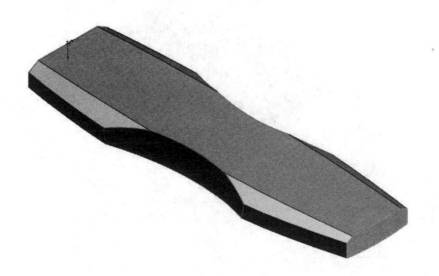

16. Creating a Surface-Knit:

- Click 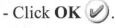 or select **Insert** / **Surface** / **Knit**.

- For Surfaces/Faces-To-Knit, select all **5** surfaces .

- Click **OK** ✓.

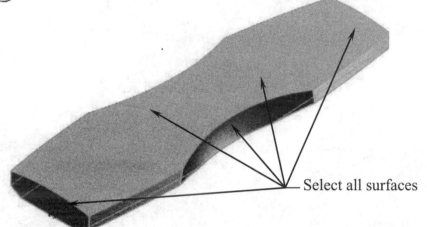

Select all surfaces

- All 5 surfaces are knitted and combined into one (Surface-Knit1).

17. Adding .500" fillets:

- Click 🔲 or select **Insert** / **Features** / **Fillet/Round**.

- Type **.500 in**. for Radius ⟋.

- Select **8** vertical edges as shown 🔲.

- Click **OK** ✓.

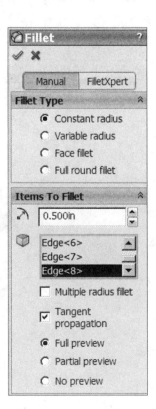

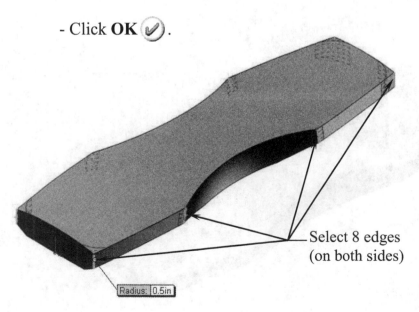

Select 8 edges
(on both sides)

18. Adding .125" fillets:

- Click 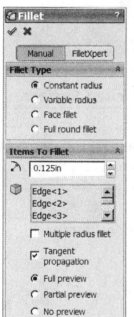 or select **Insert / Features / Fillet/ Round**.

- Type **.125 in**. for Radius .

- Select **all edges** as shown for Edges/ Faces to fillet .

- Tangent Propagation: **Enabled** .

- Click **OK** .

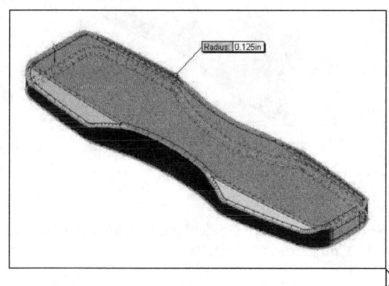

Box-Select to group all edges (on both sides)

- Compare your model with this image. Rotate the model to make sure that all edges are filleted.

19. Creating a solid from the surface model:

- Click 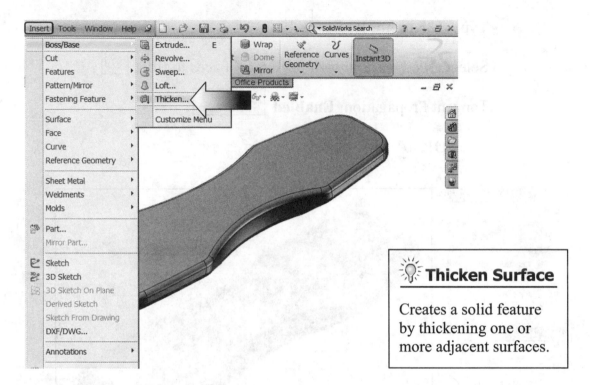 or select **Thicken** from the **Insert / Boss-Base** menu.

> 💡 **Thicken Surface**
>
> Creates a solid feature by thickening one or more adjacent surfaces.

- For **Surface-To-Thicken**: Select the face indicated 🗒 or select the **Surface-Knit1** from the Feature Tree.

- For thickness Direction: Select **Thicken Side 2** ▤ (Inside).

- For Thickness: Enter **.060 in**. `0.060in` .

- Click **OK** ✅.

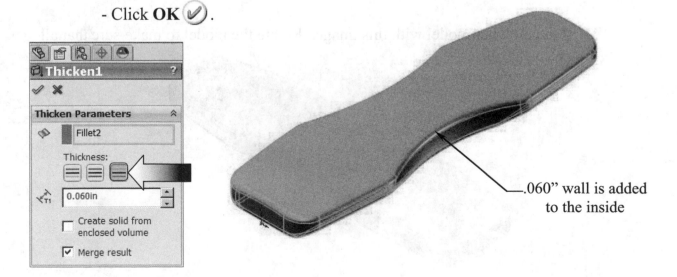

.060" wall is added to the inside

20. Sketching the cut profile: (to split the part into 2 halves)

- Select the Right plane from the FeatureManager tree.

- Click ✐ or select **Insert / Sketch**.

- Sketch a 3-Point-Arc ⌒ and add dimension ◇ as shown.

- Add a **Mid-point** relation ⊥ between the end points of the arc and the outer-most edges.

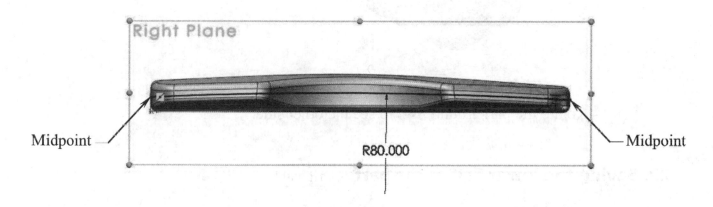

Midpoint —   —Midpoint

R80.000

21. Removing the Upper Half:

- Click ▣ or select **Insert / Cut / Extrude**.

- Extrude Type: **Through All** (default).

- Direction 2:   **Through All** (default).

- Click **OK** ✓. (use Flip-side-to-Cut if needed)

The direction of the middle arrow indicates which half is being removed…

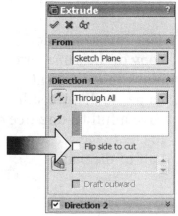

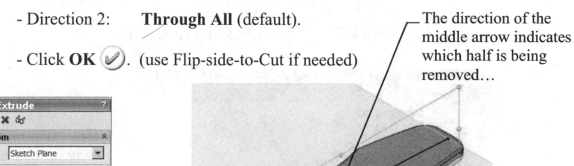

- The Upper Half of the part is removed.

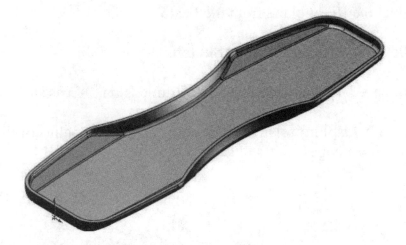

- Rotate the part around to see the other side.

22. Saving the lower half of the part: Original

- Select **File / Save As / Lower-Half / Save**.

---

23. Saving the upper half of the part: Copy

- Select **File / Save As / Upper Half**.

- Enable the **Save As Copy*** check box and click **Save**.

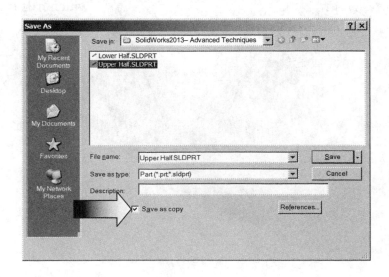

* This saves an exact
copy of the same part
but with a different
name, so that we still
have a full feature tree
to create the second
half of the part.

24. Modifying the copied file:

- Select **File / Open**.

- Select the document **Upper-Half** and click **Open**.

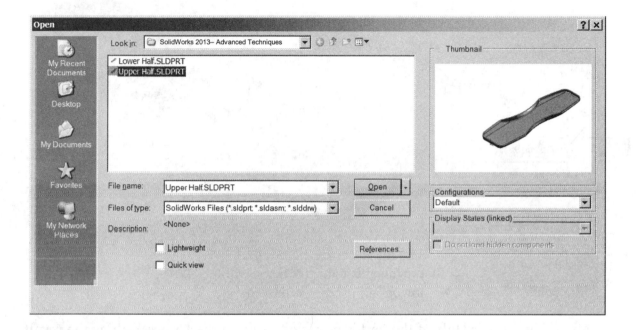

25. Changing the direction of the cut using the Flip-Side option:

- Right click the **Cut-Extrude1** (the last feature on the tree) and select:

Edit Feature  .

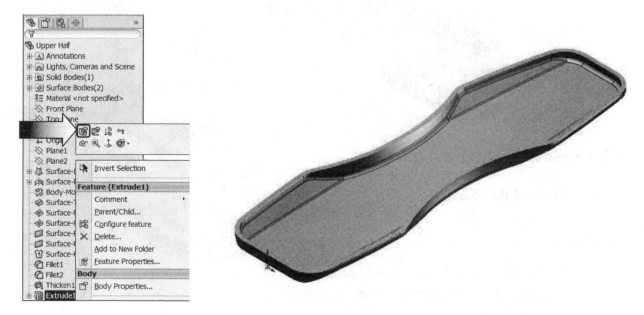

- Select **Flip Side To Cut** option ☑ Flip side to cut .

- Click **OK** ✓.

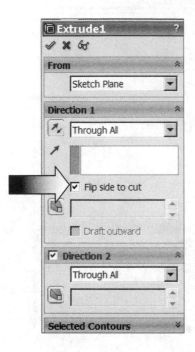

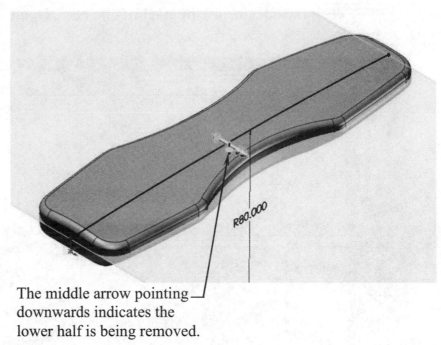

R80.000

The middle arrow pointing
downwards indicates the
lower half is being removed.

- The Lower Half of the part is removed, leaving the Upper-Half as the result
  of the Flip-Side cut.

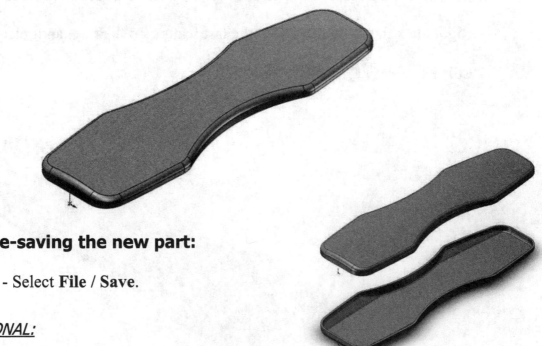

26. Re-saving the new part:

- Select **File / Save**.

OPTIONAL:

*- Insert the 2 halves into an assembly
document and assemble them as shown.*

Questions for Review

Advanced Modeling with Surfaces

1. There are no limits on how many sections you can have in a loft feature.
   - a. True
   - b. False

2. Each loft section should be modeled onto a different plane.
   - a. True
   - b. False

3. The guide curves for use in a loft feature must be Coincident or Pierced to the sections.
   - a. True
   - b. False

4. Surfaces cannot be mirrored as solid features.
   - a. True
   - b. False

5. Only two surfaces can be used for knitting at a time.
   - a. True
   - b. False

6. Fillets cannot be used with surfaces, only in solid models.
   - a. True
   - b. False

7. Surfaces can be thickened after they are knitted together.
   - a. True
   - b. False

8. Mass properties options such as volume, surface area, etc., are available for all surfaces.
   - a. True
   - b. False

9. Surfaces can be knitted into a closed volume and then thickened into a solid.
   - a. True
   - b. False

9. TRUE
7. TRUE   8. FALSE
5. FALSE   6. FALSE
3. TRUE   4. FALSE
1. TRUE   2. TRUE

Exercise: Loft_Delete Face

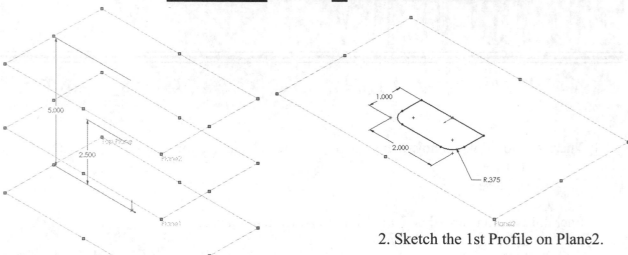

1. Create 2 new Planes, offset from Top plane.

2. Sketch the 1st Profile on Plane2.

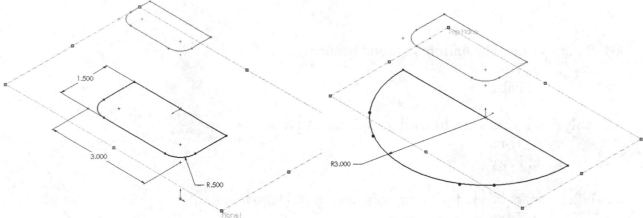

3. Sketch the 2nd Profile on Plane1.

4. Sketch the 3rd Profile on Top plane & add the connector points.

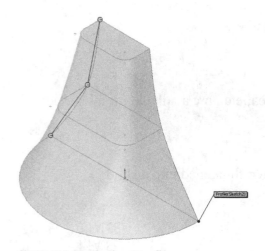

5. **Solid-Loft** the Profiles.

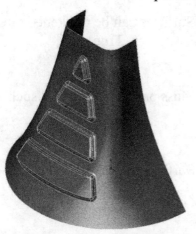

6. Add the Raised features (any size), use Delete Face command and remove 3 Faces (top, bottom & back).

CHAPTER 9

Advanced Surfaces

Using Offset Surface ⌻ & Ruled Surface ⌖

- The Offset Surface command creates a new surface from a **single face** or a **set of faces**, with a distance of zero or greater. The offset surface can be created inward or outward.

Offset Surface

Offset from a single face   *Offset from a set of faces*

- The Ruled Surface command creates a new surface from a single edge or a set of edges. The ruled surface can either be perpendicular or tapered from the selected edges.

Ruled Surface

Ruled surface from a single edge   *Ruled surface from a set of edges*

- The Offset Surface and the Ruled Surface are used to create reference surfaces that help define the solid features in a part. In most cases, these surfaces should be knitted together before the next operation of extruded cuts, fillets, etc., can be performed.

Advanced Surfaces Using
Surface Offset & Ruled

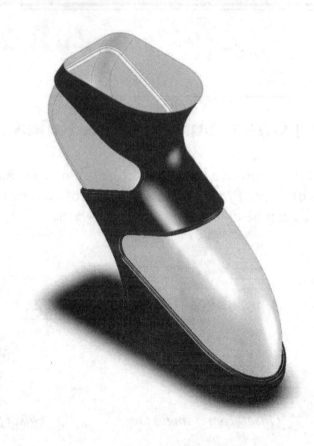

Dimensioning Standards: **ANSI**
Units: **INCHES** – 3 Decimals

Tools Needed:

Lofted Boss/Base	Split Line	Offset Surface
Ruled Surface	Knit Surface	Shell

Advanced Surface Modeling
Using Offset & Ruled Surface options

1. Opening the existing file:

- Go to: The Training CD
            and open the part document named:
            Surface_Offset_Ruled.sldprt

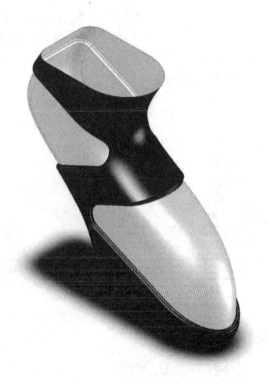

- This document contains several sketches for use
  as the Loft Profiles and 2 other sketches for use
  as the Guide Curves to help control the transition
  between each profile.

- This lesson focuses on the use of the Offset and
  Ruled Surface commands.

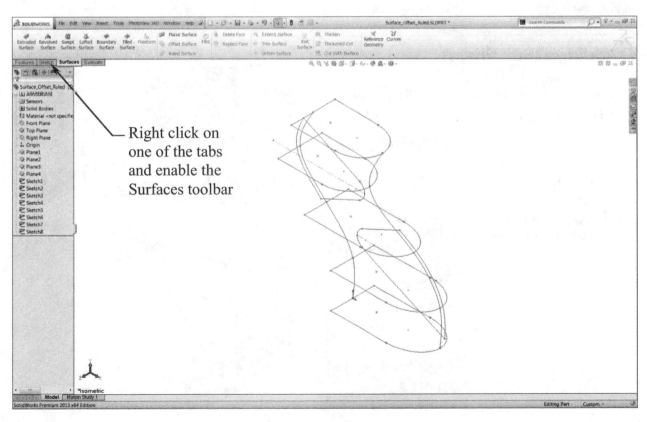

Right click on
one of the tabs
and enable the
Surfaces toolbar

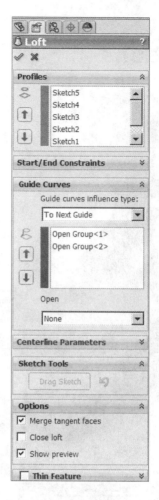

2. Creating the Base Loft:

- Click 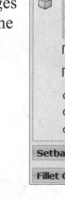 or select **Insert / Boss-Base / Loft**.

- Select the 5 Loft Profiles and the 2 Guide Curves as noted below. (The SelectionManager appears when disjointed or overlapped entities are found in the sketch).

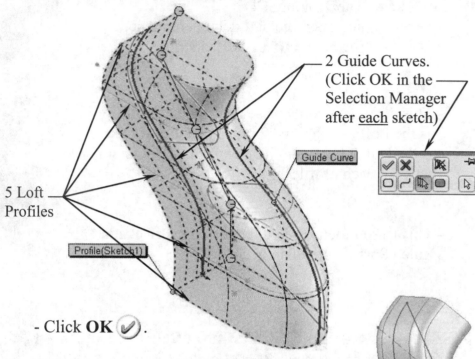

2 Guide Curves.
(Click OK in the
Selection Manager
after each sketch)

Guide Curve

5 Loft
Profiles

Profile(Sketch1)

- Click **OK** ✅.

3. Adding .250" fillets:

- Click 🔲 or select **Insert / Features / Fillet-Round**.

- Enter **.250 in**. for radius value.

- Select the 4 edges shown, to add the fillets.

- Click **OK** ✅.

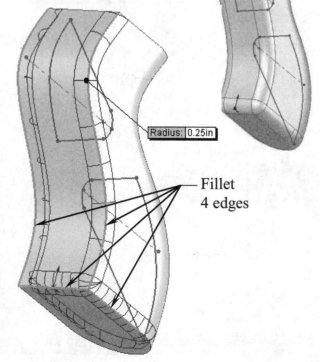

Radius: 0.25in

Fillet
4 edges

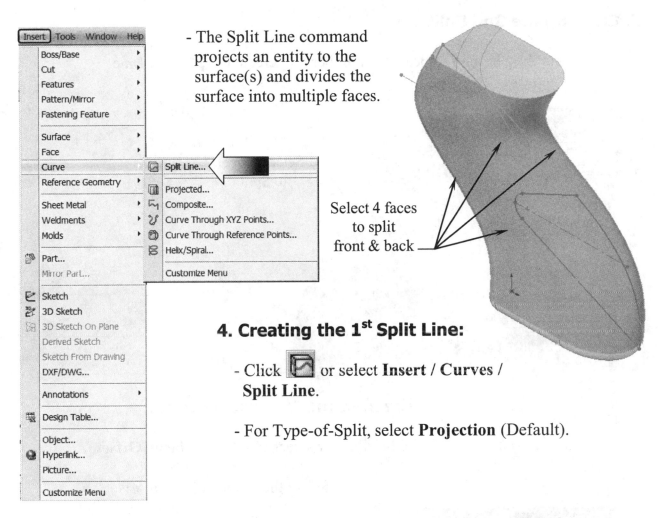

- The Split Line command projects an entity to the surface(s) and divides the surface into multiple faces.

Select 4 faces
to split
front & back

4. Creating the 1st Split Line:

- Click 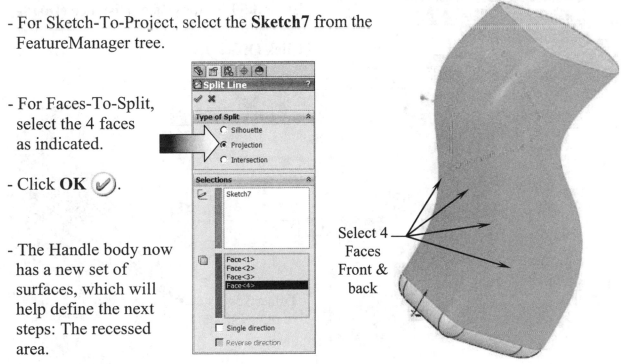 or select **Insert / Curves / Split Line**.

- For Type-of-Split, select **Projection** (Default).

- For Sketch-To-Project, select the **Sketch7** from the FeatureManager tree.

- For Faces-To-Split, select the 4 faces as indicated.

- Click **OK** ✓.

- The Handle body now has a new set of surfaces, which will help define the next steps: The recessed area.

Select 4
Faces
Front &
back

5. Creating the 2nd Split Line:

- Using the **Sketch8**, repeat step number 3 to create the 2nd Split Line.

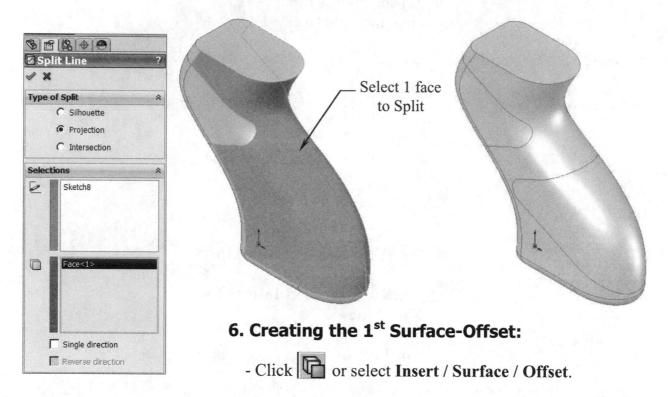

Select 1 face
to Split

6. Creating the 1st Surface-Offset:

- Click [ ] or select **Insert / Surface / Offset**.

- Select the 5 Split-Faces to offset.

- Enter **.050 in**. for Offset Distance **(Inside).**

- Click **OK** ✓.

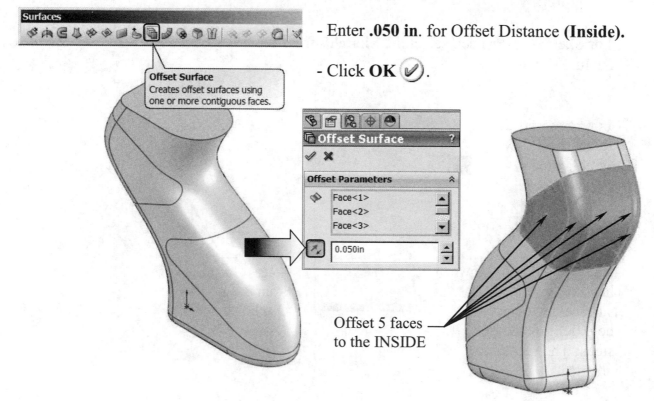

Offset 5 faces
to the INSIDE

7. Hiding the Solid Body:

- Right click on the upper surface of the solid body and select **HIDE**.

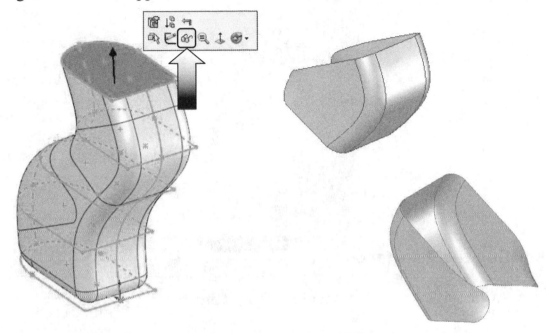

8. Creating the 1ˢᵗ Ruled Surface:

- Click the Ruled-Surface icon or select: **Insert / Surface / Ruled Surface**

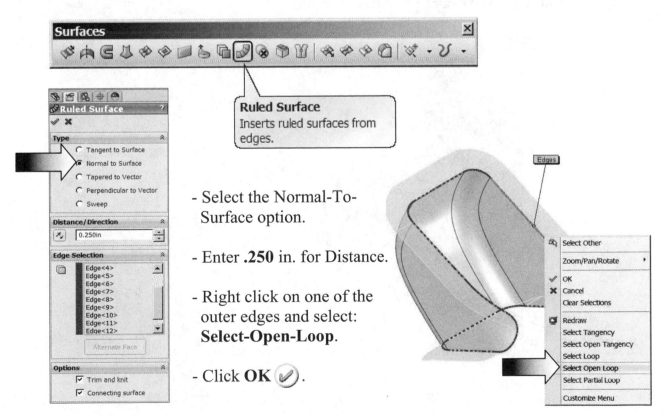

Ruled Surface
Inserts ruled surfaces from edges.

- Select the Normal-To-Surface option.

- Enter **.250** in. for Distance.

- Right click on one of the outer edges and select: **Select-Open-Loop**.

- Click **OK** ✓.

- The resulted Ruled Surfaces.

Ruled Surfaces

The Ruled Surfaces creates a set of surfaces that either perpendicular or taper from the selected edges.
These surfaces can also be used as the Interlock Surfaces in molded parts

9. Knitting the 2 surfaces:

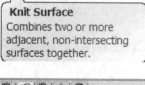

- Click  or select **Insert / Surface / Knit**.

Knit Surface
Combines two or more adjacent, non-intersecting surfaces together.

- Select the Surface-Offset and the Ruled-Surface to knit.

- Disable the **GAP CONTROL** check box.

- Click **OK** ✅.

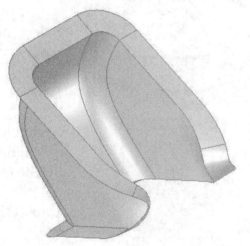

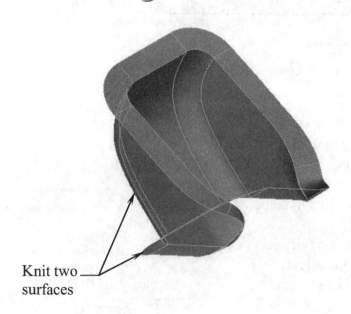

Knit two
surfaces

10. Adding .020" Fillets:

- Click  or select: **Insert / Features / Fillet-Round**.

- Enter **.020 in**. for Radius value.

- Select all Outer Edges
to fillet. (Right click /
Select Tangency).

- Click **OK** ✓.

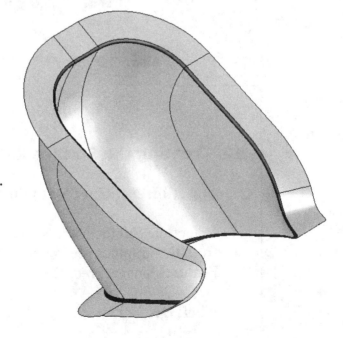

- The resulting fillets.

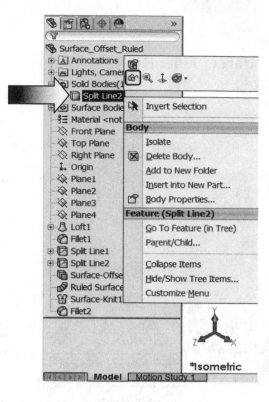

11. Showing the Solid Body:

- From the FeatureManager tree, expand the Solid Bodies folder, right click on the **Split-Line2** body, and select: **Show Solid Body**.

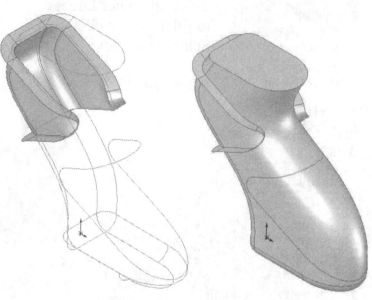

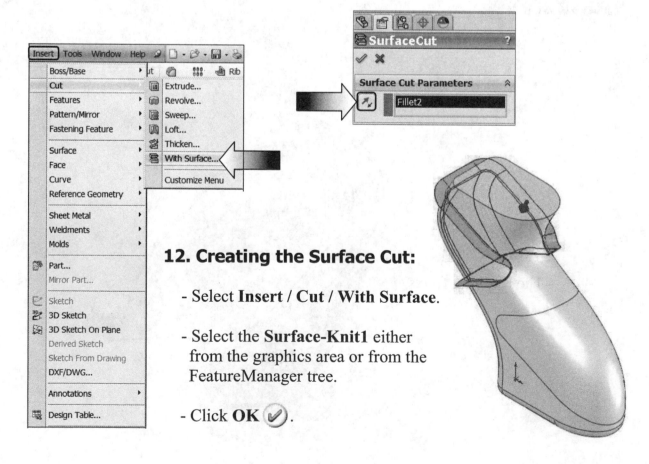

12. Creating the Surface Cut:

- Select **Insert / Cut / With Surface**.

- Select the **Surface-Knit1** either from the graphics area or from the FeatureManager tree.

- Click **OK** ✅.

13. Hiding the Knit Surface:

- Right click on the Knit Surface and select **Hide**.

R/C
and
Hide

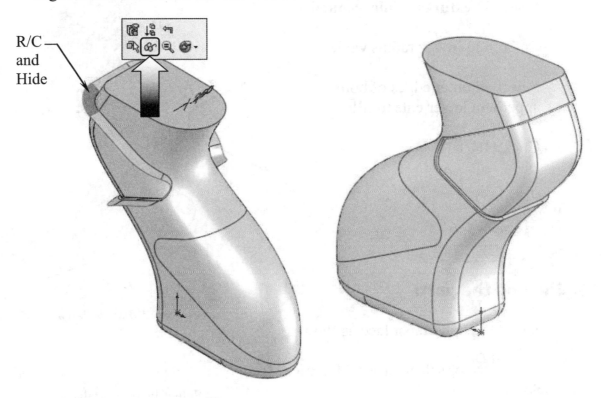

14. Creating the 2nd Ruled Surface:

- Repeat from step number 8 to create the 2nd Ruled Surface.

- Create the Surface Cut as indicated in step 12.

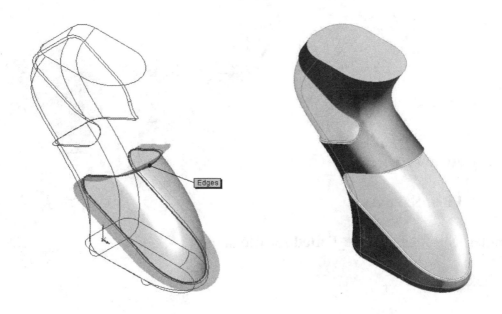

15. Adding more Fillets:

- Click 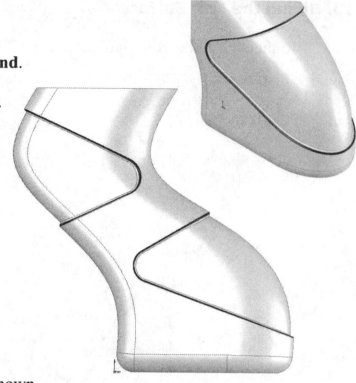 or select:
  Insert / Features / Fillet-Round.

- Enter **.020 in**. for radius value.

- Select all outer edges of both
  upper and lower cuts to fillet.

- Click **OK** ✅.

16. Shelling the part:

- Select the uppermost face as shown.

- Click 🔲 or select **Insert / Features /
  Shell**.

— Select face to Shell

- Enter **.020 in**. for thickness.

- Click **OK** ✅.

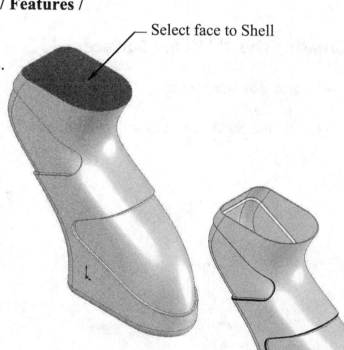

17. Saving your work:

- Click **File / Save As**.

- Enter: **Surface_Offset_Ruled** for file name.

- Click **Save**.

Exercise: Advanced Surfaces

1. Opening an Existing file:

- Go to the Training CD.

- Open the document named:
  Advanced Surfaces Exercise.

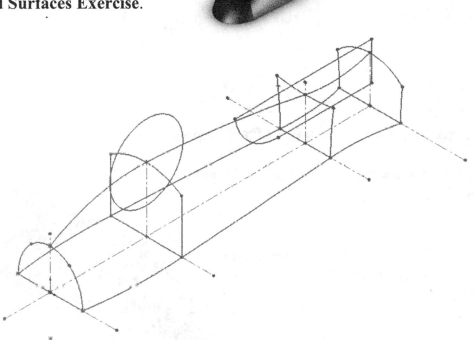

2. Creating the Loft body:

- Create a **SOLID** loft from the 4 profiles as indicated.

- Use the 2 bottom Guide Curves to control the sides.

- Use the top Guide-Curve to control the upper curvatures.

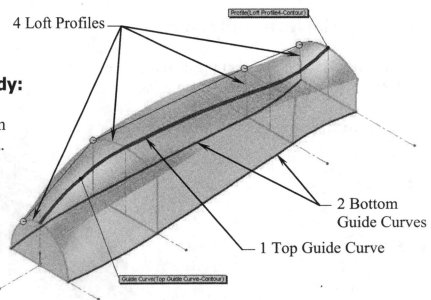

4 Loft Profiles

Profile(Loft Profile4-Contour)

2 Bottom Guide Curves

1 Top Guide Curve

Guide Curve(Top Guide Curve-Contour)

3. Adding Fillets:

- Add a **.500 in**. fillet to the upper edges, and a .250 in. fillet to the edges on the end, as shown.

* By adding the fillets in the sketches the tangent lines can be eliminated using the Merge-Tangent-Faces in the loft options.

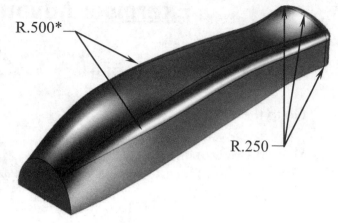

4. Creating the Split Lines & Lofted-Cuts:

- Use the 2 sketches named: Circular-Split and Side-Split to create 2 split surfaces.

- Create 2 lofted-cuts at **.093** in. deep, using either the **Offset** or **Ruled** surface options.

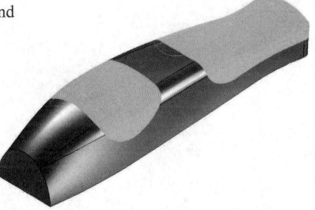

5. Adding the Nose and Fillets:

- Add the Nose feature that measured between **1.250" in** to **1.500"** from the front face.

- Remove all sharp edges with **.040 in**. fillets.

6. Saving your work:

- Save the exercise as: **Advanced_Surfaces_Exe**.

Exercise: Advanced Surfacing Techniques

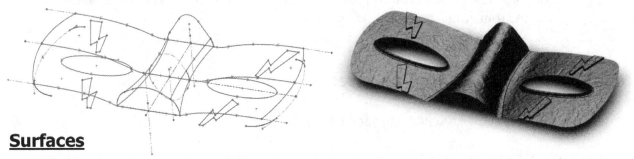

Surfaces

- Surfaces are a type of geometry that can be used to create solid features. Surfaces can be created in a variety of different ways; from a sketch or multiple sketches, a surface can be made by extruding, revolving, sweeping and lofting.
- Surfaces are normally created individually and knitted together so that an enclosed volume or a solid feature, can be generated afterwards.
- This exercise discusses some advanced techniques on surfacing such as: Lofted Surface, Boundary Surface, Trimmed Surface, Offset Surface, Extrude From, and variable fillets.

1. Opening the existing document named:

Advanced Surfacing Techniques from the training CD. Rollback below the sketch: 1st Loft Guide-Curves.

2. Creating the 1st Lofted Surface:

- Click or select:
  Insert / Surface / Loft.

- Select the **2 Loft Profiles** and the **2 Guide Curves** as indicated.

- Click **OK**.

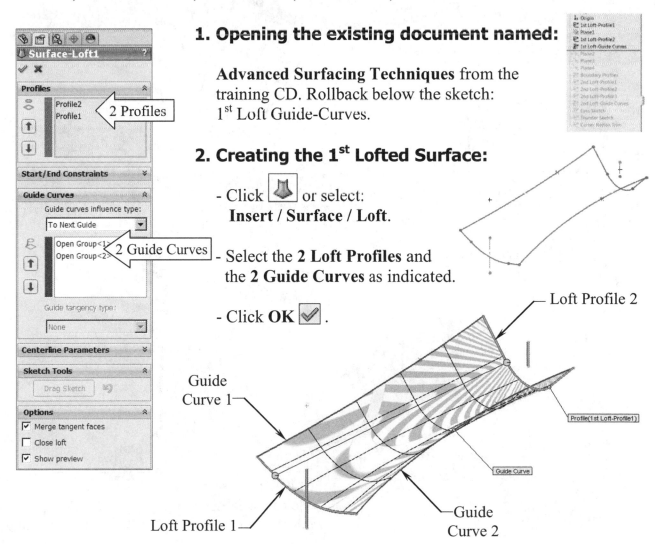

> **Lofted-Surface** creates a feature by making transitions between two or more profiles. A loft can either be a surface or solid and one or more Guide Curves can be used to guide the transitions between the profiles.

3. Creating the 2ⁿᵈ Lofted Surface:

- Click or select: **Insert / Surface / Loft**.

- Select the **3 Loft Prof**
  the **4 Guide Curves**
  as indicated.

- Click OK after each
  selection of profile and
  guide curves.

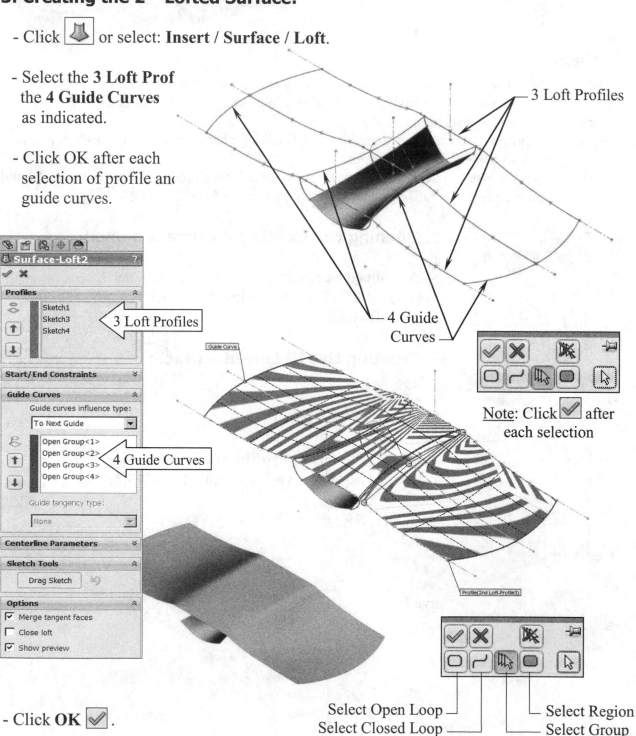

3 Loft Profiles

4 Guide
Curves

Note: Click ✓ after
each selection

- Click **OK** ✓.

Select Open Loop —
Select Closed Loop —

— Select Region
— Select Group

4. Creating the Boundary-Surfaces:

- Click 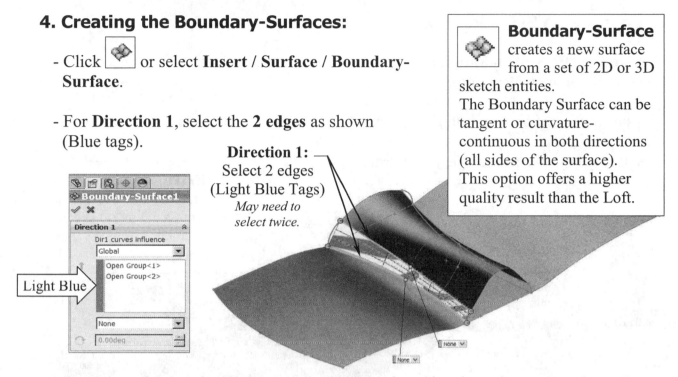 or select **Insert / Surface / Boundary-Surface**.

- For **Direction 1**, select the **2 edges** as shown (Blue tags).

> **Boundary-Surface** creates a new surface from a set of 2D or 3D sketch entities.
> The Boundary Surface can be tangent or curvature-continuous in both directions (all sides of the surface). This option offers a higher quality result than the Loft.

Direction 1:
Select 2 edges
(Light Blue Tags)
May need to select twice.

Light Blue

- For **Direction 2**, select the **3 Arcs** in the Boundary Sketch as shown (Purple tags).

Direction 2:
Select 3 Arcs
(Purple tags)
May need to select twice.

Purple

Note: Click ✓ after each selection

- Click **OK** ✓ .

5. Repeating:

- Repeat step number 4 and create another Boundary-Surface on the opposite side.

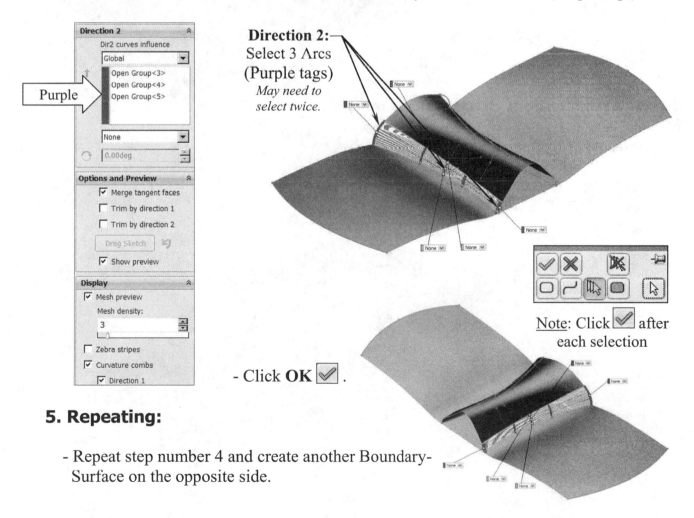

6. Creating an Extruded-Surface:

- Select the **Eyes Sketch** from the FeatureManager tree and Click [icon] or select:
Insert / Surface / Extrude.

- Change the option **Extrude From** to **Surface/Face/Plane** (Arrow).

- Select the surface as indicated, to extrude.

> [icon] **Extruded-Surface**
> creates a new surface from a 2D or 3D sketch, which protrudes normal to the sketch plane.

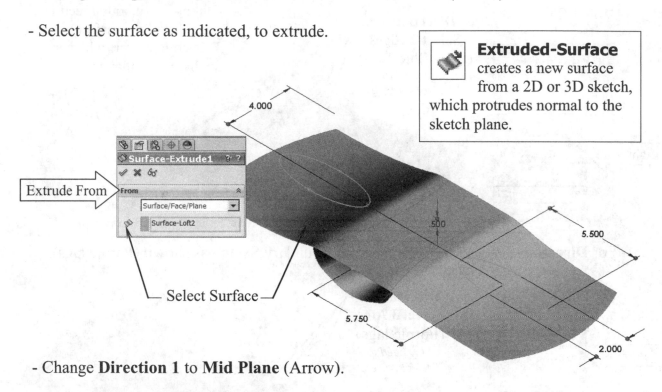

- Change **Direction 1** to **Mid Plane** (Arrow).

- Enter **.410"** for Extrude Depth.

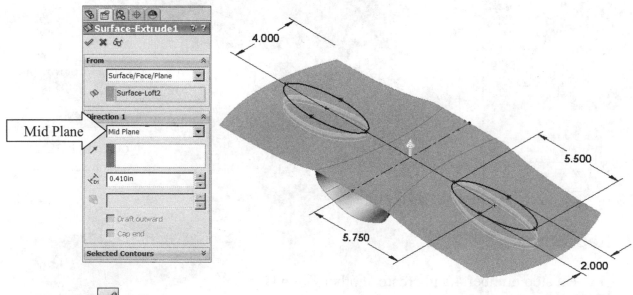

- Click **OK** [icon].

7. Creating a Trimmed Surface:

- Click 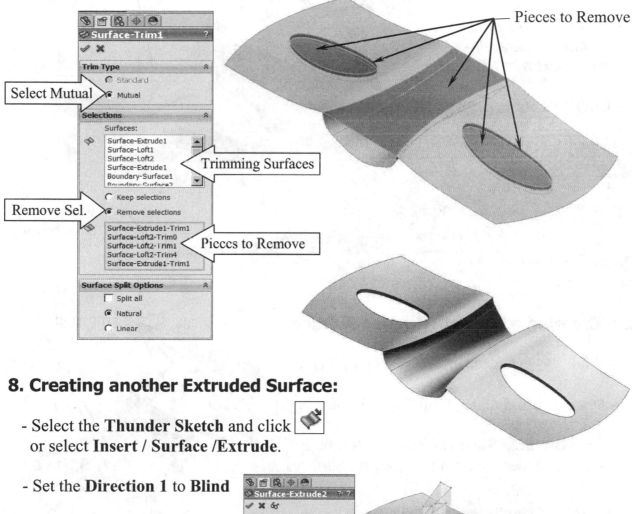 or select **Insert / Surface / Trim**.

> **Trimmed-Surface** uses a plane, a surface, or a sketch as a trim tool to trim the intersecting surfaces.

- Select **Mutual** under Trim Type (Arrow).

- For **Trimming Surfaces**, select **all surfaces** of the model.

- For **Pieces To Remove**, select the **5 Faces** as shown (Arrow).

Pieces to Remove

Select Mutual

Trimming Surfaces

Remove Sel.

Picccs to Remove

8. Creating another Extruded Surface:

- Select the **Thunder Sketch** and click 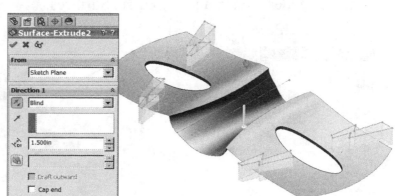 or select **Insert / Surface /Extrude**.

- Set the **Direction 1** to **Blind**

and click **Reverse Direction**.

- Set **Extrude Depth** to:
1.250”.

- Click **OK** ✓.

9. Creating an Offset-Surface:

- Click 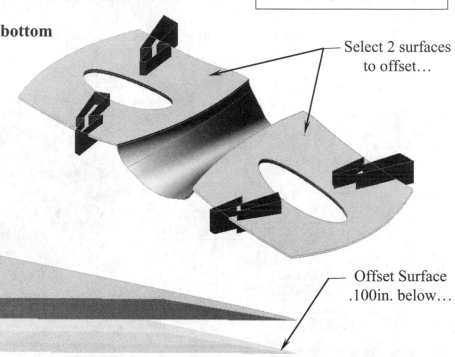 or select **Insert / Surface / Offset**.

- Select the **2 surfaces** as shown (Arrow).

- Enter **.100"** for **Offset Distance**.

- Place the copy on the **bottom** of the original.

- *Note: create 2 offset surfaces separately if the next trim failed.*

- Click **OK** ✔.

> **Offset-Surface** creates a copy of a surface in either direction, and is parallel to the selected surface(s). The offset distance can be zero or any other value.

Select 2 surfaces to offset…

Offset Surface .100in. below…

10. Creating a Mutual Trimmed Surface:

- Click 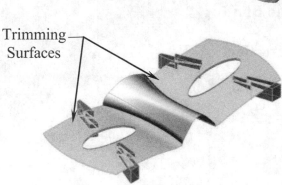 or select **Insert / Surface / Trim**.

- Select **Mutual** under Trim Type (Arrow).

- For **Trimming Surfaces**, select **all surfaces** of the Thunder Sketch and the Offset Surfaces.

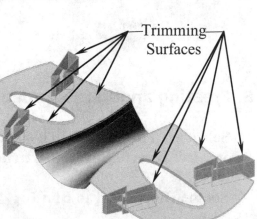

Trimming Surfaces

Trimming Surfaces

Select Mutual

- For **Remove Selection**, select the following:

* The **surfaces** of the **Thunder Sketch**,
  Keep the inside faces as noted.

* The **2 Offset Surfaces**.

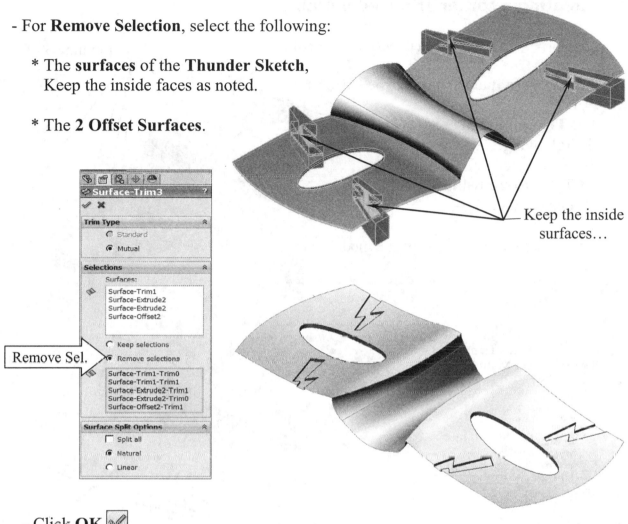

Keep the inside surfaces…

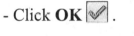

Remove Sel.

- Click **OK** .

11. Creating an Extruded Surface:

- Select the **Corner Radius Trim** Sketch
  and click or select **Insert / Surface / Extrude**.

- Set the **Direction 1** to **Blind**
  and click **Reverse Direction**.

- Set Depth to **2.000"**.

- Click **OK** .

(These new surfaces will be used to trim-off the 4 corners).

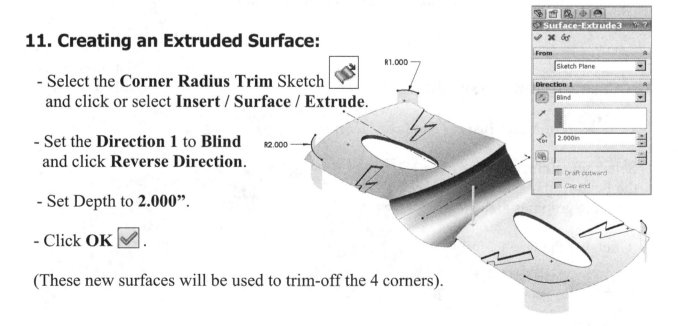

12. Creating a corner Trimmed Surface:

- Click or select **Insert / Surface / Trim**.

- Select **Mutual** under Trim Type (Arrow).

- For **Trimming Surfaces**, select the following:

    * The **4 extruded faces** and the **4 corner pieces**.

    * The **2 left/right faces** of the model.

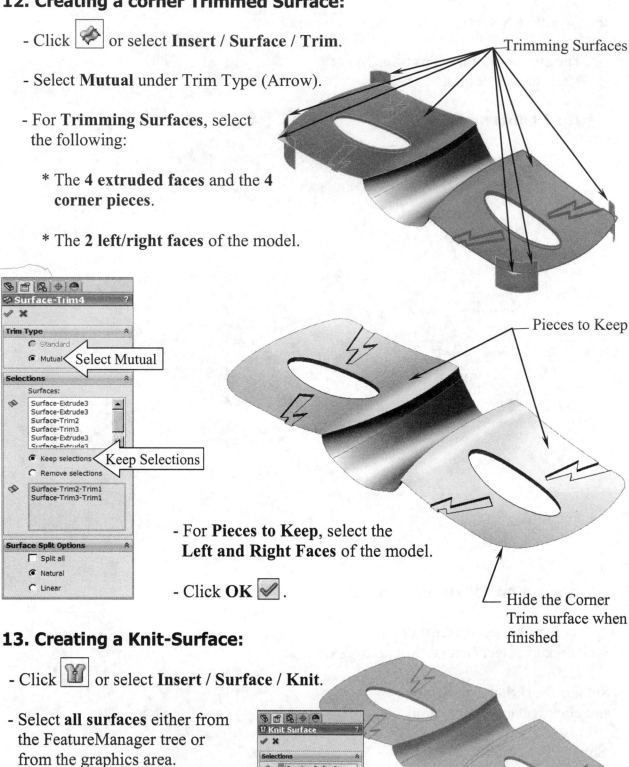

Trimming Surfaces

Pieces to Keep

- For **Pieces to Keep**, select the **Left and Right Faces** of the model.

- Click **OK**.

Hide the Corner Trim surface when finished

13. Creating a Knit-Surface:

- Click or select **Insert / Surface / Knit**.

- Select **all surfaces** either from the FeatureManager tree or from the graphics area.

- Click off the Gap Control.

- Click **OK**.

14. Adding a Variable Fillet:

- Click 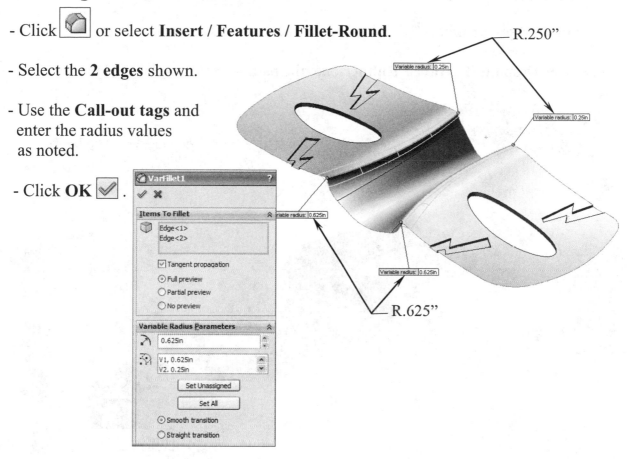 or select **Insert / Features / Fillet-Round**.

- Select the **2 edges** shown.

- Use the **Call-out tags** and
  enter the radius values
  as noted.

- Click **OK** .

R.250"

R.625"

15. Adding a Constant Fillet:

- Click 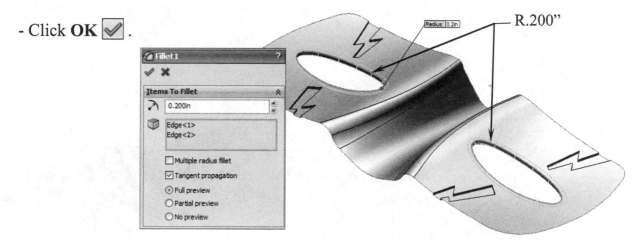 or select **Insert / Features / Fillet-Round**.

- Select the **2 edges** as shown.

- Enter **.200"** for Radius values.

- Click **OK** .

R.200"

16. Optional: Adding texture

- From the **Appearances** folder, select the **Rubber/Texture** folder.

- Drag & Drop the **Textured Rubber** onto the part, select the Apply to Part option .

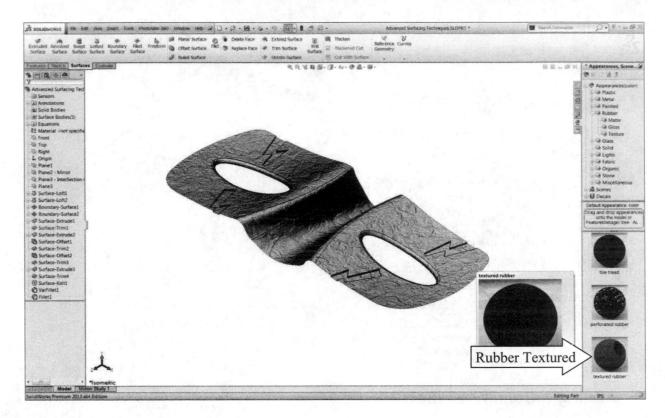

17. Saving your work:

- Click **File / Save As**.

- Enter **Advanced Surfacing Techniques** for the name of the file.

- Click **Save**.

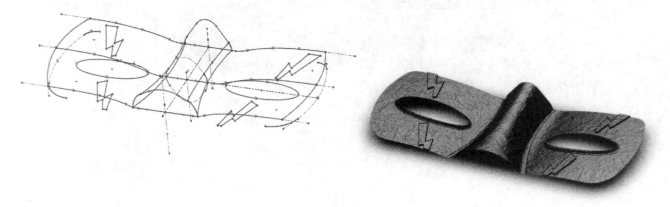

CHAPTER 10

Using Filled Surface

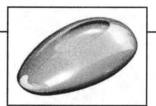

Using Filled Surface
Curvature Controls

- Use Filled Surface and Planar Surface commands to fill or patch a surface boundary with any number of sides.

- The boundary can be a set of existing model edges, sketches, or curves, including composite curves. The boundary should be closed for the patch to work properly.

- There are several options to help you control the curvatures when patching a surface boundary such as: Contact, Tangent, and Curvature. These options are explained later in the lesson.

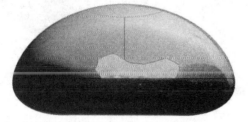 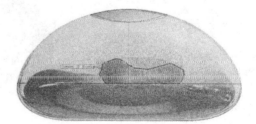

- Other than the Curvature Control options the Apply-to-All-Edges check box enables you to apply the same curvature control to all edges. If you select the function after applying both **Contact** and **Tangent** to different edges, it applies the current selection to all edges.

- If your surface model has two or four-sided surfaces try using the **Optimize surface** option. The Optimize surface option applies a simplified surface patch that is similar to a lofted surface. Potential advantages of the optimized surface patch include faster build times, and increased stability when used in conjunction with other features in the model.

- This lesson will teach us the use of the Filled Surface and Planar Surface commands.

Using Filled Surface
Patch with Curvature Controls

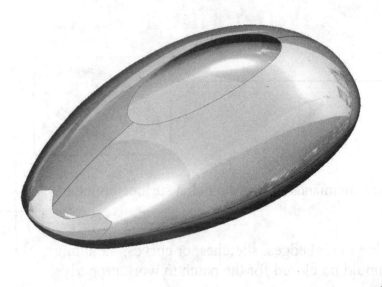

Dimensioning Standards: **ANSI**

Units: **INCHES** – 3 Decimals

Tools Needed:

 Planar Surface   Filled Surface   Knit Surface

1. Opening a part document:

- Click **File / Open**.

- Browse to the Training CD, locate and open the part document named: **Filled Surfaces**.

- This part document was previously created in another CAD software. There is no feature history available on the FeatureManager tree.

- There are three openings in the part that we will have to fill using different options within the Filled-Surface command.

- If the Feature Recognition dialog pops up, click **NO** to close it.

2. Enabling the Surfaces toolbar:

- Right click either on the Features tab or the Sketch tab and select the Surfaces tool tab.

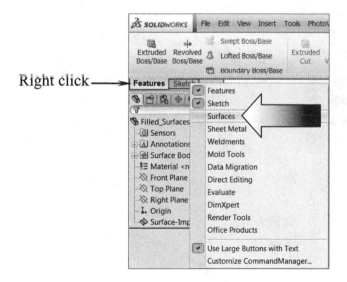

Right click

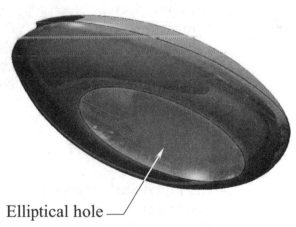

Elliptical hole

- Rotate the model and locate the elliptical-hole at the bottom of the model.

- This hole should forms a flat surface and we can use the Planar-Surface command to patch it

3. Creating a Planar surface :

- Click the **Surfaces** tool tab (arrow).

- Select the **Planar-Surface** command.

- Select the <u>edge</u> of of the elliptical hole.

- The preview of a new surface appears.

- Click **OK**.

- A planar surface can be created from a sketch, a set of closed edges, or a pair of planar entities such as curves or edges.

Select edge

4. Creating a Surface Fill with Tangent Control 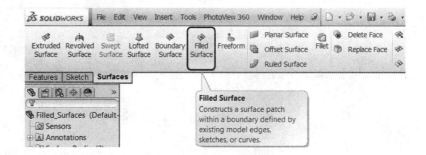 :

- Go back to the **Isometric view** (Either press Control + 7 or press the Spacebar and double click on Isometric).

- Click the **Filled Surface** command.

- The Filled Surface command is used to patch a closed boundary. You can define the boundary by selecting a set of 2D or 3D sketch entities, model edges or composite curves.

- Select the <u>two edges</u> of the elliptical hole as indicated.

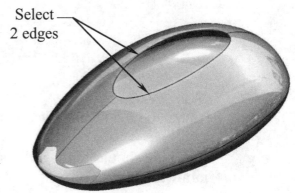

Select 2 edges

- A grid appears on the patch to help you visualize the curvature of new surface.

- Change the Curvature Control* to **Tangent**.

- Enable the checkboxes as shown.

- Click **OK**.

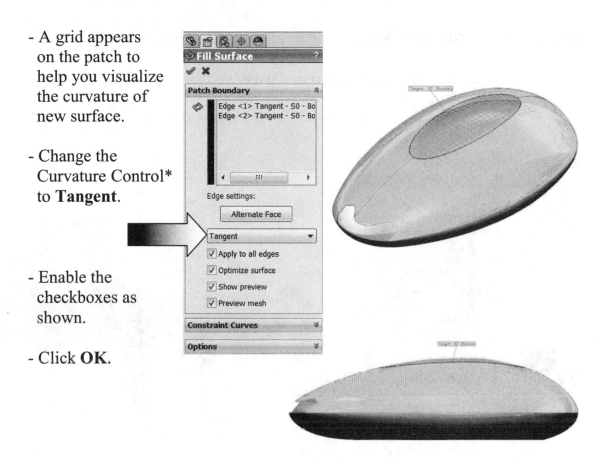

* The **Curvature Control** defines the type of control you want to exert on the patch you create. The types of **Curvature Control** include:

    Contact: Creates a surface within the selected boundary.

    Tangent: Creates a surface within the selected boundary, but maintains the tangency of the patch edges.

    Curvature: Creates a surface that matches the curvature of the selected surface across the boundary edge with the adjacent surface.

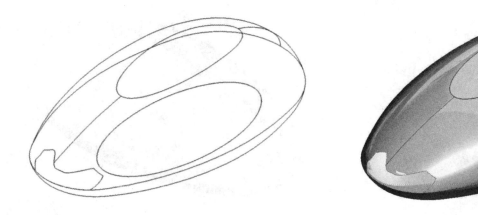

5. Creating a Surface Fill with Curvature Control :

- Click the **Filled Surface** command once again.

- Change to the Front view orientation (Press Control + 1).

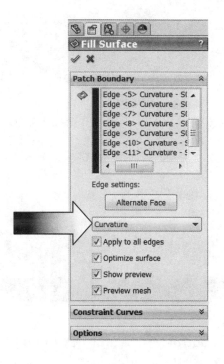

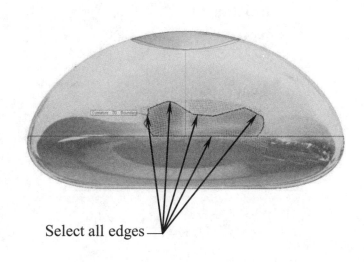

Select all edges —

- Select <u>all edges</u> of the opening in the front as noted.

- The preview mesh appears indicating a closed boundary is found. (Enable the Preview Mesh checkbox if the preview is not visible).

- Under the Curvature Control change the Contact option to **Curvature** (arrow).

- Enable the other checkbox as shown in the dialog box.

- Click **OK**.

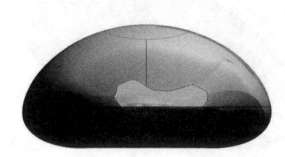

6. Knitting all surfaces 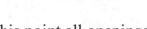 :

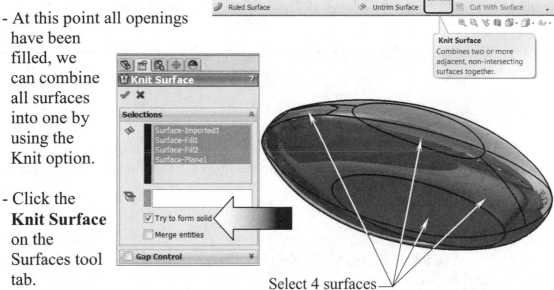

- At this point all openings have been filled, we can combine all surfaces into one by using the Knit option.

- Click the **Knit Surface** on the Surfaces tool tab.

Select 4 surfaces

- Select all for surfaces in the graphics area as indicated.

- Click the **Try To Form Solid** checkbox (arrow) to make the part solid.

- Click **OK**.

- To verify the interior of the part create a section view using the Right plane as the cutting plane. Click Cancel when done.

7. Saving your work:

- Save your work as **Using Filled Surface**.

Questions for Review

Using Filled Surface

1. When opening a part document created from another CAD software, all of its features history will appear on the FeatureManager tree.
   a. True
   b. False

2. Tool tabs can be added as needed by right clicking on one of the one of the existing tool tab and select them from the list.
   a. True
   b. False

3. A planar surface can be created from a closed sketch or a set of closed edges.
   a. True
   b. False

4. An open sketch or a set of open edges can also be patched using the Planar surface command.
   a. True
   b. False

5. The Filled Surface command is used to patch a non-planar closed boundary.
   a. True
   b. False

6. The Filled Surface command will fail if the boundary is not closed.
   a. True
   b. False

7. The Preview Mesh can be toggled on/off during the creation of the filled surface.
   a. True
   b. False

8. The Knit Surface command can only Knit the surfaces, it cannot forms a solid out of them.
   a. True
   b. False

7. TRUE   8. FALSE
5. TRUE   6. TRUE
3. TRUE   4. FALSE
1. FALSE   2. TRUE

CHAPTER 9 cont.

Boundary and Freeform Surfaces

Boundary Surface: Allows the user to create surfaces that can be tangent or curvature continuous in both directions (all sides of the surface). In most cases, this delivers a higher quality result than the loft tool.

Freeform feature: Modifies a face of a surface or a solid body. You can modify only one face at a time and the face can have any number of sides. Control curves and control points can be added to allow pushing and pulling the control points to modify the face. The triad is used to constrain the push or pull direction.

1. Opening a part file:

- Browse to the attached CD and open the part file named: **Freeform Surface**.

2. Creating the 1st Boundary Surface:

- Right click either the Features or the Sketch tab and **enable** the **Surfaces** option.

- Click the **Boundary Surface** button from the Surfaces toolbar or select: **Insert / Surface / Boundary Surface**.

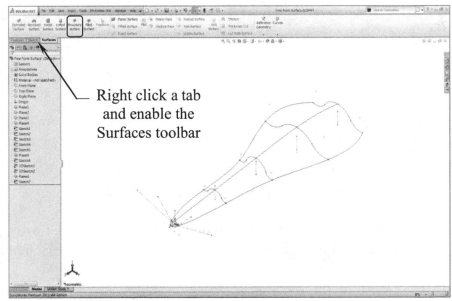

Right click a tab and enable the Surfaces toolbar

- Zoom in on the left end of the image.

- For Direction 1: select the 1st Curve approximately as shown.

- Curves are used to determine the boundary feature in Direction 1 and Direction 2.

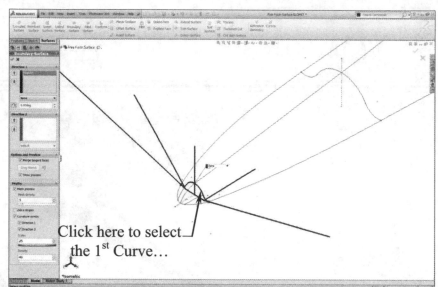

Click here to select the 1st Curve…

- For each curve, select the point from which you want the path of the boundary feature to travel.

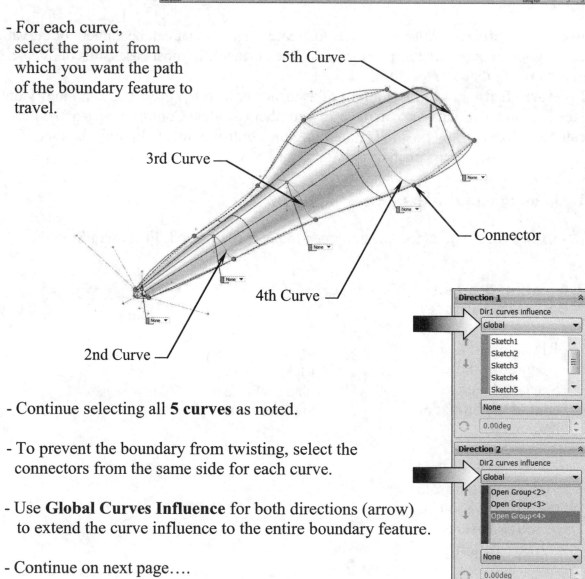

5th Curve

3rd Curve

Connector

4th Curve

2nd Curve

- Continue selecting all **5 curves** as noted.

- To prevent the boundary from twisting, select the connectors from the same side for each curve.

- Use **Global Curves Influence** for both directions (arrow) to extend the curve influence to the entire boundary feature.

- Continue on next page….

- For Direction 2: select the **3 Curves** as indicated below.

- Since both Curve6 and Curve7 were created in the same sketch, the **Selection–Manager** pops up when one of them is selected, asking to confirm your selection. Click the OK button after selecting Curve6 and Curve7.

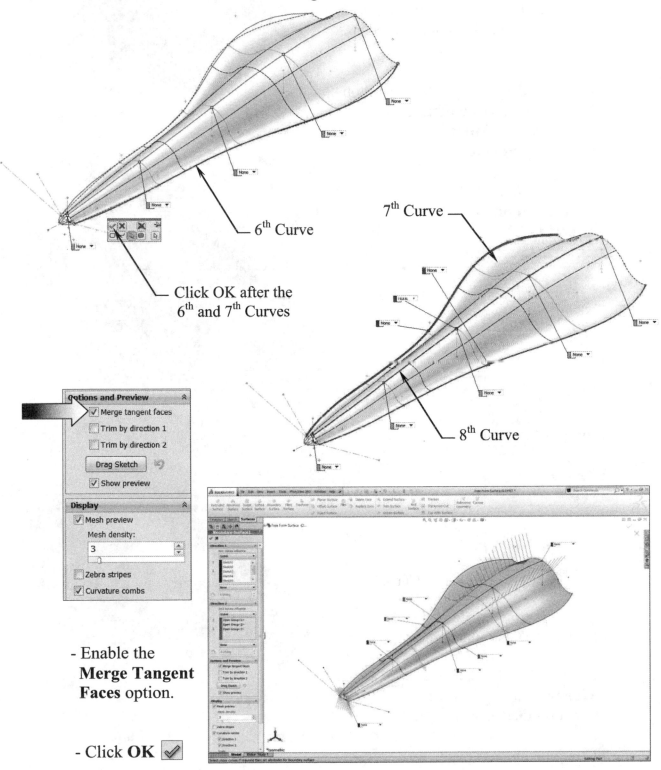

6th Curve

Click OK after the
6th and 7th Curves

7th Curve

8th Curve

- Enable the
**Merge Tangent
Faces** option.

- Click **OK**

3. Creating the 2nd Boundary Surface:

- Zoom in on the tip section of the surface.

- There are 5 other Curves on the Feature-Manager tree, 2 of them will be used as Direction 1 and the other 3, used as Direction2.

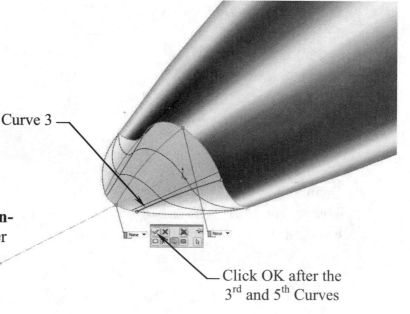

- Click the **Boundary Surface** button from the Surfaces toolbar or select: **Insert / Surface / Boundary Surface**.

- For Direction 1, select the **Curve1** and **Curve2** as noted.

Curve 1

Curve 2

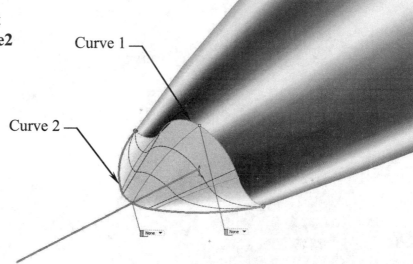

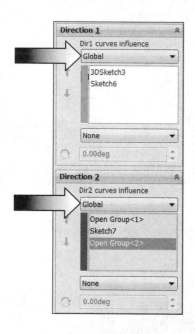

- For Direction 2, select the **Curve3** as indicated.

- Click OK in the **Selection-Manager** dialog box after selecting the Curve3.

Curve 3

Click OK after the 3rd and 5th Curves

- Continue on next page…

- For Direction2, continue selecting the Curve4 and Curve5 as noted below.
- Enable the **Merge Tangent Faces** checkbox to force the boundary feature to be tangent to the corresponding segments.

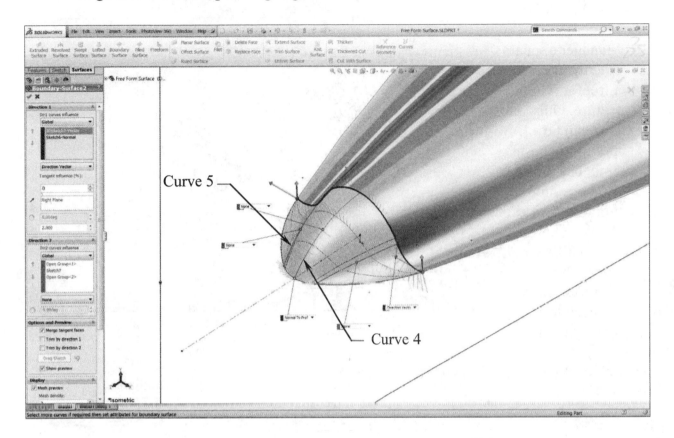

- Click **OK** ✓ .

- The resulting Boundary Surface.

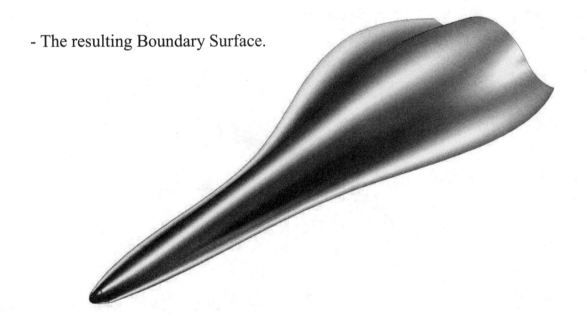

4. Creating the Freeform feature:

- From the **Insert** menus, select **Features / Freeform**.

- The **Freeform** Property-Manager appears when you create a freeform feature. Only one face can be modified at a time, but the face can have any number of sides.

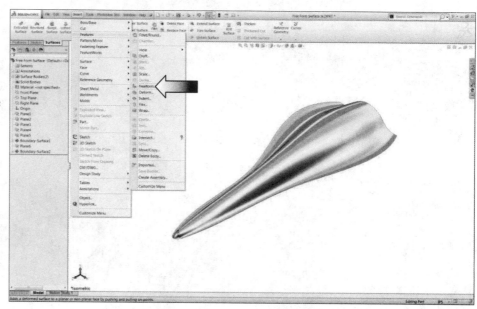

- A set of Control Curves and Control Points are used to modify the face.

- **Select the face** as indicated to modify.

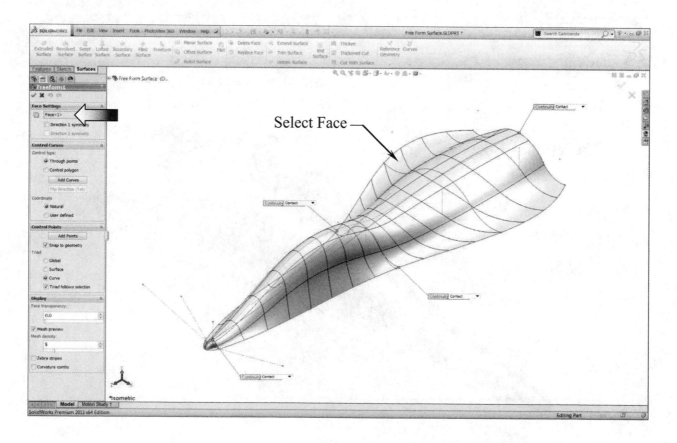

Select Face

- Go down to the **Control Curves** section and click the **Add Curves** button.

- Position the cursor approximately at the center of the face and click to **add a curve**.

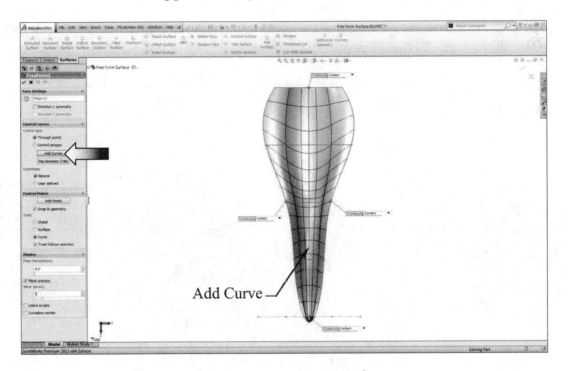

Add Curve

- Go down to the **Control Points** section and click the **Add Points** button.

- **Add 3 points** along the curve approximately as indicated.

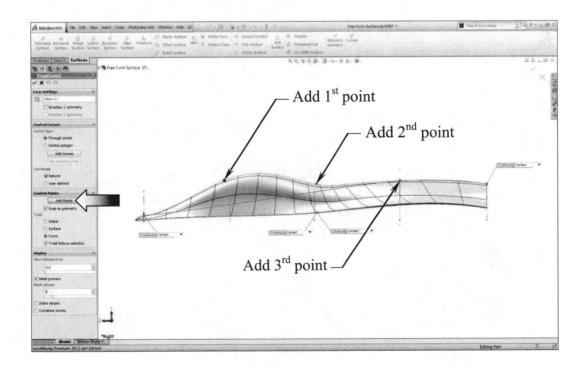

Add 1st point

Add 2nd point

Add 3rd point

- Select the 1ˢᵗ Control Point to see the Triad. The arrows on the triad are used to push or pull the surface one direction at a time. Drag the center sphere in the middle of the 3 arrows to push or pull in all directions at the same time.

- Drag the head of the green arrow slightly upward to see how the face is deformed, then change the **Triad Directions** to **X= 0.375"** and **Y= 0.500"** (arrows).

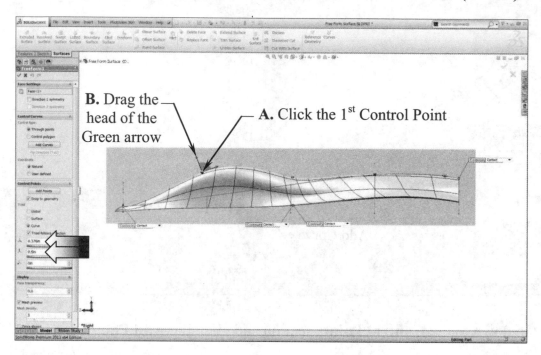

- Click the 2ⁿᵈ Control Point and set the **Triad Directions** to **X= -0.375"** and **Y= 0.050"**.

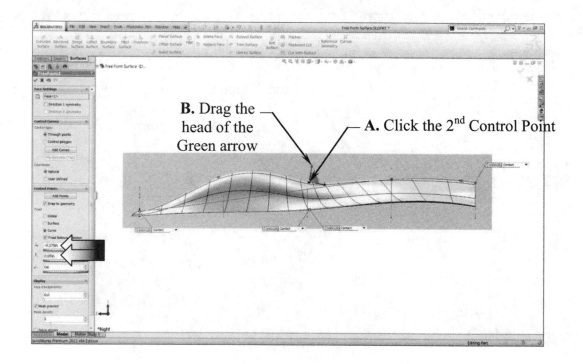

- Click the 3rd Control Point, set the **Triad Directions** to **X= -0.700"** and **Y= 0.015"**.

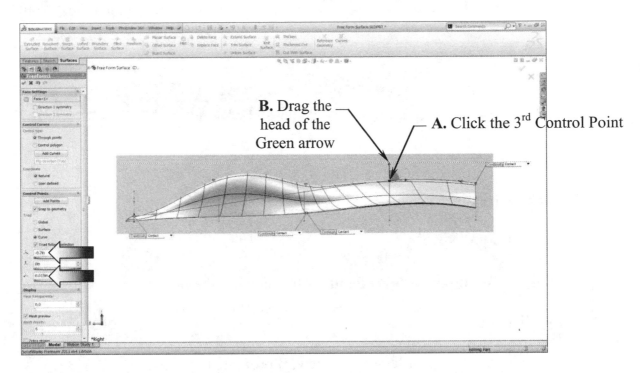

B. Drag the head of the Green arrow

A. Click the 3rd Control Point

- Click the **Curvature combs** to see a visual enhancement of the surface' curvatures.

- Set the **Scale** to adjust the size of the curvature combs and set the **Density** to adjust the number of curvature combs.

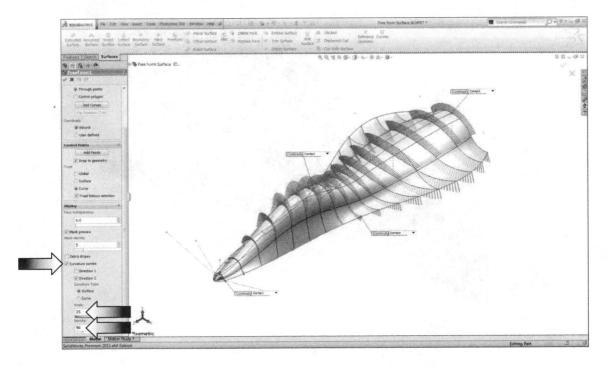

- Click **OK** ✓.

- The resulting Freeform Surface.

5. Saving your work:

- Click **File / Save As**.

- Enter **Boundary & Freeform** for the name of the file.

- Click **Save**.

- Overwrite the old file with the new, if prompted.

CHAPTER 10 Cont.

Sweep with Solid body

Sweep with Solid Body
Creating a Cam Feature

- Beside the traditional sweep using a sketch profile, we now have the option: Sweep using a solid body. It is only available for the Cut Sweep command.

- This feature is useful for end mill simulation, where a solid body is swept along a path to create cuts around cylindrical bodies, or some other cam features.

- Similar to the standard sweep using a profile and path, solid sweep requires the path to be tangent within itself and has no sharp corners.

- The path can either be an open or closed contour, and can be a set of 2D or 3D sketched lines, curves, or model edges.

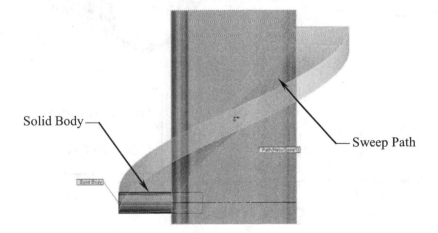

Solid Body

Sweep Path

- The profile should be a revolved feature that consists of analytical geometry only, such as lines and arcs.

- A plane perpendicular to the path is be created, and the profile gets drawn on this plane and constrained to the sweep path.

Sweep with Solid Body
Creating a Cam Part

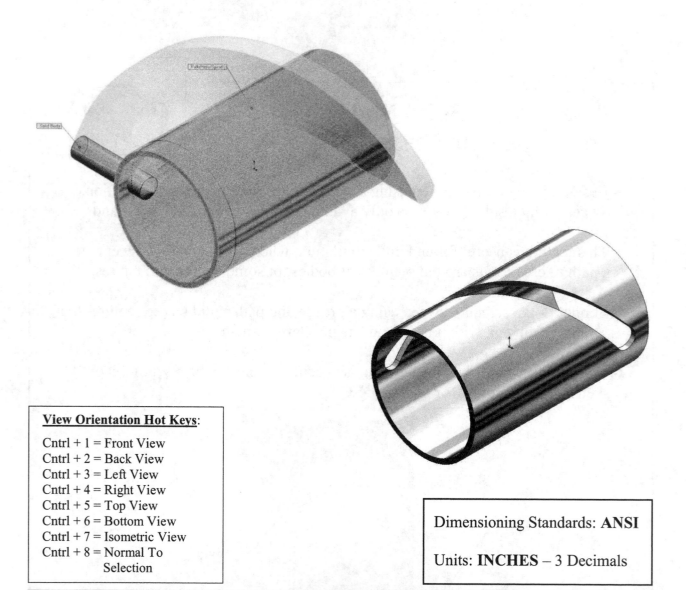

<u>View Orientation Hot Keys</u>:

Cntrl + 1 = Front View
Cntrl + 2 = Back View
Cntrl + 3 = Left View
Cntrl + 4 = Right View
Cntrl + 5 = Top View
Cntrl + 6 = Bottom View
Cntrl + 7 = Isometric View
Cntrl + 8 = Normal To
             Selection

Dimensioning Standards: **ANSI**

Units: **INCHES** – 3 Decimals

Tools Needed:

 Insert Sketch   Circle   Convert Entities

 Helix/Spiral   Plane   Swept Cut

1. Creating the main body:

- Select the <u>Front</u> plane from the Feature tree and open a new sketch .

- Sketch 2 circles centered on the origin as shown.

- Add the OD and ID dimensions to fully define this sketch.

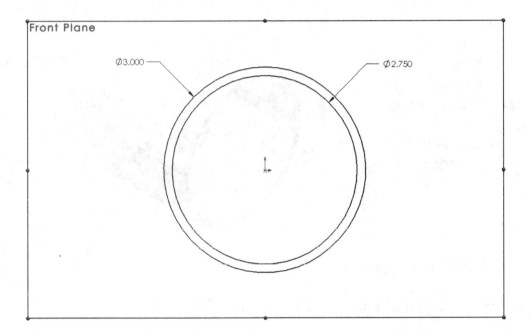

- From the Features toolbar click **Extruded Boss-Base** .

- Select the **Mid Plane** extrude option from the Direction 1 list.

- Enter **5.000**in for
  extrude depth.

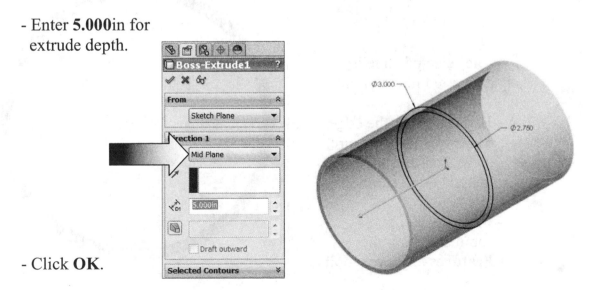

- Click **OK**.

2. Creating an Offset-Distance plane :

- Select the **Front** plane from the FeatureManager tree, hold the <u>Control</u> key <u>drag</u> the edge of the front plane to the left and release the mouse button.

- This techniques makes a parallel copy of the selected plane.

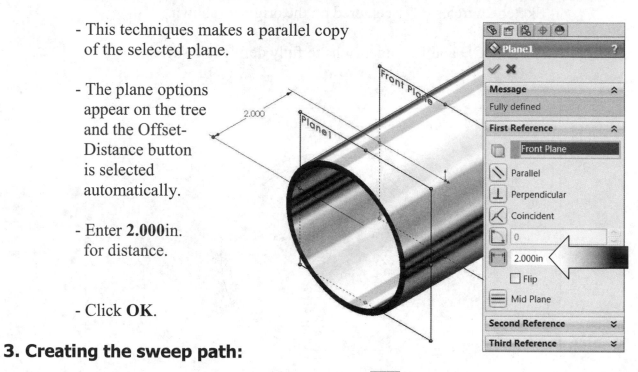

- The plane options appear on the tree and the Offset-Distance button is selected automatically.

- Enter **2.000**in. for distance.

- Click **OK**.

3. Creating the sweep path:

- Select the <u>Plane1</u> and open a new sketch 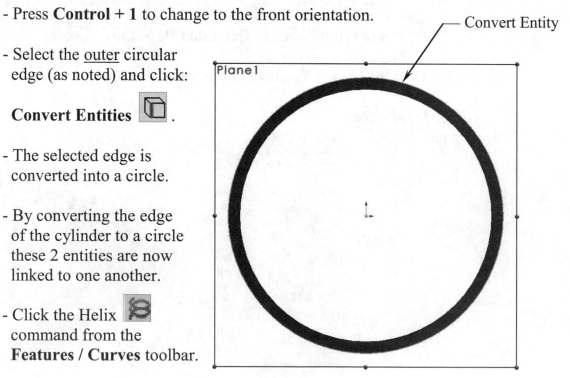.

- Press **Control + 1** to change to the front orientation.

- Select the <u>outer</u> circular edge (as noted) and click:

  Convert Entities .

- The selected edge is converted into a circle.

- By converting the edge of the cylinder to a circle these 2 entities are now linked to one another.

- Click the Helix command from the **Features / Curves** toolbar.

Convert Entity

- Use the default Pitch and Revolution under Defined By.

- Under Constant Pitch enter **7.750"** for Pitch.

- Click the **Reverse-Direction** checkbox.

- Enter **0.5** (1/2) for revolutions.

- For Start Angle, enter:**180deg**.

- Use the default **Clockwise** direction.

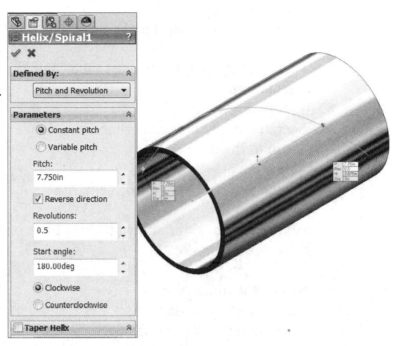

- Click **OK**.

4. Creating a plane Normal-To-Curve :

- Hold the <u>Control</u> key, select the Left endpoint of the helix <u>and</u> click the helix.

- Click the **Plane** command (or select **Insert / Reference Geometry / Plane**).

- The **Perpendicular** option should be selected already.

- Click **OK**.

- A new plane is created, normal to the helix and locked to the left end of it.

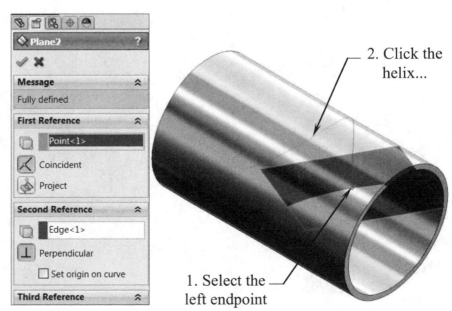

2. Click the helix...

1. Select the left endpoint

5. Creating the sweep body:

- Select the new <u>Plane2</u> and open a new sketch.

- Press <u>Control + 8</u> to change to the "Normal-To" orientation.

- Sketch a horizontal centerline from the origin to the left.

- Sketch a rectangle over the centerline.

- Add the dimensions shown to fully define the sketch.

- Notice the dimension Ø.500 is a virtual diameter dimension (dimension from the centerline to the bottom left vertex of the rectangle, and move the cursor upwards, pass the centerline to double it).

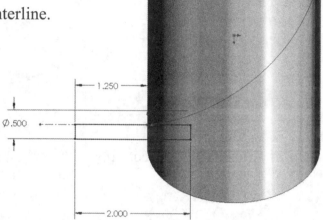

- Press **Revolve Boss-Base** from the Features toolbar.

- Use the default **Blind** and **360deg.** options.

- <u>Uncheck</u> the **Merge Result** check box (arrow) to make this feature a separate body from the first one.

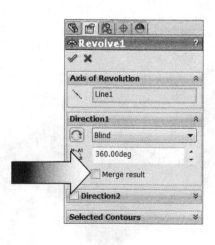

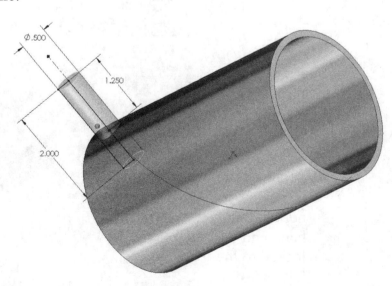

- Click **OK**.

6. Creating the sweep cut with a solid body:

- Click **Swept Cut** 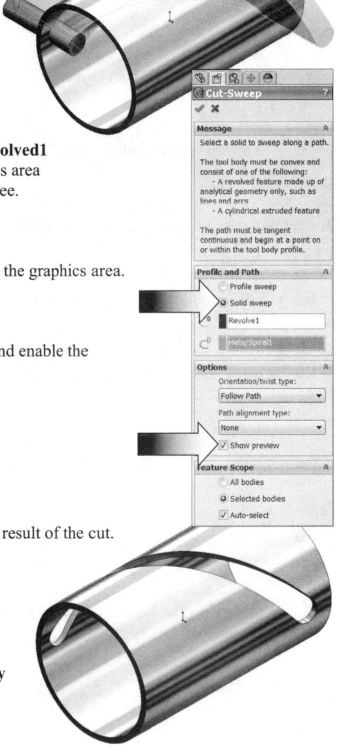 from the
  Features toolbar (or select:
  Insert / Cut / Sweep).

- Click the **Solid Sweep**
  option (arrow).

- For Tool Body, select the **Revolved1**
  feature either from the graphics area
  or from the FeatureManager tree.

- For Path, click the **Helix** from the graphics area.

- Expand the **Options** section and enable the
  Preview checkbox.

- Click **OK**.

- Rotate the model to verify the result of the cut.

7. Saving your work:

- Click **File / Save As**.

- Enter **Sweep with Solid Body**
  for the name of the file.

- Click **Save**.

Questions for Review

Sweep with Solid Body

1. A Solid Sweep uses a solid body to move along the path to create the cut feature.
  a. True
  b. False

2. The Solid Sweep option is only available for sweep cuts only, not sweep bosses.
  a. True
  b. False

3. The Convert Entities command can be found on the Features toolbar.
  a. True
  b. False

4. The converted entities are <u>not</u> linked to the original geometry, where they were converted from.
  a. True
  b. False

5. The Path used in a Solid Sweep should be continuous and tangent within itself, and have no sharp corners.
  a. True
  b. False

6. When Solid Sweep option is selected, a sketch profile can be used in place of a solid body.
  a. True
  b. False

7. The Preview option is not available when using the Solid Sweep option.
  a. True
  b. False

8. The hot-keys Control+1 thru Control+8 are default keys for changing view orientations.
  a. True
  b. False

7. FALSE   8. TRUE
5. TRUE   6. FALSE
3. FALSE   4. FALSE
1. TRUE   2. TRUE

CHAPTER 11

Surfaces vs. Solid Modeling

Surfaces vs. Solid Modeling

Surfaces are a type of geometry that can be used to create solid features. Surface tools are available on the Surfaces toolbar.

You can <u>create surfaces</u> using these methods:

- Insert a planar surface from a sketch or from a set of closed edges that lie on a plane
- Extrude, revolve, sweep, or loft, from sketches
- Offset from existing faces or surfaces
- Import a file
- Create mid-surfaces
- Radiate surfaces

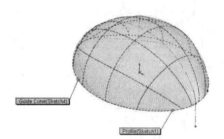

You can <u>modify surfaces</u> in the following ways:

- Extend
- Trim existing surfaces
- Un-trim surfaces
- Fillet surfaces
- Repair surfaces using Filled Surface
- Move/Copy surfaces
- Delete and patch a face
- Knit surfaces

You can <u>use surfaces</u> in the following ways:

- Select surface edges and vertices to use as a sweep guide curve and path
- Create a solid or cut feature by thickening a surface
- Extrude a solid or cut feature with the end condition Up to Surface or Offset from Surface
- Create a solid feature by thickening surfaces that have been knit into a closed volume
- Replace a face with a surface

Safety Helmet
Hybrid Modeling with Solid & Surfaces

View Orientation Hot Keys:

Cntrl + 1 = Front View
Cntrl + 2 = Back View
Cntrl + 3 = Left View
Cntrl + 4 = Right View
Cntrl + 5 = Top View
Cntrl + 6 = Bottom View
Cntrl + 7 = Isometric View
Cntrl + 8 = Normal To
            Selection

Dimensioning Standards: **ANSI**

Units: **INCHES** – 3 Decimals

Tools Needed:

Insert Sketch	Plane	Lofted Surface
Swept Surface	Planar Surface	Knit Surface
Revolve Cut	Sweep Cut	Surface Thicken

1. Opening the Existing file:

- From the Training CD, open the part document named: **Helmet**.

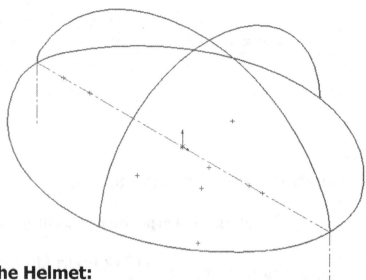

2. Constructing the Body of the Helmet:

- Click **Lofted Surface** 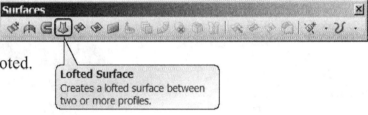 OR – select **Insert / Surface / Loft**.

- Select the 3 Sketch Profiles.

- Select the 3 Guide Curves as noted.

- Click **OK** ✅.

Lofted Surface
Creates a lofted surface between two or more profiles.

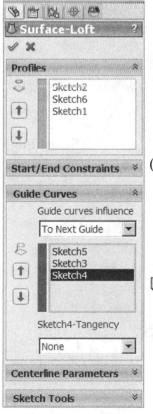

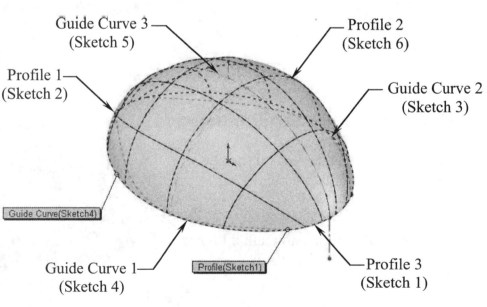

Guide Curve 3 (Sketch 5)

Profile 2 (Sketch 6)

Profile 1 (Sketch 2)

Guide Curve 2 (Sketch 3)

Guide Curve(Sketch4)

Guide Curve 1 (Sketch 4)

Profile(Sketch1)

Profile 3 (Sketch 1)

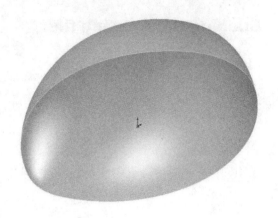

- The resulted Surface-Loft.

3. Creating a new work plane:

- Create a plane **Perpendicular** as illustrated.

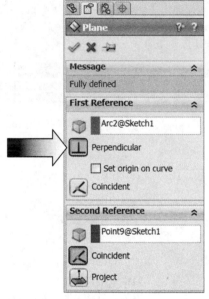

- Click **Insert / Reference Geometry / Plane** 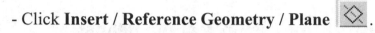.

- Select the circular edge and its endpoint as noted.

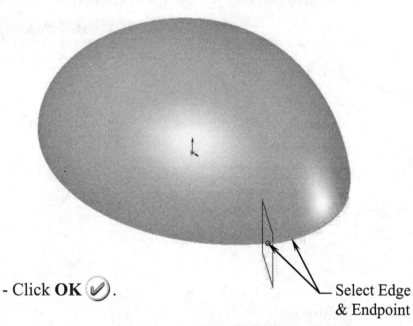

Select Edge & Endpoint

- Click **OK** ✔.

4. Sketching the Sweep-Profile:

- Open a new sketch ✏ on the new-plane and sketch a **Vertical Line** as shown.

- Add a **3.000"** dimension and a **Pierce** relation to fully define the sketch.

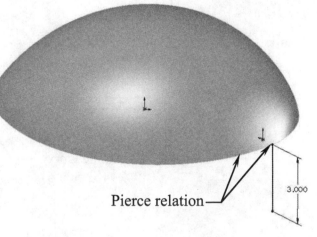

Pierce relation

3.000

- **Exit** the Sketch ✏.

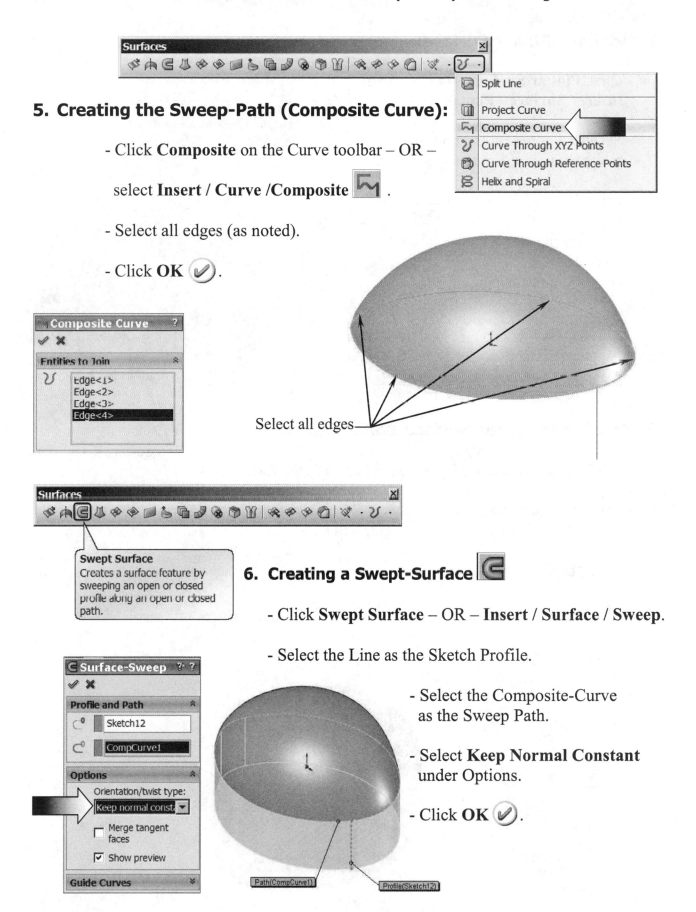

5. Creating the Sweep-Path (Composite Curve):

- Click **Composite** on the Curve toolbar – OR –

  select **Insert / Curve /Composite** .

- Select all edges (as noted).

- Click **OK** .

Select all edges

6. Creating a Swept-Surface

- Click **Swept Surface** – OR – **Insert / Surface / Sweep**.

- Select the Line as the Sketch Profile.

- Select the Composite-Curve as the Sweep Path.

- Select **Keep Normal Constant** under Options.

- Click **OK** .

Swept Surface
Creates a surface feature by sweeping an open or closed profile along an open or closed path.

7. Adding a Planar Surface:

- Click **Planar Surface** – OR – **Insert / Surface / Planar**.

- Select **all edges** on the bottom as the Bounding Entities.

- Click **OK** ✅.

- The new planar surface is created and it covers the bottom of the part.

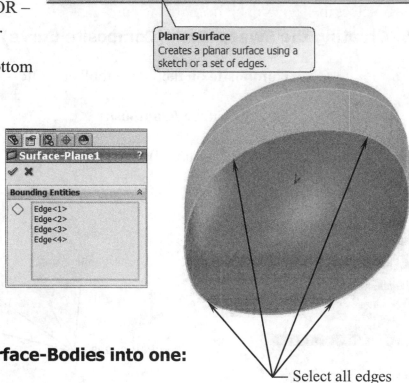

Planar Surface
Creates a planar surface using a sketch or a set of edges.

Select all edges

8. Knitting the three Surface-Bodies into one:

- Click **Knit Surface** 🎁 OR – select **Insert / Surface / Knit**.

- Select the Lofted-Surface, the Swept-Surface, and the Planar-Surface either from the FeatureManager tree or from the graphics area.

- <u>Clear</u> the Gap Control option.

- Enable the **Try To Form Solid** option, this turns the surfaces into a solid feature.

- Click **OK** ✅.

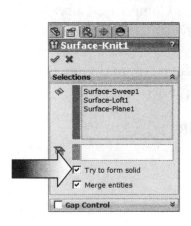

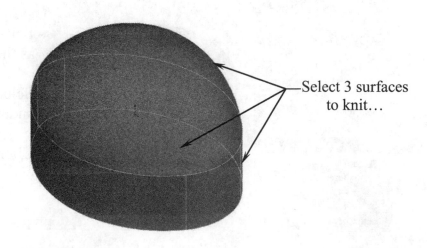

Select 3 surfaces to knit…

9. Creating a section view:

- Select the <u>Front</u> plane from the FeatureManager and click **Section View** (arrow). Click off the section view button when finished viewing.

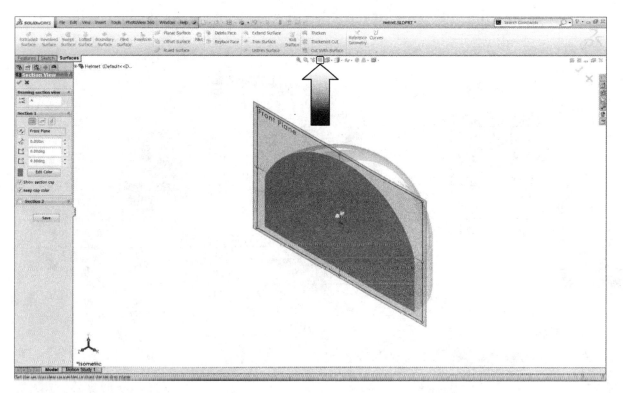

10. Adding an Extruded Cut feature:

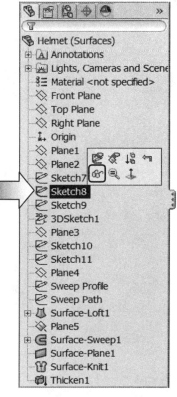

- Select the **Sketch8** from the FeatureManager Tree.

- This sketch will be used to remove the lower portion of the Helmet.

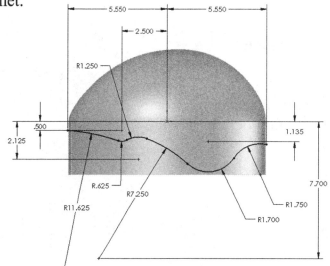

- Click **Extruded-Cut**  OR – **Insert / Cut / Extrude**.

- Use **Through-All** end conditions for both **Direction 1** and **Direction 2**.

- Enable **Flip-Side-To-Cut** if needed to remove the lower portion of the part.

- Click **OK** ✓.

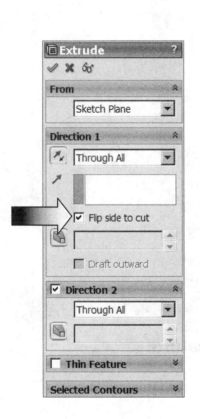

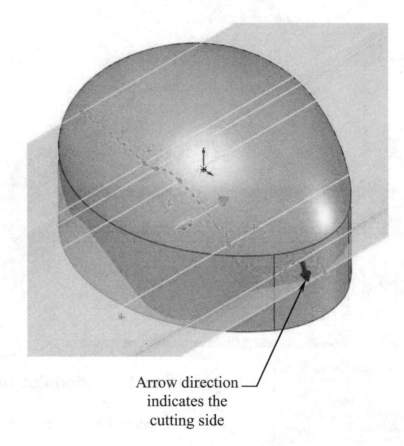

Arrow direction
indicates the
cutting side

- **Hide** the **Sketch8**.

- Compare your model with
this illustration before moving
to the next step.

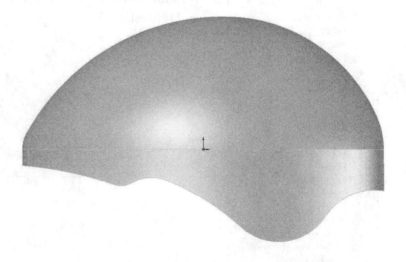

- The resulted cut.

11. Adding a Revolve-Cut feature:

- Select the **Sketch10** from the FeatureManager Tree.

- This sketch will be used to shape the <u>inside</u> of the Helmet.

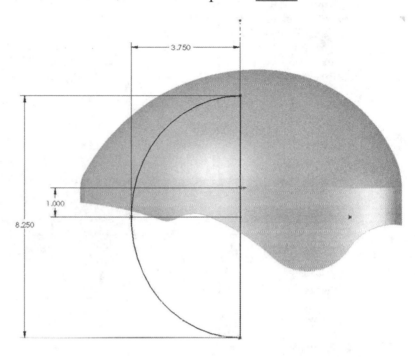

- Click **Revolve-Cut** OR – select **Insert / Cut / Revolve**.

- Select the **vertical centerline** as Revolve-Direction.

- Revolve Angle: **360.00deg**.

- Click **OK** .

- **Hide** the **Sketch10**.

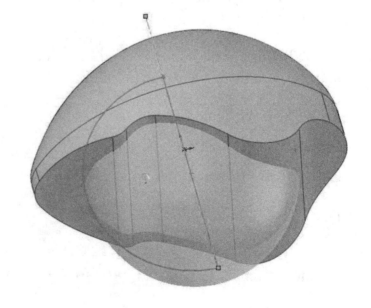

12. Adding the side cut features:

- Select the **Sketch9** from the FeatureManager Tree.

- This sketch will be used to cut from the <u>inside</u> with a **1.00deg**. draft angle.

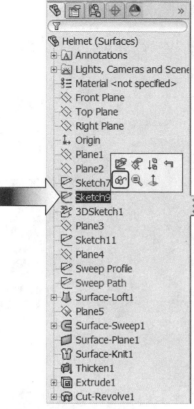

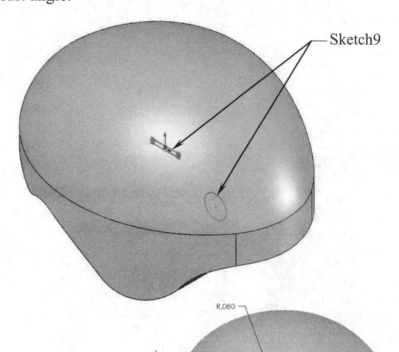

Sketch9

- Click **Extruded-Cut** OR – **Insert / Cut / Extrude**.

- Select **Through-All** for end condition.

- Enable Draft Angle and enter: **1.00deg**.

- Enable **Draft Outward** option.

- Click **OK**.

- Hide the Sketch9.

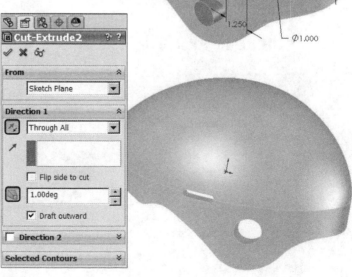

13. Creating the cut-out slot:

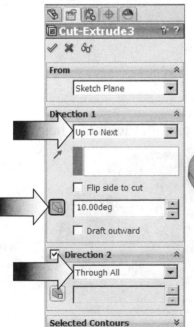

- Select the **Sketch11** from the FeatureManager Tree.

- This sketch will be used to cut a slot from the <u>outside</u> with a **10.00deg**. draft angle.

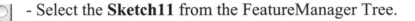

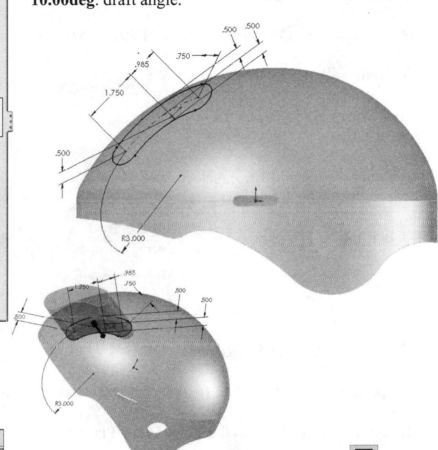

- Click **Extruded-Cut** OR – select **Insert / Cut / Extrude**.

- For Direction 1, select **Up-To- Next** end condition.

- Enable Draft Angle and enter: **10.00deg**. (inward)

- For Direction 2, select **Through-All** end condition. (No draft)

- Click **OK** .

- Hide the Sketch11.

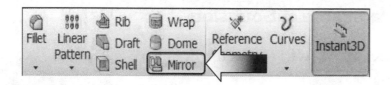

14. Mirroring the slot:

- Click **Mirror** – OR – select **Insert / Pattern-Mirror /**

Mirror .

- For Mirror Plane, select the **Right** plane.

- Under Features to Mirror, select the cut-out (Cut Extrude3).

- Click **OK** .

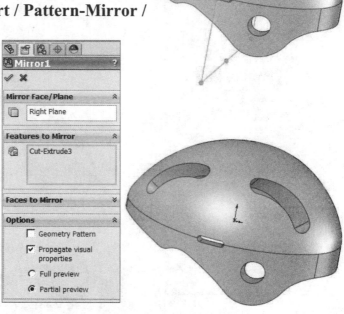

15. Mirroring the Cut Features:

- Click **Mirror** – OR – select **Insert / Pattern-Mirror / Mirror** .

- Select the **Front** plane as the Mirror Face/Plane.

- Select **both Slots** and the **Side-Holes** as Features to Mirror.

- Click **OK** .

- Compare your model with the image below.

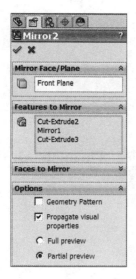

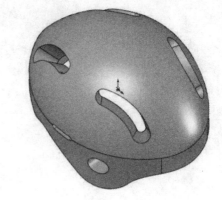

16. Creating the Sweep-Cut:

- Click **Insert / Cut / Sweep** .

- Select the sketch **Sweep-Profile** and the sketch **Sweep Path** from the FeatureManager tree.

- The preview graphics shows the proper transition of the sweep feature.

- Click **OK** .

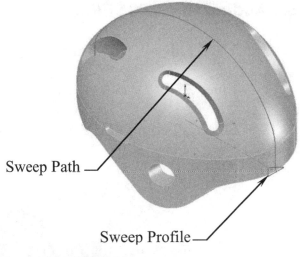

Sweep Path

Sweep Profile

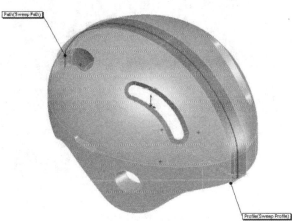

17. Adding the .500" fillets:

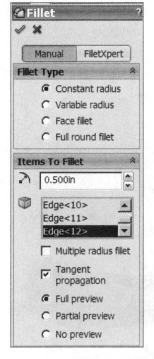

- Click **Fillet** – OR – select **Insert / Features / Fillet-Round**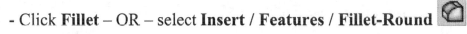

- Enter **.500"** for radius size.

- Select the edges of the Swept feature.

- Click **OK** .

18. Adding the .250" fillets:

- Click **Fillet** – OR – select: **Insert / Features / Fillet-Round**.

- Enter **.250"** for radius size.

- Select **all edges** of the part (Box Select).

- Click **OK** 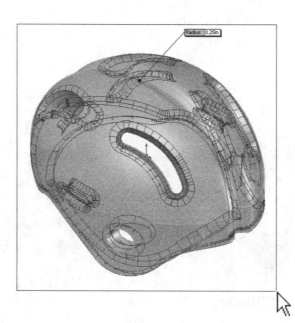.

19. Saving your work:

- Click **File / Save As / Helmet / Save**. (Save on the Desktop)

Front Isometric

Back Isometric

Exercise: Advanced Loft

1. Open the existing document:

Turbine.sldprt
From the Training CD.

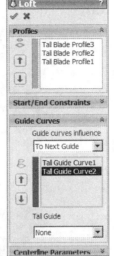

2. Create the 1st loft:
- Select the 3 Tall Blade sketches for Profiles.
- Select the Tall Guide Curve sketches for Guide Curves.

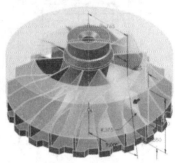

The resulted Lofts.

3. Create the 2nd loft:
- Select the 3 Short Blade sketches for Profiles.
- Select the Short Guide Curve sketches for Guide Curves.

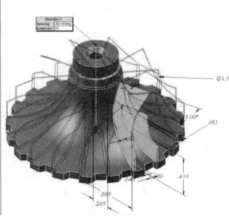

5. Create a Revolve Cut:
- Use the Blade Trim Sketch and create a Revolve-Cut.

4. Circular pattern the Blades:
- Create a circular pattern for the Lofted Blades.
- Enter **10** for number of instances.

6. Save your work as:
- Turbine Blades.

Exercise: Advanced Sweep

1. Opening the main sketch:

- From the training CD,
  locate and open the part
  document named:
  Candle Holder Sketch.

- **Edit** this sketch and verify
  that the sketch is fully defined.

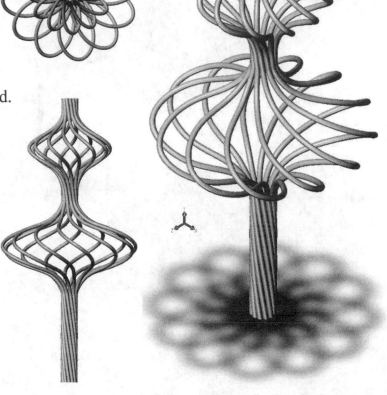

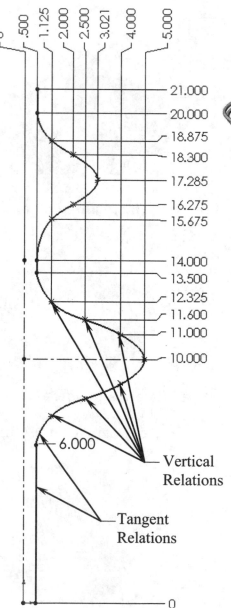

2. Revolving a surface:

- Click **Revolve Surface**.

- **Blind 360 deg**.

- Click **OK** ✅.

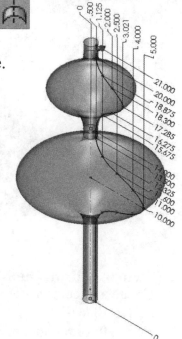

3. Creating a Helix:

- Select the Top plane and open a new sketch.

- Sketch a **10.00"** circle starting at the origin.

- Convert the Circle into a Helix using the settings as shown in the dialog box.

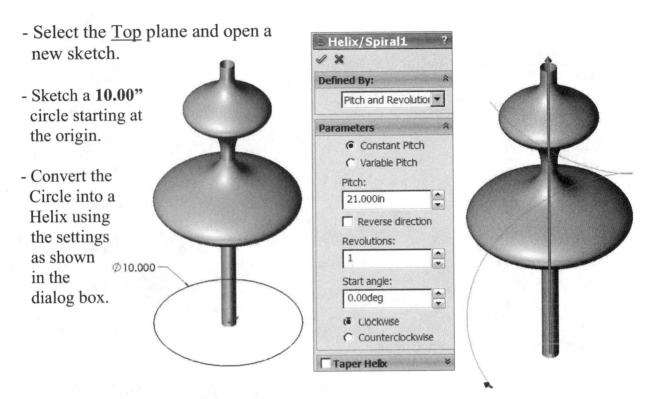

Ø10.000

Helix/Spiral1

Defined By:
Pitch and Revolution

Parameters
- ● Constant Pitch
- ○ Variable Pitch

Pitch:
21.000in

☐ Reverse direction

Revolutions:
1

Start angle:
0.00deg

- ● Clockwise
- ○ Counterclockwise

☐ Taper Helix

4. Creating a swept surface:

- Select the Top plane once again and open another sketch.

- Sketch a Line from the Origin and **Pierce** the other end of the line to the Helix.

- Click and sweep the Line along the Helix using the **Swept-Surface** option.

- Click **OK**.

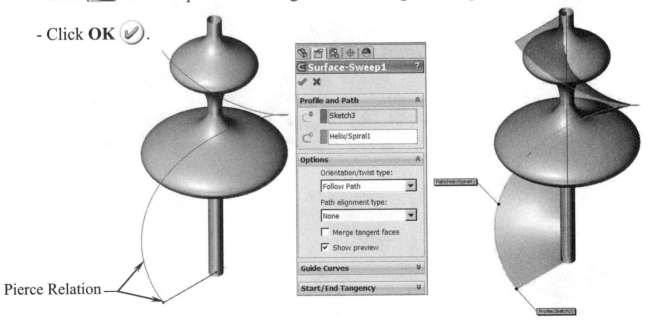

Pierce Relation

Surface-Sweep1

Profile and Path
- Sketch3
- Helix/Spiral1

Options
Orientation/twist type:
Follow Path

Path alignment type:
None

☐ Merge tangent faces
☑ Show preview

Guide Curves

Start/End Tangency

Path(Helix/Spiral1)

Profile(Sketch3)

5. Create a new Axis: (for use in step 9)

- Select **Insert / Reference Geometry / Axis** 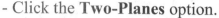.

- Click the **Two-Planes** option.

- Select the **Front** and the **Right** planes from the FeatureManager tree.

- A preview of the new axis appears in the center of the part.

- Click **OK** .

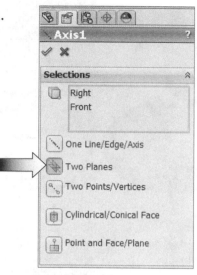

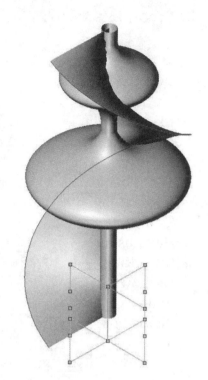

6. Create the Intersection Curve:

- Hold the CONTROL key and select the **Surface-Revolve1** and the **Surface Sweep1** from the FeatureManager tree.

- Click  or select **Tools / Sketch Tools / Intersection Curve**.

- A 3D-Sketch is created from the intersection of the two surfaces.

- **Exit** the 3D Sketch.

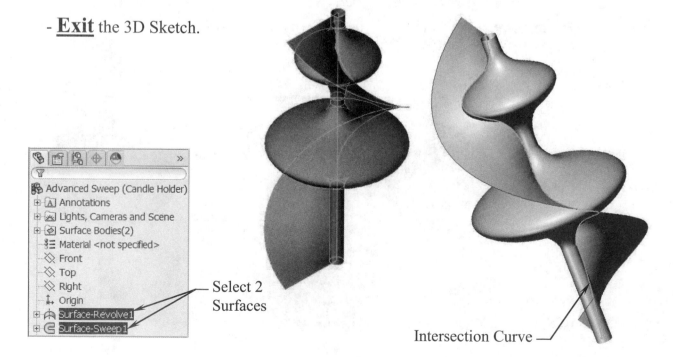

Select 2 Surfaces

Intersection Curve

7. Hide the 2 Surface Bodies:

- From the FeatureManager tree, right click on each Surface and select **Hide**.

- Select the TOP plane and open a new Sketch.

- Sketch a **Ø.260"** circle centered on the endpoint of the 3D Sketch.

- Click **OK** .

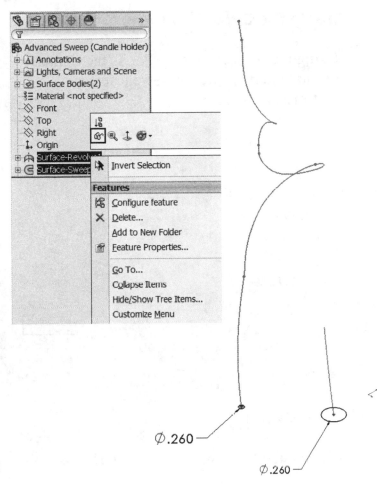

Ø.260

Ø.260

8. Create a solid swept feature:

- Click  or select **Insert / Boss-Base/ Sweep**.

- Select the Circle for Sweep Profile.

- Select the 3D-Sketch for Sweep Path.

- Click **OK** .

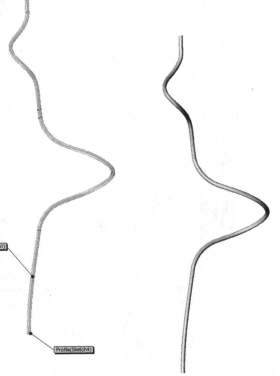

9. Create the Circular Pattern

- Using the Axis created earlier as the Center
  of the Pattern, repeat the Swept feature
  12 times.

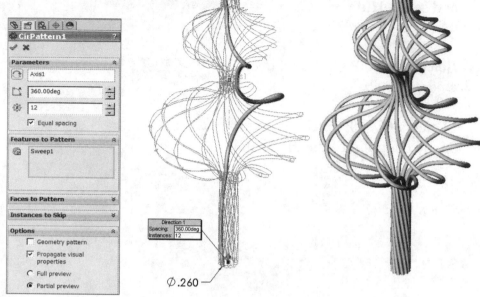

- Click **OK** ✅.

10. <u>OPTIONAL</u>:

- Create the **Base** and the **Candle Holder** solid features as shown below.

- Modify or design your own shapes if needed.

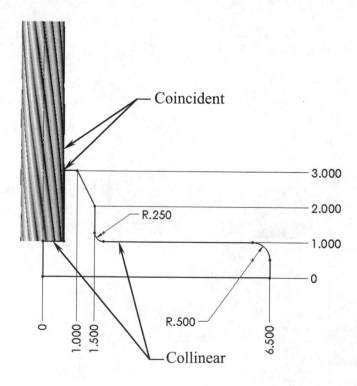

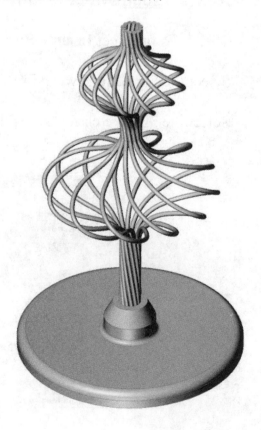

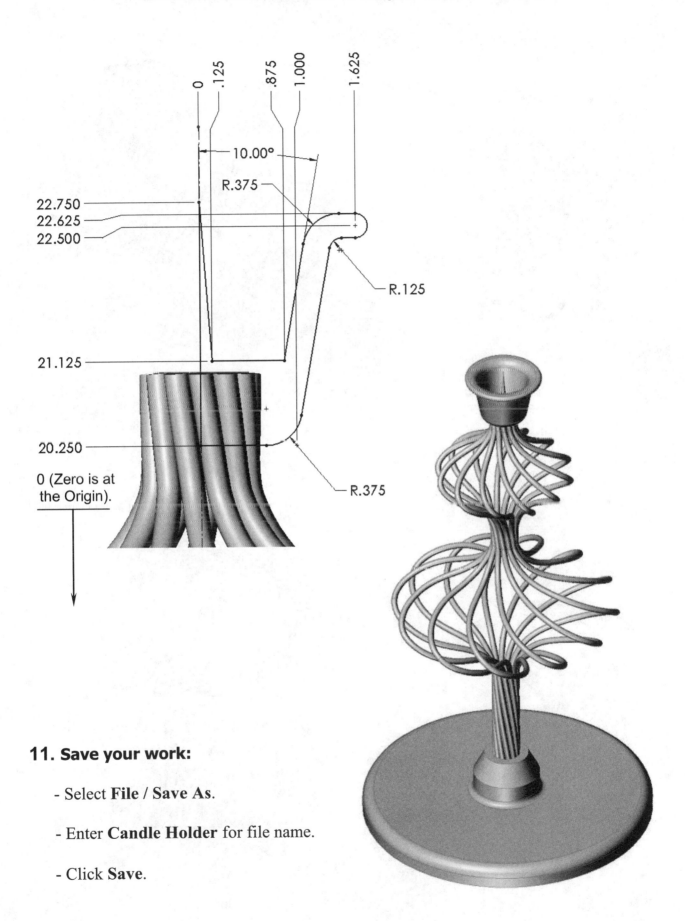

0

.125

.875

1.000

1.625

10.00°

R.375

22.750
22.625
22.500

R.125

21.125

20.250

0 (Zero is at
the Origin).

R.375

11. Save your work:

- Select **File / Save As**.

- Enter **Candle Holder** for file name.

- Click **Save**.

CHAPTER 11 cont.

Using PhotoView 360

PhotoView 360 enables the user to create photo-realistic renderings of the SolidWorks models. The rendered image incorporates the appearances, lighting, scene, and decals included with the model. PhotoView 360 is available with SolidWorks Pro or SolidWorks Premium only.

1. Enabling PhotoView 360:

- Click: **Tools / Add Ins**.

- Enable the **Photo-View 360** check-box.

- Click **OK**.

- The **PhotoView 360** program appears in the drop-down menus.

- Browse to the Training CD and open the document named: **Flying Hummer.sldprt**

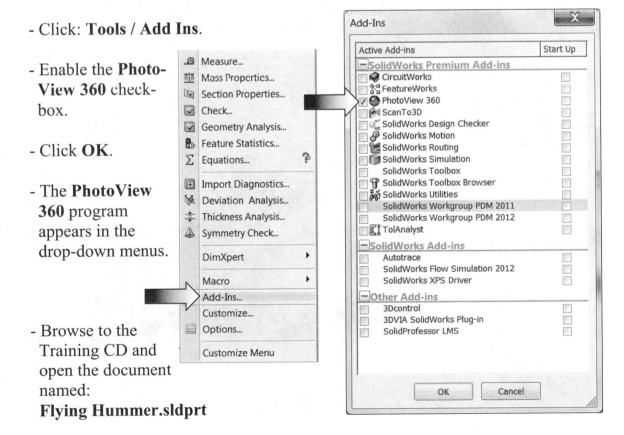

2. Setting the Appearance:

- Use Appearance to apply colors, material appearances, and transparency to parts and assembly components.

- Click **Edit-Appearance** from the PhotoView 360 pull down menu (arrow).

- From the Task Pane on the right side, Expand the **Metal** folder, the **Chrome** folder (arrows).

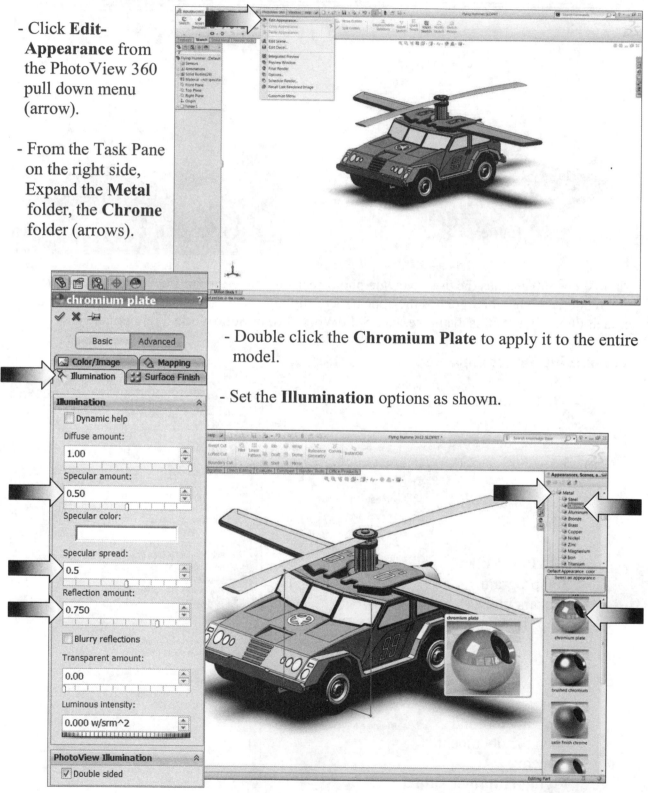

- Double click the **Chromium Plate** to apply it to the entire model.

- Set the **Illumination** options as shown.

3. Setting the Scene:

- Use Scene to create a visual backdrop behind a model, including a realistic light source, illumination, and reflections. The objects and lights in a Scene can form reflections on the model and can cast shadows on the adjustable floor.

- Click **Edit Scene** from the Photo-View 360 pull down menu (arrow).

- Expand the **Scene** folder, the **Studio Scenes** folder (arrows) and double click the **Strip Lighting** to apply to the entire model.

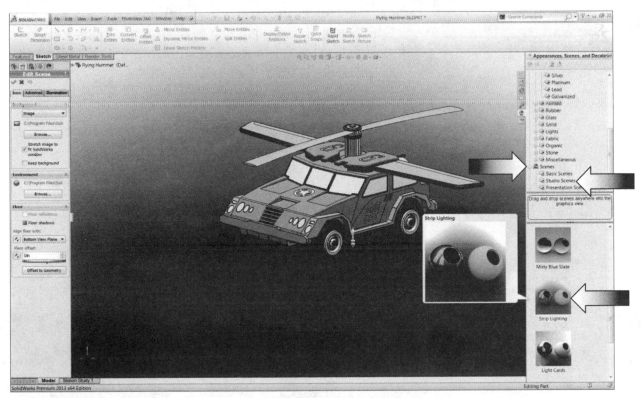

(more settings on the next page).

- The spacing between the model and the floor can be adjusted so that the shadow can look more realistic. From the **Basic tab**, set the following:

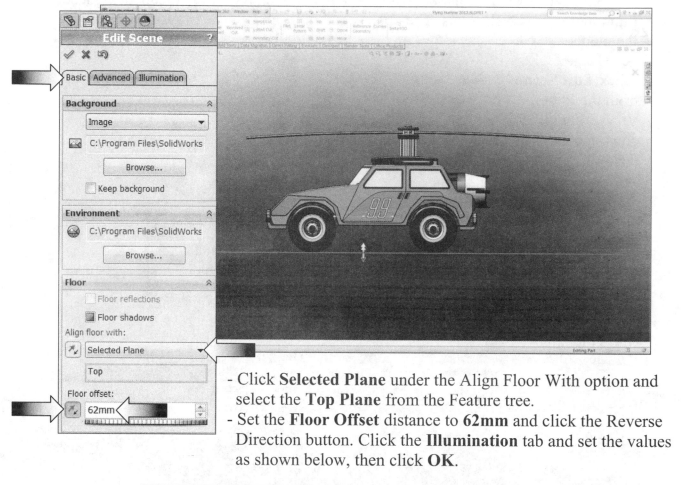

- Click **Selected Plane** under the Align Floor With option and select the **Top Plane** from the Feature tree.
- Set the **Floor Offset** distance to **62mm** and click the Reverse Direction button. Click the **Illumination** tab and set the values as shown below, then click **OK**.

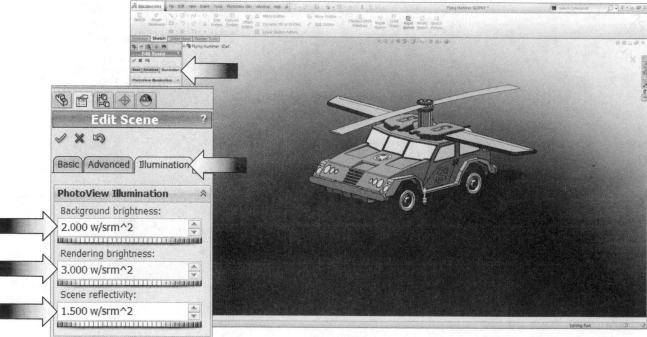

4. Setting the final rendering quality:

- Click **Final Render** from the PhotoView 360 drop down menu.

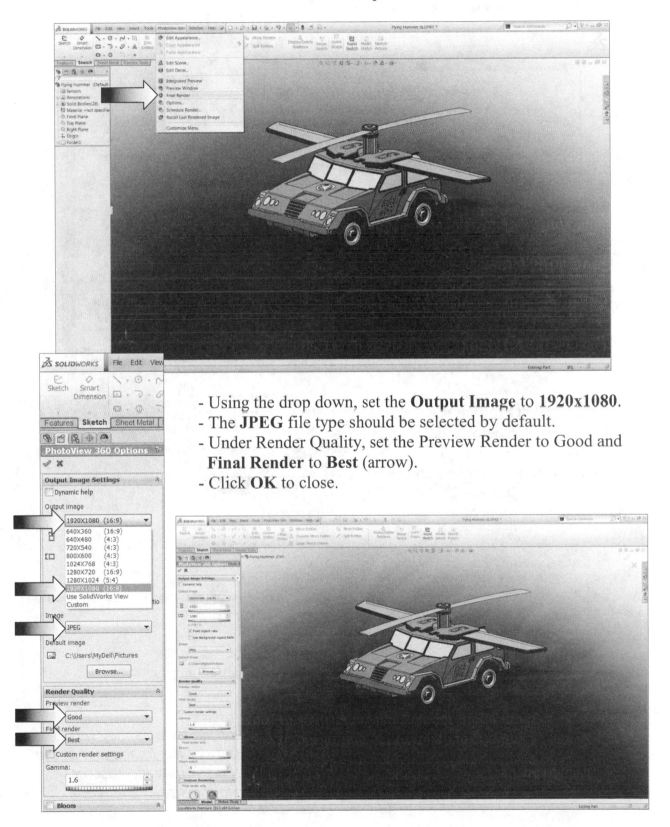

- Using the drop down, set the **Output Image** to **1920x1080**.
- The **JPEG** file type should be selected by default.
- Under Render Quality, set the Preview Render to Good and **Final Render** to **Best** (arrow).
- Click **OK** to close.

5. Saving the rendered image:

- Click **Final Render**. After the rendering is completed, set the zoom to **Best Fit** and then click **Save Image** (arrow).

- Select the **JPEG** format from the Save-as-Type drop down list.

- Enter a file name and click **OK**.

- **Save** and **close** all documents.

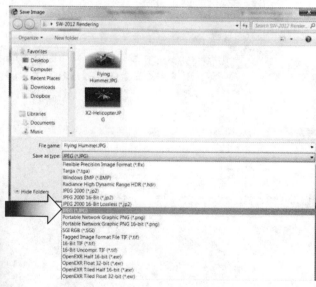

NOTE:

- *Different file formats may reduce the quality of the image and at the same time, it may increase or decrease the size of the file.*

Level 3: Final Exam

- Create the part Bottle using the LOFT and SWEEP options where noted.

- All sketch profiles must be fully defined.

- The part must have no errors when finished.

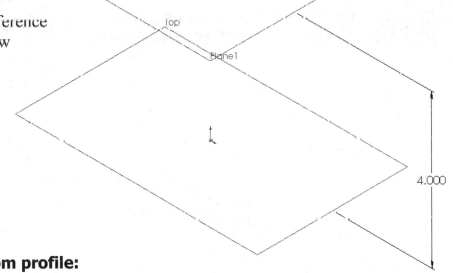

1. Create an Offset plane:

- Using the Top reference plane, create a new plane at **4.000 in**. offset distance.

2. Sketch the bottom profile:

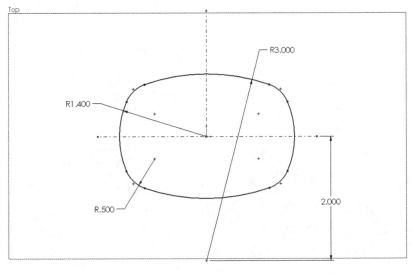

- Select the Top plane and sketch the profile as shown.

- Use the Mirror option to create the **Symmetric** relations between entities.

- **Exit** the Sketch.

3. Create the top profile:

- Using the Plane,1 sketch a Circle that centered on the Origin.

- Add a diameter dimension to fully define the sketch.

- **Exit** the sketch.

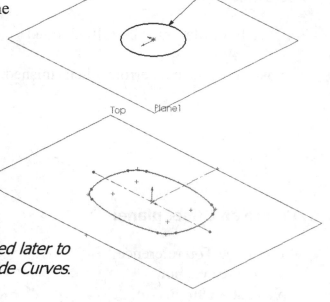

4. Create the 1ˢᵗ Guide Curve:

- Select the Front plane and sketch the profile as shown.

* *Note: The construction lines will be used later to create the Derived-Sketch and the Guide Curves.*

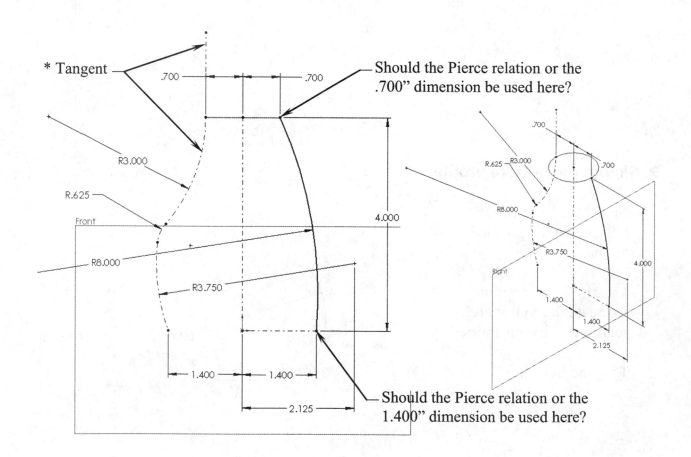

5. Create the 2nd Guide Curve:

- Using the Right plane sketch a 3-Point-Arc and add dimensions.

Should the Pierce relation or the .700" dimension be used here?

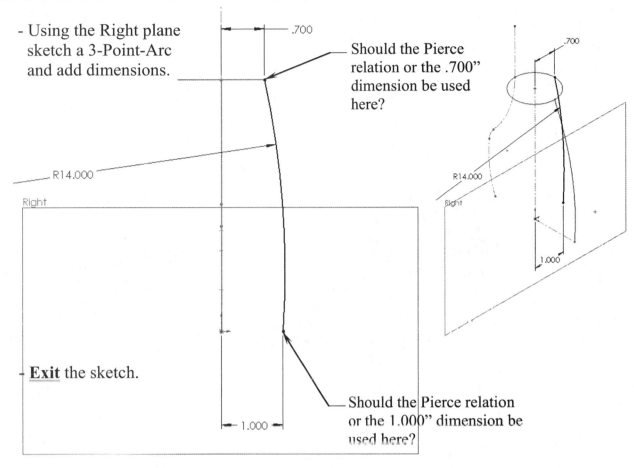

.700

R14.000

Right

- **Exit** the sketch.

1.000

Should the Pierce relation or the 1.000" dimension be used here?

6. Create the 3rd Guide Curve:

- Using the Right plane sketch a 3-Point-Arc and add dimensions.

.700

Should the Pierce relation or the .700" dimension be used here?

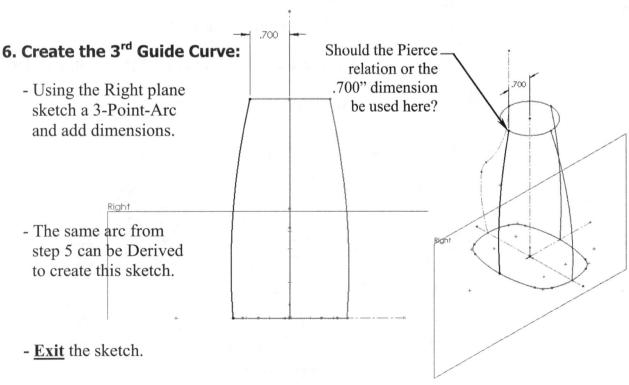

Right

- The same arc from step 5 can be Derived to create this sketch.

- **Exit** the sketch.

7. Create the 4th Guide Curve:

- Select the Front plane
  open a new sketch and
  convert the 3 entities
  as noted.

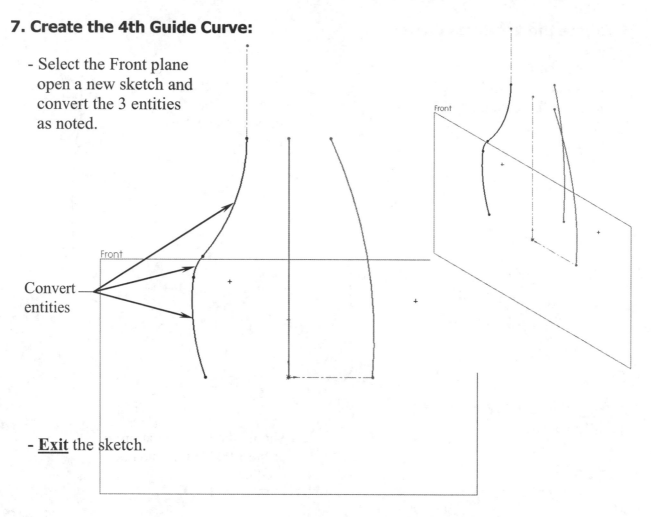

Convert
entities

- **Exit** the sketch.

8. Create the Lofted Surface:

- Use the Top and Bottom sketches as Loft Profiles.

- For Guide Curves, select the next 4 sketches.

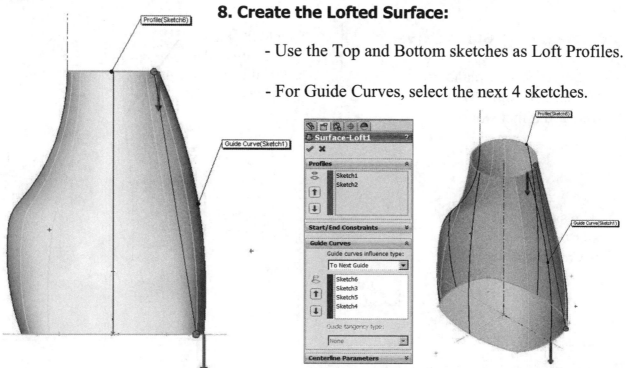

9. Fill the bottom surface:

- Select **Insert / Surface / Planar**.

- Select all of the bottom edges for this operation.

- When finished, the bottom surface should be completely covered.

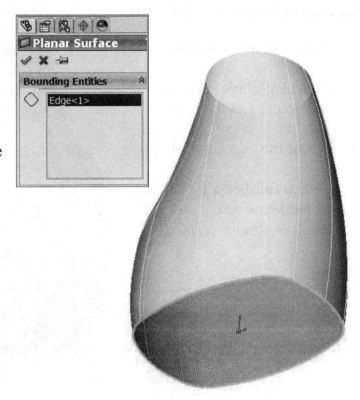

10. Sketch the Neck profile:

- Select the Front plane and sketch the profile below (2 lines).

- Revolve the sketch profile as a <u>SURFACE</u>.

- Revolve One Direction.

- Revolve a complete 360°.

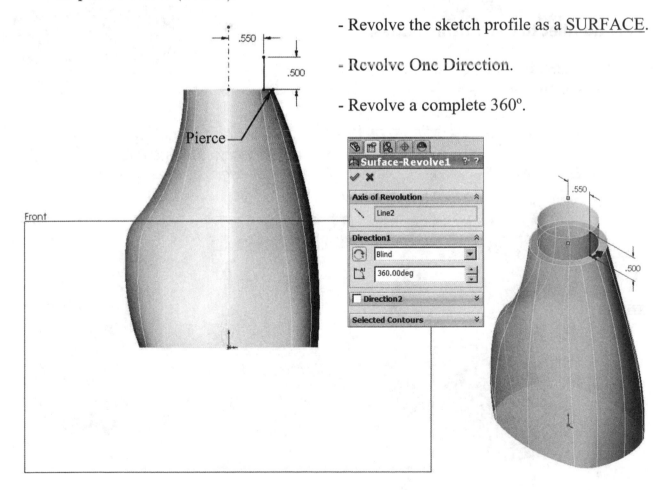

11. Knit all surfaces into one:

- Select **Insert / Surface / Knit**.

- Select all three surfaces: the body, the Neck, and the Bottom surface.

- Clear the Gap Control option.

- When finished all 3 surfaces should now be combined as one continuous surface.

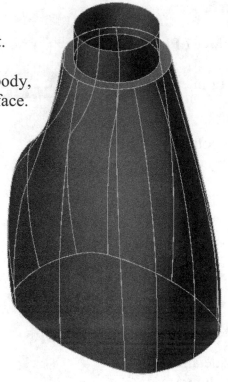

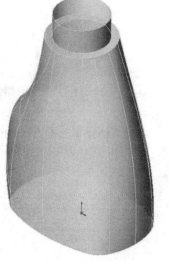

12. Add fillet to the bottom edges:

- Add a **.250 in**. fillet to the bottom edges as shown.

Tips:

- Right click on one of the edges and pick Select Tangency; this is the fastest way to select all edges at the same time.

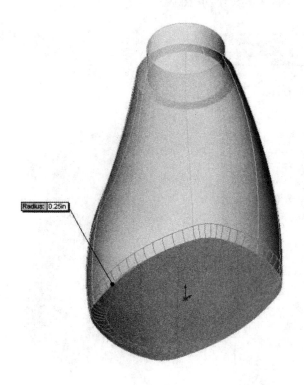

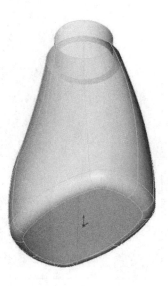

13. Add fillet to the upper part:

- Add a **.093 in**. fillet to the upper edge as indicated.

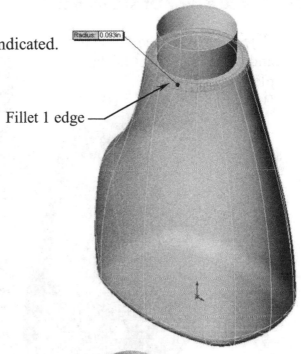

Fillet 1 edge

14. Thicken the surfaces:

- Select **Insert / Boss-Base / Thicken**.

- Enter a wall thickness of **.080 in**. to the **INSIDE** of the bottle.

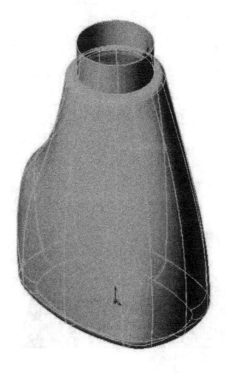

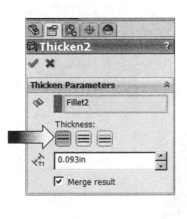

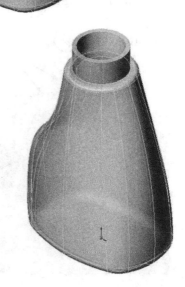

15. Create a new Offset plane:

- Select the Top face of the neck and create an Offset Distance plane at **.100 in**. <u>Below</u> it.

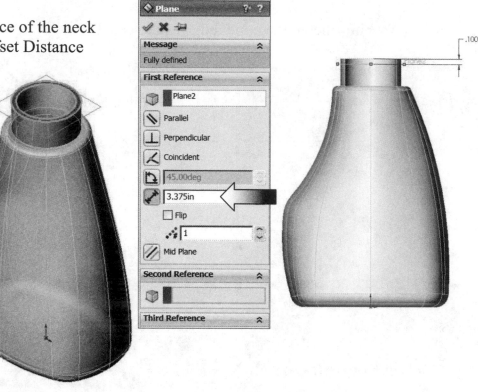

16. Create the Sweep Path of the Thread (the Helix):

- Convert the upper circular edge and click **Insert / Curves / Helix-Spiral**.

- Pitch = **.125 in**.

- Revolution = **2.5**.

- Starting Angle = **0 deg**.

- Click **OK** .

Convert Entity

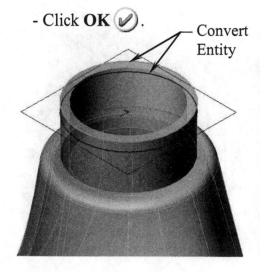

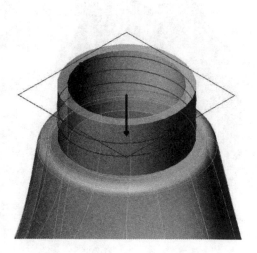

17. Create the Sweep Profile of the Thread:

- Select the Right plane and sketch the thread profile as shown.

- Add Dimensions and Relations needed to fully define the sketch.

- Add the **R.015"** fillets after the sketch is fully defined.

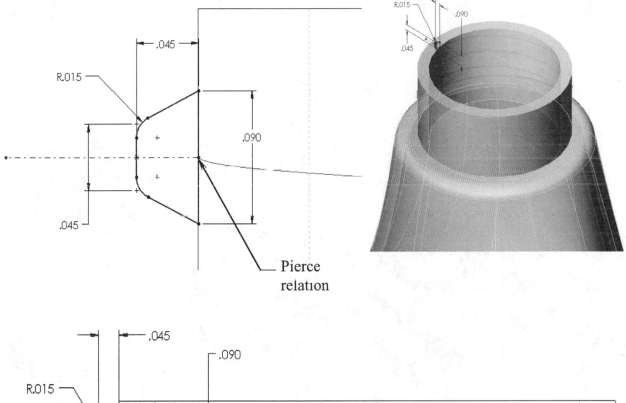

Pierce relation

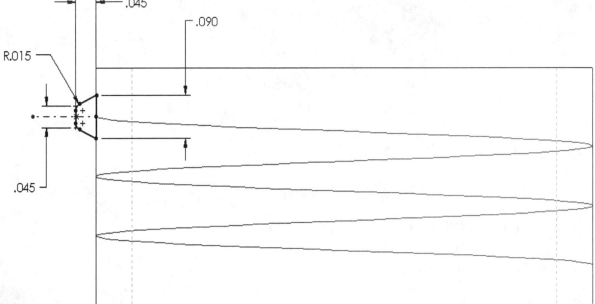

- **Exit** the sketch when finished.

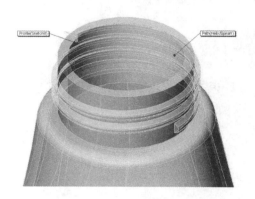

18. Sweep:

- Sweep the thread profile along the path to create the external threads.

19. Revolve:

- Convert the faces at the end of the thread and revolve them about the vertical centerlines to round off the ends.

20. Apply dimension changes:

- Change the dimension **R1.400** in the Sketch1 to **R1.500**.

- Change the **Ø1.400** in the Sketch2 to **Ø1.500**.

- Repair any errors caused by the changes.

21. Save your work:

- Save your work as: **Level 3 – Final Exam**.

Designed by a CSWP student

Designed by a CSWP student

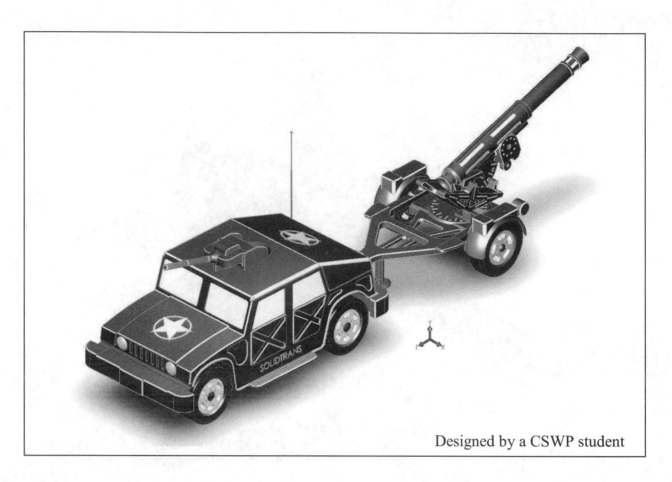

Designed by a CSWP student

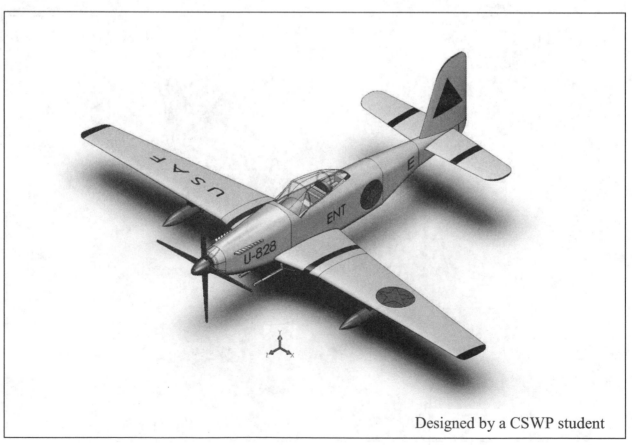

Designed by a CSWP student

CHAPTER 12

SimulationXpress

SimulationXpress is a design analysis technology that allows SolidWorks users to perform first-pass stress analysis. SimulationXpress can help you reduce cost and time-to-market by testing your 3D designs within the SolidWorks program, instead of expensive and time-consuming field tests.

There are five basic steps to complete the analysis using SimulationXpress:

1. Apply restraints (Fixture)
Users can define restraints. Each restraint can contain multiple faces. The restrained faces are constrained in all directions due to rigid body motion; you must at least restrain one face of the part to avoid analysis failure.

2. Apply loads
User inputs force and pressure loads to the faces of the model.

3. Define material of the part
* EX (Modulus of elasticity).
* NUXY (Poisson's ratio). If users do not define NUXY, SimulationXpress assumes a value of 0.
* SIGYLD (Yield Strength). Used only to calculate the factors of safety (FOS).
* DENS (Mass density). Used only to include mass properties of the part in the report file.

4. Analyze the part
SimulationXpress prepares the model for analysis, then calculates displacements, strains, and stresses.

5. View the results
After completing the analysis, users can view results. A check mark on the Results tab indicates that results exist and are available to view for the current geometry, material, restraints, and loads. A report can also be created in MS-Word format.

SimulationXpress
Using the Analysis Wizard

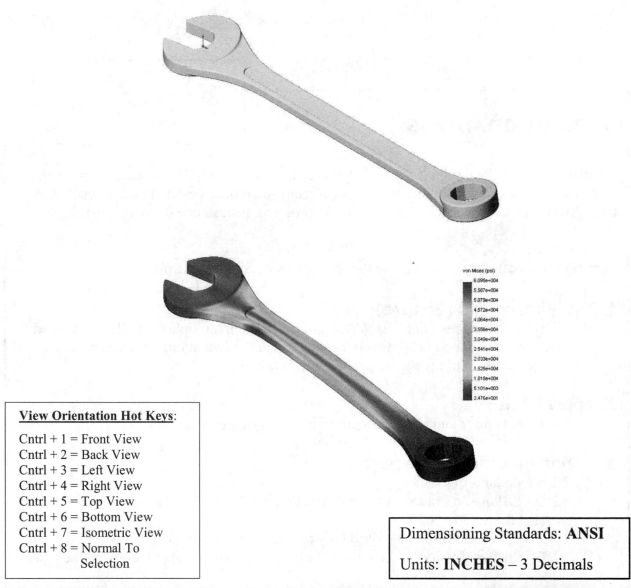

View Orientation Hot Keys:

Cntrl + 1 = Front View
Cntrl + 2 = Back View
Cntrl + 3 = Left View
Cntrl + 4 = Right View
Cntrl + 5 = Top View
Cntrl + 6 = Bottom View
Cntrl + 7 = Isometric View
Cntrl + 8 = Normal To
           Selection

Dimensioning Standards: **ANSI**

Units: **INCHES** – 3 Decimals

Tools Needed:

SimulationXpress is part of
SolidWorks 2013 Basic,
SolidWorks Office Professional,
and SolidWorks Premium.

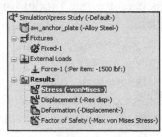

1. Starting SimulationXpress:

- Open the part document that was created earlier: **Spanner**. (or open a copy from the Training CD).

- **Suppress** the extruded text (the 5/8" and the Spanner text).

- From the **Tools** drop down menu, select **SimulationXpress** (Arrow).

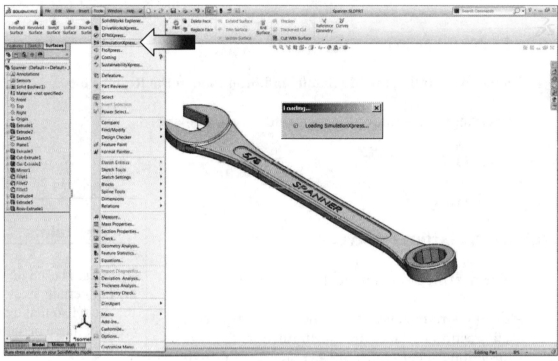

2. Setting up the Units:

- Click **Options** (arrow), to set the system of units for the analysis.

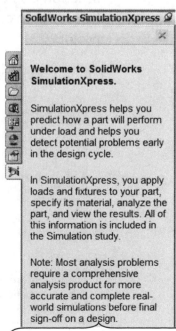

SolidWorks SimulationXpress

Welcome to SolidWorks SimulationXpress.

SimulationXpress helps you predict how a part will perform under load and helps you detect potential problems early in the design cycle.

In SimulationXpress, you apply loads and fixtures to your part, specify its material, analyze the part, and view the results. All of this information is included in the Simulation study.

Note: Most analysis problems require a comprehensive analysis product for more accurate and complete real-world simulations before final sign-off on a design.

- Select **English (IPS)** for System Of Units (Inch, Pound, Second).

- Select the folder and the location to save the analysis results.

SimulationXpress Options

System of units: English (IPS)

Results location: C:\Simulation\Temp   ...

☑ Show annotation for maximum and minimum in the result plo

OK   Cancel

- Enable the option:

Show Annotation for Maximum and Minimum in the Result Plot.

- Creating a new folder for each study is recommended.

- Click **OK**  .

- Click **Next** →.

3. Adding a Fixture (restraint):

- The next step is to create the restraint area(s).

- Each restraint can contain one or multiple faces. The restrained faces are constrained in all directions. There must at least one fixed face of the part to avoid analysis failure due to rigid body motion.

- Click **Add a Fixture** →.

☀ **Restraints**

Restraint is used to anchor certain areas of the model so that they will not move or shift during the analysis. At least one face should be restrained prior to running the analysis.

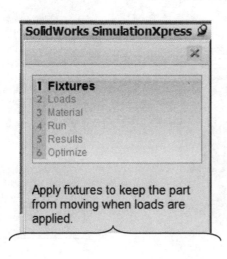

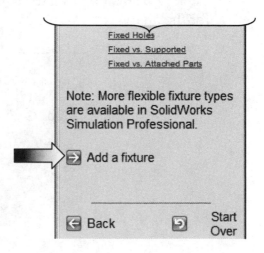

- Select the 3 faces as indicated to use as restraint faces.

- The Restraint faces are locked in all directions to avoid failure due to rigid body motion.

Restraint face 1…

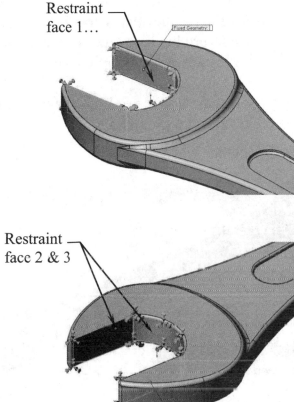

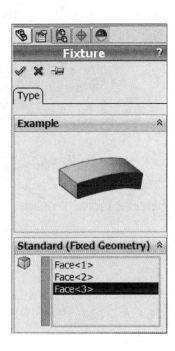

Restraint face 2 & 3

- Click **OK** .

- When the restraint faces are selected, more faces can be added to create different restraint sets. They can also be edited or deleted at anytime.

- The information regarding the settings for this study is recorded on the lower half of the Feature-Manager tree (arrows).

- These settings can be modified at anytime.

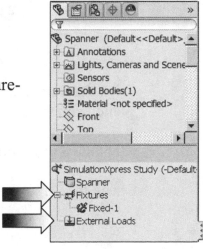

4. Applying a Force:

- Click **Add a Force** 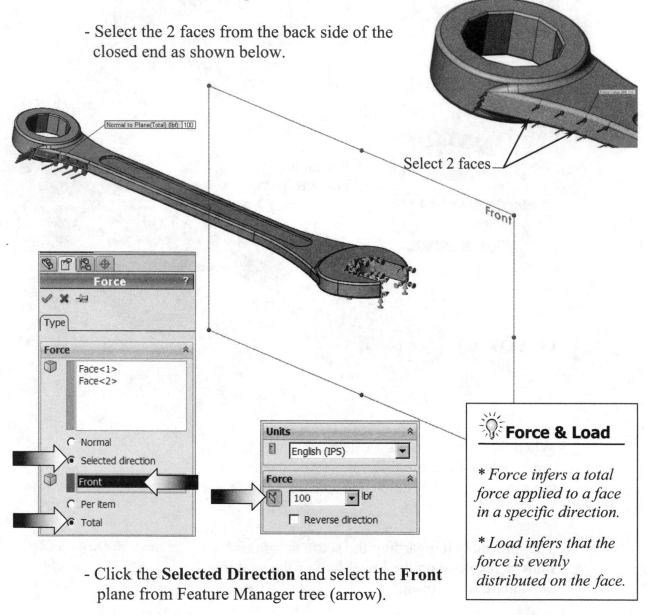.

- The **Forces** and **Pressures** options allow SolidWorks users to apply force or pressure loads to faces of the model. Multiple forces can be applied to a single face or to multiple faces.

- Select the 2 faces from the back side of the closed end as shown below.

Select 2 faces

Front

Normal to Plane(Total) (lbf): 100

Force

Face<1>
Face<2>

○ Normal
● Selected direction
Front
○ Per item
● Total

Units
English (IPS)

Force
100 lbf
☐ Reverse direction

💡 **Force & Load**

* Force infers a total force applied to a face in a specific direction.

* Load infers that the force is evenly distributed on the face.

- Click the **Selected Direction** and select the **Front** plane from Feature Manager tree (arrow).

- Click the **Total** option (arrow). Enter **100** lbs. for Total Force value (arrow).

- Check the direction arrows and click Reverse Direction if necessary.

- Click **OK** .

- At this point we will need to specify a material so that SimulationXpress can predict how it will respond to the loads.

5. Selecting the material:

- Click **Next** →.

- Select **Choose Material** →.

- Expand the **Steel** option (click the + symbol).

- Choose **Alloy Steel** from the list (arrow).

Material Editor

Material can be assigned to the part using the **Material Editor** PropertyManager. The material will then appear in Simulation- Xpress.

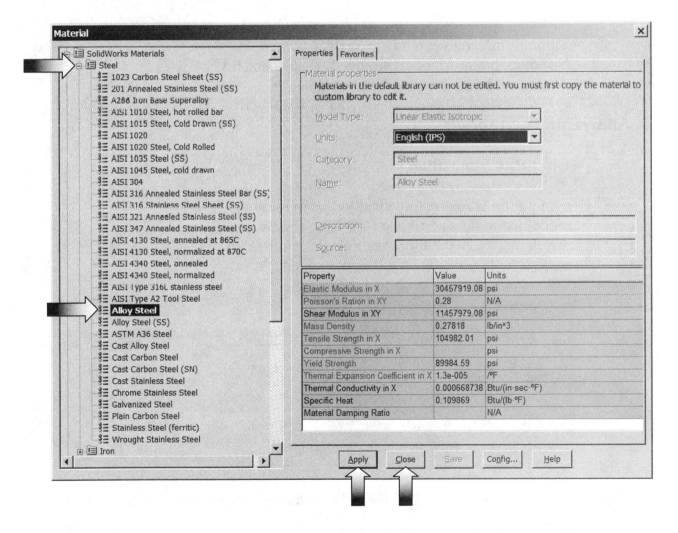

- The analysis results are dependent on the material selection. Simulation-Xpress needs to know the Visual and the Physical properties to run the analysis.

- Click **Apply** and **Close**.

- The material **Alloy Steel** is now assigned to the part. SimulationXpress assumes that the material deforms in a linear fashion with increased load. Non-Linear materials (such as many plastics) require the use of Simulation Premium.

- The Modulus of Elasticity and the Yield Strength for the selected material are reported on the right.

- Click **Next** .

- SimulationXpress is ready to analyze the model based on the information provided. Displacements, Strains, and Stresses will then be calculated.

6. Analyzing the model:

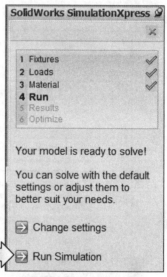

- Click **Run Simulation** .

- SimulationXpress automatically tries to mesh the model using the default element size. The smaller the element size the more accurate the results, but more time is needed to analyze the model.

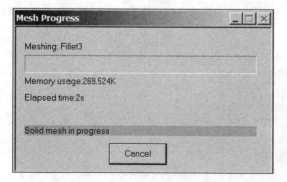

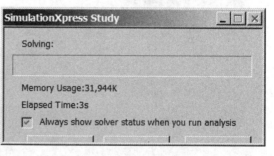

- To change mesh settings: First click **Change settings** then click **Change mesh density**.

   * Drag the slider to the right for a finer mesh (more accurate, but takes longer).

   * Drag the slider to the left for a coarser mesh (quicker).

- Select **Yes, continue** →.

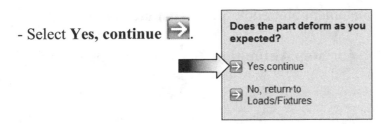

Does the part deform as you expected?

→ Yes, continue

→ No, return to Loads/Fixtures

7. Viewing the Results:

- Click **Show Von Mises Stress** →.

- SimulationXpress plots stresses on the deformed shape of the part.

- In most cases, the actual deformation is so small that the deformed shape almost coincides with the un-deformed shape, if plotted to scale.

  SimulationXpress exaggerates the deformation to demonstrate it more clearly.

- The Deformation Scale shown on the stress and deformed shape plots is the scale used to rescale the maximum deformation to **4.34794%** of the bounding box of the part.

  The **Stress Distribution Plot** is displayed below.

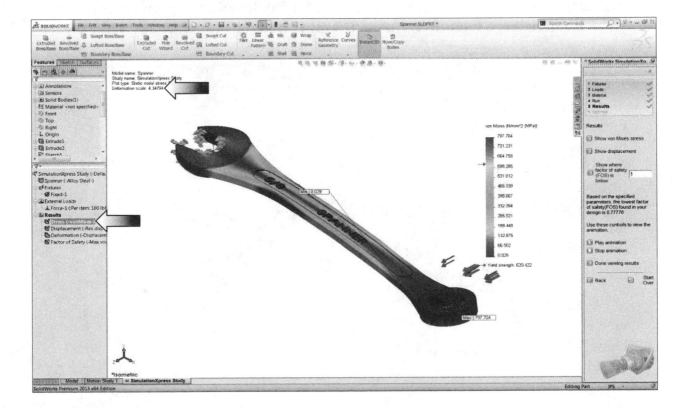

- To see the resultant displacement plot click **Show Displacement** →.

- Click **Play Animation** ▶ or **Stop Animation** ☐ when finished viewing.

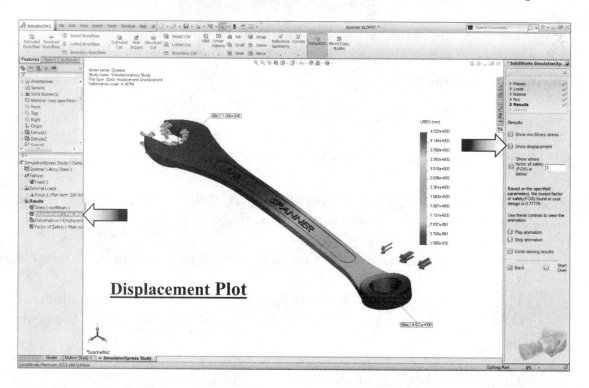

Displacement Plot

- To view regions of the model with a factor of safety less than a given value (1), click: **Show Where Factor Of Safety (FOS) Is Below: 1** (or enter any value).

- SimulationXpress displays regions of the model with factors of safety less than the specified value in red (unsafe regions) and regions with higher factors of safety in blue (safe regions).

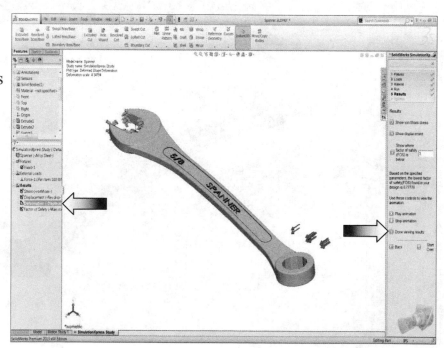

- When finished viewing click: **Done Viewing Results**.

8. Creating the report:

- Click **Generate Report** 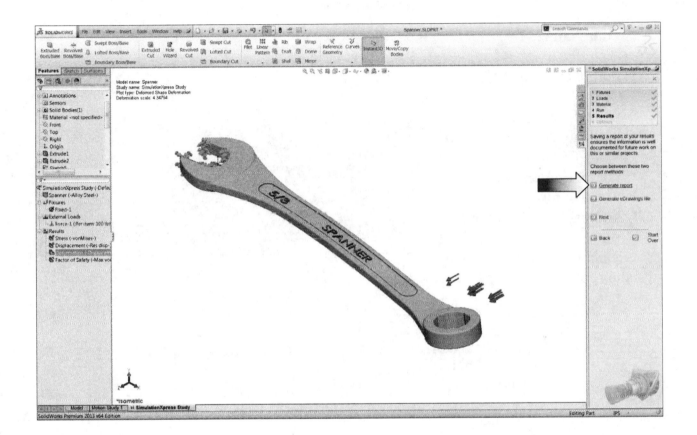 .

- SimulationXpress cycles through the results, generates a report in Word format, and the MS Word program is launched to display the full report.

- The report includes:

1. Cover Page	2. Model Information
3. Load/Fixture Details	4. Solid Mesh Information
5. Stress Results	6. Displacement Results
7. Deformation Results	8. Factor of Safety Results

- In the Report Settings dialog box, enable the Description checkbox and enter the following:

* Spanner - SimXpress Study.

* Your Name.

* Your Company Name.

* Your Web Address (if applicable).

* Your Company Logo.

* Address and Telephone.

- Select the location to save the report.

- Click **Generate**.

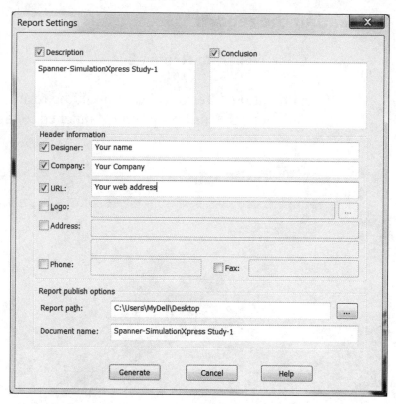

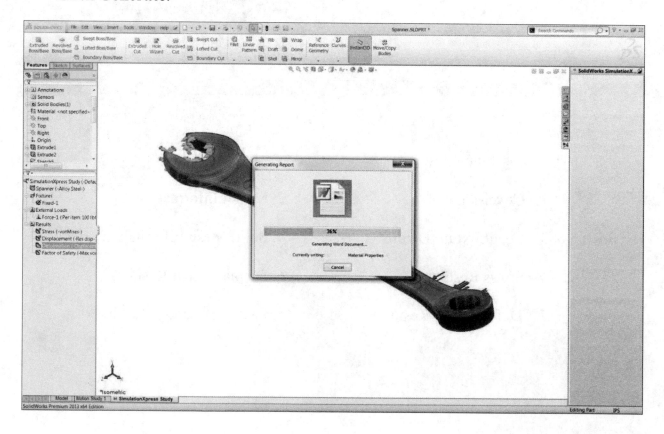

The Report Cover Page

The Model Information

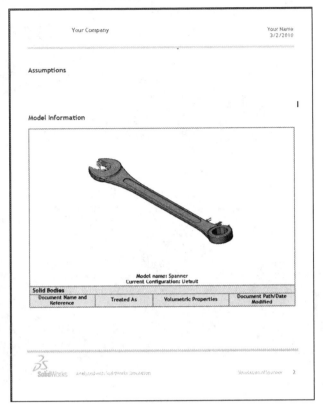

The Model Information cont.

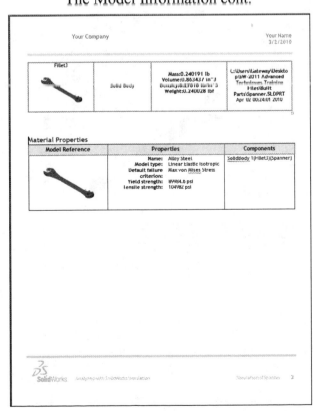

The Loads and Fixtures Details

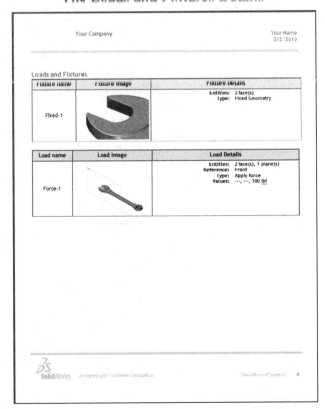

The Mesh Information

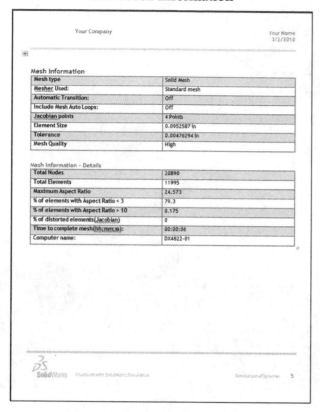

The Solid Mesh Plot

The Von Mises Stress Plot

The Displacement Plot

The Deformation Plot   The Factor of Safety Plot

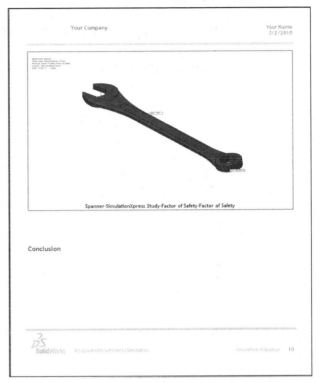

Name	Type	Min	Max
Factor of Safety	Max von Mises Stress	1.56758 Node: 1138	84263.8 Node: 19912

Conclusion

- When finished with viewing the Report, click: **Generate eDrawings File** →.

- The eDrawings program is launched automatically.

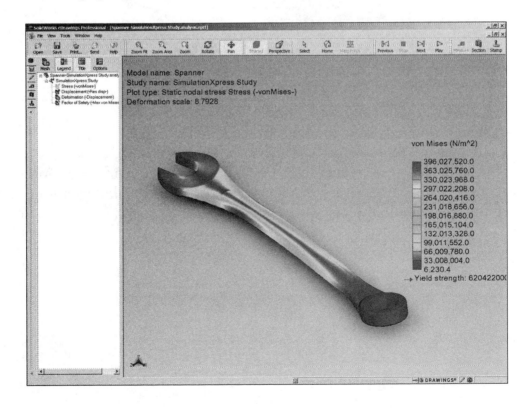

9. Generating the eDrawings file:

- An eDrawings file can be created for the SimulationXpress result plots .

- The eDrawings file allows you to view, animate and print your analysis results.

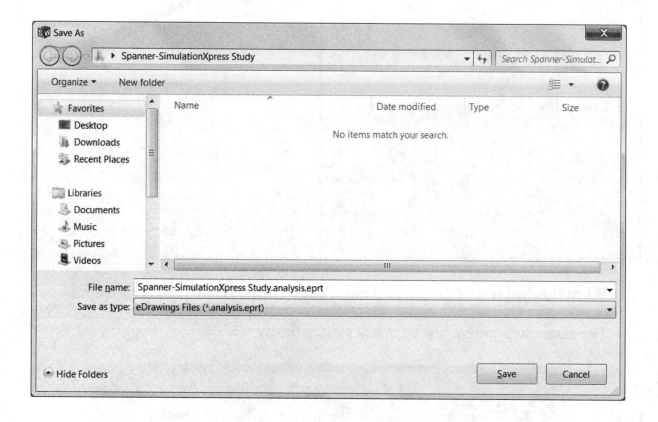

- When prompted, **Save** the analysis study in the default folder.

- SimulationXpress creates an eDrawing file with the **.eprt** extension. The file contains von Mises stress, displacement, deformation, and Factor of Safety plots. By default, the von Mises stress plot is displayed.

- Click the Play button 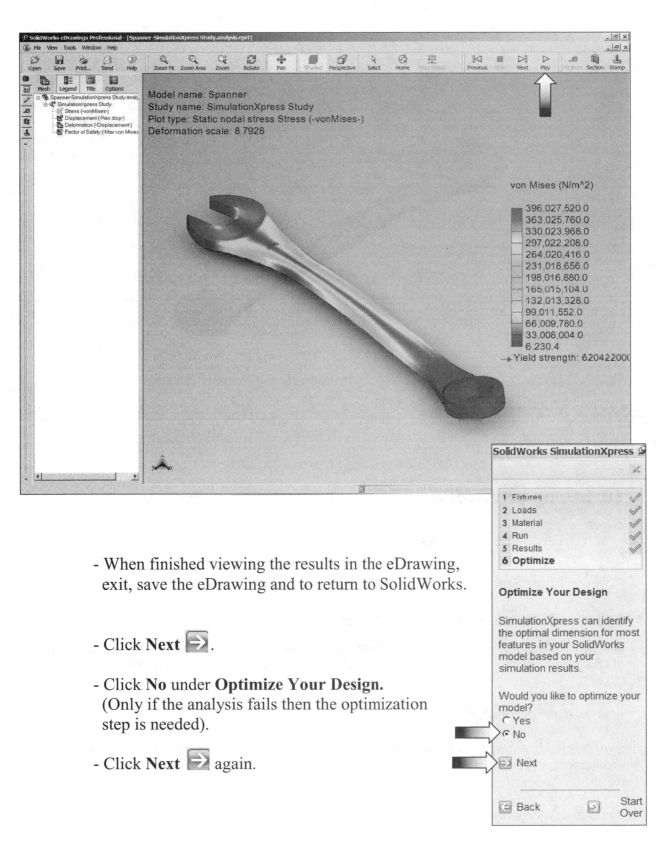 to see the animated results.

- When finished viewing the results in the eDrawing, exit, save the eDrawing and to return to SolidWorks.

- Click **Next** .

- Click **No** under **Optimize Your Design.**
  (Only if the analysis fails then the optimization step is needed).

- Click **Next** again.

- At this point, you are prompted that the analysis has been completed.

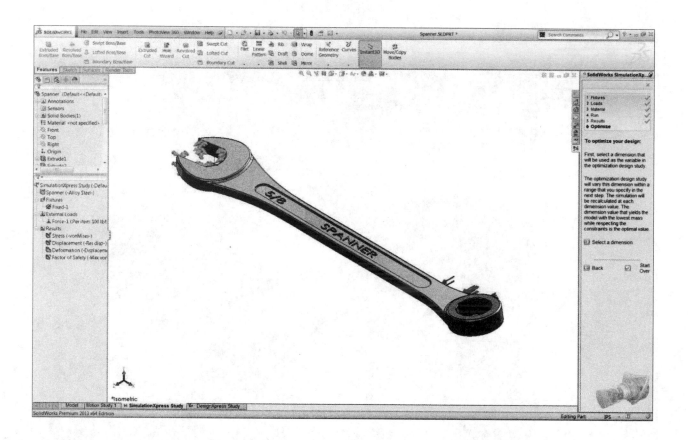

10. Saving your work:

- Click **File / Save As**.

- Enter **Spanner Study** for file name and click **Save**.

Isotropic, Orthotropic & Anisotropic Materials:

Isotropic Material: If its mechanical properties are the same in all directions. The elastic properties of an Isotropic material are defined by the Modulus of Elasticity (EX) and Poisson's Ratio (NUXY).

Orthotropic Material: If its mechanical properties are unique and independent in the directions of three mutually perpendicular axes.

Anisotropic Material: If its mechanical properties are different in different directions. In general, the Mechanical properties of the anisotropic materials are not symmetrical with respect to any plane or axis.

SimulationXpress supports Isotropic materials only.

Questions for Review

SimulationXpress

1. SimulationXpress can be accessed from the Tools pull down menu.
    a. True
    b. False

2. System Of Units SI (Joules) is the only type that is supported in SimulationXpress.
    a. True
    b. False

3. The material of the part can be selected from the built-in library or input directly by the user.
    a. True
    b. False

4. SimulationXpress supports Isotropic, Orthotropic, and Anisotropic materials.
    a. True
    b. False

5. Restraints/Fixture are used to anchor certain areas of the part so that it will not move during the analysis.
    a. True
    b. False

6. Only one surface/face should be use for restraint in each study.
    a. True
    b. False

7. The elements size (mesh) can be adjusted to a smaller value for more accurate results.
    a. True
    b. False

8. The types of results reported are:
    a. Stress Distribution
    b. Deformed Shape
    c. Deformation
    d. Factor of Safety
    e. All of the above

1. TRUE
2. FALSE
3. TRUE
4. FALSE
5. TRUE
6. FALSE
7. TRUE
8. E

Exercise 1: SimulationXpress_ Force

1. Open the existing part: **Extrude Boss & Extrude Cut.**

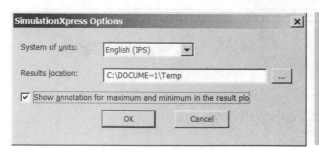

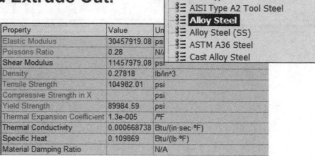

2. Set Unit to: **English (IPS).**

5. Select Material: **Alloy Steel.**

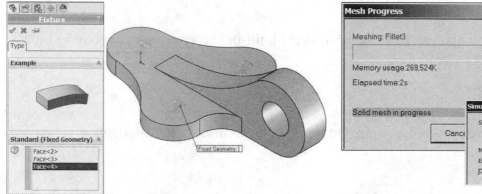

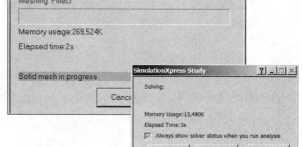

3. Apply Restraint: **to 3 Holes.**

6. Run the Analysis.

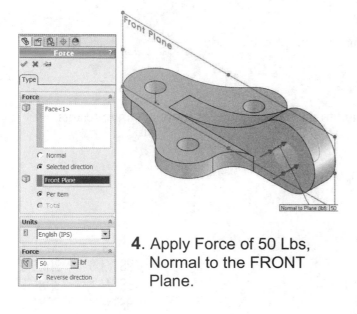

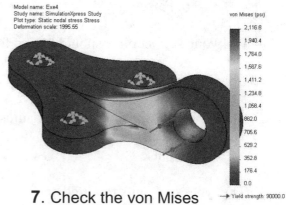

7. Check the von Mises Stress results.

4. Apply Force of 50 Lbs, Normal to the FRONT Plane.

8. Save a copy as: **Simulation_Force.**

<u>Exercise 2:</u> SimulationXpress / Pressure

1. Open the existing part: **Bottle_SimulationXpress**.

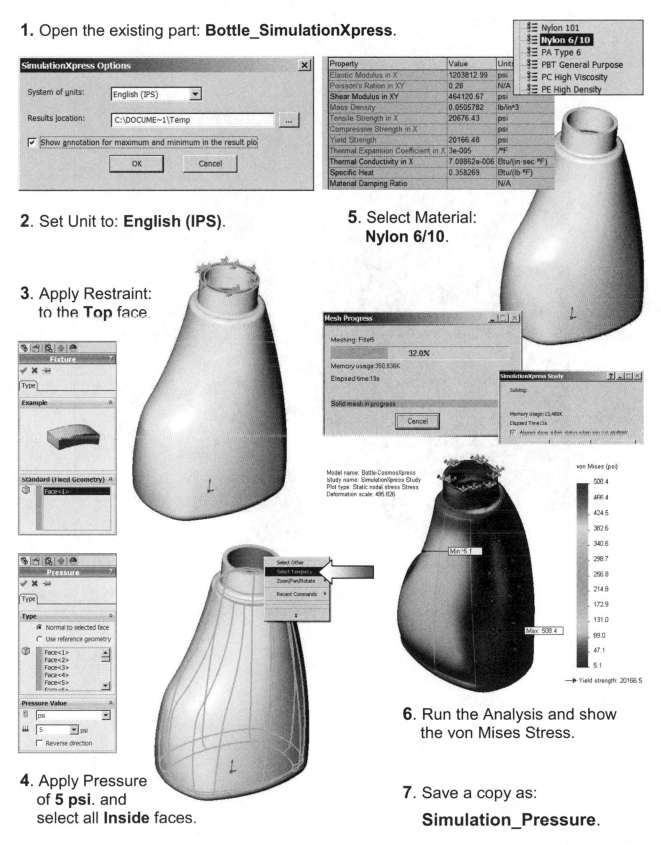

2. Set Unit to: **English (IPS)**.

5. Select Material:
 Nylon 6/10.

3. Apply Restraint:
to the **Top** face.

4. Apply Pressure
of **5 psi**. and
select all **Inside** faces.

6. Run the Analysis and show
the von Mises Stress.

7. Save a copy as:

 Simulation_Pressure.

Free SolidWorks SimulationXpress Online Tutorial:
http://www.solidworksmedia.com/SimulationXpress/index.html

CHAPTER 13

Sheet Metal Parts

Sheet Metal Parts

- This chapter discusses the introduction to designing sheet metal parts.

- Create a sheet metal part in the folded stage and add the sheet metal specific flange features such as:

  * Base Flange.
  * Edge Flanges.
  * Sketch Bends.
  * Cut with Link to Thickness.
  * Normal Cuts.

- There are at least 3 options for specifying the setback allowance, which is the difference in length when the sheet metal part is folded vs. flattened.

  * **Bend Table:** You can specify the bend allowance or bend deduction values for a sheet metal part in a bend table. The bend table also contains values for bend radius, bend angle, and part thickness.

  * **K-Factor:** Is a ratio that represents the location of the neutral sheet with respect to the thickness of the sheet metal part.
    Bend allowance using a K-Factor is calculated as follows:
    $$BA = \Pi(R + KT)\ A/180$$

  * **Use Bend Allowance:** Enter your own bend value base on your shop experience.

  * **Bend allowance Calculations:** The following equation is used to determine the total flat length when bend allowance values are used: $L_t = A + B + BA$

  * **Bend Deduction Calculations:** The following equation is used to determine the total flat length when bend deduction values are used: $L_t = A + B - BD$

Post Cap
Sheet Metal Parts

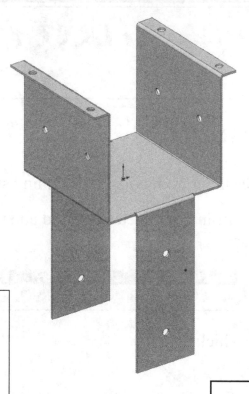

View Orientation Hot Keys:

Cntrl + 1 = Front View
Cntrl + 2 = Back View
Cntrl + 3 = Left View
Cntrl + 4 = Right View
Cntrl + 5 = Top View
Cntrl + 6 = Bottom View
Cntrl + 7 = Isometric View
Cntrl + 8 = Normal To
            Selection

Dimensioning Standards: **ANSI**

Units: **INCHES** – 3 Decimals

Tools Needed:

Insert Sketch	Line	⊕ Circle
Dimension	Add Geometric Relations	Base Flange
Edge Flange	Sketch Bend	Extruded Cut
Flat Pattern		

1. Starting with the base profile:

- Select <u>Right</u> plane from FeatureManager tree and insert a new sketch .

- Sketch the profile below using the Line tool  .

- Add dimensions  and relations needed, fully define the sketch.

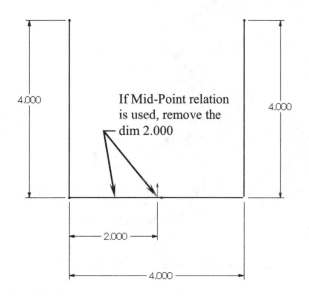

4.000

If Mid-Point relation
is used, remove the
dim 2.000

4.000

2.000

4.000

2. Extruding the Base Flange:

- Click or select **Insert / Sheet Metal / Base Flange**.

- Direction 1:   **Mid-Plane**.

- Extrude Depth: **4.00 in**.

- Use Gauge Table: **Sample Table - Steel**.

- Mat'l Thickness: **16 Gauge (.0598)** .

- Bend Radius: **.030 in**. (Override Radius) .

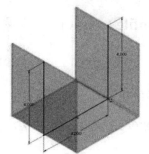

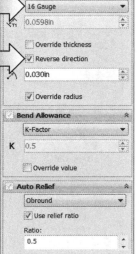

Set material
thickness to
Outside.

- Click **OK** .

3. Creating an Edge-Flange:

- Select the **model edge** as indicated.

- Click 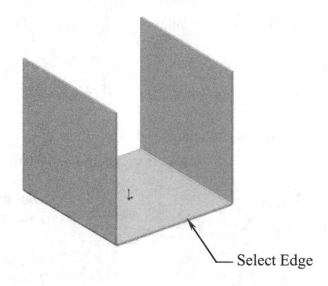 or select **Insert / Sheet Metal / Edge Flange**.

Select Edge

- Drag the cursor downwards and click to lock the preview of an Edge Flange.

- Select the 2nd edge as indicated.

- Select **Material Outside**  under the Flange Position.

- Enter **90°** for Angle (default).

- Flange Length: **Blind**.

- Enter **5.000"** for depth.

- Relief Type: **Rectangle**.

- Relief Ratio: **.500**.

- Click **Edit Flange Profile** (arrow).

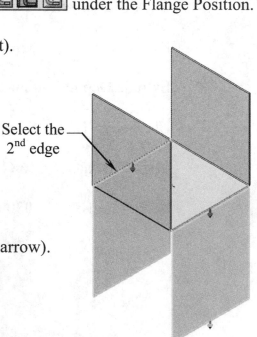

Select the 2nd edge

* The flange length will be modified in the next steps.

4. Editing the Edge Flange Profile:

- Move the Profile Sketch dialog to the upper corner.

- Drag the 2 outer lines inward as noted.

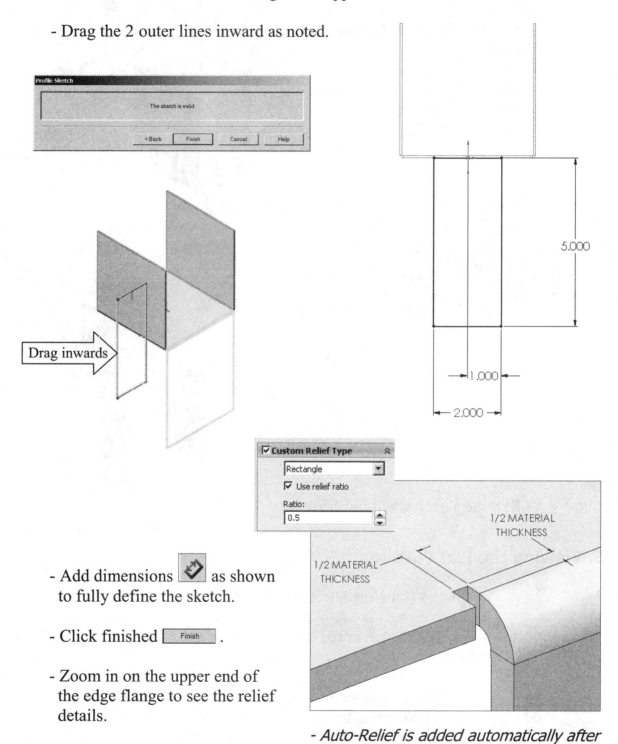

- Add dimensions as shown to fully define the sketch.

- Click finished   Finish   .

- Zoom in on the upper end of the edge flange to see the relief details.

- Beside the Rectangular relief, there are two other types available: Obround and Tear.

- *Auto-Relief is added automatically after exiting the Sketch.*
- *Relief Width and Depth are defaulted to one-half (0.5) the Material Thickness.*

- **Repeat**:

- Right click on the face of the
  2nd edge flange and select:
  Edit Sketch.

- Drag the 2 outer lines inward
  and add the dimensions to
  match the 1st flange.

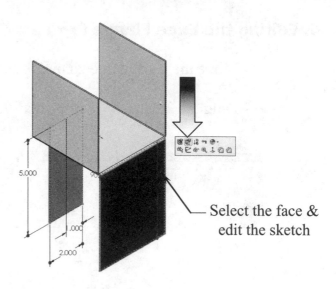

Select the face &
edit the sketch

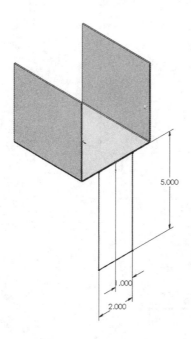

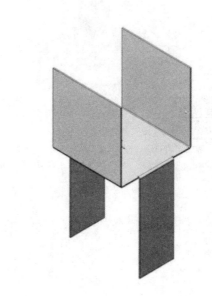

- **Exit** the sketch when finished.

5. Viewing the Flat Pattern:

- Click [icon] on the Sheet Metal toolbar:

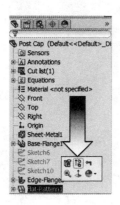

- The flat pattern of the
  Part is shown.

- Another way to view
  the flat pattern is to right
  click on the Flat-Pattern1
  feature and select
  Suppress (arrow).

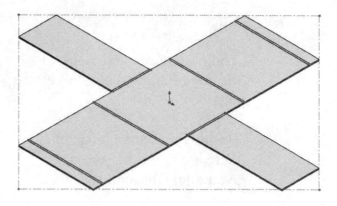

6. Changing the Fixed face:

- Edit the **Flat-Pattern** feature and select the <u>face</u> as indicated to use as the Fixed face.

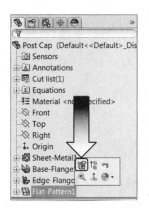

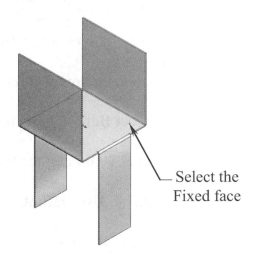

— Select the Fixed face

7. Creating a Sketch Bend:

- Select the side surface as indicated.

- Click 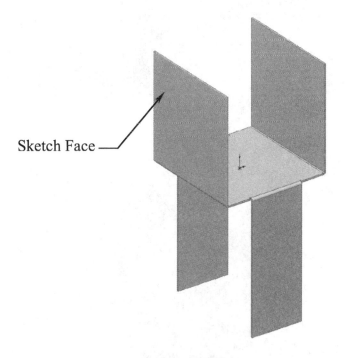 or select **Insert / Sketch**.

Sketch Face

> 💡 **Sketch Bends**
>
> This command adds Bends or Tabs to the Sheet metal part with the sketch lines.
>
> Only sketch lines are allowed, but more than one line can be used in a same sketch to create multiple bends.

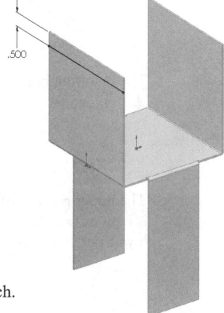

.500

- Sketch a line ╲ starting at one edge and Coincident with the other.

- Add dimensions ◇ to fully define the sketch.

- Click  or select **Insert / Sheet Metal / Sketch Bends**.

- Select the **lower portion** of the surface as Fixed Face .

- Select **Bend Centerline** (default) under Bend Position .

- Enter **90.00** deg for Bend Angle (default) `90.00deg` .

- Enable **Use Default Radius**.

- Click **OK** .

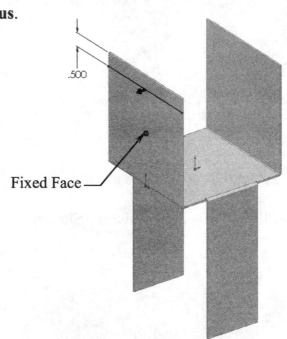

Fixed Face

- The resulting bend.

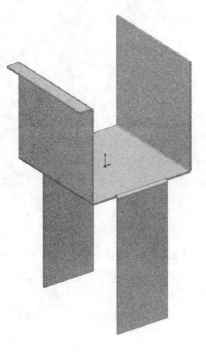

- The upper portion of the surface is bent outwards 90°, leaving the lower portion fixed.

8. Creating another Sketch Bend:

- Select the surface on the right and open a sketch ![icon] or select **Insert / Sketch**.

- Sketch a line ![icon] as shown and add dimensions ![icon] to fully define.

- Click ![icon] or select **Insert / Sheet Metal / Sketch Bend**.

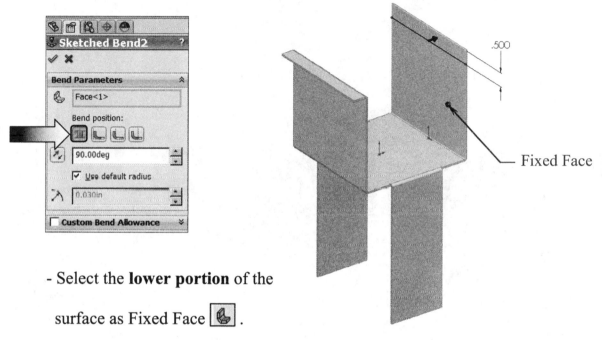

Fixed Face

.500

- Select the **lower portion** of the

  surface as Fixed Face ![icon] .

- Select **Bend Centerline** (default) ![icon] under Bend Position.

- Enter **90.00** deg for Bend Angle (default) ![icon] 90.00deg .

- Enable **Use Default Radius**.

- Click **OK** ![icon].

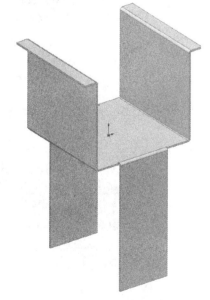

- The resulting bend.

- The upper portion of the surface is bent outwards
  90°, leaving the lower portion fixed.

9. Adding holes on the Edge Flange:

- Select the surface as shown and open a new sketch 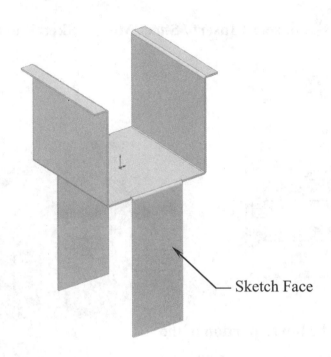 or select:
  Insert / Sketch.

Sketch Face

- Sketch two circles ⊕ on the face.

- Add dimensions ◇ as shown to
  position the circles.

- Add **Vertical** relations ⊥
  between the centers of the circles
  and the Origin, to fully define the
  sketch.

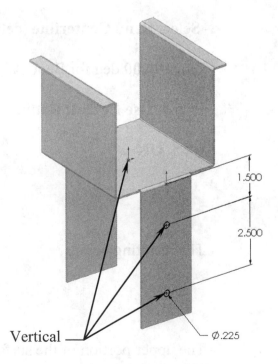

1.500

2.500

Ø.225

Vertical

- Click  or select **Insert / Cut / Extrude**.

- End Condition: **Through All**.

- Enable **Normal Cut** (default).

- Click **OK** ✔.

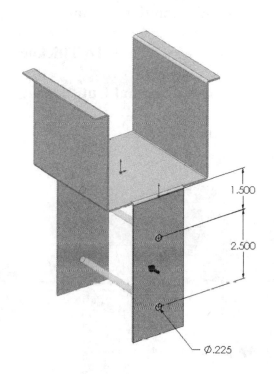

10. Adding holes on the Sketch Bend Flanges:

- Select the face as noted and open a new sketch ✏ or select **Insert / Sketch**.

- Sketch 4 circles ⊕ and add dimensions ✎ as shown.

- Add the relations ⊥ as needed to fully define the sketch.

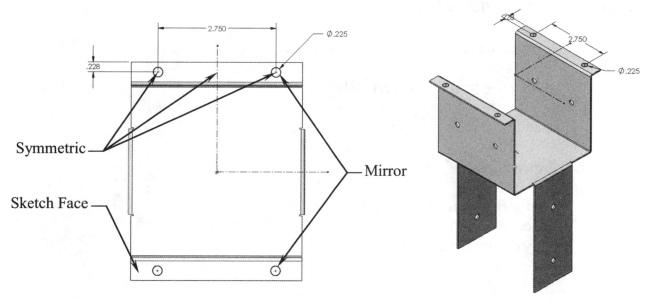

- Click 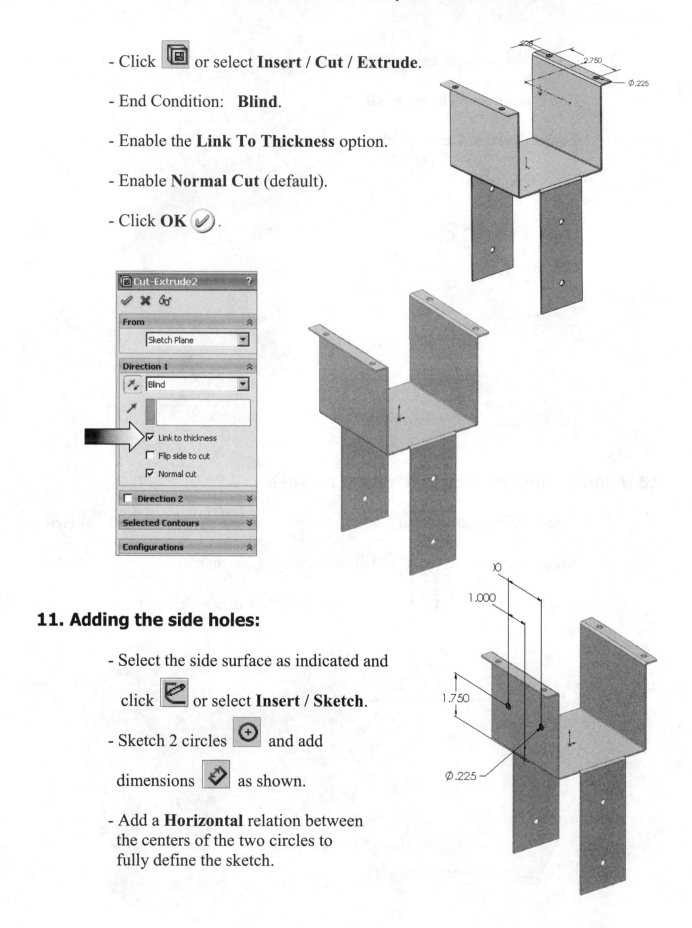 or select **Insert / Cut / Extrude**.

- End Condition: **Blind**.

- Enable the **Link To Thickness** option.

- Enable **Normal Cut** (default).

- Click **OK**.

11. Adding the side holes:

- Select the side surface as indicated and

  click or select **Insert / Sketch**.

- Sketch 2 circles and add

  dimensions as shown.

- Add a **Horizontal** relation between
  the centers of the two circles to
  fully define the sketch.

- Click  or select **Insert / Cut / Extrude**.

- End Condition: **Through All**.

- Enable **Normal Cut** (default).

- Click **OK** ✓.

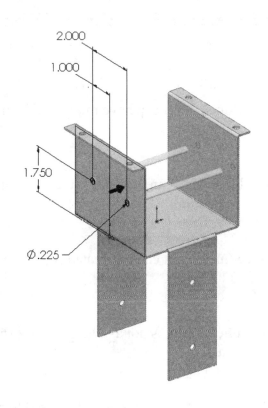

12. Making the Flat Pattern:

- Click **Flat Pattern** 🔲 on the Sheet Metal toolbar.

- The part is flattened with the bend lines shown (centerlines).

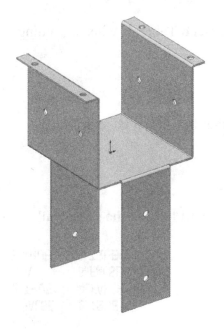

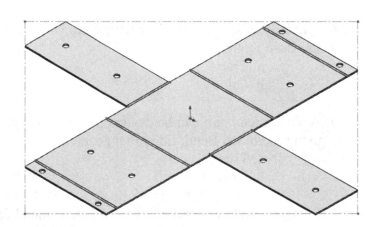

13. Saving your work:

- Select **File / Save As / Post Cap / Save**.

Questions for Review

Sheet Metal

1. A sheet metal part can have multiple thicknesses.
   a. True
   b. False

2. An Edge Flange can be mirrored just like any other feature.
   a. True
   b. False

3. A sheet metal part can be created right from the beginning using the Base flange option.
   a. True
   b. False

4. Auto relief option is not available when extruding a Base Flange.
   a. True
   b. False

5. When the Sketched Bend option is used to create a bend, you'll have to specify at least two parameters:
   a. A fixed side and a sketched line.
   b. Fixed side and a bend angle value.
   c. A bend radius and a bend angle value.

6. The only time when the K-Factor option can be changed to Bend Table, is when extruding the Base Flange.
   a. True
   b. False

7. A sheet metal part can be designed from a flat sheet and other bends can be added later using Sketched Bend, Edge Flange, etc..
   a. True
   b. False

8. Link-to-Thickness option allows all sheet metal features in a part to have the same wall thickness and they can all be changed at the same time.
   a. True
   b. False

1. FALSE   2. TRUE
3. TRUE   4. FALSE
5. A   6. FALSE
7. TRUE   8. TRUE

CHAPTER 13 cont.

Sheet Metal Parts

Sheet Metal Parts

Sheet metal parts can be created using one of the following methods:

- Create the part as a solid and then insert the sheet metal parameters such as rips, bend radius, material thickness, bend allowance, and cut relief so that the part can be flattened.

- Create the part as a sheet metal part from the beginning by using the Base Flange command to extrude the first feature.

- Sheet metal parameters can be applied onto the sheet metal part during the extrusion or after the fact.

This chapter will guide you through some techniques of creating a sheet metal part as well as the use of the sheet metal and forming tool commands to create some features in a sheet metal part and some other sheet metal features such as:

- Creating the parent feature with the Base Flange command.
- Using the Miter-flange command.
- Create a sheet metal part in the flat or folded stage.
- Create Revolved features.
- Accessing the Design Library.
- Using the forming tool to form the louvers.
- Create a Linear pattern of features.
- Create a Circular pattern of features.
- Create a pattern of patterned features.

Vents
Sheet Metal Parts

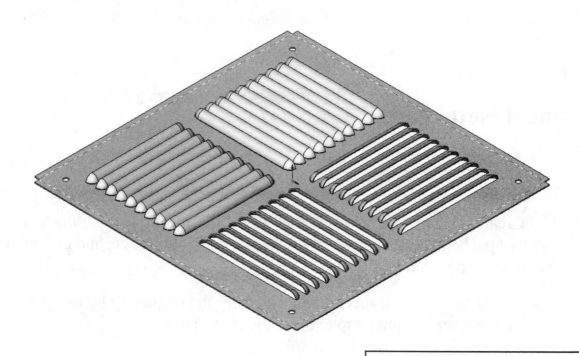

Dimensioning Standards: **ANSI**

Units: **INCHES** – 3 Decimals

Tools Needed:

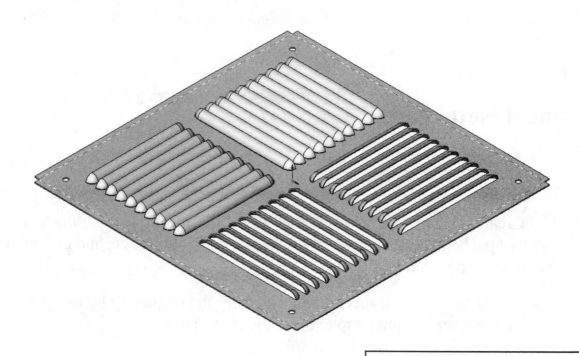 Insert Sketch	Line	Dimension
Rectangle	Add Geometric Relations	Linear Pattern
Base Flange	Miter Flange	Circular Pattern
Flat Pattern	Extruded Cut	Design Library

1. Sketching the first profile:

- Select <u>Front</u> plane from the FeatureManager tree.

- Click 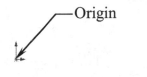 from Sketch toolbar OR select **Insert / Sketch**.

- Click ＼ and sketch a horizontal line **below the Origin**.

- Click ◇ and dimension the length of the line to **18.00 in**.

—Origin

18.000

2. Adding a Midpoint relation:

- Click └┴ from the Sketch toolbar OR select **Tools / Relations /Add**.

- Click on the Origin point and select the line as shown.

- Select **Midpoint** option from the Add Geometric Relation dialog box.

- Click **OK** ⊘.

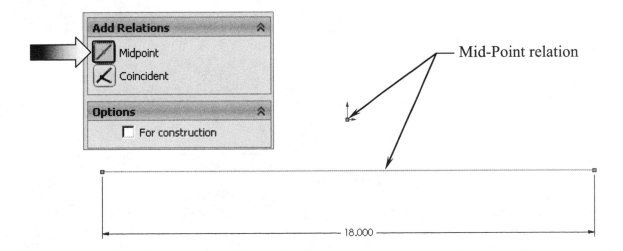

Mid-Point relation

18.000

3. Extruding the Base-Flange:

- Click 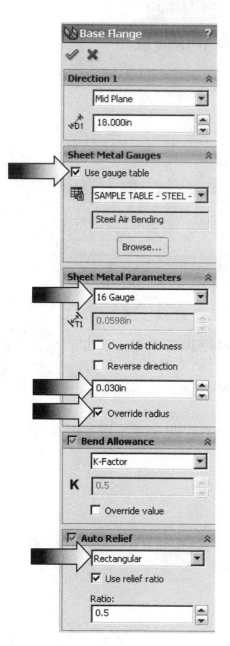 (Base Flange) from the Sheet Metal toolbar OR select:
Insert /Sheet Metal / Base Flange.

- Enter / select the following:

Direction 1:	**Mid-plane**.
Extrude Depth:	**18.00 in**.
Use Gauge table:	**Sample Table – Steel**.
Thickness:	**16 Gauge (.0598")**.
Bend Radius:	**.030 in**. (Override radius).
Bend Allowance:	**K-Factor / Ratio: 0.5**.
Auto Relief:	**Rectangular / Ratio: 0.5**.

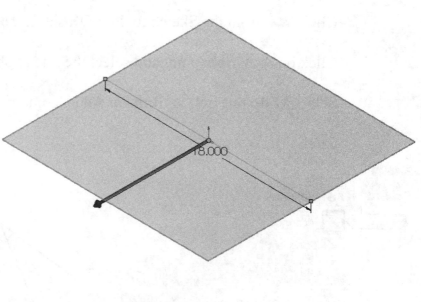

- Click **OK** ✓.

4. Creating the Miter-Flanges:

- Hold the control key, select the <u>Edge</u> and the vertex as indicated below, and click 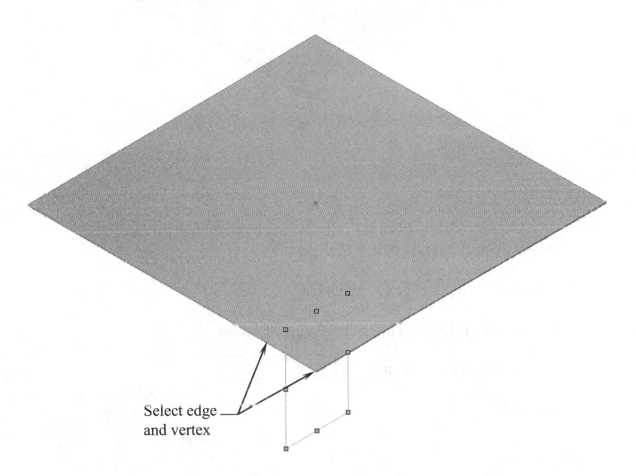 OR select: **Insert / Sketch**.

- SolidWorks automatically creates a new plane <u>normal</u> to the selected edge.

Select edge
and vertex

- Click **Zoom-to-Area** 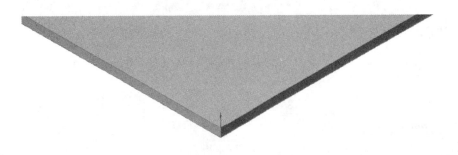 from the View toolbar and zoom in on the corner as shown below.

- Sketch a vertical line 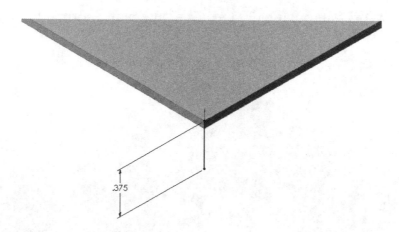 staring at the upper corner.

- Click (Dimension) and make the length of the line **.375 in**.

.375

- Click **(Miter-Flange)** from the Sheet Metal toolbar OR select:
Insert / Sheet Metal / Miter Flange.

- Select the **4** upper edges as indicated.

- Choose **Material Outside** under Flange Position.

- Set Gap Distance to **.010 in** `0.010in`.

- Click **OK**.

Select the top
4 edges

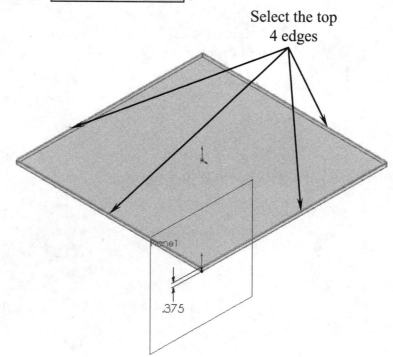

.375

5. Flattening the part:

- The Flat Pattern can be toggled at anytime during or after the part is created.

- Click ▦ (Flatten) from the Sheet Metal toolbar to flatten the part.

6. Switching back to the folded-model:

- Click ▦ (Flatten) again to return it back to the folded stage.

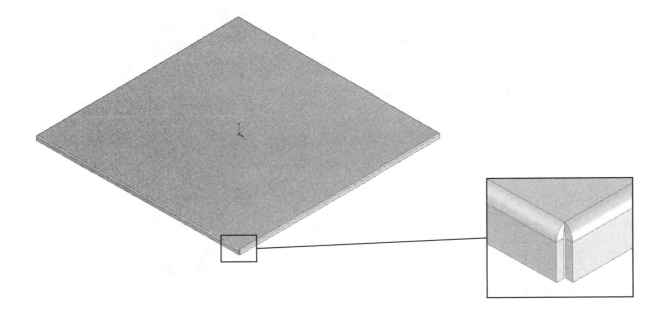

7. Saving your work: Select **File / Save As / Sheet Metal Vent / Save**.

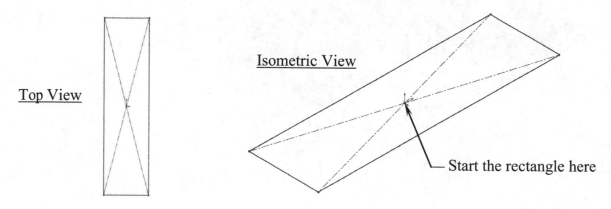

8. Creating a new Forming Tool – The Louver:

- Start a new Part file: click **File / New / Part / OK**.

- Set Units to Inches – 3 Decimal (Tools/Options/Document Properties/ Units).

9. Sketching on the TOP reference plane:

- Select the Top plane and click 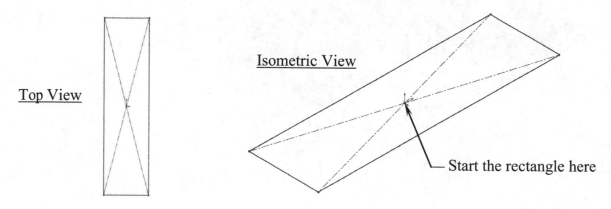 **Insert / Sketch** from the Sketch toolbar.

- Select the (Center Rectangle) from the Sketch-Tools toolbar.

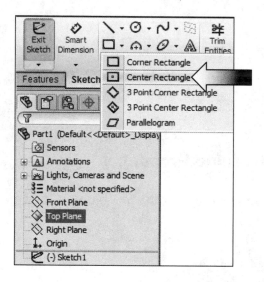

- Sketch a rectangle that starts from the Origin, as shown below.

Top View

Isometric View

Start the rectangle here

10. Other Rectangle options:

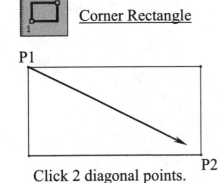 <u>Corner Rectangle</u>

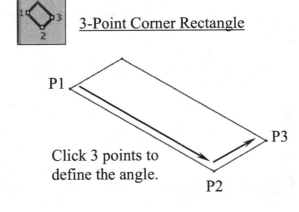 <u>3-Point Corner Rectangle</u>

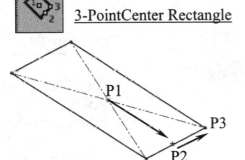

Click 2 diagonal points.

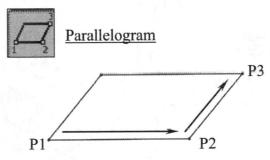

Click 3 points to
define the angle.

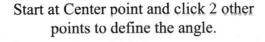 <u>3-PointCenter Rectangle</u>

<u>Parallelogram</u>

P3

P1 ——→ P2

Click 3 points to define the parallelogram.

Start at Center point and click 2 other
points to define the angle.

11. Adding dimensions:

- Click (Smart Dimension) and add the dimensions shown below.

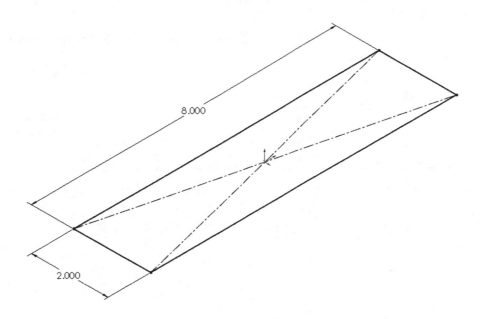

8.000

2.000

12. Extruding the Base:

- Click 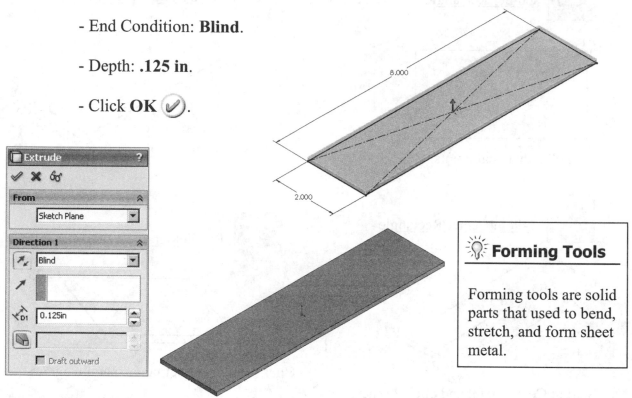 (**Extruded Boss/Base**) and fill in the following parameters:

- End Condition: **Blind**.

- Depth: **.125 in**.

- Click **OK** ✓.

> 💡 **Forming Tools**
>
> Forming tools are solid parts that used to bend, stretch, and form sheet metal.

13. Building the louver body:

- Select the <u>upper face</u> of the part and open a new sketch.

- Change to the Top View Orientation (Cntrl+5).

- Sketch the profile of the Louver-Forming tool and add Dimensions as illustrated below:

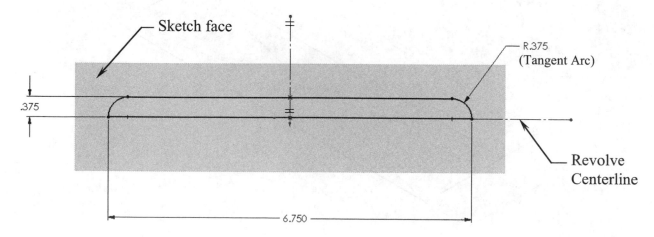

Sketch face

R.375 (Tangent Arc)

.375

Revolve Centerline

6.750

- Select the horizontal Centerline and click 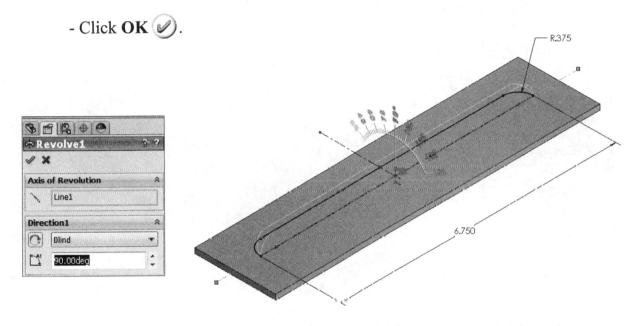 (**Revolve Boss/Base**).

- Use **Blind** for Revolve Type.

- For revolve Angle, enter **90°**.

- Toggle (Reverse) and make sure the preview looks like the one below.

- Click **OK**.

- The resulting of a 90° revolved.

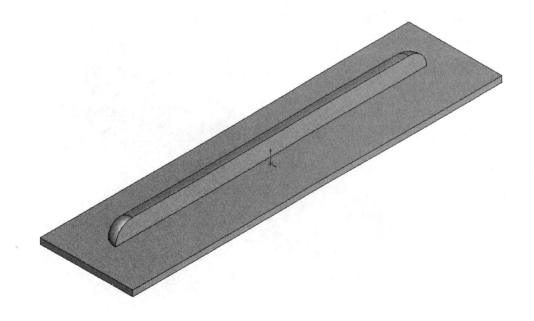

14. Adding a fillet at the base:

- Click Fillet 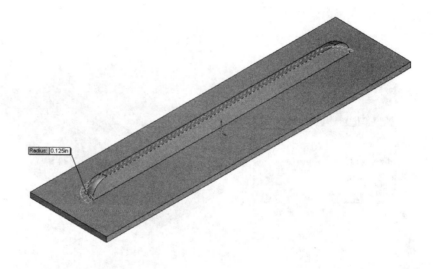 and enter **.125** in. under Radius [0.125in].

- Select the edge as indicated ▢.

- Select **Tangent Propagation** check box (default), the system applies the same fillet to all connected tangent edges [☑ Tangent propagation] .

- Click **OK** ✓.

- The revolved feature viewed from the backside.

- The resulting fillet also viewed from the backside.

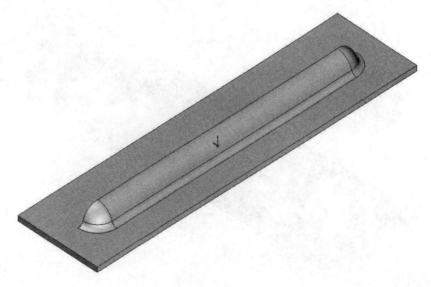

15. Removing the base:

- The Rectangular block was created to
  help creating the fillet between
  itself and the revolved feature.
  We no longer need it at
  this point.

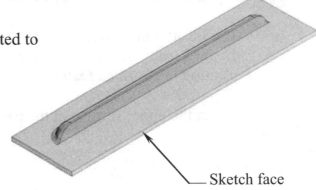

Sketch face

- Select the <u>side surface</u> of the part and
  open a new sketch.

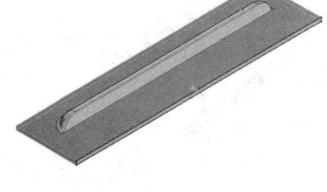

- While the side surface is still highlighting
  press the **Convert Entities** command.
  The selected face is converted to a
  rectangle.

- Switch to the **Features** tool tab
  and click the **Extruded Cut** command.

- Change the End Condition to **Through All**.

- Click **OK** .

- The base is removed and
  only the form portion
  is kept.

16. Creating the Positioning Sketch:

- The Positioning Sketch displays the preview of the Form tool while it is being dragged from the Design Library. Its sketched entities can be dimensioned to position the Formed feature.

- Select the upper surface of the part and click 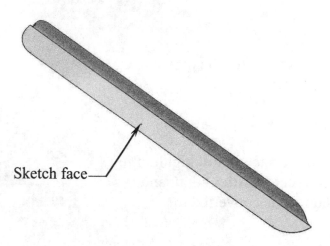 to insert a new sketch.

Sketch face—

- Select the bottom face of the part (or the outer edges of the louver) and click **Convert Entities**   .

- Add a Centerline ⋮ as shown to help position the tool when it is placed on a sheet metal part.

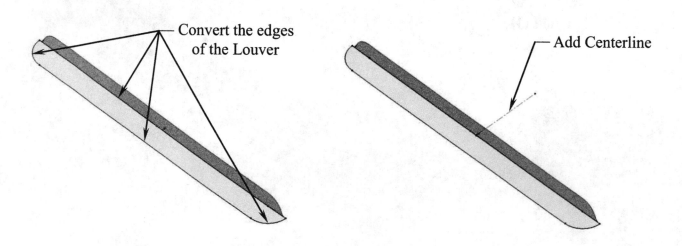

Convert the edges of the Louver

Add Centerline

- **Exit** the sketch or click 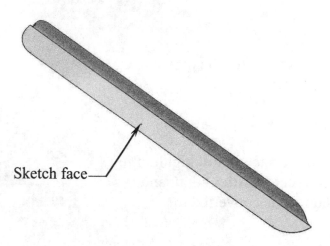 .

- Re-name the sketch to **Position Sketch** from the FeatureManager tree.

17. Establishing the Stop and Remove faces:

- In order for the forming tools to work properly, a set of Stopping Face and Removing Faces will have to be established prior to saving as a forming tool.

- Switch to the Sheet metal tool tab and click the **Forming Tool** command.

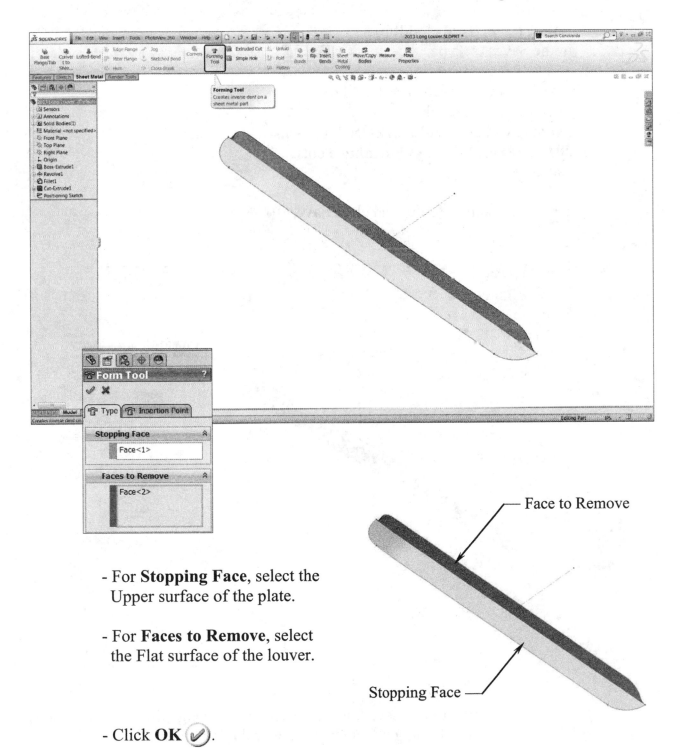

Face to Remove

Stopping Face

- For **Stopping Face**, select the Upper surface of the plate.

- For **Faces to Remove**, select the Flat surface of the louver.

- Click **OK** .

18. Saving the Forming Tool:

- Click: **File / Save As.**

- Enter **Long Louver** for the name of the file.

- Select **Form Tool** (*.sldftp) in the Save As Type.

- The following directories should be selected automatically:
Program Files\ SolidWorks\ SolidWorks 2013\ Design Library\ Forming Tools\ Louvers.

- Select the Louver folder and click **Save**.

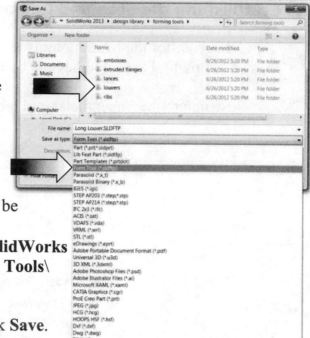

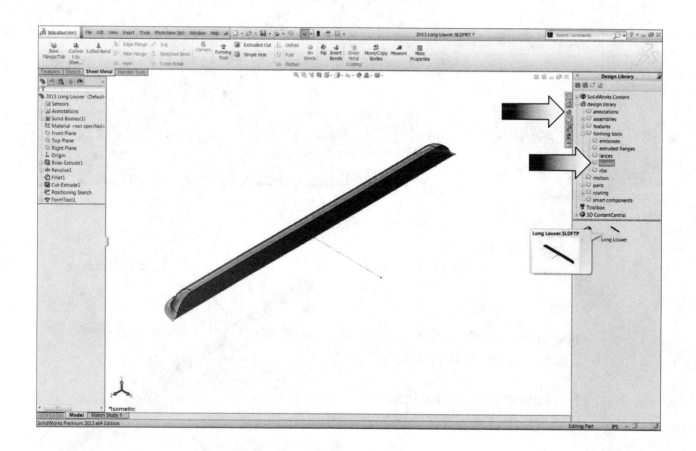

- After the forming tool is saved, it can be accessed through the Task pane, and by dragging and dropping it from the Design Library folder.

19. Opening the previous part:

- Open the Sheet Metal Vent that was saved earlier. (**Alt+Tab**)

- Click the push pin to lock the Task Pane in place (arrow).

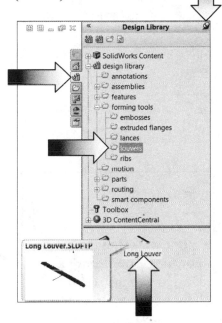

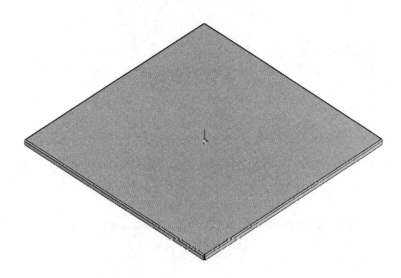

- Click the **Design Library** icon  .

- Expand the Forming Tool folder and double click on the Louvers folder to see its content.

- Hover the mouse cursor over the name Long Louver to see the preview of the Forming tool.

20. Applying the form tool:

- **Drag** the Long Louver form tool from the Design Library and **drop** it approximately as indicated.

Forming Tools

Forming tools should be inserted from the Design Library window and applied onto parts with sheet metal parameters such as material thickness, bend allowance, fixed face, cut relief, etc…

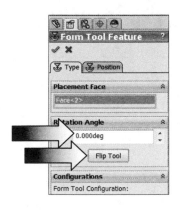

- Change the Angle to **180°** and click **Flip Tool**.

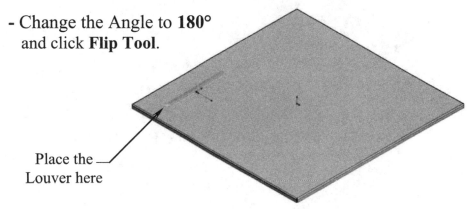

Place the Louver here

21. Positioning the form tool:

- Click the **Position** tab (arrow).

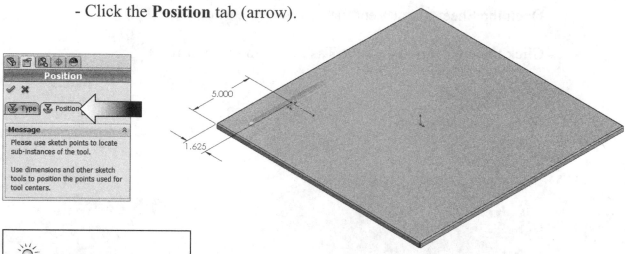

- Add the locating dimensions  as shown to fully define this sketch.

- Use the <u>outer edges</u> of the sheet metal part when adding the dimensions.

- Click **OK** ⊘.

Push / Pull

While dragging the Forming Tool from the Design Library, (still holding the mouse button) press the TAB key to reverse the direction from push to pull.

- The Louver is formed.

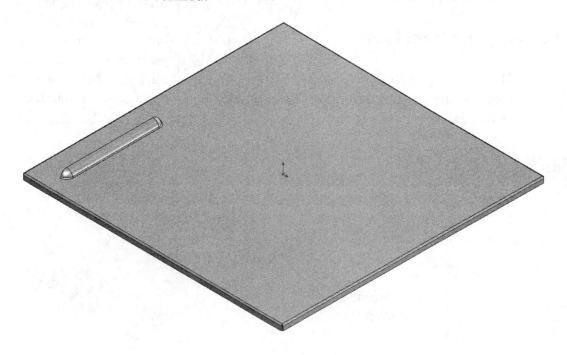

22. Adding a mounting hole:

- Select the <u>upper face</u> of the part as indicated.

- Click 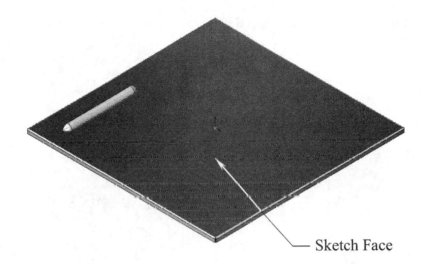 or select **Insert / Sketch**.

Sketch Face

Sketch a circle ⊕ on the left side of the louver.

- Add dimensions ✎ to define the circle.

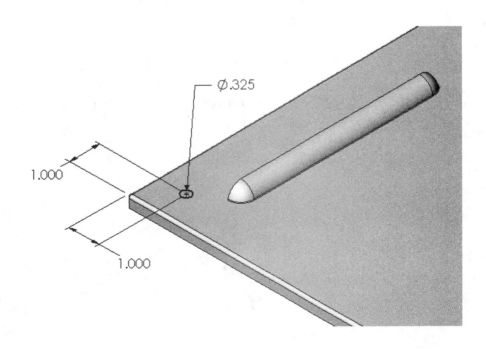

Ø.325

1.000

1.000

23. Extruding a cut:

- Click  or select **Insert / Cut / Extrude**.

- End Condition: **Blind**.

- Link to Thickness: **Enabled**.

- Normal Cut: **Enabled**.

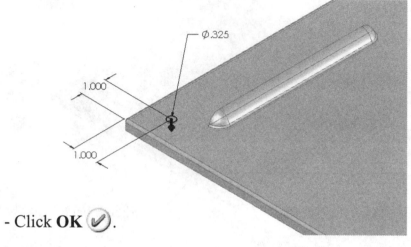

- Click **OK** ✓.

24. Creating a Linear Pattern:

- Click 📦 or select **Insert / Pattern Mirror / Linear Pattern**.

- Select the bottom edge as Pattern Direction 🔼.

- Enter **.703 in**. as Spacing.

- Enter **10** as Number of Instances.

- Select the Long Louver as Features to Pattern.

- Click **OK** ✓.

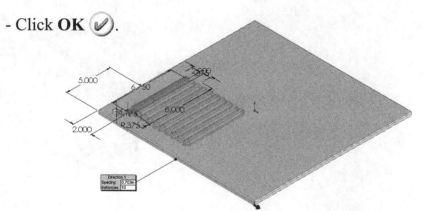

- The completed Linear Pattern.

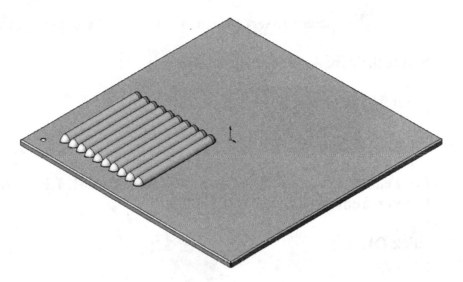

25. Creating an Axis:

- An axis can be created at anytime so features can be arrayed around it. In this case, an axis in the center of the part will be made and used as the center of the next Circular Pattern.

- Click [icon] or select **Insert / Reference Geometry / Axis**.

- Click **Two Planes** option [icon].

- Select **Front** and **Right** planes from FeatureManager tree.

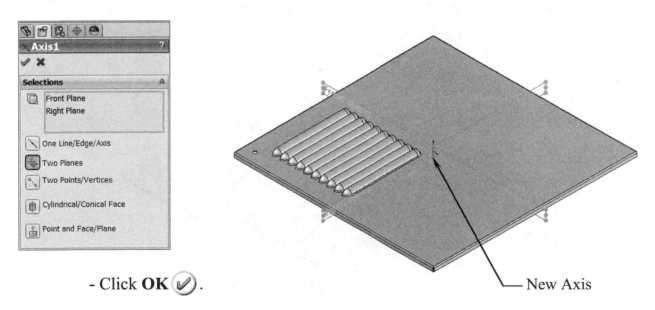

New Axis

- Click **OK** ✓.

26. Creating a Circular Pattern:

- Click ⬕ or select **Insert / Pattern Mirror / Circular Pattern**.

- Select the new Axis for Pattern Axis 🔄 .

- Enter **360 deg**. for Pattern Angle 🔲 .

- Enter **4** for Number of Instances ❖ .

- For Feature to Pattern 🗐 select the **Cut-Extrude1**, **LPattern1** and the **Long Louver** from the FeatureManager tree.

- Click **OK** ✅ .

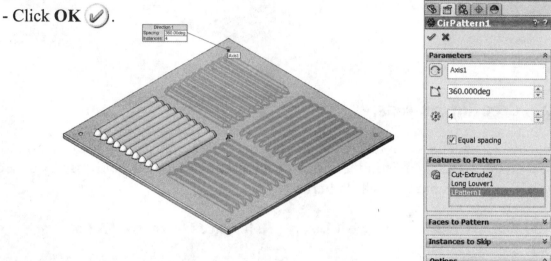

27. Saving your work:

- Either click on the Save icon 💾 to save and override the previous file – or – select **File / Save As / Sheet Metal Vent / Save**.

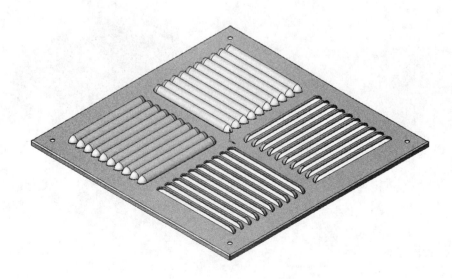

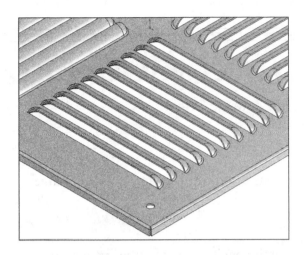
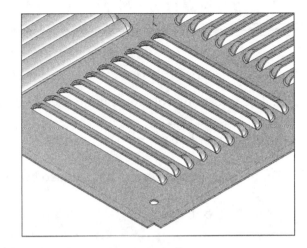

Finished Part (Folded)   **Flat Pattern***

* After the formed features are created they will remain their formed shapes even when toggled back and forth between Folded or Flattened.

Questions for Review

Sheet Metal Parts

1. The mid-point relation can be used to center a line onto the Origin.
    a. True
    b. False

2. The base flange command can also be selected from Insert / Sheet Metal / Base Flange.
    a. True
    b. False

3. When a linear model edge is selected and the sketch pencil is clicked, the system creates a NORMAL TO CURVE plane automatically.
    a. True
    b. False

4. The Miter Flange feature can create more than one flange in the same operation.
    a. True
    b. False

5. The Flat and the Folded patterns cannot be toggled until the part is completed and saved.
    a. True
    b. False

6. An existing forming tool cannot be edited or changed; forming tools are fixed by default.
    a. True
    b. False

7. When applying a form tool onto a sheet metal part, the push or pull direction can be toggled when pressing:
    a. Up arrow
    b. Tab
    c. Control

8. The Modify Sketch command can be used to rotate or translate the entire sketch.
    a. True
    b. False

9. A formed feature(s) cannot be copied or patterned.
    a. True
    b. False

	9. FALSE
8. TRUE	7. B
6. FALSE	5. FALSE
4. TRUE	3. TRUE
2. TRUE	1. TRUE

CHAPTER 14

Sheet Metal Forming Tools

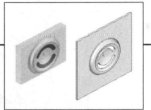

Sheet Metal Forming Tools

- Forming tools act as dies that bend, stretch, or otherwise form sheet metal.

- SolidWorks includes some sample forming tools to get you started. They are stored in: ***Installation_Directory\Data\Design Library\Forming Tools\folder_name***.

- Some types of form features, such as louvers and lances, create openings on sheet metal parts. To indicate which forming tool faces create openings, the system changes the color of these faces to **red (255,0,0)**.

- The user can only insert (drag & drop) forming tools from the **Design Library** window and apply them only to sheet metal parts. The Design Library window gives you quick access to the parts, assemblies, library features, and form tools that are used most often.

- Users can create their own forming tools and apply them to sheet metal parts to create form features such as louvers, lances, flanges, and ribs.

- The Design Library window has several default folders. Each folder contains a group of palette items, displayed as Thumbnail Graphics.

- Design Library can include:
    - Parts (.sldprt)
    - Assemblies (.sldasm)
    - Sheet Metal Forming Tools (.sldftp)
    - Library Features (.sldlfp)

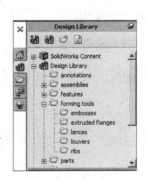

- In this 1st half of the chapter we will learn how to create and save a forming tool.

Button with Slots
Forming Tools

Dimensioning Standards: **ANSI**

Units: **INCHES** – 3 Decimals

Tools Needed:

Insert Sketch	Boss/Base Revolve	Convert Entities
Dimension	Add Geometric Relations	Extrude Cut
Split Line	Fillet/Round	Forming Tool

1. Creating the base block:

- Select the <u>Right</u> plane and Insert a new Sketch .

- Sketch a Center-Rectangle ▣ that centers on the origin.

- Add the width and height dimensions ◈ as shown.

(The sketch should be fully defined at this point)

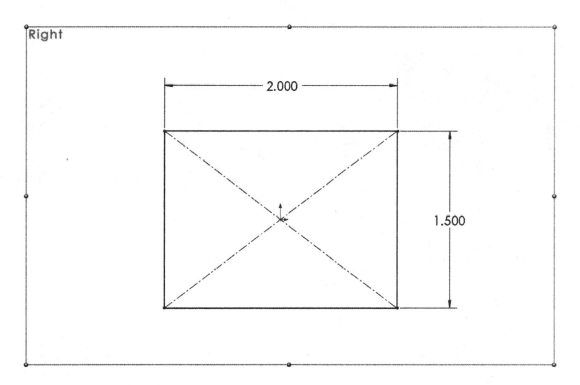

2. Extruding the base:

- Click **Extruded Boss/Base** 📦 .

- Enter the following:

- Direction 1: **Blind**.

- **Reverse** Direction.

- Depth: **.250in**.

- Click **OK** ✅ .

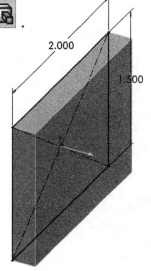

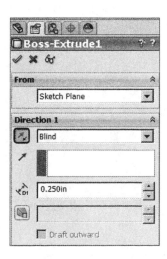

3. Creating the forming tool body:

- Select the <u>Front</u> plane and open a new sketch 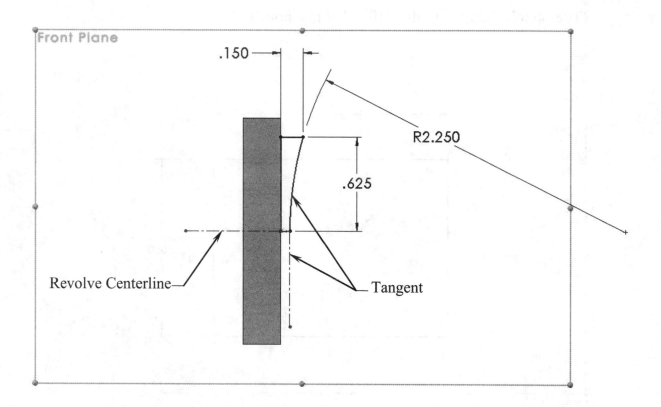.

- Sketch the profile as shown.

- Add dimensions and relations to fully define the sketch.

Front Plane

.150

R2.250

.625

Revolve Centerline

Tangent

4. Revolving the body:

- Click **Revolved Boss/Base** .

- Revolve **Blind** with a full **360 deg**.

- Click **OK** .

Revolve

Axis of Revolution
Line1

Direction1
Blind
360.00deg
☑ Merge result

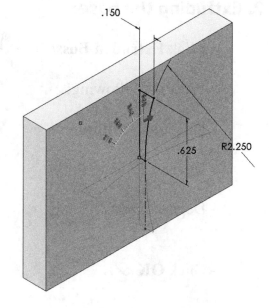

.150

.625 R2.250

5. Adding fillet:

- Click **Fillet** 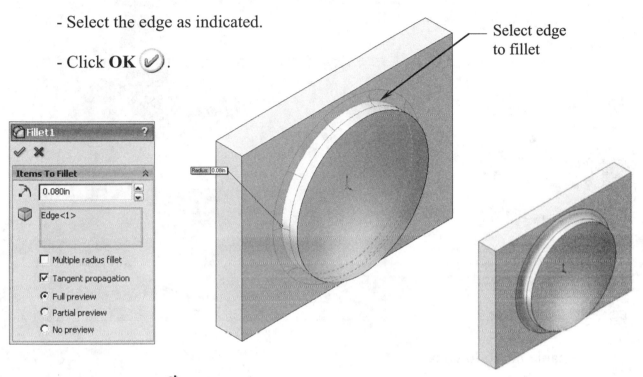 and enter **.080 in.** for Radius.

- Select the edge as indicated.

- Click **OK**.

Select edge
to fill

6. Sketching the 1ˢᵗ slot profile:

- We will look at two different methods to create the slots. For the 1ˢᵗ Arc Slot, let us try out the **Offset Entities** option.

- Select the face as indicated and open a new sketch. Draw a Center-Point-Arc approximately as shown.

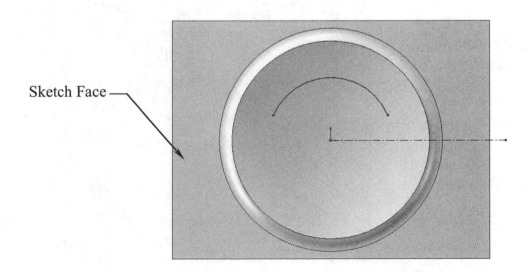

Sketch Face

- While the arc is still
highlighting, click the
Offset Entities command.

- Enter **.0625 in**. under
Offset Distance.

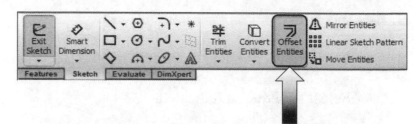

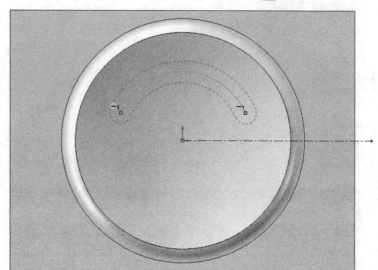

- Enable the following:

    * **Select Chain**   * **Bi-Directional**

    * **Make Base Construction**   * **Cap End / Arcs**.

- Click **OK** ✓.

Note:

- _We will use the Arc-Slot
command to create the 2nd slot._

- Add dimensions ◈ and the

horizontal relations ⌐ shown
to fully define the sketch.

135.00°

.063
.063

R.388

Horizontal

7. Creating the 1st Split Line:

- Click Split Line  from the **CURVES** toolbar or select: **Insert / Curve / Split Line.**

- Select the <u>face</u> as indicated to split .

- Click **OK** .

> 💡 **Split Line**
>
> The Split Line command projects an entity to the face and divides it into multiple faces.

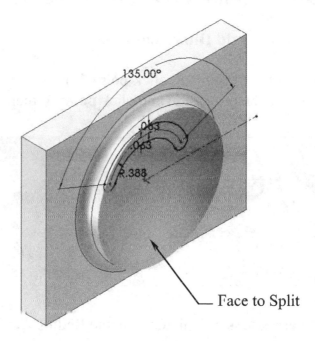

Face to Split

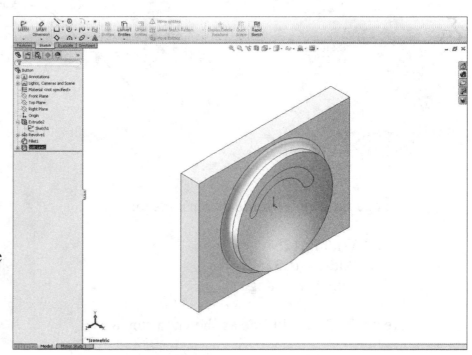

- The selected face is split into a new, separate surface.

- This new surface can now be used as Faces-to-Remove, when the form tool is inserted into a sheet metal part.

- The Faces to Remove option specifies what features/area will get a through cut.

8. Creating the 2nd slot profile:

- Next, we will try another method to create the 2nd curved slot.

- Select the **Face** as noted and open a new sketch.

- Select the **Center Arc Slot** under the Straight-Slot button.

- Enable the **Add Dimensions** checkbox.

- Start at the Origin and click **point 1**, move outward and click **point 2**, swing the cursor to the other side and click **point 3**, then drag down or upward to **point 4**.

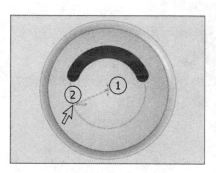 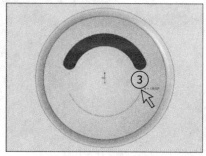 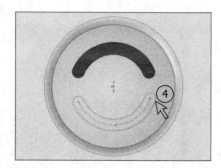

- The arc-slot is completed with the Radius, Width, and Angular dimensions.

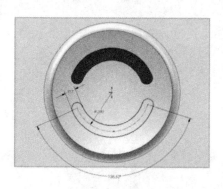 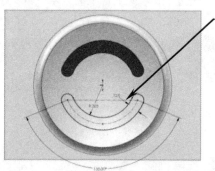

Add a horizontal centerline

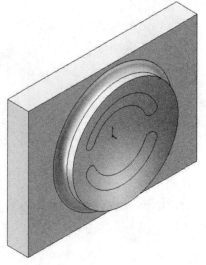

- Change the values of the dimensions to:

      * Width: **.125"**
      * Radius: **R.325"**
      * Angle: **135 deg.**

- Create the 2nd split line as shown in step 8.

9. Adding more fillets:

- Click **Fillet** 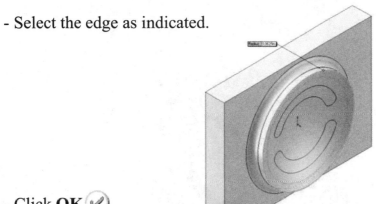 and enter **.0625 in**. for Radius.

- Select the edge as indicated.

- Click **OK** .

10. Inserting the Forming Tool feature:

- Select **Insert / Sheet Metal / Forming tool** from the pull down menu

- Select the **Stopping-Face** and the **Faces-to-Remove** as indicated.

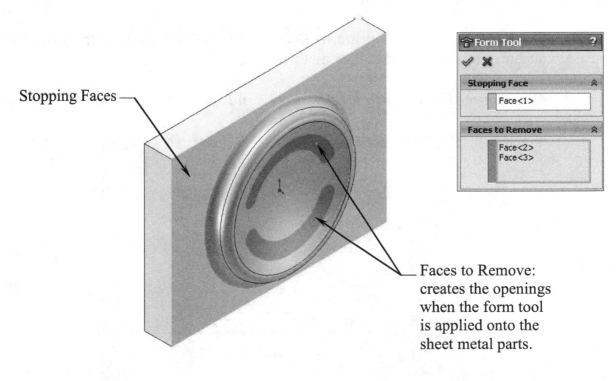

Stopping Faces

Faces to Remove: creates the openings when the form tool is applied onto the sheet metal parts.

- Click **OK** .

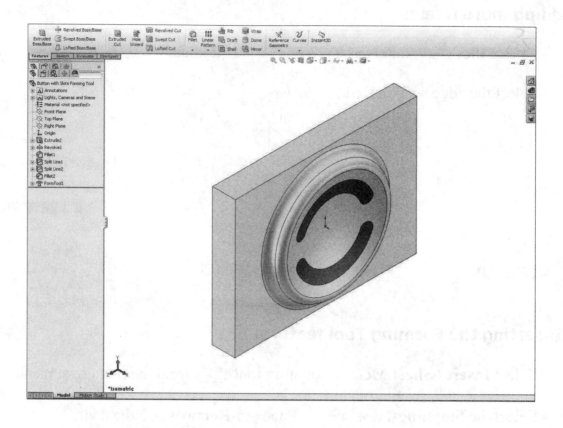

11. Saving the Forming tool:

- Click **File / Save As / Button w-Slots**, change the Save as Type to **Form Tool** and save the part in the following directories:

C:\Program Files\SolidWorks\Data\Design Library\Forming Tools\File Name

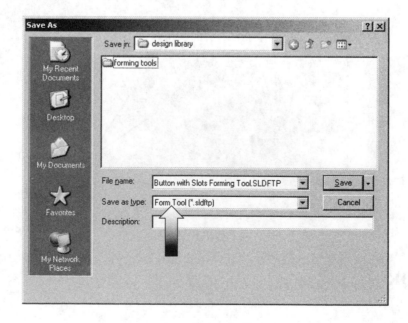

Note:

> - *The Sheet metal forming tools can also be saved by dragging and dropping from the FeatureManager tree to a folder (i.e. Forming Tools) inside the Design Library.*

> - *The file name, file type, and path can be selected to save the forming tool at this time.*

12. Applying the new forming tool: (Optional)

> - Create a sheet metal part using the drawing below and test out your new forming tool.

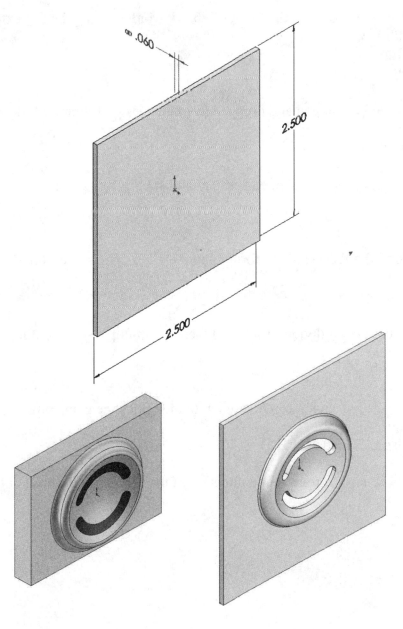

Questions for Review

Forming Tools

1. Forming tools can bend or stretch sheet metal parts.
    a. True
    b. False

2. Forming tools can be stored in the Design Library window using the file extension:
    a. slddrw
    b. sldftp
    c. dwg

3. Forming tools can be dragged and dropped from the Design Library window.
    a. True
    b. False

4. Forming tools can be used to formed surfaces and solid parts as well.
    a. True
    b. False

5. The Red color on the face(s) of the forming tool creates openings on the sheet metal parts.
    a. True
    b. False

6. The Split Line command divides a selected face into multiple separate faces.
    a. True
    b. False

7. Only one single closed sketch can be used with the Split Line command.
    a. True
    b. False

8. The _____ key is used to reverse the direction of the forming tool (push/pull):
    a. Shift
    b. Tab
    c. Alt

7. TRUE   8. b
5. TRUE   6. TRUE
3. TRUE   4. FALSE
1. TRUE   2. B

CHAPTER 14 (cont.)

Designing Sheet Metal Parts

Designing Sheet Metal Parts

- Sheet metal components are normally used as a housing or enclosures for parts or to strengthen and support other parts.

- A Sheet Metal part can be created as a single part or it can also be designed in the context of an assembly that has enclosed components.

- Forming tools are dies that can bend, stretch, or form sheet metal.

- In SolidWorks, forming tools are applied using the "Positive Half" (the raised side) to form features.

- When inserting a forming tool, its direction can be reversed using the TAB key (Push or Pull).

- The Sheet Metal part can be flattened either by using the Unfold [icon] or Flattened [icon] button, and drawings can be made to show views of the bent or flattened part. Bend lines are also visible in the drawing views.

- By default, only the Bend-Lines are visible at all time, but not the Bend-Regions. To show the Bend Regions, right click on the Flat Pattern1 icon at the bottom of the FeatureManager tree, then select Edit Feature and clear the Merge Faces check box.

- In this 2nd half of the chapter, besides learning how to create a sheet metal part, we will also learn how to apply the form tool that was created earlier in the 1st half of the lesson.

Mounting Tray
Designing Sheet Metal Parts

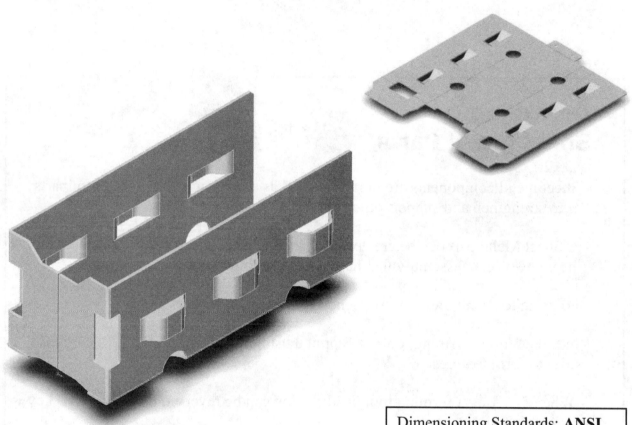

| Dimensioning Standards: **ANSI** |
| Units: **INCHES** – 3 Decimals |

Tools Needed:

Insert Sketch		Base Flange		Edge Flange	
Unfold		Fold		Extruded Cut	
Linear Pattern		Flattened		Break Corner	

1. Starting with the base sketch:

- Select the Front plane from FeatureManager Tree.

- Click 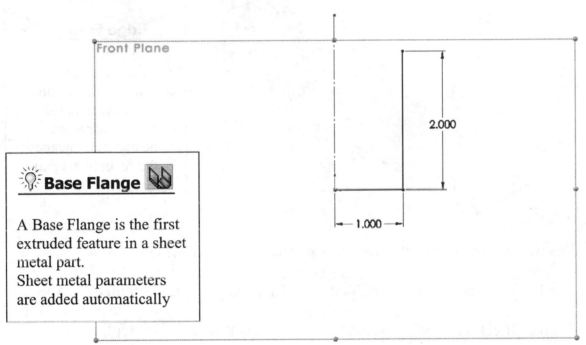 or select **Insert / Sketch**.

- Sketch the profile below and add dimensions to fully define the sketch.

Base Flange

A Base Flange is the first
extruded feature in a sheet
metal part.
Sheet metal parameters
are added automatically

2. Extruding the Base Flange:

- Click on the Sheet Metal toolbar, or select:

Insert / Sheet Metal / Base Flange.

- End Condition: **Blind**.

- Extrude Depth: **5.000**.

- Thickness: **18 Gauge**.

- Override Radius: **Enabled**.

- Bend Radius: **.010**.

- Click **OK** .

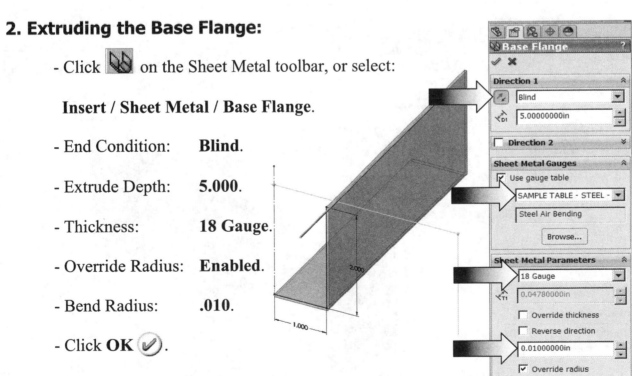

3. Creating an Edge Flange:

- Select the outer edge as shown and click 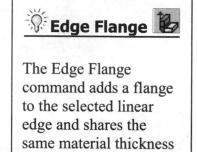 on the Sheet Metal toolbar or select:
Insert / Sheet Metal / Edge Flange.

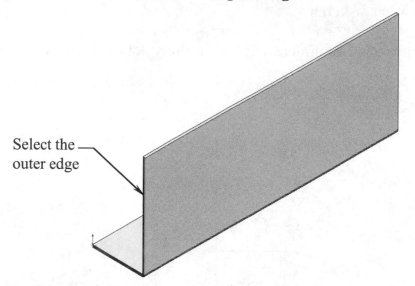

Select the outer edge

Edge Flange

The Edge Flange command adds a flange to the selected linear edge and shares the same material thickness as the sheet metal part.

- Position the flange towards the left side and set the following:

- Use Default Radius: **Enabled**.

- Flange Direction: **Blind**.

- Bend Angle: **90deg**.

- Flange Depth: **.985**.

- Use **Inner Virtual Sharp** .

- Flange Position: **Material Outside** .

- Click **OK** .

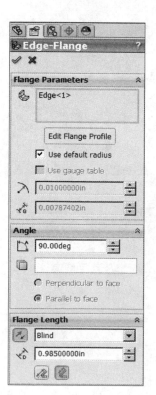

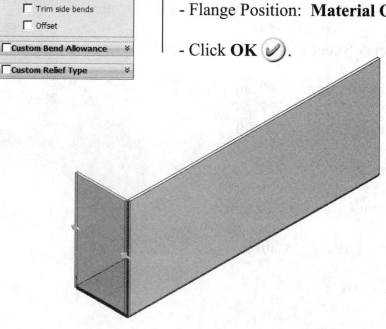

4. Adding cut features:

- Select the <u>face</u> as shown and insert a new sketch 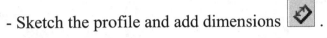.

- Sketch the profile and add dimensions .

- The horizontal dimensions are measured from the Centerline.

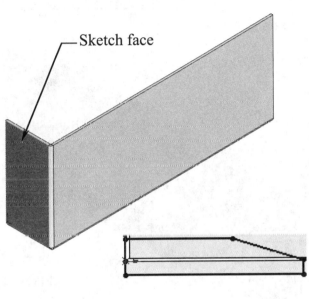

—Sketch face

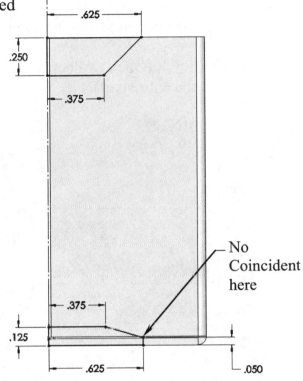

.625

.250

.375

.375

.125

.625

.050

No Coincident here

5. Extruding a cut:

- Click  or select **Insert / Cut / Extrude**.

- End Condition: **Blind**.

- Extrude Depth: **.165 in.**

- Click **OK** .

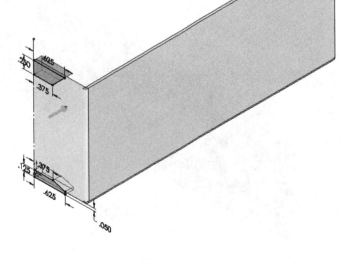

6. Using the Unfold command:

- Click 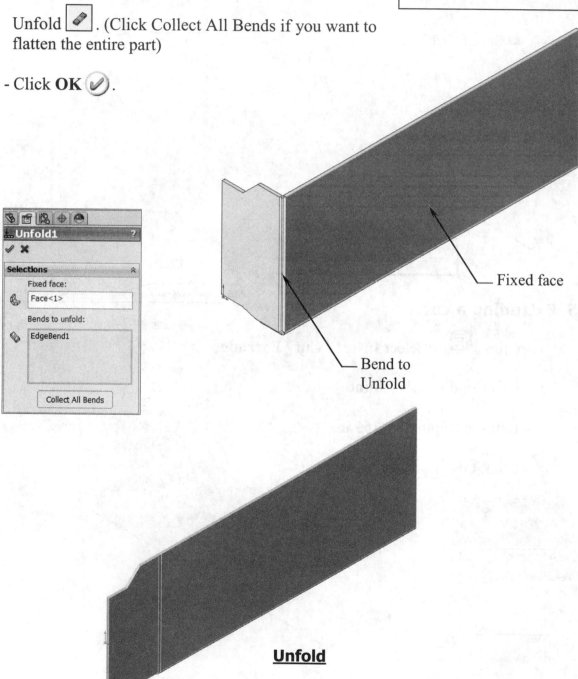 on the Sheet metal toolbar or select:
Insert / Sheet Metal / Unfold.

- Select the right face as Fixed face .

- Select the bend radius as indicated for Bends to

Unfold . (Click Collect All Bends if you want to
flatten the entire part)

- Click **OK** .

> ⌖ **Unfold**
>
> ───────────────
>
> When adding cuts across
> a bend, the Unfold
> command flattens one or
> more bend(s) in a sheet
> metal part.

Unfold1

Selections

Fixed face:
Face<1>

Bends to unfold:
EdgeBend1

Collect All Bends

Fixed face

Bend to
Unfold

Unfold

7. Creating a Rectangular Window:

- Select the <u>face</u> as indicated and insert a new sketch  .

- Sketch a rectangle ▢ as shown below.

- Add dimensions ◈ and Sketch Fillets ⌐ .

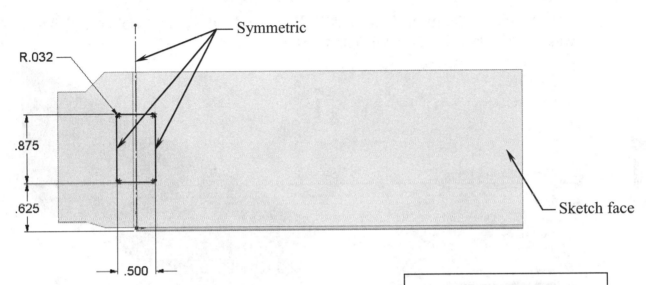

R.032

Symmetric

.875

.625

.500

Sketch face

8. Extruding a Cut:

- Click 🔲 or select **Insert / Cut / Extrude**.

- End Condition: **Blind**.

- Link to Thickness: **Enabled** (default) .

- Normal Cut: **Enabled**.

- Click **OK** ✓ .

Cut-Extrude2

From
Sketch Plane

Direction 1
Blind

☑ Link to thickness
☐ Flip side to cut
☑ Normal cut

💡 **Link To Thickness**

- The Link-to-Thickness option is only available in sheet metal parts.

- When this option is enabled, the extruded depth is automatically linked to the part thickness.

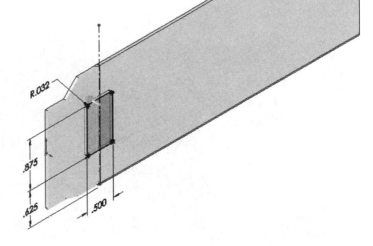

R.032

.875

.625

.500

9. Using the Fold command:

- Click 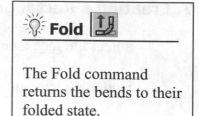 on the Sheet metal toolbar or select:

Insert / Sheet Metal / Fold.

- Select the right face as Fixed face ⬡ .

- Select the bend radius as indicated for Bends to Fold 🔲 . (If Collect All Bends was selected last time, click it again this time)

- Click **OK** ✓.

> ⚲ **Fold**
>
> The Fold command returns the bends to their folded state.

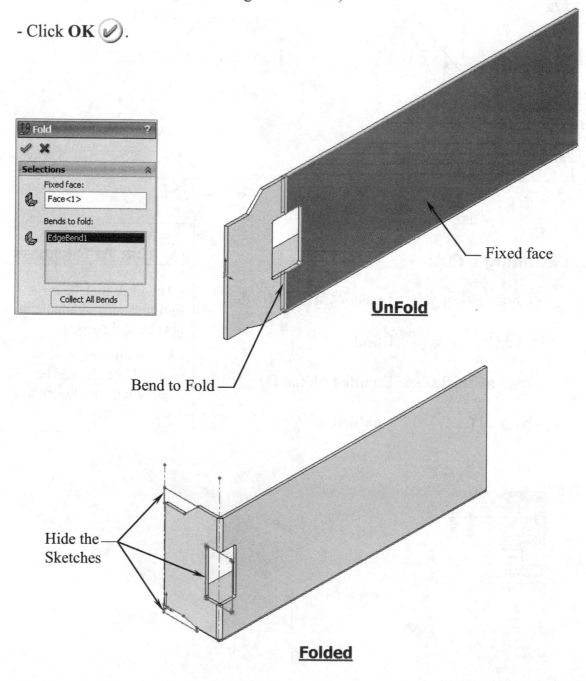

UnFold

Fixed face

Bend to Fold

Hide the Sketches

Folded

10. Unfolding multiple bends:

- Click  or select **Insert / Sheet Metal / Unfold**.

- Select the <u>bottom face</u> as Fixed face .

- Select the faces of the 2 bends as shown for Bends To Unfold .

- Click **OK** .

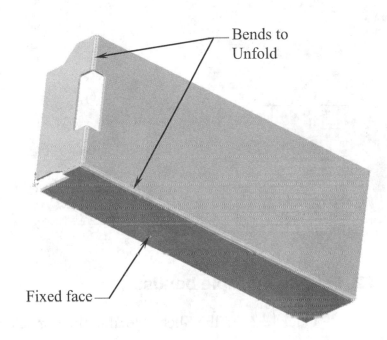

Bends to Unfold

Fixed face

11. Adding more Cuts:

- Select the upper face as noted and insert a new sketch .

- Sketch 2 Circles and add dimensions for size and position.

- Add an Equal and a Vertical relation between the circles.

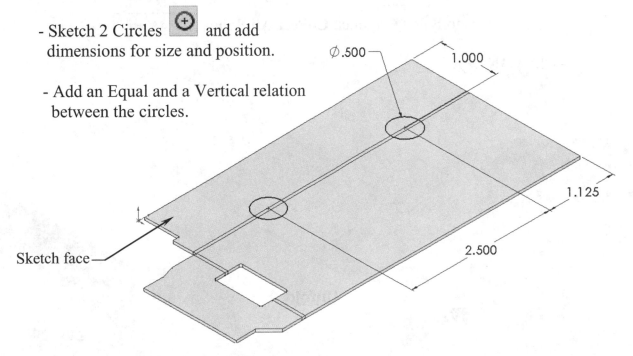

Ø.500 1.000 1.125 2.500

Sketch face

- Click 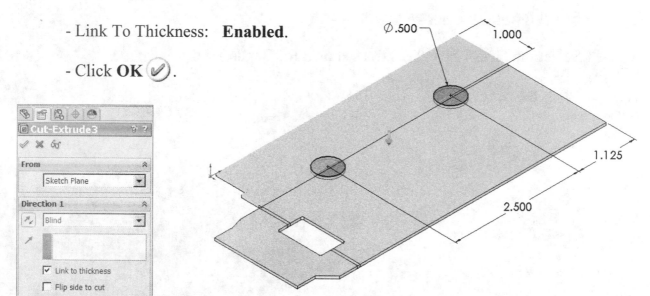 or select **Insert / Cut / Extrude**.

- End Condition: **Blind**.

- Link To Thickness: **Enabled**.

- Click **OK** ✓.

12. Folding multiple bends:

- Click 📐 on the Sheet Metal toolbar or select: **Insert / Sheet Metal / Fold**.

- The Fixed face 🔲 is still selected by default.

- Under Bends to Fold 🔲, click **Collect All Bends** [Collect All Bends].

- Click **OK** ✓.

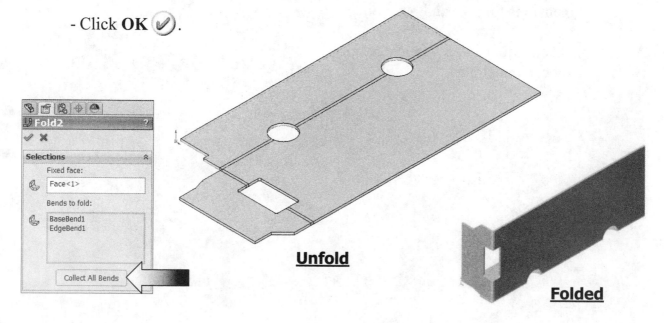

Unfold

Folded

13. Inserting a Sheet Metal Forming Tool:

- Click the **Design Library** icon and click the push pin to lock.

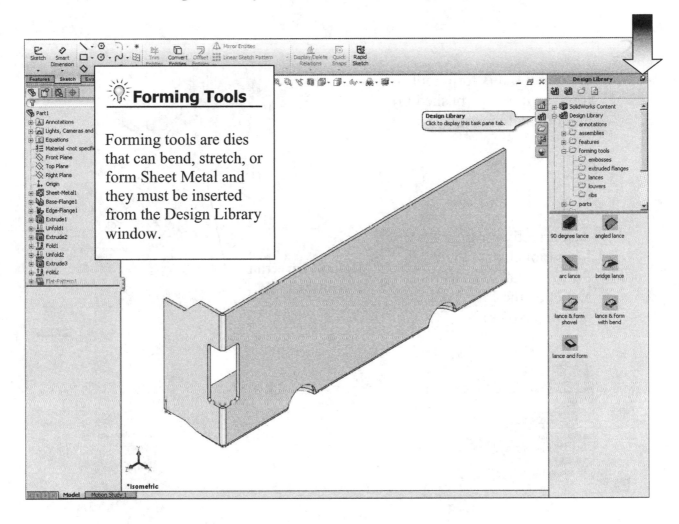

Forming Tools

Forming tools are dies that can bend, stretch, or form Sheet Metal and they must be inserted from the Design Library window.

- Click the Design Library folder to expand it.

- Click on the **Forming Tools** folder forming tools .

- Click on the **Lances** folder lances .

- Locate the **Bridge Lance** form tool.

- Hover the mouse cursor over the Bridge Lance icon to see its preview graphics.

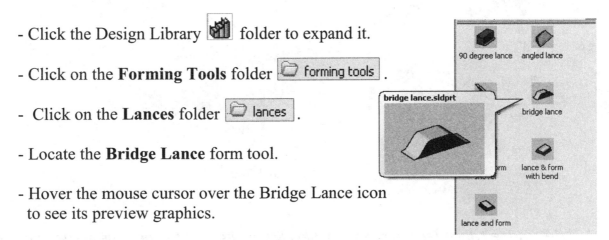

bridge lance.sldprt

- SolidWorks includes some sample forming tools to get you started.

- Drag the Bridge Lance from the Task Pane and drop it on the sheet metal part approximately as shown.

- By default, this form tool is inserted inwards (pushed in) and orientated vertically.

- To correctly position the form tool change the Rotation Angle to **180°** and click the **Flip Tool** button (arrows).

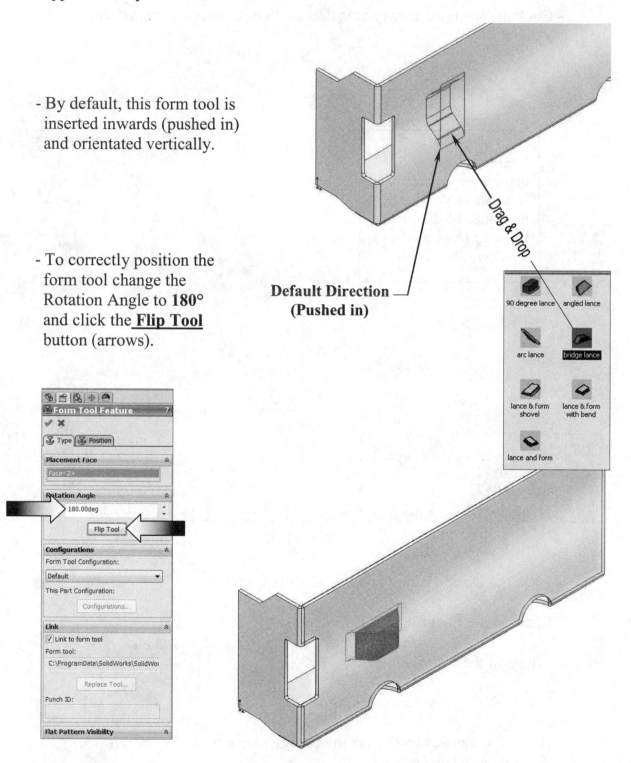

Default Direction (Pushed in)

* If the Bridge Lance fails to form, double click on its icon to open the actual part, and re-save it in the same location, but using the new Forming Tool extension (.sldftp)

14. Locating the Bridge Lance:

- At the next pop-up screen, add the dimensions 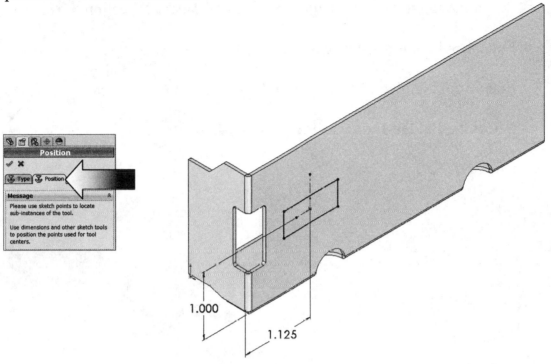 as shown below to correctly position the formed feature.

- Add dimensions from the centerlines to the outer-most edges of the part.

- Click Finish .

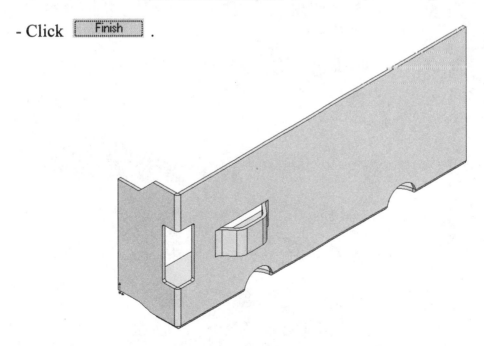

- Un-pin the Design Library Tree ⊞ to put it away temporarily.

15. Creating the Linear Pattern of the Bridge Lance:

- Click ⣿ or select **Insert / Pattern Mirror / Linear Pattern**.

- Select the top **horizontal edge** of the part as Pattern Direction 🡕 .

- Enter **1.500** in. for Instance Spacing 📏 .

- Enter **3** for Number of Instances ⠿# .

- Select the **Bridge-Lance** as Features to pattern 📑 .

- Click **OK** ✅ .

Direction arrow

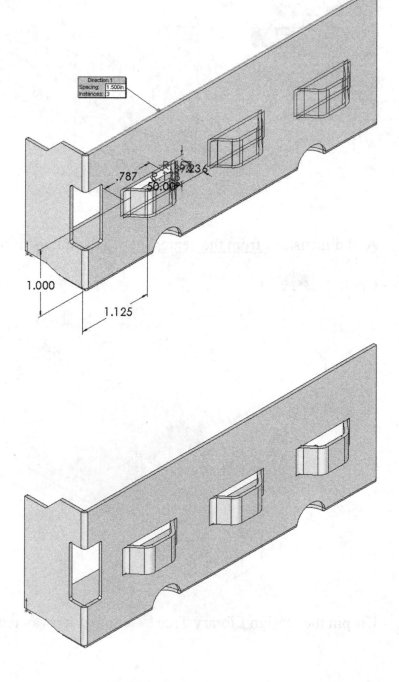

16. Mirroring the body:

- Rotate the part and select the face as indicated (for mirror face).

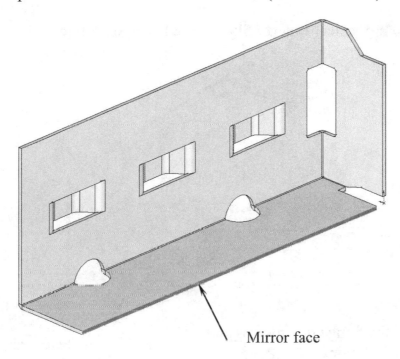

Mirror face

- Select **Insert / Pattern Mirror / Mirror**.

- Expand the Bodies to Mirror section and select the body as shown.

- Click **OK** ✅.

Body to mirror

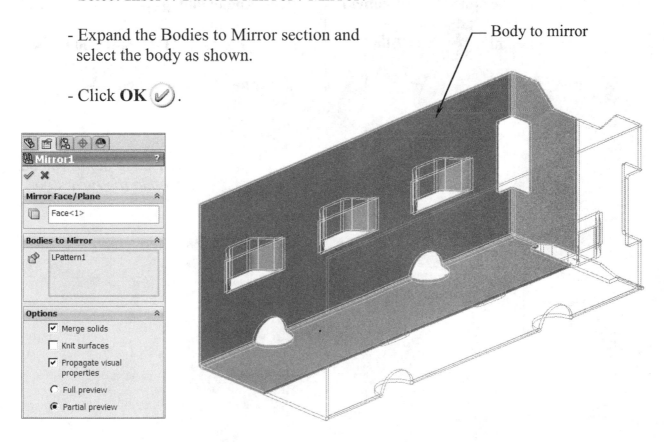

17. Adding the rear Edge Flange:

- Select the <u>edge</u> as indicated.

- Click or select **Insert / Sheet Metal / Edge Flange**.

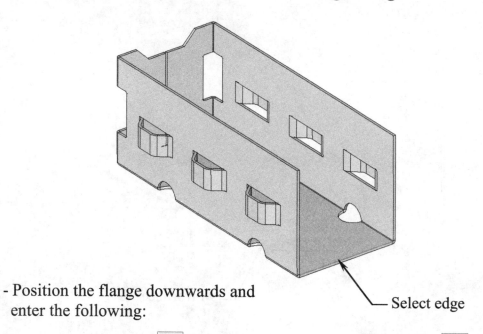

Select edge

- Position the flange downwards and enter the following:

- Use Default Radius: **Enabled**.

- Flange Length: **Blind**.

- Bend Angle: **90deg**.

- Flange Position: **Material Inside**.

- Use **Inner Virtual Sharp**.

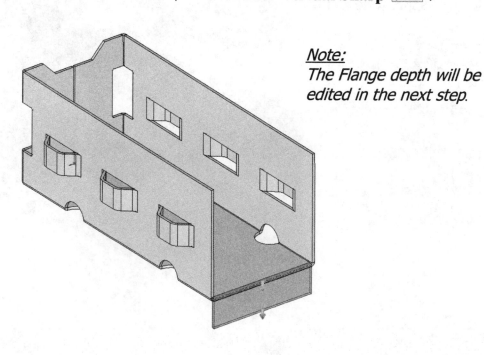

Note:
The Flange depth will be edited in the next step.

18. Resizing the Edge Flange:

- Click the **Edit Flange Profile** button (arrow).

- This option goes back to the 2D sketch of the flange so that its shape and size can be altered.

- Drag the 2 outer-most vertical lines inward (pictured).

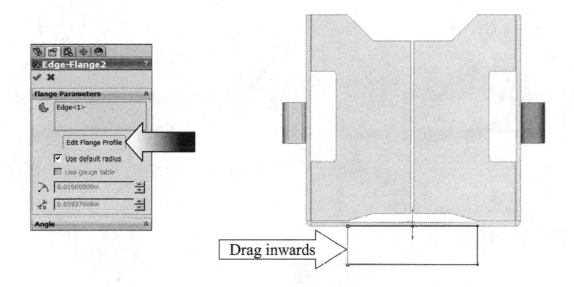

- Sketch 2 Circles 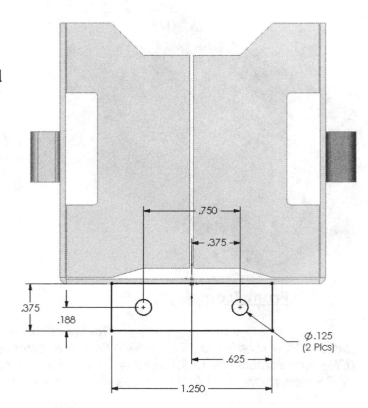 and add the Dimensions as shown.

- Click ✏ to <u>exit</u> the sketch

  or click Rebuilt 🔘 .

19. Adding Chamfers:

- Click 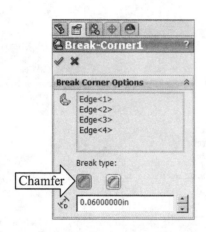 or select **Insert / Sheet Metal / Break-Corner**.

- Break Type: **Chamfer** .

- Enter **.060** for chamfer depth.

- Select the **4 Edges** as shown.

- Click **OK** .

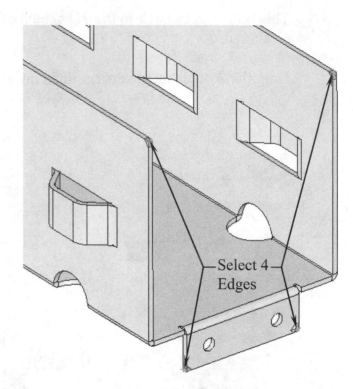

Select 4 Edges

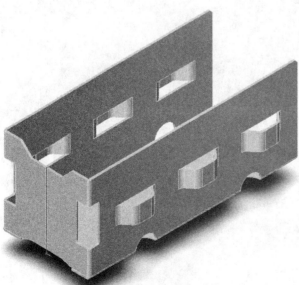

Front Isometric

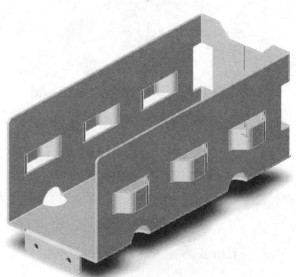

Back Isometric
See note below

Rotation Options:
*(Set the View rotation to 15 degrees – Press the **Right** arrow 12 times and **Down** arrow 4 times).*
*(OR - View rotation set to 30 degrees – Press the **Right** arrow 6 times and **Down** arrow 2 times).*
*(OR - View rotation set to 60 degrees – Press the **Right** arrow 3 times and **Down** arrow 1 time).*

20. Switching to the Flat Pattern:

- Click 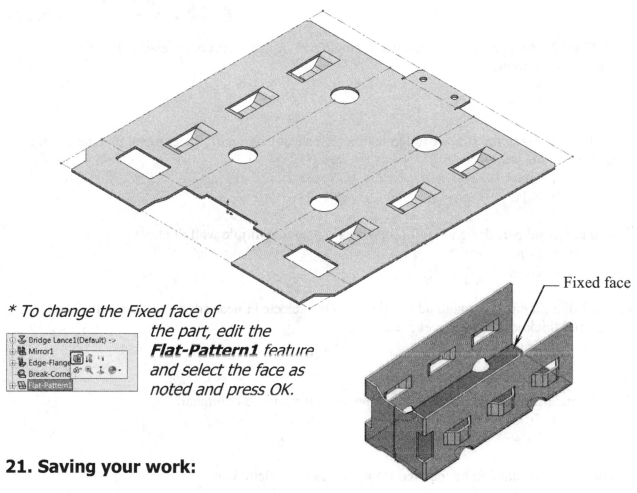 or select **Insert / Sheet Metal / Flattened***.

- Verify that the part is flattened properly and there are no rebuild errors.

* To change the Fixed face of
the part, edit the
Flat-Pattern1 feature
and select the face as
noted and press OK.

Fixed face

21. Saving your work:

- Select **File / Save As / Mounting Tray / Save**.

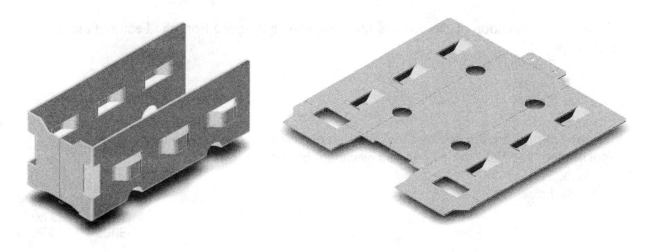

Questions for Review

1. A Sheet Metal part can be created as a single part or in context of an assembly with enclosed components.
   - a. True
   - b. False

2. A Base Flange is the first extruded feature in a sheet metal part. Sheet metal parameters are added automatically.
   - a. True
   - b. False

3. A sheet metal part designed in SolidWorks can have multiple wall thickness.
   - a. True
   - b. False

4. The Edge Flange command adds a flange to the selected linear edge and shares the same material thickness of the sheet metal part.
   - a. True
   - b. False

5. Only one bend can be flattened at a time using the Unfold command.
   - a. True
   - b. False

6. Forming tools have to be inserted from the Feature Palette window.
   - a. True
   - b. False

7. To reverse the direction of the forming tool while being dragged from the Feature Palette window, press:
   - a. Tab
   - b. Control
   - c. Shift

8. After the features are created by the forming tools, their sketches can only be moved or re-positioned, and their dimension values cannot be changed.
   - a. True
   - b. False

1. TRUE	2. TRUE
3. FALSE	4. TRUE
5. FALSE	6. TRUE
7. A	8. TRUE

CHAPTER 15

Sheet Metal Conversions

Sheet Metal Conversions
From IGES to SolidWorks

- Parts created from other CAD systems (using IGES or **I**nitial **G**raphics **E**xchange **S**pecification) can be imported and converted into SolidWorks Sheet Metal.

- When importing other CAD formats into SolidWorks, read them in as follows:

  - If there are blank surfaces, they are imported and added to the Feature Manager design Tree as surface features.
  - If the attempt to knit the surfaces into a solid succeeds, the solid appears as the base feature (named **Imported1**) in a new part file.
  - If the surfaces represent multiple closed volumes, then one part is generated for each closed volume.
  - If the attempt to knit the surfaces fail, the surfaces are grouped into one or more surface features (named **Surface-Imported1...**) in a new part file.
  - If you import a **.dxf** or **.dwg** file, the **DXF/DWG import wizard** appears to guide you through the import process.

- The imported parts must be of uniform thickness to fold and unfold properly.
- After the part is opened in SolidWorks, sheet metal parameters such as Rip 🔧 , Fixed face or edge 🔧 , Bend radius 🔧 , etc., should be added before the Flat Pattern can be created.

- The converted part appears on the Feature Manager Design tree, it contains the features Sheet Metal1 🔲 , Flatten Bend1 🔲 , and Process Bend1 🔲 .

- The sheet metal part can now be Flattened and Folded by toggling the Suppression state 🔲 of the Process Bends.

Sheet Metal Conversions
From IGES to SolidWorks Flat Pattern

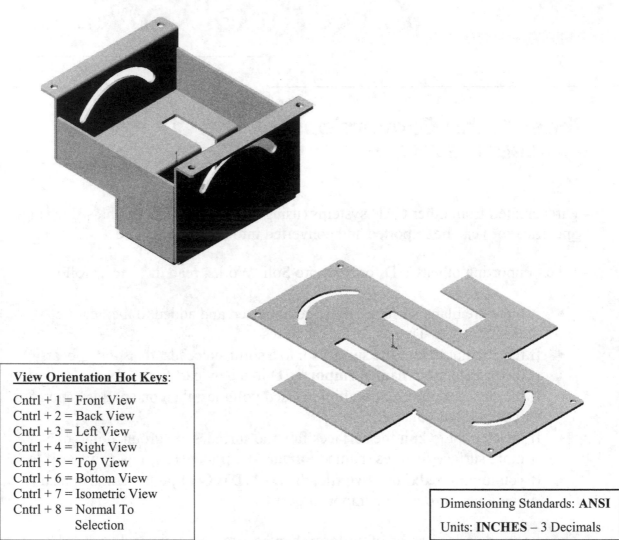

View Orientation Hot Keys:

Cntrl + 1 = Front View
Cntrl + 2 = Back View
Cntrl + 3 = Left View
Cntrl + 4 = Right View
Cntrl + 5 = Top View
Cntrl + 6 = Bottom View
Cntrl + 7 = Isometric View
Cntrl + 8 = Normal To
                 Selection

Dimensioning Standards: **ANSI**

Units: **INCHES** – 3 Decimals

Tools Needed:

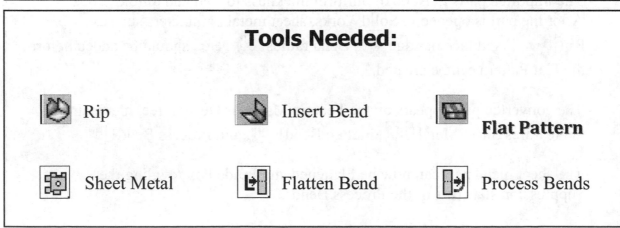

Rip   Insert Bend   **Flat Pattern**

Sheet Metal   Flatten Bend   Process Bends

1. Opening an IGES document:

- From the training CD select **File / Open** and change Files of Type to **IGES**.

- Select: **Sheet Metal Conversion** and click **Open**.

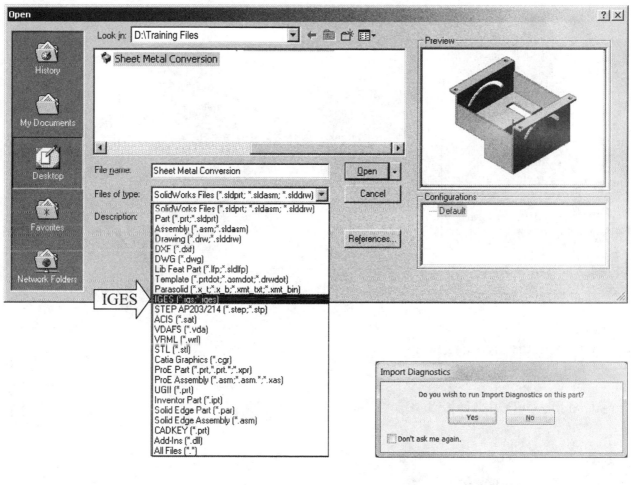

- Click NO  to skip the Import-
Diagnosis option.

- Click NO to skip the Feature-
Recognition option.

- The part is imported
into **Solid**Works as
the base feature with
no history.

2. Creating the Rips:

- Click **Rip** on the sheet metal toolbar or select **Insert / Sheet Metal / Rip**.

- Select the **inner edge** as shown.

- The 2 arrows indicate that the Rip command is going to cut both walls.

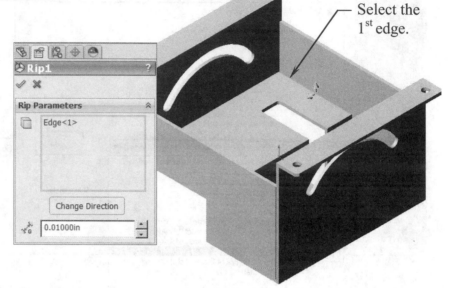

RIP

The RIP command creates a tear between the 2 walls. A Gap is entered and the rip direction can be toggled to achieve the Butt, Over-lapped, or Under-lapped results.

Select the 1st edge.

- Click on the arrow as noted, to keep the correct sides from being ripped.

- Use the **Default Gap** (.010).

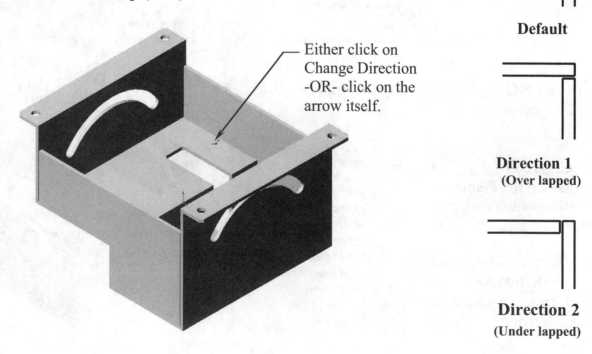

Either click on Change Direction -OR- click on the arrow itself.

Default

Direction 1
(Over lapped)

Direction 2
(Under lapped)

- Select a total of 4 edges (2 on each side) as indicated.

- Click **OK** ✅.

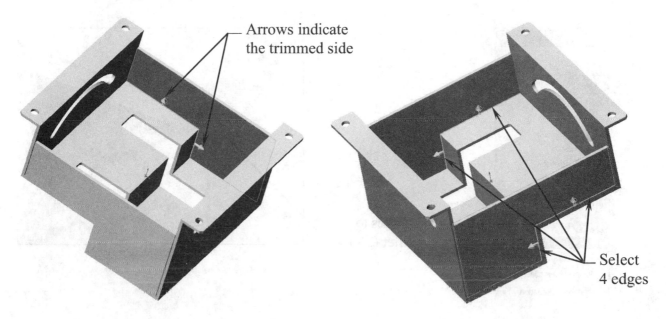

Arrows indicate
the trimmed side

Select
4 edges

3. Inserting the Sheet Metal Parameters:

- Click **Insert Bends** ⬚ command or select **Insert / Sheet Metal / Bends**.

- Select the inside face for use as the Fixed Face ⬚ .

- Enter **.015 in.** for inside Bend-Radius ⬚ .

- Click **C** ✅ .

- The system reports some Auto Relief Cuts were made for some bends.

- Click OK .

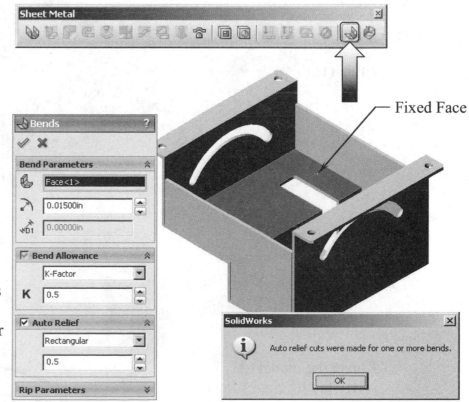

Fixed Face

4. Adding Fillets:

- Click **Fillet** command 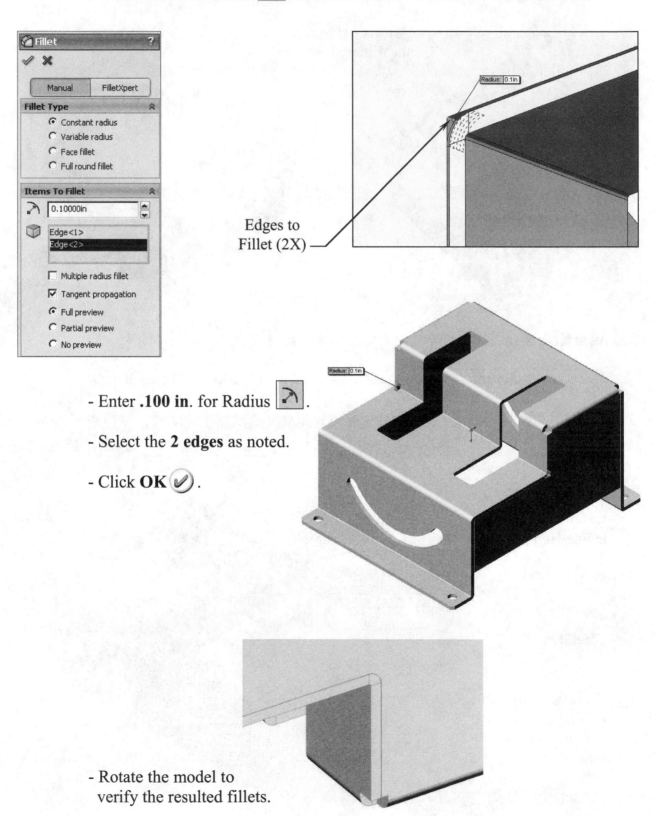 or select **Insert / Features / Fillet/Round**.

Edges to
Fillet (2X) —

- Enter **.100 in**. for Radius .

- Select the **2 edges** as noted.

- Click **OK** .

- Rotate the model to
verify the resulted fillets.

5. Switching to the Flat pattern:

- To examine the part in the

flattened view; click **Flatten** 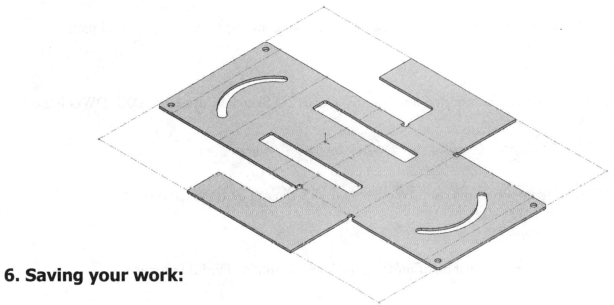 on the Sheet Metal toolbar.

6. Saving your work:

- Click **File / Save As**.

- Enter **Sheet Metal Conversion** for file name.

- Click **Save**.

Questions for Review

Sheet Metal Conversions

1. An IGES file can be imported into SolidWorks and converted into a sheet metal part.
    a. True
    b. False

2. DXF and DWG are imported into SolidWorks as 2D Sketches, using the DXF/DWG Import-Wizard.
    a. True
    b. False

3. After being imported into SolidWorks, the IGES file can be flattened instantly.
    a. True
    b. False

4. The imported parts must be of uniform thickness to fold and unfold properly.
    a. True
    b. False

5. The Rip feature removes 1 material thickness based on the side of the direction arrow that you select.
    a. True
    b. False

6. When applying the sheet metal parameters you do not have to specify a fixed face.
    a. True
    b. False

7. The width and depth of the relief cuts are fixed and cannot be changed.
    a. True
    b. False

8. The Folded and the Flat pattern can be toggled by moving the Rollback Line up or down.
    a. True
    b. False

7. FALSE   8. TRUE
5. TRUE   6. FALSE
3. FALSE   4. TRUE
1. TRUE   2. TRUE

CHAPTER 15 Cont.

Flat Pattern Stent

Flat Pattern Stent
A Different Approach

- Using the built-in Sheet Metal features in SolidWorks you can flatten or roll solid models such as wire mesh screens, grill meshes, or stent patterns.

- When designing a sheet metal part, the material setback is something we must keep in mind: The Bend allowance and bend deduction calculations are methods you can choose to determine the flat length of sheet stock to give the desired dimension of the bent part. This lesson uses the default settings of the K-Factor to calculate the bend allowance (BA=P(R + KT) A/180).

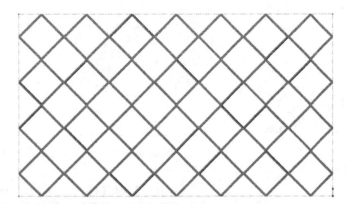

- K-Factor is a ratio that represents the location of the neutral sheet with respect to the thickness of the sheet metal part. When you select K-Factor as the bend allowance, you can specify a K-Factor bend table. The SolidWorks application also comes with a K-Factor bend table in Microsoft Excel format.

- There are several known methods for creating this types of patterns, this lesson will walk you through the use of rolling and unrolling a cylinder and its pattern, using the Sheet Metal functions in Solidworks.

Flat Pattern Stent
A Different Approach

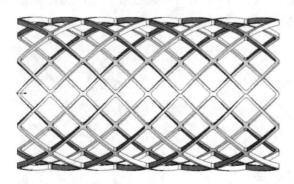

| Dimensioning Standards: **ANSI** |
| Units: **INCHES** – 3 Decimals |

Tools Needed:

Revolve Boss-Base	Flatten	Unfold
Fold	Extruded Cut	Fillet / Round

1. Starting with a part document:

- Click **File / New / Part**, set the units to **Inches, 3 decimal** places.

- Select the <u>Front</u> plane and open a new sketch.

- Create the sketch and add the dimensions / relation shown below. (The dimensions are scaled up for ease of modeling purposes).

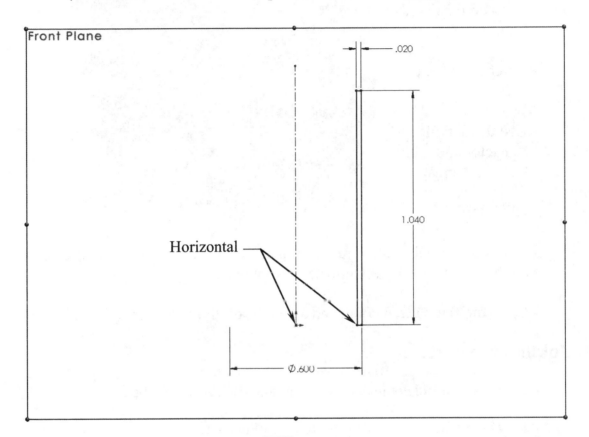

Front Plane

Horizontal

.020

1.040

Ø.600

- Click **Revolve / Boss-Base**  .

- The revolve centerline is selected automatically.

- Use the default **Blind** type.

- Enter **359.9deg** for angle.

- Click **OK**.

(The gap is needed to flatten the part later on).

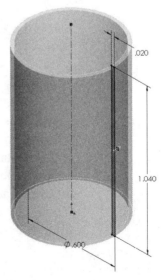

2. Converting to Sheet Metal :

- Click the **Insert-Bends** command on the Sheet Metal toolbar.

- Select the left <u>edge</u> as noted for Fixed-Edge/Face.

- Enter **0** for bend radius.

- Use the default K-Factor and Auto Relief settings.

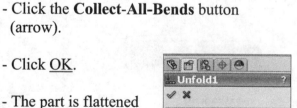

Select the Fixed edge

- Click **OK**.

- The solid model is converted to a Sheet Metal part. Press the Flatten command on the Sheet Metal toolbar to see its flat pattern.

- Click the flat pattern command again to roll the part back to its default shape.

3. Unfolding the part:

- Select the **Unfold** command ⬇ from the Sheet Metal toolbar.

- Select the same <u>edge</u> to keep as the Fixed Edge/Face.

- Click the **Collect-All-Bends** button (arrow).

- Click <u>OK</u>.

- The part is flattened but this time new features can be added and they will roll back when the part is folded.

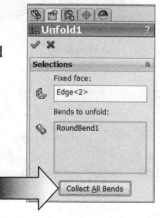

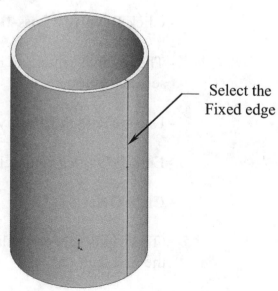

Select the Fixed edge

4. Adding the sketch pattern:

- Select the face as noted and open a new sketch.

- Sketch a couple of squares (notice the upper square is slightly larger than the lower one by .006").

- Add the dimensions and relations shown to fully define the sketch.

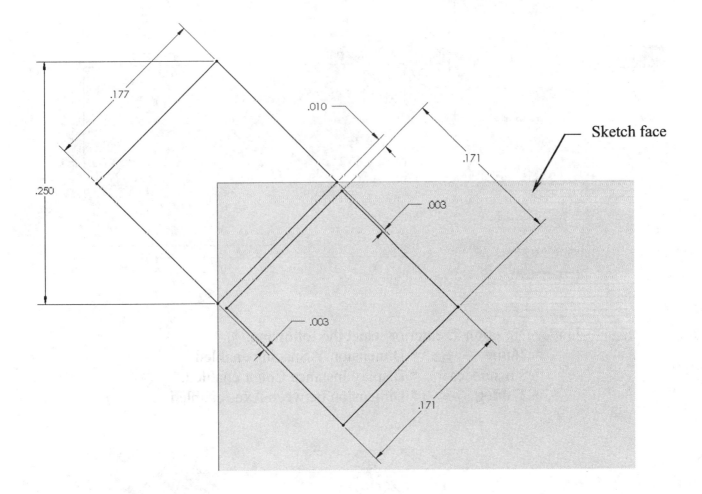

- Additional relations such as Parallel, Equal, or Perpendicular can also be used to help eliminate some of dimensions

- We are going to use the Linear Sketch Pattern command to repeat the two squares several times, so there are a few things to keep in mind:

    * Pre-select the entities to pattern.   *Auto add spacing dimensions.
    * Pattern along 2 directions, use angle (0deg and 270deg for directions).

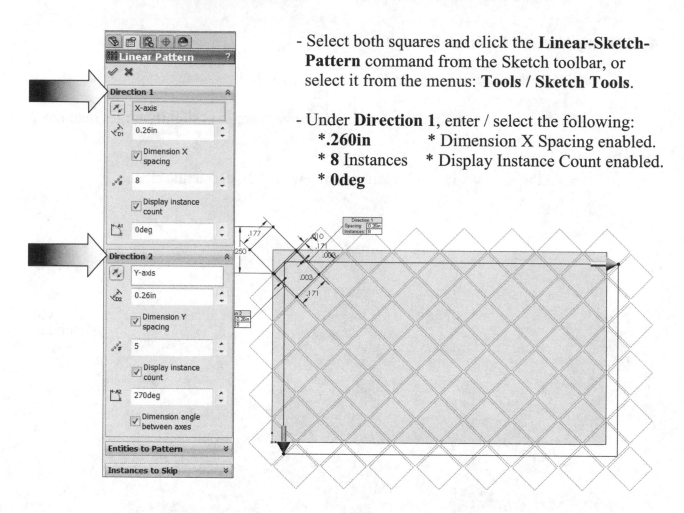

- Select both squares and click the **Linear-Sketch-Pattern** command from the Sketch toolbar, or select it from the menus: **Tools / Sketch Tools**.

- Under **Direction 1**, enter / select the following:
  * **.260in**   * Dimension X Spacing enabled.
  * **8** Instances   * Display Instance Count enabled.
  * **0deg**

- Under Direction 2, enter or select the following:
  * **.260in**   * Dimension Y Spacing enabled.
  * **5** Instances   * Display Instance Count enabled.
  * **270deg**   * Dimension between Axes enabled.

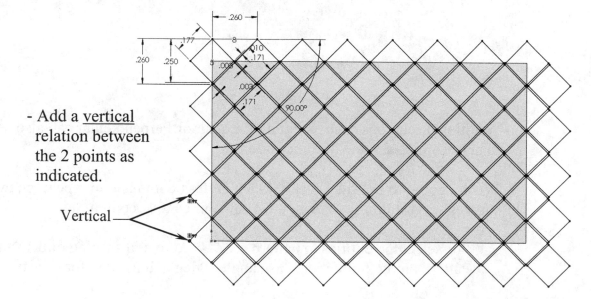

- Add a <u>vertical</u> relation between the 2 points as indicated.

Vertical

5. Creating a cut Link to Thickness:

- Select the **Extruded Cut** command from the Sheet Metal toolbar.

- Us the default **Blind** option and enable the **Link To Thickness** checkbox.

- Click **OK**.

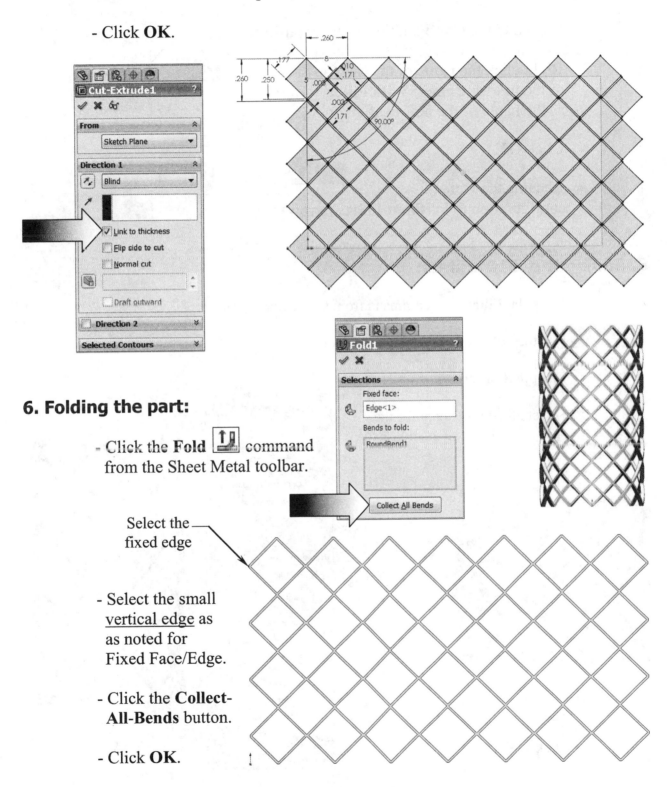

6. Folding the part:

- Click the **Fold** command from the Sheet Metal toolbar.

Select the fixed edge

- Select the small <u>vertical edge</u> as as noted for Fixed Face/Edge.

- Click the **Collect-All-Bends** button.

- Click **OK**.

7. Creating a new configuration:

- Before adding the fillets to all the intersections, we will
  need to create a configuration so that the fillets can be
  added and captured in a separate configuration.

- Switch to the ConfigurationManager (arrow).

- Right click the name of the part (on the top
  of the tree) and enter: **With Fillets** (arrow)
  as the name of the new configuration.

- Click **OK**.

- Rename the Default
  configuration to **Without Fillets** (arrow).

8. Adding the .010" fillets:

- Click the **Fillet** command from the Features toolbar.

- Use the default Constant radius option.

- Enter **.010in** for radius.

- Select all edges <u>except</u> for the
  ones at the two end as indicated.

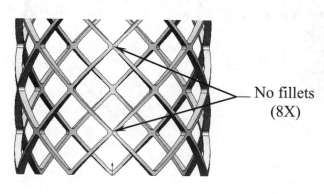

No fillets
(8X)

- Click **OK**.

9. Switching to Flatten mode:

- Click **Flatten** on the Sheet Metal toolbar.

- The part is flattened and the cut pattern is unrolled with it.

- Use the Flatten command to flatten the sheet metal part to check its dimensions, get a print out from it, or export it as a DXF or DWG for use in manufacturing.

- Use the Fold and Unfold commands to flatten the part and add new features, so that these features can roll or unroll with the part.

10. Switching configuration:

- Switch back to the **Without Fillets** configuration by double clicking on its name.

- Click the **Flatten** command again to verify the pattern.

- At this point, the pattern can be exported or a print can be made from it for inspection or documentation purposes.

11. Saving your work:

- Click **File / Save As**.

- Enter **Flat Pattern Stent** for the name of the file.

- Click **Save**.

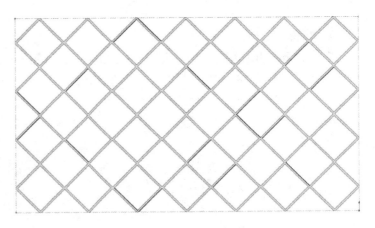

Questions for Review

Flat Pattern Stent

1. Using Solidworks, a cylinder or a cone can be unrolled into a Sheet Metal flat pattern.
   - a. True
   - b. False

2. There must be a gap or a slit, along the length of the cylinder for it to flattened.
   - a. True
   - b. False

3. A sheet metal part can have more than one thickness.
   - a. True
   - b. False

4. A sheet metal part must have one uniform thickness.
   - a. True
   - b. False

5. The Link to Thickness option links the depth-of-cut to the thickness of the part.
   - a. True
   - b. False

6. The K-Factor value is locked to .5, this ratio cannot be changed.
   - a. True
   - b. False

7. Use the Flatten command to flatten the part and add new features.
   - a. True
   - b. False

8. Use the Unfold command to flatten the part and add new features.
   - a. True
   - b. False

7. FALSE   8. TRUE
5. TRUE   6. FALSE
3. FALSE   4. TRUE
1. TRUE   2. TRUE

Exercise: Stent Sample - Sheet Metal Approach

- There are many known methods for creating the shapes of stents. This exercise will show one that uses of the combination of Patterns, Ribs and Combine Common options to create the model shown above. (The dimensions in the model are scaled up for visual purposes).

1. Creating the main sketch:

- Select the <u>Front</u> plane and open a new Sketch.

- Sketch a line centered on the origin, and two center-lines as shown.

- Add the dimensions to fully define the sketch.

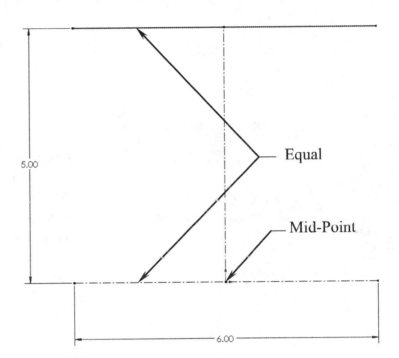

2. Revolving the main body:

- From the Features toolbar, click **Revolve Boss-Base**.

- Set Direction 1 to: **Mid-Plane**.

- Set Revolve Angle to: **90deg**.

- Set Thickness under Thin-Feature to: **.040in**.

- Click **OK**.

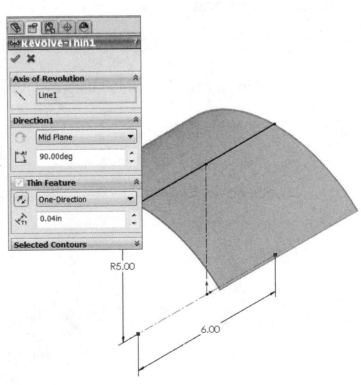

3. Creating a 2nd body:

- Select the **Top** plane and open a new sketch.

- Sketch a **Center Rectangle** and add the dimension shown.

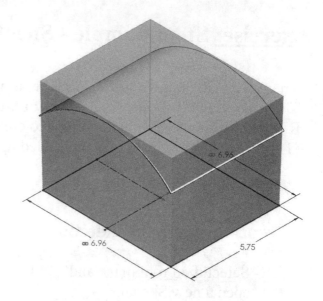

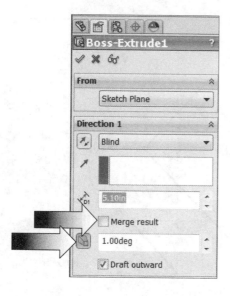

- **Extrude Boss-Base**:
  - Blind: **5.10in**
  - Merge Result: Cleared (arrow).
  - Draft: **1deg**
  - Draft Outward **Enabled** (arrow).

- Click **OK**.

4. Shelling the body:

- Click the **Shell** command from the Features toolbar.

- Select the **upper face** of the **body2** to remove.

- Enter **.040in.** for thickness.

- Click **OK**.

Remove the upper face

<u>Note:</u>

Only the Body2 is shelled. The Body1 is set below the top surface by .100".

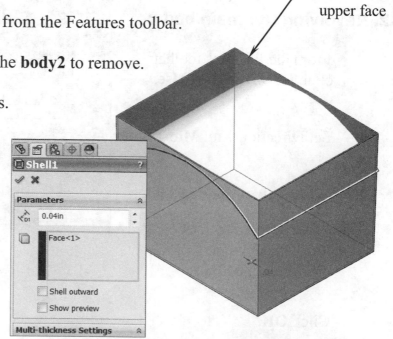

5. Creating an offset plane:

- Select the <u>uppermost face</u> of the part and create an offset plane at **.040in**.

- Click the **Flip** checkbox to place the new plane **<u>below</u>** the surface.

- Click **OK**.

6. Creating a Rib feature:

- Open a new sketch on the <u>new plane</u>.

- Add a line across the walls, at the upper left corner of the part.

- Sketch a centerline that is coincident to the 2 diagonal corners.

- Add the dimension and relations as noted.

- Click the **Rib** command from the Features toolbar.

- Set the thickness to **Mid Plane**.

- Set the wall to: **.040in**.

- Click the **Normal To Sketch** button (arrow).

- Under the Selected Body section, click the **Shelled** body (arrow).

- Click **OK**.

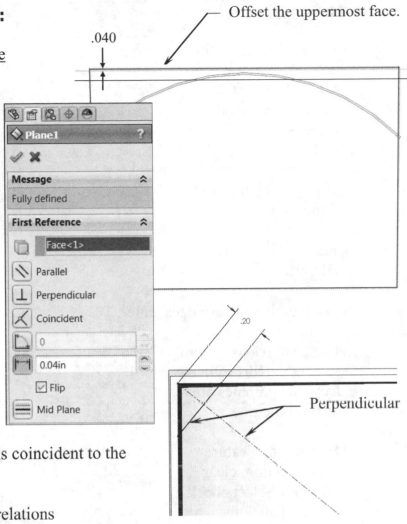

Offset the uppermost face.

.040

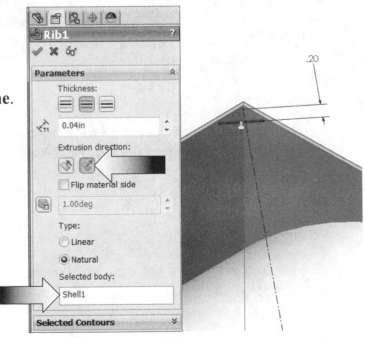

Perpendicular

.20

7. Patterning the Rib:

- Click **Linear Pattern**.

- Click the **front face** of the rib to see its dimensions.

- For Pattern Direction: double click the **.200in** dimension.

- For Spacing, enter: **.502**in.

- For Number of Instances, enter: **18**.

- For Features to Pattern, select the **Rib1** either from the graphics area or from the tree.

- Expand the Feature-Scope section, clear the Auto-Select check box, and click the face of the Rib as noted.

- Click **OK**.

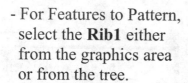

Double click this dimension for direction

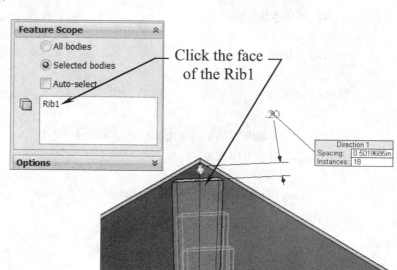

Click the face of the Rib1

- The rib feature is repeated 18 times along the direction that was specified by the .200in dimension.

- This is the 1st set of the ribs. We'll repeat the steps 6 and 7 again to create the similar ribs on the opposite side.

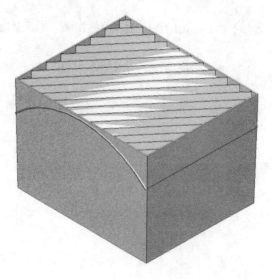

8. Creating another rib:

- Select the <u>upper face</u> of the part and open a new sketch.

- Sketch a line across the walls as shown.

- Add a centerline that is coincident to the 2 diagonal corners.

- Add the dimension and relations as indicated.

- Create another rib using the <u>same settings</u> as the first one.

- Click **OK**.

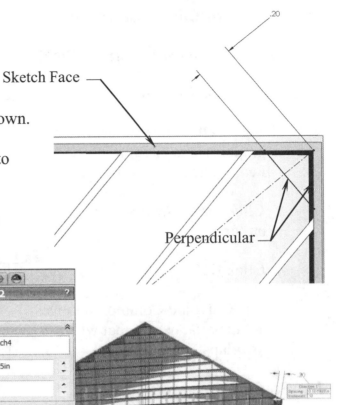

9. Patterning the 2nd set of the ribs:

- Click **Linear Pattern**

- Click the front face of the rib to see its dimensions.

- For Pattern Direction: <u>double click</u> the .**20**in. dimension.

- For Spacing, enter: **.502in**.

- For Number of Instances, enter: **18**.

- For Features to Pattern, select the **Rib1**.

- Expand the Feature-Scope section, <u>clear</u> the Auto-Select checkbox, and click the <u>face of the Rib</u>.

- Click **OK**. The Rib is repeated 18 times.

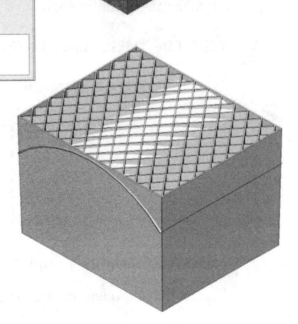

10. Using Combine Common:

- Select **Insert / Features / Combine**.

- Click the **Common** option.

- Select **all bodies** either from the graphics area or from the Feature tree.

- Click the **Show Preview** button.

- Click **OK**.

- The Combine-Common removes all material except that which overlaps.

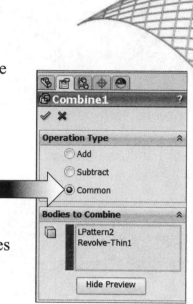

11. Saving the part:

- Save the part as **Stent Sample.sldprt**

12. Making an assembly from the part:

- The first one-quarter of the part is finished. We are going to place it in an assembly document and create 3 more instances to make the complete part.

- Click **File / Make Assembly From Part**.

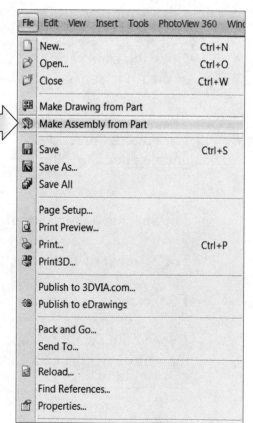

- Select the **Assembly Template** and click **OK**.

- Place the component on the Origin as noted.

13. Creating a Circular Component pattern:

- Enable the <u>Temporary Axis</u> under the **View** pull down menu.

- On the Assembly tool tab, select: **Circular Component Pattern** (arrow).

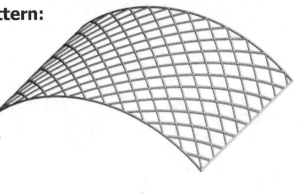

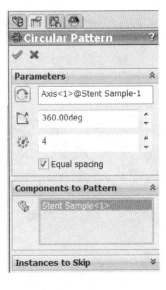

Place the part on the Origin

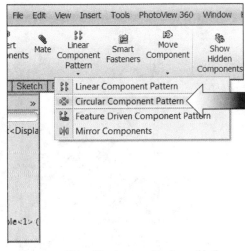

- For Pattern Axis, click the **Temporary Axis**.

- Enable the **Equal Spacing** checkbox.

- Enter **4** for number of instances.

- Under Components to Pattern, select the component in the graphics area.

- Click **OK**.

14. Saving the assembly:

- Click **File / Save As**.

- Enter **Stent Sample Assembly.sldasm** for the name of the file.

- Click **Save**.

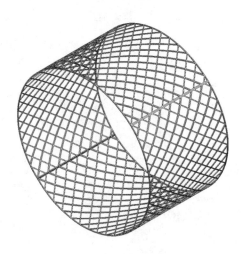

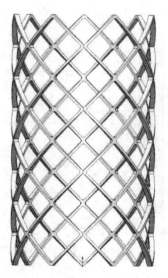

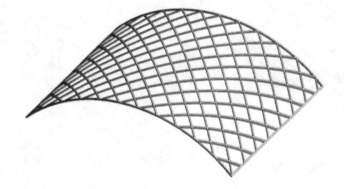

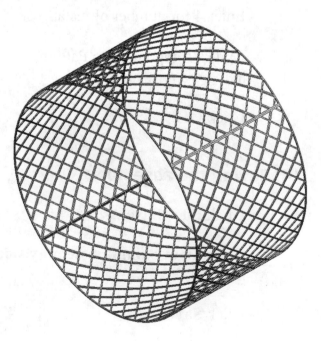

CHAPTER 16

Working with Sheet Metal STEP Files

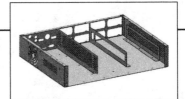

Working with Sheet Metal STEP Files

- <u>STEP</u> file extension is short for: **ST**andard for the **E**xchange of **P**roduct data.

- The STEP translator supports <u>import and export</u> of body, face, and curve colors from STEP AP214 files.

- The STEP AP203 standard does not have any color implementation.

- The STEP translator <u>imports</u> STEP files as SolidWorks part or assembly documents.

- The STEP translator <u>exports</u> SolidWorks part or assembly documents to STEP files. You can select to export individual parts or subassemblies from an assembly tree, limiting export to only those parts or subassemblies. If you select a subassembly, all of its components are automatically selected. If you select a component, its ascendants are partially selected, preserving the assembly structure.

- This lesson discusses one of the methods to convert an Assembly STEP file into SolidWorks Sheet Metal parts.

- After the components are converted, some of the Assembly Features such as the Hole Series and Hole Wizards are used to add the new holes in the assembly mode; then the Fasteners are inserted automatically using the Smart Fasteners feature (required SolidWorks Toolbox).

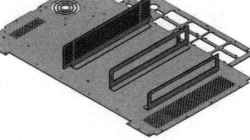

Working with
Sheet Metal STEP Files

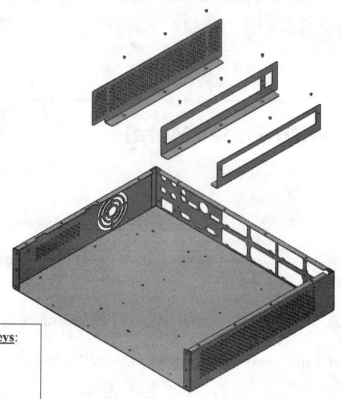

Dimensioning Standards: **ANSI**

Units: **INCHES** – 3 Decimals

Tools Needed:

 Dimension   Insert Bends   Flat Pattern

 Hole Series   Hole Wizard   Smart Fasteners

Sheet Metal **STEP Files** and **Smart Fasteners**

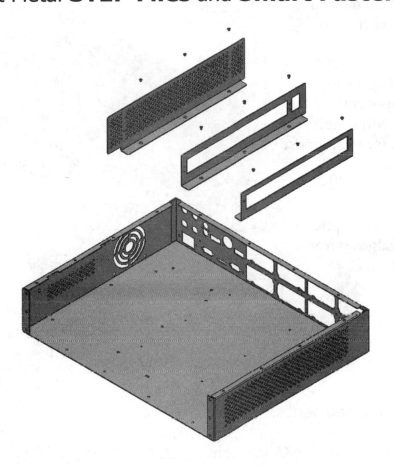

1. Opening an Assembly Step file:

- Change the Files of Type to STEP and open the STEP document named: **SM-Assembly.step**, from the Training CD.

- The part files from the STEP document will appear as SolidWorks documents on the FeatureManager tree.

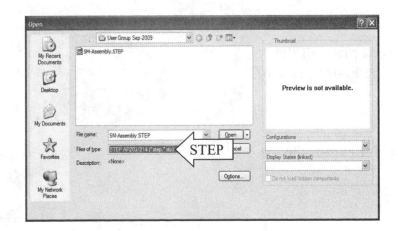

- There are 4 components in this assembly and they have not yet been constrained.

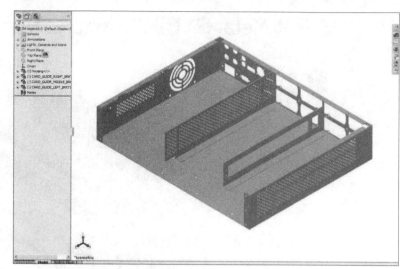

- The Housing will be used as the Fixed Component and the 3 Card Guides will be left un-constrained for the purpose of this exercise.

- Change the Shading option to: **Shaded with Edges** (arrow).

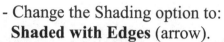

Shaded with Edges

2. Mating the components:

- In order to mate the Housing Component to the assembly's Origin, we'll need to align the 3 Front, Top & Right planes.

Coincident 2 Front Planes

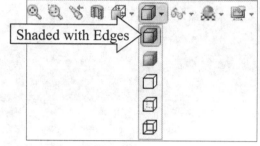

- Click the **Mate** command from the Assembly toolbar.

- Select the **Front** plane of the Housing and the **Front** plane of the Assembly.

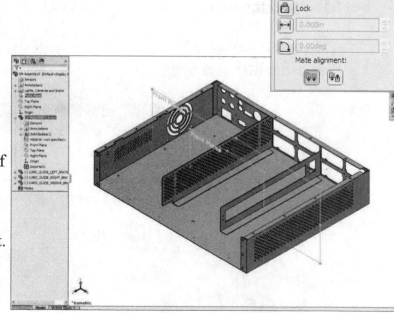

- Select **Coincident** from the list.

- Click **OK** .

- Add the same Coincident mate to the **Top** plane of the Housing and the **Top** plane of the Assembly.

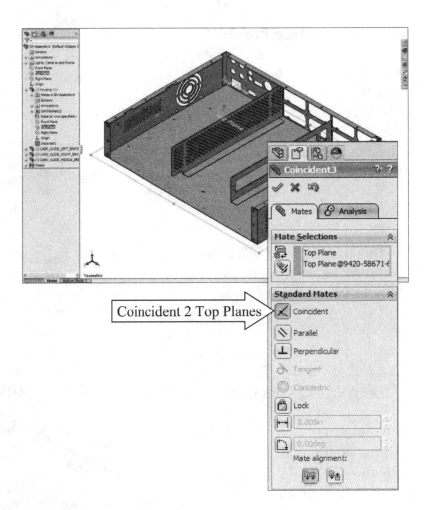

Coincident 2 Top Planes

- Repeat the Coincident mate for the **Right** plane of the Housing and the **Right** plane of the Assembly.

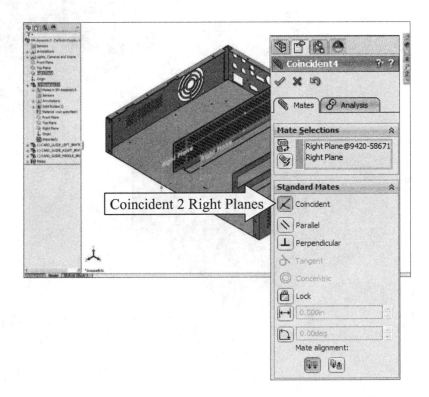

Coincident 2 Right Planes

- The Housing component should be **Fixed** (f) at this time.

3. Adding other Mates:

- Other mates can be added to constrain the other components, but later on they'll need to be suppressed so that the final sheet metal components can be flattened properly.

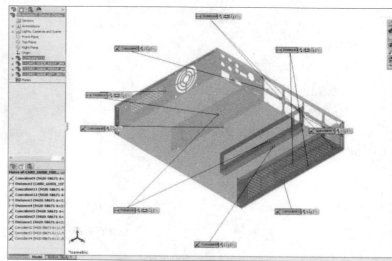

- In this exercise we will leave the components un-constrained to help focus on other areas.

4. Examining the components:

- The imported components have **Sharp corners** all around, which is not suitable for the Sheet Metal processes.

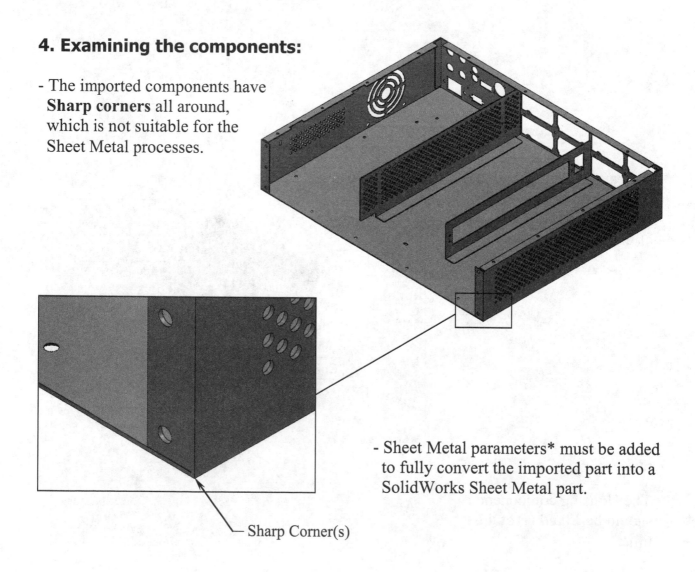

- Sheet Metal parameters* must be added to fully convert the imported part into a SolidWorks Sheet Metal part.

Sharp Corner(s)

5. Adding the Sheet Metal tool tab:

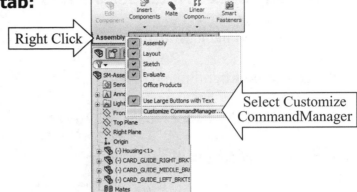

- In an assembly, if the Sheet Metal tool tab is not visible on the CommandManager, do the following to add it:

- Right click on the Assembly tool tab and select the **Customized CommandManager** option (arrow).

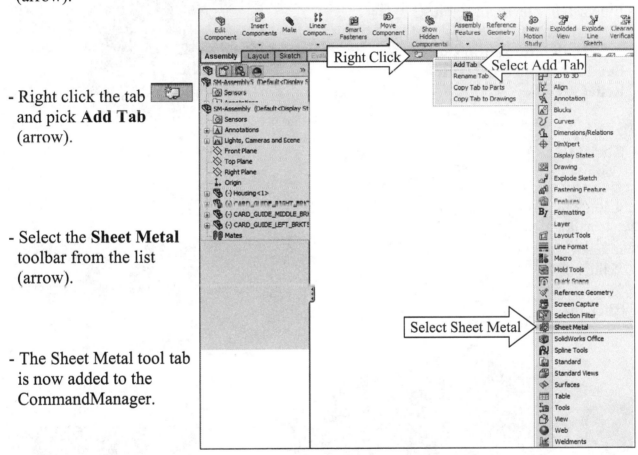

- Right click the tab and pick **Add Tab** (arrow).

- Select the **Sheet Metal** toolbar from the list (arrow).

- The Sheet Metal tool tab is now added to the CommandManager.

- Switch to the Sheet Metal tool tab (arrow).

6. Inserting Sheet Metal parameters*:

- Select the component **Housing** and click the

Edit Component command.

- From the Sheet Metal tool tab

click the **Insert Bends** command.

- Select the **Fixed face** as noted.

- Enter **.010"** for Bend Radius.

- Use the **default settings** for **Bend Allowance** and **Auto-Relief**.

- Click **OK**.

- A message appears indicating that Auto Relief Cuts were added to some of the corners of the part.

- Click OK.

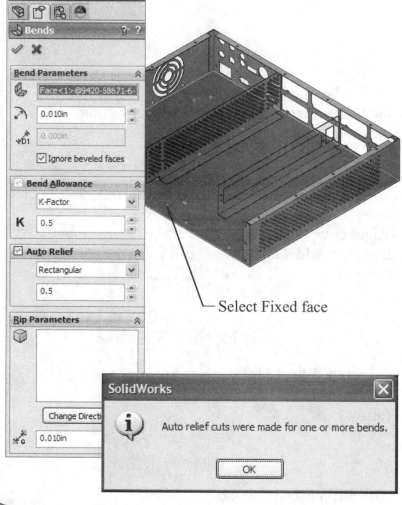

Select Fixed face

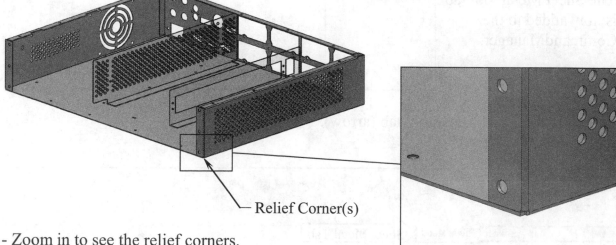

Relief Corner(s)

- Zoom in to see the relief corners.

7. Viewing the Flat Pattern:

- From the Sheet Metal tool tab, click the

Flatten command 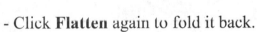 .

- The Housing is flattened. The orientation of the flattened view is based on the Fixed face that was specified in step number 6.

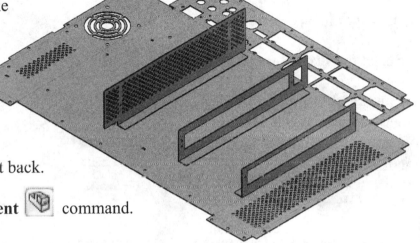

- Click **Flatten** again to fold it back.

- Click-off the **Edit Component** command.

8. Converting the 2nd component:

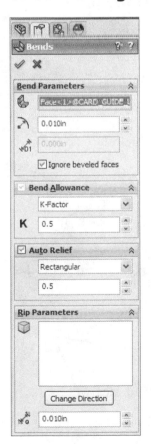

- Select the **Card Guide Left** as shown and click the

Edit Component command.

- From the Sheet Metal tool tab, select **Insert Bends** command.

- Select the **Fixed face** as noted.

- Enter **.010"** for Radius.

- Click **OK** .

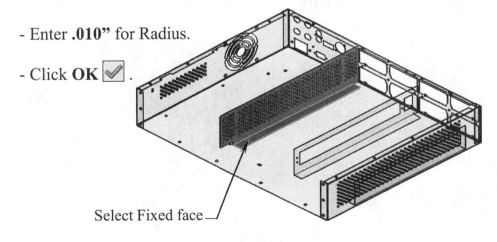

Select Fixed face

- Click off the **Edit Component** command.

9. Converting the 3rd component:

- Select the **Card Guide Middle** as shown and click the **Edit-Component** command.

- From the Sheet Metal tool tab select **Insert Bends** .

- Select the **Fixed face** as noted.

- Enter **.010"** for Bend Radius and use the **default settings** for the Bend Allowance and K-Factor.

- Click **OK** .

- Click-off the **Edit Component** command.

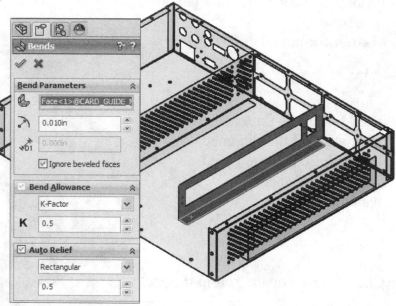

10. Converting the 4th component:

- Select the **Card Guide Right** as shown and click the **Edit Component** command.

- From the Sheet Metal tool tab, click: **Insert Bends** .

- Select the **Fixed face** as noted.

- Enter **.010"** for Bend Radius.

- Click **OK** .

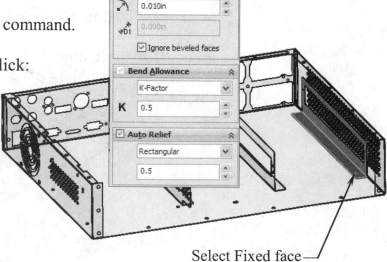

Select Fixed face

- Click-off the **Edit Component** command.

11. Using the Hole-Series:

- The hole series is an Assembly Feature, used to create a series of holes through the individual parts of an assembly.

- Unlike other assembly features, the holes are contained in the individual parts as externally referenced features. If you edit a hole series within an assembly, the individual parts are modified.

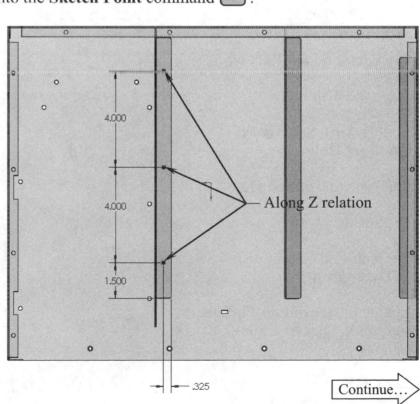

- From the Assembly tool tab, select **Assembly Features / Hole Series** .

- From the FeatureManager, click **Create New Hole**.

- The mouse cursor changes into the **Sketch Point** command .

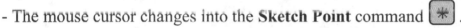

- Create **3 points** approximately as shown.

- Each point will become the center of a hole.

- Add an **ALONG Z** relation (Vertical) between the 3 points.

- Add the dimensions as indicated to fully define the positions of the points.

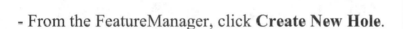

Along Z relation

4.000

4.000

1.500

.325

Continue...

- Click the **First Part** tab.

- Click the **Countersink** option.

- Select the following:

Standard: **Ansi Inch**

Type: **Flat Head Screw**

Size: **#4**

Fit: **Normal**

- Use the default settings for Custom Sizing.

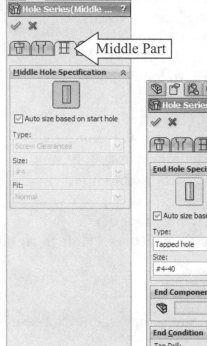

- Click the **Middle Part** tab.

- Enable the check box:

Auto Size based on Start Hole.

- Click on the **Last Part** tab.

- Click the **Tap** button.

- Enable **Auto Size Based On Start Hole**.

- Set Type to **Tapped Hole**.

- Set Size to **#4-40**.

- Set both End Conditions to **Through All**.

- Enable the **Cosmetic Thread** and **With Thread Callout**.

- Click **OK** .

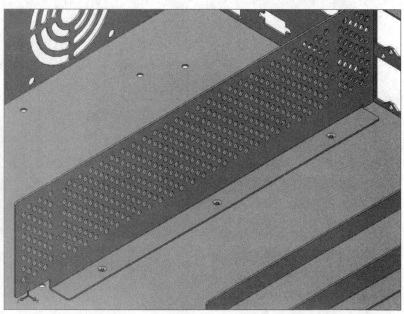

12. Using the Hole Wizard:

- Hole wizard is an Assembly Feature, which creates these types of holes:

- Counterbore
- Countersink
- Hole
- Straight Tap
- Tapered Tap
- Legacy

- From the Assembly tool tab, click **Assembly Features / Hole Wizard**.

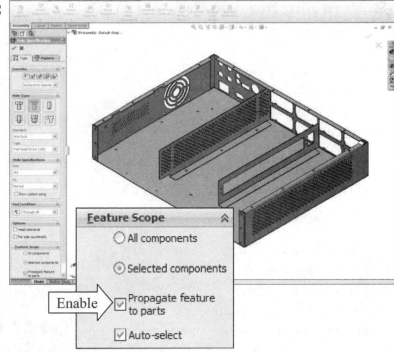

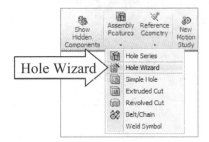

- Select the **Countersink** option under the **Type** tab.

- Set the options **to match** the last 3 holes in step number 11.

- Switch to the **Positions** tab.

- Click approximately as shown to create **3 points**.

- Each point represents the center for that hole.

- Add relation and dimensions as indicated.

- Click **OK** ✓.

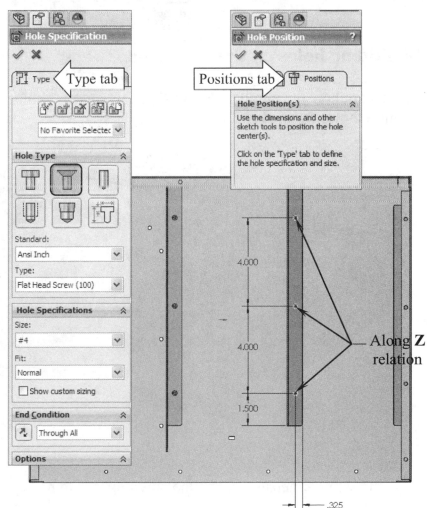

13. Verifying the two hole types:

- Even though the 6 holes were created with 2 different hole options, they are exactly identical.

- Open the Card Guide Middle to verify that the holes are actually there on the part.

- The new feature in step 12 (propagate feature to parts) allows these Assembly Features to appear in the part mode as well.

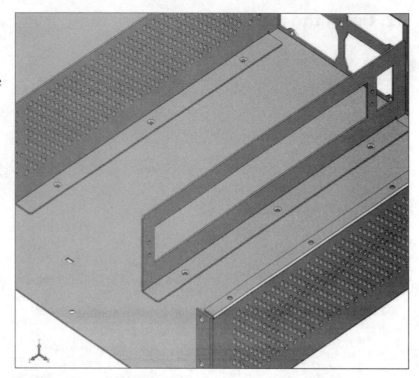

14. Adding holes on the Card Guide Right:

- Repeat either step number 11 (Hole Series) or step number 12 (Hole Wizard) and create 3 more holes for the last Card Guide.

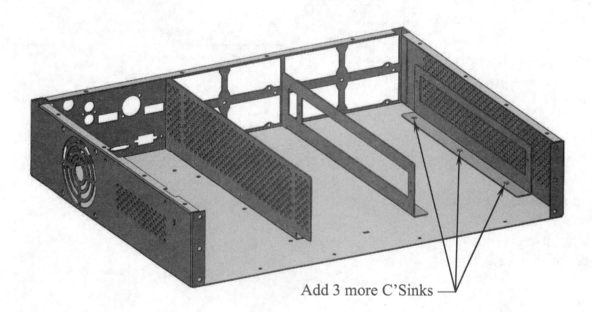

Add 3 more C'Sinks ⎯

- Use the same dimensions from the previous step to position the holes.

15. Adding the Smart Fasteners:

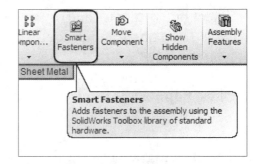

- Click **Smart Fasteners**  from the Assembly tool tab.

- An error message appears asking for SolidWorks Toolbox to be activated** (Required SolidWorks Office Professional or SolidWorks Premium).

** To activate Toolbox, go to:

       - **Tools / Add Ins**.

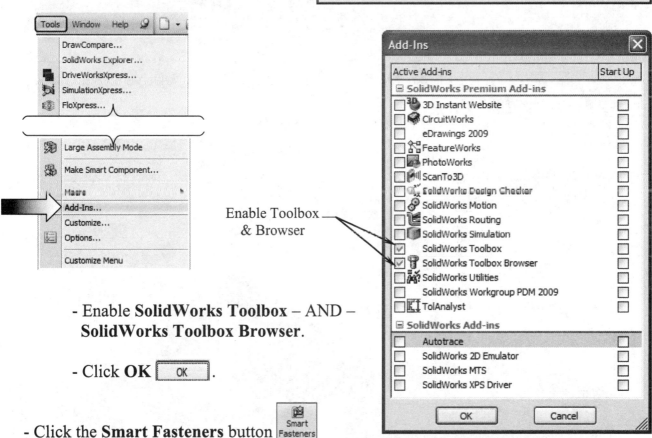

Enable Toolbox & Browser

- Enable **SolidWorks Toolbox** – AND – **SolidWorks Toolbox Browser**.

- Click **OK**.

- Click the **Smart Fasteners** button once again.

- Another message pops up indicating that the Smart Fasteners calculation may take extra time, click **OK**.

- Select one of the C'sink
  holes from the graphics area.

- Click **Populate All** (arrow).

- The system searches for the
  best matched screws from
  its Toolbox library and
  automatically inserts them
  into each hole.

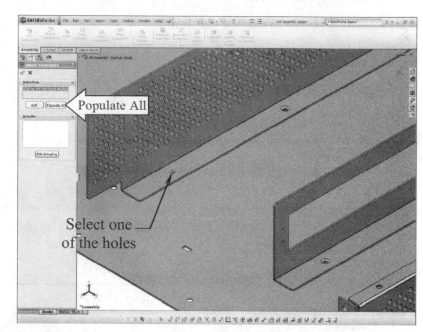

- Set the following properties:

- Size: **#4-40**   Length: **.125"**   Drive Type: **Cross**

- Thread Display: **Simplified**

- Click **OK** ☑ .

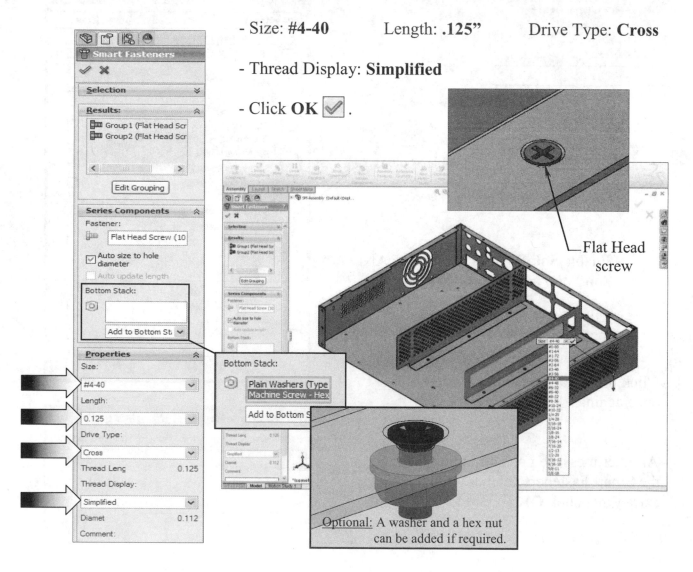

Flat Head
screw

Optional: A washer and a hex nut
can be added if required.

16. Creating an Exploded View:

Option 1

- Create an exploded view with all 4 parts
  show in folded stage as shown.

- When an exploded view is created, SolidWorks
  also creates an animated configuration, which
  can be played back and saved as an AVI
  file format.

Option 2

- Create a 2nd exploded view with all
  4 parts as shown in the Flatten view below.

NOTES:

- *Edit each component in order to switch from the
  Folded to flatten stage).*

- *Configurations can also be used to capture
  the flat pattern of each component.*

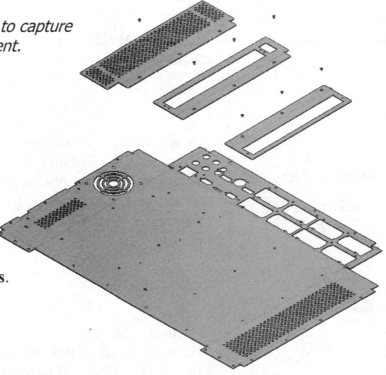

17. Saving your work:

- Click **File / Save As**.

- For the name of the file enter:
  SM_Assembly_Smart Fasteners.

- Click **Save**.

- Close all documents.

Weldments – Structural Members

The options in Weldments allows you to develop a weldment structure as a single multibody-part. The basic framework is defined using a 2D or a 3D sketch, then structural members like square or round Tubes are added by sweeping the tube profile along the framework. Gussets, end caps, and weld-beads can also be added using the tools on the **Weldments** toolbar.

1. Opening an existing document:

- Open a file named **Weldment Frame** from the Training CD.

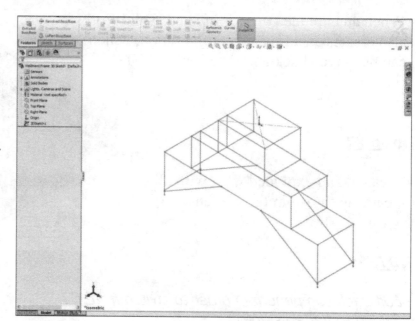

2. Enabling the Weldment toolbar:

- Click **View / Toolbar** and select the **Weldment toolbar** from the list (arrow).

- Click the **Weldment button** from the weldment toolbar.

Weldment
Creates a weldment feature to enable the weldment environment.

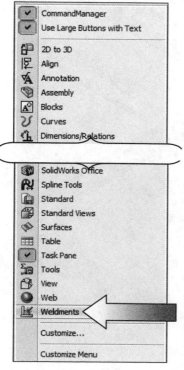

- A Weldment Feature appears on the feature tree along with a Weldment Cut List (arrows), which indicates the items from the model to include in this cut list.

- A single 3D Sketch is created for the purpose of this exercise. In reality, multiple sketches (2D & 3D) can be used to work with weldments.

3. Adding Structural Members:

- Click the **Structural Member** button from the Weldment toolbar.

- Select the following:

- **Ansi Inch.**
- **Square Tube**
- **4 X 4 X 0.25**

- Click the **4 lines** on the top of the frame.

- Select the **MITER** under Apply Corner-Treatment.

- Click **OK**.

- By default, the profile of the tube is automatically centered on the end of each line.

- Try out all 3 options for corner treatments: End Miter, End Butt,1and End Butt2.

- Switch back to the End Miter option when finished.

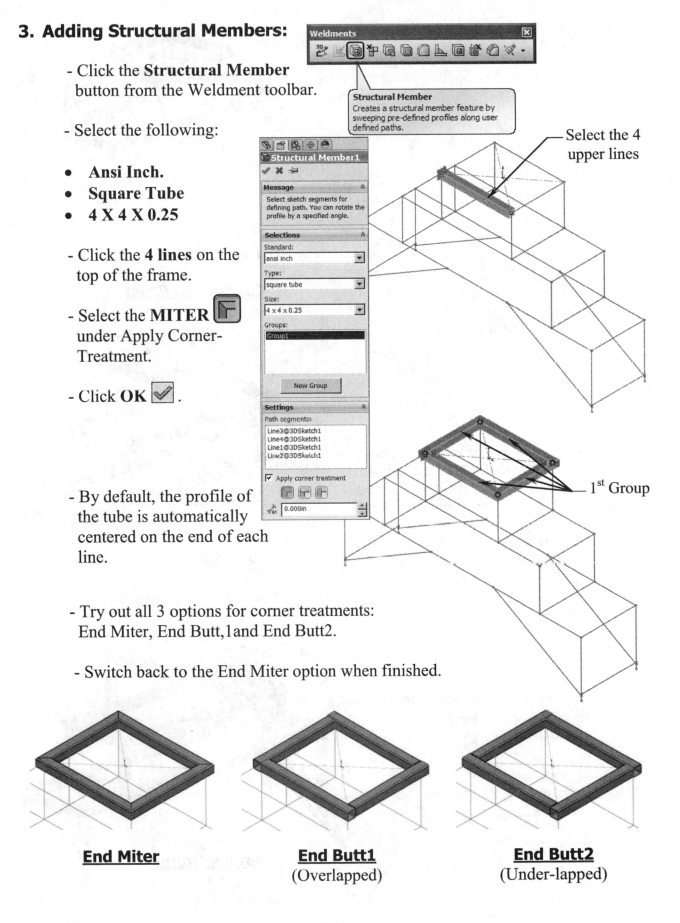

| **End Miter** | **End Butt1**
(Overlapped) | **End Butt2**
(Under-lapped) |

4. Adding Structural Members to Contiguous Groups*:

- Repeat the previous Step and add another 4 square tubes to the 2nd group as shown.

- Use these same settings:

- **Ansi Inch.**
- **Square Tube**
- **4 X 4 X 0.25**

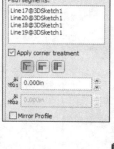

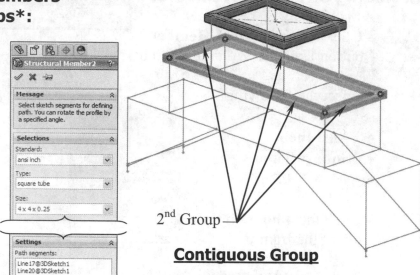

2nd Group——

Contiguous Group

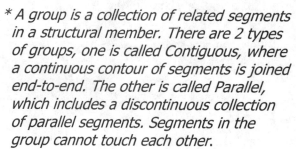

* A group is a collection of related segments in a structural member. There are 2 types of groups, one is called Contiguous, where a continuous contour of segments is joined end-to-end. The other is called Parallel, which includes a discontinuous collection of parallel segments. Segments in the group cannot touch each other.

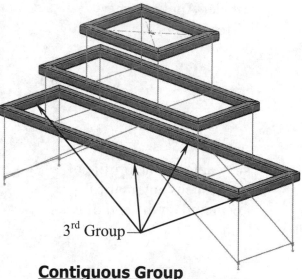

3rd Group——

Contiguous Group

- Repeat the same step for the 3rd group.

- Follow the same procedure and add the same size tubing to the vertical members as note for the 4th group.

Note: Select the exact same members on both sides (total of 12).

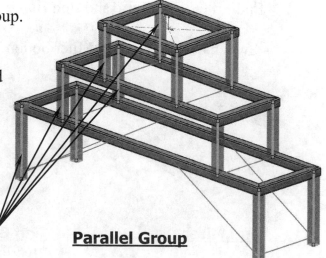

4th Group——
(both sides)

Parallel Group

5. Adding Structural Members to the Parallel Groups:

- Repeat the previous step and add the same structural members to the 5th group as indicated.

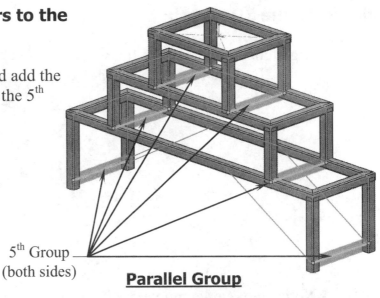

5th Group
(both sides)

Parallel Group

 Note

You can define a group in a single plane or in multiple planes. A 3D sketch is best suited for weldment designs since all entities can be drawn and controlled in the same sketch.

- Create the same type of structural Members for the 6th and 7th group, which has only 2 lines in each group...

6th Group
Rotate 30 deg.

- Rotate the profile to **30 deg.** for the 6th group and **60 deg.** for the 7th group.

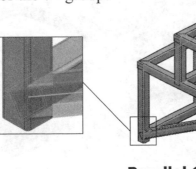

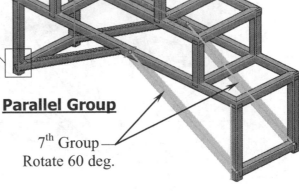

Parallel Group

7th Group
Rotate 60 deg.

- There are several over-lapped areas that need trimming, we will look into that in the next steps.

6. Hiding the 3D sketch:

- Right click on one of the lines
  in the 3D sketch and select **Hide**.

- Notice the overlapping areas in the enlarged view below?
  For practice purposes, we will learn to use different trim
  options to cut the tubes to their exact lengths and angles.

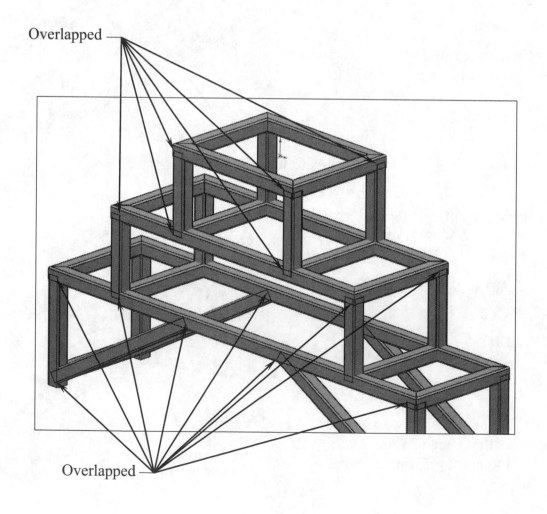

Overlapped

Overlapped

7. Trimming the Structural Members:

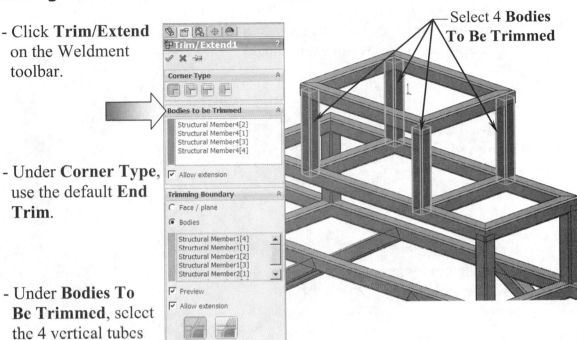

- Click **Trim/Extend** on the Weldment toolbar.

- Under **Corner Type**, use the default **End Trim**.

- Under **Bodies To Be Trimmed**, select the 4 vertical tubes as shown.

Select 4 **Bodies To Be Trimmed**

- Under **Trimming Boundary**, select the **Body** option (arrow).

- Select the 6 horizontal tubes as indicated, for use as trimming bodies.

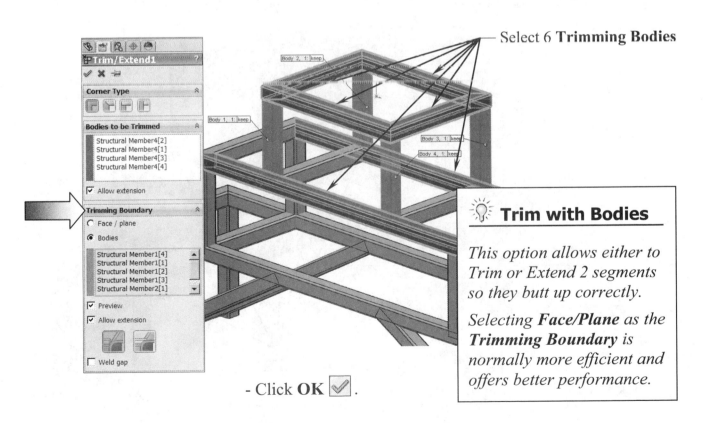

Select 6 **Trimming Bodies**

Trim with Bodies

This option allows either to Trim or Extend 2 segments so they butt up correctly.

*Selecting **Face/Plane** as the **Trimming Boundary** is normally more efficient and offers better performance.*

- Click **OK**.

8. Trimming the Parallel Groups:

- Select the **Trim/Extend** command once again from the weldment toolbar.

- Click in the **Bodies To Be Trimmed**

dialog to activate it and select the next 4 vertical tubes as noted.

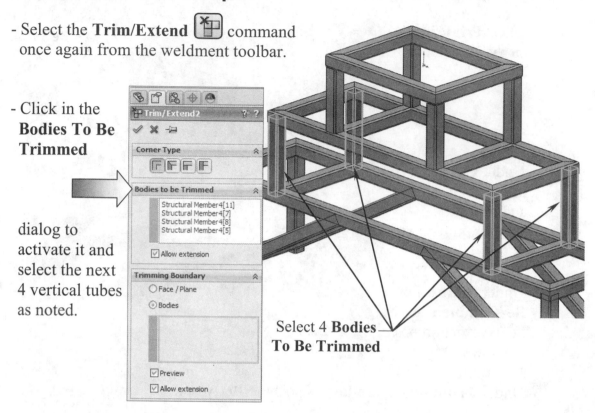

Select 4 **Bodies To Be Trimmed**

- For **Trimming Boundary**, select the **Body** option again (Arrow).

- Select the 6 horizontal tubes as shown, for use as trimming bodies.

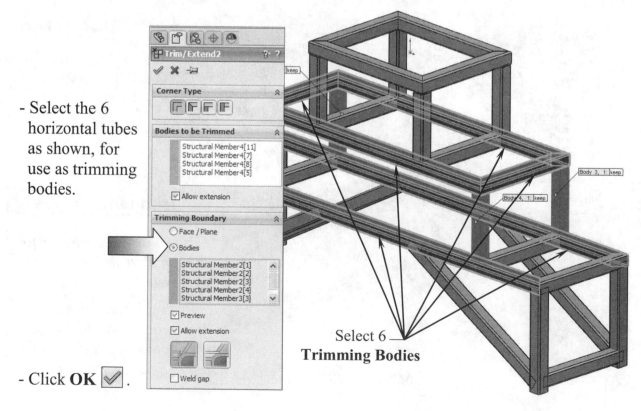

Select 6 **Trimming Bodies**

- Click **OK**.

9. Trimming the next sets of Parallel Groups:

- Select the **Trim/Extend** 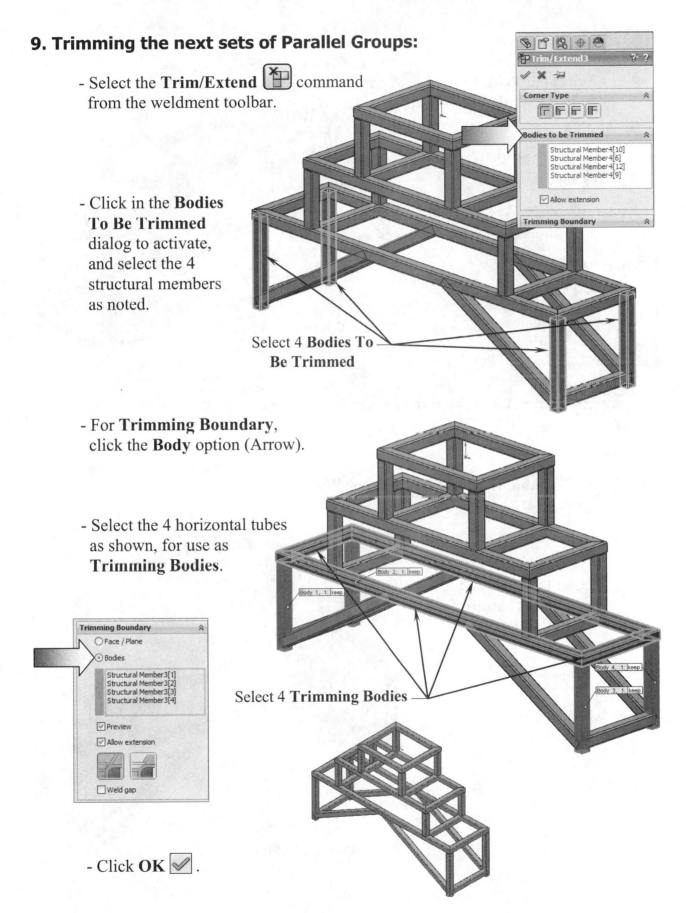 command from the weldment toolbar.

- Click in the **Bodies To Be Trimmed** dialog to activate, and select the 4 structural members as noted.

Select 4 **Bodies To Be Trimmed**

- For **Trimming Boundary**, click the **Body** option (Arrow).

- Select the 4 horizontal tubes as shown, for use as **Trimming Bodies**.

Select 4 **Trimming Bodies**

- Click **OK** .

10. More Trimming:

- Select the **Trim/Extend**  command from the weldment toolbar.

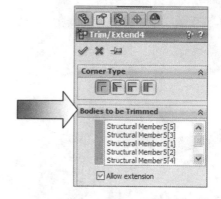

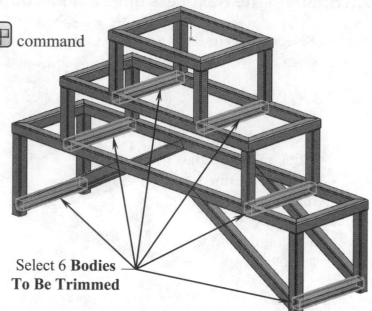

Select 6 **Bodies To Be Trimmed**

- For **Bodies To Be Trimmed** select the 6 structural members as indicated.

- For **Trimming Boundary**, click the **Body** option (Arrow).

- Select the 8 horizontal structural members as shown, for **Trimming Bodies**.

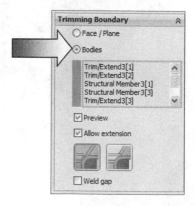

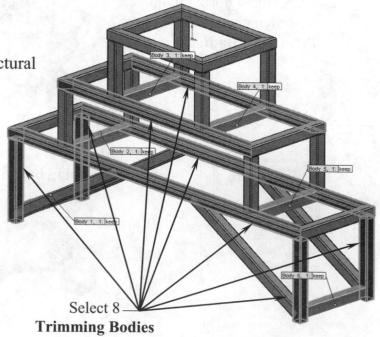

Select 8 **Trimming Bodies**

- Click **OK** ✓.

11. Trimming with Face/Plane:

- Select the **Trim/Extend** 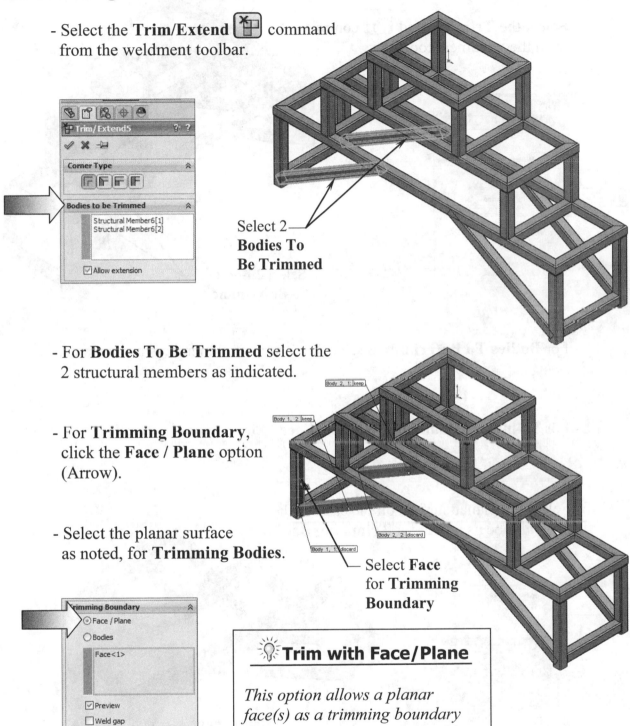 command from the weldment toolbar.

Select 2
**Bodies To
Be Trimmed**

- For **Bodies To Be Trimmed** select the 2 structural members as indicated.

- For **Trimming Boundary**, click the **Face / Plane** option (Arrow).

- Select the planar surface as noted, for **Trimming Bodies**.

Select **Face**
for **Trimming
Boundary**

💡 Trim with Face/Plane

This option allows a planar face(s) as a trimming boundary to trim one or more solid bodies.

*Selecting **Face/Plane** as the **Trimming Boundary** is normally more efficient and offers better performance.*

- Click **OK** .

12. More Trimming with Face/Plane:

- Select the **Trim/Extend** command from the weldment toolbar.

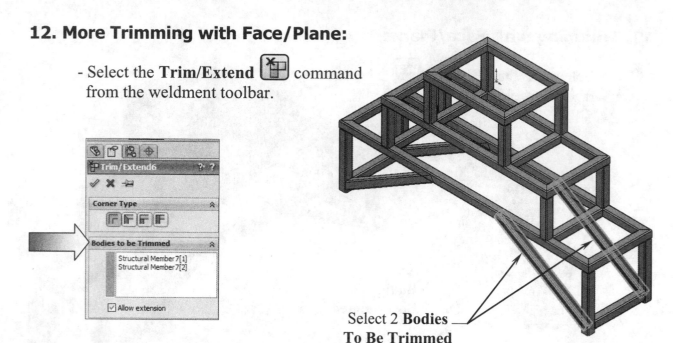

Select 2 **Bodies**
To Be Trimmed

- For **Bodies To Be Trimmed** select the 2 structural members as indicated.

- For **Trimming Boundary**, click the **Face / Plane** option (Arrow).

- Select the planar surface on the back of the vertical tube as noted, for **Trimming Bodies**.

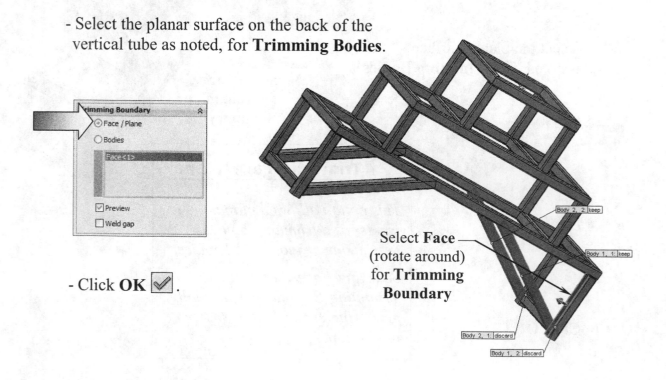

Select **Face**
(rotate around)
for **Trimming**
Boundary

- Click **OK** .

13. Trimming the last 4 structural members:

- Select the **Trim/Extend** 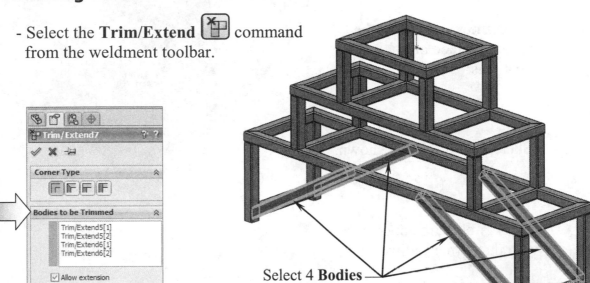 command from the weldment toolbar.

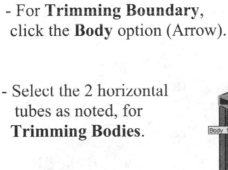

Select 4 **Bodies To Be Trimmed**

- For **Bodies To Be Trimmed** select the 4 structural members as shown.

- For **Trimming Boundary**, click the **Body** option (Arrow).

- Select the 2 horizontal tubes as noted, for **Trimming Bodies**.

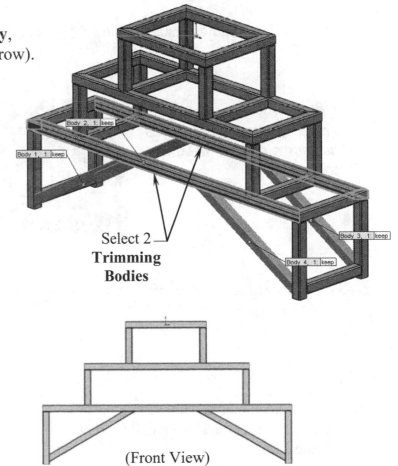

Select 2 **Trimming Bodies**

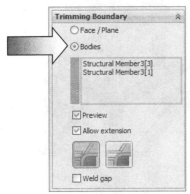

- Click **OK** .

(Front View)

14. Adding the foot pads:

- Insert a new sketch on the bottom surface of one of the 4 legs.

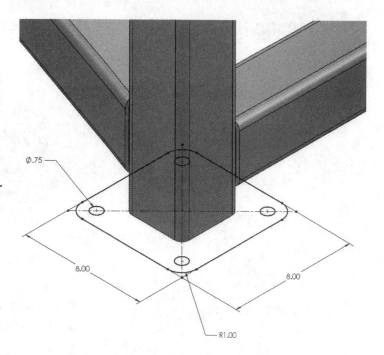

- Sketch the profile as shown.

- The 4 circles are concentric with the corner radius.

- Add the dimensions and relations needed to fully define the sketch.

- Mirror the sketch to make a total of 4 foot pads.

<u>Note:</u>
Add a couple of centerlines as shown prior to making the mirror.

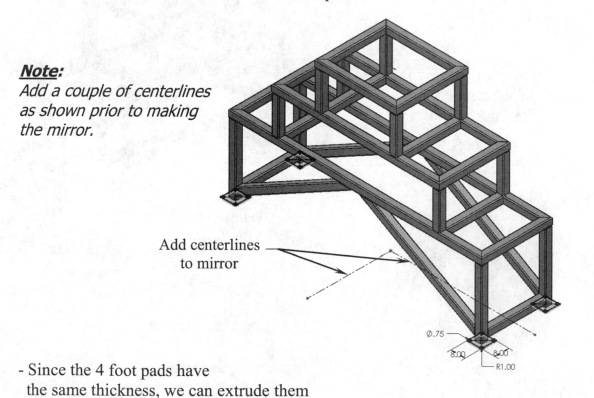

Add centerlines to mirror

- Since the 4 foot pads have the same thickness, we can extrude them at the same time.

- Click **Extruded Boss/ Base**.

- Enter the following:

  * Type: **Blind**

  * Depth: **1.000**

- Click **OK** ✓ .

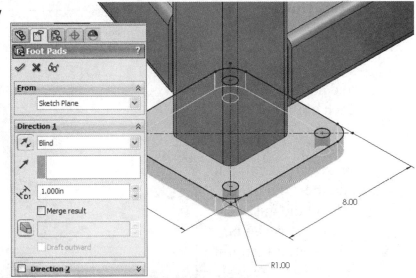

15. Adding the Gussets:

- Rotate and zoom to an orientation that looks similar to the view below.

- Click the **Gusset** Command.

- For **Supporting Faces**, Select the **2 faces** as indicated.

- Enter the following:

  * Distance1: **5.00 in.**

  * Distance2: **5.00 in.**

  * Distance3: **.500 in.**

  * Thickness: **.500"**
    (Both Sides)

  * Location: **Midpoint**

- Click **OK** ✓ .

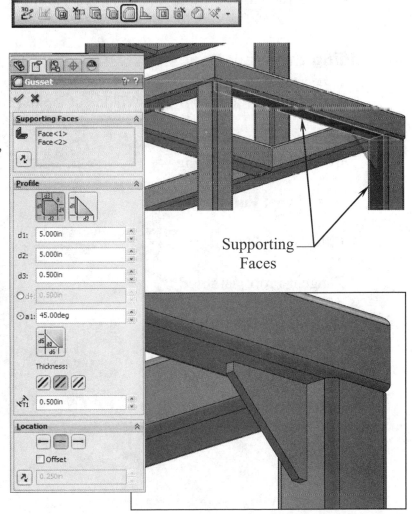

Supporting Faces

16. Adding more Gussets:

- Repeat the step 15 and add a gusset to each corner of the frame.

- Next, we're going to add the weld beads around the gussets. Weld beads can be added as full length, intermittent, or staggered fillet weld beads between any intersecting weldment entities such as structural members, plate weldments, or gussets.

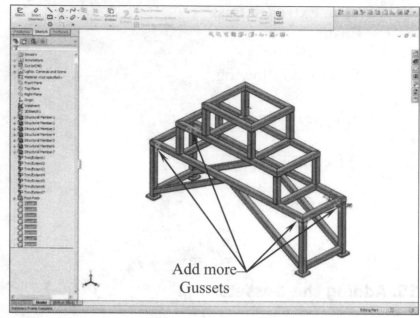

Add more Gussets

17. Adding the Weld Beads:

- Click Fillet Bead  on the Weldment toolbar.

- From the Weld Bead properties tree, enter the following:

* Bead Type: **Full Length**

* Fillet Size: **.250 in.**

* Tangent Prop: **Enabled**

* Face Set1: **Select the 2 faces** as noted.

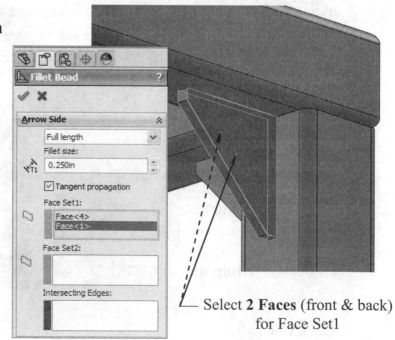

Select **2 Faces** (front & back) for Face Set1

(continue on next page...)

- For **Face Set2**, select the next 2
faces as indicated.

*(Intersecting Edges.
Highlights edges where
Face Set1 and Face Set2
intersect. You can right-
click an edge and select
Delete to remove from
the weld bead).*

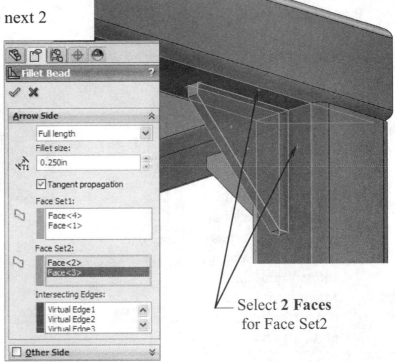

- Enable the **Other
Side** check box
and apply the
same settings
to the back
end of the gusset.

Select **2 Faces**
for Face Set2

- Different bead type
or fillet size can be
added to the other
side, but we are going
to use the same settings
as the first side.

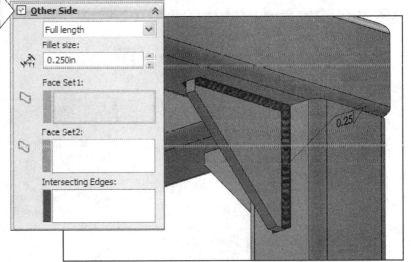

- Click **OK** ✅.

- A bead call out is added automatically (see example
below).

Example: *0.25 = Length of the leg of the fillet bead.*
0.375 = Length of each bead segment.
0.7 = Distance between the start of each bead.

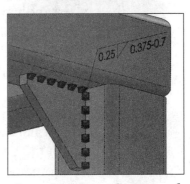

Intermittent or Staggered

18. Adding more Fillet Beads:

- Repeat step 17 and add a set of fillet beads to each gusset that was created earlier.

- When adding the fillet beads, try using the different types of beads: Full Length, Intermittent, and Staggered to see the different results and callouts.

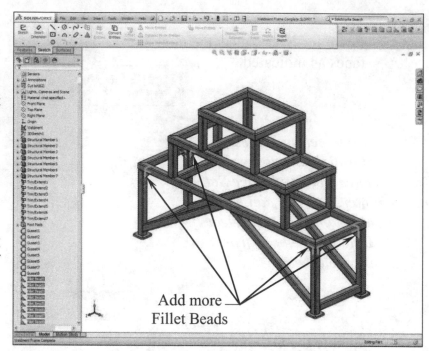

Add more Fillet Beads

19. Viewing the Weldment Cut List:

- Locate the **Cut List** on the FeatureManager tree and click the Plus (+) sign to expand.

- The Cut List needs to be updated every time something is added to the model.

- An icon in front of the cut list indicates that it needs updating and the icon indicates the list is up to date.

- The current list displays all items in the order that they were created. We will update the list in the next step.

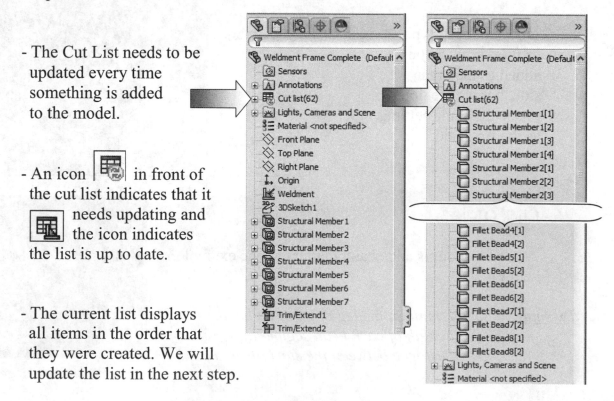

20. Updating the Cut List:

- Right click on the cut list and select **Update** (arrow).

- Notice the option **Automatic** is on by default? This option organizes all of the weldment entities in the cut list for the new weldment parts.

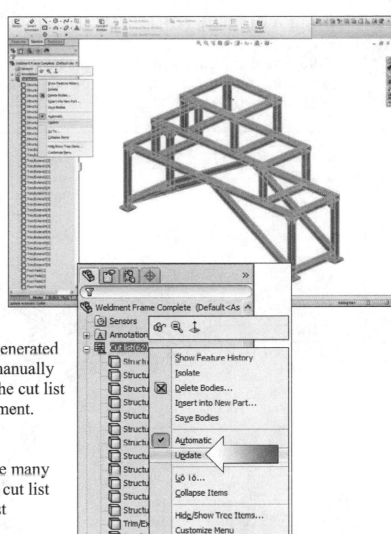

- Although the cut list is generated automatically, you can manually specify when to update the cut list in a weldment part document.

- This enables you to make many changes, then update the cut list once; however the cut list updates automatically when you open a drawing that references the list.

- At this time, the icon in front of the cut list is changed to which indicates the cut list is now up to date.

- The cut list Table can now be viewed by accessing the Properties of one of the item folders.

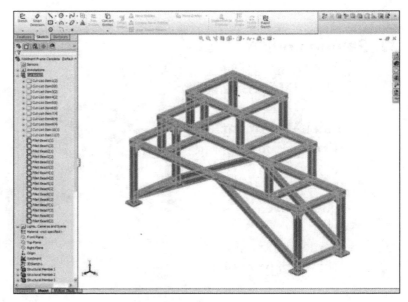

21. Creating a drawing (OPTIONAL):

- A drawing that includes the cut list can be generated. (Refer to the part 2 of the Basic Tools textbook for more information on how to create a detail drawing in SolidWorks 2012).

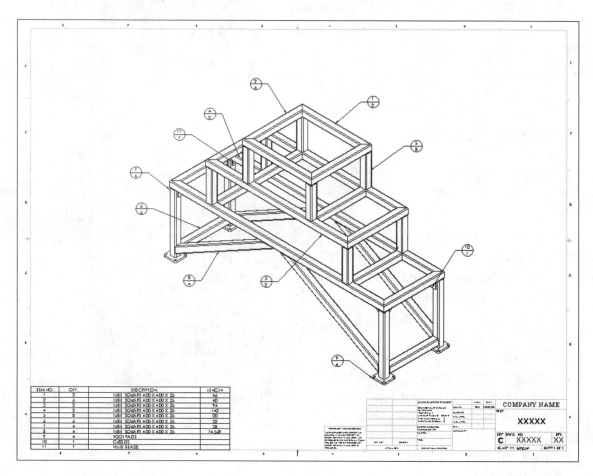

22. Saving your work:

- Click **File / Save As**.

- Enter **Weldment Frame** for the name of the file.

- Click **Save**.

- Replace the existing file when prompted.

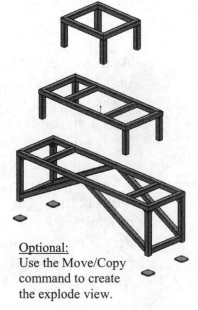

Optional:
Use the Move/Copy command to create the explode view.

CHAPTER 17

Core & Cavity – Assembly Level

Creating a Core & Cavity Assembly Level

- Creating new parts in the context of an assembly by using the existing geometry and positions of other parts. To build and reference the new parts allows the components involved to be fully associated with each other.

- In the Top down Assembly mode (also called In-Context Assembly), when a face or plane is selected as a sketch plane for the new part, the system creates an INPLACE mate to reference the new part. (Only one Inplace mate is generated for each component)

- When active the Inplace mate keeps the component fixed, but when it is suppressed the component can be moved or re-positioned.

- When a component is being edited, the Edit Component icon is selected and the part's color on the Feature tree is changed to Blue (or Magenta, depending on the color settings selected by the user).

- In Top Down Assembly mode, the active component remains its default color while other components are turned to transparent. (This option can be changed under: *Tools/Options/Display Selection/Assembly Transparency For In Context Edit*, by dragging the transparency slider back or forth.

- The Scale feature is used when creating the core and cavity. To increase the overall size of the part to accommodate the shrinkage; the scale feature changes the part's size, but not its dimensions and changes done to the engineered part will pass onto the 2 halves automatically.

Creating a Core and Cavity
Assembly Level

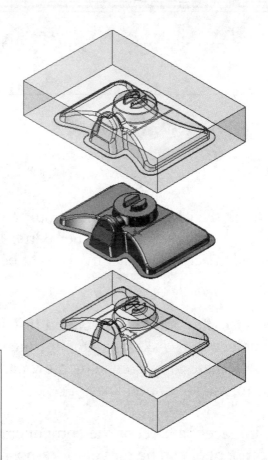

Dimensioning Standards: **ANSI**

Units: **INCHES** – 3 Decimals

Tools Needed:

Insert Sketch	Convert Entities	Scale
Radiate Surface	Knit Surface	Plane
Base/Boss Extrude	Edit Component	Exploded View

1. Opening the existing IGES document:

- Click **File / Open**. Change the File Type to **IGS**.

- Browse to the Training CD and open a document named: **Tooling.IGS**.

- Click **No** to close the Import Diagnostics box.

2. Scaling the part*:

- Click 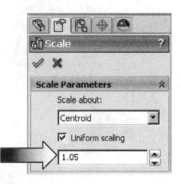 or select **Insert / Features / Scale**.

- Scale About: **Centroid**.

- Uniform Scaling: **Enabled**.

- Scale Factor: **1.05%**

- Click **OK** ⊘.

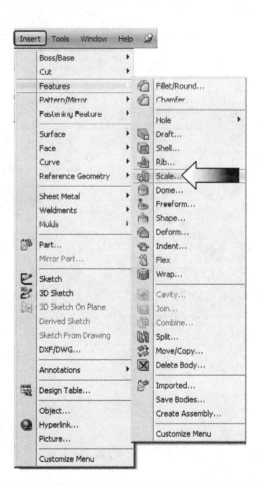

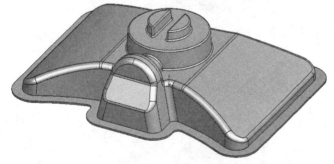

__Scale:__

- *The scale feature changes the part's size, but not its dimensions to accommodate for the material shrinkage.*
- *When a drawing is made from the scaled part, the original dimensions will be shown in the drawing views.*
- *The scaled feature appears in the Feature Manager tree, its value and type can be altered.*

---

3. Creating the Radiate Surface:

- Click  or select **Insert / Surface / Radiate**.

- Select the **upper face** for Radiate Direction.

- Select the **bottom edges** for Edges to Radiate.

- Enter **1.750 in**. for Radiate Distance.

Radiate Surfaces

A radiate surface is a surface created from the parting lines, an edge, or a set of continuous edges inwards or outwards, and parallel to a selected plane (or Perpendicular with the direction of pull).

Radiate Surface
Radiates a surface originating from an edge parallel to a plane.

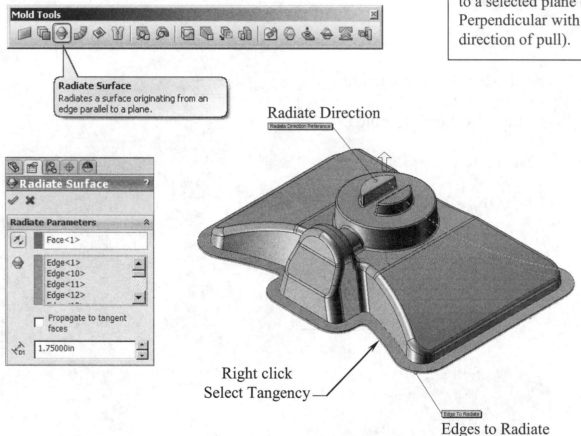

Radiate Direction

Right click
Select Tangency

Edges to Radiate

- Click **OK**.

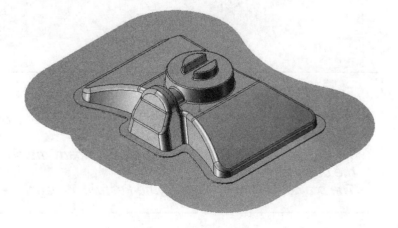

- The resulted Radiate Surface.

4. Transferring the part to Assembly:

- Click the **Make Assembly From Part** button or select: **File / Make-Assembly From Part**.

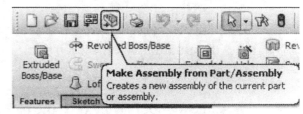

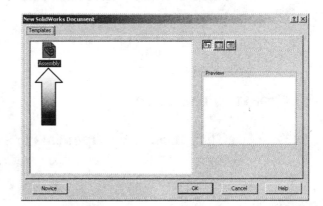

- Select an **Assembly** template and click **OK**.

- If the origin is not visible, select it from the View pull down menu.

- The part Tooling is automatically attached to the mouse cursor.

- Place the part on the Origin as indicated.

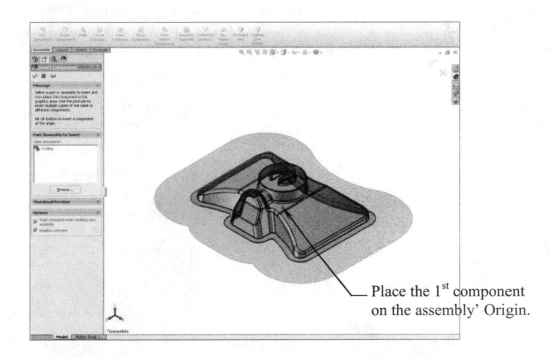

Place the 1st component on the assembly' Origin.

5. Saving the assembly:

- Save the assembly document as **<u>Core and Cavity</u>**.

- The 1st part (Tooling part) is fixed automatically on the Origin.

- The symbol **(f)** next to the part's name indicates that it has been fixed and cannot be moved or rotated.

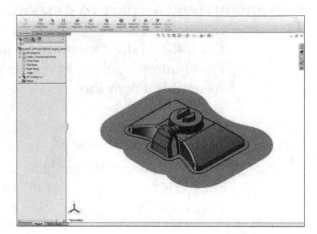

6. Creating the Core:

- Click **Insert / Components / New Part**.

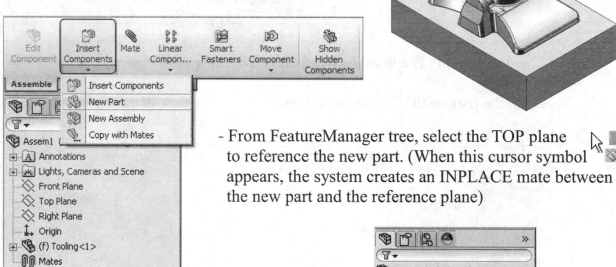

- From FeatureManager tree, select the TOP plane to reference the new part. (When this cursor symbol appears, the system creates an INPLACE mate between the new part and the reference plane)

- From the FeatureManager tree, right click the part:[Part1^Assem]<1> and select **Rename**.

- Enter: **Core** for the new name.

- **Exit** the Sketch (the Knit surface must be created first).

- The Knit option is only available when the sketch mode is not active.

7. Knitting the surfaces to form a new part:

- Click ⬚ or select **Insert / Surface / Knit**.

- First, select the Radiated surface for Faces to Knit ⬚ .

- Second, select one of the faces on the <u>Inside</u> as indicated for Seed Faces ⬚ . Clear the Gap Control checkbox.

- Click **OK** ✓.

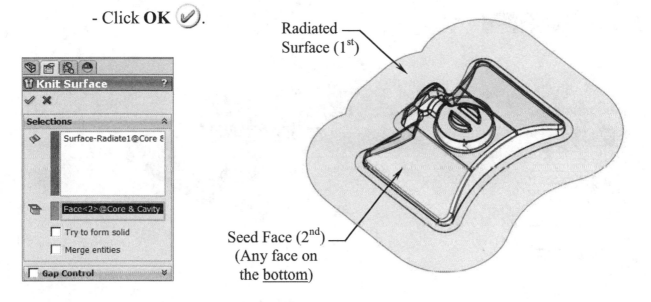

Radiated Surface (1st)

Seed Face (2nd) (Any face on the <u>bottom</u>)

8. Hiding the engineered part:

- Right click over the part **Tooling** and select **Hide Components** ⬚ .

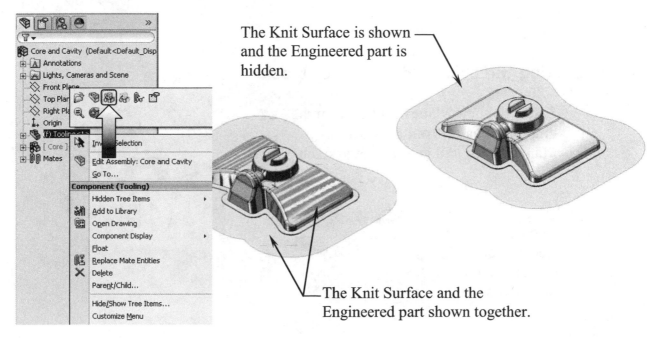

The Knit Surface is shown and the Engineered part is hidden.

The Knit Surface and the Engineered part shown together.

9. Creating a new work plane:

- Click 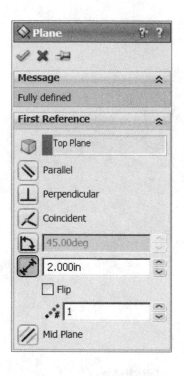 or select **Insert / Reference Geometry / Plane**.

- Select the **Offset Distance** option and enter **2.00 in**.

- Select the TOP plane of the assembly (or the part's Front plane) for offset.

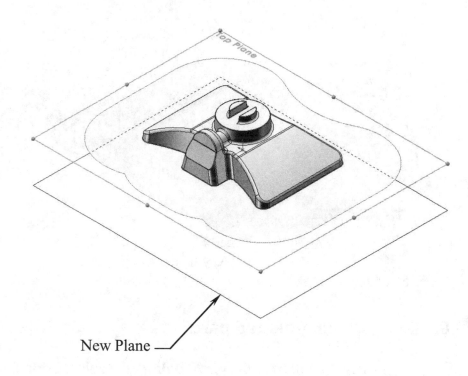

New Plane

- Click **OK** ✓.

10. Sketching the profile of the lower block:

- Select the new Plane1, either from the graphics area or from the Feature-Manager tree and insert a new sketch.

- Sketch a Corner-Rectangle that is centered on the origin as shown.

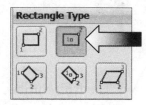

- Add the width and height dimensions shown.

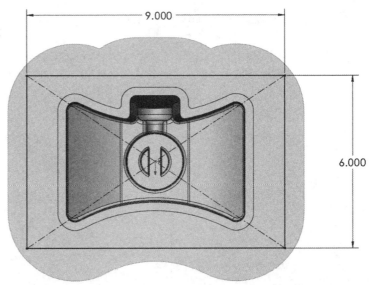

- The sketch should be fully defined at this point.

11. Extruding the lower block:

- Click  or select **Insert / Boss-Base / Extrude**.

- Direction 1: **Up to Surface**.

- Click the **Radiated** surface as Face/Plane end condition.

- Click **OK** ✓.

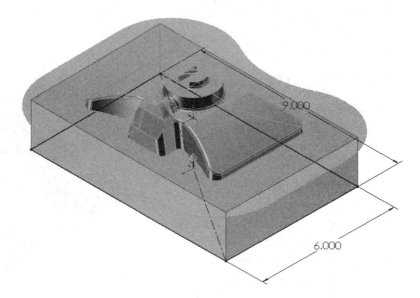

- The Core is created; this is the 1st half of the mold.

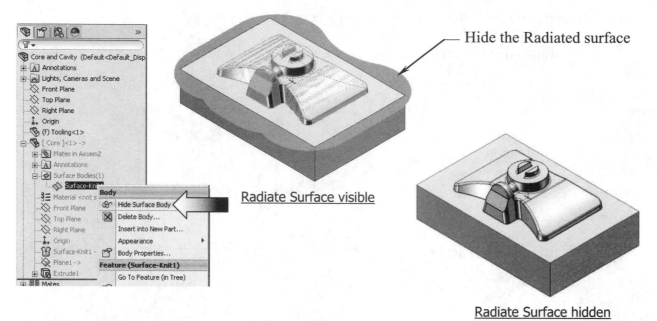

Hide the Radiated surface

Radiate Surface visible

Radiate Surface hidden

12. Returning to the assembly mode:

- Click ⬛ or right-click the part and select **Edit Assembly** to exit the part mode.

13. Showing the hidden part:

- Right click over the name **Tooling** and select **Show**.

- The engineered part reappears. It will be used again to help create the upper half of the mold (the cavity).

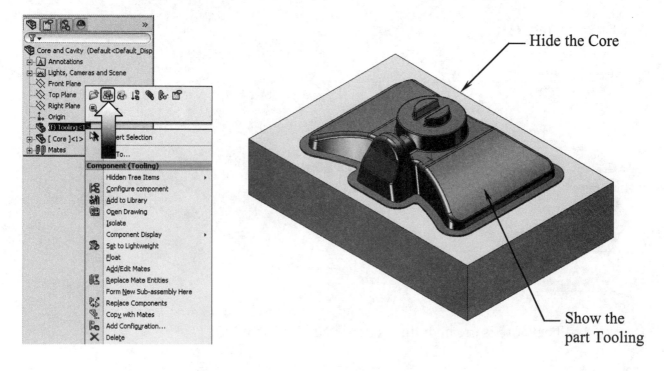

Hide the Core

Show the part Tooling

14. Creating the Cavity: (Repeat from step 5)

- Select **Insert / Components / New Part**.

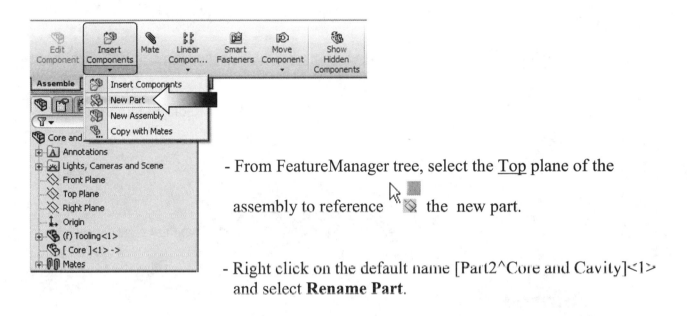

- From FeatureManager tree, select the <u>Top</u> plane of the assembly to reference the new part.

- Right click on the default name [Part2^Core and Cavity]<1> and select **Rename Part**.

- Enter: **Cavity** for the new name.

- The system creates an INPLACE mate between the new part and the Top reference plane. The new part is fixed.

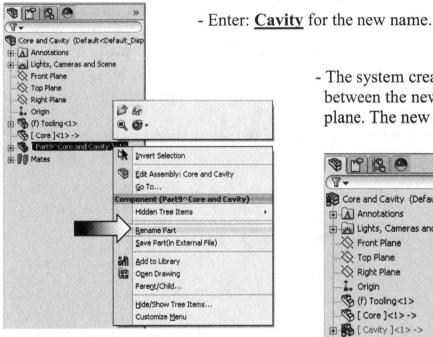

- **Exit** the Sketch or select **Insert / Sketch**; the Knit-Surface must be created first.

15. Knitting the surfaces to form a new part:

- Click 📖 or select **Insert / Surface / Knit**.

- Select the **Radiated** surface as Surfaces and Faces to Knit 📖 .

- Select the face indicated as Seed Faces 📦 . Clear the Gap Control checkbox.

- Click **OK** ✅ .

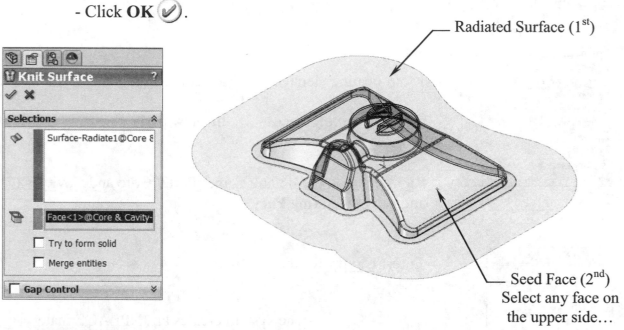

Radiated Surface (1ˢᵗ)

Seed Face (2ⁿᵈ)
Select any face on
the upper side…

16. Hiding the engineered part:

- Right click over the part named **Tooling** and select **Hide**.

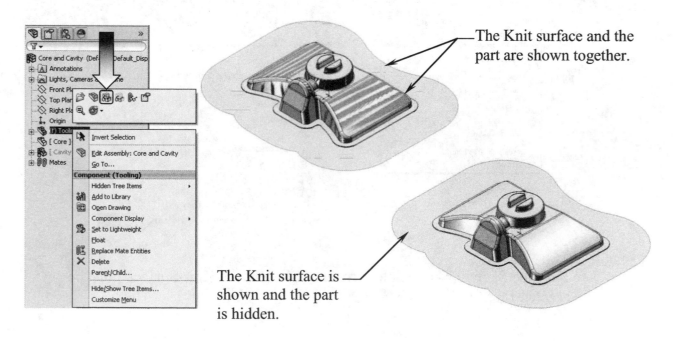

The Knit surface and the
part are shown together.

The Knit surface is
shown and the part
is hidden.

17. Creating a new work plane:

- Click 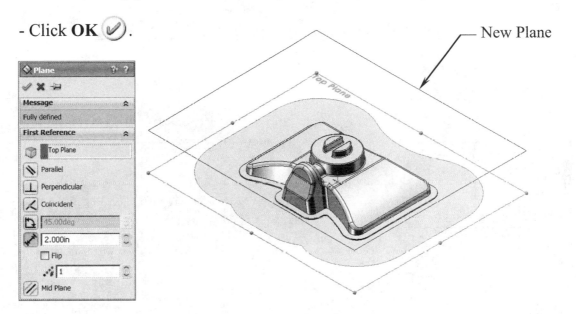 or select **Insert / Reference Geometry / Plane**.

- Select **Offset Distance** option and enter **2.00 in**.

- Select the **Top** plane of the assembly from FeatureManager tree.

- Click **OK** .

New Plane

18. Sketching the profile of the upper block:

- Select the <u>new plane</u> either from the graphics area or from the Feature tree.

- Click or select **Insert / Sketch**.

- Convert the Rectangle from the

previous sketch .

Convert from the previous sketch

Note: From the Feature-
Manager tree, **show**

the part Core
and then **show** the

Sketch1 of the
Extruded1 feature.

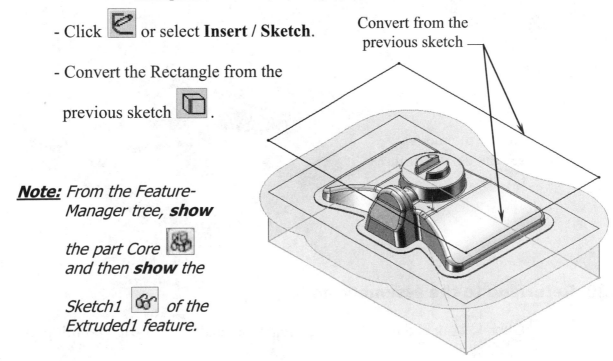

19. Extruding the upper block:

- Hide the Sketch1 and the part Core, from the previous step.

- Click 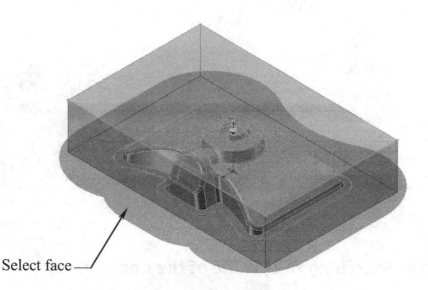 or select **Insert / Boss-Base / Extrude**.

- End Condition: **Up To Surface** .

- Select the Radiated surface as Face/Plane .

- Click **OK** .

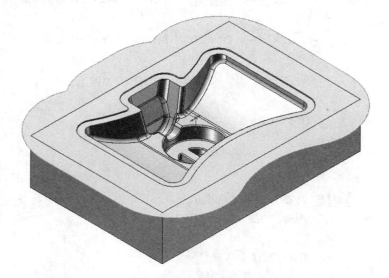

Select face —

- Rotate the model to
  see the details of the
  Cavity.

20. Returning to the assembly mode:

- Click or right-click on the component and select **Edit Assembly** to exit.

21. Showing all components:

- Right click on the part named **Tooling** and select **Show** .

- Right click on the part named **Core** and select **Show**  .

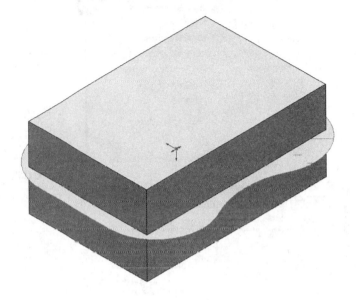

22. Hiding the Surface Bodies:

- Expand the part Tooling and click the plus symbol (+) next to the **Surface Bodies** folder to open.

- Right click on Surface Radiate1and select: **Hide-Surface Body**.

Hide the
Surface Radiate

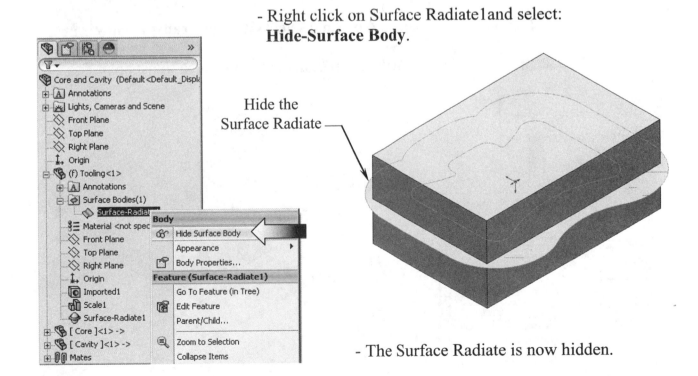

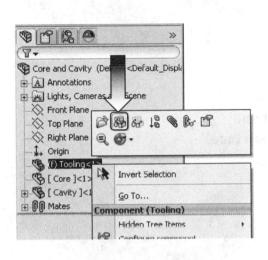

- The Surface Radiate is now hidden.

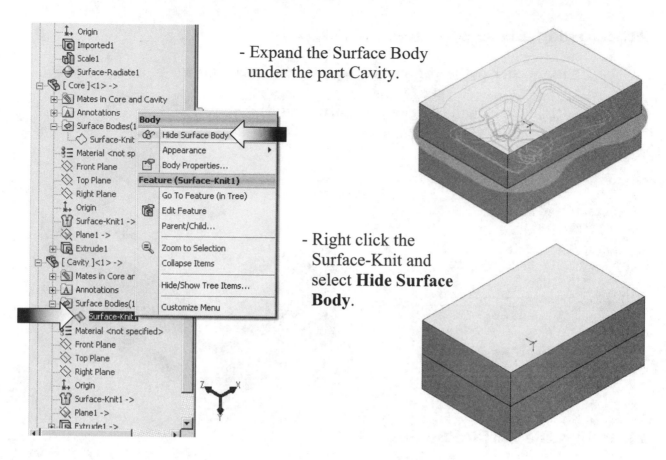

- Expand the Surface Body under the part Cavity.

- Right click the Surface-Knit and select **Hide Surface Body**.

- The Surface-Knit1 is now hidden.

23. Making the parts transparent:

- Right click on the part named **Core** and select **Change Transparency** .

- Repeat the same step and make the part named Cavity also transparent.

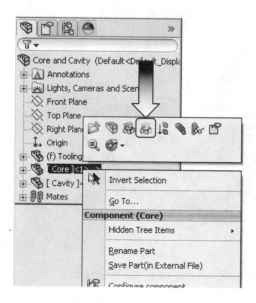

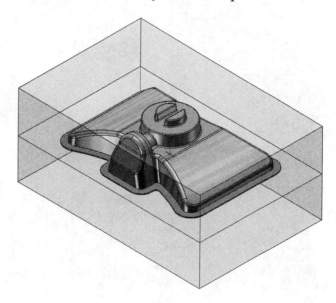

24. Creating an assembly Exploded view:

- Select **Exploded View** 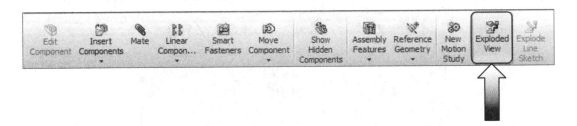 from the **Insert** menu OR click the Exploded-View Icon from the Assembly toolbar.

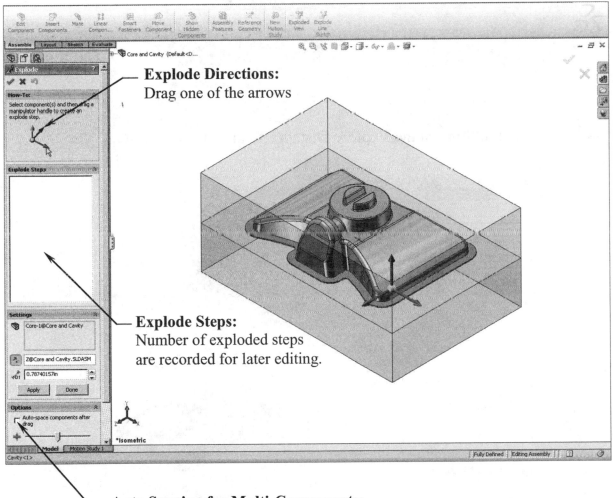

Explode Directions:
Drag one of the arrows

Explode Steps:
Number of exploded steps
are recorded for later editing.

Auto Spacing for Multi-Components:
Select several components, enable Auto-Space check box, drag one
of the arrows to move the components, and release the mouse cursor.
The components are automatically evenly spaced.

- Select the part **Cavity** either from the Feature tree or in the graphics area.

- For Direction, click the GREEN arrow (Y axis).

1. Select the component

2. Select Green Arrow (Y axis)

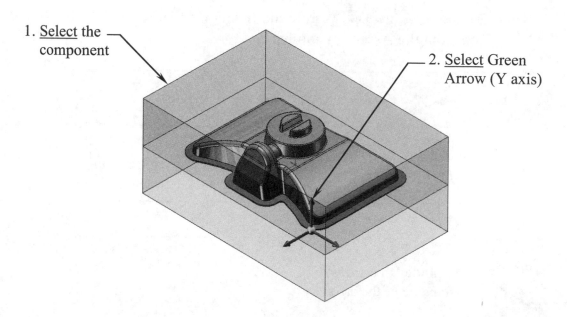

- Enter **6.00in.**, in the Explode Distance field and click **Apply** Apply .

Explode Step1

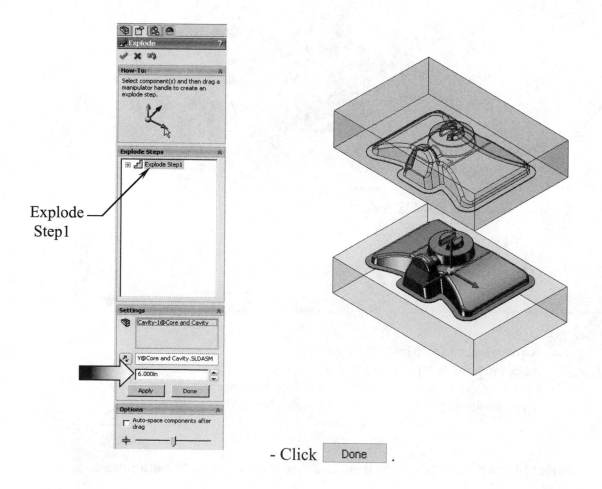

- Click Done .

- Select the part **Core** either from the Feature tree or in the graphics area.

- Click the GREEN arrow (Y Axis)

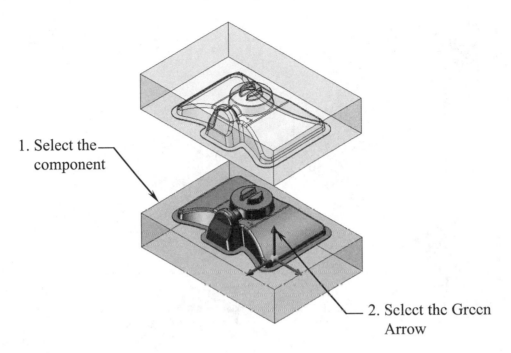

1. Select the component

2. Select the Green Arrow

- Enter **-6.00in.**, in the Explode Distance field (circled).

Click **Apply**   Apply   and then click **Done**   Done   .

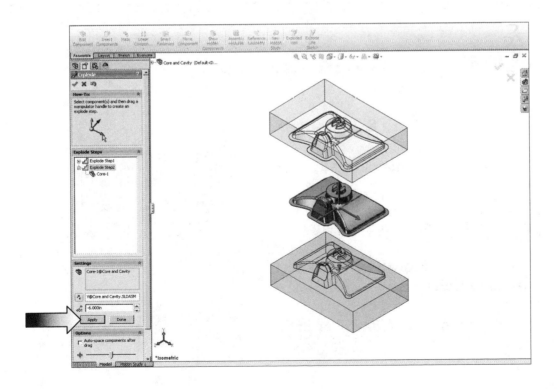

- The Explode Step2 is completed and recorded in the Explode Steps dialog.

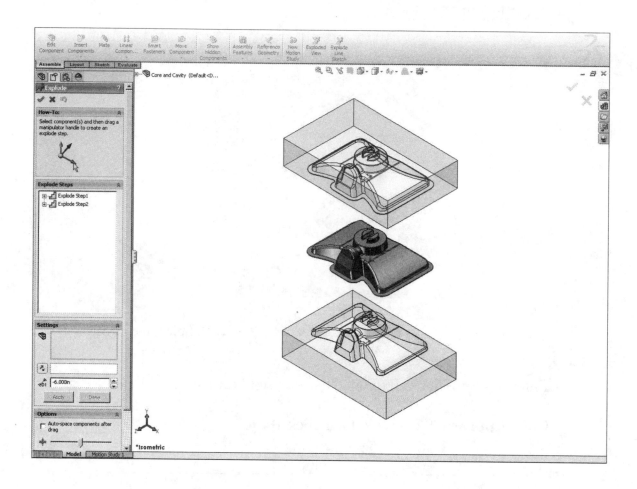

- Click **OK** ✅ to close out of the Explode mode.

25. Animating the Explode & Collapse:

- Switch to the ConfigurationManager Tree (arrow).

- Expand the Default configuration.

- Right click on **ExplView1** and select: **Animate Collapse**.

- See the **Animation Controller** in the next step.

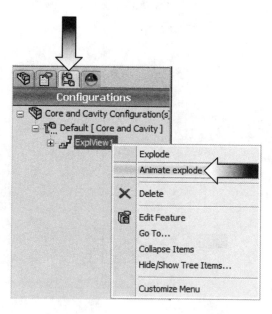

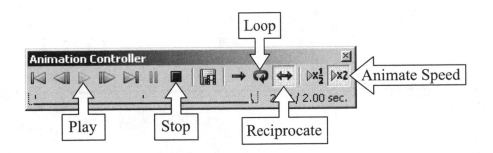

Loop · Play · Stop · Reciprocate · Animate Speed

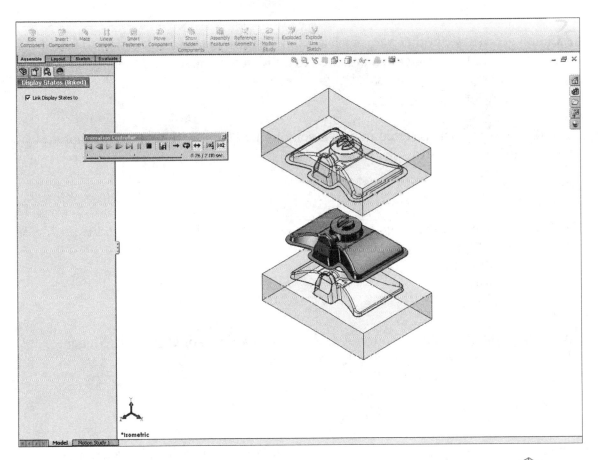

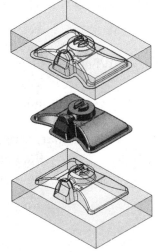

- Stop the animation when finished viewing.

26. Saving your work:

- The document was saved once before.

- Select **File / Save**.

- (Replace the previous
  document when prompted).

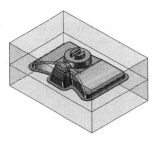

Questions for Review

Top Down Assembly

1. Existing geometry of other parts such as model edges, hole sizes, locations, sketches, surfaces, etc., can be converted and used to build new parts in the assembly level.
    a. True
    b. False

2. The first existing part inserted into an assembly document will be fixed (anchored) by the system automatically.
    a. True
    b. False

3. In Top-Down assembly, when selecting a plane or a model face to sketch the profile of a new part, the system creates the mate:
    a. Coincident
    b. Concentric
    c. Inplace

4. When the Edit Component button is selected, the part's color changes to Magenta (or Blue, depending on color settings), which means:
    a. The part is over defined
    b. The part is being edited
    c. The part is out of context

5. The Scale feature not only scales the part, but all of its dimensions as well.
    a. True
    b. False

6. When a radiate surface is created from a solid model, it can have thickness as well.
    a. True
    b. False

7. When a part is built in Top-Down assembly, it can only be moved when:
    a. Its mates are suppressed
    b. Its mates are deleted
    c. Create an exploded view
    d. All of the above

1. TRUE   2. TRUE
3. C   4. B
5. FALSE   6. FALSE
7. D

CHAPTER 17 (cont.)

Core & Cavity – Part Level

Creating a Core and Cavity Part Level

- A mold is normally designed in SolidWorks using a sequence of intergraded tools that control the mold creation process. Using the finished model, these mold tools can be used to analyze and correct deficiencies in the part.

- The process usually follows these steps: Draft analysis, Undercut Detection, Parting Lines, Shut-Off Surfaces, Parting Surfaces, Interlock Surfaces (Ruled Surfaces), and Tooling Split.

- The Parting Lines ⬡ lie along the edge of the molded part, between the core and the cavity surfaces. They are used to create the Parting Surfaces and to separate the surfaces.

- The Shut-Off Surfaces ⬡ are created after the Parting Lines. A shut-off surface closes up a through hole by creating a surface patch along the Edges that form a continuous loop -OR- a parting line you previously created, to define a loop.

- After the Parting Lines and the Shut-Off Surfaces are determined, the Parting Surfaces ⬡ are created. The Parting Surfaces extrude from the parting lines and are used to separate the mold cavity from the core.

- After a parting surface is defined, the Tooling Split tool ⬡ is used to create the core and cavity blocks for the model. To create a tooling split, at least three surface bodies are needed in the Surface Bodies folder ⬡ Surface Bodies.

- With most mold parts, the interlock surfaces ⬡ need to be created. The interlock surfaces help prevent the core and cavity blocks from shifting, and are located along the perimeter of the parting surfaces. Usually they have a 5-degree taper.

Creating a Core and Cavity
In the Part Level

Dimensioning Standards: **ANSI**
Units: **INCHES** – 3 Decimals

Tools Needed:

 Parting Lines

 Parting Surfaces

 Shut-Off Surfaces

 Tooling Split

 Planes

 2D Sketch

1. Opening an existing Parasolid document:

- Select **File / Open**.

- Change the Files of Type to **Parasolid**.
  (Go to the Training CD)

- Select **Remote Control.x_b** and click **Open**.

Scale

The Parasolid part has already been scaled to 1.05%, about its Centroid.

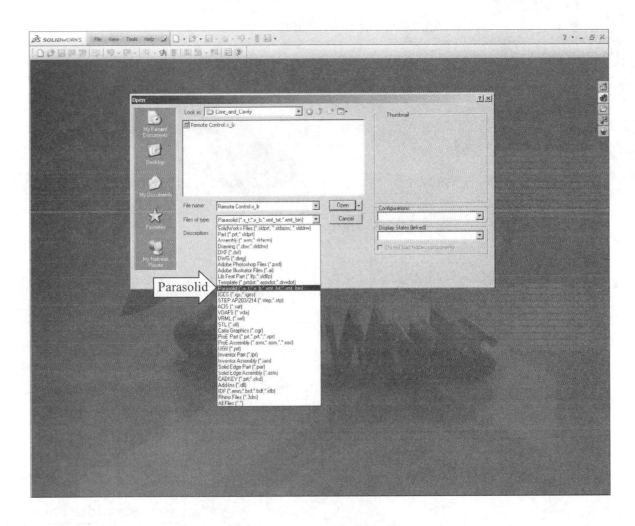

Parasolid

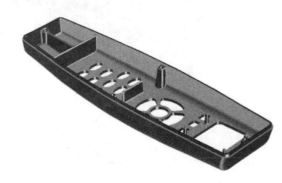

2. Creating the Parting Lines:

- Click 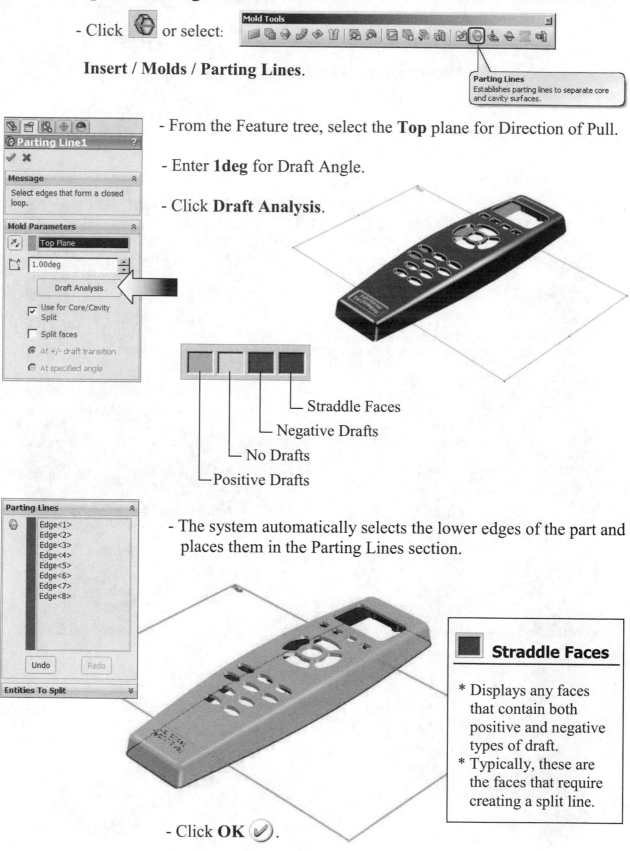 or select:

Insert / Molds / Parting Lines.

Mold Tools

Parting Lines
Establishes parting lines to separate core and cavity surfaces.

- From the Feature tree, select the **Top** plane for Direction of Pull.

- Enter **1deg** for Draft Angle.

- Click **Draft Analysis**.

Parting Line1

Message
Select edges that form a closed loop.

Mold Parameters
Top Plane
1.00deg
Draft Analysis
☑ Use for Core/Cavity Split
☐ Split faces
◉ At +/- draft transition
○ At specified angle

Straddle Faces
Negative Drafts
No Drafts
Positive Drafts

- The system automatically selects the lower edges of the part and places them in the Parting Lines section.

Parting Lines
Edge<1>
Edge<2>
Edge<3>
Edge<4>
Edge<5>
Edge<6>
Edge<7>
Edge<8>

Undo   Redo

Entities To Split

Straddle Faces

* Displays any faces that contain both positive and negative types of draft.
* Typically, these are the faces that require creating a split line.

- Click **OK** ✅.

3. Creating the Shut-Off Surfaces:

- Click 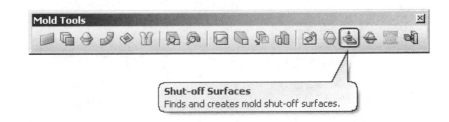 or select **Insert / Molds / Shut-Off Surfaces**.

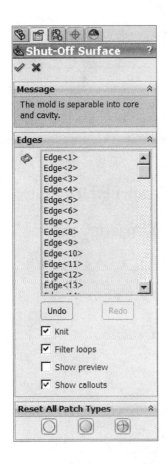

- The system automatically picks up all of the openings and labels them as Loop/Contacts.

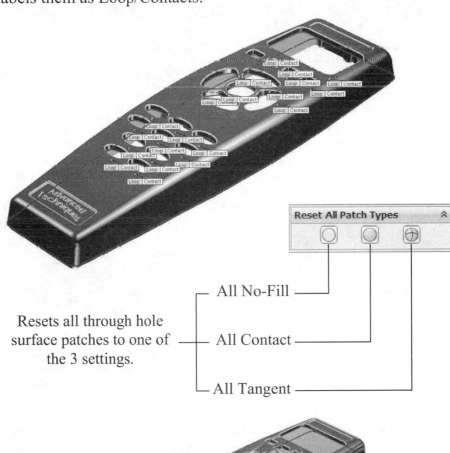

- Resets all through hole surface patches to one of the 3 settings.

  — All No-Fill

  — All Contact

  — All Tangent

💡 Patch Types

Only one Shut-Off Surface feature is allowed in a model. Therefore, within the one feature, you must assign a fill type of **Contact**, **Tangent**, or **No Fill** to every hole.

- Click **OK** ✓.

4. Creating the Parting Surfaces:

- Click 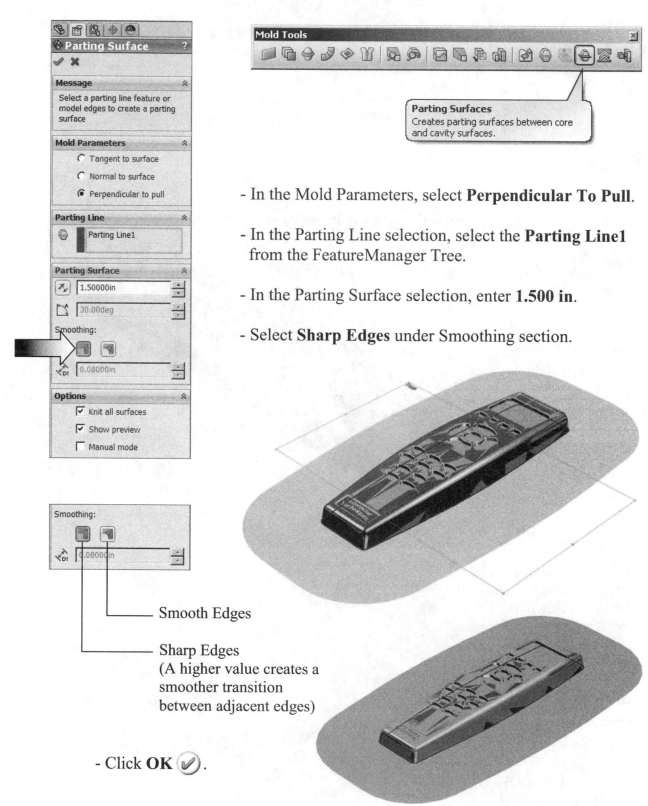 or select **Insert / Molds / Parting Surfaces**.

Parting Surfaces
Creates parting surfaces between core and cavity surfaces.

- In the Mold Parameters, select **Perpendicular To Pull**.

- In the Parting Line selection, select the **Parting Line1** from the FeatureManager Tree.

- In the Parting Surface selection, enter **1.500 in**.

- Select **Sharp Edges** under Smoothing section.

Smooth Edges

Sharp Edges
(A higher value creates a smoother transition between adjacent edges)

- Click **OK**.

5. Sketching the profile of the mold-blocks:

- Select the <u>Top</u> plane and open a new sketch 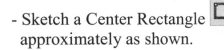 .

- Sketch a Center Rectangle 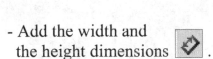 approximately as shown.

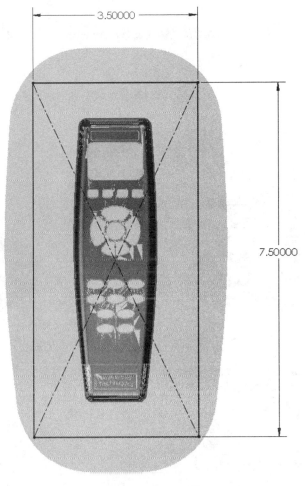

- Add the width and the height dimensions ⬦ .

- The sketch should be fully defined at this point.

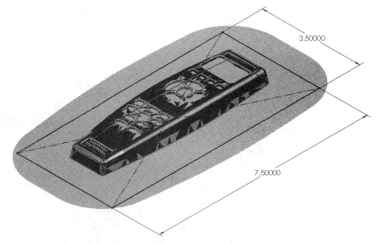

- **Exit** the Sketch 🖉 .

(The next step is to create the upper and lower blocks using the Tooling Split command. This is only available when the Sketch is off)

6. Creating the Tooling Split:

- Click 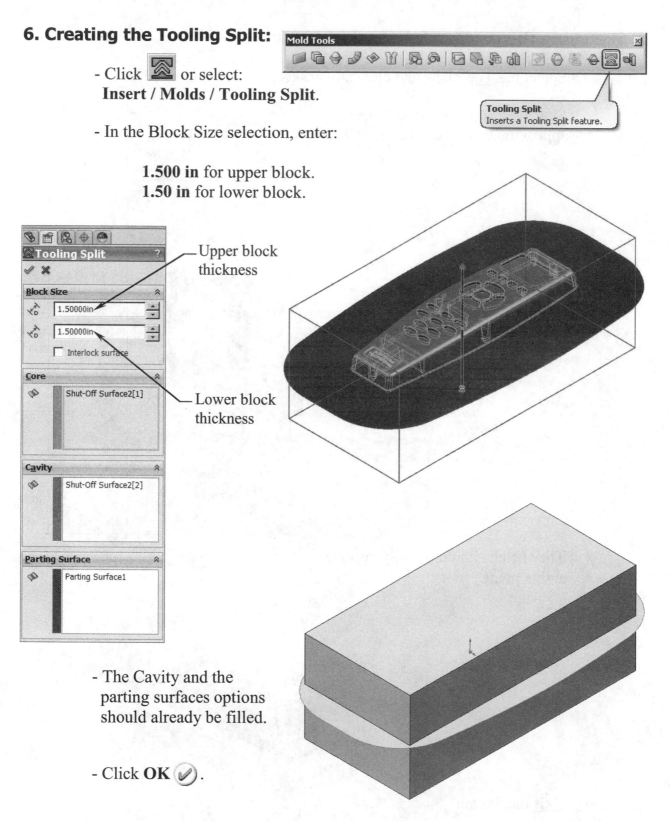 or select:
Insert / Molds / Tooling Split.

- In the Block Size selection, enter:

1.500 in for upper block.
1.50 in for lower block.

Upper block thickness

Lower block thickness

- The Cavity and the parting surfaces options should already be filled.

- Click **OK**.

* The Interlock Surface surrounds the perimeter of the parting lines in a slight tapered direction, it helps seal the mold to prevent resins from leaking, prevents shifts, and maintains alignment between the tooling entities.

7. Hiding the Solid Bodies:

- From the FeatureManager Tree, expand the Surface Bodies folder.

- Hold the CONTROL key and select all **3 surfaces** in the folder.

- Right click over one of the 3 surfaces and select **Hide Bodies**.

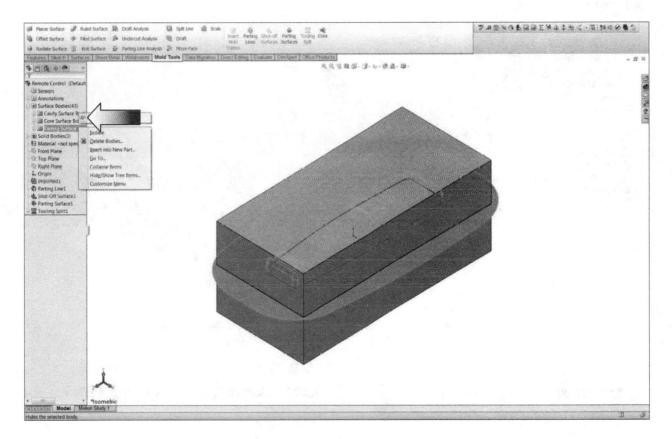

- The 3 surfaces that were created in the previous steps are temporarily removed from the graphics display.

- Change to the Wireframe mode to see the inside details of the blocks.

- Right click on the blue parting lines to hide.

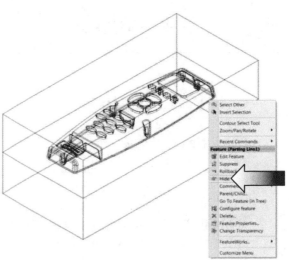

8. Saving the parts:

- Expand the **Solid Bodies folder**, right click on **Tooling Split [1]** and select: **Insert into New Part**.

- Enter: **Remote_Control_Core**, for the name of the file.

- Click **Save**.

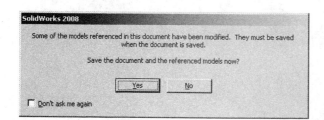

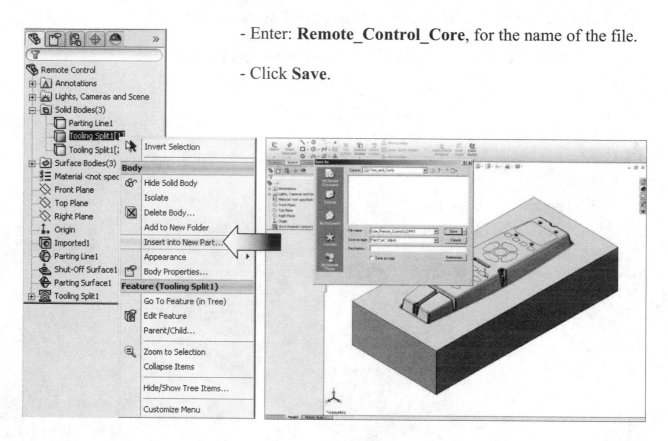

- Click **Yes** to confirm the References.

- Click **Save** to save the original part.

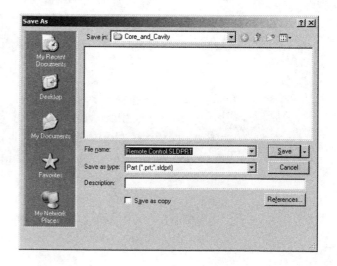

- Repeat the same step to save the Tooling Split[2], enter **Remote_Control_Cavity**, for the name of the 2nd block.

9. Separating the 2 blocks:

- Select **Insert / Feature / Move-Copy**.

- Select the upper block in the graphics.

- Click the vertical Green arrow to define the direction.

- Under the Translate section, enter **6.00in** and press ENTER.

- Click **OK**.

- The upper block moves 6 inches upward from its original position.

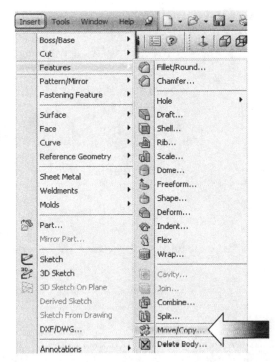

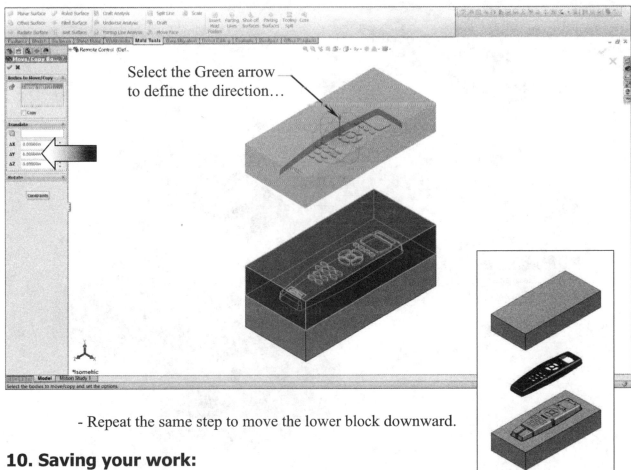

Select the Green arrow to define the direction...

- Repeat the same step to move the lower block downward.

10. Saving your work:

- Save a copy of your work as **Remote Control Tooling**.

11. Optional:

- Start a new Assembly document and assemble the 3 components.

- Create an Assembly Exploded View as a separate configuration.

- Add Injector hole.

- Ejector holes.

- Alignment Pins.

- Make copies of the components and create an exploded view as shown.

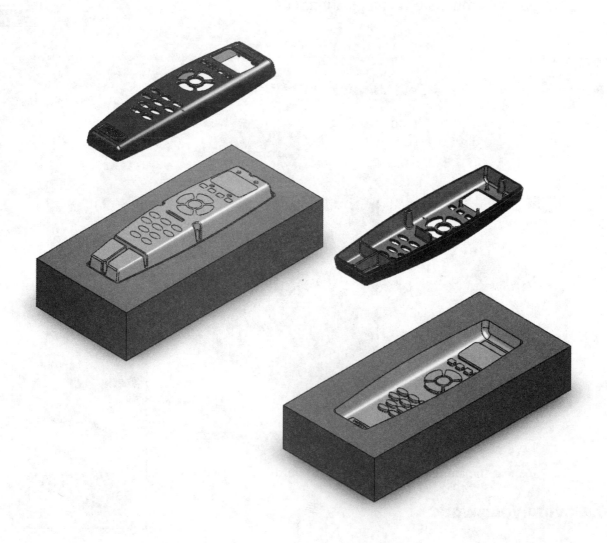

Questions for Review

Core & Cavity

1. Using the finished model, the mold tools can be used to analyze and correct the deficiencies such as undercuts, draft angles, shut-off surfaces, etc.
   - a. True
   - b. False

2. The Parting Lines are used to create the Parting Surfaces and to separate the surfaces.
   - a. True
   - b. False

3. A shut-off surface closes up a through hole by creating a surface patch along the edges that form a continuous loop.
   - a. True
   - b. False

4. The Parting Surfaces extrude from the parting lines and are used to separate the mold cavity from the core.
   - a. True
   - b. False

5. To create a tooling split, what surface bodies are needed for this operation?
   - a. The Core
   - b. The Cavity
   - c. The Parting Surface
   - d. All of the above

6. The Interlock surfaces help prevent the core and cavity blocks from shifting and are located along the perimeter of the parting surfaces.
   - a. True
   - b. False

7. The solid bodies can be hidden or shown just like any other features in SolidWorks.
   - a. True
   - b. False

7. TRUE
5. D   6. TRUE
3. TRUE   4. TRUE
1. TRUE   2. TRUE

CHAPTER 18

Top-Down Assembly

Top-Down Assembly

- This chapter will guide us through some techniques of creating new parts in the context of an assembly or Top Down mode.

- By using the existing geometry of other parts such as their locations, features, and sizes to construct new components is referred to as In Context Assembly. This option greatly helps capture your design intent and reduces the time it takes to do a design change, having the parts update within themselves based on the way they were created.

- While working in the top down assembly mode, every time a face or a plane is selected as a sketch plane to create a feature of the new part, the system automatically creates an INPLACE mate to reference the new part.

- The Inplace mates can be suppressed so that components can be moved or repositioned and the Inplace mates can also be deleted as well, new mates can be added to establish new relationships with other components.

- When a part is being edited in the Top Down Assembly mode, the Edit-Component icon is selected and the part's color changes to Blue (or Magenta depending on the color settings in the system options).

- Upon the successful completion of this lesson, you will have a better understanding of the 2 assembly methods in SolidWorks: the traditional Bottom Up assembly (where parts are created separately, then inserted into an assembly document and mated together) and the dynamic Top-Down assembly (where parts can be created together, in the context of an assembly).

Miniature Vise
Top-Down Assembly

Dimensioning Standards: **ANSI**

Units: **INCHES** – 3 Decimals

Tools Needed:

Insert Sketch	Rectangle	Circle
Dimension	Add Geometric Relations	Sketch Mirror
Offset Entities	Planes	Fillet/Round
Base/Boss Extrude	Loft	Edit Component

1. Starting with a new assembly:

- Select **File / New / Assembly**.

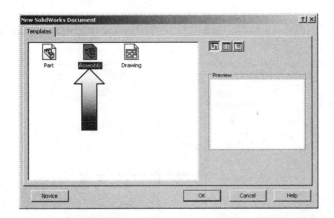

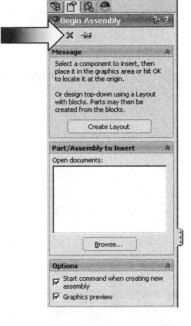

- Click **Cancel** ✖ to exit the **Begin Assembly** mode.

- **Save** the new assembly document as **Mini Vise.sldasm**.

2. Creating the Base part:

- Select **Insert / Component / New Part**.

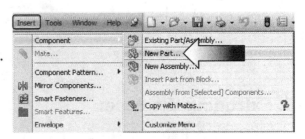

- Select the <u>Front</u> plane from the FeatureManager tree to reference the new part (Inplace1).

- The system creates a new part using a default name **[Part1^Assembly]<1>**.

- To rename the part, right click on the default name and select **Rename Part**.

- Enter: **Base** as the new name for the 1st part.

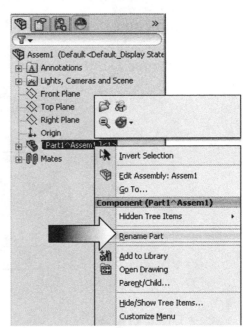

- The new part has the default Blue color.

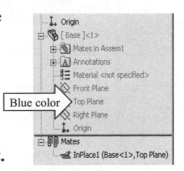

- To change the part's color, go to: **Tools/ Options / System Options / Colors / Assembly Edit Part.**

- A new sketch is created automatically when a new component is inserted .

- Sketch the profile shown below; keep the Origin at the lower right corner.

- Add the Dimensions ⬦ or Relations ⊥ needed to fully define the sketch.

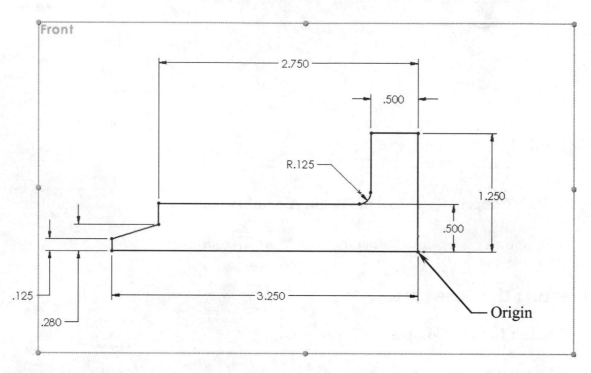

3. Extruding the Base:

- Click 🔲 or select **Insert / Boss-Base / Extrude**.

- Direction 1:   **Mid-Plane**.

- Extrude Depth: **.750 in.**

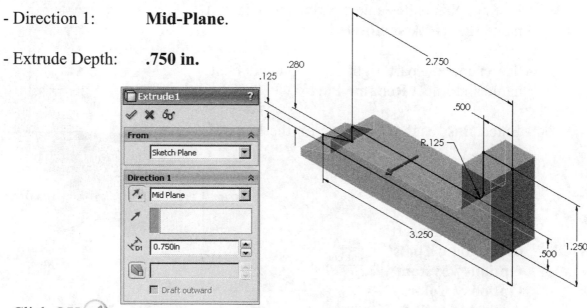

- Click **OK** ✅ .

4. Adding the side flanges:

- Select the <u>bottom face</u> of the base and open a new sketch  .

- Sketch the profile below; use the Mirror option to keep the sketch entities symmetrical with the Centerline.

- Add dimensions as shown. (Hold the Shift key when adding the .625 dim.)

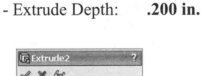

Sketch Face

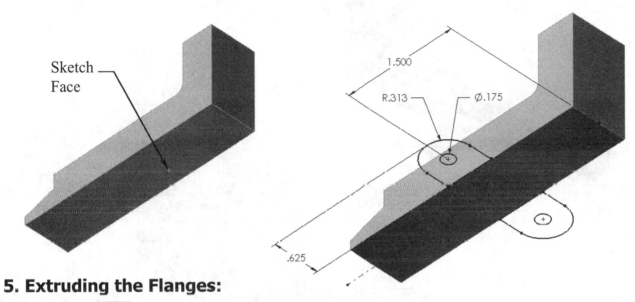

1.500

R.313   Ø.175

.625

5. Extruding the Flanges:

- Click or select **Insert / Boss-Base / Extrude**.

- Direction 1:   **Blind** (Reverse).

- Extrude Depth: **.200 in.**

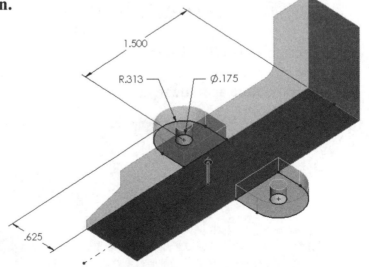

1.500

R.313   Ø.175

.625

- Click **OK** .

6. Adding the side cuts:

- Select the <u>face</u> as indicated and click 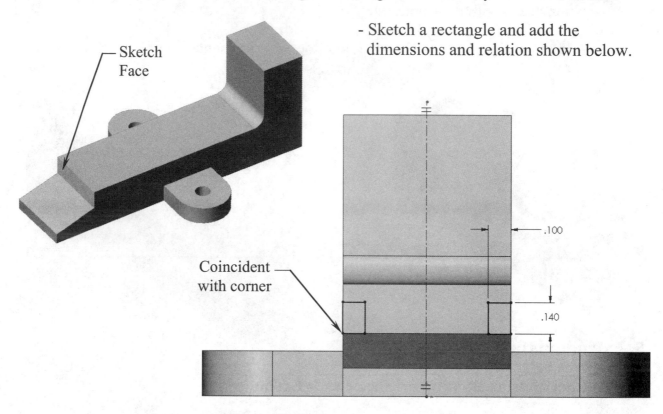or select **Insert / Sketch**.

- Sketch a Centerline starting at the Origin and click Dynamic Mirror.

- Sketch a rectangle and add the dimensions and relation shown below.

Sketch Face

Coincident with corner

.100

.140

7. Extruding the side cuts:

- Click or select **Insert / Cut / Extrude**.

- Direction 1: **Up-To-Surface**.

- Select the **face** as indicated.

Select Face

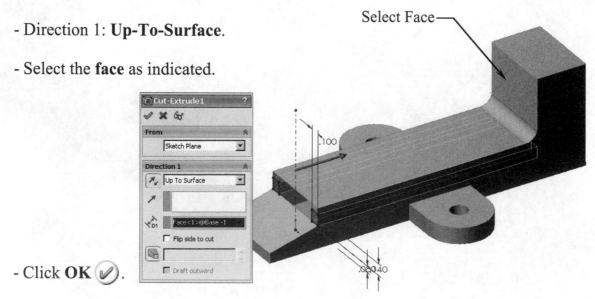

Cut-Extrude1

From
Sketch Plane

Direction 1
Up To Surface

Face<1>@Base -1

Flip side to cut

Draft outward

.100

- Click **OK**.

8. Creating an offset distance plane:

- Select the <u>face</u> as shown and click 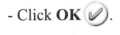 or select **Insert / Reference Geometry / Plane**.

- Click **Offset Distance** option .

- Enter **.150 in**. (the new plane is placed **away** from the face)

- Click **OK** .

Select Face

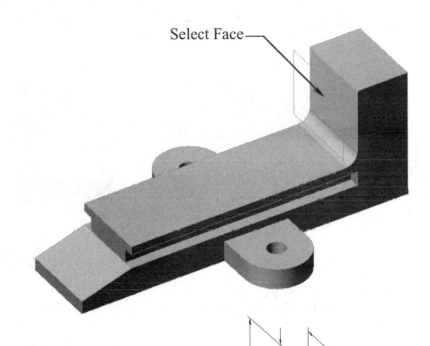

9. Creating the Fixed Jaw, sketch 1 of 4:

- Select the <u>new plane</u> and click or select **Insert / Sketch**.

- Sketch a rectangle approx. 2 inches above the origin.

<u>NOTE:</u> *The dimension .450 can be replaced with a centerline and a symmetric relation.*

More...

- Add dimensions 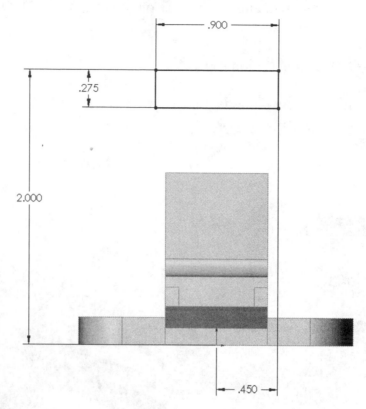 to fully position the sketch.

- **Exit** the sketch ✏ or select **Insert / Sketch**.

10. Creating the 2nd profile, sketch 2 of 4:

- Select the <u>face</u> as indicated and click ✏ or select **Insert / Sketch**.

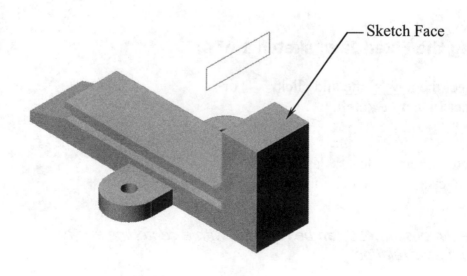

Sketch Face

- Hold the CONTROL key and select the 4 edges as shown (or simply select the rectangular face and click the Convert Entities command).

- Click **Convert Entities** on the Sketch-Tools toolbar.

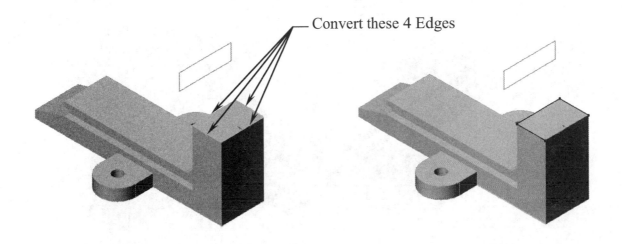

Convert these 4 Edges

- The 4 selected edges are converted into a new 2D rectangle.

- **Exit** the sketch or select **Insert / Sketch**.

11. Creating the 3D Guide Curves:

- Select **3D Sketch** from the Sketch tool tab or select **Insert / 3D Sketch**.

- Sketch a 3-Point-Arc approximately as shown and add the **Coincident** relation between the ends of the arc and the corners of the rectangles.

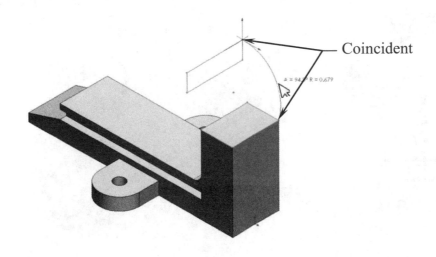

Coincident

- Add a **Perpendicular** relation between the <u>endpoint</u> of the arc and the <u>upper face</u> of the part as noted.

- Repeat the last step and create the other 3 arcs the same way.

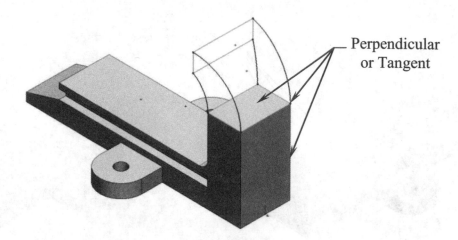

Perpendicular
or Tangent

- **Exit** the 3D Sketch or select **Insert / 3D Sketch** (Control + Q).

12. Creating the Fixed Jaw loft:

- Click or select **Insert / Boss-Base / Loft**.

- Select the 2 sketch profiles as labeled (Profile 1 and Profile 2) . (Click near the ends of the rectangles will work just fine. SolidWorks will select the nearest endpoints automatically).

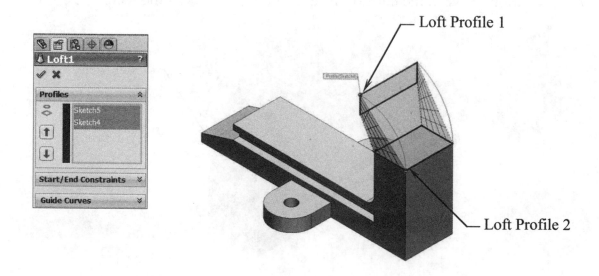

Loft Profile 1

Loft Profile 2

- Expand the **Guide Curve** section and select one of the guide curves 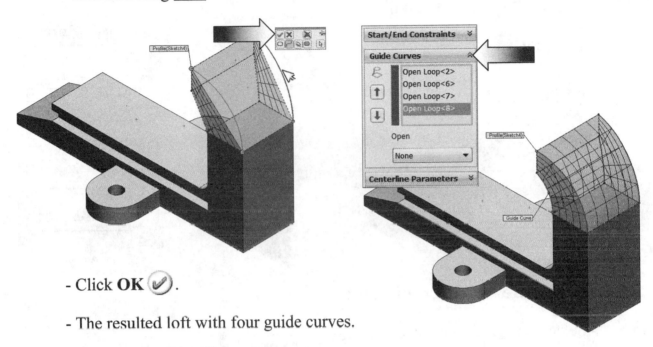 in the 3D Sketch.

- Because this sketch has multiple entities that are not connected with one another, you will have to click the OK button (the check mark) on the SelectionManager after selecting <u>each</u> arc.

- Click **OK** ✓.

- The resulted loft with four guide curves.

13. Creating the Fixed Jaw Clamp:

- Select the <u>Front</u> plane from the FeatureManager tree and click 📝 or select **Insert / Sketch**.

- Sketch a Rectangle ⬜ and add Dimensions ◇ and Relations ⊥ as indicated. *(Add a horizontal centerline and a midpoint relation between the right endpoint and the model edge).*

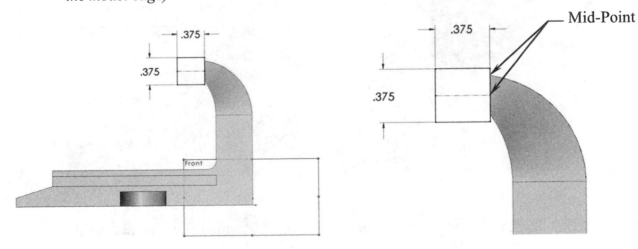

14. Extruding the Fixed Jaw Clamp:

- Click 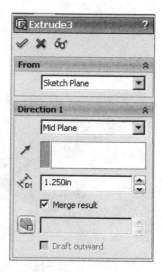 or select **Insert / Boss-Base / Extrude**.

- Direction 1:   **Mid-Plane**.

- Extrude Depth: **1.250 in**.

- Click **OK** ✓.

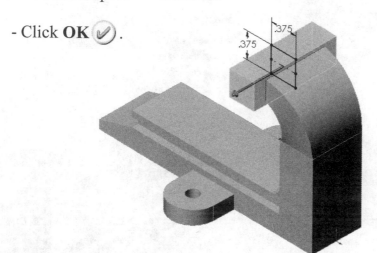

.375
.375

Extrude3

From
Sketch Plane

Direction 1
Mid Plane

1.250in

☑ Merge result

☐ Draft outward

15. Creating the Lead Screw Hole:

- Select the <u>face</u> as indicated

  and open a new sketch ✎ .

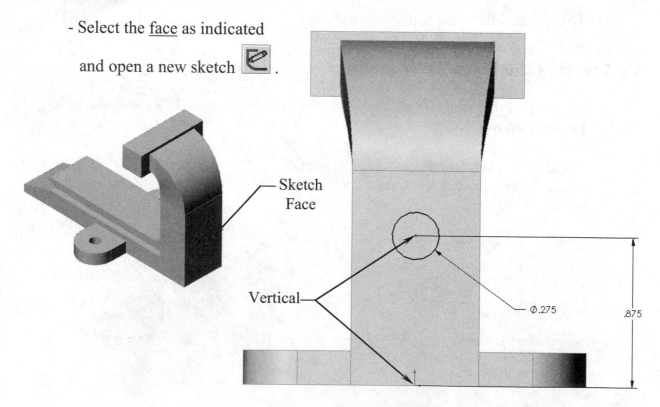

Sketch
Face

Vertical

Ø.275

.875

- Sketch a Circle ⊕ and add the dimensions ◇ and relations └ as shown.

16. Extruding the Hole:

- Click 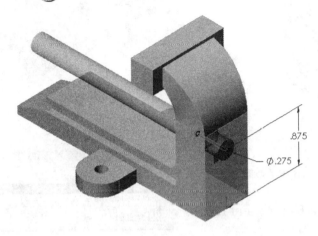 or select **Insert / Cut / Extrude**.

- Direction 1: **Through All**.

- Click **OK** ✅.

17. Adding Fillets:

- Click Fillet  or select **Insert / Features /Fillets-Rounds**.

- Enter **.032 in**. for Radius.

- Select the edges as shown for Edges to Fillet.

- Click **OK** ✅.

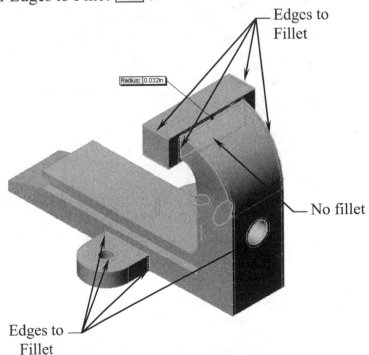

Edges to Fillet

No fillet

Edges to Fillet

- The Base part is shown in Front and Back Isometric views.

18. Saving your work:

- Select **File / Save As / Base / Save**.

- Click  to exit the Edit Component mode.

19. Creating a new component: the Slide Jaw

- Select **Insert / Component / New Part**.

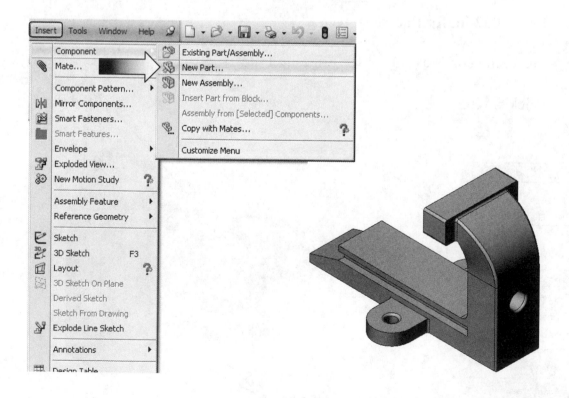

- Rotate the model to the right, the planar surface on the left side will be used next.

- Select the <u>face</u> indicated as sketch plane for the new component (Inplace2). A new part and a new sketch are created in the FeatureManager tree.

- **Rename** the component to **Slide Jaw**.

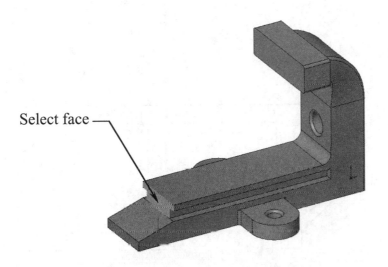

Select face

- A new part is created in the FeatureManager tree and the sketch pencil is activated.

- An INPLACE mate is also created for the new component to reference its location.

20. Using the Offset Entities command:

- Select the **4 edges** of the model (as shown) and click **Offset Entities** .

- Enter **.010 in**. for offset value. This offset distance between 4 the lines and the model edges will remain locked and get updated at the same time when the value is changed.

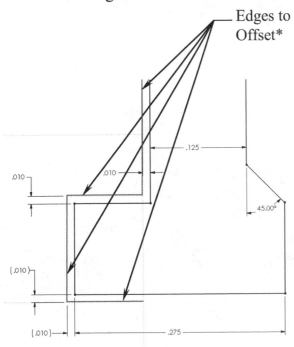

Edges to Offset*

┌───┐
│ 💡 **Offset Entities**   │
│   │
│ * The geometry of a model such as   │
│   edges, faces, and other sketch   │
│   entities can be offset or converted   │
│   to use in the new part.   │
│ * The offset entities can be set to   │
│   one direction or bidirectional.   │
│ * An On-Edge relation is created   │
│   for each converted sketch entity.   │
└───┘

- Sketch the rest of the profile and add the dimensions or relations needed to fully define the sketch.

Note:

The mirror option 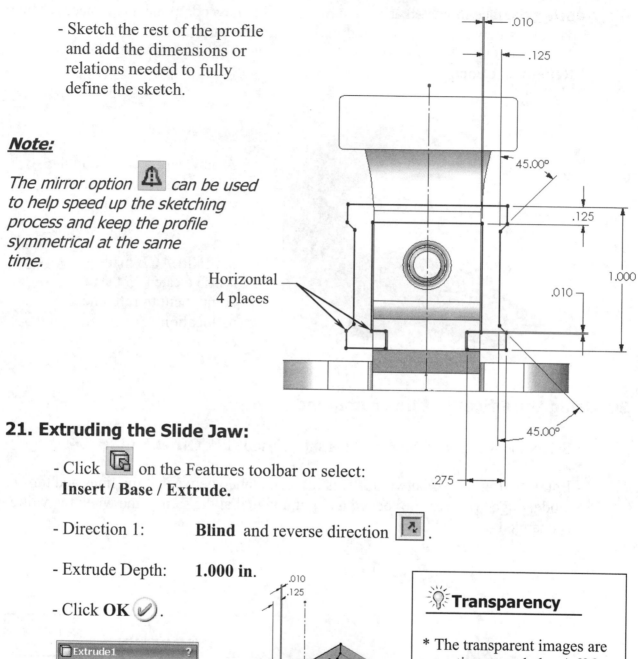 *can be used to help speed up the sketching process and keep the profile symmetrical at the same time.*

Horizontal
4 places

21. Extruding the Slide Jaw:

- Click [icon] on the Features toolbar or select:
Insert / Base / Extrude.

- Direction 1:   **Blind** and reverse direction [icon].

- Extrude Depth: **1.000 in**.

- Click **OK** ✓.

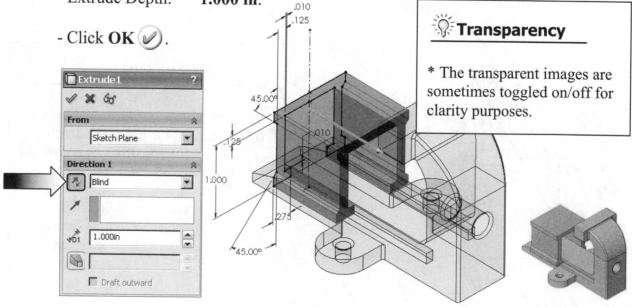

Transparency

* The transparent images are sometimes toggled on/off for clarity purposes.

22. Adding the support wall:

- Select the <u>face</u> indicated and open a new sketch 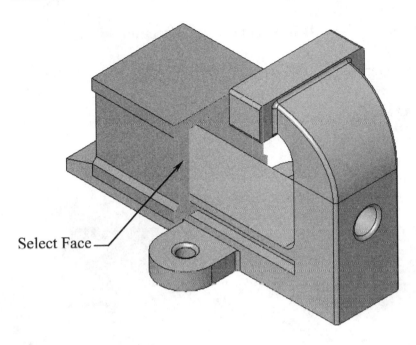 or select **Insert / Sketch.**

Select Face

- Sketch the profile and add the dimensions and relation as shown below to fully define the sketch.

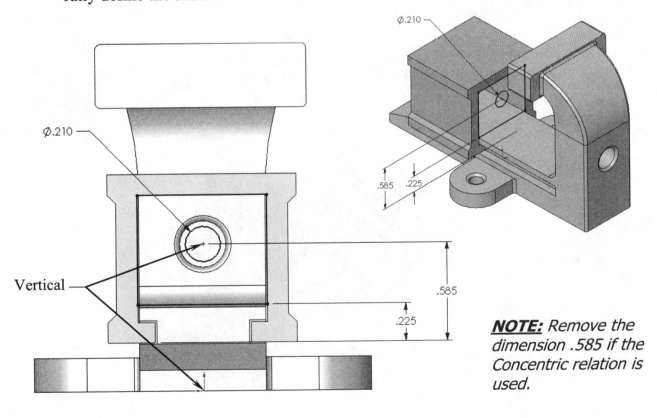

Ø.210

Vertical

.585

.225

Ø.210

.585   .225

NOTE: Remove the dimension .585 if the Concentric relation is used.

23. Extruding the Support Wall:

- Click 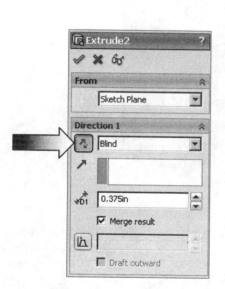 on the Features toolbar or select **Insert / Base / Extrude.**

- Direction 1: **Blind** and reverse direction .

- Extrude Depth: **.375 in**.

- Click **OK** .

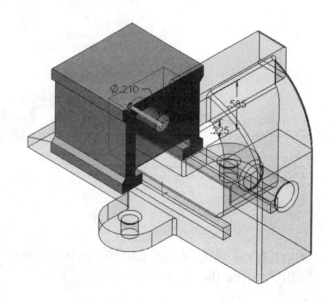

- The Support wall is built with a guide hole.

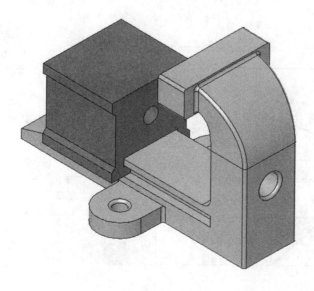

24. Creating a new work plane:

- Select the face as indicated and click 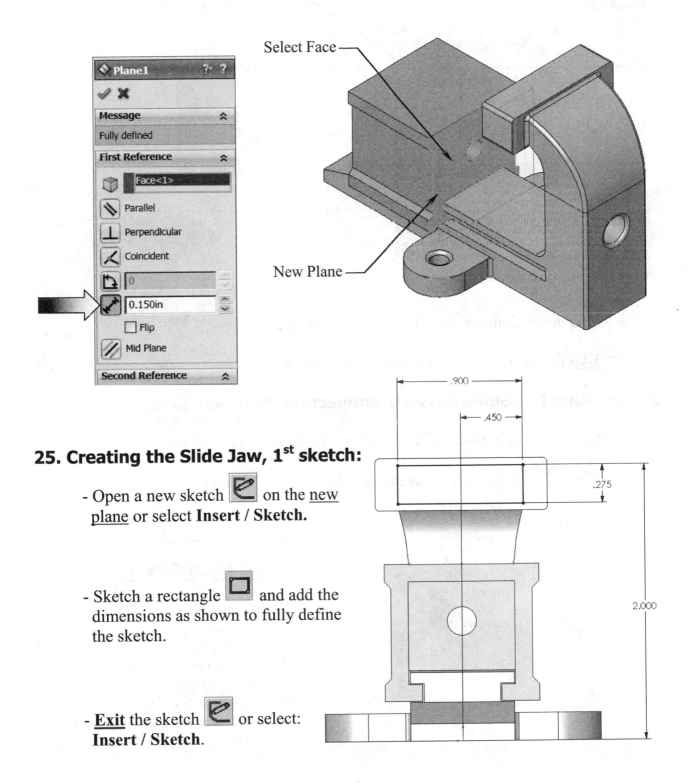 or select: **Insert / Reference Geometry / Plane.**

- Enter **.150 in**. in the Offset Distance box and place the new plane on the **outside**.

25. Creating the Slide Jaw, 1st sketch:

- Open a new sketch on the new plane or select **Insert / Sketch.**

- Sketch a rectangle and add the dimensions as shown to fully define the sketch.

- **Exit** the sketch or select: **Insert / Sketch.**

26. Creating the Slide Jaw, 2nd sketch:

- Select the <u>face</u> indicated and open a new sketch 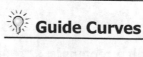 or select: **Insert / Sketch.**

- Sketch a rectangle 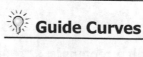 as shown.

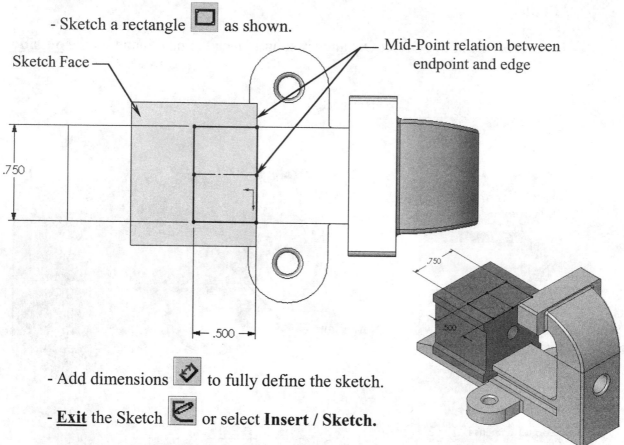

Sketch Face

Mid-Point relation between endpoint and edge

.750

.500

.750

.500

- Add dimensions 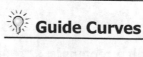 to fully define the sketch.

- **Exit** the Sketch 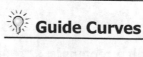 or select **Insert / Sketch.**

27. Creating the Guide Curve to connect the two sketches:

- Select the <u>Right</u> plane of the part from the FeatureManager tree.

- Click 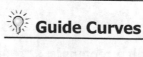 to open a new sketch or select: **Insert / Sketch.**

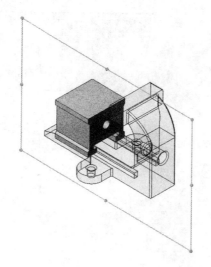

💡 Guide Curves

* Guide curves are used to control the profile from twisting as the sketch is swept along the path.
* Guide curves are also used in Sweep to shape the 3D Features.
* Each profile is PIERCED or coincident with the guide curve.

- Sketch either a **Centerpoint Arc** 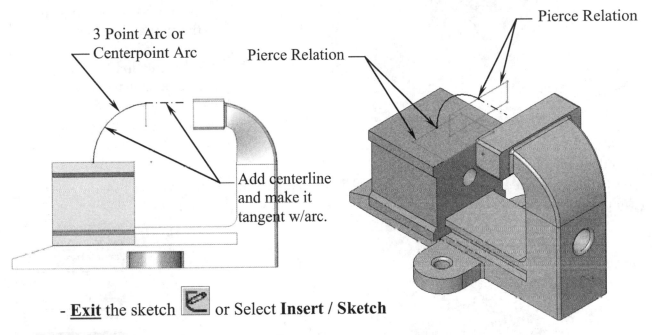 or a **3-Point Arc** that connects the two sketches.

- Add the Relations as shown below to fully define the sketch.

3 Point Arc or
Centerpoint Arc

Pierce Relation

Pierce Relation

Add centerline and make it tangent w/arc.

- **Exit** the sketch or Select **Insert / Sketch**

28. Creating the Slide Jaw Loft:

- Click on the Features toolbar or select **Insert / Boss / Loft.**

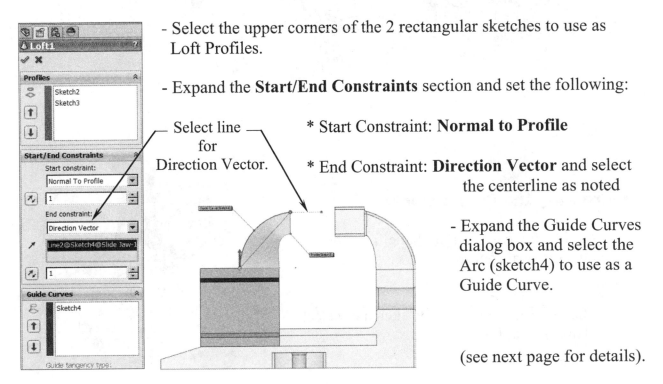

- Select the upper corners of the 2 rectangular sketches to use as Loft Profiles.

- Expand the **Start/End Constraints** section and set the following:

Select line for Direction Vector.

* Start Constraint: **Normal to Profile**

* End Constraint: **Direction Vector** and select the centerline as noted

- Expand the Guide Curves dialog box and select the Arc (sketch4) to use as a Guide Curve.

(see next page for details).

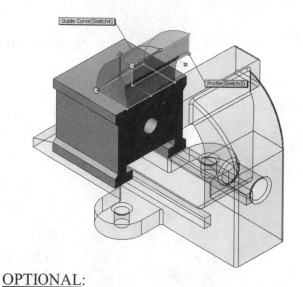

💡 Start/End Constraints

* The Start constraint and End constraint option applies a constraint to control tangency to the start and end profiles.

* The Direction Vector option applies a tangency constraint based on a selected entity used as a direction vector.

OPTIONAL:
4 Guide Curves
(in one 3D Sketch)

Tangent —

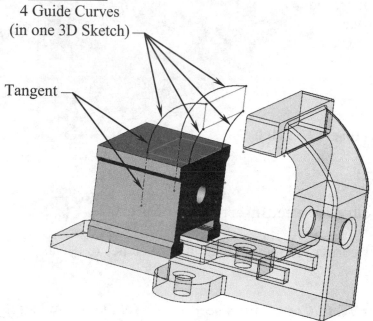

- Click **OK** ✓.

29. Creating the Clamp block:

- Select the part's <u>Right</u> plane from the FeatureManager tree.

- Click 📝 to open a new sketch or select:
Insert / Sketch.

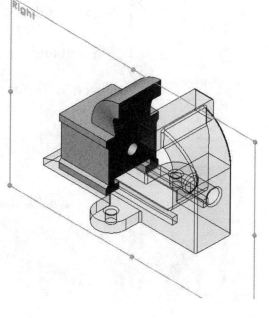

- Sketch a Rectangle and add Dimensions as shown.

- Add a Centerline in the middle of the rectangle and position it on the Mid-Point of the vertical edge.

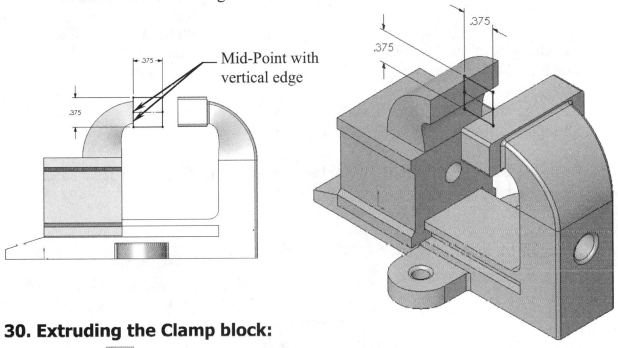

Mid-Point with vertical edge

30. Extruding the Clamp block:

- Click or select **Insert / Boss-Base Extrude**.

- Direction 1:   **Mid-Plane**.

- Extrude Depth: **1.250 in**.

- Merge Result: **Enabled**.

- Click **OK**.

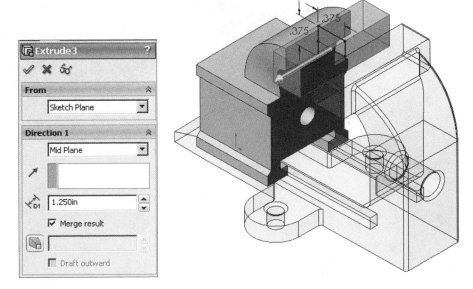

31. Which option is better?

- Instead of using the Mid-Plane extrude, the **Up-To-Surface** option can be used to link the length dimensions of the 2 Clamp Blocks together.

- Right click on the last Extruded feature and select **Edit Feature**.

- Change **Direction 1** from Mid-Plane to **Up-To-Surface** and select the face on the left side.

- Change **Direction 2** to **Up-To-Surface** and select the face on the right side as indicated.

- Click **OK** ✓.

> ### ☀ Up-To-Surface
>
> * Extends the feature from the sketch plane to the selected surface.
> * When the driving surface is changed in length, the referenced extruded feature will also be reflected.

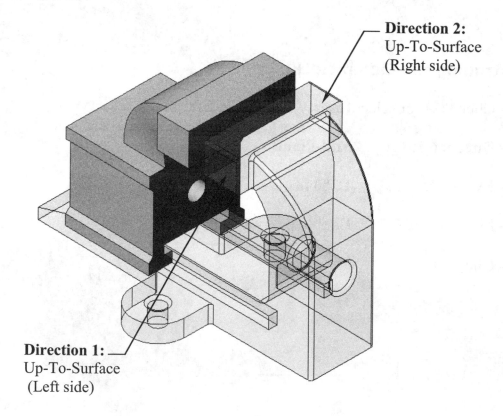

Direction 2:
Up-To-Surface
(Right side)

Direction 1:
Up-To-Surface
(Left side)

32. Adding fillets:

- Click ⬡ or select **Insert / Features / Fillet-Round.**

- Enter **.032** for Radius value ⟋ .

- Select the edges as shown ⬚ .

- Click **OK** ✓ .

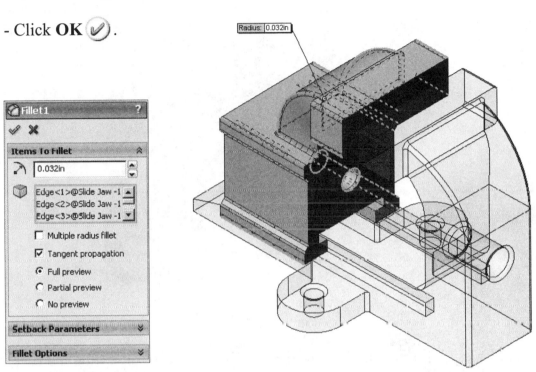

- The fillets are shown in the Front and Back Isometric views for clarity.

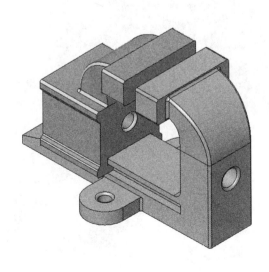
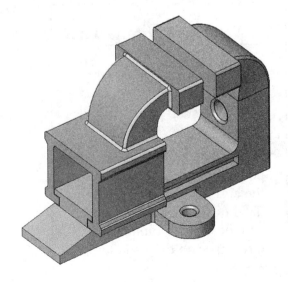

33. Creating the internal threads:

- Starting with the sweep path.

- Select the <u>face</u> indicated and open a new sketch 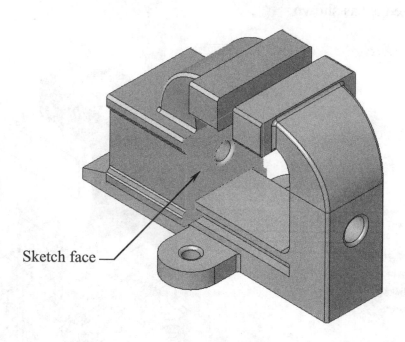 or select: **Insert / Sketch.**

Sketch face —

- Sketch a Circle ⊕ that is Concentric with the hole. (Converting the ID of the hole is another good way to link the diameter of the circle to the hole's diameter)

- Add a **Ø.210** dimension 🗹 to fully define.

💡 **Wake up Center Points**

* Center-points of existing geometry can be "woke-up" for use as snap points in a sketch.

* With a Circle tool selected, position the mouse cursor over the circumference of the hole; the 4 quadrant points appear, and the center-point of the circle is visible for snapping.

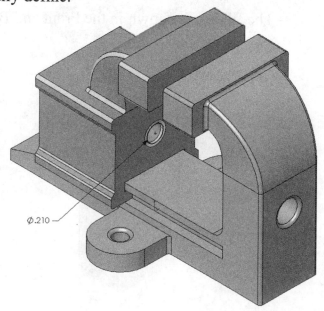

Ø.210 —

- Select **Insert / Curve / Helix-Spiral.**

- Enter the following parameters:

Defined by:	**Pitch and Revolution**.
Pitch:	**.080 in**.
Revolution:	**5.000**.
Starting Angle:	**90.00 deg**.
Reverse Direction:	**Enabled**.
Clockwise:	**Selected**.

- Click **OK** 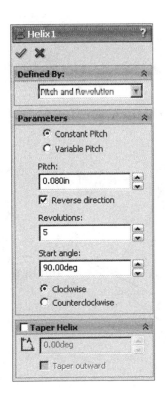.

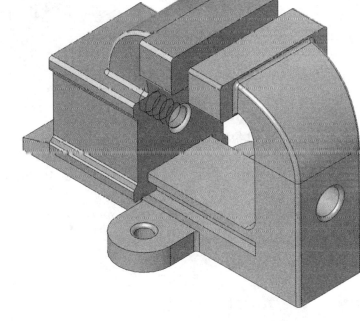

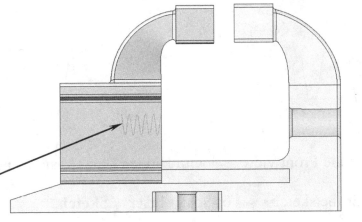

Click **View / Curves** if
the helix is not visible.

- **Sketching the Sweep Profile:**

- Select the part' <u>Right</u> plane from the Feature tree and open a new sketch 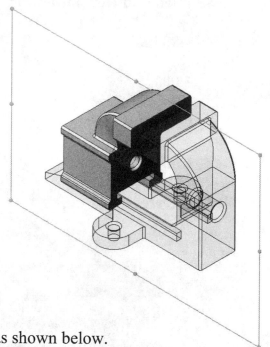 or select: **Insert / Sketch.**

- Sketch the profile as shown below.
  (Use Mirror to keep the entities symmetrical)

- Add Dimensions 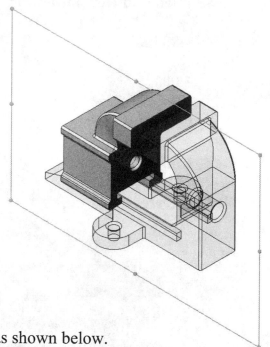 and Relations 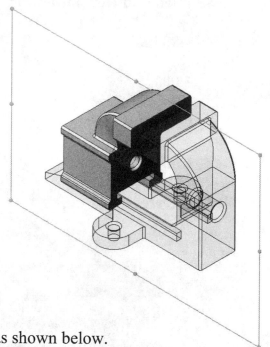 to fully define the sketch.

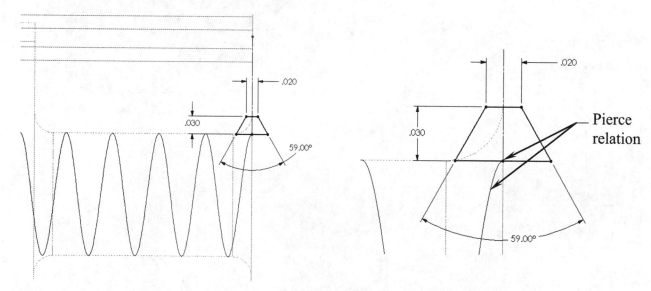

- Use the Front view 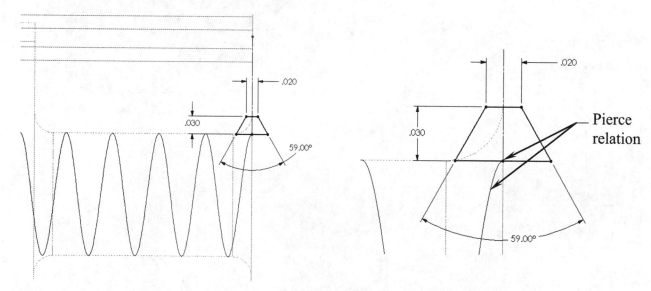 with Hidden Lines Visible option 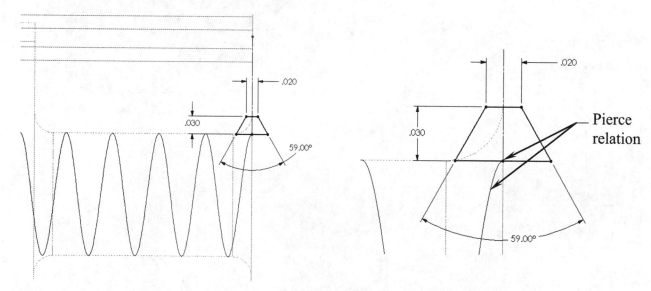 .

- <u>**Exit**</u> the sketch or Select **Insert / Sketch**.

34. Sweeping the thread Profile along the Helix:

- Click  or select **Insert / Cut / Sweep.**

- Select the thread profile to use as Sweep Profile .

- Select the Helix to use as Sweep Path .

- Click **OK** .

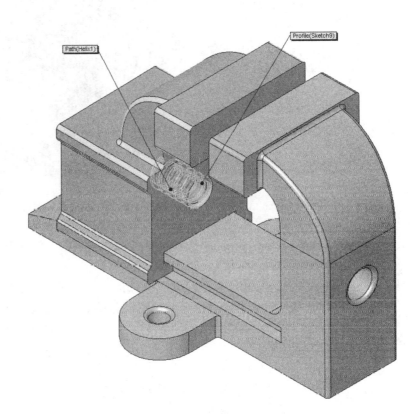

35. Creating a Section View:

- Click the **Section View** command or select **View / Display / Section View**.

- Use the **Right** plane for cutting.

- Verify the details of the threads.

- Click the **Section View** icon again to turn it off.

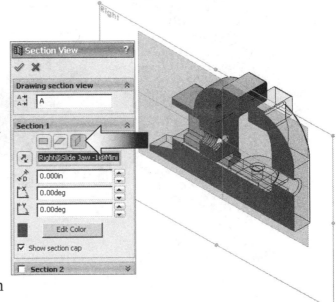

36. Saving your work.

- Save your work once again using the same file name: **Mini-Vise.sldasm**

- Overwrite the old file when prompted.

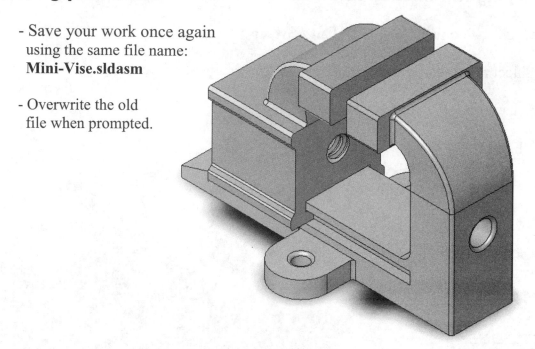

37. Assembly Exploded view (Optional):

- Create the additional components: Lead Screw, Crank Handle, and Crank Knob. Using the Top Down Assembly method, create an assembly exploded view as shown. (Details on next page)

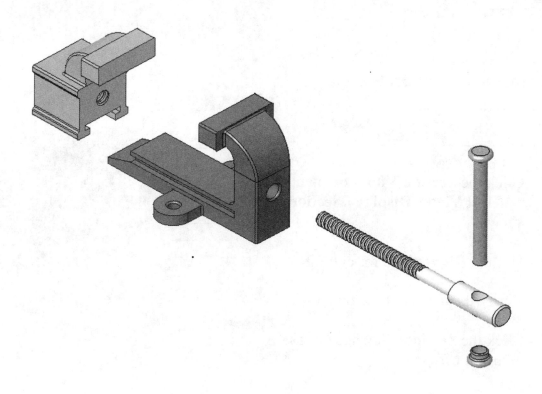

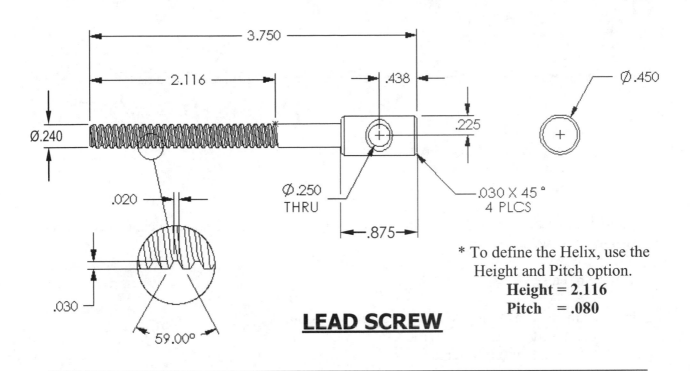

* To define the Helix, use the
Height and Pitch option.
Height = 2.116
Pitch   = .080

LEAD SCREW

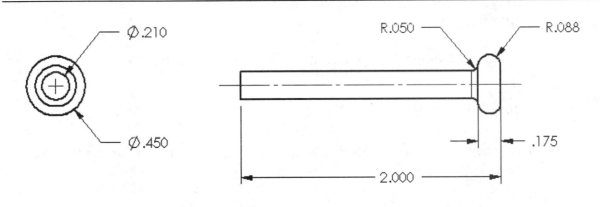

CRANK HANDLE

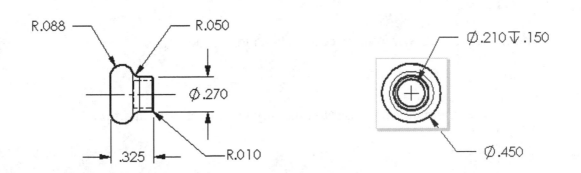

CRANK KNOB

Questions for Review

Top-Down Assembly

1. New parts can be created in context of an assembly.
   - a. True
   - b. False

2. Geometry of other components such as model edges, hole diameters, and locations etc., can be used to construct a new part.
   - a. True
   - b. False

3. Part documents can be inserted into an assembly using:
   - a. Insert menu
   - b. Windows Explorer
   - c. Drag and drop from an open window
   - d. All of the above

4. The suffix (f) next to the first part's name in the FeatureManager tree stands for:
   - a. Fail
   - b. Fixed
   - c. Float

5. When inserting new components into an assembly, the Inplace mates are created by the user.
   - a. True
   - b. False

6. Either in the part or assembly mode, the guide curves are used to help control the profiles from twisting, as they are swept along the path.
   - a. True
   - b. False

7. Centerpoint Arcs are drawn from its center, then radius, and angle.
   - a. True
   - b. False

8. The Link Values option allows a user to link only two dimensions at a time.
   - a. True
   - b. False

7. TRUE   8. FALSE
5. FALSE   6. TRUE
             4. B
3. D
1. TRUE   2. TRUE

CHAPTER 19

Top Down Assembly

Top Down Assembly
Water Control Valve

- When a component is built in the context of an assembly external references are created to reference how it was constructed, and which plane or surface was used to create it with. Starting from the very <u>Top</u> level assembly, information regarding the new component are added and flow <u>Down</u> to the component level, and gets repeated every time a new component is added.

- For example: The mounting holes in the second part can be converted from the first, so that the hole diameters and the location dimensions are the same for both parts. When the holes in the 1st part are changed, the holes in the 2nd part would also changed. Thus the sketch of the holes in the 2nd part is defined in the assembly, not by sketching and dimensioning them as in the part mode.

- Using the Top Down assembly design, one of the better approaches is to use the geometry of the existing parts to create the new. This way several parts can be controlled and changed at the same time.

- There are many advantages for creating parts in Top Down mode, and just to mention a few: not only this method is much quicker than the others due to the ability to use existing geometry to reference the new parts, but because all the parts are always visible in the assembly to help developing the <u>Form</u> of the new part, how it supposed to <u>Fit</u> with other parts , and therefore, it is more predictable how it is going to <u>Function</u>. Interference, friction and or clearance fits can be created and controlled within the very same screen.

- However, there are a few thing to consider when designing in Top Down mode:
    * External references are created to the geometry that the new part is referenced, and that means:
    * When changes occurred, the assembly updates all of its internal parts, and if drawings were made from these parts earlier, they will get updated as well.

Top Down Assembly
Water Control Valve

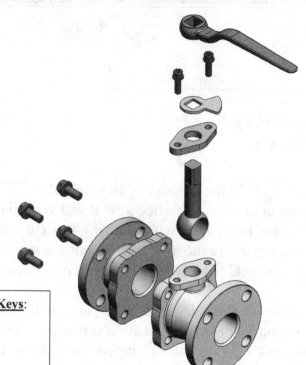

View Orientation Hot Keys:

Cntrl + 1 = Front View
Cntrl + 2 = Back View
Cntrl + 3 = Left View
Cntrl + 4 = Right View
Cntrl + 5 = Top View
Cntrl + 6 = Bottom View
Cntrl + 7 = Isometric View
Cntrl + 8 = Normal To
      Selection

Dimensioning Standards: **ANSI**

Units: **INCHES** – 3 Decimals

Tools Needed:

Insert Sketch	Line	Circle
Add Geometric Relations	Sketch Fillet	Trim
Dimension	Centerline	Fillet/Round
Base/Boss Revolve	Extruded Boss/Base	Assembly

1. Starting with a new Assembly Template:

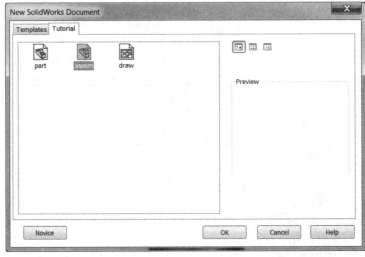

- Click **File / New**.

- Select an **Assembly** template either from the Template or the Tutorial tab.

- Click the **Advance** button at the lower left corner of this dialog box if you do not see the similar templates.

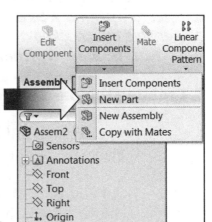

- The **Begin Assembly** dialog appears on the left side, click **Cancel**. We're going to use a different approach to create the new components.

- At the bottom right of the screen, set the Units to **IPS (Inch, Pound, Second).**

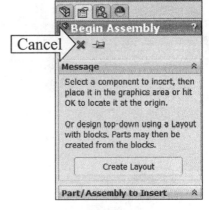

- From the **Assembly tab**, click the **drop arrow** below the Insert Components command and select: **New Part**.

- Creating components in context of an assembly will requires a few additional steps:

    a/. A new part is inserted into an Assembly and the Part's name is entered.

    b/. A plane is selected at this time to reference the new part.

    c/. The Edit Component command is activated and the Sketch mode is enabled for the plane selected in step b.

    d/. The Active part will have the color blue assigned to it automatically.

2. Creating the 1st component:

- When the symbol √ appears next to your mouse cursor, click the <u>Front</u> plane from the Feature tree. An Inplace mate is created to reference the new part.

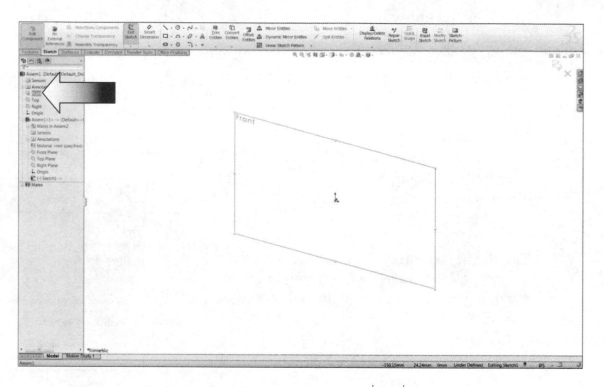

- Press **Control + 1** to switch to the Front orientation.

<u>NOTE:</u> *To automatically rotate normal to the sketch plane, go to System* **Options / Sketch,** *and enable the checkbox:* **Auto Rotate View Normal to**...

3. Creating the Base Profile:

- Sketch the profile <u>above</u> the origin.

- Add the dimensions shown. Notice the diameter dimensions are created as Virtual Diameters.

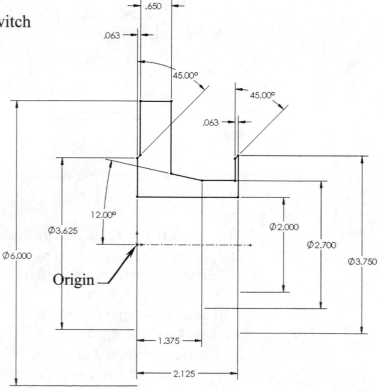

- Click **Revolve** .

- The centerline should be selected automatically.

- Use the default Blind option and revolve the sketch one complete revolution.

- Click **OK**.

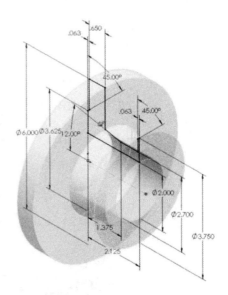

4. Adding the Inlet Flange:

- Select the <u>face</u> indicated and open a new sketch.

- Sketch the profile shown below. Use the Dynamic Mirror option to help speed up the sketching process.

- Add the dimensions and relations needed to fully define the sketch.

- The number of places are added to help clarify the sketch, you do not have to add them.

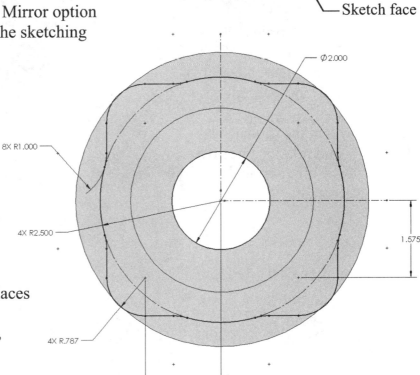

Sketch face

- Click **Extruded Boss-Base**.

- Use the **Blind** extrude option.

- Enter **.650"** for thickness.

- Enable the Merge Result checkbox.

- Click **OK**.

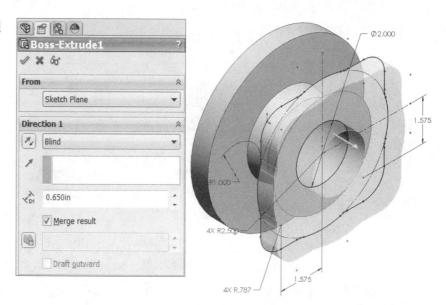

5. Adding the mounting holes:

- Select the <u>face</u> indicated and open a new sketch.

- Sketch a couple of center-lines to help locate the center and directions for this sketch.

- Add a circle and either mirror it or circular pattern it 4 times around.

- Add the dimensions and relations needed to fully define the sketch.

- Press **Extruded Cut**.

- Select the **Up-To-Next** extrude option.

- Click **OK**.

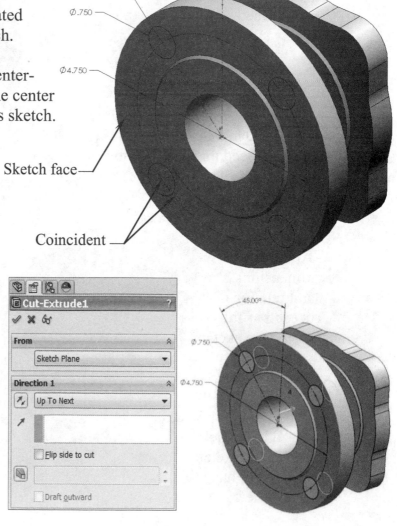

6. Adding other mounting holes:

- Select the <u>face</u> as noted and open a new sketch.

- Sketch a circle and **convert** it to **construction** (click the For-Construction checkbox on the Feature tree).

- Add a couple of **centerlines** as shown.

- Sketch a **smaller circle** that's coincident with the construction circle and the endpoint of the centerline.

- Use the **Circular-Sketch-Pattern** option to array the small circle 4 times around.

- Add the dimensions and relations needed to fully define this sketch.

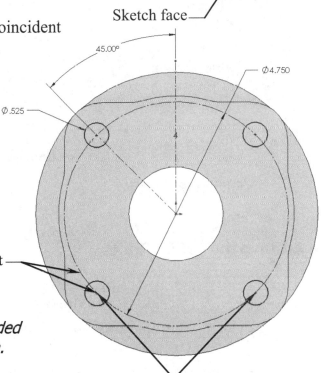

The center of the circle is coincident with the construction circle and the endpoint of the angled centerline.

Sketch face—

Coincident—

Horizontal

NOTE: *An additional Vertical or Horizontal relation between the centers of the small circles is needed when using the 2D sketch pattern.*

- Click **Extruded Cut**.

- Use the **Up-To-Next** extrude option to ensure that the cut only goes through the thickness of the flange.

- Click **OK**.

- Rotate the view to verify the cut result.

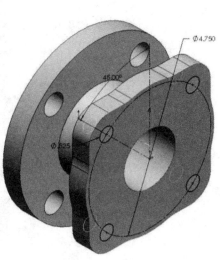

7. Adding the .032" chamfers:

- Click **Chamfer** (below the Fillet command).

- Enter **.032"** for Depth and use the default **45°** angle.

- Select the edges of the 8 holes and the 2 edges of the round flange.

- To un-select an edge simply click it once again.

- Click **OK**.

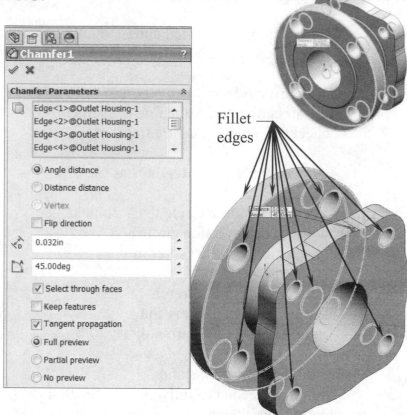

Fillet edges

8. Adding the .060" fillets:

- Click the **Fillet** command.

- Enter **.060"** for radius size.

Fillet edges

- Select the **3 edges** of the transition body.

- Enable the Full Preview checkbox.

- Change to the Top orientation (Control + 5) to verify the selection.

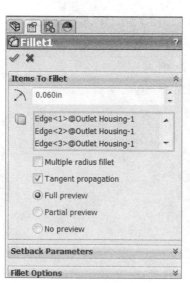

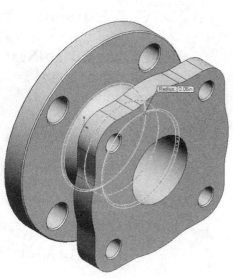

- Click **OK**.

9. Adding the .125" chamfers:

- Click **Chamfer** once again.

- Enter **.125"** for Depth and use the default **45°** angle.

- Select the **2 edges** of the center hole.

- Selecting the face of the hole would be the same as selecting its 2 edges.

- Click **OK**.

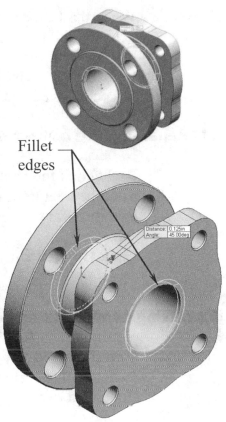

Fillet edges

10. Exiting the Edit Component mode:

- Click off the **Edit Component** button to return to the Edit Assembly mode.

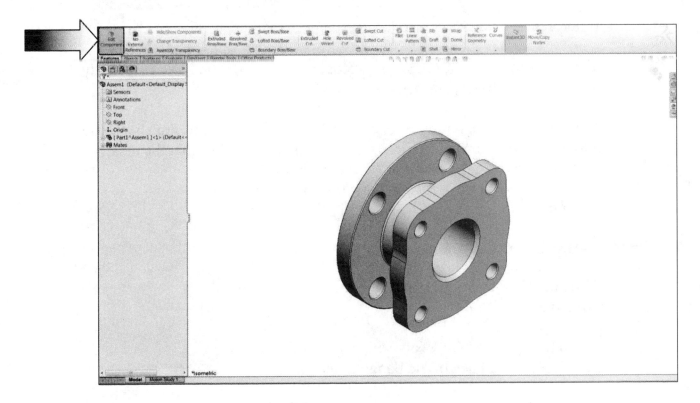

- When the Edit Component command is <u>not active</u>, the part's color goes back to its default color (grey).

- In the Edit Assembly mode, new components can be created or existing parts can be inserted and mated to others.

11. Renaming the component:

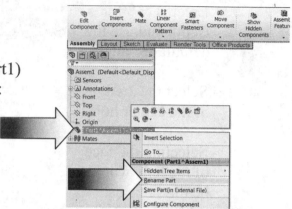

- Right click the name of the part (Part1) from the FeatureManager and select: **Rename Part** (arrow).

- Enter **Outlet Housing** and press enter.

12. Saving as Virtual Component:

- Virtual component are quite useful in the Top-Down Assembly mode. These components are saved internally, or embedded in the assembly document, instead of as separate part or sub-assembly documents.

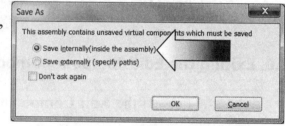

- Click **File /Save As**.

- Enter **Water Control Valve** for the file name and press **Save**.

- The Save As Virtual Component dialog appears, click the **Save Internally** (Inside the Assembly) option and click **OK**.

- When the parent assembly is opened, all virtual components are also loaded into RAM. The virtual components can then be opened so that the detail drawings can be generated from them, or they can simply be saved as external part documents to share with others.

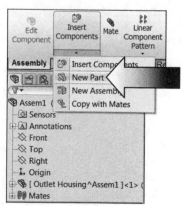

13. Creating the 2nd component:

- Click the **New Part** command from below the Insert-Components button (arrow).

- When the symbol √ appears next to your mouse cursor, click the <u>Face</u> of the flange as indicated.

- At this point, another Inplace
  mate is create for the new part.

- A new (blank) component
  is inserted on the Feature
  tree.

- The Outlet Housing turns
  to transparent (inactive).

- The **Edit Component** command
  is activated.

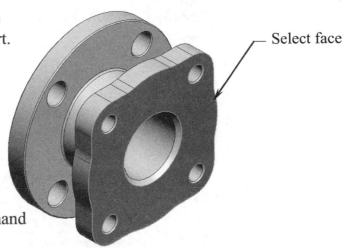

Select face

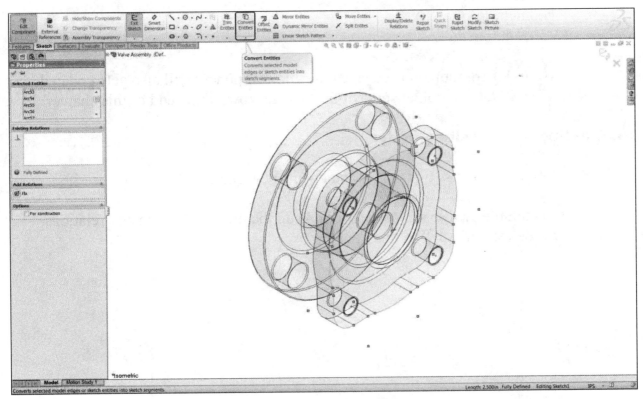

- The Sketch pencil is also enabled automatically.

  a/. Right click on one of the outer edges and
      pick **Select Tangency**.

  b/. Press **Convert Entities**. The selected
      edges are converted to new sketch entities.

- Convert also the **circular edges** of the 4 holes.

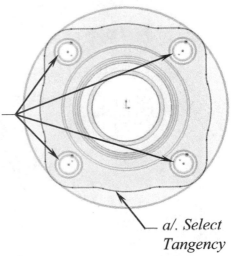

b/. Convert Entities

*a/. Select
Tangency*

- Click **Extruded Boss-Base**.

- Use the default **Blind** extrude option.

- Enter **.650"** for thickness.

- Click **OK**.

- The new flange is created using the geometry of the 1st component.

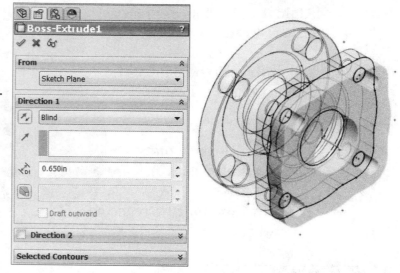

- If the 1st component is changed the 2nd component will also gets updated. We will take a look at some of the changes toward the end of this chapter.

14. Creating the transition body:

- Select the part's <u>Right</u> plane and open a new sketch.

- Sketch the profile shown below and add the dimensions and any relations needed to fully define this sketch.

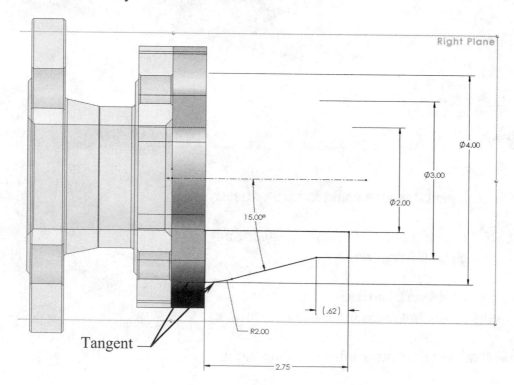

- Click **Revolve Boss-Base**.

- The revolve centerline is selected by default.

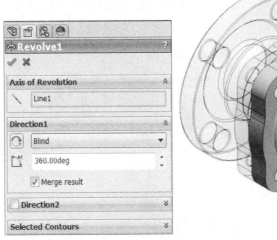
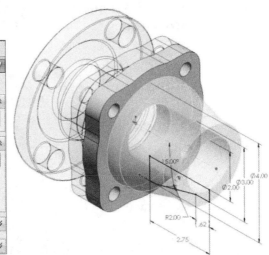

- Use the default settings:
  * **Blind**
  * **360deg**

- Click **OK**.

15. Adding another mounting flange:

- Select the <u>face</u> as indicated and open a new sketch.

- Hold the control key and select the circular edge of the round flange <u>and</u> the 4 edges of its mounting holes (arrow).

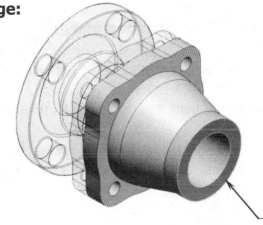

Sketch face

- Click **Convert Entities**.

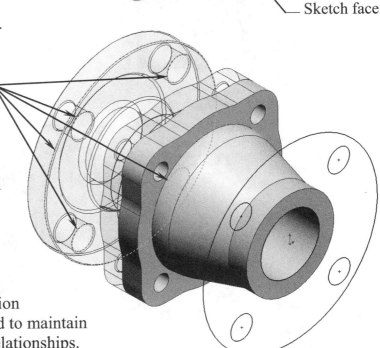

Convert 5 edges

- The selected edges are converted and projected onto the sketch face.

- Each sketch entity is linked to the original geometry where it was converted from. A relation called On-Edge is added to maintain their parent and child relationships.

- Click **Extruded Boss-Base**.

- Use the default **Blind** option.

- Enter **.650"** for depth.

- Extrude direction is outward.

- Click **OK**.

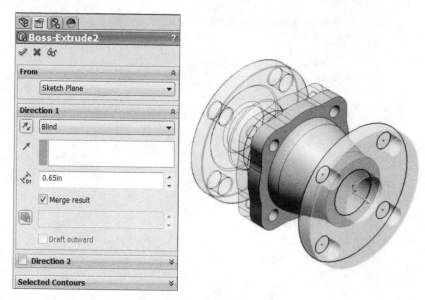

16. Adding an Offset-Distance plane:

- Select the Top plane of the part from the FeatureManager tree.

- From the Features tab, click **Reference Geometry / Plane**.

- The Offset Distance option should be selected already, enter **1.625"** for distance, and place the new plane above the Top plane.

- Click **OK**.

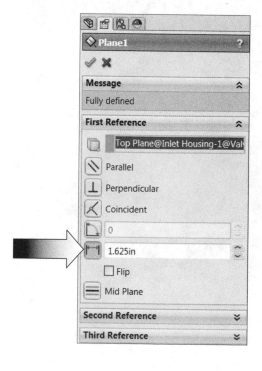

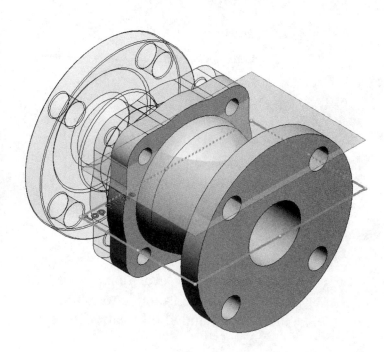

17. Adding a circular boss:

- Select the new <u>Plane1</u> and open a new sketch.

- Sketch a **circle** approx. as shown.

- Add the **1.50"** diameter dimension and the **1.00"** locating dimension.

- Add the **horizontal** relation as noted to fully define the sketch.

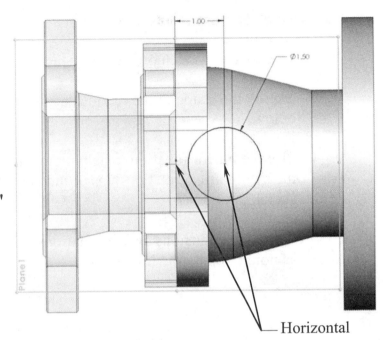

Horizontal

- Click **Extruded Boss-Base**.

- Use the default **Blind** option.

- Enter: **.875"** for depth.

- Click **OK**.

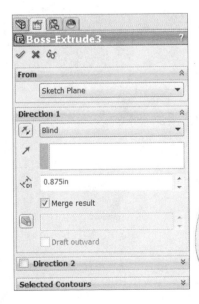

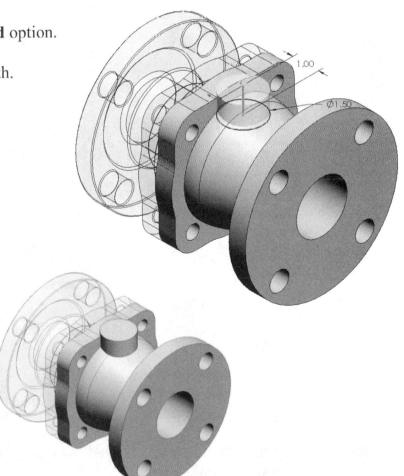

18. Adding a thermostat valve mount:

- Open a new sketch on the <u>upper face</u> of the boss.

- Sketch the shape of the thermostat shown below.

- Use the mirror function to help maintain the symmetrical relationships of the sketch entities.

- Add the dimensions and the relations as noted in the drawing below.

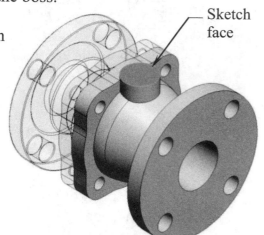

Sketch face

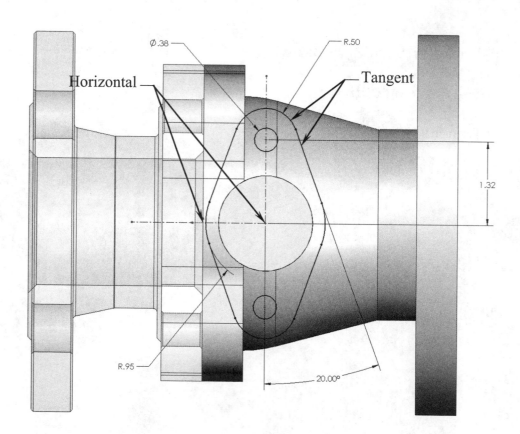

- The centers of the circles should be vertical with each other.

- If the mirror feature was not used, then be sure to add the symmetric relations to fully define this sketch.

- Click **Extruded Boss-Base**.

- For **Direction 1**: Use **Blind** and the depth of **.250"**.

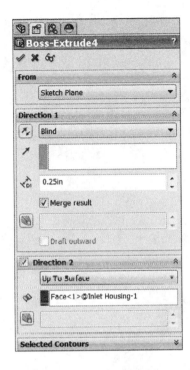

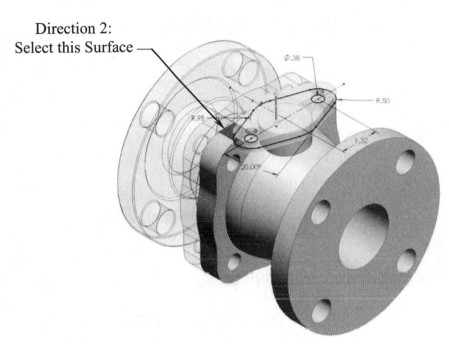

Direction 2:
Select this Surface

- For **Direction 2**: Use **Up-To-Surface** option and select the planar face of the square mount as indicated.

- Click **OK**.

19. Adding a hole:

- Open a new sketch on the upper face of the thermostat.

- Sketch a **Ø1.00 circle** and add a **concentric** relation to center it.

Sketch face

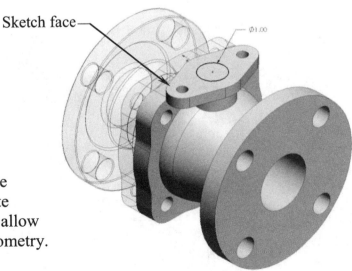

- Make use of the "Wake up the Entities Snap Mode". With the Circle command selected, hover the mouse cursor over the circular edge of the radius, the appropriate snap-entities will appear to allow snapping to the existing geometry.

- Click **Extruded Cut**.

- Click the **Reverse** direction button.

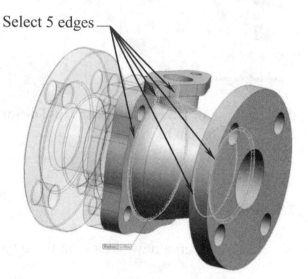

- Select the option **Up-To-Next** from the list

- Click **OK**.

20. Adding the .080" fillets:

- From the Features tab, click **Fillet**.

- Enter **.080"** for radius size.

- Select the **5 edges** as indicated.

- The Tangent Propagation checkbox should be selected.

Select 5 edges

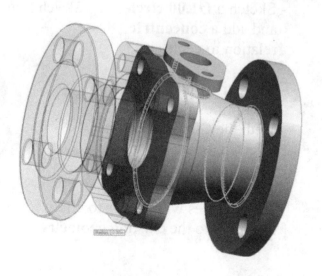

- Click **OK**.

21. Adding the .032" chamfers:

- Click **Chamfer** below the Fillet command.

- Enter **.032"** for depth.

- Use the default **45deg** angle.

- Select the **edges** of the holes as shown in the preview image. (23 edges total).

- The same result can be achieved by selecting the inner faces of the holes.

- Click **OK**.

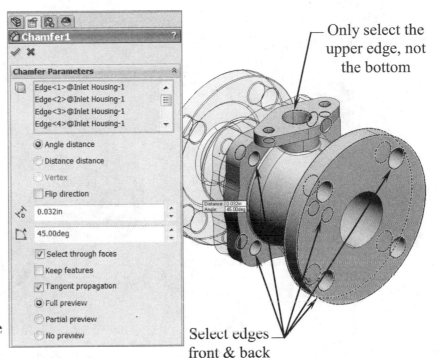
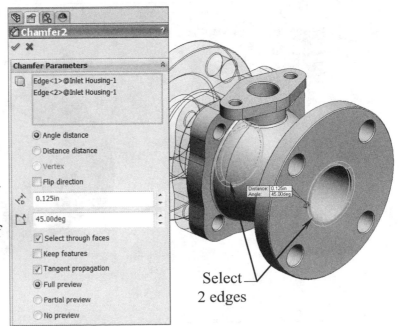

Only select the upper edge, not the bottom

Select edges front & back

22. Adding the .125" chamfers:

- Click **Chamfer** once again.

- Enter **.125"** for depth.

- Use the same **45deg** angle.

- Select the **2 edges** of the center hole. (Selecting the face of the hole would get the same result).

- Click **OK**.

Select 2 edges

23. Exiting the Edit Component mode:

- On the Assembly toolbar, click off the **Edit Component** command (arrow).

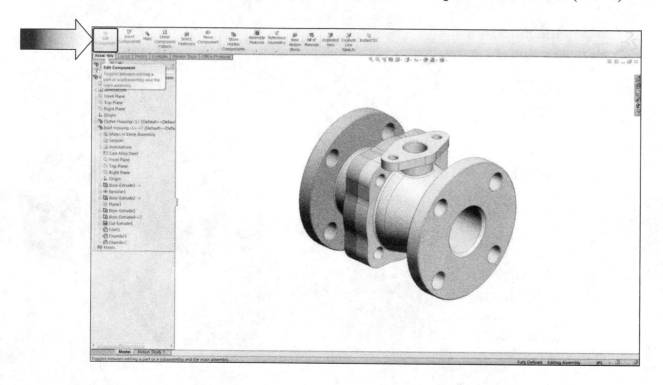

24. Applying dimensions changes:

- Expand the part Outlet Housing and double click on the feature **Revolve1**.

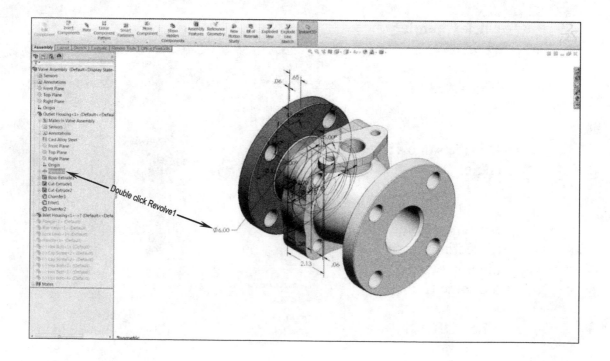

- Change the flange diameter **from 6.00" to 7.00"**

- Click the **Rebuild** (the green traffic light) to execute the change*.

- Notice the dimension change also updates the flange diameter on the right.

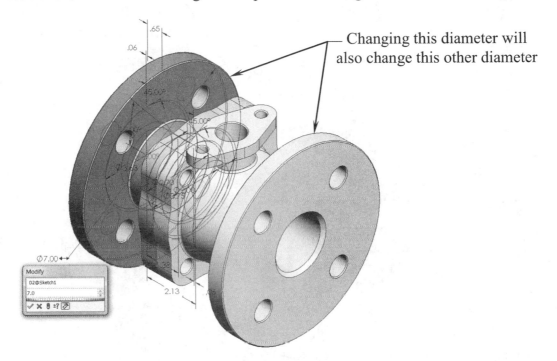

Changing this diameter will also change this other diameter

* Press <u>undo</u> to switch the dimension back to its original value, or double click the same dimension, re-enter the previous value, and click Rebuild again.

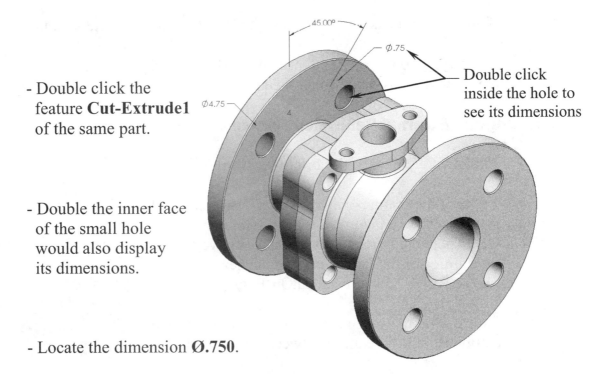

- Double click the feature **Cut-Extrude1** of the same part.

Double click inside the hole to see its dimensions

- Double the inner face of the small hole would also display its dimensions.

- Locate the dimension **Ø.750**.

- Change the hole diameter **from .750" to .500"**.

- Click the **Rebuild** green traffic light to execute the change*.

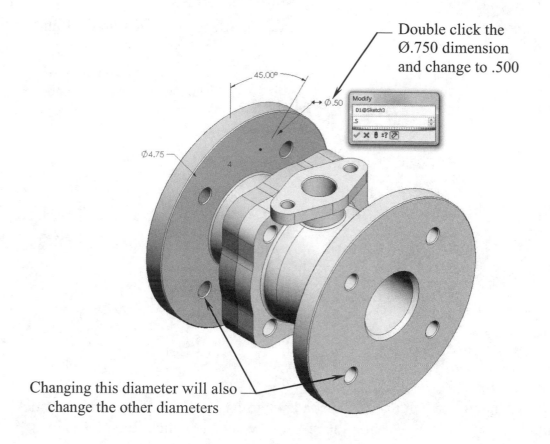

Double click the
Ø.750 dimension
and change to .500

Changing this diameter will also
change the other diameters

- Notice the dimension change also updates the hole diameters on the right.

* Press <u>undo</u> to switch the dimension back to its original value, or double click
the same dimension, re-enter the previous value, and click Rebuild again.

25. Viewing the External Reference Symbols:

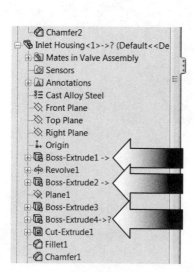

- Expand the 2nd part, the **Inlet Housing**.

- Some of the features have the External reference
symbols next to their names. These references
were created automatically when we converted
the entities of the Part1 to create the new sketch
for the Part2. They are called On-Edge relations.

- An external reference is also created when we add
a dimension or a relation between Part1 and Part2.

26. Inserting other components:

- Due to the length of this lesson, we are going to insert and mate the rest of the components that belong to this assembly.

- Go to the Training CD and insert the components as labeled below.

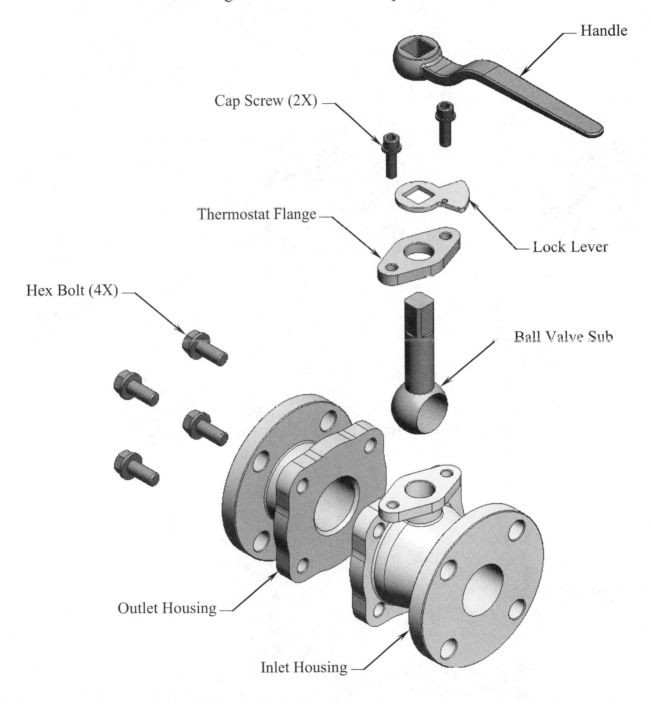

- Create the mates that are appropriate for each component. The non-moving components will get 3 mates, and the moving components will need only two.

27. Optional:

a/. Create a section view to verify how the components were mated.

b/. To center the 2 components, it is best to use the Width mate option.

c/. Change / correct any mates or geometry that would cause the interferences.

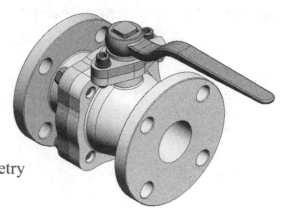

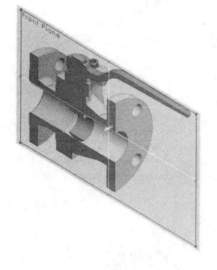

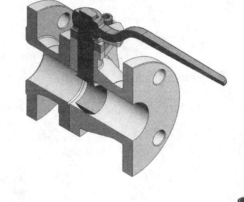

- Add the Explode-Line Sketch as shown.

- When adding the explode lines, pay attention to the direction arrows, flip or reverse them before completing each line.

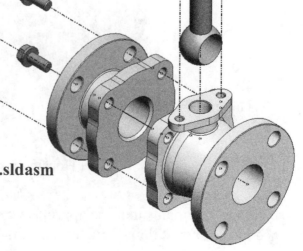

28. Saving your work:

- Click **File / Save As**.

- Enter **Water Control Valve.sldasm** for the name of the file.

- Press **Save**.

Questions for Review

Top Down Assembly

1. In Top Down mode, when a plane is selected to sketch the new part, SolidWorks will create an Inplace mate to reference the new part.
   - a. True
   - b. False

2. After the plane is selected, SolidWorks will also activate the Edit Component command and the Sketch mode at the same time.
   - a. True
   - b. False

3. The option Auto-Rotate Normal to the Sketch is not available to set as the default.
   - a. True
   - b. False

4. The Convert Entities command can only be used when the Sketch pencil is turned off.
   - a. True
   - b. False

5. The Virtual part is saved / embedded inside an assembly document.
   - a. True
   - b. False

6. When editing a part in Top Down mode, both the current part and other parts can be filleted at the same time.
   - a. True
   - b. False

7. The Edit Component command should be left active prior to inserting a new part.
   - a. True
   - b. False

8. When a dimension is changed, any reference geometry of other parts should also changed.
   - a. True
   - b. False

7. FALSE 8. TRUE
5. TRUE   6. FALSE
3. FALSE 4. FALSE
1. TRUE   2. TRUE

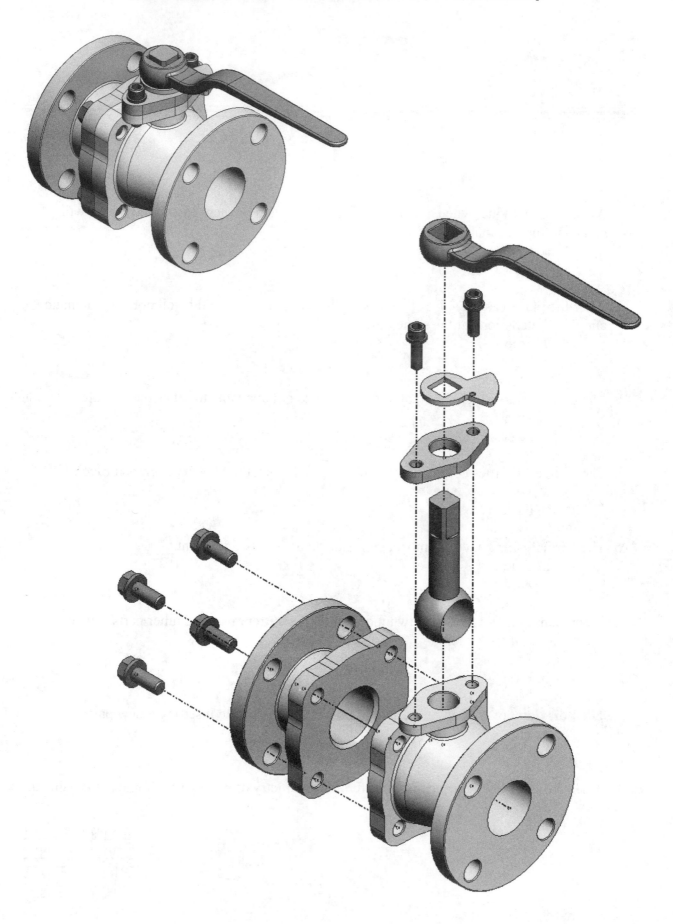

Top Down Assembly
Using the Lip & Groove option

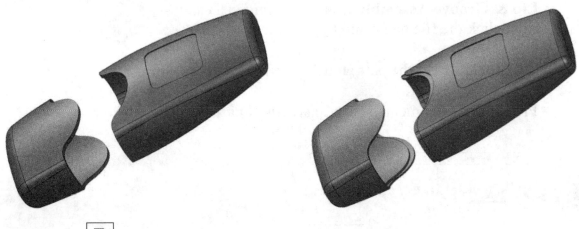

Lip & Groove

- You can create lip and groove fastening features to align, mate, and hold together two plastic parts.
    * The Lip option adds material to the part
    * The Groove option removes material from the part

- This session discusses the in-depth details of creating a set of Lip & Groove for the two plastic parts.

Fastening features streamline the creation of common features for plastic and sheet metal parts. You can create: **Lips and Grooves**. Align, mate, and hold together two plastic parts. Lip and groove features support multibodies and assemblies.	
Mounting bosses. Create a variety of mounting bosses. Set the number of fins and choose a hole or a pin.	
Snap hooks and **snap hook grooves**. Customize the snap hook and snap hook groove. You must first create a snap hook before you can create a snap hook groove.	
Vents. Create a variety of vents using a sketch you create. Set the number of ribs and spars. Flow area is calculated automatically. *(Images Courtesy of the SolidWorks Online Help)*	

Using the Lip & Groove option

1. Opening the existing assembly document named:
Lip & Groove Assembly from the training CD and
right click the file name and <u>Collapse</u> the assembly.

2. Editing Part: Select the part **Housing** and click **Edit Component**.

    - From the **Insert** menu, select **Fastening Feature / Lip /Groove**.

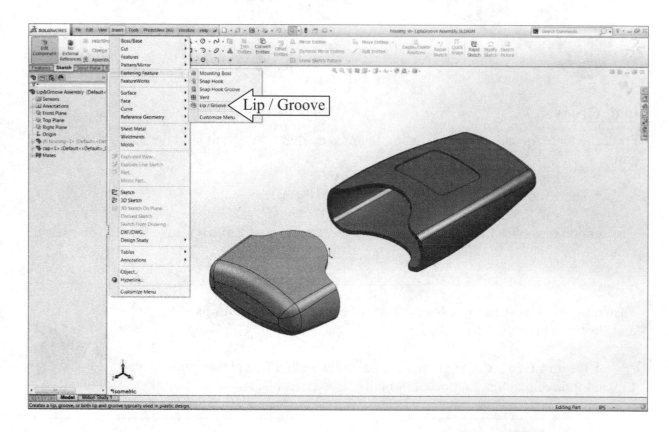

- Select the following from
the FeatureManager tree:

Cap: Lip

Direction: Front

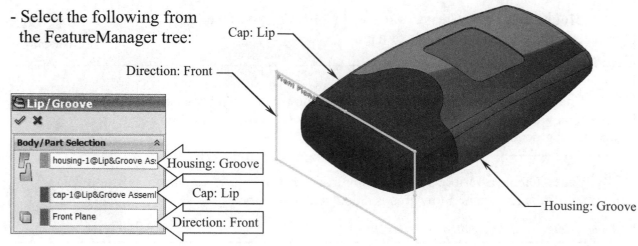

Housing: Groove

Lip/Groove

Body/Part Selection

housing-1@Lip&Groove As: Housing: Groove

cap-1@Lip&Groove Assem| Cap: Lip

Front Plane   Direction: Front

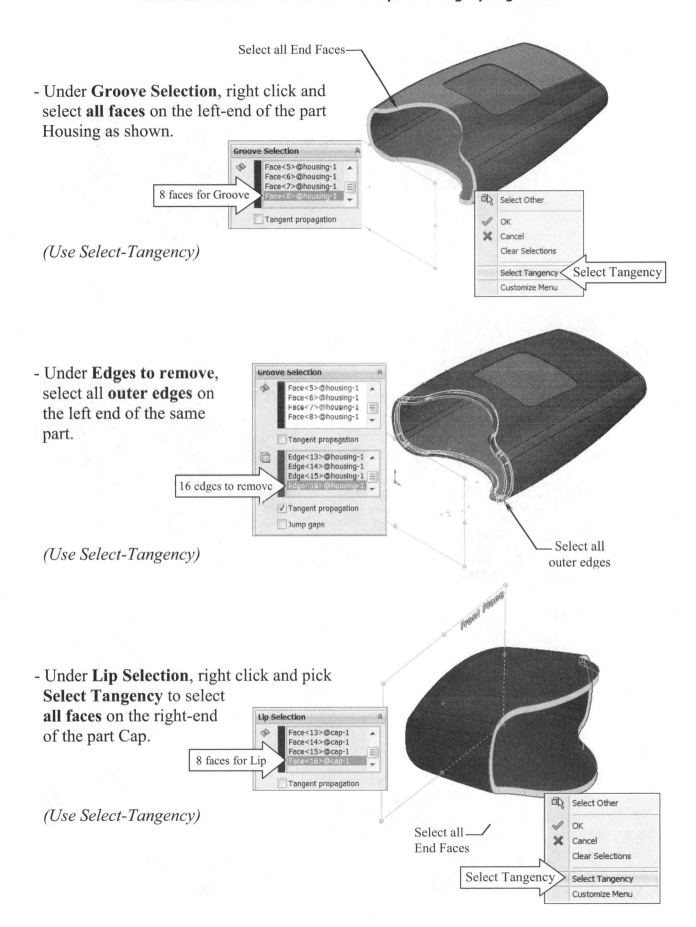

- Under **Groove Selection**, right click and select **all faces** on the left-end of the part Housing as shown.

Select all End Faces

(Use Select-Tangency)

8 faces for Groove

Select Tangency

- Under **Edges to remove**, select all **outer edges** on the left end of the same part.

16 edges to remove

(Use Select-Tangency)

Select all outer edges

- Under **Lip Selection**, right click and pick **Select Tangency** to select **all faces** on the right-end of the part Cap.

8 faces for Lip

(Use Select-Tangency)

Select all End Faces

Select Tangency

- Under **Edges To Add Material**, select all **outer edges** on the right-end of the same part.

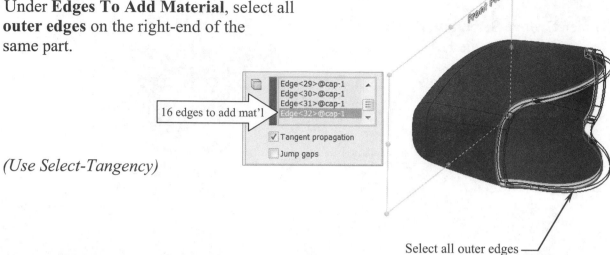

16 edges to add mat'l

(Use Select-Tangency)

Select all outer edges

- Under **Parameters**, set the followings:

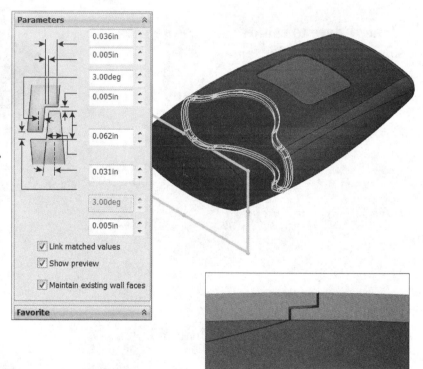

* Groove Width: **.031in.**

* Spacing : **0.005in.**

* Groove Draft: **3.00deg.**

* Upper Gap: **0.005in.**

* Lip Height: **.062in.**

* Lip Width: **.031in.**

* Lower Gap: **0.005in.**

- Click **OK** ✅.

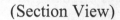

(Section View)

3. Saving your work:

- Save your work using the same file name and overwrite the old document.

Top Down Assembly
Using the Mounting Boss Option

Mounting Boss

You can create common mounting features for plastic parts like Mounting Bosses, Snap Hooks, Snap Hook Grooves, Vents, and Lips/Grooves.

The mounting bosses come with a variety of options to help streamline the creation of common Fastening features.

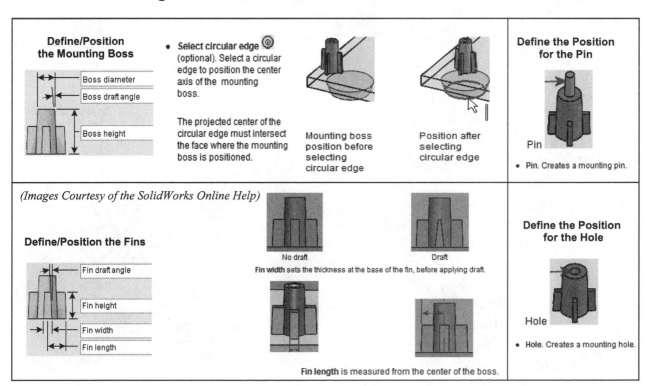

Using the Mounting Boss option

1. Opening the existing assembly document named:
Mounting Boss Assembly from the Training CD folder,
right click the file name, and <u>Collapse</u> the Assembly.

2. Editing Part: Select the part **Lower Half** and click **Edit Component** .

- From the **Insert** menu, select **Fastening Feature / Mounting Boss**.

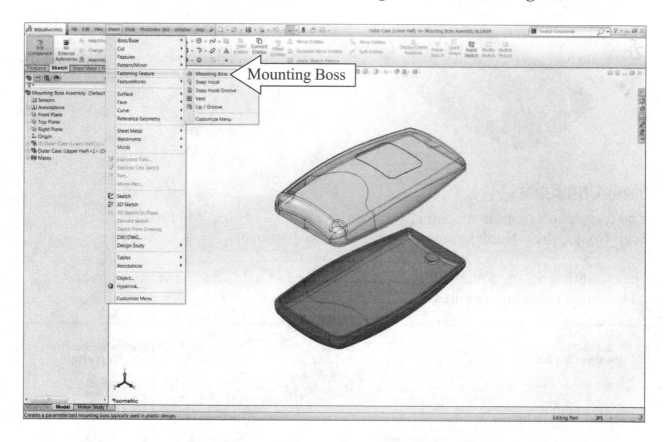

3. Setting the Parameters:

- The options to set
the parameters for
the mounting boss
appear on the tree.

- For **Position Face**
of the Mounting-
Boss, select the
face as shown.

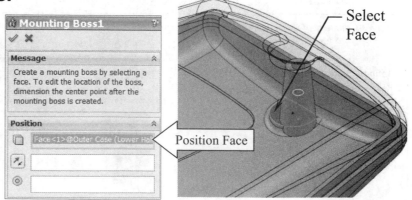

Select
Face

Mounting Boss1

Message

Create a mounting boss by selecting a
face. To edit the location of the boss,
dimension the center point after the
mounting boss is created.

Position

Face<1>@Outer Case (Lower Half) ← Position Face

- For **Position Edge** to line up the Mounting Boss, select the **circular edge** as shown.

(Use the Top plane here for direction only when required)

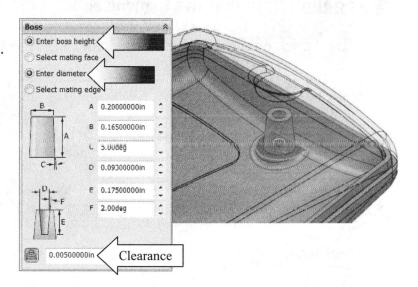

Position Edge

Select Edge

- Under the **Boss Type** section, select the **Pin Boss** and the **Hole** option.

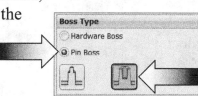

- Under the Boss section, click the **Enter Boss Height** and **Enter Diameter** options.

- Enter the following dimensions:

    * **A = .200in**.

    * **B = .165in**.

    * **C = 5.00deg**.

    * **D = .093in**.

    * **E = .175in**.

    * **F = 2.00deg**

    * **Clearance = .005in**.

Clearance

- Under the **Fins** section, change the number of fins to **0** (zero).

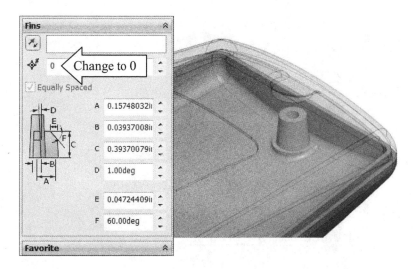

Change to 0

- Click **OK** ✓.

4. Adding 2 more mounting bosses:

- Repeat the steps above and create two other Mounting Bosses on the opposite side.

- Exit the **Edit Component** 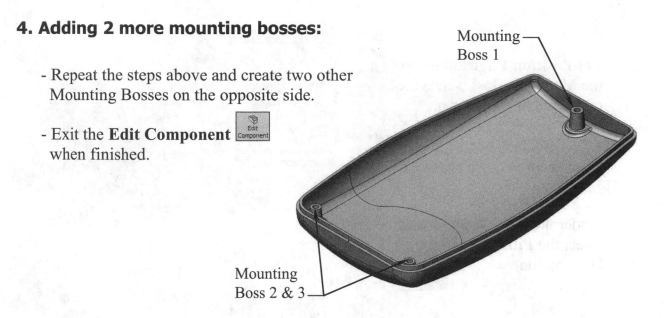 when finished.

Mounting Boss 1

Mounting Boss 2 & 3

5. Toggling between the Explode and the Collapse views:

- Right click on the name of the assembly and select **Explode***.

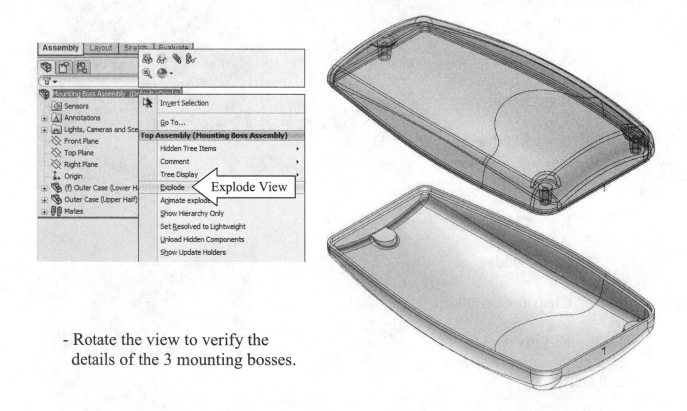

- Rotate the view to verify the details of the 3 mounting bosses.

* Remember to **Collapse** the assembly prior to editing the next component.

6. Creating the Mating Bosses:

- Select the part **Outer-Case (Upper Half)** and click the **Edit Component** 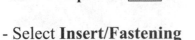 command.

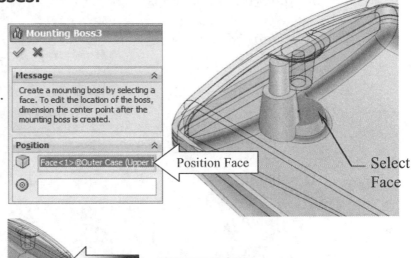

Position Face   Select Face

- Select **Insert/Fastening Feature/ Mounting Boss**.

- For **Position Face**, select the **Face** as indicated. (To select the hidden face, right click in the area where the surface is under and pick **Select Other** then select the face from the list.

- For **Direction**, select the **Top** plane from the Feature tree (use only if required).

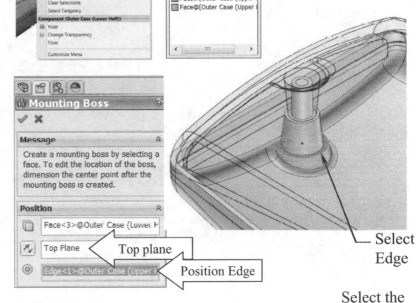

Top plane   Position Edge   Select Edge

- For **Position Edge**, select the **Edge** as noted to align the center of the mounting boss to the center of the circular edge.

- Under the **Boss Type** section, select the **Pin Boss** option.

Select the Mating Face

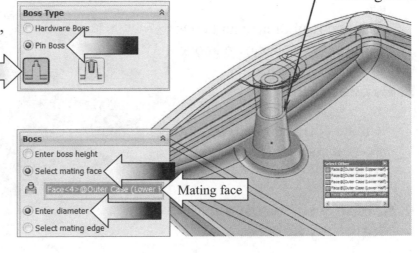

Mating face

- Select the options **Select-Mating Face** and **Enter-Diameter**.

- Select the **upper surface** of the mounting boss as noted.

- Enter the following dimensions:

    * **A = Defined by mating face**.

    * **B = .157 in.**

    * **C = 5.00deg.**

    * **D = .080in.**

    * **E = .165in**.

    * **F = 2.00deg.**

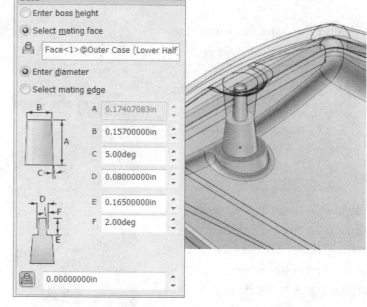

- Click **OK** when finished.

- Click off the **Edit Component** button.

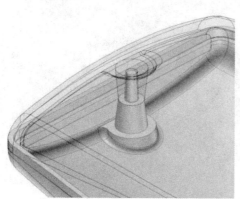

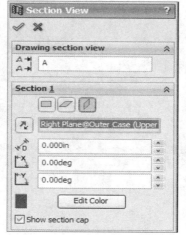

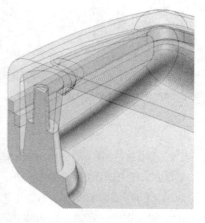

Section View

7. Creating a Section View:

- Use the <u>Right</u> plane and create a section view as shown above.

8. Repeating:

- Create two additional Mounting-Bosses, use the same settings as the first one.

9. Saving your work as: Mounting Bosses.

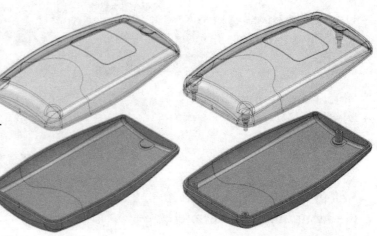

CHAPTER 20

External References

External References & Repair Errors

An **external reference** is created when one document is dependent on another document for its solution. If the referenced document changes, the dependent document changes also.

In an assembly, you can create an **in-context** feature on one component that references the geometry of another component. This in-context feature has an external reference to the other component. If you change the geometry on the referenced component, the associated in-context feature changes accordingly.

The External Symbols:

-> .... External Reference   ? .... Out Of Context

(+) .... Over Defined   * .... Reference Locked

X .... Reference Broken

a. External Reference ->:
The part itself or some of its entities are depending on the geometry of other parts for their solutions.

b. Out Of Context ?:
The part or its features are not solved, not up-to-date or disconnected from its assembly.

c. Over Defined (+):
The Dimensions or Relations of the sketch are conflicting; redundant dimensions or wrong relations were used.

d. Reference Locked *:
Lock the external references on a part, the existing references no longer update and the part will not accept any new references from that point.

e. Reference Broken X:
The references between the part and the others are broken.
Changes done to the part will not affect the others.

External References & Repair Errors

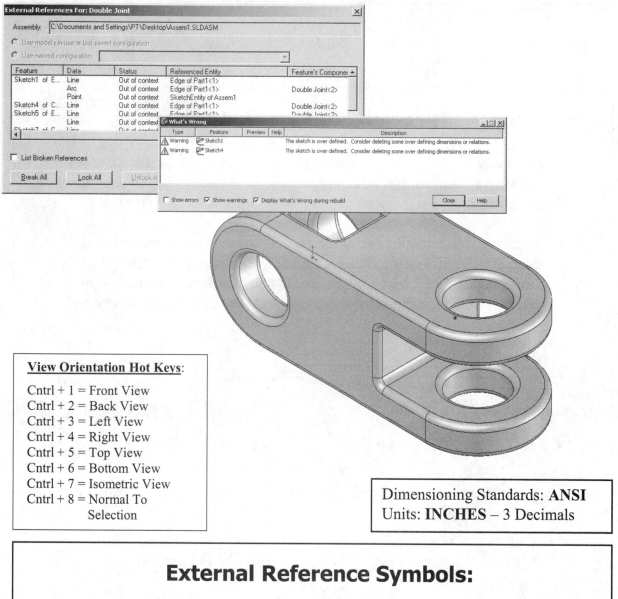

View Orientation Hot Keys:

Cntrl + 1 = Front View
Cntrl + 2 = Back View
Cntrl + 3 = Left View
Cntrl + 4 = Right View
Cntrl + 5 = Top View
Cntrl + 6 = Bottom View
Cntrl + 7 = Isometric View
Cntrl + 8 = Normal To
               Selection

Dimensioning Standards: **ANSI**
Units: **INCHES** – 3 Decimals

External Reference Symbols:

Symbol	Meaning	Symbol	Meaning
->	External Reference	?	Out of Context
(+)	Over Defined	*	External Reference Locked
X	External Reference Broken		Display/Delete Relations

Understanding & Removing External References

1. Opening an existing part: Double Joint

- <u>Go to:</u>

    Training CD
    Repair Errors folder.

- Open the part named: **Double Joint**.

- The What's Wrong dialog appears displaying the current errors.

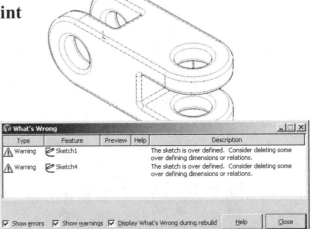

2. Listing the External References:

- Right click on the part's name and select **List External Refs**.

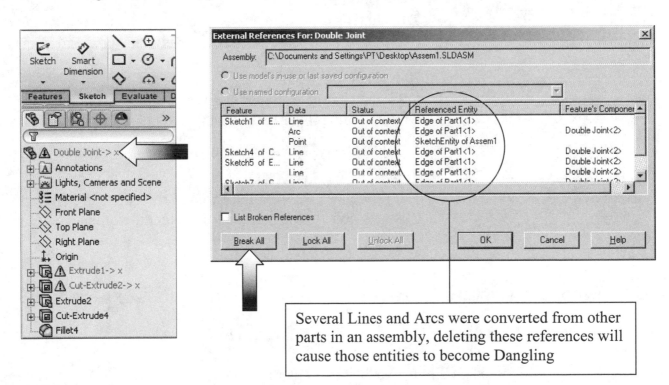

Several Lines and Arcs were converted from other parts in an assembly, deleting these references will cause those entities to become Dangling

3. Removing External References:

- Click Break All to remove the external references.

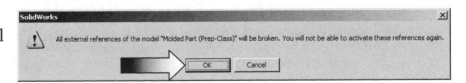

- Click OK [OK] .

4. Understanding the External Symbols:

-> .... External Reference
? .... Out Of Context
(+) .... Over Defined
∗ .... Reference Locked
X .... Reference Broken

💡 **Error Colors**

- **Olive Green:** Dangling

- **Red:** Over Defined

- **Yellow:** Not Solved

(From the Feature-Manager tree, expand the first two features, to see their sketches)

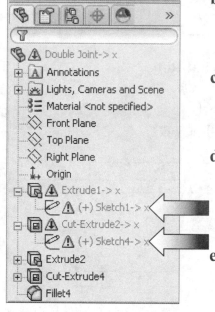

a. External Reference ->:
The part itself or some of its entities are depending on the geometry of other parts for their solutions.

b. Out Of Context ?:
The part or its features are not solved, not up-to-date, or disconnected from its assembly.

c. Over Defined (+):
The Dimensions or Relations of the sketch are conflicting; Redundant dimensions or wrong relations were used.

d. Reference Locked ∗:
Lock the external references on a part, the existing references no longer update - and - the part will not accept any new references from that point.

e. Reference Broken X:
The references between the part and the others are broken. Changes done to the part will not affect the others.

5. Viewing the existing Relations:

- Right-click on the 1st sketch and select **Edit-Sketch** ✎ .

- Click 🔲 or select **Tools / Relations / Display/Delete.**

- The Ø.325 is shown in Olive Green color; this indicates either a relation is wrong or the sketch is over dimensioned.

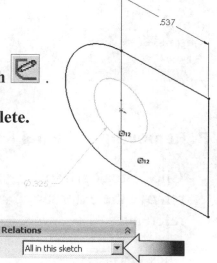

- Change the Relations Filter to **All In This Sketch**

6. Repairing the 1st sketch:

- Click **Display / Delete Relations** and delete the **Coradial** relation (the Circle is Coradial with an entity that is no longer exists).

- Delete all relations that have the External Relations (->X) next to their names.

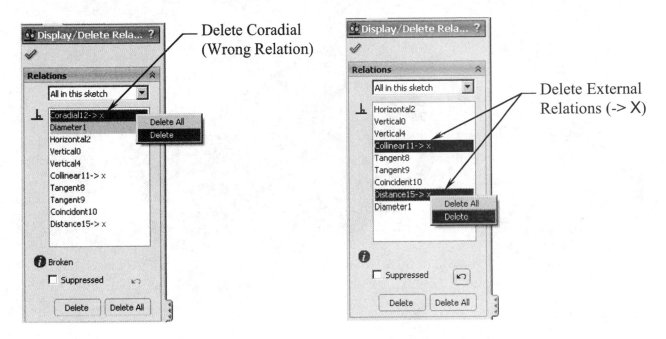

Delete Coradial (Wrong Relation)

Delete External Relations (-> X)

- Add the new Dimensions as noted to fully define the sketch.

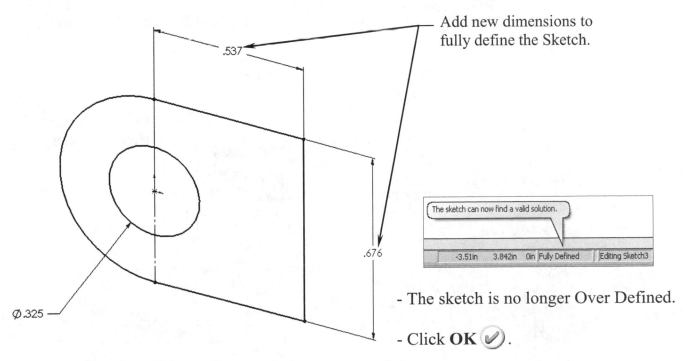

Add new dimensions to fully define the Sketch.

- The sketch is no longer Over Defined.

- Click **OK** .

- **Exit** the sketch. There are still some errors in the part.

7. Repairing the 2nd sketch:

- Right click on the 2nd sketch and select **Edit-Sketch** and click the **Display- / Delete Relations** command once again.

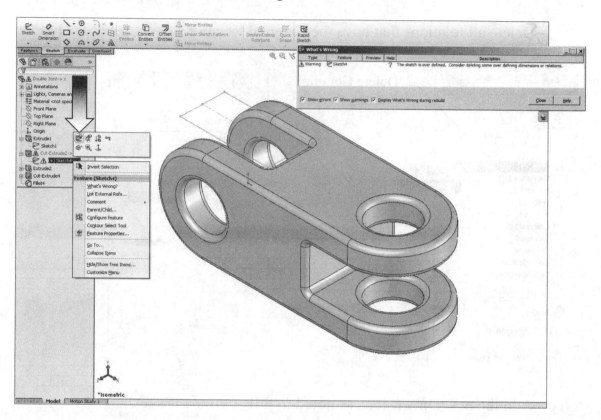

- Delete the External Dimensions and Relations that were created in context of other parts.

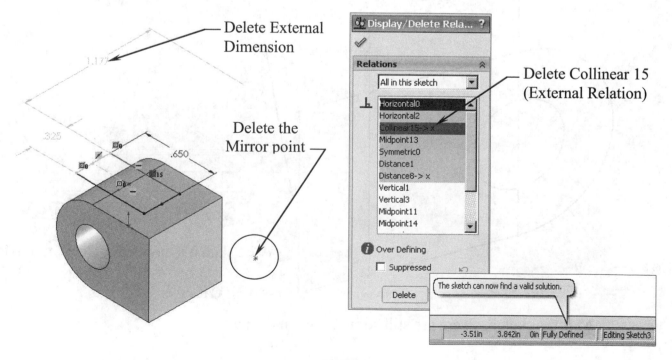

Delete External Dimension

Delete the Mirror point

Delete Collinear 15 (External Relation)

The sketch can now find a valid solution.

8. Rebuilding the model:

- Press Rebuild 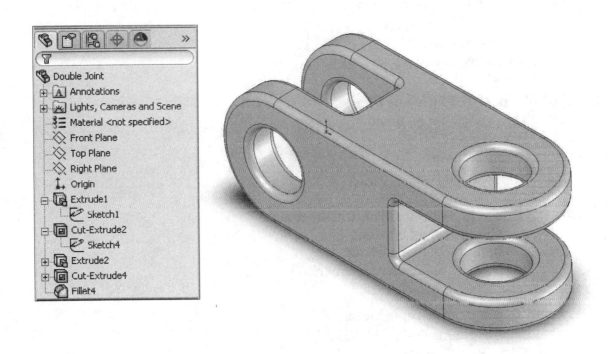 to re-generate the model.

- Verify that the part has no rebuild errors and there should not be any external reference symbols in the FeatureManager tree.

9. Saving your work:

- Select **File / Save As / Breaking External References / Save**.

Questions for Review

External References

1. The symbol -> next to a file name means:
    - a. Dangling dimension
    - b. External reference
    - c. Not solved

2. The symbol ? next to a file name means:
    - a. The part cannot be found
    - b. Wrong mates
    - c. Wrong relations
    - d. Out of context

3. The symbol **X** next to a file or a feature name means:
    - a. The part or feature is wrong
    - b. The part or feature is deleted
    - c. The external references are broken

4. The symbol * next to a file name means:
    - a. External references are locked
    - b. Select all references
    - c. Deselect all references

5. The symbol *X next to a feature name means:
    - a. The feature is fully defined
    - b. The feature is over defined
    - c. The feature is under defined
    - d. None of the above.

6. The Olive-Green color in a sketch means:
    - a. The sketch entity is selected
    - b. The sketch entity is being copied.
    - c. The sketch has dangling entities, relations or dimensions.

7. The dangling dimensions can be "re-attached" simply by dragging its handle point to a sketch line or a model edge.
    - a. True
    - b. False

7. TRUE
5. D   6. C
3. C   4. A
1. B   2. D

Repair Errors & External References

1. Opening an existing part:

- <u>Go to</u>:

  The Training CD.
  Repair Errors folder.

- Open the document named:
  Molded Part.

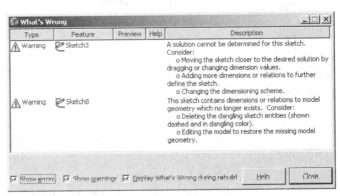

- The What's Wrong dialog pops
  up displaying the current errors.

- Click **Close**. We are going to
  take a look at breaking the
  external references first.

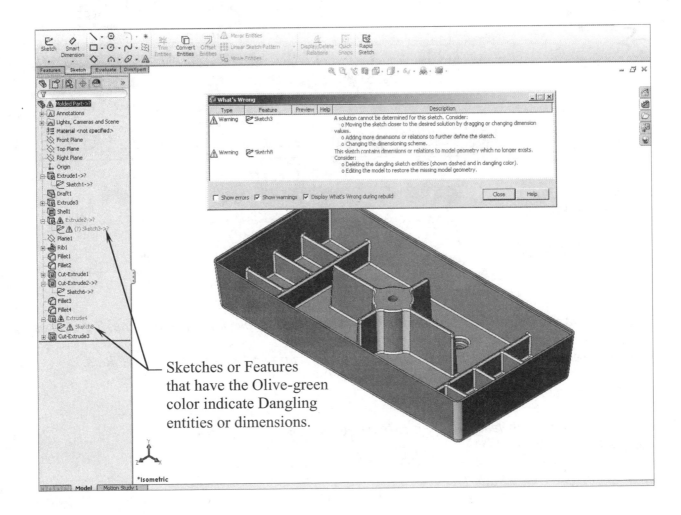

Sketches or Features
that have the Olive-green
color indicate Dangling
entities or dimensions.

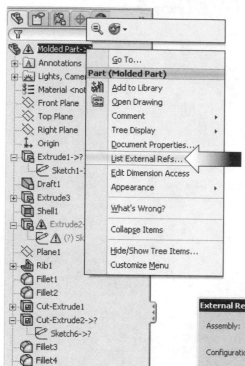

2. Breaking all External References:

- Right click on the part's name and select: **List External Refs**.

- All of the Out of Context entities are displayed in the dialog box along with the names of the component parts in which they were related.

- Click **Break All** (Arrow).

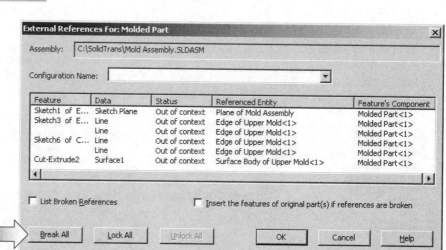

- Click **OK** [OK] to confirm the deletion of all External References.

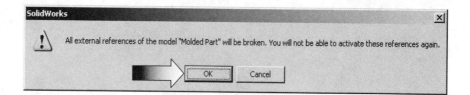

💡 **_TIPS:_** _**4 basic steps** should be done, in most cases, to repair or replace External References:_

1. Break all External references (Right click on the part's name and select List External Refs.).

2. Replace the sketch Plane or Face (if missing).

3. Delete or replace any Relation with an External Reference symbol next to it (Display/Delete Relations).

4. Repair or replace the extrude type.

3. Replacing the Sketch Plane:

- Expand the **Extrude1** feature to see the **Sketch1** below.

- Right click on **Sketch1** and select **Edit Sketch Plane**  .

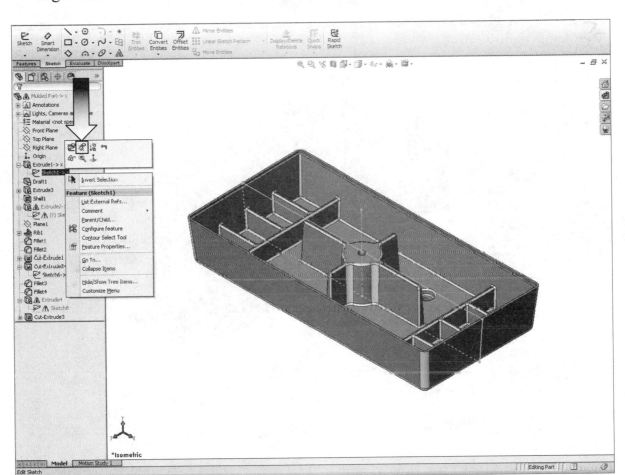

- The Sketch Plane is missing, its dialog box is empty

- Select the **Front** plane from the Feature tree.

- After replacing the plane, click **OK** ⊘.

- The system displays the warning on other errors along with the solutions for repairing.

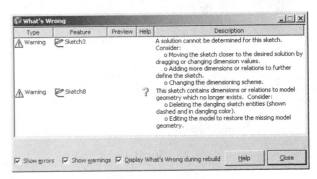

- Click **Close** Close .

4. Repairing the sketch Relations and Dimensions:

- Right click on **Sketch1** and select **Edit Sketch**.

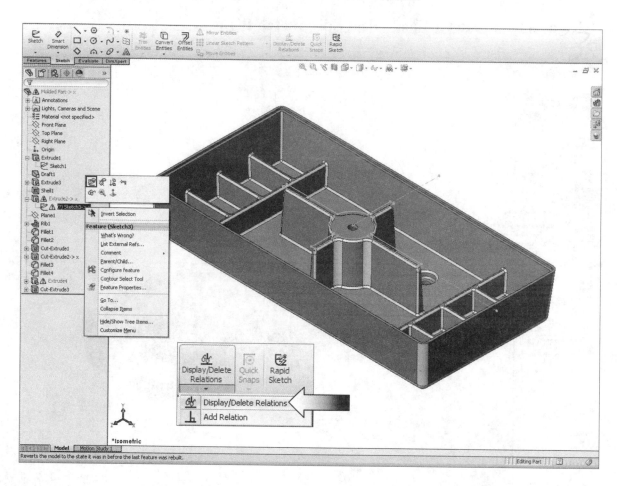

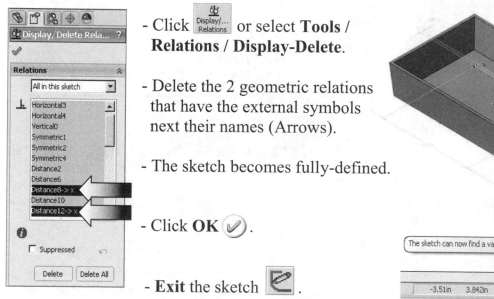

- Click [Display/... Relations] or select **Tools / Relations / Display-Delete**.

- Delete the 2 geometric relations that have the external symbols next their names (Arrows).

- The sketch becomes fully-defined.

- Click **OK**.

- **Exit** the sketch.

The sketch can now find a valid solution.

| -3.51in | 3.842in | 0in | Fully Defined | Editing Sketch3 |

5. Repairing the next sketch errors:

- Right click on **Sketch6** (under Cut-Extrude2) and select:

Edit Sketch .

- Two dimensions are no longer attached to the part (Circled).

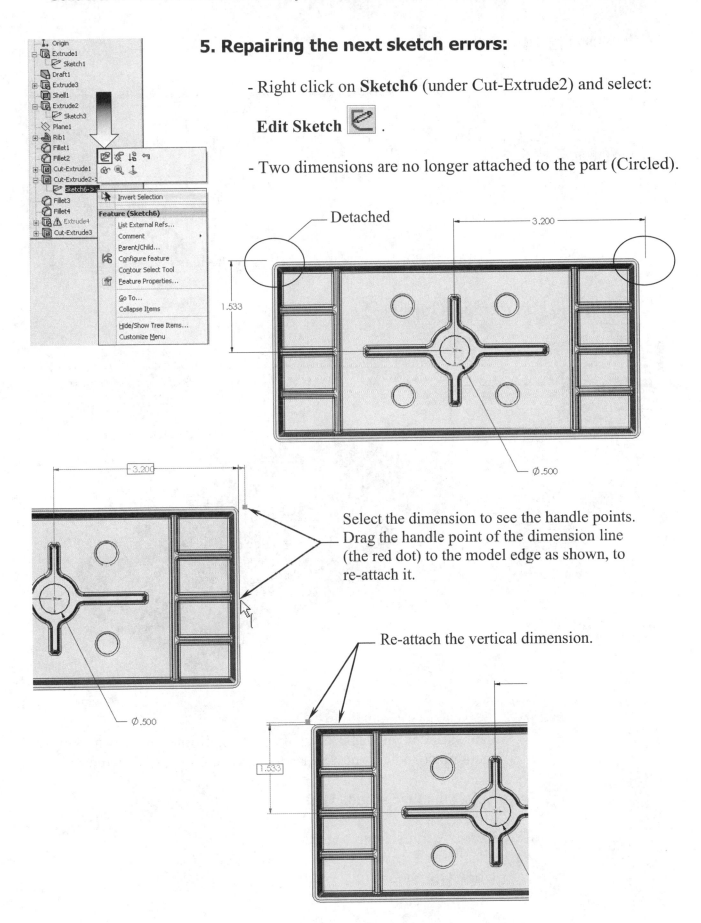

Detached

3.200

1.533

Ø.500

Select the dimension to see the handle points. Drag the handle point of the dimension line (the red dot) to the model edge as shown, to re-attach it.

Re-attach the vertical dimension.

3.200

Ø.500

1.533

- The sketch becomes fully defined;
the two dimensions are
attached to locate the
center of the circle.

- **Exit** the sketch .

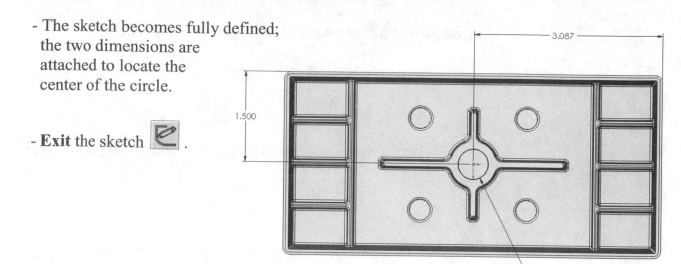

6. Repairing the extrude type:

- Right click on **Cut-Extrude2** and select **Edit Feature**.

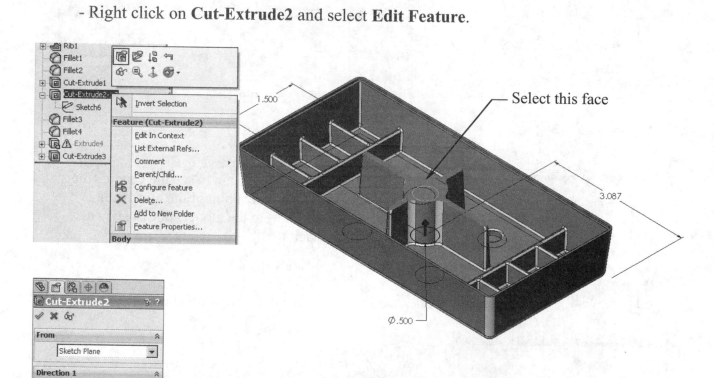

Select this face

- The surface that was used as the end condition option is no longer
recognized, a new surface has to be selected for replacement.

- Select the **face** as indicated.

- Leave extrude depth as **.100**in.

- Click **OK** .

7. Repairing the errors in the last sketch:

- Right click on the **Sketch8** and select **Edit Sketch**.

- Change to the Bottom orientation, or press Control + 6 to switch to the bottom view.

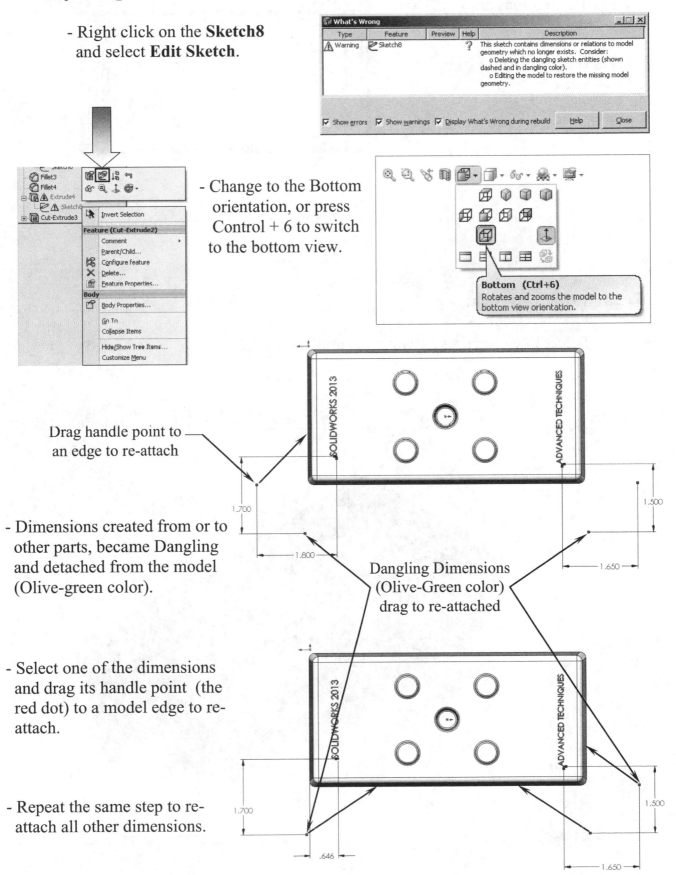

Drag handle point to an edge to re-attach

- Dimensions created from or to other parts, became Dangling and detached from the model (Olive-green color).

Dangling Dimensions (Olive-Green color) drag to re-attached

- Select one of the dimensions and drag its handle point (the red dot) to a model edge to re-attach.

- Repeat the same step to re-attach all other dimensions.

- The sketch becomes fully defined after all dimensions are re-attached.

- The text color is set to Blue by default.

- **Exit** the sketch 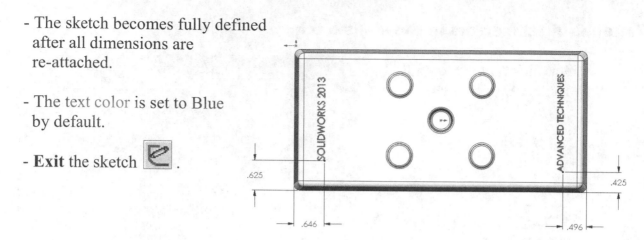 .

- The reference symbols and the error colors on the FeatureManager tree should now be all removed.

8. Saving your work:

- Select **File / Save As / Repair Errors / Save**.

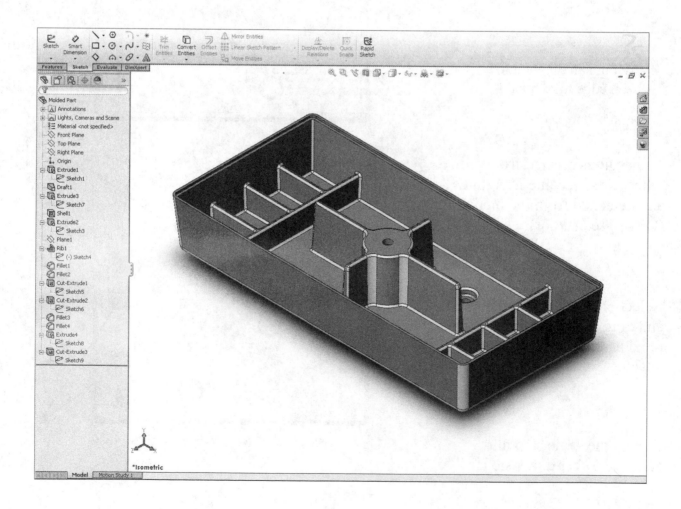

Level 4 – Final Exam:

1. Open an existing part document:

<u>Go to:</u>

Training CD
Tooling Design folder
L4 Final Exam.sldprt.

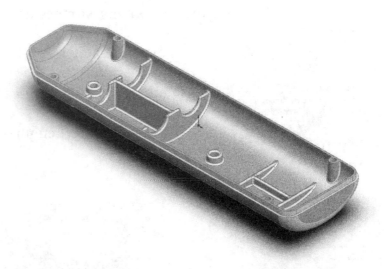

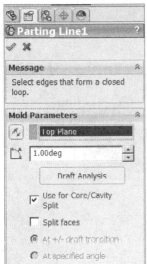

2. Create a **Parting Line** using:

- Direction of Pull = **TOP plane**.

- Draft Angle   = **1deg.****

- Parting Lines   = **All outer edges** as shown.

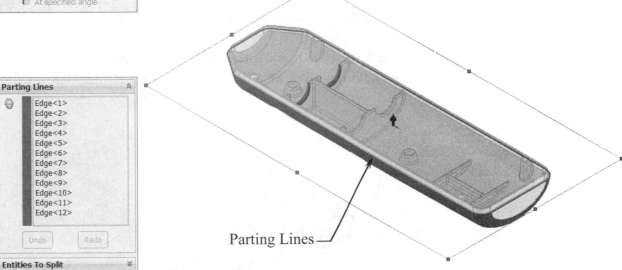

Parting Lines

** <u>**Important** - Roll back before the Loft feature and:</u>

a/ Add 1º drafts to all Yellow faces, including the 4 holes, this change will create some errors in the part.

b/ <u>Re-order</u> or <u>re-create</u> the fillets, if necessary, after adding the drafts.

3. Create a **Parting Surface** using:

- **Perpendicular to Pull**.

- Parting Line: **Parting Line1**.

- Parting Surface Length = **.250 in**.

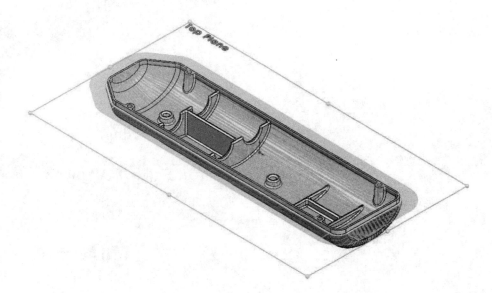

4. Create a new **Offset Distance plane** using:

- The **Top** reference plane and **.375 in**. distance.

- The new plane is placed **above** the Top plane.
(This new plane will also be use to create the Interlock Surfaces)

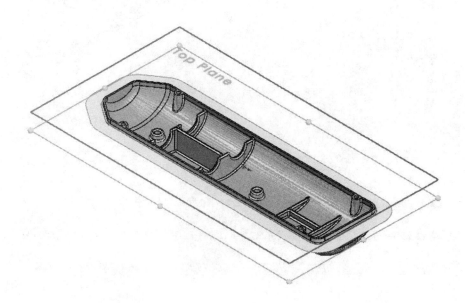

5. Sketch a **Rectangle** on the new plane (Plane1) and add dimensions* shown.

Adjust the dimensions if needed to center the rectangle around the part.

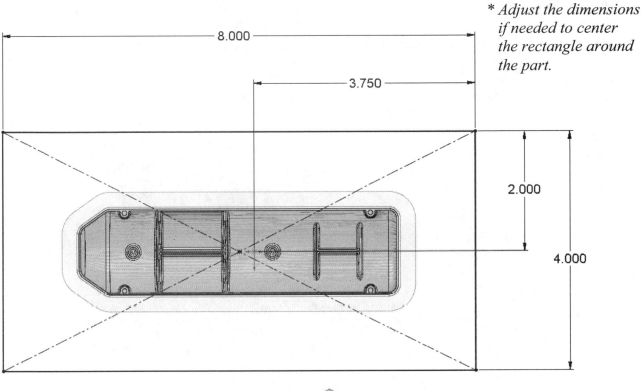

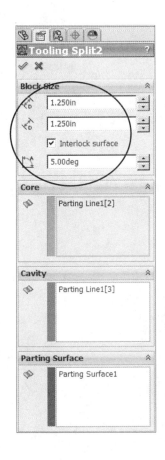

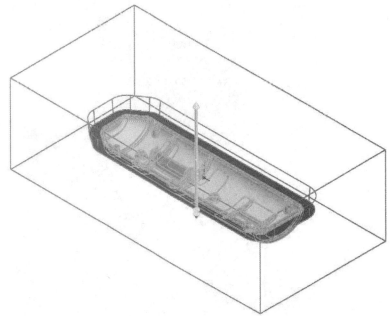

6. Exit the Sketch and create a **Tooling split** using:
- **1.250in.** (upper block)
- **1.250in.** (lower block)
- Use **Interlock Surface** with **5° Draft**.

7. Re-order or **re-create** the fillets if necessary.

8. Use the **Move/Copy** command to separate the two halves.

**** <u>OPTIONAL</u>: Make the upper and lower solid bodies transparent for clarity.

9. Save your work as L4-Final.

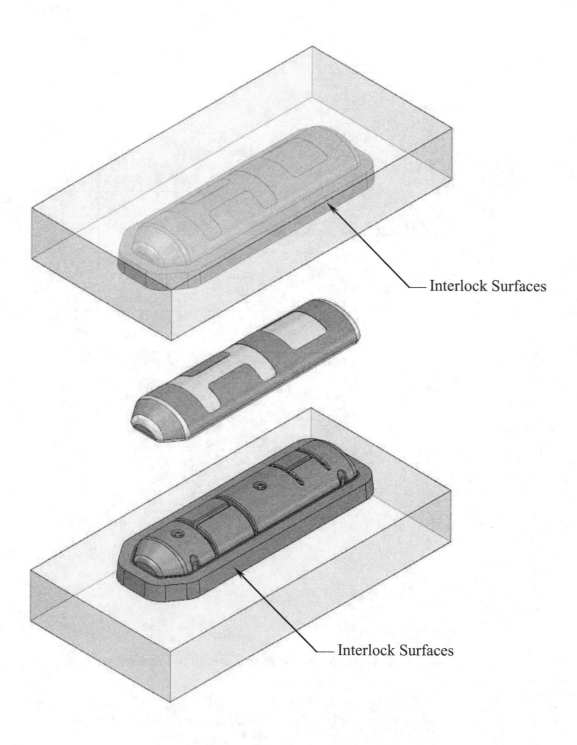

Interlock Surfaces

Interlock Surfaces

SolidWorks 2013

Certified SolidWorks Professional (CSWP)

Certification Practice for the Core Examination

Courtesy of Paul Tran, Sr. Certified SolidWorks Instructor

Certified-SolidWorks-Professional program (CSWP)
Certification Practice for the Core-Exam

Complete this challenge within 90 minutes

(The following examples are intended to assist you in familiarizing yourself with the structures of the exams and the method in which the questions are asked).

- Create this part in SolidWorks   - Unit: **Inches, 3 decimals**   - Origin: **Arbitrary**

- Drafting Standards: **ANSI**   - Material: **Cast Alloy Steel**   - Density: **0.264 lb/in^3**

1. Creating the 1st revolve body:

- Using the <u>Front</u> plane, sketch the profile shown below.

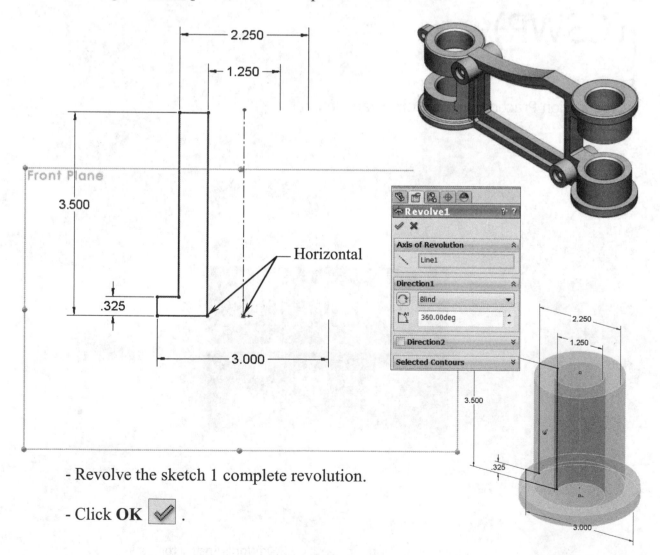

Horizontal

- Revolve the sketch 1 complete revolution.

- Click **OK** ✓ .

2. Creating the 2nd revolve body:

- Open a new sketch on the <u>Front</u> plane.

- Sketch a rectangle on the left side of the vertical centerline.

- Add the dimensions shown.

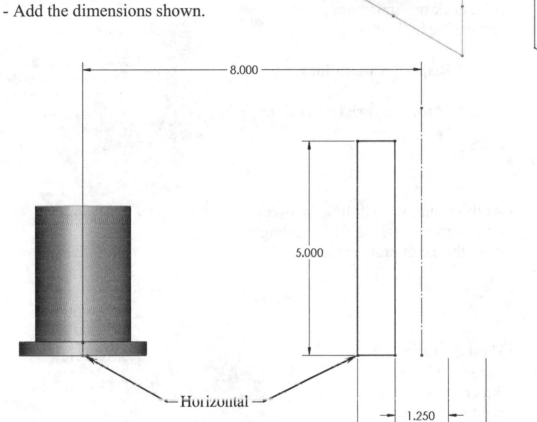

8.000

5.000

← Horizontal →

1.250

3.000

- Add a horizontal relation to fully define the sketch.

- Revolve the sketch 360 degrees.

Revolve

Axis of Revolution

Line1

Direction1

Blind

360.00deg

☑ Merge result

Direction2

- Click **OK** .

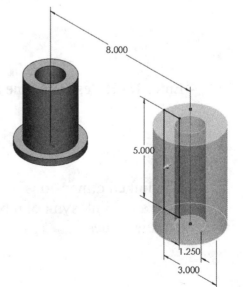

8.000

5.000

1.250

3.000

3. Linking the dimension values:

- To save time on editing features later on, we will link some of the dimensions together.

- From the FeatureManager tree, right click on Annotations and enable both options:

  * **Display Annotations**

  * **Show Feature Dimensions**

- At this point, we will link the two ID dimensions (Ø1.250), by giving them the exact same name.

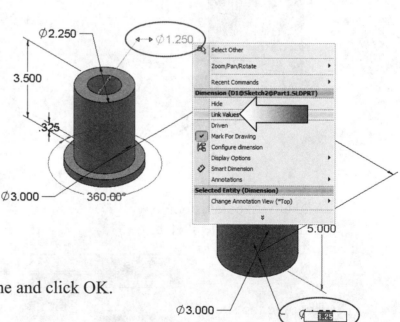

- Hold the Control key and select both ID dimensions (circled), right click on one of them and select: **Link Values** (arrow).

- Enter **ID Holes** for Name and click OK.

- The linked dimensions now have a red link symbol next to their values.

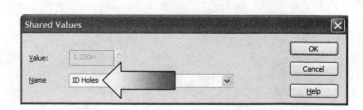

4. Creating the transition wall:

- Select the <u>Front</u> plane and open a new sketch.

- Sketch the profile as shown.

- Add the dimensions and the relations as indicated.

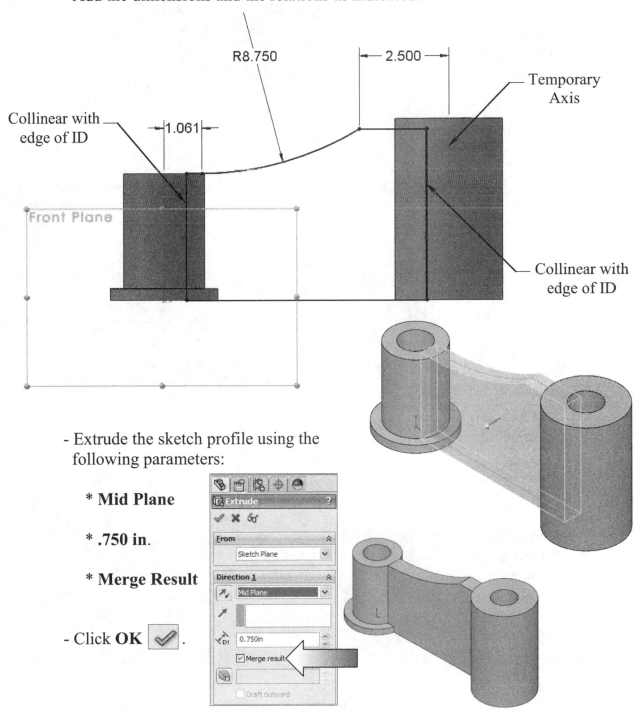

- Extrude the sketch profile using the following parameters:

    * **Mid Plane**

    * **.750 in**.

    * **Merge Result**

- Click **OK**.

5. Creating a recess feature:

- Select the <u>face</u> as indicated and open a new sketch.

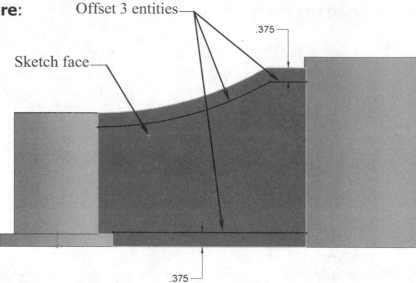

Offset 3 entities

Sketch face

.375

.375

- Select the arc, the 2 lines, and click **Offset Entities**.

- Enter **.375"** for offset distance and click OK.

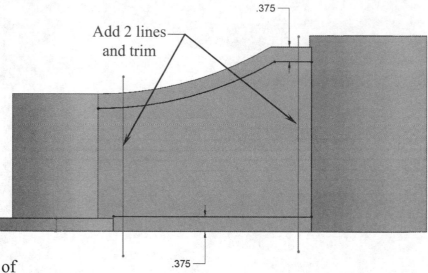

Add 2 lines and trim

.375

.375

- Add 2 more lines as shown and trim them to their nearest intersections.

- Add a sketch fillet of **R.125** to 5 places.

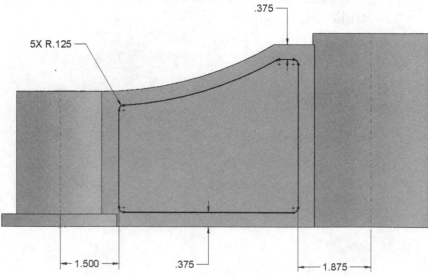

5X R.125

.375

- Enable the Temporary Axis and add the dimensions as shown to fully define this sketch.

1.500   .375   1.875

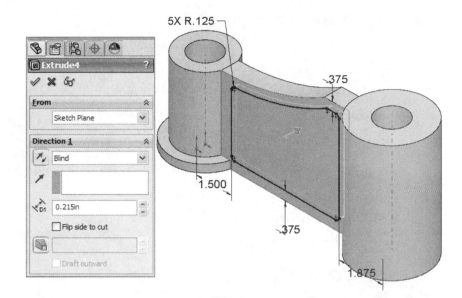

- Click **Extruded Cut** and use the following parameters:

  * Blind

  * .215 in.

- Click **OK** ✓.

6. Mirroring the recess feature:

- Select the <u>Front</u> plane for use as the Mirror plane and click the **Mirror** Command from the Features toolbar.

- Click the recess feature either from the graphics area or from the FeatureManager tree.

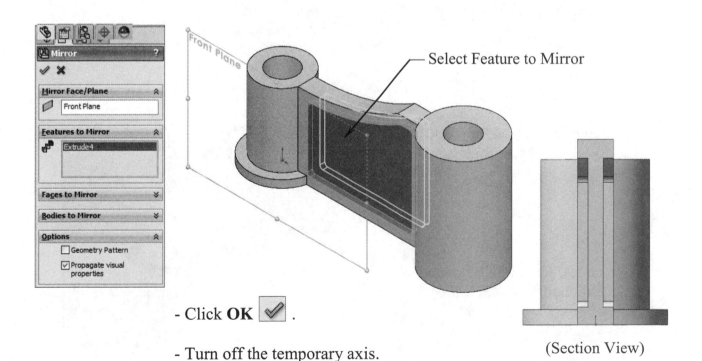

Select Feature to Mirror

- Click **OK** ✓.

- Turn off the temporary axis.

(Section View)

7. Adding Fillets:

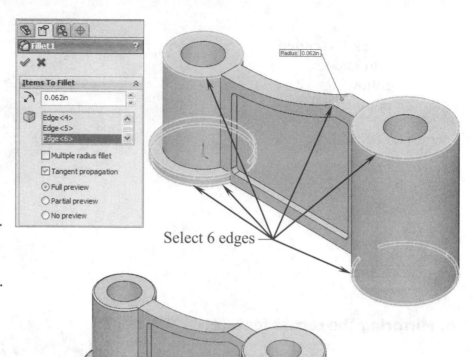

- Click the **Fillet** command and enter **.062"** for radius value.

- Select the **6 edges** as shown.

Select 6 edges

- Click **OK** .

8. Changing dimension values:

- The grading scores are based on the mass of the part after certain changes. At this point, we will change several dimensions and see what the final mass may be.

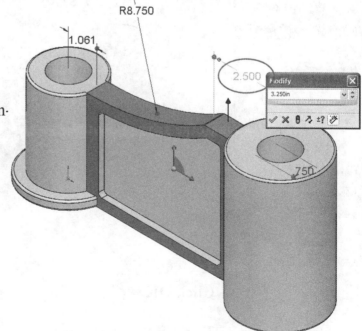

- Double click on the Transition Wall to see its dimensions.

- Locate the **2.500"** dimension and change it to **3.250"**.

- Change the dimension
  8.000" to **8.750"**

- Click Rebuild
  or **Control + Q**.

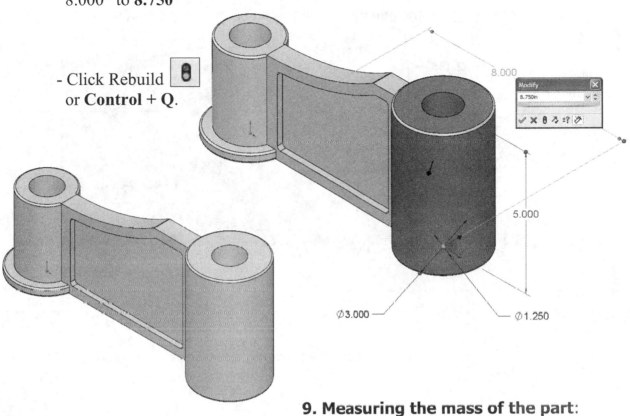

9. Measuring the mass of the part:

- Select **Tools / Mass Properties**.

- Enter the Mass here: _____ pounds.

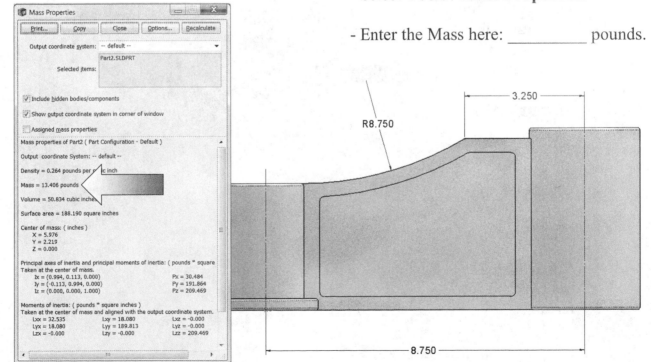

10. Adding the cut features:

- Select the <u>Front</u> plane and open a new sketch.

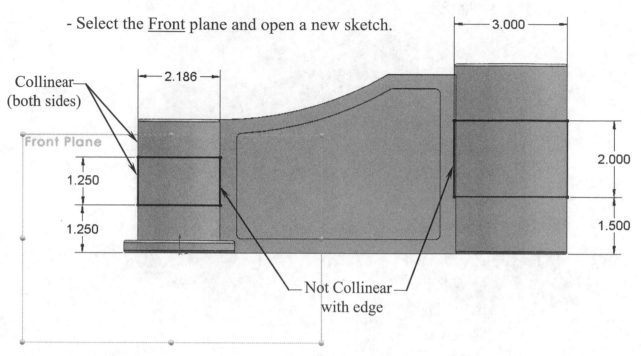

Collinear
(both sides)

Front Plane

3.000

2.186

1.250

1.250

2.000

1.500

Not Collinear
with edge

- Sketch the 2 rectangles as shown, and add dimensions/relations to fully define the sketch.

- Click **Extruded Cut**.

- Under Direction1, select: **Through All**.

- For Direction2 also select: **Through All**.

- Click **OK** .

- Rotate the part to verify the cut feature.

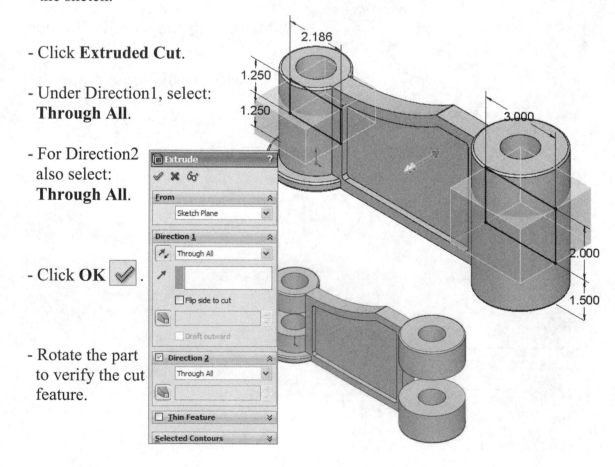

2.186

1.250

1.250

3.000

2.000

1.500

Extrude

From

Sketch Plane

Direction 1

Through All

Flip side to cut

Draft outward

Direction 2

Through All

Thin Feature

Selected Contours

11. Adding fillets and chamfers:

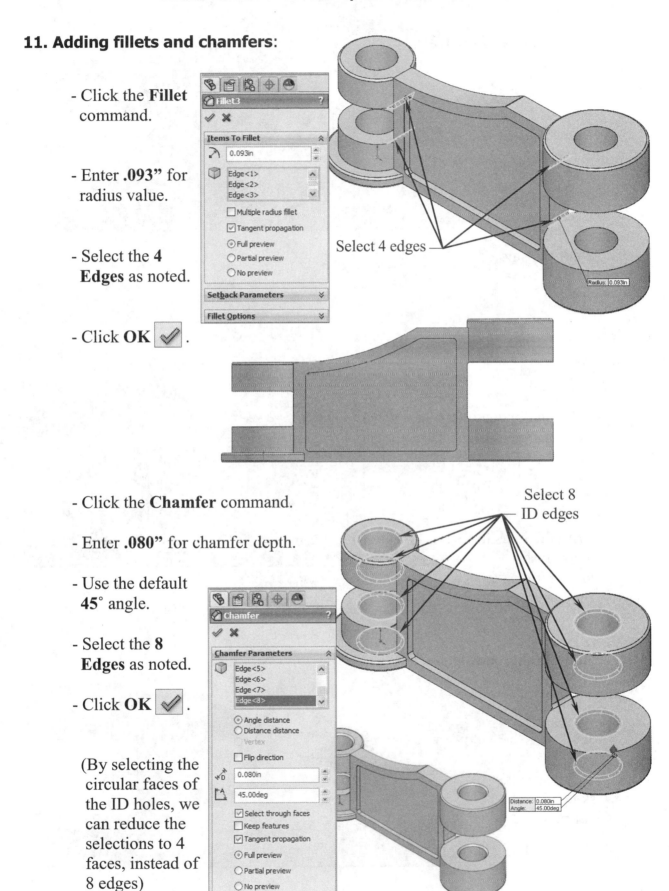

- Click the **Fillet** command.

- Enter **.093"** for radius value.

- Select the **4 Edges** as noted.

- Click **OK**.

Select 4 edges

Radius: 0.093in

Select 8 ID edges

- Click the **Chamfer** command.

- Enter **.080"** for chamfer depth.

- Use the default **45°** angle.

- Select the **8 Edges** as noted.

- Click **OK**.

(By selecting the circular faces of the ID holes, we can reduce the selections to 4 faces, instead of 8 edges)

Distance: 0.080in
Angle: 45.00deg

12. Adding a recess feature:

- Select the <u>face</u> as indicated and open a new sketch.

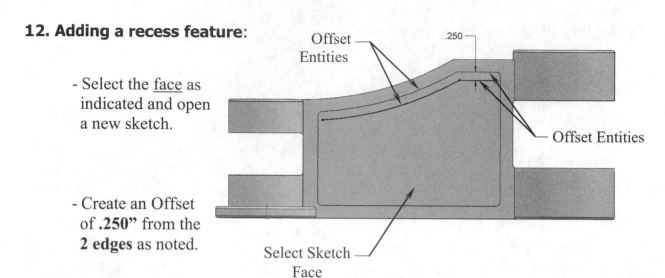

- Create an Offset of **.250"** from the **2 edges** as noted.

- Add **3 lines** approximately as shown.

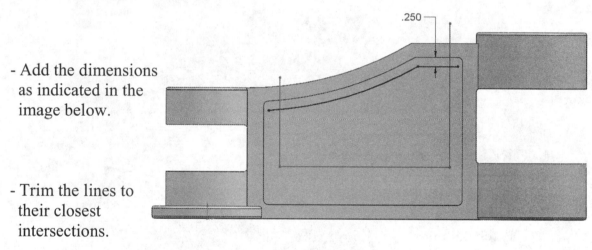

- Add the dimensions as indicated in the image below.

- Trim the lines to their closest intersections.

- Add the **sketch fillets** of **R.093"** to **5 places**.

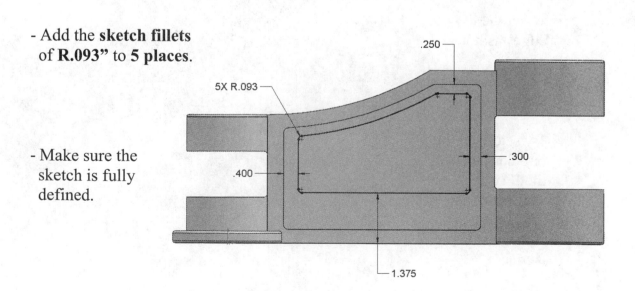

- Make sure the sketch is fully defined.

- Click **Extruded Cut**.

- Under Direction1, select:
  Through All.

- For Direction2
  also select:
  Through All.

- Click **OK** 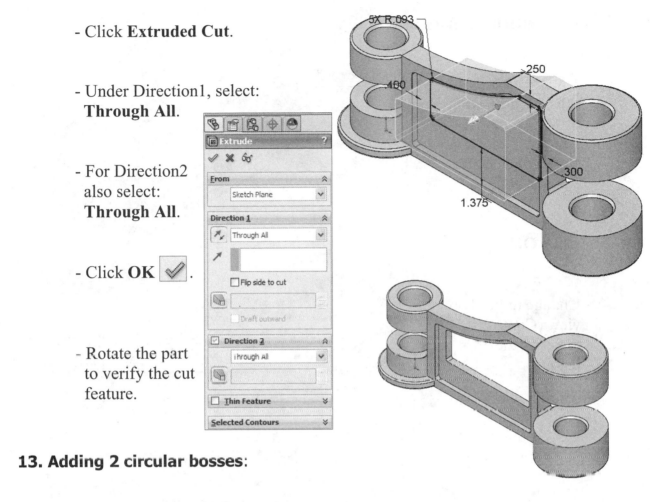.

- Rotate the part
  to verify the cut
  feature.

13. Adding 2 circular bosses:

- Select the Front plane from the FeatureManager tree and open a new sketch.

- Sketch 2 circles and add the dimensions as shown to fully define them.

- Link the diameter dimensions using the Link Values option. Rename them to:
  Cir_Bosses.

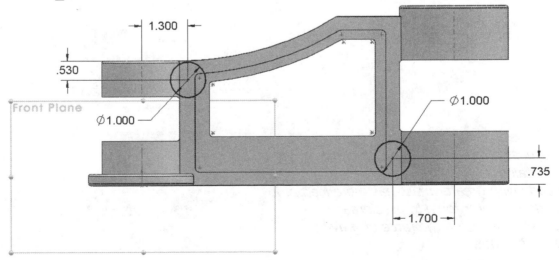

- Click **Extruded Boss/Base**.

- Under Direction1, select: **Mid Plane**.

- For extrude depth enter: **2.000in**.

- Click **OK** .

- Change to the Top view (Control + 5) to verify the boss feature.

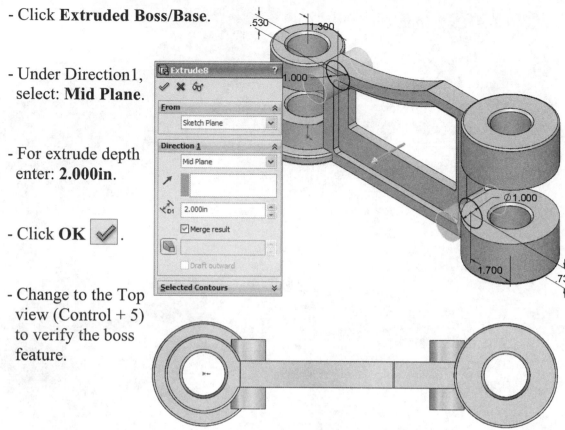

14. Measuring the mass of the part*:

- Click **Tools / Mass Properties**.

- Locate the mass* (arrow) and enter

it here _____ lbs.

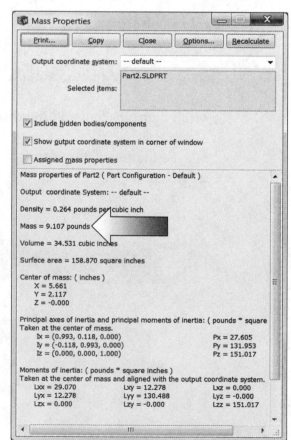

* *The mass of an object is the amount of material it contains.
A body with greater mass has more inertia; it needs a greater force to accelerate.
Weight depends on the force of gravity, but mass does not.*

15. Modifying the feature dimensions:

- Locate the diameter
  dimensions for the
  2 ID holes (circled)
  and change them
  from: Ø1.250
  to Ø **1.500"**.

- Click **Rebuild**
  or press **Control + Q**.

- Locate the OD dimension (Ø3.000) for the
  Circular boss on the right side (circled) and change it
  from Ø3.000" to Ø**2.750"**.

- Click **Rebuild**
  or press **Control + Q.**

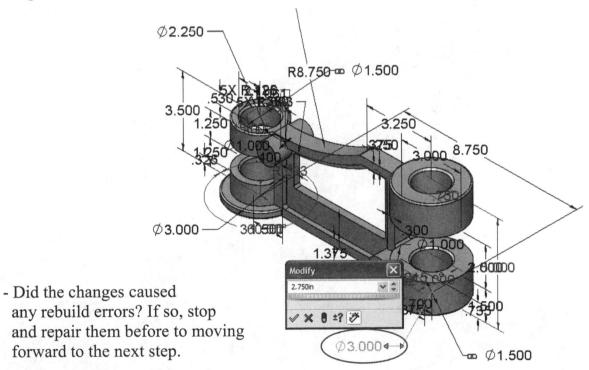

- Did the changes caused
  any rebuild errors? If so, stop
  and repair them before to moving
  forward to the next step.

- Locate the OD dimension for the circular boss on the left (circled) and change it from Ø2.250 to **2.500"**.

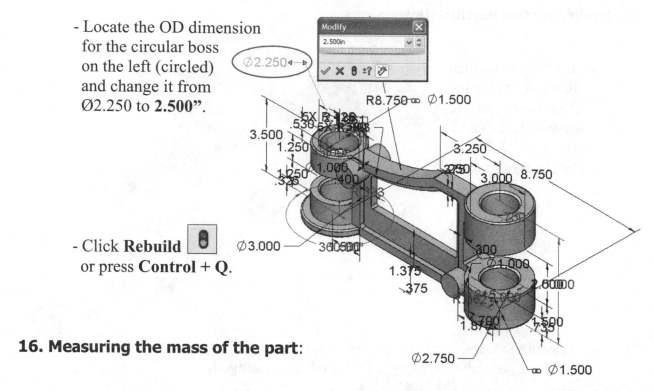

- Click **Rebuild** or press **Control + Q**.

16. Measuring the mass of the part:

- Click **Tools / Mass Properties**.

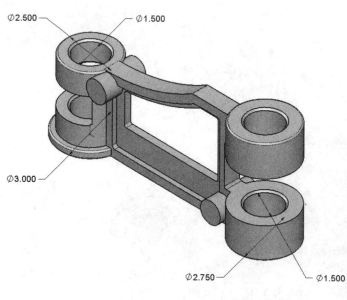

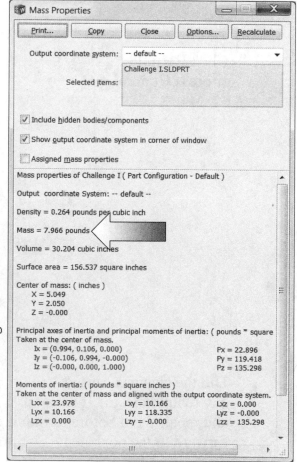

- Locate the mass (arrow) and enter it

here: _____ lbs.

17. Creating the Counter-Bores:

- Click the **Hole-Wizard** command from the Features toolbar.

- Select the following:

     * Hole Type: **Counterbore**

     * Standard: **Ansi Inch**

     * Type: **Binding Head Screw**

     * Size: **1/4**

     * Fit: **Normal**

     * End Condition: **Through All**

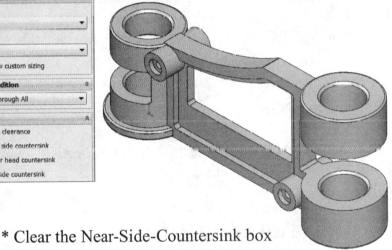

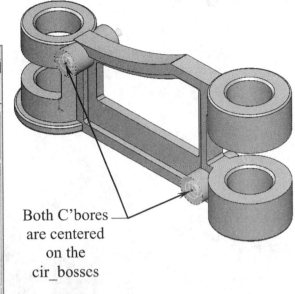

Both C'bores are centered on the cir_bosses

* Clear the Near-Side-Countersink box

- Change to the **Positions** tab (circled) and place 2 Counter-bores on the same centers as the circular boss features, click OK when finished.

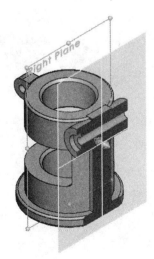

- Create a **Section View** similar to the one shown below to verify the 2 counter bores.

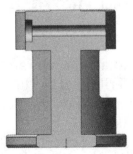

18. Adding a side tab:

- Open a new sketch on the <u>Front</u> plane.

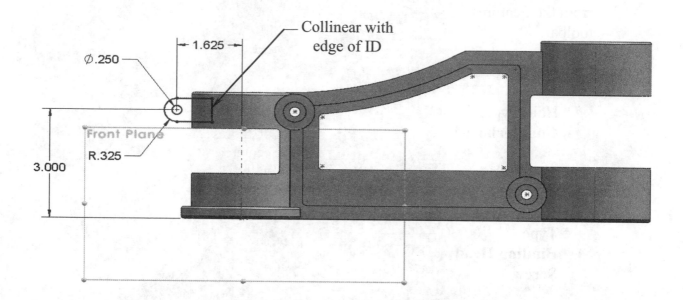

- Sketch the profile of the tab as show.

- Add the dimensions and relations needed to fully define the sketch.

- Click **Extruded Boss/Base**.

- Under Direction1, select: **Mid Plane**.

- For extrude depth enter: **.425 in**.

- Click **OK** .

- Rotate the part and Verify that the tab is centered on the Front plane.

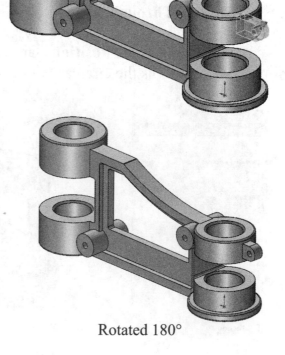

Rotated 180°

19. Modifying the recess feature:

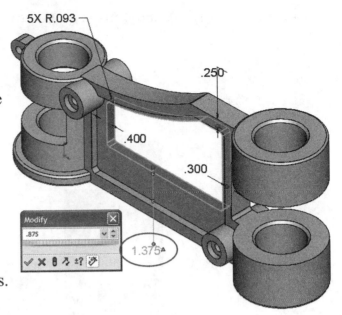

- Locate the spacing dimension of the recess (1.375") and change to **.875"**.

- Click **Rebuild** .

- Find the final mass of the part and enter it here: _____ lbs.

20. Modifying the Revolved feature:

- Edit the sketch of the **Revolved2** feature.

- Add 3 new lines as indicated.

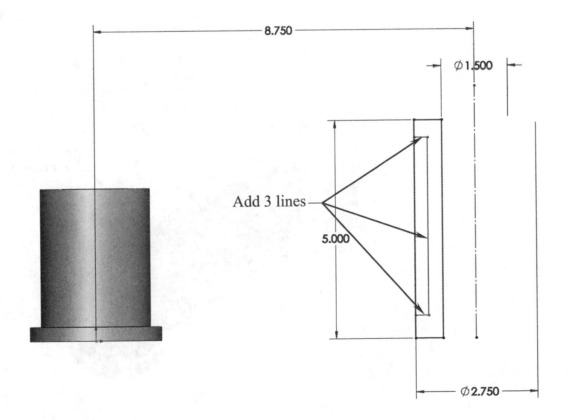

Add 3 lines

- Add the 3 dimensions (circled) to fully define this sketch.

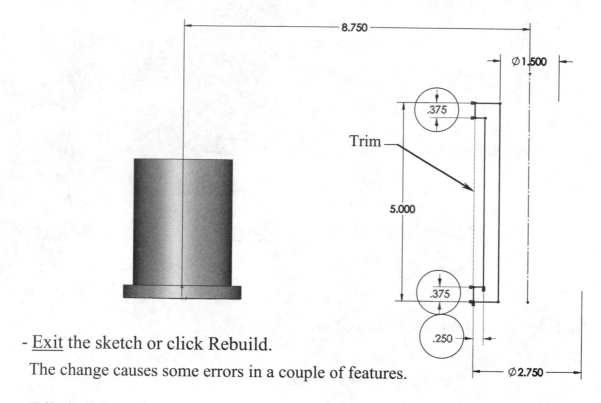

- <u>Exit</u> the sketch or click Rebuild.

The change causes some errors in a couple of features.

- <u>Edit</u> the **Fillet1** feature and select the missing edge as noted.

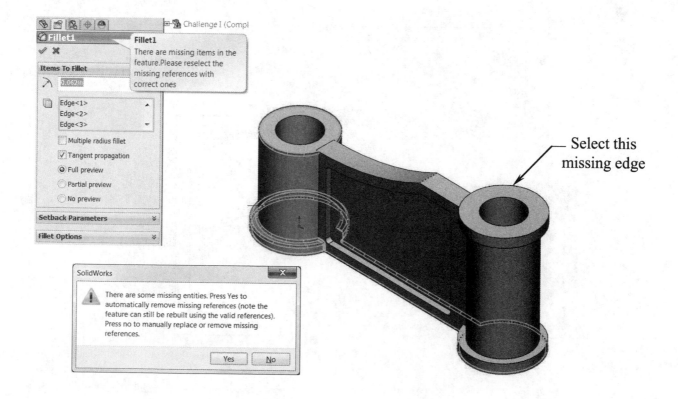

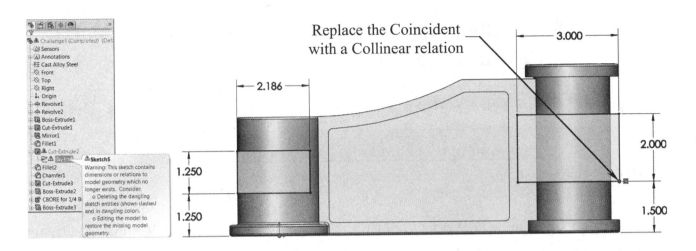

- <u>Edit the Sketch5</u> under the Cut-Extrude2. Replace the relation as noted. Click Rebuild.

- Measure the final mass of the part and enter it here: _____ lbs.

21. Saving your work:

- Save your work as **Challenge1** and close the document when done.

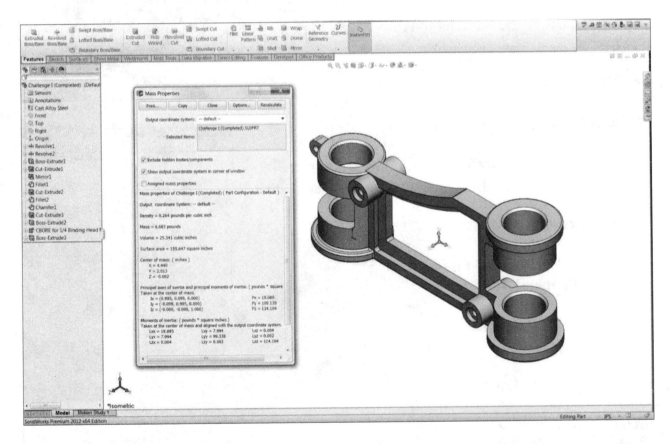

- Use the example file from the included CD to review the construction of the part, if needed.

Certified-SolidWorks-Professional program (CSWP)
Certification Practice for the Core-Exam

Challenge II-A: Part Configurations & Design Tables

Complete this challenge (A&B) within 45 minutes

(The following examples are intended to assist you in familiarizing yourself with the structures of the exams and the method in which the questions are asked).

- Modify this part in SolidWorks
- Drafting Standards: **ANSI**
- Unit: **Millimeter, 2 decimals**
- Material: **Alloy Steel**
- Origin: **Arbitrary**
- Density: **0.008 /mm^3**

1. Opening a part document:

- Browse to the Training CD, locate and open the part **Challenge II-A**.

2. Setting the options:

- Change the material to **Alloy Steel**.

- Change the system options to match the settings above.

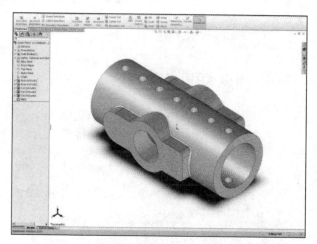

3. Switching Configuration:

- Switch to the ConfigurationManager tree, double click the **Configuration A** to activate it.

4. Measuring the Mass:

- Select **Tools/ Mass Properties**.

- Enter the mass in grams:

_____ grams.

<u>NOTE:</u> *Material must be selected before calculating the mass of the part.*

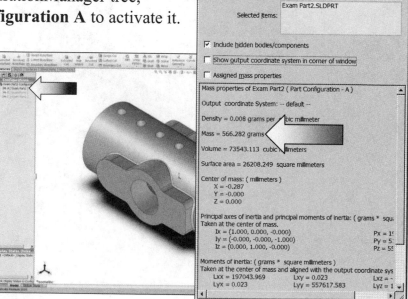

5. Adding a New Configuration:

- Create a <u>new configuration</u> named **D**, and enter the comment:
  Added a 10mm hole.

- Select the face shown below and open a new sketch.

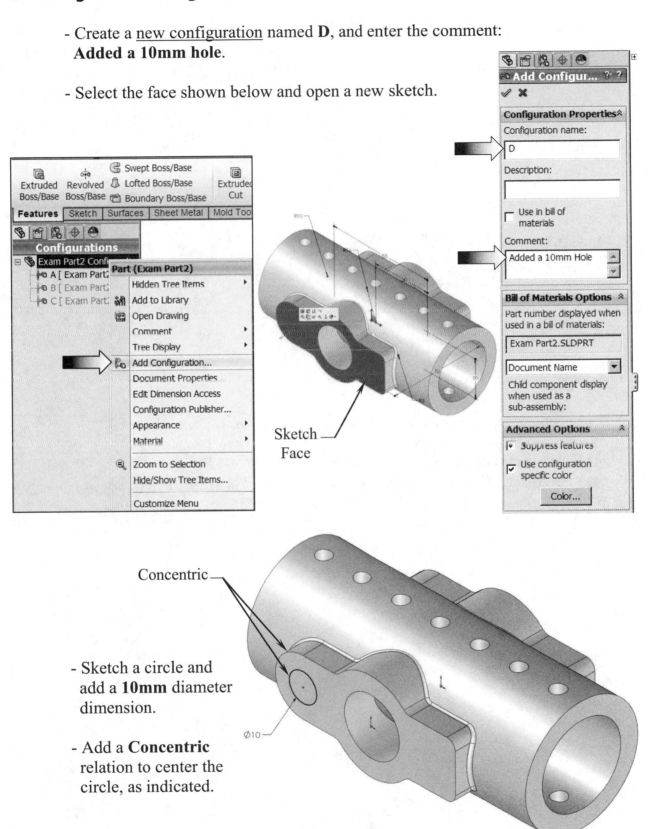

Sketch Face

Concentric

- Sketch a circle and add a **10mm** diameter dimension.

- Add a **Concentric** relation to center the circle, as indicated.

6. Extruding a cut:

- Click **Extruded Cut**.

- Set Direction1 to:

Through All.

- Click **OK** ✓.

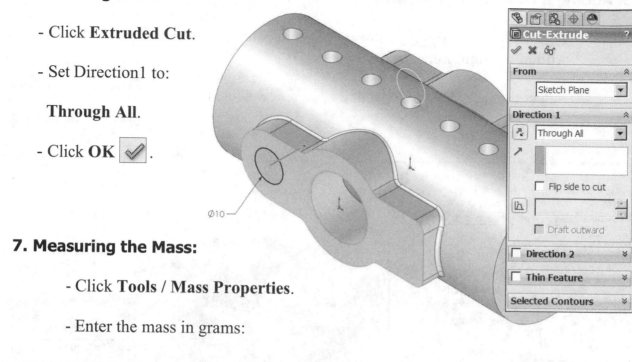

Ø10

7. Measuring the Mass:

- Click **Tools / Mass Properties**.

- Enter the mass in grams:

_____ grams.

Note: *The center of mass shown in the dialog boxes are examples for use with this text only. The actual mass properties of the part is based on the material specified for each challenge in the actual exam.*

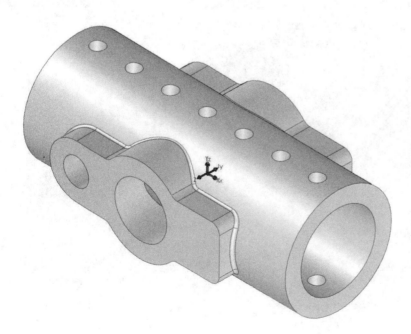

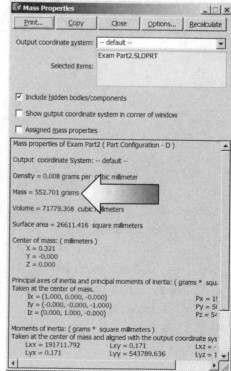

8. Switching configuration:

- Double click on **Configuration B** to make it active.

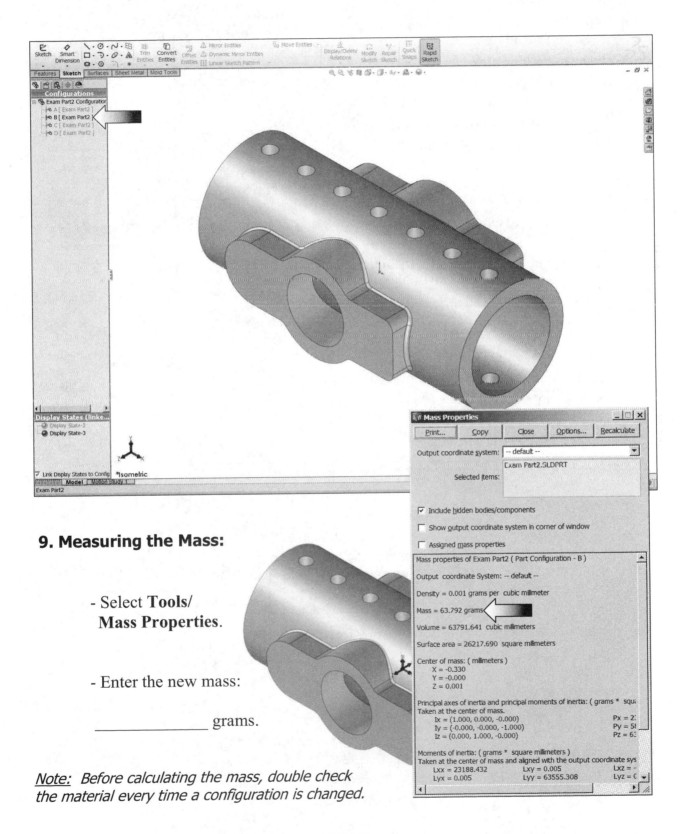

9. Measuring the Mass:

  - Select **Tools/
    Mass Properties**.

  - Enter the new mass:

    _____ grams.

Note: _Before calculating the mass, double check
the material every time a configuration is changed._

10. Creating a Design Table:

- Double click the configuration **B** to activate it.

- Select **Insert/ Tables /Design Tables**.

- Click the **Auto Create** option and leave all other options as defaults.

11. Adding new Configurations:

- Right click on **Row4** and select **Copy**.

- Right click on **Row7** and select **Paste**.

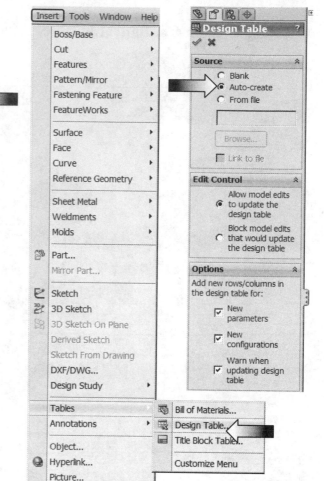

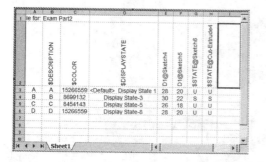

The Default Design Table

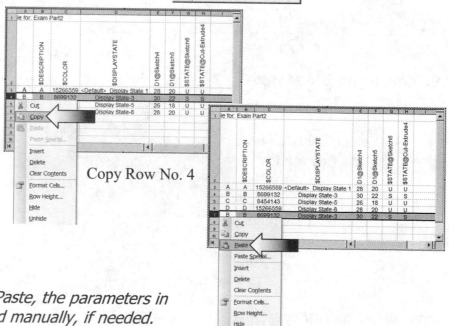

Copy Row No. 4

Note: Instead of Copy/Paste, the parameters in Row7 can also be entered manually, if needed.

12. Modifying the new configurations:

- Change the name of the new config. to **E**.

- Change the ID dimension on the body to **24**.

- Change the hole Diameter to **16**.

- Leave the Suppression States at Suppressed (S).

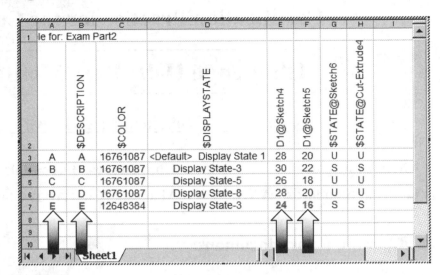

	A	B	C	D		E	F	G	H	I
1	le for: Exam Part2									
2	$DESCRIPTION	$COLOR		$DISPLAYSTATE		D1@Sketch4	D1@Sketch5	$STATE@Sketch6	$STATE@Cut-Extrude4	
3	A	A	16761087	\<Default\>	Display State 1	28	20	U	U	
4	B	B	16761087		Display State-3	30	22	S	S	
5	C	C	16761087		Display State-5	26	18	U	U	
6	D	D	16761087		Display State-8	28	20	U	U	
7	E	E	12648384		Display State-3	**24**	**16**	S	S	

Sheet1

- Click anywhere in the background to return to SolidWorks.

- Double click on **Configuration E** to activate. *Uncheck the Link to Display State option and click Rebuild to update the color).*

13. Measuring the final Mass:

- Select **Tools/ Mass Properties**.

- Enter the final mass: _____ grams

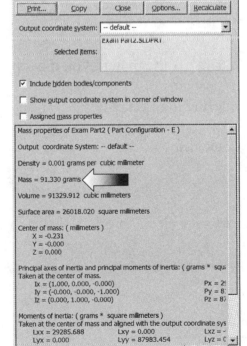

14. Save your work as Challenge 2-A.

Certified-SolidWorks-Professional program (CSWP)
Certification Practice for the Core-Exam

Challenge II-B: Part Modifications

Complete this challenge (A&B) within 45 minutes

- Modify this part in SolidWorks
- Drafting Standards: **ANSI**

- Unit: **Inches, 3 decimals**
- Material: **Cast Alloy Steel**

- Origin: **Arbitrary**
- Density: **0.008 /mm^3**

1. Opening a part document:

- Browse to the training CD, locate and open the part named **Challenge II-B**.

2. Setting the options:

- Change the material to **Cast Alloy Steel**.

- Change the system options to match the settings above.

3. Adding the 1st cut:

- Select the <u>Top</u> plane and open a new sketch.

- Sketch the profile shown below, it will be used to trim off the material on the top.

- Add the dimensions and relations needed to fully define the sketch.

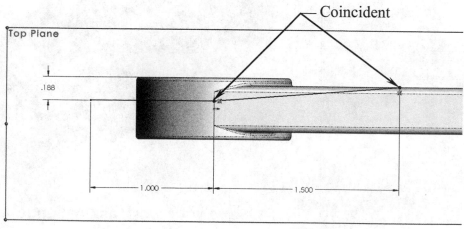

- Click **Extruded Cut**.

- Set Direction 1 to: **Through All**.

- Set Direction 2 also to: **Through All**.

- Click **OK** .

4. Measuring the Mass:

- Select **Tools/ Mass Properties**.

- Enter the mass here: _____ pounds.

5. Adding the 2nd cut:

- Select the Face as indicated and open a new sketch.

Convert Entity

Sketch face

- Create the circle by using the **Convert Entities** option.

- Extrude Cut using the **2 Directions** as shown.

- Click **OK** .

6. Reversing the extruded cut:

- <u>Edit</u> the Sketch2 (under the Cut-Extude1 feature).

- Delete the coincident relation and the two dimensions as indicated.

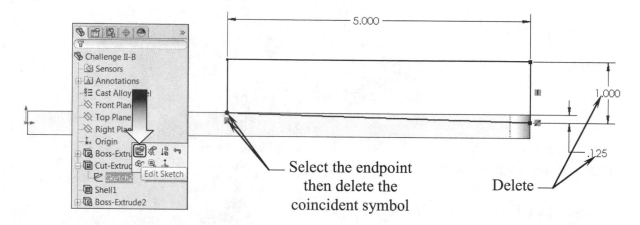

Select the endpoint
then delete the
coincident symbol

Delete

- Drag the horizontal line downward, recreate the coincident relation and the two deleted dimensions.

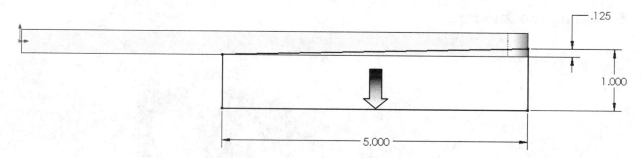

- The change causes some errors in the model. Click **Continue** to close the error dialog box (arrow).

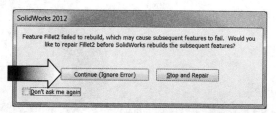

7. Editing the Shell feature:

- One of the faces in the shell feature is missing due to the last change. There should be a total of <u>three faces</u> in the Faces-To-Remove selection box.

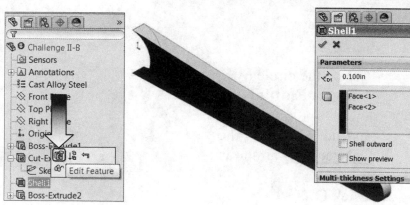

- Click inside the **Faces-to-Remove** selection box to active this option, then <u>select the planar face</u> on the right as noted.

- Click **OK** 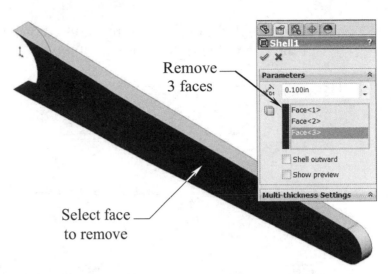.

8. Editing the parent sketch:

- <u>Edit</u> the Sketch1 below the Boss-Extrude1 feature.

Remove 3 faces

Select face to remove

- This is the parent sketch, changing its geometry will cause errors in some of the children features.

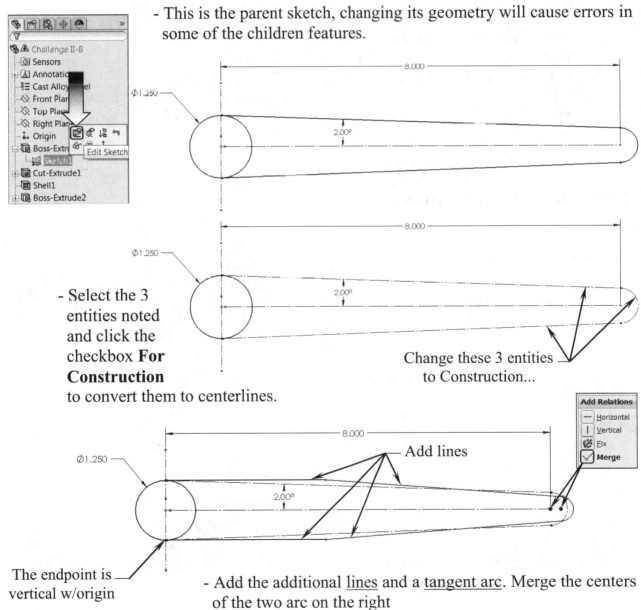

- Select the 3 entities noted and click the checkbox **For Construction** to convert them to centerlines.

Change these 3 entities to Construction...

Add lines

The endpoint is vertical w/origin

- Add the additional <u>lines</u> and a <u>tangent arc</u>. Merge the centers of the two arc on the right

- Hold the <u>Shift</u> key and add the **5.00"** dimension that measures from the endpoint of the line to the right-quadrant of the arc. This sketch becomes fully defined.

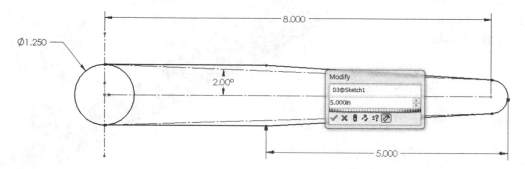

- <u>Exit</u> the sketch.

- The change causes some errors in the model once again. Select the option: **Exit the Sketch and Rebuild anyway**.

- The right end of the model disappeared. To correct this, we need to re-select the contour of the extruded feature.

9. Editing the parent feature:

- Click the Boss-Extrude1 feature and **Edit Feature** (arrow).

- Expand the <u>Selected Contour</u> section, click inside the area as noted and click **OK** ✔.

- The highlighted area will used as the contour for the handle body.

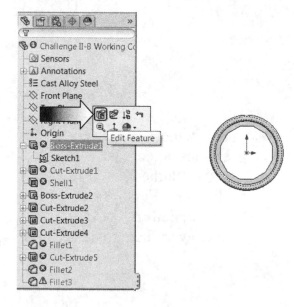

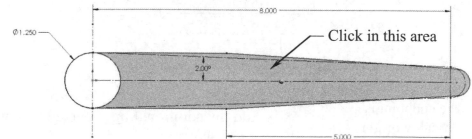

Click in this area

10. Correcting the dangling relations:

- The new contour causes the dependent sketch to become dangling.

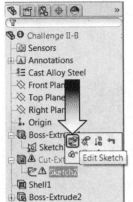

- Edit the Sketch2 below the Cut-Extrude1 feature to fix this error.

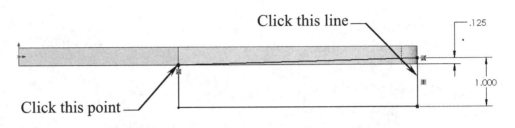

Click this line ⎯

Click this point ⎯

.125

1.000

- Click the endpoint of the line to see the dangling relation, displayed in <u>Olive-Green</u> color, under the Existing relations box.
Right click the Coincident8 and select **Delete**.

- Repeat the last step and delete the collinear relation and also the dimension **.125**, they both have the dangling color.

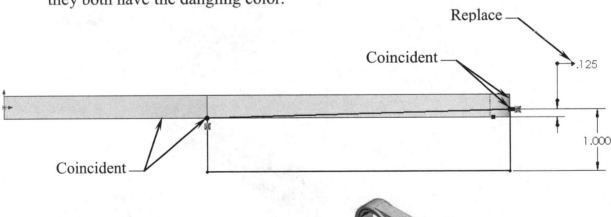

Replace ⎯

Coincident ⎯

Coincident ⎯

.125

1.000

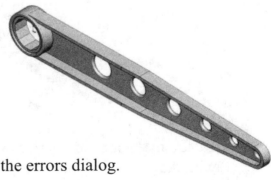

- Re-create the Coincident relations and the dimension .125" as indicated above.

- The status of the sketch should change to Fully Defined at this point.

- <u>Exit</u> the sketch and click <u>continue</u> to close the errors dialog.

11. Editing the .125" fillets:

- Click the **Fillet1** on the feature tree and select **Edit Feature** (arrow).

- Delete the 2 missing edges from the Edges to Fillet selection box.

- Select the 2 inner edges, behind the circular boss to replace with the missing ones.

- Click **OK** .

- The model should have no errors at this point.

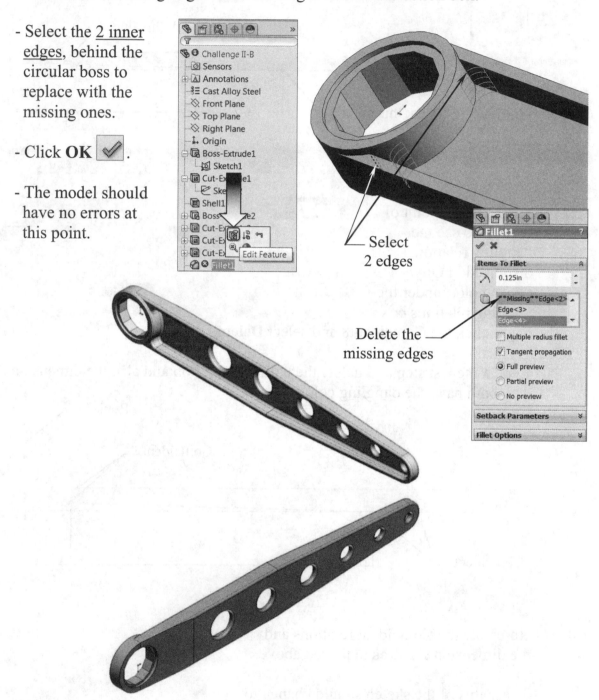

Select 2 edges

Delete the missing edges

- Rotate the model and verify the correction to the fillets and compare your model with the one shown above.

12. Correcting the wall thickness:

- Select the <u>Top</u> plane and open a new sketch. (The section view is created for clarity only, use the Wireframe display mode for this sketch).

- The wall thickness needs to be corrected. Reordering the Shell feature would cause a lot of errors which will take extra time to repair. We are going to create a boss to correct this error instead.

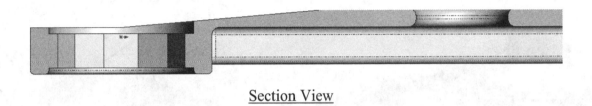

Section View

- Create a sketch below and add the dimensions / relations needed to fully define it.

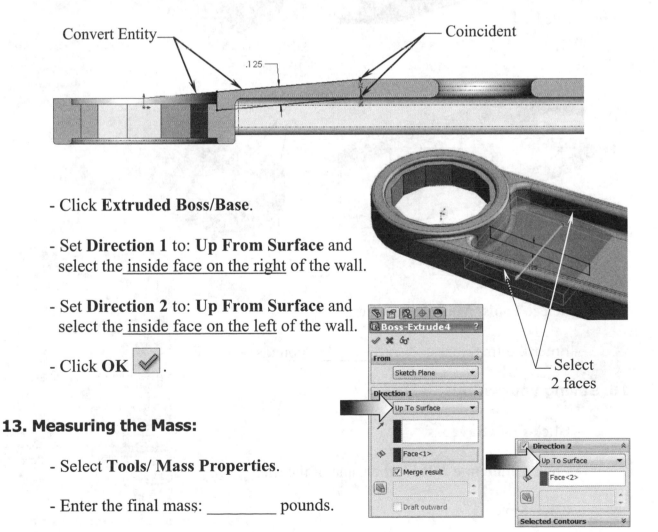

- Click **Extruded Boss/Base**.

- Set **Direction 1** to: **Up From Surface** and select the <u>inside face on the right</u> of the wall.

- Set **Direction 2** to: **Up From Surface** and select the <u>inside face on the left</u> of the wall.

- Click **OK**.

13. Measuring the Mass:

- Select **Tools/ Mass Properties**.

- Enter the final mass: _____ pounds.

14. Correcting the fillets:

- Some of the fillets got disconnected due to newly added features in the last few steps. One quick way to correct this is to add some new fillets to the missing edges.

- Click the **Fillet** command from the Features toolbar.

- Add the 2 fillets, **R.040** and **R.010**, as indicated in the images below.

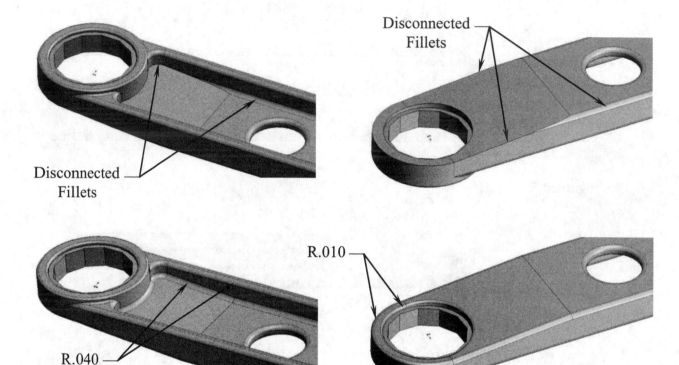

Disconnected Fillets

Disconnected Fillets

R.010

R.040

15. Measuring the Mass:

- Select **Tools/ Mass Properties**.

- Enter the final mass: _____ pounds.

16. Saving your work:

- Click **File / Save As**.

- Enter **Challenge 2-B** for the name of the file.

- Click **Save**.

Certified SolidWorks Professional program (CSWP)
Certification Practice for the Core-Exam

Challenge III: Bottom Up Assembly

Complete this challenge within 90 minutes

(The following examples are intended to assist you in familiarizing yourself with the structures of the exams and the method in which the questions are asked).

1. Assemble the components using mates.
2. Create a new coordinate system in the Assem.
3. Units: IPS (Inch/Pound/Second).

4. Detect and repair all interferences.
5. Mate modifications.
6. Decimal: 3 places.

1. Opening the 1st part document:

- Open the document named: **Base** from the Challenge 3 folder.

- This part will be used as the Parent component in the assembly.

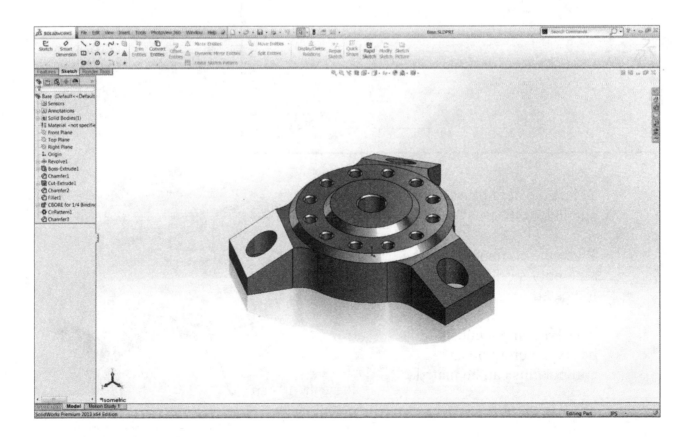

2. Transferring the part to Assembly:

- Select **Make Assembly From Part** from the **File** pull down menu (arrow).

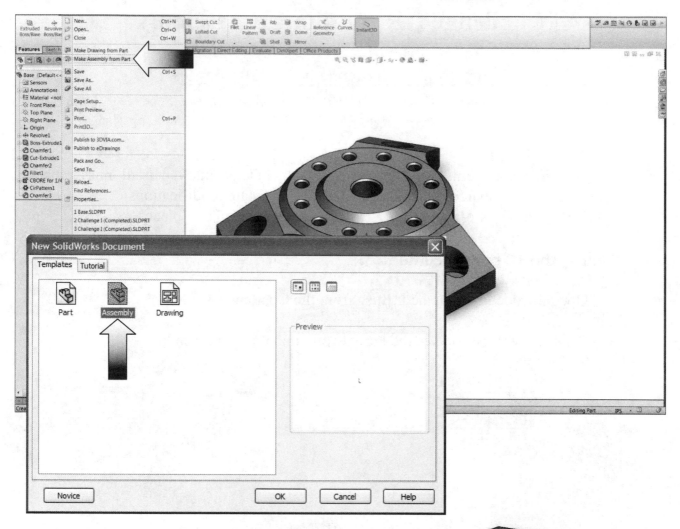

- Select the default **Assembly Template** and click **OK** [OK] .

- Place the component on the assembly's origin as indicated.

- The 1st component should be fixed before other components can be mated.

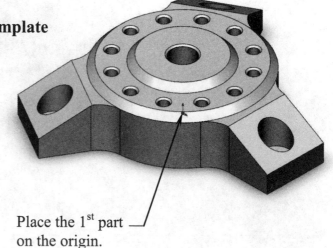

Place the 1st part on the origin.

3. Creating a Coordinate System:

- From the Assembly toolbar, click the Reference Geometry button and select the **Coordinate System** command – OR –

- From the pull down menu select: **Insert / Reference Geometry / Coordinate System**.

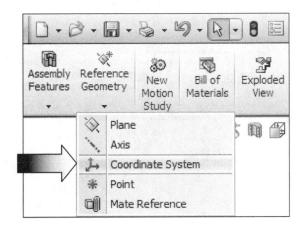

- Select the Corner-Vertex for **Origin**.

- Select the **X** and **Y** axis as indicated. Click Reverse Direction if needed.

- Leave the Z direction blank.

- Click **OK** .

- This Coordinate System will be used to calculate the Center of Mass for all questions from here on.

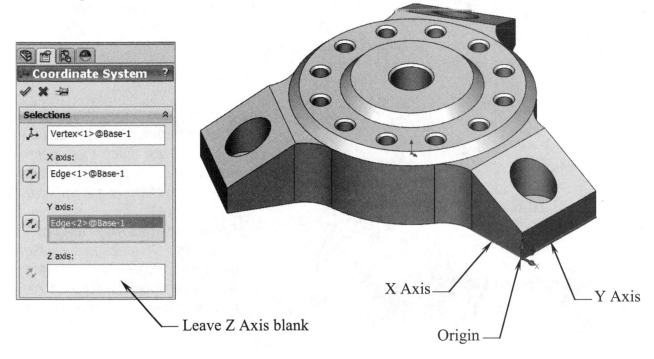

Leave Z Axis blank

X Axis

Y Axis

Origin

4. Inserting the 2ⁿᵈ component:

- From the Assembly toolbar, click the **Insert Component** command.

- Click Browse Browse... and open the component named: **Pivot**.

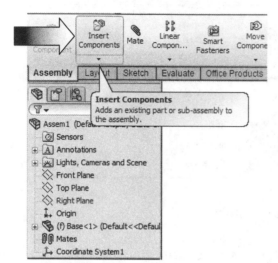

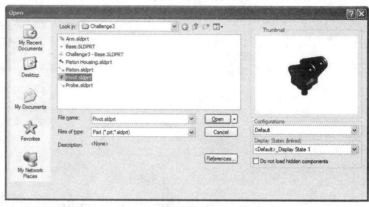

- Place the component approx. as shown below.

5. Adding the 1ˢᵗ mate:

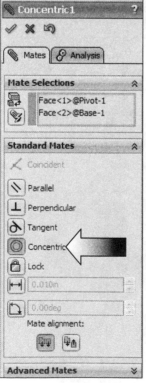

- From the Assembly toolbar, click **Mate**.

- Select the Circular Boss and the Hole as indicated.

- The **Concentric** mate is automatically created by default.

- Click **OK** ✓ .

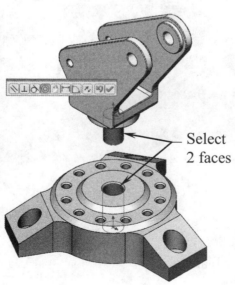

Select
2 faces

NOTE:

Most components will receive only 2 mates, since they were designed to move and rotate after everything is assembled.

Sometimes you may need to create the 3ʳᵈ mate just to align the components. These mates should be suppressed prior to mating other components.

6. Adding the 2nd mate:

- Click **Mate** again if you are not already there.

- Select the <u>bottom face</u> of the Circular Boss and the <u>upper face</u> of the Base.

- The **Coincident** mate is added automatically.

- Click **OK** .

Coincident

7. Adding the 3rd mate:

- Click **Mate** again.

- Select the FRONT of the Base and the FRONT plane of the Pivot.

- Click the **Parallel** mate option.

- Click **OK** .

NOTE:
This parallel mate will align the 2 components for the time being, it will get changed to an Angle mate later on.

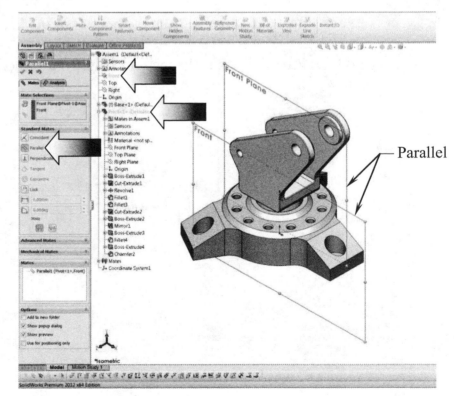

Parallel

8. Measuring the Center Of Mass:

- Select **Tools / Mass Properties**.

- Change the default output coordinate to: **Coordinate System1**.

- Enter the Center Of Mass (in Inches).

X = _____

Y = _____

Z = _____

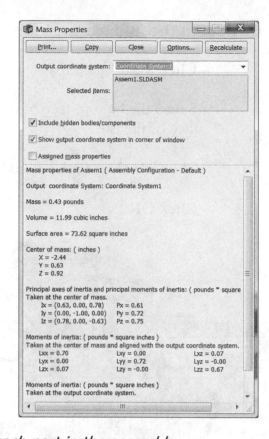

NOTE:
The center of mass shown in the dialog boxes are examples for use with this text only.

The actual mass properties of the components and the center of mass of the assembly depend upon the materials and the locations specified for each part in the assembly.

9. Creating an Angle mate:

- Expand the **Mate Group** from the bottom of the FeatureManager tree.

- Edit the **Parallel** mate, change it to **Angle** mate and enter **30.00deg**. Click **OK**.

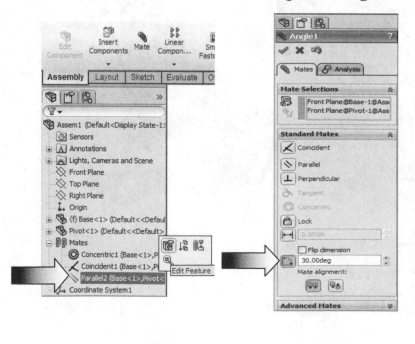

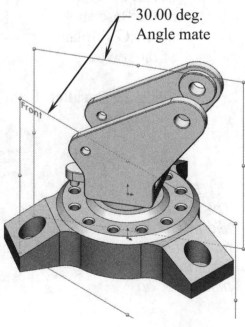

30.00 deg. Angle mate

10. Measuring the new Center Of Mass:

- Select **Tools / Mass Properties**.

- Use the same output **Coordinate System1**.

- Enter the Center Of Mass (in Inches).

X = _____

Y = _____

Z = _____

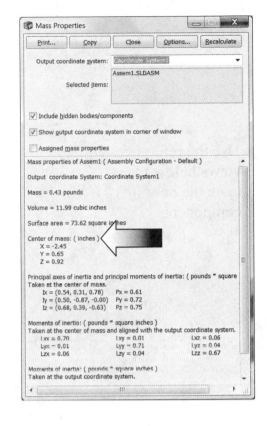

11. Inserting and mating other components:

- Click the **Insert Component** command from the Assembly toolbar.

- **Insert** and **Mate** the following components:

* **Arm**   * **Probe**   * **Piston**   * **Piston Housing**

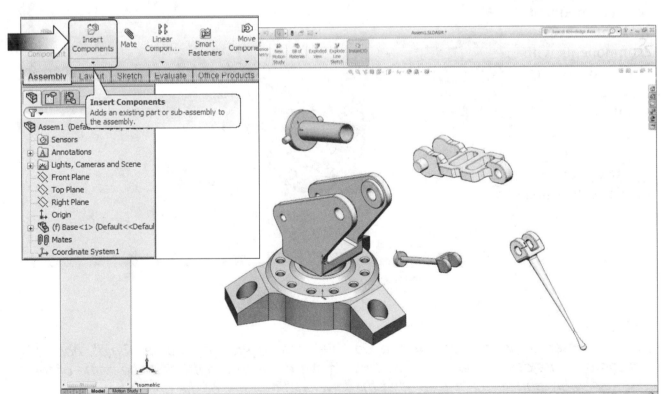

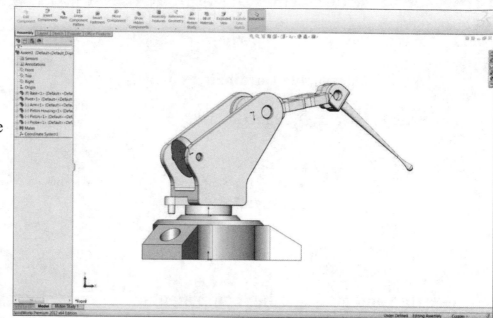

FRONT VIEW

- Use the reference views below to mate the new components.

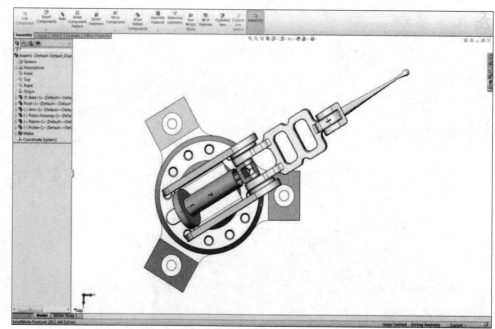

TOP VIEW

- Use either of the Front planes on each component to center the components with Coincident mates

– OR –

use the **Width mate** option to achieve the same results.

<u>NOTE:</u>
If a sub-assembly is inserted into the top-level assembly it will become "Rigid", none of its components can be moved or rotated. To overcome this, right click the name of the sub-assembly and select "Flexible" at the lower right corner of the dialog box.

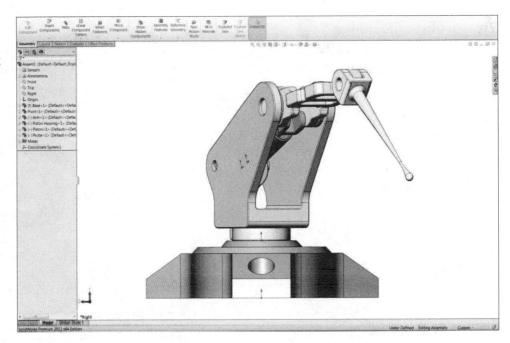

- Most component should have at least 1 degree of freedom left.

- You should be able to rotate the assembly back and forth, or up and down at this point.

RIGHT VIEW

12. Measuring the new Center Of Mass:

- Select **Tools / Mass Properties**.

- Use the same output **Coordinate System1**.

- Enter the Center Of Mass (in Inches).

$$X = \underline{\hspace{5cm}}$$

$$Y = \underline{\hspace{5cm}}$$

$$Z = \underline{\hspace{5cm}}$$

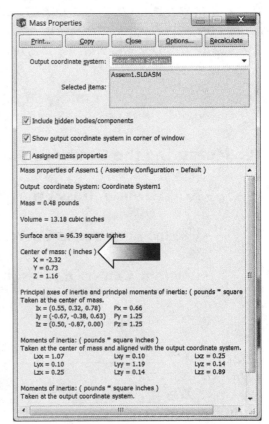

NOTE:
The current angle between the Base and the Pivot is still set at 30 degrees.

13. Changing the mate angle:

- Edit the **30deg** mate and change it to **180deg**.

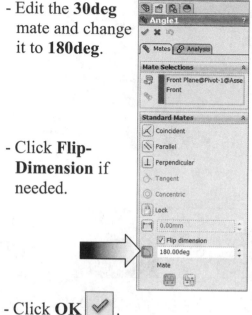

- Click **Flip-Dimension** if needed.

- Click **OK** ✓.

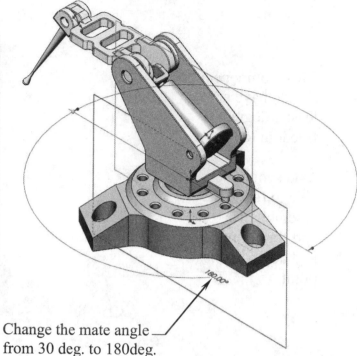

Change the mate angle from 30 deg. to 180deg.

NOTE:
If the angle mate causes an error, expand the mates group and suppress any red mates, especially the parallel mates, if any.

14. Measuring the Center Of Mass:

- Select **Tools / Mass Properties**.

- Use the same output **Coordinate System1**.

- Enter the Center Of Mass (in Inches).

X = _____

Y = _____

Z = _____

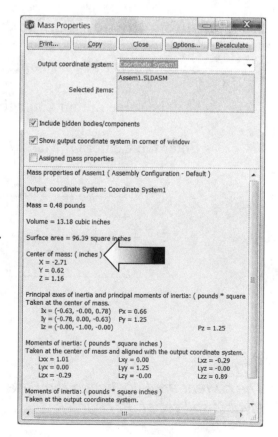

15. Replacing the Base:

- From the FeatureManager tree, right click the component Base and select: **Replace Component** (Arrow).

- Browse to the Training CD locate and open the part named: **Base B**.

- Under the Options dialog box, leave all default options as they were.

- Click **OK** ✓.

- The Base B does not have the features needed to re-attach the existing mates. The Mated-Entities dialog appears, asking for the new entities to replace with the old ones.

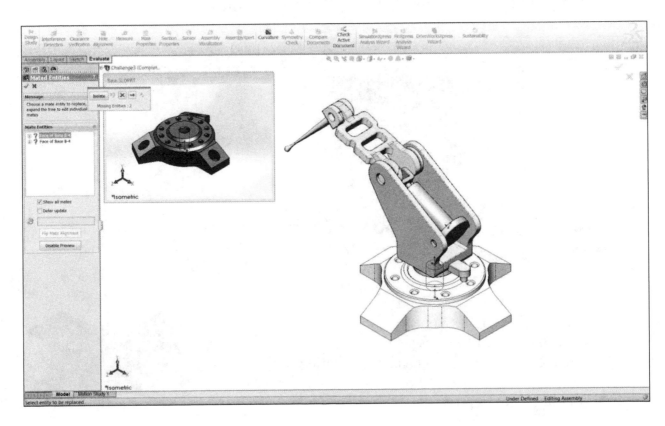

16. Replacing mate entities:

- The first error shows <u>the hole</u> that was used to create the <u>concentric</u> mate is being missing.

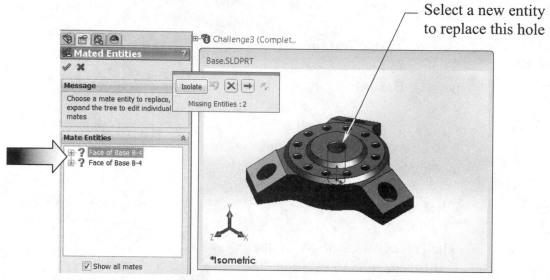

Select a new entity
to replace this hole

- Rotate the assembly and <u>select the main hole</u> in the center of the Base B as noted.

- All components (except the Base B) got flipped 180 degrees, click the **Flip-Mate-Alignment** button (arrow) to re-align the components.

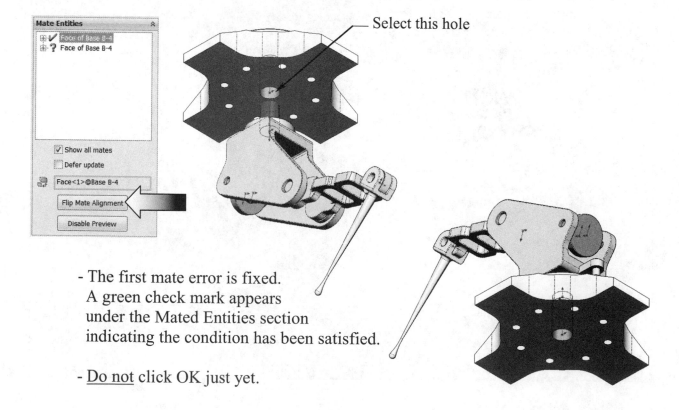

Select this hole

- The first mate error is fixed.
A green check mark appears
under the Mated Entities section
indicating the condition has been satisfied.

- <u>Do not</u> click OK just yet.

- Click the second error (the red question mark) in the Mated Entities dialog box.

- The second error shows the upper face the base is missing.

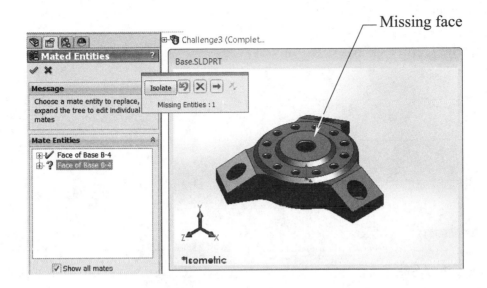

Missing face

- Switch back to the Isometric view (Control + 7) and <u>select the planar face</u> as indicated to replace with the missing one.

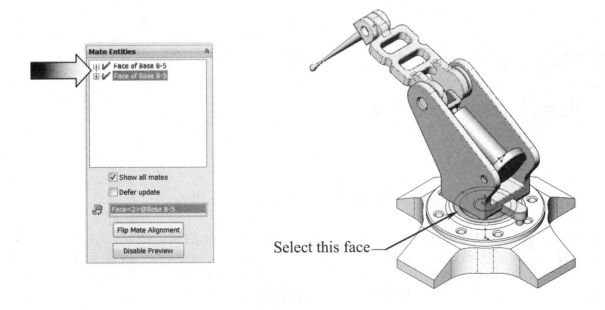

Select this face

- The second error is corrected.

- A green check mark appears again indicating the last condition has been satisfied.

- Click **OK** ✓.

17. Measuring the final Center Of Mass:

- Select **Tools / Mass Properties**.

- Use the same output **Coordinate System1**.

- Enter the Center Of Mass (in Inches).

X = _____

Y = _____

Z = _____

18. Saving your work:

- Click **File / Save As**.

- Enter **Challenge 3** for the name of the assembly.

- Click **Save**.

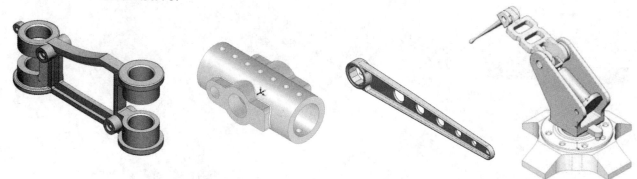

<u>NOTE</u>: When you're ready to take the actual examination, log on to:

www.solidworks.com/sw/mcad-certification-programs.htm, click on the CSWP option and select **purchase exam**. After the registration is completed, you will receive 2 emails from SolidWorks; one of them is the receipt for the purchase of the exam and the other have the instruction on how to download and take the online exam.

If you passed all 3 parts, an email will be sent to you from the Grading server notifying you of the results and instructing you on how to print out your certificate.

But if you failed, there is a 14-day waiting period, you will need to register and pay for the segment that you did not pass, and start the process over again.

Glossary

Alloys:

An Alloy is a mixture of two or more metals (and sometimes a non-metal). The mixture is made by heating and melting the substances together.
Example of alloys are Bronze (Copper and Tin), Brass (Copper and Zinc), and Steel (Iron and Carbon).

Gravity and Mass:

Gravity is the force that pulls everything on earth toward the ground and makes things feel heavy. Gravity makes all falling bodies accelerates at a constant 32ft. per second (9.8 m/s). In the earth's atmosphere, air resistance slow acceleration. Only on airless Moon would a feather and a metal block fall to the ground together.
The mass of an object is the amount of material it contains.
A body with greater mass has more inertia; it needs a greater force to accelerate.
Weight depends on the force of gravity, but mass does not.

When an object spins around another (for example: a satellite orbiting the earth) it is pushed outward. Two forces are at work here: Centrifugal (pushing outward) and Centripetal (pulling inward). If you whirl a ball around you on a string, you pull it inward (Centripetal force). The ball seems to pull outward (Centrifugal force) and if released will fly off in a straight line.

Heat:

Heat is a form of energy and can move from one substance to another in one of three ways: by Convection, by Radiation, and by Conduction.

- Convection takes place only in liquids like water (for example: water in a kettle) and gases (for example: air warmed by a heat source such as a fire or radiator). When liquid or gas is heated, it expands and become less dense. Warm air above the radiator rises and cool air moves in to take its place, creating a convection current.
- Radiation is movement of heat through the air. Heat forms a match sets molecules of air moving and rays of heat spread out around the heat source.

- Conduction occurs in solids such as metals. The handle of a metal spoon left in boiling liquid warms up as molecules at the heated end moves faster and collide with their neighbors, setting them moving. The heat travels through the metal, which is a good conductor of heat.

Inertia:

A body with a large mass is harder to start and also to stop. A heavy truck traveling at 50mph needs more power breaks to stop its motion than a smaller car traveling at the same speed.
Inertia is the tendency of an object either to stay still or to move steadily in a straight line, unless another force (such as a brick wall stopping the vehicle) makes it behave differently.

Joules:

The Joules is the SI unit of work or energy.
One Joule of work is done when a force of one Newton moves through a distance of one meter. The Joule is named after the English scientist James Joule (1818-1889).

Materials:

- Stainless steel is an alloy of steel with chromium or nickel.

- Steel is made by the basic oxygen process. The raw material is about three parts melted iron and one part scrap steel. Blowing oxygen into the melted iron raises the temperature and gets rid of impurities.

- All plastic are chemical compounds called polymers.

- Glass is made by mixing and heating sand, limestone, and soda ash. When these ingredients melt they turn into glass, which is hardened when it cools. Glass is in fact not a solid but a "supercooled" liquid, it can be shaped by blowing, pressing, drawing, casting into molds, rolling, and floating across molten tin, to make large sheets.

- Ceramic objects, such as pottery and porcelain, electrical insulators, bricks, and roof tiles are all made from clay. The clay is shaped or molded when wet and soft, and heated in a kiln until it hardens.

Machine Tools:

Are powered tools used for shaping metal or other materials, by drilling holes, chiseling, grinding, pressing or cutting. Often the material (the workpiece) is moved while the tool stays still (lathe), or vice versa, the workpiece stayed while the tool moves (mill).
Most common machine tools are: Mill, Lathe, Saw, Broach, Punch press, Grind, Bore and Stamp break.

Newton's Law:

1. Every object remains stopped or goes on moving at a steady rate in a straight line unless acted upon by another force. This is the inertia principle.
2. The amount of force needed to make an object change its speed depends on the mass of the object and the amount of the acceleration or deceleration required.
3. To every action there is an equal and opposite reaction. When a body is pushed on way by a force, another force pushes back with equal strength.

Polymers:

A polymer is made of one or more large molecules formed from thousands of smaller molecules. Rubber and Wood are natural polymers. Plastics are synthetic (artificially made) polymers.

Speed and Velocity:

- Speed is the rate at which a moving object changes position (how far it moves in a fixed time).
- Velocity is speed in a particular direction.
- If either speed or direction is changed, velocity also changed.

Absorbed
A feature, sketch, or annotation that is contained in another item (usually a feature) in the FeatureManager design tree. Examples are the profile sketch and profile path in a base-sweep, or a cosmetic thread annotation in a hole.

Align
Tools that assist in lining up annotations and dimensions (left, right, top, bottom, and so on). For aligning parts in an assembly.

Alternate position view
A drawing view in which one or more views are superimposed in phantom lines on the original view. Alternate position views are often used to show range of motion of an assembly.

Anchor point
The end of a leader that attaches to the note, block, or other annotation. Sheet formats contain anchor points for a bill of materials, a hole table, a revision table, and a weldment cut list.

Annotation

A text note or a symbol that adds specific design intent to a part, assembly, or drawing. Specific types of annotations include note, hole callout, surface finish symbol, datum feature symbol, datum target, geometric tolerance symbol, weld symbol, balloon, and stacked balloon. Annotations that apply only to drawings include center mark, annotation centerline, area hatch, and block.

Appearance callouts

Callouts that display the colors and textures of the face, feature, body, and part under the entity selected and are a shortcut to editing colors and textures.

Area hatch

A crosshatch pattern or fill applied to a selected face or to a closed sketch in a drawing.

Assembly

A document in which parts, features, and other assemblies (sub-assemblies) are mated together. The parts and sub-assemblies exist in documents separate from the assembly. For example, in an assembly, a piston can be mated to other parts, such as a connecting rod or cylinder. This new assembly can then be used as a sub-assembly in an assembly of an engine. The extension for a SolidWorks assembly file name is .SLDASM.

Attachment point

The end of a leader that attaches to the model (to an edge, vertex, or face, for example) or to a drawing sheet.

Axis

A straight line that can be used to create model geometry, features, or patterns. An axis can be made in a number of different ways, including using the intersection of two planes.

Balloon

Labels parts in an assembly, typically including item numbers and quantity. In drawings, the item numbers are related to rows in a bill of materials.

Base

The first solid feature of a part.

Baseline dimensions

Sets of dimensions measured from the same edge or vertex in a drawing.

Bend

A feature in a sheet metal part. A bend generated from a filleted corner, cylindrical face, or conical face is a round bend; a bend generated from sketched straight lines is a sharp bends.

Bill of materials
A table inserted into a drawing to keep a record of the parts used in an assembly.

Block
A user-defined annotation that you can use in parts, assemblies, and drawings. A block can contain text, sketch entities (except points), and area hatch, and it can be saved in a file for later use as, for example, a custom callout or a company logo.

Bottom-up assembly
An assembly modeling technique where you create parts and then insert them into an assembly.

Broken-out section
A drawing view that exposes inner details of a drawing view by removing material from a closed profile, usually a spline.

Cavity
The mold half that holds the cavity feature of the design part.

Center mark
A cross that marks the center of a circle or arc.

Centerline
A centerline marks, in phantom font, an axis of symmetry in a sketch or drawing.

Chamfer
Bevels a selected edge or vertex. You can apply chamfers to both sketches and features.

Child
A dependent feature related to a previously-built feature. For example, a chamfer on the edge of a hole is a child of the parent hole.

Click-release
As you sketch, if you click and then release the pointer, you are in click-release mode. Move the pointer and click again to define the next point in the sketch sequence.

Click-drag
As you sketch, if you click and drag the pointer, you are in click-drag mode. When you release the pointer, the sketch entity is complete.

Closed profile
Also called a closed contour, it is a sketch or sketch entity with no exposed endpoints; for example, a circle or polygon.

Collapse

The opposite of explode. The collapse action returns an exploded assembly's parts to their normal positions.

Collision Detection

An assembly function that detects collisions between components when components move or rotate. A collision occurs when an entity on one component coincides with any entity on another component.

Component

Any part or sub-assembly within an assembly

Configuration

A variation of a part or assembly within a single document. Variations can include different dimensions, features, and properties. For example, a single part such as a bolt can contain different configurations that vary the diameter and length.

ConfigurationManager

Located on the left side of the SolidWorks window, it is a means to create, select, and view the configurations of parts and assemblies.

Constraint

The relations between sketch entities, or between sketch entities and planes, axes, edges, or vertices.

Construction geometry

The characteristic of a sketch entity that the entity is used in creating other geometry but is not itself used in creating features.

Coordinate system

A system of planes used to assign Cartesian coordinates to features, parts, and assemblies. Part and assembly documents contain default coordinate systems; other coordinate systems can be defined with reference geometry. Coordinate systems can be used with measurement tools and for exporting documents to other file formats.

Cosmetic thread

An annotation that represents threads.

Crosshatch

A pattern (or fill) applied to drawing views such as section views and broken-out sections.

Curvature

Curvature is equal to the inverse of the radius of the curve. The curvature can be displayed in different colors according to the local radius (usually of a surface).

Cut

A feature that removes material from a part by such actions as extrude, revolve, loft, sweep, thicken, cavity, and so on.

Dangling

A dimension, relation, or drawing section view that is unresolved. For example, if a piece of geometry is dimensioned, and that geometry is later deleted, the dimension becomes dangling.

Degrees of freedom

Geometry that is not defined by dimensions or relations is free to move. In 2D sketches, there are three degrees of freedom: movement along the X and Y axes, and rotation about the Z axis (the axis normal to the sketch plane). In 3D sketches and in assemblies, there are six degrees of freedom: movement along the X, Y, and Z axes, and rotation about the X, Y, and Z axes.

Derived part

A derived part is a new base, mirror, or component part created directly from an existing part and linked to the original part such that changes to the original part are reflected in the derived part.

Derived sketch

A copy of a sketch, in either the same part or the same assembly, that is connected to the original sketch. Changes in the original sketch are reflected in the derived sketch.

Design Library

Located in the Task Pane, the Design Library provides a central location for reusable elements such as parts, assemblies, and so on.

Design table

An Excel spreadsheet that is used to create multiple configurations in a part or assembly document.

Detached drawing

A drawing format that allows opening and working in a drawing without loading the corresponding models into memory. The models are loaded on an as-needed basis.

Detail view

A portion of a larger view, usually at a larger scale than the original view.

Dimension line

A linear dimension line references the dimension text to extension lines indicating the entity being measured. An angular dimension line references the dimension text directly to the measured object.

DimXpertManager

Located on the left side of the SolidWorks window, it is a means to manage dimensions and tolerances created using DimXpert for parts according to the requirements of the ASME Y.14.41-2003 standard.

DisplayManager

The DisplayManager lists the appearances, decals, lights, scene, and cameras applied to the current model. From the DisplayManager, you can view applied content, and add, edit, or delete items. When PhotoView 360 is added in, the DisplayManager also provides access to PhotoView options.

Document

A file containing a part, assembly, or drawing.

Draft

The degree of taper or angle of a face, usually applied to molds or castings.

Drawing

A 2D representation of a 3D part or assembly. The extension for a SolidWorks drawing file name is .SLDDRW.

Drawing sheet

A page in a drawing document.

Driven dimension

Measurements of the model, but they do not drive the model and their values cannot be changed.

Driving dimension

Also referred to as a model dimension, it sets the value for a sketch entity. It can also control distance, thickness, and feature parameters.

Edge

A single outside boundary of a feature.

Edge flange

A sheet metal feature that combines a bend and a tab in a single operation.

Equation

Creates a mathematical relation between sketch dimensions, using dimension names as variables, or between feature parameters, such as the depth of an extruded feature or the instance count in a pattern.

Exploded view

Shows an assembly with its components separated from one another, usually to show how to assemble the mechanism.

Export

Save a SolidWorks document in another format for use in other CAD/CAM, rapid prototyping, web, or graphics software applications.

Extension line

The line extending from the model indicating the point from which a dimension is measured.

Extrude

A feature that linearly projects a sketch to either add material to a part (in a base or boss) or remove material from a part (in a cut or hole).

Face

A selectable area (planar or otherwise) of a model or surface with boundaries that help define the shape of the model or surface. For example, a rectangular solid has six faces.

Fasteners

A SolidWorks Toolbox library that adds fasteners automatically to holes in an assembly.

Feature

An individual shape that, combined with other features, makes up a part or assembly. Some features, such as bosses and cuts, originate as sketches. Other features, such as shells and fillets, modify a feature's geometry. However, not all features have associated geometry. Features are always listed in the FeatureManager design tree.

FeatureManager design tree

Located on the left side of the SolidWorks window, it provides an outline view of the active part, assembly, or drawing.

Fill

A solid area hatch or crosshatch. Fill also applies to patches on surfaces.

Fillet

An internal rounding of a corner or edge in a sketch, or an edge on a surface or solid.

Forming tool

Dies that bend, stretch, or otherwise form sheet metal to create such form features as louvers, lances, flanges, and ribs.

Fully defined

A sketch where all lines and curves in the sketch, and their positions, are described by dimensions or relations, or both, and cannot be moved. Fully defined sketch entities are shown in black.

Geometric tolerance

A set of standard symbols that specify the geometric characteristics and dimensional requirements of a feature.

Graphics area

The area in the SolidWorks window where the part, assembly, or drawing appears.

Guide curve

A 2D or 3D curve used to guide a sweep or loft.

Handle

An arrow, square, or circle that you can drag to adjust the size or position of an entity (a feature, dimension, or sketch entity, for example).

Helix

A curve defined by pitch, revolutions, and height. A helix can be used, for example, as a path for a swept feature cutting threads in a bolt.

Hem

A sheet metal feature that folds back at the edge of a part. A hem can be open, closed, double, or tear-drop.

HLR

(Hidden lines removed) a view mode in which all edges of the model that are not visible from the current view angle are removed from the display.

HLV

(hidden lines visible) A view mode in which all edges of the model that are not visible from the current view angle are shown gray or dashed.

Import

Open files from other CAD software applications into a SolidWorks document.

In-context feature

A feature with an external reference to the geometry of another component; the in-context feature changes automatically if the geometry of the referenced model or feature changes.

Inference

The system automatically creates (infers) relations between dragged entities (sketched entities, annotations, and components) and other entities and geometry. This is useful when positioning entities relative to one another.

Instance

An item in a pattern or a component in an assembly that occurs more than once. Blocks are inserted into drawings as instances of block definitions.

Interference detection

A tool that displays any interference between selected components in an assembly.

Jog

A sheet metal feature that adds material to a part by creating two bends from a sketched line. (2)

Knit

A tool that combines two or more faces or surfaces into one. The edges of the surfaces must be adjacent and not overlapping, but they cannot ever be planar. There is no difference in the appearance of the face or the surface after knitting.

Layout sketch

A sketch that contains important sketch entities, dimensions, and relations. You reference the entities in the layout sketch when creating new sketches, building new geometry, or positioning components in an assembly. This allows for easier updating of your model because changes you make to the layout sketch propagate to the entire model.

Leader

A solid line from an annotation (note, dimension, and so on) to the referenced feature.

Library feature

A frequently used feature, or combination of features, that is created once and then saved for future use.

Lightweight

A part in an assembly or a drawing has only a subset of its model data loaded into memory. The remaining model data is loaded on an as-needed basis. This improves performance of large and complex assemblies.

Line

A straight sketch entity with two endpoints. A line can be created by projecting an external entity such as an edge, plane, axis, or sketch curve into the sketch.

Loft

A base, boss, cut, or surface feature created by transitions between profiles.

Lofted bend

A sheet metal feature that produces a roll form or a transitional shape from two open profile sketches. Lofted bends often create funnels and chutes.

Mass properties

A tool that evaluates the characteristics of a part or an assembly such as volume, surface area, centroid, and so on.

Mate

A geometric relationship, such as coincident, perpendicular, tangent, and so on, between parts in an assembly.

Mate reference

Specifies one or more entities of a component to use for automatic mating. When you drag a component with a mate reference into an assembly, the software tries to find other combinations of the same mate reference name and mate type.

Mates folder

A collection of mates that are solved together. The order in which the mates appear within the Mates folder does not matter.

Mirror

(a) A mirror feature is a copy of a selected feature, mirrored about a plane or planar face.
(b) A mirror sketch entity is a copy of a selected sketch entity that is mirrored about a centerline.

Miter flange

A sheet metal feature that joins multiple edge flanges together and miters the corner.

Model

3D solid geometry in a part or assembly document. If a part or assembly document contains multiple configurations, each configuration is a separate model.

Model dimension

A dimension specified in a sketch or a feature in a part or assembly document that defines some entity in a 3D model.

Model item
A characteristic or dimension of feature geometry that can be used in detailing drawings.

Model view
A drawing view of a part or assembly.

Mold
A set of manufacturing tooling used to shape molten plastic or other material into a designed part. You design the mold using a sequence of integrated tools that result in cavity and core blocks that are derived parts of the part to be molded.

Motion Study
Motion Studies are graphical simulations of motion and visual properties with assembly models. Analogous to a configuration, they do not actually change the original assembly model or its properties. They display the model as it changes based on simulation elements you add.

Multibody part
A part with separate solid bodies within the same part document. Unlike the components in an assembly, multibody parts are not dynamic.

Native format
DXF and DWG files remain in their original format (are not converted into SolidWorks format) when viewed in SolidWorks drawing sheets (view only).

Open profile
Also called an open contour, it is a sketch or sketch entity with endpoints exposed. For example, a U-shaped profile is open.

Ordinate dimensions
A chain of dimensions measured from a zero ordinate in a drawing or sketch.

Origin
The model origin appears as three gray arrows and represents the (0,0,0) coordinate of the model. When a sketch is active, a sketch origin appears in red and represents the (0,0,0) coordinate of the sketch. Dimensions and relations can be added to the model origin, but not to
a sketch origin.

Out-of-context feature
A feature with an external reference to the geometry of another component that is not open.

Over defined

A sketch is over defined when dimensions or relations are either in conflict or redundant.

Parameter

A value used to define a sketch or feature (often a dimension).

Parent

An existing feature upon which other features depend. For example, in a block with a hole, the block is the parent to the child hole feature.

Part

A single 3D object made up of features. A part can become a component in an assembly, and it can be represented in 2D in a drawing. Examples of parts are bolt, pin, plate, and so on. The extension for a SolidWorks part file name is .SLDPRT.

Path

A sketch, edge, or curve used in creating a sweep or loft.

Pattern

A pattern repeats selected sketch entities, features, or components in an array, which can be linear, circular, or sketch-driven. If the seed entity is changed, the other instances in the pattern update.

Physical Dynamics

An assembly tool that displays the motion of assembly components in a realistic way. When you drag a component, the component applies a force to other components it touches. Components move only within their degrees of freedom.

Pierce relation

Makes a sketch point coincident to the location at which an axis, edge, line, or spline pierces the sketch plane.

Planar

Entities that can lie on one plane. For example, a circle is planar, but a helix is not.

Plane

Flat construction geometry. Planes can be used for a 2D sketch, section view of a model, a neutral plane in a draft feature, and others.

Point

A singular location in a sketch, or a projection into a sketch at a single location of an external entity (origin, vertex, axis, or point in an external sketch).

Predefined view

A drawing view in which the view position, orientation, and so on can be specified before a model is inserted. You can save drawing documents with predefined views as templates.

Profile

A sketch entity used to create a feature (such as a loft) or a drawing view (such as a detail view). A profile can be open (such as a U shape or open spline) or closed (such as a circle or closed spline).

Projected dimension

If you dimension entities in an isometric view, projected dimensions are the flat dimensions in 2D.

Projected view

A drawing view projected orthogonally from an existing view.

PropertyManager

Located on the left side of the SolidWorks window, it is used for dynamic editing of sketch entities and most features.

RealView graphics

A hardware (graphics card) support of advanced shading in real time; the rendering applies to the model and is retained as you move or rotate a part.

Rebuild

Tool that updates (or regenerates) the document with any changes made since the last time the model was rebuilt. Rebuild is typically used after changing a model dimension.

Reference dimension

A dimension in a drawing that shows the measurement of an item, but cannot drive the model and its value cannot be modified. When model dimensions change, reference dimensions update.

Reference geometry

Includes planes, axes, coordinate systems, and 3D curves. Reference geometry is used to assist in creating features such lofts, sweeps, drafts, chamfers, and patterns.

Relation

A geometric constraint between sketch entities or between a sketch entity and a plane, axis, edge, or vertex. Relations can be added automatically or manually.

Relative view

A relative (or relative to model) drawing view is created relative to planar surfaces in a part or assembly.

Reload

Refreshes shared documents. For example, if you open a part file for read-only access while another user makes changes to the same part, you can reload the new version, including the changes.

Reorder

Reordering (changing the order of) items is possible in the FeatureManager design tree. In parts, you can change the order in which features are solved. In assemblies, you can control the order in which components appear in a bill of materials.

Replace

Substitutes one or more open instances of a component in an assembly with a different component.

Resolved

A state of an assembly component (in an assembly or drawing document) in which it is fully loaded in memory. All the component's model data is available, so its entities can be selected, referenced, edited, used in mates, and so on.

Revolve

A feature that creates a base or boss, a revolved cut, or revolved surface by revolving one or more sketched profiles around a centerline.

Rip

A sheet metal feature that removes material at an edge to allow a bend.

Rollback

Suppresses all items below the rollback bar.

Section

Another term for profile in sweeps.

Section line

A line or centerline sketched in a drawing view to create a section view.

Section scope

Specifies the components to be left uncut when you create an assembly drawing section view.

Section view

A section view (or section cut) is (1) a part or assembly view cut by a plane, or (2) a drawing view created by cutting another drawing view with a section line.

Seed

A sketch or an entity (a feature, face, or body) that is the basis for a pattern. If you edit the seed, the other entities in the pattern are updated.

Shaded

Displays a model as a colored solid.

Shared values

Also called linked values, these are named variables that you assign to set the value of two or more dimensions to be equal.

Sheet format

Includes page size and orientation, standard text, borders, title blocks, and so on. Sheet formats can be customized and saved for future use. Each sheet of a drawing document can have a different format.

Shell

A feature that hollows out a part, leaving open the selected faces and thin walls on the remaining faces. A hollow part is created when no faces are selected to be open.

Sketch

A collection of lines and other 2D objects on a plane or face that forms the basis for a feature such as a base or a boss. A 3D sketch is non-planar and can be used to guide a sweep or loft, for example.

Smart Fasteners

Automatically adds fasteners (bolts and screws) to an assembly using the SolidWorks Toolbox library of fasteners.

SmartMates

An assembly mating relation that is created automatically.

Solid sweep

A cut sweep created by moving a tool body along a path to cut out 3D material from a model.

Spiral

A flat or 2D helix, defined by a circle, pitch, and number of revolutions.

Spline

A sketched 2D or 3D curve defined by a set of control points.

Split line

Projects a sketched curve onto a selected model face, dividing the face into multiple faces so that each can be selected individually. A split line can be used to create draft features, to create face blend fillets, and to radiate surfaces to cut molds.

Stacked balloon

A set of balloons with only one leader. The balloons can be stacked vertically (up or down) or horizontally (left or right).

Standard 3 views

The three orthographic views (front, right, and top) that are often the basis of a drawing.

Stereolithography

The process of creating rapid prototype parts using a faceted mesh representation in STL files.

Sub-assembly

An assembly document that is part of a larger assembly. For example, the steering mechanism of a car is a sub-assembly of the car.

Suppress

Removes an entity from the display and from any calculations in which it is involved. You can suppress features, assembly components, and so on. Suppressing an entity does not delete the entity; you can un-suppress the entity to restore it.

Surface

A zero-thickness planar or 3D entity with edge boundaries. Surfaces are often used to create solid features. Reference surfaces can be used to modify solid features.

Sweep

Creates a base, boss, cut, or surface feature by moving a profile (section) along a path. For cut-sweeps, you can create solid sweeps by moving a tool body along a path.

Tangent arc

An arc that is tangent to another entity, such as a line.

Tangent edge

The transition edge between rounded or filleted faces in hidden lines visible or hidden lines removed modes in drawings.

Task Pane
Located on the right-side of the SolidWorks window, the Task Pane contains SolidWorks Resources, the Design Library, and the File Explorer.

Template
A document (part, assembly, or drawing) that forms the basis of a new document. It can include user-defined parameters, annotations, predefined views, geometry, and so on.

Temporary axis
An axis created implicitly for every conical or cylindrical face in a model.

Thin feature
An extruded or revolved feature with constant wall thickness. Sheet metal parts are typically created from thin features.

TolAnalyst
A tolerance analysis application that determines the effects that dimensions and tolerances have on parts and assemblies.

Top-down design
An assembly modeling technique where you create parts in the context of an assembly by referencing the geometry of other components. Changes to the referenced components propagate to the parts that you create in context.

Triad
Three axes with arrows defining the X, Y, and Z directions. A reference triad appears in part and assembly documents to assist in orienting the viewing of models. Triads also assist when moving or rotating components in assemblies.

Under defined
A sketch is under defined when there are not enough dimensions and relations to prevent entities from moving or changing size.

Vertex
A point at which two or more lines or edges intersect. Vertices can be selected for sketching, dimensioning, and many other operations.

Viewports
Windows that display views of models. You can specify one, two, or four viewports. Viewports with orthogonal views can be linked, which links orientation and rotation.

Virtual sharp

A sketch point at the intersection of two entities after the intersection itself has been removed by a feature such as a fillet or chamfer. Dimensions and relations to the virtual sharp are retained even though the actual intersection no longer exists.

Weldment

A multibody part with structural members.

Weldment cut list

A table that tabulates the bodies in a weldment along with descriptions and lengths.

Wireframe

A view mode in which all edges of the part or assembly are displayed.

Zebra stripes

Simulate the reflection of long strips of light on a very shiny surface. They allow you to see small changes in a surface that may be hard to see with a standard display.

Zoom

To simulate movement toward or away from a part or an assembly.

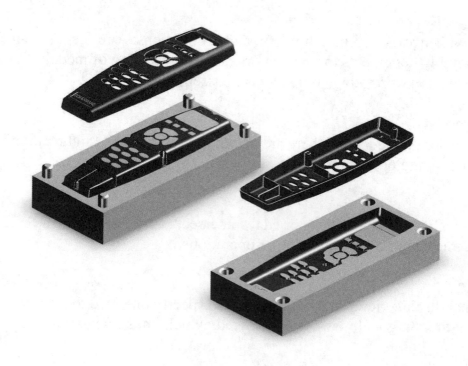

Index

Images Designed and Rendered with Solidworks 2013

SolidWorks® Quick-Guide

Quick Reference Guide To SolidWorks® 2013 Command Icons & Toolbars

The STANDARD Toolbar

Creates a new document.

Opens an existing document.

Saves an active document.

Make Drawing from Part/Assembly

Make Assembly from Part/Assembly

Prints the active document.

Displays full pages as they are printed.

Cuts the selection & puts it on the clipboard.

Copies the selection & puts it on the clipboard.

Inserts the clipboard contents.

Deletes the selection.

Reverses the last action.

Redo the last action that was undone.

Rebuilds the part / assembly / drawing.

Saves all documents.

Changes the color of the current selection(s).

Edits material.

Closes an existing document

Shows or hides the Selection Filter toolbar.

Shows or hides the Web toolbar.

Displays Help topics for SolidWorks.

Displays full pages as they will be printed.

The STANDARD Toolbar (Cont.)

Loads or unloads the 3D instant website add-in

Select tool.

Reloads the current document from disk.

Places an online order for a rapid prototype part.

Checks read-only files for write access.

Show/Edit the properties of the current selection.

Changes options settings for SolidWorks.

Tiles windows vertically, as non-overlapping.

Tiles windows horizontally, as non-overlapping.

Opens another window for the active document.

The SKETCH TOOLS Toolbar

Sketches a rectangle from the center.

Sketches a centerpoint arc slot.

Sketches a 3-point arc slot.

Sketches a straight slot.

Sketches a centerpoint straight slot.

Stretches sketch entities and annotations.

Inserts an Equation Driven Curve.

Sketches a 3-point arc.

Inserts a picture into the sketch background.

Creates sketched ellipses.

Quick Reference Guide To SolidWorks® 2013 Command Icons & Toolbars

The SKETCH TOOLS Toolbar

 Selects items for commands to act on.

 Sets up Grid parameters.

 Creates a sketch on a selected plane or face.

 Creates a 3D sketch.

 Scales/Translates/Rotates the current sketch.

 Moves or copies sketch entities and annotations.

 Scales sketch entities and annotations.

 Sketches an angle rectangle from the center.

 Sketches a parallelogram.

 Sketches a line.

 Creates a center point arc: center, start, end.

 Creates an arc tangent to a line.

 Sketches splines on a surface or face.

 Sketches a circle.

 Sketches a circle by its perimeter.

 Sketches a partial ellipse.

 Makes a path of sketch entities.

 Mirrors entities dynamically about a

 Insert a plane into the 3D sketch.

 Rotates sketch entities and

 Copies sketch entities and

 Sketches on a plane in a 3D sketch.

 Moves sketch entities without solving dimensions or relations.

The SKETCH TOOLS Toolbar (Cont.)

 Partial ellipses.

 Adds a Parabola.

 Creates sketched splines.

 Sketches a polygon.

 Sketches a rectangle.

 Sketches a parallelogram.

 Creates points.

 Creates sketched centerlines.

 Adds text to sketch.

 Converts selected model edges or sketch entities to sketch segments.

 Creates a sketch along the intersection of multiple bodies.

 Converts face curves on the selected face into 3D sketch entities.

 Mirrors selected segments about a centerline.

 Fillets the corner of two lines.

 Creates a chamfer between two sketch entities.

 Creates a sketch curve by offsetting model edges or sketch entities at a specified distance.

 Fits a spline to selected entities.

 Trims a sketch segment.

 Extends a sketch segment.

 Splits a sketch segment.

 Construction Geometry.

 Creates linear steps and repeat of sketch entities.

 Creates circular steps and repeat of sketch entities.

Quick Reference Guide To SolidWorks® 2013 Command Icons & Toolbars

The SHEET METAL

Inserts a FlattenBends & a ProcessBends feature, A sheet metal feature will be added.

Shows flat pattern for this sheet metal part.

Shows part without inserting any bends.

Inserts a rip feature to a sheet metal part.

Inserts a Sheet Metal Base Flange or a Tab feature.

Inserts a Sheet Metal Miter Flange feature.

Folds selected bends.

Unfolds selected bends.

Inserts bends using a sketch line.

Inserts a flange by pulling an edge.

Inserts a sheet metal corner feature.

Inserts a Hem feature by selecting edges.

Breaks a corner by filleting/chamfering it.

Inserts a Jog feature using a sketch line.

Inserts a lofted bend feature using 2 sketches.

Creates inverse dent on a sheet metal part.

Trims out material from a corner, in a sheet metal

Inserts a fillet weld bead.

Converts a solid/surface into a sheet metal part.

Adds a Cross Break feature into a selected face.

The SURFACES Toolbar

Deletes a face or a set of faces.

Creates mid surfaces between offset face pairs.

Patches surface holes and external edges.

The SURFACES Toolbar (cont.)

Creates an extruded surface.

Creates a revolved surface.

Creates a swept surface.

Creates a lofted surface.

Creates an offset surface.

Radiates a surface originating from a curve, parallel to a plane.

Knits surfaces together.

Creates a planar surface from a sketch or A set of edges.

Creates a surface by importing data from a file.

Extends a surface.

Trims a surface.

Generating MidSurface(s).

Deletes Face(s).

Replaces Face with Surface.

Patches surface holes and external edges by extending the surfaces.

Creates parting surfaces between core & cavity surfaces.

Inserts ruled surfaces from edges.

The WELDMENTS Toolbar

Creates a weldment feature.

Creates a structure member feature.

Adds a gusset feature between 2 planar adjoining faces.

Creates an end cap feature.

Adds a fillet weld bead feature.

Trims or extends structure members.

The DIMENSIONS/RELATIONS Toolbar

Inserts dimension between two lines.

Creates a horizontal dimension between selected entities.

Creates a vertical dimension between selected entities.

Creates a reference dimension between selected entities.

Creates a set of ordinate dimensions.

Creates a set of Horizontal ordinate dimensions.

Creates a set of Vertical ordinate dimensions.

Creates a chamfer dimension.

Adds a geometric relation.

Automatically Adds Dimensions to the current sketch.

Displays and deletes geometric relations.

Fully defines a sketch.

Scans a sketch for elements of equal length or radius.

Automatically recognize tolerance features.

Creates linked, unlinked, or collection pattern feature.

Paints faces of toleranced features in different colors.

Adds DimXpert location dimension.

Adds DimXpert datum.

Copies existing tolerance scheme to current configuration.

Adds DimXpert size dimension.

Adds DimXpert geometric tolerance.

Deletes all tolerance data base.

Adds new Tol Analyst.

The STANDARD VIEWS

Front view.

Back view.

Left view.

Right view.

Top view.

Bottom view.

Isometric view.

Trimetric view.

Dimetric view.

Normal to view.

Links all views in the viewport together.

Displays viewport with front & right views

Displays a 4 view viewport with 1st or 3rd Angle of projection.

Displays viewport with front & top

Displays viewport with a single

The Block Toolbar

Makes a new block.

Edits the selected block.

Inserts a new block to a sketch or drawing.

Adds/Removes sketch entities to/from blocks.

Updates parent sketches effected by this block.

Saves the block to a file.

Explodes the selected block.

Inserts a belt.

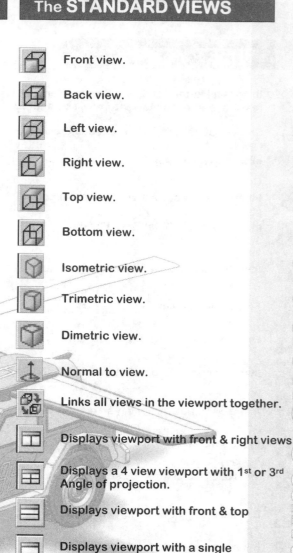

Did you know??
* Ctrl+Q will force a rebuild on all features of a part.
* Ctrl+B will rebuild the feature being worked on and its dependants.

SolidWorks Quick-Guide

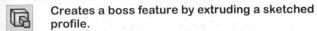

The FEATURES Toolbar

Creates a boss feature by extruding a sketched profile.

Creates a revolved feature based on profile and angle parameter.

Creates a cut feature by extruding a sketched profile.

Creates a cut feature by revolving a sketched profile.

Creates a sweep feature by sweeping a profile along a path curve.

Creates a cut by sweeping a closed profile along an open or closed path.

Creates a cut by removing material between two or more profiles

Creates a cut by thickening one or more adjacent surfaces.

Adds a deformed surface by push or pull on

Creates a lofted feature between two or more profiles.

Creates a solid feature by thickening one or more adjacent surfaces.

Creates a filled feature.

Chamfers an edge or a chain of tangent edges.

Inserts a rib feature.

Scales model by a specified factor.

Creates a shell feature.

Applies draft to a selected surface.

Creates a cylindrical hole.

Inserts a hole with a pre-defined cross section.

Puts a dome surface on a face.

Puts a shape feature on a face.

Applies global deformation to solid or surface bodies.

Wraps closed sketch contour(s) onto a face.

Moves / Sizes features.

Suppresses the selected feature or component.

Un-suppresses the selected feature or component.

Flexes solid and surface bodies

Creates a linear pattern using the selected feature(s).

Creates a circular pattern using the selected feature(s).

Mirrors a feature about a plane.

Creates a Curve Driven Pattern.

Creates a Sketch Driven pattern.

Creates a Table Driven Pattern.

Inserts a split Feature.

Combines two or more solid bodies.

Joins bodies from one or more parts into a single part in the context of an assembly.

Deletes a solid or a surface.

Inserts solid(s) or surface(s) into an existing open document.

Inserts a part from file into the active part document.

Moves/Copies solid and surface bodies or moves graphics bodies.

Merges short edges on faces

Pushes solid / surface model by another solid / surface model

Moves face(s) of a solid

Area fills faces or bodies into one or more contours.

Inserts holes into a series of parts.

Returns suppressed items with dependents to the model.

Cuts a solid model with a surface.

Adds material between profiles in two directions to create a solid feature.

Cuts a solid model by removing material between profiles in two directions.

Did you know??

* Right-mouse drag a component in an assembly rotates it.
* Left- mouse drag a component in an assembly moves it.

The MOLD TOOLS Toolbar

 Extracts core(s) from existing tooling split

 Constructs a surface patch

 Moves face(s) of a solid

 Finds & creates mold shut-off surfaces

 Inserts cavity into a base part.

 Scales a model by a specified factor.

 Applies draft to a selected surface.

 Inserts a split line feature.

 Creates an offset surface.

 Creates parting lines to separate core & cavity surfaces

 Creates a planar surface from a sketch or A set of edges.

 Knits surfaces together.

 Analyzes draft angles of faces, based on a mold pull direction.

 Inserts ruled surfaces from edges.

 Creates parting surfaces between core & cavity surfaces

 Creates multiple bodies from a single body.

 Inserts a tooling split feature.

 Identifies faces that form undercuts.

 Creates parting surfaces between the core & cavity.

 Inserts surface body folders for mold operation.

The SELECTION FILTERS

 Turns selection filters on and off.

 Clears all filters.

 Selects all filters.

 Inverts current selection.

The SELECTION FILTERS cont.

 Allows selection of edges only.

 Allows selection of faces only.

 Adds filter for Surface Bodies.

 Adds filter for Solid Bodies.

 Adds filter for Axes.

 Adds filter for Planes.

 Adds filter for Sketch Points.

 Adds filter for Sketch Segments.

 Adds filter for Midpoints.

 Adds filter for Center Marks.

 Adds filter for Centerline.

 Adds filter for Dimensions and Hole Callouts.

 Adds filter for Surface Finish Symbols.

 Adds filter for Geometric Tolerances.

 Adds filter for Notes / Balloons.

 Adds filter for Weld Symbols.

 Adds filter for Datum Targets.

 Adds filter for Cosmetic Threads.

 Adds filter for blocks.

 Adds filter for Dowel pin symbols.

 Adds filter for connection points.

 Allows selection filter for vertices only.

 Allows selection of weld symbols only.

 Allows selection of blocks only.

 Adds filter for routing points.

SolidWorks Quick-Guide

The **FLYOUT** Toolbar

2D to 3D.

Align.

Annotation.

Assemblies.

Curves.

Dimensions / Relation.

Drawings.

Features.

Fonts.

Line Formats.

Macros.

Molds.

Reference Geometry.

Quick snap filters.

Selection Filters.

Sheet Metal.

Simulation.

Sketch.

SolidWorks Office.

Splines.

Standard.

Standard Views.

Surfaces.

Tools.

View.

Web.

Weldments.

Block commands.

Explode sketch commands.

Table commands.

Fastening feature commands.

Creates a rounded internal or external fillet.

Linear Patterns Features, Faces and Bodies.

Creates various corner treatments.

Displays Deletes geometric relations.

Creates dimensions for one or more entities.

Adds an existing part or assembly.

Linear Patterns components in assembly.

Moves components in assembly.

Adds section view with a section line.

Creates various assembly features.

Toggles various view settings.

The **SCREEN CAPTURE** Toolbar

 Copies the current graphics window to the clipboard.

 Records the current graphics window to an AVI file.

Stops recording the current graphics window to an AVI file.

The **Explode Line Sketch** Toolbar

Adds a route line that connect entities.

Adds a jog to the route lines.

The LINE FORMAT Toolbar

Changes layer properties.

Changes line color.

Changes line thickness.

Changes line style.

Hides a visible edge.

Shows a hidden edge.

Changes line display mode.

The 2D-To-3D Toolbar

Makes a Front sketch from the selected entities.

Makes a Top sketch from the selected entities.

Makes a Right sketch from the selected entities.

Makes a Left sketch from the selected entities.

Makes a Bottom sketch from the selected entities.

Makes a Back sketch from the selected entities.

Makes an Auxiliary sketch from the selected entities.

Creates a new sketch from the selected entities.

Repairs the selected sketch.

Aligns a sketch to the selected point.

Creates an extrusion from the selected sketch segments, starting at the selected sketch point.

Creates a cut from the selected sketch segments, optionally starting at the selected sketch point.

The ALIGN Toolbar

Aligns the left side of the selected annotations with the leftmost annotation.

Aligns the right side of the selected annotations with the rightmost annotation.

Aligns the top side of the selected annotations with the topmost annotation.

Aligns the bottom side of the selected annotations with the lowermost annotation.

Evenly spaces the selected annotations horizontally.

Evenly spaces the selected annotations vertically.

Centrally aligns the selected annotations horizontally.

Centrally aligns the selected annotations vertically.

Compacts the selected annotations horizontally.

Compacts the selected annotations vertically.

Aligns the center of the selected annotations between

Creates a group from the selected items

Deletes the grouping between these items

Aligns & groups selected dimensions along a line or an arc

Aligns & groups dimensions at a uniform distances

The SIMULATION Toolbar

Stops Record or Playback.

Records Simulation.

Replays Simulation.

Resets Components.

Adds Linear Motor.

Adds Rotary Motor.

Adds Spring.

Adds Gravity.

The MACRO Toolbar

Runs a Macro.

Stops Macro recorder.

Records (or pauses recording of) actions to create a Macro.

Launches the Macro Editor and begins editing a new macro.

Opens a Macro file for editing.

Creates a custom macro.

The TABLE Toolbar

 Adds a hole table of selected holes from a specified origin datum.

 Adds a Bill of Materials.

 Adds a revision table.

 Displays a Design table in a drawing.

 Adds a weldments cuts list table.

Adds a Excel based of Bill of Materials

Adds a general table to a drawing sheet.

The REFERENCE GEOMETRY

 Adds a reference plane

 Creates an axis.

 Creates a coordinate system.

 Adds a reference point

 Specifies entities to use as references using SmartMates.

The SPLINE TOOLS Toolbar

 Adds a point to a spline.

 Displays points where the concavity of selected spline changes.

 Displays minimum radius of selected spline.

 Displays curvature combs of selected spline.

 Reduces numbers of points in a selected spline.

 Adds a tangency control.

 Adds a curvature control.

 Adds a spline based on selected sketch entities & edges.

 Displays all handles of selected splines.

 Displays the spline control polygon.

The ANNOTATIONS Toolbar

 Inserts a note.

 Inserts a surface finish symbol.

 Inserts a new geometric tolerancing symbol.

 Attaches a balloon to the selected edge or face.

 Adds balloons for all components in selected view.

 Inserts a stacked balloon.

 Attaches a datum feature symbol to a selected edge / detail.

 Inserts a weld symbol on the selected edge / face / vertex.

 Inserts a datum target symbol and / or point attached to a selected edge / line.

 Selects and inserts block.

 Inserts annotations & reference geometry from the part / assembly into the selected.

 Adds center marks to circles on model.

 Inserts a Centerline.

 Inserts a hole callout.

 Adds a cosmetic thread to the selected cylindrical feature.

 Inserts a Multi-Jog leader.

 Selects a circular edge or and arc for Dowel pin symbol insertion.

 Toggles the visibility of annotations & dimensions.

 Inserts latest version symbol.

 Adds a cross hatch patterns or solid fill.

 Adds a weld symbol on a selected entity.

 Adds a weld bead caterpillar on an edge.

The "Feathers"

 Lightweight component.

 Out-of-Date component.

 Hidden Lightweight component.

 Hidden, Out-of-Date and Lightweight.

The DRAWINGS Toolbar

Updates the selected view to the model's current stage.

Creates a detail view.

Creates a section view.

Inserts an aligned section using the selected line or section line.

Unfolds a new view from an existing view.

Generates a standard 3-view drawing (1st or 3rd angle).

Inserts an auxiliary view of an inclined surface.

Adds an Orthogonal or Named view based on an existing part or assembly.

Adds a Relative view by two orthogonal faces or planes.

Adds a Predefined orthogonal projected or Named view with a model.

Adds an empty view.

Adds vertical break lines to selected view.

Crops a view.

Creates a Broken-out section.

Inserts an Alternate Position view.

The QUICK SNAP Toolbar

Snap to points.

Snap to center points.

Snap to midpoints.

Snap to quadrant points.

Snap to intersection of 2 curves.

Snap to nearest curve.

Snap tangent to curve.

Snap perpendicular to curve.

Snap parallel to line.

Snap horizontally / vertically.

Snap horizontally / vertically to points.

Snap to discrete line lengths.

Snap to grid points.

Snap to angle.

The LAYOUT Toolbar

Creates the assembly layout sketch.

Sketches a line.

Sketches a rectangle.

Sketches a circle.

Sketches a 3 point arc.

Rounds a corner.

Trims or extends a sketch.

Adds sketch entities by offsetting faces, Edges curves.

Mirrors selected entities about a centerline.

Adds a relation.

Creates a dimension.

Displays / Deletes geometric relations.

Makes a new block.

Edits the selected block.

Inserts a new block to the sketch or drawing.

Adds / Removes sketch entities to / from a block.

Saves the block to a file.

Explodes the selected block.

Creates a new part from a layout sketch block.

Positions 2 components relative to one another.

Moves a component within the degrees of freedom defined by its mates.

The CURVES Toolbar

- Projects sketch onto selected surface.
- Inserts a split line feature.
- Creates a composite curve from selected edges, curves and sketches.
- Creates a curve through free points.
- Creates a 3D curve through reference points.
- Helical curve defined by a base sketch and shape parameters.

The VIEW Toolbar

- Displays a view in the selected orientation.
- Reverts to previous view.
- Zooms out to see entire model.
- Zooms in by dragging a bounding box.
- Zooms in or out by dragging up or down.
- Zooms to fit all selected entities.
- Dynamic view rotation.
- Scrolls view by dragging.
- Displays image in wireframe mode.
- Displays hidden edges in gray.
- Displays image with hidden lines removed.
- Controls the visibility of planes.
- Controls the visibility of axis.
- Controls the visibility of parting lines.
- Controls the visibility of temporary axis.
- Controls the visibility of origins.
- Controls the visibility of coordinate systems.

- Controls the visibility of reference curves.
- Controls the visibility of sketches.
- Controls the visibility of 3D sketch planes.
- Controls the visibility of 3D sketch
- Controls the visibility of all annotations.
- Controls the visibility of reference points.
- Controls the visibility of routing points.
- Controls the visibility of lights.
- Controls the visibility of cameras.
- Controls the visibility of sketch relations.
- Redraws the current window.
- Rolls the model view.
- Turns the orientation of the model view.
- Dynamically manipulate the model view in 3D to make selection.
- Changes the display style for the active view.
- Displays a shade view of the model with its edges.
- Displays a shade view of the model.
- Toggles between draft quality & high quality HLV.
- Cycles through or applies a specific scene.
- Views the models through one of the model's cameras.
- Displays a part or assembly w/different colors according to the local radius of curvature.
- Displays zebra stripes.
- Displays a model with hardware accelerated shades.
- Edits the real view appearance of entities in the model.
- Applies a texture to entities in a model.
- Changes the visibility of items in the graphics area.
- Controls visibility of the sketch grid.

The **TOOLS** Toolbar

Calculates the distance between selected items.

Adds or edits equation.

Calculates the mass properties of the model.

Checks the model for geometry errors.

Inserts or edits a Design Table.

Evaluates section properties for faces and sketches that lie in parallel planes.

Reports Statistics for this Part/Assembly.

Deviation Analysis.

Runs the COSMOSXpress analysis wizard Powered by COSMOS.

Checks the spelling.

Import diagnostics.

Runs the DFMXpress analysis wizard.

Runs the DriveWorkXpress wizard.

Runs the COSMOSFloXpress analysis wizard.

The **ASSEMBLY** Toolbar

Creates a new part & inserts it into the assembly.

Adds an existing part or sub-assembly to the assembly.

Creates a new assembly & inserts it into the assembly.

Turns on/off large assembly mode for this document.

Hides / shows model(s) associated with the selected model(s).

Toggles the transparency of components.

Changes the selected components to suppressed or resolved.

Toggles between editing part and assembly.

Inserts a belt.

Inserts a new part into an

 Smart Fasteners.

 Positions two components relative to one.

 External references will not be created.

 Moves a component.

 Rotates an un-mated component around its center point.

 Replaces selected components.

 Replaces mate entities of mates of the selected components on the selected Mategroup.

 Creates a New Exploded view.

 Creates or edits explode line sketch.

 Interference detection.

 Changes assembly transparency.

 Shows or Hides the Simulation toolbar.

 Patterns components in one or two linear directions.

 Patterns components around an axis.

 Toggles the transparency of components Between 0 and 75 percent.

 Toggles between editing a Part and Assembly.

 Adds fasteners to the assembly using Toolbox.

 Displays statistics and check the health of The current assembly.

 Patterns components relative to an existing Pattern in a part.

 Shows hidden components.

 Toggles large assembly mode for this document.

 Checks assembly hole alignments.

 Mirrors subassemblies and parts.

To add or remove an icon
to or from the toolbar, first select:

Tools/Customize/Commands

Next select a **Category**, click a button to see its description and then drag / drop the command icon into any toolbar.

Standard Keyboard Shortcuts

Rotate the model

* Horizontally or Vertically: _____ Arrow keys

* Horizontally or Vertically 90°: _____ Shift + Arrow keys

* Clockwise or Counterclockwise: _____ Alt + left or right Arrow

* Pan the model: _____ Ctrl + Arrow keys

* Zoom in: _____ Z (shift + Z or capital Z)

* Zoom out: _____ z (lower case z)

* Zoom to fit: _____ F

* Previous view: _____ Ctrl+Shift+Z

View Orientation

* View Orientation Monu: _____ Space bar

* Front: _____ Ctrl+1

* Back: _____ Ctrl+2

* Left: _____ Ctrl+3

* Right: _____ Ctrl+4

* Top: _____ Ctrl+5

* Bottom: _____ Ctrl+6

* Isometric: _____ Ctrl+7

Selection Filter & Misc.

* Filter Edges: _____ e

* Filter Vertices: _____ v

* Filter Faces: _____ x

* Toggle Selection filter toolbar: _____ F5

* Toggle Selection Filter toolbar (on/off): _____ F6

* New SolidWorks document: _____ F1

* Open Document: _____ Ctrl+O

* Open from Web folder: _____ Ctrl+W

* Save: _____ Ctrl+S

* Print: _____ Ctrl+P

* Magnifying Glass Zoom _____ g

* Switch between the SolidWorks documents _____ Ctrl + Tab

SolidWorks Quick-Guide

SolidWorks 2013 Quick-Guide©
Customized Keyboard Shortcuts

SW 2013 Sample Customized Hot Keys

Function Keys

F1	SW-Help
F2	2D Sketch
F3	3D Sketch
F4	Modify
F5	Selection Filters
F6	Move (2D Sketch)
F7	Rotate (2D Sketch)
F8	Measure
F9	Extrude
F10	Revolve
F11	Sweep
F12	Loft

Sketch

C	Circle
P	Polygon
E	Ellipse
O	Offset Entities
Alt + C	Convert Entities
M	Mirror
Alt + M	Dynamic Mirror
Alt + F	Sketch Fillet
T	Trim
Alt + X	Extend
D	Smart Dimension
Alt + R	Add Relation
Alt + P	Plane
Control + F	Fully Define Sketch
Control + Q	Exit Sketch

Part of SolidWorks 2013 – Basic Tools and Advanced Techniques

SolidWorks® Quick-Guide by Paul Tran – Sr. Certified SolidWorks Instructor
© Issue 9 / Jan-2013 - Printed in The United State of America – All Rights Reserved